The Book in History, The Book as History:
New Intersections of the Material Text

THE BEINECKE SERIES
IN THE HISTORY OF THE BOOK

Kathryn James, series editor

The volumes in this series illuminate the study of literature through the examination of the material forms in which it circulates and is experienced. Intended for an audience of students and scholars, each volume focuses on a specific aspect of practice or production, made visible in a canonical text. In engaging with the materiality of the literary canon, the series extends our understanding of literature's mediated pasts, presents, and, inevitably, futures.

The Book in History, The Book as History:
New Intersections of the Material Text
Edited by Heidi Brayman, Jesse M. Lander, and Zachary Lesser

The Book in History, The Book as History: New Intersections of the Material Text

ESSAYS IN HONOR OF
DAVID SCOTT KASTAN

Edited by Heidi Brayman, Jesse M. Lander, and Zachary Lesser

Beinecke Rare Book & Manuscript Library, Yale University
Distributed by Yale University Press, New Haven and London

Published by Beinecke Rare Book & Manuscript Library, Yale University

Distributed by Yale University Press, P.O. Box 209040,
New Haven, Connecticut 06520-9040 www.yalebooks.com/art

Library of Congress Control Number: 2016933933
ISBN 978-0-300-22316-3

Yale

Contents

Acknowledgments

This volume is itself an acknowledgment, and it would be superfluous to rehearse here the intellectual debts and affiliations that led to its creation. But all such projects are also an opportunity to make new friends and incur new debts. As the book was nearing completion, the contributors were able to participate in a conference on the futures of historicism, convened at Yale by Ivan Lupić, Aaron Pratt, and Kathryn James, and also in honor of David Kastan. A model of intellectual exchange, the occasion was galvanizing, provoking a burst of activity that moved the project over the finish line, and we are grateful to Ivan, Aaron, and Kathryn for organizing and moderating the event. Committed as we are to Roger Stoddard's now familiar insight, "Whatever they may do, authors do not write books," we thank Kathryn James as well for her help in making this book, which would not have been possible without her creativity, energy, and support. At the Beinecke Library, Eve Houghton provided crucial editorial and production assistance at every phase, and Bob Halloran did the superb photography for the images. It was also a pleasure to work with Rebecca Martz, the book designer, who created the beautiful material text you are now holding. We are also indebted to the acuity of Lesley Baier, proof that the art of copyediting is not dead. Any errors that remain are of course our responsibility, but the book, whatever its deficiencies, stands as a wonderful example of the still formidable collaborations made possible by print.

To the Reader.

his Figure, that thou here ſeeſt
It vvas for gentle Shakeſpeare
Vherein the Grauer had a ſtrife
vvith Nature, to out-doo the
, could he but haue dravvne his
As vvell in braſſe, as he hath h

INTRODUCTION

HEIDI BRAYMAN, JESSE M. LANDER,
AND ZACHARY LESSER

The essays in this collection form part of what we think of as a second wave of early modern literary studies in book history and the materiality of the text. At the same time, and very much constitutive of this second wave, they reach beyond book history to address fundamental questions about historicism as critical theory and method, while exploring connections with a broad range of issues such as gender and sexuality, religion, political theory, economic history, adaptation and appropriation, and quantitative analysis and digital humanities. The extent and depth of these "new intersections" both set this work apart from and demonstrate its indebtedness to the first wave of early modern English book history in the 1980s and 1990s. Inspired both by early work in the field of print culture by Marshall McLuhan, Elizabeth Eisenstein, and others, and by poststructuralist theories of textuality epitomized by Foucault's "What Is an Author?" and Barthes's "From Work to Text," that "first-wave" scholarship addressed itself to large philosophical questions about the nature of authorship, the text, and reading. The revisionist bibliographical program of "unediting," for example, sought to examine the early editions of the drama of Shakespeare and his contemporaries in all of their material multiplicity.[1] Rather than reading *behind* these books to find the authorial *work*, these critics reveled in the oddities and variations of the early *documents:* from variant spellings to speech prefixes to multiple versions of plays.[2] Others sought to trace the winding path through the London book trade that plays followed from popular stage entertainment to enduring literary works; to explore the importance of the Shakespeare folio (and the Jonson folio before it) to the inculcation of the idea that plays might be worthy of authors; to write a genealogy of Shakespeare's works as they had been transformed and reified over the centuries by a parade of editors intent on fixing his texts and rooting them in his intention; and to explore models of authorship beyond the dominant one afforded by Shakespeare, such as those presented by Thomas Middleton or John Milton.[3]

The history of the book and the material text saw a remarkable efflorescence in the last decade of the twentieth century, thanks to this first wave of scholarship that effectively made its concerns central to the study of early modern literature. A new attention to the mechanics of culture led to work on the history of reading and the recovery of scribal culture, both of which were understood as providing a corrective to earlier work that was too preoccupied with authors, print, and production.[4] Feminist work similarly drew attention to material texts that disrupted established ideas about literary culture, to books as objects circulating within households, to the words embroidered on bed curtains and as samplers, and to the expectations and practices of women readers, both early modern and modern. Further, editing took on new urgency for feminist scholars who wanted to teach recovered texts to undergraduates; these projects, in turn, introduced a new generation of students to the materiality of the text and the challenges facing editors and bibliographers.[5]

We can see the impact of this movement in the difference between three anthologies, produced at either end of the 1990s, all intended for use in undergraduate survey classes or introductory graduate courses. The hugely influential *Staging the Renaissance: Reinterpretations of Elizabethan and Jacobean Drama* (1991), which most of the contributors to this collection can vividly remember encountering in college and graduate school, was largely a dissemination and institutionalization of the New Historicism. Edited by David Scott Kastan and Peter Stallybrass, it included foundational essays on the place of the stage (Steven Mullaney), on "Playing and Power" (Leonard Tennenhouse), on boy actors and cross-dressing (Lisa Jardine), and other important topics, alongside a series of readings of Renaissance plays excerpted from influential New Historical books and articles. Nestled among this New Historicist canon, however, were an essay by Stephen Orgel on "What is a Text?" and one by Random Cloud (Randall McLeod) on "Editing and the Invention of Dramatick Character." The presence, but decidedly minority status, of these "New Textual" essays in this important collection heralded the emergence of this strand of criticism that would rapidly come to seem inescapable in early modern studies.

The issues that Orgel and McLeod addressed in *Staging the Renaissance* – the nature of textuality; the difference between reading plays in early editions or facsimiles as opposed to modern edited texts – can be seen to share important concerns with the New Historicism that surrounded them, as indeed is also suggested by their shared debt to Foucault (whether the Foucault of *Discipline and Punish* and *The History of Sexuality* or the Foucault of "What Is an Author?"). And yet they also mark out a new direction for the field: a concern with texts at the literal level (the level of the letter, of the word, of the typeface) rather than the discursive; a concern with local specificity of a very different kind than the New Historical anecdote; a concern with questions more properly literary than the more diffuse "culture" that the New Historicism tended to take as its object. The subsequent reinvigoration of textual studies, which had often been treated as merely preliminary to the work of scholarly editing, has reshaped our understanding of the entire range of early modern discourses and their circulation.

By the time of *A New History of Early English Drama* (1997) and *A Companion to Shakespeare* (1999), both also edited by Kastan (the former with John D. Cox), the textual materiality of early modern drama in particular, and early modern writing in general, had become far more central.[6] Essays on the mechanics of printing, the organization of the London book trade, scriptwriting, censorship, the publication of playbooks, authorship and collaboration, play readers, libraries, manuscript drama, and similar concerns make up a sizable proportion of these anthologies. These essays influenced not only scholars working on print culture but also performance critics and theater historians, a field in which they also helped to spark innovation, as in the work of Tiffany Stern on the material documents of performance.[7] We might see the culmination of this first wave of book history in Kastan's magisterial monograph, *Shakespeare and the Book* (2001), which not only offered new theories on the publication of Shakespeare's early quartos and the First Folio but also, more importantly, captured in a single compelling narrative an entire way of thinking about Shakespeare, a bibliographic habit of mind, that Kastan had done much to make available to the field.

If the last decade of the twentieth century saw the rapid ascent of this way of thinking, we believe that the first decade and a half of the twenty-first has seen a second wave of studies that build on this earlier work but push it in new directions. The earlier concerns with the nature of authorship and the construction of a more material theory of textuality, with the legacy of editorial history and the variant versions of literary works, and with the transformation of drama into literature, have by no means disappeared: indeed, they are addressed throughout this collection. The relation of the second to the first wave is hardly agonistic; despite Kastan's tongue-in-cheek labeling of many of our contributors as "Young Turks," they do not set out to overthrow the earlier work.

Rather, the very success of that work seems to us to be a precondition of the essays in this collection; it is precisely because we no longer need to make the argument that early modern literary works exist always and only in their material instantiations that the contributors to this volume can treat the history of the book less as a *topic* than as a *methodology*. Attention has thereby shifted from a fundamental concern with establishing the materiality of the text to an effort to make book history speak to a wide variety of critical agendas. The transformation of this subfield from a topic to a methodology has meant that book history has now become enmeshed with a host of other approaches to early modern studies, from feminism to postcolonialism to political theory. As the New Historicism has faded from its dominant position, the history of the book has come to seem more and more central precisely because, thanks to the first wave of work, the materiality of texts can never be ignored, regardless of the particular topic under investigation. The diversity of this engagement can be seen clearly in the range of essays included here.

It was again Kastan who did much to push the field forward, in his much-debated (if often, in our view, misunderstood) polemic *Shakespeare after Theory* (1999).[8] Kastan's call for a return to history "after theory" has been widely endorsed and critiqued; indeed, as Mario DiGangi observes in this volume, it sometimes seems as if the "presentist" movement includes an unwritten law that every essay must include a denunciation of the book.[9] Whether praised or blamed, however, *Shakespeare after Theory* is the rare book that has provoked the kind of field-setting discussion about methodological and theoretical concerns that has often seemed missing in our current disciplinary moment.[10] Here Kastan urges a "sharper focus on the material relations of discourse to the world in which it circulated," in order to give our "cultural analysis more historical purchase, fixing it more firmly in relation to the actual producers and consumers of those discourses, locating it, that is, in the world of lived history. Only then is discourse truly enlivened, recognized as a product of human desire and design."[11] In practice, this often means attending to the materiality of the texts in which these discourses circulate so that we can better understand their meanings to their "producers and consumers."

The history of the book thus provides an alternative to the New Historicist mode of reading text as discourse, shifting attention from the freeform "circulation of social energy" to a more rooted understanding of texts as objects produced by particular people in particular circumstances to speak to particular audiences. While his co-edited *Staging the Renaissance* did much to bring New Historicism to a generation of students, in *Shakespeare after Theory* Kastan launches a powerful critique of New Historicism as a masked formalism – dependent for its often pyrotechnical effects on the formal unity of "culture."[12] This critique echoes Alan Liu's brilliant argument that the New Historicism "is an ultimate formalism so 'powerful' that it colonizes the very world as its 'text.'" In place of the New Historicism's "Geertzian 'symbolic' of culture," Liu wants a "*renewed rhetoric,*" and what he means by this rhetoric sounds very similar to Kastan's "material relations of discourse": "a method or 'language' of contextualization founded upon some *historically-realized* philosophy of discourse – i.e., some notion of rhetoric, or more broadly, of language as historically situated event."[13] While Liu himself does not engage with the methodology or critical concerns of the history of the book, nonetheless we would argue that it is precisely this idea of language as *rhetoric,* as *historically situated event,* that the study of the materiality of the text can offer.

In various ways, the essays in this collection – and more generally the second wave of early modern book historical scholarship – seek to explicate how texts work rhetorically in the world, as events rather than discourses. On the one hand, such an approach narrows the critical field of vision: rather than taking in all of "culture" in sweeping New Historicist fashion, these essays address the circulation of meaning among specific authors, stationers, readers, book buyers, dedicatees, and others, by means of the specific rhetorical genres of early modern textual culture – the book *in* history. They do so through a close attention to the book itself as a material embodiment of these rhetorical situations: the book *as* history. On the other hand, while the focus may narrow – or, as Kastan would have it, sharpen – the critical *purchase* deepens, we would argue. For such studies can illuminate the multifarious ways that people made meaning from the literary and nonliterary texts that confronted them in "the world of lived history."[14]

PAST IMPOSITIONS

The essays in part 1, "Past Impositions," employ a range of recent and emerging theoretical lenses to explore how the present makes meaning of the past, and how the past may at times resist those efforts. The three essays do not share a theoretical approach – they work with formalism, queer theory, and bibliographic theory, respectively – but each seeks to bring "theory" and "history" together in sympathy with Kastan's agenda in *Shakespeare after Theory*. While the "after" of Kastan's title was often misunderstood to suggest that we ought to leave theory behind, in fact it signaled Kastan's desire to incorporate the lessons of theory into historicism.[15] Each of these essays does so in innovative ways.

In "The Matter of Form: Book History, Formalist Criticism, and Francis Bacon's Aphorisms," András Kiséry and Allison Deutermann point to recent scholarship that combines a renewed formalism with an engagement with the material text. Kiséry and Deutermann advocate this approach but insist upon its theorization and uncover its long history in their reading of Francis Bacon's *The Advancement of Learning* (1605). In Bacon's understanding of the interdependence of form and matter, Kiséry and Deutermann find conceptual compatibility between formalism and historicism in literary studies, as they propose a critical practice that "refuses to distinguish sharply between literary and bibliographical form." Tracing the development of formalist and historicist approaches, Kiséry and Deutermann note Richard Helgerson's aspiration to be a "historical formalist" in his *Forms of Nationhood* (1992). In his first book, *Shakespeare and the Shapes of Time* (1982), David Kastan reached toward a similar articulation when practicing a historicized genre theory to understand the plays in historical time: "genre becomes a way of imagining time as it shapes and is shaped by humankind."[16] As Kiséry and Deutermann argue, genre has long been a site of convergence for formalist and historicist approaches; with the case study of Bacon's *Advancement of Learning,* they model a way of thinking about genre, in this case the aphorism, that is embedded in both historical formalism and the materiality of the text.

Like the new formalism, a new presentism has recently emerged in opposition to a dominant and, for some of its critics, alienating historicism. In "Shakespeare after Queer Theory," Mario DiGangi plays on Kastan's famous title and shares his insistence that historicist scholars incorporate the lessons of theory. Pushing back against the claims in Hugh Grady and Terence Hawkes's influential collection, *Presentist Shakespeares* (2007), and working against what Valerie Traub has recently termed "the new unhistoricism in queer studies," DiGangi reminds us that queer historiography has powerfully modeled a way to reach back into the early modern past from a self-reflective place of present investments and desires.[17] DiGangi draws inspiration from Kastan's insistence on reading "the specific material and institutional conditions of the discursive exchanges" in early modern culture, offering a nuanced account of how Antonio's position as a merchant allows for the recovery of queer affects in *The Merchant of Venice*. As his survey of late-sixteenth-century secular and religious texts demonstrates, merchants were cast as emotionally transparent types, moved only by financial loss and gain. Antonio's sadness and affective opacity, accordingly, are all the more striking in this context. Shakespeare's refusal to reveal Antonio's interiority extends, too, to any display of direct causality in the romantic relationships in the play. "The origins of romantic desire" in this play, DiGangi argues, "are almost entirely obscured in the past." Only once the queer circuit of desire between Bassanio and Antonio is taken out of the equation does Antonio revert to the type of "the merchant whose emotional life can be reduced to the easily legible antipathies of joy and despair." In DiGangi's essay, we see a fully theorized historicism make available to queer studies "the world of lived history" to which Kastan urges us to be responsible.

In "Playbooks and the Question of Ephemerality," Alan Farmer undertakes a very different historical method, but one equally inspired by Kastan's call to situate discourse in its material conditions. Unlike DiGangi, Farmer does not read any single play in depth; instead he "reads" all of them statistically through the quantitative lens of the emerging field he terms "Literary and Bibliographical Big Data." A central intervention of Farmer's essay is to historicize bibliographical categories like "ephemera"; and by attending to size, format, genre, bindings, and edition-sheets, Farmer explores the various factors that contributed to the survival or loss rates of early modern printed sheets. Early modern ephemerality exists on a continuum, Farmer insists; further, he is careful to distinguish between cultural ephemerality as a discursive category and bibliographic ephemerality as a material category. Working with an archive of numbered editions and considering both form and matter, Farmer concludes that playbooks were not the ephemeral objects that critics have often imagined. And in pointing to genres that were indeed ephemeral in the period – catechisms, schoolbook grammars, corantos, and pamphlets of two sheets or less – Farmer enacts precisely the refusal to "distinguish sharply between literary and bibliographical form" that Kiséry and Deutermann advocate for historicist practice.

TEXTUAL INCARNATIONS

One of the critiques of book history has always been that it is antiquarian, that it fetishizes "materiality" (understood as mere physicality) above the broader concerns of literature or history. The essays in part 2, "Textual Incarnations," historicize this critique: they investigate the intersection of economics, religion, and the material text in the creation of the book as fetish object. In "Book Fetishes," Benedict Robinson explores how early modern English writers understood Muslim reverence for the Qur'an as a perverse bibliophilia. The insistence that Muslims idolatrously worshipped their holy book appears at first glance to be a predictable bit of xenophobia, a way of denigrating the practitioners of an alien faith as childlike and simpleminded. But Robinson quickly complicates the picture, demonstrating that early modern European descriptions of the Qur'an were informed by post-Reformation controversies over the status and authority of Christian scripture. As Robinson suggests, the problems are particularly acute in a Protestant context in which the adoption of *sola scriptura* as a principle and a battle cry invited the charge of bibliolatry. Consequently, English descriptions of Islamic textual practices are not simply the stereotypical dismissal of an alien culture but also the working out of conflicts central to Protestant worship and culture. The dichotomy between letter and spirit, physical form and meaning, proved to be a durable problem for the Abrahamic religions, and Robinson concludes by suggesting that Spinoza's account of scripture, which reduces the assemblage of biblical texts to a simple moral imperative "to love God above all things and one's neighbor as oneself," is haunted by the specter of the Qur'an. According to Spinoza, those who preoccupy themselves with the troubled textual history of the scriptures "verge…on adoring images and pictures, i.e. paper and ink."

In "Spenser's Thaumaturgy: 'Mental Space' and the Material Forms of *The Faerie Queene* (1590)," Thomas Festa pays close attention to the physical form of the book as he discusses Spenser's representational strategies as a form of thaumaturgy, a wonder-working that produces enchanting images that always threaten to become idols or fetishes. Festa explores Spenser's ambivalence about his art, a concern registered in the figure of Archimago, who specializes in the creation of deceptive simulacra such as the false Una. Spenser "turns our attention to the irreducible paradox of materialism," Festa suggests, concluding his account with a consideration of the woodcut of St. George that appears in both the 1590 and 1596 editions of *The Faerie Queene*. While the woodcut initially appears to offer an image of holiness achieved, an iconic representation of Redcrosse Knight, its powers of signification are complicated by its earlier appearance in a variety of other books. Instead, the woodcut manages to present "in visual form Spenser's complex status as both iconoclast and thaumaturge."

In his essay, "Indicating Commodities in Early English Discovery Narratives," Daniel Vitkus asks what a consideration of book history can add to our understanding of the emergence and promulgation of discovery narratives. In his telling, books describing and promoting the newly "discovered" spaces of the globe efface the labor of travel in order to present a seemingly frictionless world in which commodities are presented as ready and waiting for the adventurous trader. While scholars have discussed in detail the shifting cartographic imaginary of early modern Europe, Vitkus draws attention to often neglected elements of these books such as the table and the index. Unlike attempts to represent topography, these lists serve as inventories, presenting the lands under consideration as warehouses stocked with valuable goods. The elements of the book that Ann Blair has considered in connection with early modern information overload are here understood as an integral part of a colonial enterprise.[18] Even as these books promote the value of overseas expansion and trade, they also serve more immediately as entrants within the domestic market for print. In a "double commodity fetishization," the travel book becomes a "fetish that fetishizes."

Milton has been increasingly recognized as an acute student and critic of the material book. In "'His Idoliz'd Book': Milton, Blood, and Rubrication," Bianca Calabresi demonstrates that the use of red ink in *Eikonoklastes* is a deliberate attempt to revise the semiotics of rubrication established in Royalist books, especially William Dugard's edition of *Eikon Basilike* (1649). Calabresi identifies John Foxe's *Actes and Monuments* as initiating a debate about the significance of rubrication in English. The first English edition of the book (1563) included a Calendar that listed Protestant martyrs using red ink, an act of iconoclasm that was attacked by Catholic controversialists, who saw its color-coding as an underhanded attempt to create new saints. Foxe's attempt to appropriate red letter for a Protestant purpose informed Dugard's later presentation of King Charles as "The Martyr of the People"; at the same time, Calabresi argues, Dugard presented his edition as a "manual" – a term with Roman Catholic associations – that would guide readers in "the ordering and enacting of sacred rituals around a holy body." Milton's hostility to the book's visual strategies extends beyond the idolatry of the famous frontispiece to include its typography. The otherwise puzzling use of red ink on the title page of *Eikonoklastes* makes sense when it is understood as an attempt to model a correct, humanist form of rubrication. Milton's careful handling of his own red letters confirms the claim that he was attentive to the material attributes of the book, and it serves as an important reminder that the gray-scale images available on EEBO (*Early English Books Online*) provide only partial access to the remarkable legacy of early modern print.

GLOSSING THE TEXT AND THE SELF

Just as it effaces color, so too EEBO erases the histories of particular copies of books by effectively reducing every edition to a single, paradigmatic copy, whichever copy happened to have been microfilmed by UMI beginning in the early twentieth century. As a result, the copy-specific aspects of early modern books, marginalia among the most important of them, can become invisible, and much recent work has sought to recover these readers' marks. The first two essays in part 3, "Glossing the Text and the Self," take up another form of marginal comment, not readers' manuscript notes but printed marginalia designed to guide reading itself. In Sarah Kelen's reading of the *Shepheardes Calender*, E.K.'s glosses work to blur the boundary between old and new, medieval and early modern. The gloss, itself a classical form, serves in the first instance to place the text in a defined tradition, a textual succession that is limned by the glosser, who alerts the reader to connections between the *Calender* and its illustrious predecessors both classical and medieval. While the glosses consecrate the work, establishing its literary value and authority, they also open up a series of unsettling and unsettled questions about the pastness of literary history. In particular, the glossing of Middle English oscillates between explaining the obvious and assuming familiarity with medieval verse, especially Chaucer. Kelen finds this unsteadiness suggestive: by belaboring the obvious, the glosses encourage the reader to feel superior; by leaving allusions to be discovered by the attentive reader, the glosses anticipate and encourage a sense of readerly independence and accomplishment. Seen in this light, the glosses in the *Shepheardes Calender* display an ambivalent early modern sense of simultaneous proximity to and distance from the medieval.

Chloe Wheatley likewise explores the strategic use of marginal notes to guide reading, in this case in Milton's *The Reason of Church-governement*. Deriding the excessive use of citations as a form of false learning in which ostentation exceeds substance, Milton sets out to "reform the very act of citation itself." While he arraigns his opponents for cluttering their margins with irrelevant citations, he does not himself entirely reject the marginal note. Usually Milton identifies scriptural citations within the body of his text, but there are four conspicuous cases where a scriptural quotation is highlighted in the margins. These cases, Wheatley argues, function almost as hyperlinks intended to direct the reader to a particular passage of Scripture, which when read in its own wider context will yield additional, supportive meanings that demonstrate the biblical basis of Presbyterianism. Rather than functioning to protect his text from assault, Milton's minimal notes are an encouragement to further reading. Like Calabresi, Wheatley shows how attuned Milton was to the affordances of the printed book: his marginalia reveal him as at once confident in the harmony of Scripture and skeptical of the normal procedures of print controversy. Milton thus becomes one of Kiséry and Deutermann's ideal critics who refuse to demarcate literary from bibliographical form.

Claire McEachern's essay extends the concept of the gloss beyond the material margins of a text and into the more abstract realm of godly self-examination, which functions as a kind of marginal commentary on the state of one's soul. The "religious turn" in Shakespeare studies is now decades old, but the notion that Shakespeare might have an affinity for what has been called "hot Protestantism" has not featured largely in the conversation. Instead, recent examinations of Shakespeare's religious affiliations have tended to focus on Catholicism. As Kastan shows in *A Will to Believe,* the argument for a "Catholic Shakespeare" has long focused on the material text, the archival documents that are thought to provide unique access into Shakespeare's faith: from the discovery of John Shakespeare's "Spiritual Testament" in the 1750s, through William Henry Ireland's forged Shakespearean "professione of fayth" in the 1790s, through the twentieth-century investigation of the Lancashire recusant Alexander Hoghton's will, with its reference to "William Shakeshafte."[19] As Kastan rightly observes, such documents provide a false assurance, and would do so even if we found a legitimately Shakespearean "profession of faith": "Shakespeare nowhere says anything explicitly about what he believes, but even if he did it would tell us only what he believed when he said it or what he was willing to say about what he believed."[20] Rather, Kastan argues for a renewed exploration, not of Shakespeare's religion, but of religion *in Shakespeare,* of the multifarious ways in which the plays handle an aspect of life that was central to early modern culture.

Like Kastan, McEachern eschews biography, offering no speculation on Shakespeare's own beliefs. Instead, she begins with a basic element of drama, spectatorship, arguing that this formal structure provides a fruitful analogue to the procedures associated with Calvinist practical divinity. Using William Perkins as her primary case study, McEachern suggests that the cultivation of doubt about one's salvation could paradoxically become confirmation of one's election. While McEachern concedes that the efficacy of such mental judo is surprising, there is evidence that it was successful for many. Perhaps more importantly, the practices of introspection enjoined by Perkins and other advocates of the Protestant conscience encouraged a sense that one was a spectator, viewing and assessing the workings of grace in one's life. What McEachern calls "soteriological self-study" has, she argues, a deep connection with dramatic irony. Especially in the English history plays, in which the final outcome is always known in advance, the prospects for dramatic irony are so strong that deliberate efforts must be made in order to create suspense. In *Richard II,* the central source of suspense is the monarch's tortured subjectivity, and the concluding phase in which Richard is un-kinged presents "a state of ambivalence that borders on the soteriological." For McEachern, the play does not simply *represent* a case of conscience, staging an exemplar of anxious introspection; instead, the play engages the audience by forcing it to watch, with excruciating suspense, the unfolding of what is already written.

RECOMPOSING SHAKESPEARE

Our final section, "Recomposing Shakespeare," extends this hermeneutical focus from readers and audience members to editors and translators. It returns as well to the concerns of the opening section, the imbrication of the past and the present, by exploring the materiality of Shakespeare's texts across the centuries since the first quartos, exploring the ways in which choices by editors and translators have shaped the reading and performance of Shakespeare. The essays do so by focusing on one particularly charged moment in the history of Shakespeare, the early twentieth century. In "Early Modern Punctuation and Modern Editions: Shakespeare's Serial Colon," William Sherman turns an editorial eye to "pointing," considering the serial colon first in the 1609 *Sonnets* and then in the 1623 First Folio as integral to their argumentative, rhetorical, and generic structures. Like Kiséry and Deutermann and Farmer in Part I, Sherman enacts a practice that assumes the interdependence of literary and bibliographical form. And as in the other essays in this final section, Sherman's critical practice is to juxtapose modern versions of Shakespeare, here the Tercentenary and Quatercentenary editions of the *Sonnets,* both with the early editions and with each other. In modern editing, Sherman demonstrates, punctuation has not received the scholarly attention or the methodological guidance granted most other aspects of Shakespeare's texts. As a result, no two independent modern editions agree; every mark of punctuation might in fact be considered a textual crux. The silent, ubiquitous, and various modernization of punctuation, he argues, has profound implications for our Shakespeare. At least for the serial colon, no modern equivalent quite captures both its grammatical and rhetorical effects. To translate it into another mark is to reduce the interpretative range and literary evidence available to actors and readers – to refuse the possibility that mere points have histories worth preserving.

Zoltán Márkus continues this attention to our modern Shakespeares in "*Unser Shakespeare* in 1940," examining the competing nationalistic constructions of Shakespeare in Britain and Germany during World War II. He begins from the premise, which underlies all the essays in the volume, that "the changing materiality and past significance of Shakespeare and his plays determine their present uses." Márkus notes the strong revival in 1930s Nazi Germany of the nineteenth-century idea of a "German" Shakespeare, which by 1940 presented the English press with the problem of a Shakespeare who was published and produced more widely in Germany than "at home." The German sense of kinship and even ownership of Shakespeare as "*unser Shakespeare*" produced a corollary unease in the German wartime press. Márkus explores this tension between national Shakespeares and a universal Shakespeare, arguing that "as a function or myth of the text, Shakespeare is continuously conjured up in the process of dealing with his plays." The meaning of Shakespeare is thus produced dialectically by the history of our engagement with the plays – the ways we have adapted them to contemporary agendas – and by their materiality both in print and performance tradition, which sets limits on those acts of appropriation.

In "Making Histories; or, Shakespeare's *Ring*," Adam Hooks traces this same dialectic across the *longue durée* of Shakespeare's life in print and performance. Hooks follows the shifting presentations, perceptions, and performances of Shakespeare's ten English chronicle history plays from their first quartos through the first English production of the full cycle in 1906, inspired in part by Wagner's *Ring*. Though the cycle finds its fullest expression on stage in the twentieth century, the notion that the histories constitute a unified national epic emerges from book rather than theater history. The plays were not performed as a sequence or even in pairs in Shakespeare's time; further, the contemporary titles make no effort to link the plays. Rather, it is Shakespeare's first editors, Heminge and Condell, and their successors – most notably, Samuel Johnson – who forge a sequence out of these individual plays. The view of the histories as a single, national epic emerged, however, not in England but in late-eighteenth-century Germany with A.W. Schlegel's translations. Inspired by Schlegel's view of the history plays, the first performance of the complete cycle was staged in Weimar as part of the tercentenary celebration of Shakespeare's birth in 1864. Shakespeare's influence on German culture was then reciprocated by German scholarship's impact on modern Shakespeare when the full cycle was performed in Stratford-upon-Avon. Only by traveling to Germany and back did Shakespeare's histories become a quintessentially "English" epic. Exploring the long history of the Shakespearean history play as book and as performance, as the plays were put to use in different historical moments, Hooks returns us to the central dialectic of this volume as a whole, between the book *in* history and the book *as* history.

When Robert Darnton proposed his model of the communication circuit in 1982, he hoped to provide coherence to an emergent field marked by "interdisciplinarity run riot."[21] Darnton's account is an admitted and admired classic, but his attempt to impose order on the vibrant variety of scholarship that marched under the banner of book history was unsuccessful, and subsequently the field (understood in a loose sense) has witnessed a proliferation of approaches, all of which testify to the extraordinary range of work made possible by an attention to both the material and linguistic means of communication. Rather than cohering into a unified whole with clearly defined boundaries, this field has instead turned outward, reaching into every area of early modern studies. It is defined more by habits of thinking and ways of seeing than by any particular model or set of principles. It is this turn outward, rather than the taming of interdisciplinary riot in order to consolidate an already defined landscape, that has given studies of the material text such force in recent years, as the essays in this volume amply demonstrate.

NOTES

1 On unediting, see Steven Urkowitz, *Shakespeare's Revision of King Lear* (Princeton: Princeton University Press, 1980); Randall McLeod, "UN *Editing* Shak-speare," *SubStance* 10/11 (1981–82): 26–55; Gary Taylor and Michael Warren, eds., *The Division of the Kingdoms: Shakespeare's Two Versions of* King Lear (Oxford: Clarendon Press, 1983); Stanley Wells and Gary Taylor, "The Oxford Shakespeare Re-viewed by the General Editors," *AEB: Analytical and Enumerative Bibliography*, n.s., 4 (1990): 6–20; Leah S. Marcus, *Unediting the Renaissance: Shakespeare, Marlowe, Milton* (London: Routledge, 1996).

2 See, for example, Margreta de Grazia and Peter Stallybrass, "The Materiality of the Shakespearean Text," *Shakespeare*

Quarterly 44 (1993): 255–83; Random Cloud (Randall McLeod), "'The very names of the Persons': Editing and the Invention of Dramatick Character," in *Staging the Renaissance: Reinterpretations of Elizabethan and Jacobean Drama*, ed. David Scott Kastan and Peter Stallybrass (New York: Routledge, 1991), 88–96; Random Clod (Randall McLeod), "Information on Information," *Text* 5 (1991): 241–81; and Marcus, *Unediting the Renaissance*.

3 Important early examples of work on the cultural history of dramatic literature and the dramatic author include Joseph Loewenstein, "The Script in the Marketplace," *Representations* 12 (1985): 101–14; Gary Taylor, *Reinventing Shakespeare: A Cultural History, from the Restoration to the Present* (New York: Weidenfeld and Nicolson, 1989); Margreta de Grazia, *Shakespeare Verbatim: The Reproduction of Authenticity and the 1790 Apparatus* (Oxford: Clarendon Press, 1991). On Middleton as alternative model to Shakespeare, see Gary Taylor and John Lavagnino, eds., *Thomas Middleton and Early Modern Textual Culture: A Companion to the Collected Works* (Oxford: Oxford University Press, 2007); on Milton, see Sharon Achinstein, *Milton and the Revolutionary Reader* (Princeton: Princeton University Press, 1994); Stephen B. Dobranski, *Milton, Authorship, and the Book Trade* (Cambridge: Cambridge University Press, 1999).

4 Landmark early work in this area includes Harold Love, *Scribal Publication in Seventeenth-Century England* (Oxford: Clarendon Press, 1993); Arthur F. Marotti, *Manuscript, Print, and the English Renaissance Lyric* (Ithaca: Cornell University Press, 1995); and Henry Woudhuysen, *Sir Philip Sidney and the Circulation of Manuscripts, 1558–1640* (Oxford: Oxford University Press, 1996).

5 See Anne M. Haselkorn and Betty S. Travitsky, eds., *The Renaissance Englishwoman in Print: Counterbalancing the Canon* (Amherst: University of Massachusetts Press, 1990); Mary Ellen Lamb, *Gender and Authorship in the Sidney Circle* (Madison: University of Wisconsin Press, 1990): Margaret J.M. Ezell, *Writing Women's Literary History* (Baltimore: Johns Hopkins University Press, 1993); Victoria Burke, "Women and Early Seventeenth-Century Manuscript Culture: Four Miscellanies," *The Seventeenth Century* 12 (1997): 135–50; Juliet Fleming, "Wounded Walls: Graffiti, Grammatology, and the Age of Shakespeare," *Criticism* 39 (1997): 1–30; Juliet Fleming, *Graffiti and the Writing Arts of Early Modern England* (Philadelphia: University of Pennsylvania Press, 2001). Influential early editing projects include Betty S. Travitsky, ed., *The Paradise of Women: Writings by Englishwomen of the Renaissance* (Westport, Conn.: Greenwood Press, 1981), and the Brown Women Writers Project.

6 John D. Cox and David Scott Kastan, eds., *A New History of Early English Drama* (New York: Columbia University Press, 1997); David Scott Kastan, ed., *A Companion to Shakespeare* (Oxford: Blackwell Publishers, 1999).

7 Stern cites *A New History* and Kastan's monograph *Shakespeare and the Book* (Cambridge: Cambridge University Press, 2001) as two of the books that most influenced her own groundbreaking work. See Michael P. Jensen, "Talking Books with Tiffany Stern," *Shakespeare Newsletter* 62 (2012): 9–17 (10).

8 David Scott Kastan, *Shakespeare after Theory* (New York: Routledge, 1999).

9 See, for example, Terence Hawkes, *Shakespeare in the Present* (London: Routledge, 2002), 1–2; Linda Charnes, "Shakespeare, and Belief, in the Future," in *Presentist Shakespeares*, ed. Hugh Grady and Terence Hawkes (London: Routledge, 2007), 64–78 (64–65); and Linda Charnes, *Hamlet's Heirs: Shakespeare and the Politics of a New Millennium* (New York: Routledge, 2006), 21–23.

10 See Diana E. Henderson's astute comment that the dichotomy of Kastan and Hawkes has "initiated a debate of heuristic usefulness, although the claims of difference between them in critical practice have been exaggerated" – claims largely made by others, not by the principals themselves, it should be noted. Diana E. Henderson, *Collaborations with the Past: Reshaping Shakespeare across Time and Media* (Ithaca: Cornell University Press, 2006), 238n80.

11 Kastan, *Shakespeare after Theory*, 18.

12 Ibid., 30–31.

13 Alan Liu, "The Power of Formalism: The New Historicism," *ELH* 56 (1989): 721–71 (756).

14 Kastan, *Shakespeare after Theory*, 18.

15 Ibid., 31.

16 David Scott Kastan, *Shakespeare and the Shapes of Time* (Hanover, N.H.: University Press of New England, 1982), 173.

17 Valerie Traub, "The New Unhistoricism in Queer Studies," *PMLA* 128 (2013): 21–39.

18 Ann M. Blair, *Too Much to Know: Managing Scholarly Information before the Modern Age* (New Haven: Yale University Press, 2010).

19 David Scott Kastan, *A Will to Believe: Shakespeare and Religion* (Oxford: Oxford University Press, 2014), 17–26.

20 Ibid., 18.

21 Robert Darnton, "What Is the History of Books?" *Daedalus* 111, no. 3 (1982): 65–83 (67).

AN HOMILIE AGAINST disobedience and wilfull rebellion.

The first part.

S GOD the Creatour and Lord o
things appointed his Angels and h
uenly creatures in all obedience to se
and to honour his maiesty : so wa
his will that man, his chiefe creat
vpon the earth, should liue vnder
obedience of his Creatour and Lo
and for that cause, GOD [illegible] also
as hee had created ma[illegible]nto
a certaine prece[illegible]hich
(being ye[illegible]ncy,
remayni[illegible] obse
as a ple[illegible]oue
inden obedience, with denunciatio[illegible]ansgr
breake the sayd Law and comma[illegible]D wo
e man to be his obedient subiect, [illegible] creatu
iect vnto man, who kept their d[illegible] so long
n remayned in his obedience vn[illegible]h obedien
n had continued still, there had[illegible]ases, no si
e, no death, nor other miserie[illegible]s now infin
nd most miserably afflicted a[illegible]e appeareth
ginall kingdome of GOD o[illegible]n, and vniuers
r all things, and of man ou[illegible] which GOD
e subiect vnto him, and with [illegible]o blessed state, wh
gels, man, and all creatures had rema[illegible]in, had they continue

PAST
IMPOSITIONS

of the proficience and aduancement of Learning, diuine and
humane.

To the King.

At London,

Printed for *Henrie Tomes*, an[d]
are to be sould at his shop at Graies Inne

The Matter of Form: Book History, Formalist Criticism, and Francis Bacon's Aphorisms

ANDRÁS KISÉRY, WITH ALLISON DEUTERMANN

Although the easy opposition of formalism and materialism can make such connections still appear paradoxical, in recent years scholars have increasingly combined the analysis of literary form with the exploration of the material text. Through this conjunction, they have begun to address some of the criticisms that have been lobbed at formalism and book history, respectively: that "form" is an overly elastic or baggy term without precise – and precisely historicized – definition, and that the study of the material text prioritizes books (and the people who make them and read them) over literature. The often untheorized linking of the two approaches has important implications for our assumptions about the relationship between form and matter as well as between the material texts that instantiate literary and nonliterary writing and the forms that are produced by, with, and among them. A significant body of this work has emerged in medieval and early modern studies, perhaps because these periods predate the emergence of "literature" and "the literary" as stable categories, and these fields have therefore long been troubled by conflicting retrospective articulations of the field of writing according to formal and material features.[1]

In the pages that follow, we attempt to grasp some of the conceptual and disciplinary implications of this conjunction of literary formalism and textual materialism. We begin with a look at Francis Bacon's eclectic considerations of form and matter for a schematic framework within which to capture the connection between these two approaches. After considering their compatibility in the light of some of the contemporary arguments about them, our essay concludes with an amphibious—material as well as literary—exploration of the form that enables the Baconian project, namely, the aphorism, whose portability may stand as a figure of testing intellectual divisions and of enabling methodological transfers between disciplines.

WHAT'S THE MATTER? BACON AND THE VARIETY OF FORMS

> ...the Inuention of Formes is of al other Parts of Knowledge the worthiest to bee sought, if it bee Possible to bee found. As for the possibilitie, they are ill discouerers, that thinke there is no land when they can see nothing but Sea.[2]

For Bacon, forms are the true objects of scientific knowledge, the goal toward which all investigation and observation of the natural world should tend. Which of them are to be explored, however, is for Bacon far from self-evident: the infinite variety of the forms of specific substances is "so perplexed," as he puts it, that "they are not to be inquired." The analogy Bacon uses to explain his way out of this quandary is a linguistic one. He likens the variety of substances in the world to the sheer variety of words, "which by the composition and transposition of letters are infinite":

> But on the otherside, to enquire *the forme of those Soundes or Voices which make simple Letters* is easily comprehensible, and being knowen, induceth and manifesteth *the formes of all words,* which consist, & are compounded of them; in the same maner to enquire *the forme* of a Lyon, of an Oake, of Gold: Nay of Water, of Aire, is a vaine pursuit: But to enquire *the formes* of Sence, of voluntary Motion, of Vegetation, of Colours, of Grauitie and Leuitie, of Densitie, of Tenuitie, of Heate, of Cold, & al other Natures and qualities, which like an *Alphabet* are not many, & of which the essences (vpheld by Matter) of all creatures do consist: To enquire I say *the true formes* of these, is that part of METAPHYSICKE, which we now define of. (2G3v)

Underpinning this argument is the familiar metaphor of the world as a book or text,[3] but Bacon's analogy between the intelligibility of the world and the intelligibility of a text—his idea that not only are forms the units of intelligibility of the world, but they are also written in an alphabet waiting to be deciphered—seems to anticipate a dispersal of the classical and medieval analytic of forms into a Lucretian atomism, and asserts that the natural philosopher, like the linguist, ought to start by enumerating and describing the elementary forms underlying and constituting more complex ones.[4]

If the forms to be investigated seem to elude the inquirer, this difficulty is due to the complexity of the relationship between forms and what they are forms of, or what they are "upheld" by—that is, matter. The conceptualization of this relationship constitutes one of the main threads of the history of Western thought, and Bacon recognizes it as the crucial question on which the success or failure of the entire philosophical enterprise depends. According to Bacon, it is the aloofness of Plato's attempt to imagine forms or ideas as extricable from their material determinations, that upends his philosophical project:

> But it is manifest, that *Plato* in his opinion of *Ideas,* as one that had a wit of eleuation scituate as vpon a Cliffe, did descry, *that formes were the true obiect of knowledge;* but lost the reall fruite of his opinion by considering of formes, as absolutely abstracted from Matter, & not confined and determined by Matter. (2G3r)

By insisting that forms and matter cannot be understood apart from each other—and that rather than determining matter, forms are in fact themselves bound up and determined by it—Bacon not only turns against Plato, but also articulates a departure from the Aristotelian tradition.[5] Bacon's emphasis on matter as not only an underlying but also a determining factor would later compel Marx's attention: he thought Bacon was "the real founder of English materialism and all modern experimental science," adding that in his work "matter smiled at man with a poetical sensuous brightness," since Bacon had not yet reduced the sensuousness of the physical world to geometrical abstractions.[6] But Marx's own elated vision of the "poetical sensuous brightness" (or "luster") with which matter "smiles" at the observer[7] also recalls Bacon's rapturous discussion, in his account of First Philosophy, of the analogies among the principles of the various "partitions of knowledge" – analogies that seem to challenge a deterministic understanding of the matter-form relationship. The correspondences among the various forms of human creativity, and their correspondences with the phenomena of the natural world, prove them all to be identical:

> Is not the Trope of Musicke, to auoyde or slyde from the close or Cadence, common with the Trope of Rhetoricke of deceyuing expectation? Is not the delight of the Quavering vppon a stoppe in Musicke the same with playing of Light vppon the water? – *Splendet tremulo sub Lumine Pontus.* (2F1v–2F2r)

Taken from book 7 of the *Aeneid,* the Latin that closes Bacon's carefully wrought sequence of parallel questions does more than merely restate the preceding phrase – although it also does that. In this instance of Baconian analogical argument, a particular modulation of light in nature is described as analogous to a particular modulation of sound in music, and then we are presented with an instance of the analogous modulation of language in poetry. Virgil's phrase does not merely describe a natural effect, but at the same time also captures and reproduces it in its own, textual and acoustic, medium, thus embodying the analogy and exemplifying how poetry, like music, and like the sea, can directly reflect and project the light of sensuous experience.[8]

Baconian analogy is a formal similarity, a sameness of certain aspects of various materially different entities, a sameness in their modulation, shaping, making.[9] How poetry in particular is capable of doing what Bacon's example shows it does – that is, how it creates a sensuous, aesthetic effect – is, of course, a question that the formal analysis of literature is supposed to be asking, as an inquiry into what is specifically literary about literary works.[10] In poetic or rhetorical contexts, Bacon uses the word "form" to refer to style and *elocutio,* as well as genre. So in his account of the effects of the rediscovery of ancient authors, Bacon writes about the "delight" the moderns were taking

> in their manner of Stile and Phrase, and an admiration of that kinde of writing; which was much furthered & precipitated

> by the enmity...against the Schoole-men:...whose Writings were altogether in a differing Stile and fourme, taking libertie to coyne and frame new tearms of Art...without regard to the purenesse, pleasantnesse, and (as I may call it) lawfulnesse of the Phrase or word. (E3r)

Here, "form" means the choice of words, the intricacies of expression—in short, the manner of making. Later, in his account of historiography, Bacon introduces a different usage when he mentions

> a forme of Writing, which some graue and wise men haue vsed, containing a scattered History of those actions, which they haue thought worthy of memorie, with politic discourse and observation thereupon. (2D2v–2D3r)

Such books—"rvminated history," i.e., historical commentaries like those of Machiavelli's on Livy—he calls "Bookes of policie" rather than history proper, because

> it is the true office of History to represent the euents themselues... and to leaue the obseruations, and conclusions thereupon, to the liberty and facultie of euery mans iudgment. (2D3r)

The mixing of narrative with reflection on the narrative thus defines a particular kind or form of writing (books of policy), a group of texts with a shared purpose and shared characteristics—in short, a genre.

These notions of "form" as a term referring to aspects of texts—as style or as structure—still haunt our own literary-critical vocabulary. Like the metaphysical notion of form, they denote the underlying logic and ordered disposition of matter. What disrupts the seeming continuity between literary and metaphysical forms is precisely the difference in the nature of their matter, the matter they form or inform—which is not surprising, given that the literary and metaphysical uses of the term derive from different classical notions. But trying to bring the metaphysical concept of form to bear on the rhetorical or literary seems to us an illuminating move. Such conceptual violence, which exploits what is effectively a homonymy, enables a rethinking of the very "matter" of literature itself: of what it is as well as what it does, and how it does it.

Bacon's discussion of First Philosophy and Metaphysics in *The Advancement of Learning* follows hard upon his brief treatment of poesy, which he finds, of the three parts of "Man's Understanding," the one with "no deficience. For being as a plant that commeth of the lust of the earth, without a formall seede, it hath sprung vp, and spread abroad, more than any other kinde" (2E3v). The perfection and proliferation of poesy have to do with the fact that it is "extreamely licensed: and doth truly referre to the Imagination: which beeing not tyed to the Lawes of Matter; may at pleasure ioyne that which Nature hath seuered: & seuer that which Nature hath ioyned" (2E1v). The "matter" of literature here is the *res* that are represented through the *verba* – or, as Sir Philip Sidney explains the relationship between the Englished pair of terms, requiring a closer relationship between them, "matter to be expressed by words, and words to express the matter."[11] Bacon's understanding of the relationship between form and matter changes rather radically, however, when he turns his attention from poesy to the natural world and metaphysics. Whereas in poesy, he found a realm unconstrained by matter, a realm of writing that may consist, presumably, of pure forms; in metaphysics and in the study of nature, he stresses the interdependence of form and matter – and the matter that is opposed to form in metaphysics is *materia*. If we now transfer this metaphysical binary of matter and form, and specifically, of tangible matter and form, to literature, we conceive of literature as a material product, as a thing of the physical world, and its matter as the materials of which it is made: paper and parchment, glue and ink – that is, the *materia* by which literary forms are constrained.

As David Kastan puts it, "matter is both conceptual and artefactual."[12] The two versions of the matter-form relationship, with two kinds of matter upholding and confining their respective form, reflect the dual nature of writing and the dual nature of literature as both an imaginary and a material object, and the two versions of writing thus constituted are the objects, respectively, of formalist criticism and of textual-materialist scholarship. The traditions and practices of literary studies may at first sight suggest that these two perspectives on literature are complementary – i.e., that as critics and scholars, we can consider a literary work from either perspective, but cannot see it both ways at the same time. This dual nature of the text/book is by no means a necessary or inevitable given; rather, it is the result of abstraction and idealization. As Leah Price has suggested, "the book's Janus-faced potential" – manifested in its conflicting medieval etymologies, as a word that was understood to come either from the word for the bark on which texts were written, or from the verb "liberare," "to liberate" – is to a large extent produced by an ideological investment in their opposition.[13] It is the result of the efforts of "text-lovers" to distinguish themselves from "book-lovers," as Price puts it, or, in other words, the outcome of the very insistence that an attention to the ideal object should either block out, or be blocked out by, an attention to the thing.

Bacon may provide a way to resolve this conventional divide within our discipline. Once we regard literature's duality not as a simple opposition between matter and form, or between materialism and idealism, but rather as a duality constituted by two distinct types of matter, each with its own formal determinations and ramifications, the two natures of literature and the two disciplinary approaches they inspire may turn out to be conceptually compatible after all. The concept of "form" would then mediate between the two natures of literature – that is, between literature as a textual (or imaginary) and as a physical object.

DISCIPLINES AND THE STUDY OF FORMS

Characterized by Marjorie Levinson as more of a "movement than a theory or method," the new formalism calls for a shift in focus from the content of a given work to its form: to the structures in which that content is produced and contained, and through which it is given meaning.[14] Though by no means a unified approach, its proponents seem to share a sense of urgency, as well as the belief that only a return to form will restore what the discipline is missing – be it an appreciation of the aesthetic, the recognition that not all "texts" are created equal or read the same way, or even (we might say especially) the uniqueness and distinctness of literary studies itself.[15]

This case is made, frequently, by invoking such aphoristic statements as Roland Barthes's "a little formalism turns one away from History, but...a lot brings one back to it,"[16] William Empson's "a profound enough criticism could extract an entire cultural history from a simple lyric,"[17] or Theodor Adorno's "the unsolved antagonisms of reality return in art-works as immanent problems of form."[18] Although the very form of these claims, the pointedly paradoxical aphorism, depends on the immediately recognizable binary opposition between history and form, or between reality and literature, the claims themselves are now deployed to signal the logical compatibility of an attention to form with historical inquiry. These sound bites of "theory" (made portable by being extracted from their contexts) are used to suggest that the division between formalist and historicist critical practices has never been particularly deep or clear-cut, and, at the same time, to sound a call to arms. The task these pointed statements urge us to perform is the work of connecting the two poles of a binary, while asserting that this work has somehow already been done; which is to say that the project of connecting the two poles of the binary will be completed when we no longer consider these aphorisms neatly paradoxical. As Geoffrey Hartman suggested in a seminal essay, the sharp, pointed, epigrammatic style of the aphoristic observation works by pretending "as if truth were here or there, as if life could be localized, as if revelation were a property.... Pointing is to encapsule something.... It is to overobjectify, to overformalize."[19] The knowingness of these aphoristic statements registers an anxiety originating in the context of their circulation in journals and essay collections on English literature, and reflects the tensions of the discipline.

Schematic accounts of a field are less likely to be neutral depictions of a state of affairs than polemical interventions into it. The organizing binary of history versus form, as articulated in emblematic skirmishes like Trotsky's indictment of the Russian formalists or the storied exchange between Cleanth Brooks and Douglas Bush, has always been used strategically to assert priorities and positions in the study of literature. One of the more surprising features of new versions of formalism, however, is their apparent avoidance of engaging in such conflicts and contradictions. Not only do the various overviews of new and historical formalist criticism insist on the supplementary nature of their intervention, and their unwillingness to "replace other critical approaches to Renaissance literature with the various formalisms they advocate,"[20] but they also tend to present this intervention as an update of, or a return to, earlier positions that admitted and theorized the interplay between the two poles of the binary. The work of Raymond Williams and Fredric Jameson, as well as of the 1980s New Historicists, the Russian formalists, and even the New Critics, has been referred to as signposts toward which the enterprise of literary studies ought to retrace its steps in search for a formal instruction – all without abandoning the insights gained through cultural studies. Simultaneously iconoclastic and traditional, brand new and very old, new formalisms often turn out to be something we all already know how to do and, apparently, have been doing all along.[21]

The conciliatory rhetoric that envelops such historical formalisms could betoken a larger, and long-standing, worry about the dissolution of the specificity and identity of the discipline, of the profession, or of whatever else we may want to call the academic study of literature. The present moment in literary studies seems, in fact, to be characterized less by explicit conflicts among various modes of critical practice than by all of us minding our own business, quietly worrying about how to justify our continued existence in a rapidly changing environment. How are we to reconcile the institutional requirement that we read and teach literary texts with our wide-ranging interests in the worlds of the past? As several critics have observed, the current attention to form seems to be motivated at least in part by the hope that it will reconsolidate a specific expertise in which the discipline can be anchored – one which the discipline can use, moreover, to help balance the mounting deficit it has supposedly built up in interdisciplinary exchange.[22] For such a balancing act to be successful, a mode of analysis specific to literary scholarship needs to be imagined both as applicable to textual objects other than strictly literary ones, and as productive in ways other disciplines will recognize as useful.

New formalist approaches in early modern literary studies are especially concerned with the relationship between the disciplines of history and literary scholarship, and seek to identify the specific ways in which forms relate to history or historical reality, sometimes revising and expanding the notion of form to include not only the patterning of literary artifacts but also the patterns that organize social and cultural existence.[23] Other scholars seek to define the interdisciplinary work of formalism while focusing on specifically literary forms. Stephen Cohen suggests we begin to think about form in terms of "mediation" – acknowledging "the various roles that form may play in the historical study of literature" without "reduc[ing]" that relationship to one of "reflection," allowing "instead for mutual influence and adjustment." Cohen's emphasis is on the ideological work and significance of forms as practices, which frame and interpret the text for its audience by providing it with "a socially produced meaning or function…to be reproduced, contested, or appropriated."[24] This active, socialized understanding of form as a knowable, shaping force underpins much recent formalist work that seeks to study the entanglement of literature in life.[25]

One of the things with which literature is entangled, of course, is matter – specifically, reading matter. Parallel with the gradual reemergence of formalism in Renaissance scholarship,[26] another area of study promised to bridge the divide that Paul de Man sarcastically described as separating "the internal law and order of literature" and its "foreign affairs" or "external politics"[27] – namely, book history, also known as the study of the material text. These two approaches (the new formalisms on the one hand, and book history on the other) appear to fall precisely on the two sides of the internal-external divide. The former is a trend within literary studies, a not-so-new approach to the defining object of the discipline: the literary work, studied at departments of literature. The latter is a field of study making an increasingly clear claim on a separate disciplinary identity. It, too, has a specific object of study, the material book. In some of its foundational texts, book history has been presented as an approach that is, because of its rigorous focus on the matter of reading, on the material text, diametrically opposed to formalist criticism, which is considered as dealing with supposedly abstract, purely semiotic entities.[28] But beyond their radical dissimilarity and complementarity, striking convergences between the concepts in which the two approaches are couched suggest the possibility of their more deliberate conjunction.

The implications of the history of the book as a field of study for literary scholarship have repeatedly been expressed in language strikingly similar to that used by Cohen and other "new formalists," insisting on the role of "form" in mediating between text and its contexts: its production, reproduction, circulation, and reception. In fact, "form" turns out to be the central term not only of formalism but also of book history, along with "the basic assumption that form effects sense."[29] In their studies, which laid the foundations for the current proliferation of research in book history, Donald McKenzie and, building on him, Roger Chartier, effectively reappropriated the term "form" to mean the text's typography, layout, paper, binding, etc.—that is, "the forms of the representation of the text."[30] As Chartier has repeatedly suggested, for example, "forms produce meaning and…a text, stable in its letter, is invested with a new meaning and status when the mechanisms that make it available to interpretation change."[31] A rigorous attention to the structures of circulation allows us to restore historical specificity to the works by reconstructing "their conditions of possibility and intelligibility."[32]

The division between new formalists and book historians might be seen as a function of their attention to the two types of Baconian matter determining literary form: new formalists to the *res* and book historians to the *materia* that shape and are shaped by the forms of writing. And it is this shared attention to form, directed at the two matters of literature, that enables a shared agenda of crossing disciplinary boundaries and bridging methodological divides. While Cohen argued that form should be understood as a mediating agent in the historical study of literature, David Kastan influentially claimed that the history of the book provides "a possible interface of literary studies and history."[33] The shared aim suggests the parallel nature of the two enterprises; at the same time, their radically different methodologies (functions of a different form-matter conjunction) hold the promise of a fruitful and mutually beneficial exchange.[34] As Alexandra Gillespie argued in her excellent survey of the state of the field,[35] the history of the book has a tendency to look "through" its purported object of study, and use it to make discoveries about the people using the books and their culture: to anchor meanings in the intentions and desires of historical agents. Gillespie suggests that this tendency can be corrected, and the study of the book as a material object redirected at the book itself, by learning from formal analysis—that is, precisely from the theoretically informed close reading practices advocated by the new formalists. Conversely, the historical relationships among various forms can also be studied through linking literary forms to their material texts. To use Hartman's example of the dominance of the pointed style in the seventeenth and eighteenth centuries, the function and the popularity of the sharp epigrammatic style (or, as Hartman puts it, "the point of the point") may be understood through a study of the social life of the short form in manuscript circulation and in printed anthologies of witty discourse, anchoring the form in material and social practices.[36]

The emphasis on form has in fact been enabling explorations attentive to both the *res* and the *materia* of writing from the start. As Gillespie has suggested, McKenzie's own work on Congreve, while the classic example of an essay in "the sociology of texts," is at the same time also an exemplary instance of a "formalist" reading of a material text – that is, a reading in which it is indeed the forms that effect the meaning, and in which intentions are discussed as in fact "internal to textual form" rather than as residing in some extra-textual reality.[37] And to offer an example from the opposite end of the apparent divide: long before the terms "new formalism" or "historical formalism" attained their present currency, in the introduction to his 1992 *Forms of Nationhood* Richard Helgerson wrote as follows: "My literary training may have made me a formalist, but I have tried, even when looking at literary texts, to be a historical formalist." Like more recent proponents of a renewed, historically and culturally attuned attention to form, Helgerson carefully distanced himself from a reductive understanding of "formalism" by denying "that certain forms have an intrinsic or universal meaning, an ineradicable aesthetic appeal":

> On the contrary, I assume that meanings and aesthetic affinities are historically established and historically maintained. They arise from the quite specific relations in which particular texts and forms are enmeshed at some particular time and place.[38]

This attention to the texts' embeddedness in their context also required an attention to the material book. Helgerson's understanding of "formal differences" includes differences not only in genre, but also in how writing appeared and circulated: as he emphatically states up front, *Forms of Nationhood* is about books "massive in size and scope," about the "discursive kinds embodied in the fat books younger Elizabethans wrote about England."[39] Although his focus on such works as Coke's *Reports* or Hakluyt's *Principal Navigations* is motivated by his interest in the discursive differences and political meanings of these works, the fact that around the turn of the century these discourses came to be codified in just such "fat books" is central to Helgerson's argument about the importance of this moment in the formation of English nationhood.

While the study of the material text and literary formalism have a long history of interaction and interference, the links between them have mostly been made at the level of practice, not of sustained and widely disseminated metacritical reflection. But it is striking how well their conjunction promises to address perceived limitations within each of these critical practices. The project of book history is often considered as a reductive and, from the point of view of literary reading, superficial (not to say tedious) exercise, one that uses the material book as evidence in uncovering the various agencies involved in the making and remaking of texts and their external and public effects. The new or historical formalism, on the other hand, attentive as it is to verbal structures, lacks a sophisticated and rigorously theorized interface through which to relate the formal to the historical and the material, and is thus open to the accusation that it is picking and choosing analogies and homologies at will.[40] Their combination promises a critical practice that provides the analysis of literary form with material and historical specificity, and the analysis of material form with literary traction. Literary texts subjected to the close reading that is still the hallmark of our discipline allow us perhaps more readily than any other resource to meditate on written (whether printed, manuscript, or otherwise inscribed) objects as the nonhuman actors of our histories – on agents that are in turn invested with agency through the social, cultural, and literary fictions they participate in.[41] While material forms clearly do effect meaning, we also need to ask how literary forms shape the perception and use of the medium, not only reflecting but also affecting the material form.[42] Such a practice refuses to distinguish sharply between literary and bibliographical form – to consider the study of the *res* and the *materia* of writing as separate branches of learning. Instead it links the literary with the bibliographical, verse with vellum, typology with typography, developing a more precise language of interface and influence.[43]

One early site for the development of such language was the study of genre, particularly within the fields of medieval and Renaissance literature. As we noted above, in 1992 Richard Helgerson was already arguing for an understanding of form that included not only genre but also how various kinds of books were presented in print. Genre continues to be a key concept for new formalist scholarship – indeed, the predominant (although by no means exclusive) concern of early modern work of "new formalist" or "historical formalist" bent has been with generic forms[44] – and it is here that once again a more precise vocabulary of interface becomes possible. Not only size and format, but also typography may serve as generic markers. So, too, may methods of circulation. Recent research on the book trade – on the specialization of individual booksellers, for example – has helped us to discern textual linkings and groupings obscured by later transmission. And although an attention to genre is fundamentally literary (poetical or rhetorical) in nature, it is also applicable and active outside the field of literature; after all, it is in the study of the early modern news market that the conditions and forms of circulation and the "content" of what is circulating have been most obviously and inseparably linked.[45]

In the remaining pages, we return to Bacon's *Advancement of Learning* as the object of a case study. Not one of Helgerson's "big books," Bacon's book is a materially modest quarto that employs the distinctive genre of the aphorism not only to argue for but also to perform a particular mode of intellectual exchange. In our attention to Bacon's aphoristic form, we further explore the key terms of analysis touched on above – namely form, matter, literature, and the literary – and highlight potential payoffs and pitfalls of that exchange for our discipline.

FORMING LITERATURE

The Twoo Bookes of Francis Bacon. Of the proficience and aduancement of Learning, diuine and humane is part of the outpouring of learned writing that marked the accession of James, and the most voluminous product of Bacon's extended campaign to advance himself through his learning and advice, offering his services as a propagandist and political adviser to the new king.[46] The text, addressed "To the King" on the title page and framed as an address to him throughout, opens with an extended compliment to James on the breadth of his knowledge: "there hath not beene since Christs time any King or temporall Monarch which hath ben so learned in all literature & erudition, diuine and humane" (A3v). It is James's "literature" that distinguishes him from both "the succession of the Emperours of Rome" and "the lines of *Fraunce, Spaine, England, Scotland,* and the rest" (A3v). For Bacon, as for his contemporaries, "literature" is an expansive rather than an exclusive category, and "literary history" still means "the general state of learning...described and represented from age to age" (2B3v), and thus the remembrance of past efforts at the advancement of learning. Works of imagination, on the other hand, would constitute a specific branch of learning, called "fained historie" or poesy, distinguished from other branches either by its matter (imaginary stories) or by its metrical form, or perhaps by both. The question of whether or not a work "counts" as literature is itself a relatively new one, emerging in the mid-to-late eighteenth century: it was around this time that the term "literature" ceased to refer to writing of all sorts, to letters, or (as with the Roman *litteratura*) to the state or quality of being lettered, and began instead to refer only to works of the imagination,[47] although the reorganization of the field of writing arguably begins earlier, and the elevation of the prestige of commercial plays has been discussed as part of the early modern invention of English literature.[48] This broad understanding of literature, of the arts of writing, arguably contributes to the mobility of literary – that is, textual – forms across different fields of study that would later be separated not only by their subject matter, but also by their formal features.

James was, of course, also a poet, and even authored "A treatise of the airt of Scottis poësie," but James's poetical works are – perhaps tactfully – left unmentioned in *The Advancement of Learning*. This does not, however, mean that Bacon neglected to refer to the king's writings – and to refer to his most recent work, the anonymously printed *Counter-blaste to Tobacco,* from which he paraphrases "one of your Maiesties owne most wise and Princely Maximes" early in the second book of *The Advancement* – a maxim concerning the origins of what we would now call social and cultural practices and institutions, which demands

> *that in all vsages, and Presidents, the Times be considered wherein they first beganne, which if they were weake, or ignorant, it derogateth from the Authoritie of the Vsage, and leaueth it for suspect.* (2A4v)

The maxim appears in italic—as do many other passages in the text—which marks it as notable, sententious material (fig. 1). This typographic feature points to a key formal feature of Bacon's project. The aphorism or maxim is Bacon's preferred form of articulation: a portable distillation of knowledge, a standalone insight isolated and abstracted from observation. As Bacon explains, the isolation of the aphorism makes its content (the observation) plainly visible, unobstructed by the facade of rhetorical architecture, and instead of giving a sense of satisfaction and closure, it encourages further investigation (2Q3r–v). The advantage of aphoristic writing is its versatility: it allows both for application in new contexts and for easy revision in the light of new experience. Bacon's *Novum Organum,* his attempt to lay down the foundations for the new science, will accordingly be written as a sequence of aphorisms.[49] By presenting the king as a source of aphoristic wisdom, the book establishes the legitimacy and authority of Bacon's own aphoristic method, even as it flatteringly parallels James with Solomon, the book's most frequently quoted authority.[50] And the true greatness of Solomon, whom both Bacon and James invoked as a model of wise authority, lies in his ability to bridge the gap between moral and natural philosophy. On the one hand, Solomon's political aphorisms, his "sentences pollitique" (3A3r), serve as models for the "wisedome touching negotiation or businesse" (2Z3v)—i.e., for prudent action in political affairs. But on the other hand, "Salomon became inabled, not onely to write those excellent Parables, or Aphorismes concerning diuine and morall philosophie; but also to compile a natural Historie of all verdor, from the cedar upon the Mountaine, to the mosse upon the wall,...and also of all things, that breath or move" (H3r).

For Bacon, the maxim or aphorism is the form that unifies all areas of learning: Solomon's wisdom takes sententious, aphoristic form in policy as well as in natural history, a form that enables the fluid circulation of insights, not only from one book or one context to another, but also, more generally, among fields and disciplines of study. The adaptability of the form to all contexts means that it becomes the vehicle of transfer among contexts, allowing the observations to be moved among various fields and disciplines, and thus allowing the analogical operation of different fields of study—different because of their subject matter, but analogous in their protocols of observation.

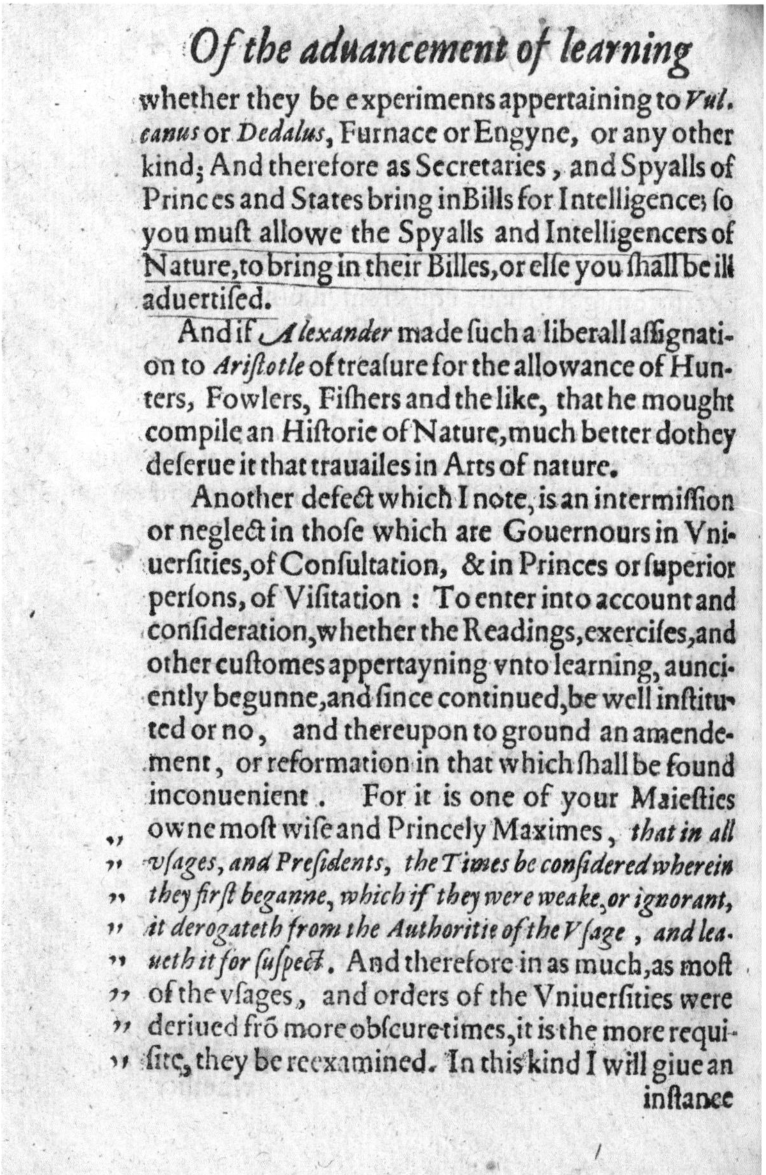

Of the aduancement of learning

whether they be experiments appertaining to *Vulcanus* or *Dedalus*, Furnace or Engyne, or any other kind; And therefore as Secretaries, and Spyalls of Princes and States bring in Bills for Intelligence; ſo you muſt allowe the Spyalls and Intelligencers of Nature, to bring in their Billes, or elſe you ſhall be ill aduertiſed.

And if *Alexander* made ſuch a liberall aſſignation to *Ariſtotle* of treaſure for the allowance of Hunters, Fowlers, Fiſhers and the like, that he mought compile an Hiſtorie of Nature, much better do they deſerue it that trauailes in Arts of nature.

Another defect which I note, is an intermiſſion or neglect in thoſe which are Gouernours in Vniuerſities, of Conſultation, & in Princes or ſuperior perſons, of Viſitation: To enter into account and conſideration, whether the Readings, exerciſes, and other cuſtomes appertayning vnto learning, auncientIy begunne, and ſince continued, be well inſtituted or no, and thereupon to ground an amendement, or reformation in that which ſhall be found inconuenient. For it is one of your Maieſties owne moſt wiſe and Princely Maximes, *that in all vſages, and Preſidents, the Times be conſidered wherein they firſt beganne, which if they were weake, or ignorant, it derogateth from the Authoritie of the Vſage, and leaueth it for ſuſpect.* And therefore in as much, as moſt of the vſages, and orders of the Vniuerſities were deriued frō more obſcure times, it is the more requiſite, they be reexamined. In this kind I will giue an

inſtance

Fig. 1. Francis Bacon, *The Twoo Bookes of Francis Bacon. Of the proficience and aduancement of Learning* (London, 1605), 2A4v. Cambridge University Library Rare Books, LE 7.45, the copy of Isaac Dorislaus

As Solomon's example shows, the knowledge transfer between political observation and the study of nature is of particular importance here. In an earlier tract addressed to the king about the projected union of the Kingdoms, Bacon argued that there is "a great affinity and consent between the rules of nature, and the true rules of policy."[51] That the true laws of nature, and wisdom in matters of the state of nature, are of practical political application is, in Julian Martin's view, a crucial part of the Baconian idea that "knowledge is power."[52] But when we examine the genetics of his thought, we may observe Bacon himself proceeding in the opposite direction, relying on his political education and political erudition in approaching nature and natural philosophy.[53] Lisa Jardine and Alan Stewart have argued that the intelligence-gathering work performed in his youth informed Bacon's later work practices: in other words, his conception of the methodology of the study of nature was defined by the methodologies of political service.[54] Attention to the historical and material contexts of the Baconian aphorism offers an important example of the genres and textual technologies of political analysis modeling and informing Bacon's natural philosophy.[55]

Alongside Solomon's own moral and political wisdom, a whole body of "sentences pollitique" quoted in the *Advancement of Learning* points us in the direction of a distinctly nonbiblical source of aphoristic political learning: the late-sixteenth-century neohumanist historical and political scholarship Bacon was in close contact with, and a practitioner of, in the 1590s when he was working for Essex.[56] Machiavelli's *Prince* and *Discorsi* were canonical texts of this tradition, which provided much of the ammunition for collections of political maxims or aphorisms that codified political prudence in a flexible form, aimed at future application. Late-sixteenth- and early seventeenth-century political writing in manuscript and increasingly also in print is dominated by collections of political maxims that depended on Machiavelli's writings as sources and models for experience-based political observations. Examples include not only Gentillet's *Anti-Machiavelli* and Lipsius's *Six Books of Politics,* but also Robert Dallington's *Aphorismes Civill and Militarie,* dedicated (in manuscript) to Prince Henry, and (in print) to Prince Charles,[57] as well as the late-sixteenth-century *Obseruations Political and Civill,* compiled by one T.B., dedicated to the Privy Councillor Lord North, and later published by John Milton as Raleigh's *Cabinet-Council* (fig. 2). Bacon's close

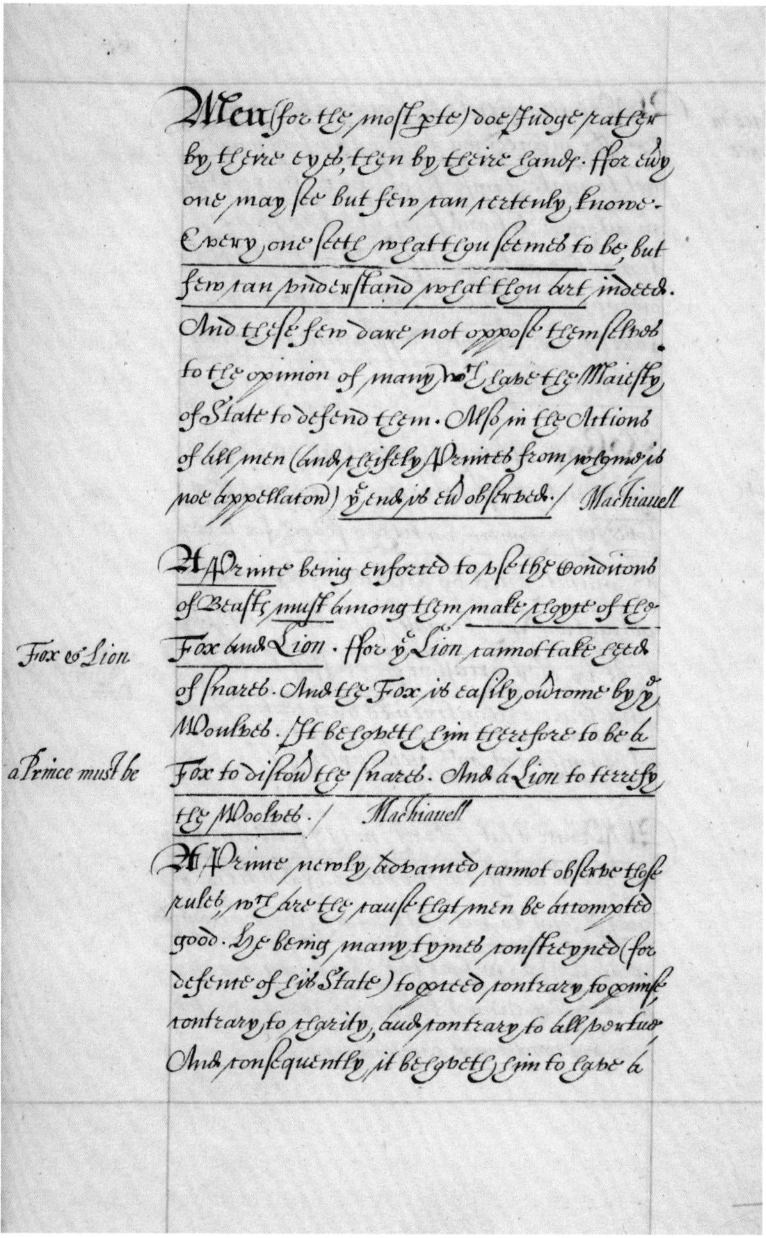

Men (for the most parte) doe Judge rather
by theire eyes, then by theire handes. ffor every
one may see but few can certenly knowe.
Every one seeth what thou seemest to be, but
few can understand what thou art indeed.
And these few dare not oppose themselves
to the opinion of many wch have the Maiesty
of State to defend them. Also in the Actions
of all men (and cheifely Princes from whome is
noe appellation) ye end is ever observed./ Machiavell

A Prince being enforced to use the Conditions
of Beastes, must among them make choyce of the
Fox & Lion — Fox and Lion. ffor ye Lion cannot take heed
of snares. And the Fox is easily overcome by ye
Woulves. It behoveth him therefore to be a
a Prince must be — Fox to discover the snares. And a Lion to terrefy
the Woolves./ Machiavell

A Prince newly advanced cannot observe those
rules, wch are the cause that men be accompted
good. He being many tymes constreyned (for
defence of his State) to proceed contrary to promise,
contrary to charity, and contrary to all vertue.
And consequently it behoveth him to have a

Fig. 2. T.B., *Obseruations Political and Civill* (ca. 1596–1600), f. 65v. Huntington Library, San Marino, California, HM EL 1174

familiarity with the aphoristic mode of political advice clearly informs all of his writing, as indicated already by his first published work, the 1597 *Essays,* whose pragmatic guidance in various aspects of a courtly, political life is typographically divided into short, standalone observations (fig. 3).[58] In the *Advancement of Learning* Bacon specifically singles out Machiavelli for praise – as he puts it, for writing "what men doe and not what they ought to do" (2V4r) – that is, for instituting the mode of experiential, observation-based study of the practice of politics that was conducted through such collections of aphorisms. And in what is his most emphatic plea for the analogical structure of all fields of knowledge – directly preceding the passage, quoted early in our essay, about the analogies of sensuous perception in various media – he identifies him as the exemplary thinker in the field of civil science, someone whose work and methodology can serve as a model for the natural sciences as well: "Is not the ground which *Machiavill* wisely and largely discourseth concerning Gouernments, That the way to establish and preserve them, is to reduce them *ad Principia:* a rule in Religion and Nature, aswell as in Ciuill administration?" (2F1v)

While the textual form of Bacon's aphorisms illuminates their intellectual ramifications, their material form reveals the textual culture and the technologies that uphold them. The book's deployment of the aphoristic insights of Machiavelli, alongside marked or unacknowledged quotations from Tacitus, Commines, and other key sources of the maxim-based discourse about the reason of state,[59] are indications of the contents of Bacon's own commonplace books. In the hands of the book's early users, *The Advancement of Learning* was itself read for aphoristic material to be put to use elsewhere. One early reader of *The Advancement of Learning* was the Dutch historian Isaac Dorislaus, who is most famous for having been forbidden to continue to lecture at Cambridge after delivering just two lectures on Tacitus. The fame of his advocacy of republicanism and regicide accompanied him through the rest of his life: in 1649 he was appointed as counsel to the prosecution in the trial of Charles I, and he was murdered by a group of English Royalists while on a diplomatic mission in The Hague in May 1649.[60] In his copy of *The Advancement,* Dorislaus marked Bacon's distillation of James's suggestion into a maxim (the royal prose being by no means as clear, concise, and

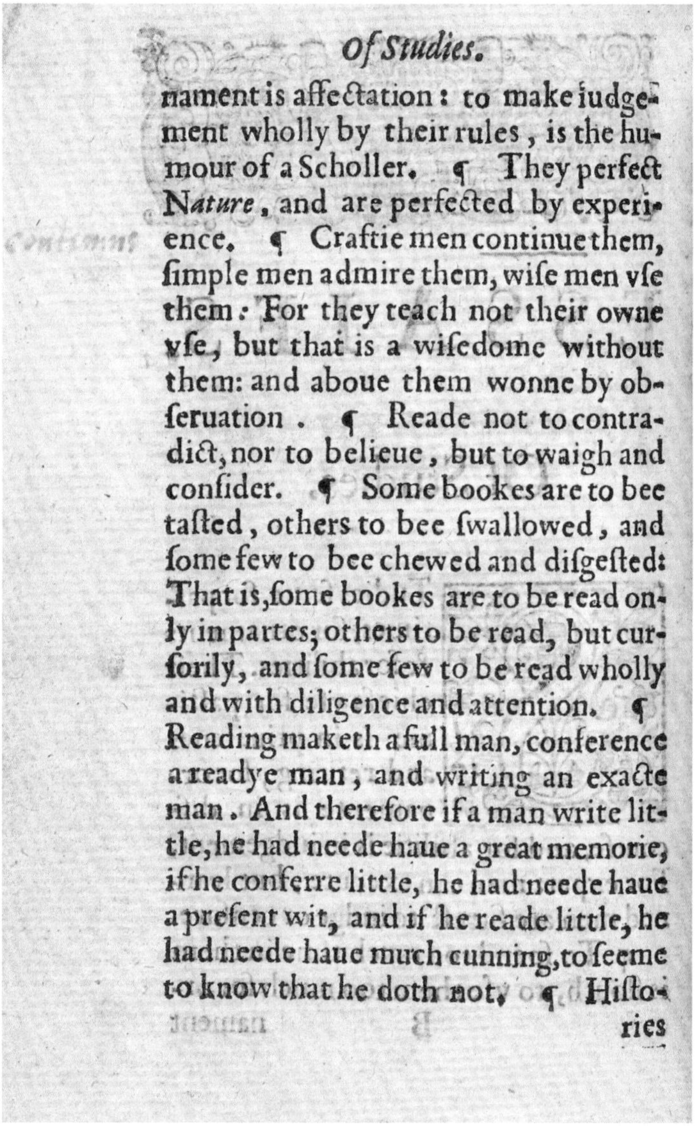

Of Studies.

nament is affectation: to make iudgement wholly by their rules, is the humour of a Scholler. ¶ They perfect *Nature*, and are perfected by experience. ¶ Craftie men continue them, ſimple men admire them, wiſe men vſe them: For they teach not their owne vſe, but that is a wiſedome without them: and aboue them wonne by obſeruation. ¶ Reade not to contradict, nor to belieue, but to waigh and conſider. ¶ Some bookes are to bee taſted, others to bee ſwallowed, and ſome few to bee chewed and diſgeſted: That is, ſome bookes are to be read only in partes; others to be read, but curſorily, and ſome few to be read wholly and with diligence and attention. ¶ Reading maketh a full man, conference a readye man, and writing an exacte man. And therefore if a man write little, he had neede haue a great memorie, if he conferre little, he had neede haue a preſent wit, and if he reade little, he had neede haue much cunning, to ſeeme to know that he doth not. ¶ Hiſto-

ries

Fig. 3. Francis Bacon, *Essayes. Religious Meditations. Places of perswasion and disswasion* (London, 1597), B1v. Beinecke Rare Book and Manuscript Library, Yale University, Eliz 6

than my writings, if choise may be had in so worthlesse things. This also happeneth vnto me,that where I seeke my selfe,I finde not my selfe : and I finde my selfe more by chaunce, than by the search of mine owne judgement. I shall perhappes have cast-forth some suttletie in writing, happily dull and harsh for another, but smoothe and curious for my selfe.Let vs leave all these complements and quaintnesse. That is spoken by every man, according to his owne strength. I have so lost it, that I wot not what I would have saide, and strangers have sometimes found it before me. Had I alwaies a razor about me, where that happeneth, I should cleane raze my selfe out. Fortune may at some other time make the light thereof appeare brighter vnto me, than that of mid-day, and will make mee wonder at mine owne faltring or sticking in the myre.

The eleuenth Chapter.

Of Prognostications.

As touching Oracles it is very certaine, that long before the comming of our Sauiour *Iesus Christ*, they had begunne to loose their credit : for we see that *Cicero* laboureth to finde the cause of their declination : And these be his words : *Cur isto modo iam oracula Delphis non eduntur non modo nostra ætate, sed iamdiu, vt nihil possit esse contemptius? Why in like sorte are not Oracles now vttered, not onely in our times, but a good while since, so as now nothing can be more contemptible?* But as for other prognostikes, that were drawne from the anatomie of beasts in sacrifices, to which *Plato* doth in some sorte ascribe the naturall constitution of the internall members of them, of the scraping of chickins, of the flight of birds, *Aues quasdam rerum augurandarum causas natas esse putamus. We are of opinion, certaine birdes were even bred to prognosticate some things of thunders, of turnings aud back-recourse of rivers. Multa cernunt aruspices: multa augures prouident: multa oraculis declarantur: multa vaticinationibus: multa somnijs: multa portentis. Soothsayers see much: bird-prophets fore-see as much; much is foretold by Oracles; much by prophesies; much by dreames; much by portentuous signes*, and others, vpon which antiquitie grounded most of their enterprises, as well publike as private : our religion hath abolished them. And albeit there remaine yet amongst vs some meanes of divination in the starres, in spirits, in shapes of the body, in dreames, and elsewhere a notable example of the mad and fond curiositie of our nature, ammusing it selfe to preoccupate future things, as if it had not enough to doe to digest the present.

Cic.diuin.lib.2

——cur hanc tibi rector Olympi
Sollicitis visum mortalibus addere curam,
Noscant venturas vt dira per omnia clades?
Sit subitum quodcunque paras, sit cæca futuri
Mens hominum fati, liceat sperare timenti.
Why pleas'd it thee, thou ruler of the spheares,
To adde this care to mortalls care-clog'd minde,
That they their miserie know, ere it appeares?
Let thy drifts sodaine come; let men be blinde
T'wards future fate: oh let him hope that feares.

Lucan.lib.2 4.

Ne vtile quidem est scire quid futurum sit: Miserum est enim nihil proficientem angi. It is not so much as profitable for vs, to know what is to come, for it is a miserable thing, a man should fret and be vexed, and doe no good. Yet is it of much lesse authoritie, loe here wherefore the example of *Francis Marquis* of *Saluzzo* hath seemed remarkeable vnto me: who being Lieutenant Generall vnto *Francis* our King, and over all his forces, which hee then had beyond the Mountaines in *Italie*, a man highly favoured in all our court, and otherwise infinitly beholding to the King for his owne Marquisate, which his brother had forfeited : and having no occasion to doe it, yea and his minde and affections contradicting the same, suffered himselfe to be frighted and deluded (as it hath since been manifestly prooved) by the fond prognostications, which then throughout all *Europe* were given out to the advantage of the

pointed as the Baconian paraphrase), using the period's standard markers of sententious passages: gnomic points, i.e., double inverted commas, a marker well established in continental print by the late sixteenth century that came to prominence in English vernacular print around the turn of the seventeenth century (see fig. 1).[61] This is the only passage in the book Dorislaus highlights with this sign, which originated in medieval manuscript culture, was transferred to print by Aldus Manutius, and (as the mark of passages deserving to be copied out into a commonplace book) served as the tool for reconverting print into manuscript, for exporting passages from one text and context into another. The marks in Dorislaus's copy indicate the aphorism's life and mobility in the technology of early modern note-taking, of which the typography, the book's use of italic to signal aphorisms, is a material part. Characteristically, italic was used to highlight aphorisms in Florio's translation of Montaigne's *Essais* – a feature not found in the early French editions, thus reflecting a reading of Montaigne particularly attentive to the aphoristic structure of reflection and advice,[62] and obliging readers who want to *not-read* the book to use it while avoiding its linear intentions (fig. 4).[63] Bacon's *Novum Organum,* the central, theoretical part of the *Instauratio magna,* follows a different pattern: instead of presenting aphorisms woven into essays – that is, continuous, thematically connected groupings – it presents them as an ordered series of distinct units, numbered for easier navigation. While the highlighting of individual aphorisms embedded in continuous texts is a register of the technologies of their manipulation, the typography of the collection of aphorisms reveals a formal and intellectual connection to collections of observation-based political aphorisms, like the collection by Guicciardini best known as the *Ricordi,* which were clearly intended as manuals for political action (figs. 5 and 6). The Baconian assertion that both the truth and utility of things are inherent in their objective reality[64] finds an anticipation in the realm of political interpretation, where "what men doe" offers both the truth of politics and the only kind of useful guidance to the conduct of political activity.

Fig. 4. Michel de Montaigne, *The Essayes; or, Morall, Politike and millitarie Discourses of Lo: Michaell de Montaigne* (London, 1603), C4r. Beinecke Rare Book and Manuscript Library, Yale University, 1977 +54

48 Nouum Organum. LIB. I.

cient, aut regunt; Ita & instrumenta Mentis, Intellectui aut ſuggerunt, aut cauent.

III.

SCientia & Potentia humana in idem coincidunt, quia ignoratio cauſæ destituit effectum. Natura enim non niſi parendo vincitur: Et quod in Contemplatione, instar cauſæ eſt; Id in Operatione, instar Regulæ eſt.

IV.

AD opera nil aliud poteſt Homo, quàm vt corpora naturalia admoueat, & amoueat: reliqua, Natura intùs tranſigit.

V.

SOlent ſe immiſcere Naturæ (quoad Opera) Mechanicus, Mathematicus, Medicus, Alchymiſta, & Magus: ſed omnes (vt nunc ſunt res) conatu leui, ſucceſſu tenui.

VI.

INſanum quiddam eſſet, & in ſe contrarium, exiſtimare ea, quæ adhuc nunquàm facta ſunt, fieri poſſe, niſi per modos adhuc nunquàm tentatos.

VII.

GEnerationes Mentis & Manûs numeroſæ admodùm videntur in libris, & Opificijs. Sed omnis iſta varietas ſita eſt in ſubtilitate eximiâ, & deriuationi-

LIB. I. Nouum Organum. 49

tionibus paucarum rerum, quæ innotuerunt; non in numero Axiomatum.

VIII.

ETiam Opera, quæ iam inuenta ſunt, Caſui debentur, & Experientiæ, magìs quàm Scientijs: Scientiæ enim, quas nunc habemus, nihil aliud ſunt quàm quædam Concinnationes rerum anteà inuentarum; non modi inueniendi, aut deſignationes nouorum Operum.

IX.

CAuſa verò & radix ferè omnium malorum in Scientijs ea vna eſt; quòd dum Mentis humanæ vires falſò miramur & extollimus, vera eius auxilia non quæramus.

X.

SVbtilitas Naturæ ſubtilitatem Senſûs & Intellectûs multis partibus ſuperat; vt pulchræ illæ meditationes, & ſpeculationes humanæ, & Cauſationes, res male-ſana ſint, niſi quòd non adſit, qui aduertat.

XI.

SIcut Scientiæ, quæ nunc habentur, inutiles ſunt ad inuentionem Operum: Ita & Logica quæ nunc habetur, inutilis eſt ad inuentionem Scientiarum.

XII.

LOgica, quæ in vſu eſt, ad errores (qui in notionibus vulgaribus fundantur) ſtabiliendos & figendos

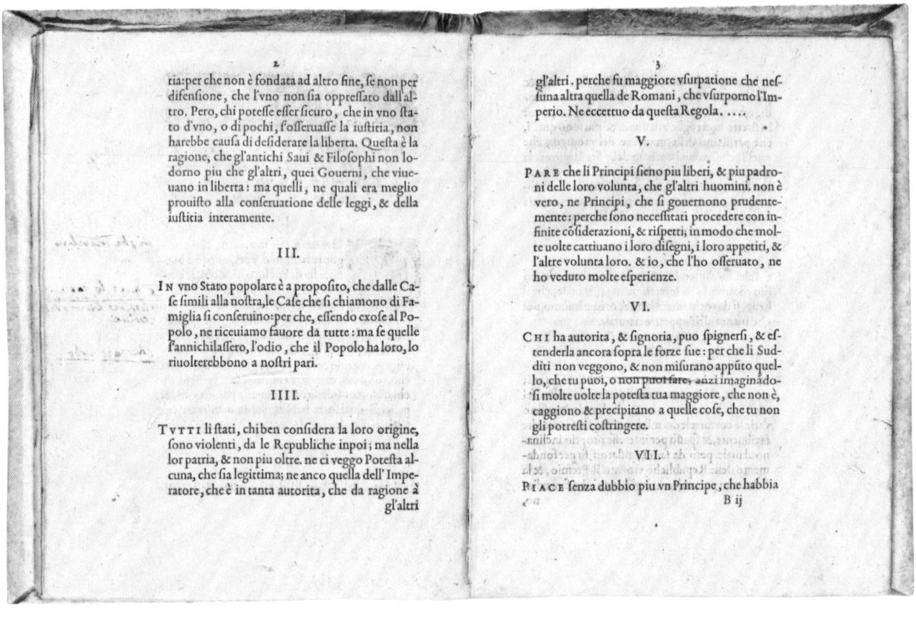

2

tia: per che non è fondata ad altro fine, ſe non per difenſione, che l'vno non ſia oppreſſato dall'altro. Pero, chi poteſſe eſſer ſicuro, che in vno ſtato d'vno, o di pochi, ſ'oſſeruaſſe la iuſtitia, non harebbe cauſa di deſiderare la liberta. Queſta è la ragione, che gl'antichi Saui & Filoſophi non lodorno piu che gl'altri, quei Gouerni, che viueuano in liberta: ma quelli, ne quali era meglio prouiſto alla conſeruatione delle leggi, & della iuſtitia interamente.

III.

IN vno Stato popolare è a propoſito, che dalle Caſe ſimili alla noſtra, le Caſe che ſi chiamono di Famiglia ſi conſeruino: per che, eſſendo exoſe al Popolo, ne riceuiamo fauore da tutte: ma ſe quelle ſ'annichilaſſero, l'odio, che il Popolo ha loro, lo riuolterebbono a noſtri pari.

IIII.

TVTTI li ſtati, chi ben conſidera la loro origine, ſono violenti, da le Republiche inpoi; ma nella lor patria, & non piu oltre. ne ci veggo Poteſta alcuna, che ſia legittima; ne anco quella dell' Imperatore, che è in tanta autorita, che da ragione à gl'altri

3

gl'altri. perche fu maggiore vſurpatione che neſſuna altra quella de Romani, che vſurporno l'Imperio. Ne eccettuo da queſta Regola. . . .

V.

PARE che li Principi ſieno piu liberi, & piu padroni delle loro volunta, che gl'altri huomini. non è vero, ne Principi, che ſi gouernono prudentemente: perche ſono neceſſitati procedere con infinite cõſiderazioni, & riſpetti; in modo che molte uolte cattiuano i loro diſegni, i loro appetiti, & l'altre volunta loro. & io, che l'ho oſſeruato, ne ho veduto molte eſperienze.

VI.

CHI ha autorita, & ſignoria, puo ſpignerſi, & eſtenderla ancora ſopra le forze ſue: per che li Sudditi non veggono, & non miſurano appũto quello, che tu puoi, o non puoi fare, anzi imaginãdoſi molte uolte la poteſta tua maggiore, che non è, caggiono & precipitano a quelle coſe, che tu non gli potreſti coſtringere.

VII.

PIACE ſenza dubbio piu vn Principe, che habbia

B ij

The typography and the manuscript markers establish the historical context, connotations, and genealogies of the Baconian aphorism – help us to trace it, in other words, to its "*vsages, and Presidents*." Bacon's intense reliance on the humanist technology and culture of the commonplace book throughout his career, including in his works on natural philosophy, is well documented.[65] But as we have argued here, rather than being a manifestation of a general late-humanist practice, *The Advancement of Learning* is shaped by its specialized application in political reading and note-taking.[66] Bacon's conception of scientific research proceeding through the formulation of distinct, self-contained insights that can be reconfigured according to our evolving understanding of the observed phenomena is informed by the culture of action-oriented political reading and writing.[67] The Baconian interpretation of the book of nature is enabled by the experience of political note-taking.

The political aphorism Bacon attributes to James points to the sometimes problematic authority of old customs and precedents in government. It is a maxim which, in an exemplary prudential application of a generalized observation to a new context, Bacon redirects to question "whether the Readings, exercises, and other customes appertayning vnto learning… be well instituted or no, and thereupon to ground an amendement, or reformation in that which shall be found inconuenient" (2A4v). Bacon's aphoristic practice, presented as an alternative of the systematic treatise or "method" of school philosophy, is in fact such a practical reformation of the "Readings, exercises, and other customes appertayning vnto learning," a reformation that consists in the extension of neohumanist prudential reading and writing to all areas of learning. And it is James himself who provides the textual and intellectual authority for this project.

The greatness of the royal patron is signaled by his authorship of quotable and redeployable advice in the prudential tradition. But in the

Fig. 5. Francisci de Verulamio [Francis Bacon], *Summi Angliae Cancellarii, Instauratio magna* (London, 1620), E2v–E3r. Beinecke Rare Book and Manuscript Library, Yale University, 1988 +163

Fig. 6. *Piv consigli et avvertementi di m. Fr. Gvicciardini gentilhvomo fior. in materia di repvblica et di privata* (Paris, 1576), B1v–B2r. Beinecke Rare Book and Manuscript Library, Yale University, Ocg30 G942 576

logic of the praise lavished on the king, James's possession of "the power and fortune of a King; the knowledge and illumination of a Priest, and the learning and vniuersalitie of a Philosopher" deserves further fame and tribute. As Bacon puts it,

> This propriety inherent and indiuiduall attribute in your Maiestie deserueth to be expressed, not onely in the fame and admiration of the present time, nor in the Historie or tradition of the ages succeeding; but also in some solide worke, fixed memoriall, and immortall monument, bearing a Character or signature, both of the power of a king, and the difference and perfection of such a king. Therefore I did conclude with my selfe, that I could not make vnto your Maiesty a better oblation, then of some treatise tending to that end. (A3v–A4r)

In an effort to celebrate the unique "literature" of his monarch, Bacon's plain quarto book revises the classical monument *topos,* the idea that poetry is a commemorative form more lasting than marble or gilded monument.[68] Recent work in early modern literature and on Shakespeare especially has argued that, although the term "literature" may not have come into modern usage until much later, this is precisely the moment when certain kinds of English vernacular writing were beginning to be classed alongside celebrated classical works. Such claims of value were frequently encoded in the material form of the work.[69] Yet Bacon's own *Advancement of Learning,* his most important vernacular philosophical work, is published as a modest volume seemingly careful not to aspire to monumental status for itself. It seeks instead to advise the king on how to build such a monument by presiding over a collaborative project of research. What Bacon's introductory words to James suggest is that a permanent work, a "work immortall" is to be performed by the monarch himself—but a work more general in its ambition and scope than a poetic achievement. The project of the advancement, patronage, and promotion of learning is envisaged as an appropriate monument to James's poly-historic capabilities. Best embodied in the mobile, provisional collection of aphorisms, its monumentality and permanence consist in its endless adaptability and its openness to prudent revision.

Ultimately, then, the advancement of learning proceeds by the application of forms of writing strongly associated with a specific cultural field to new areas of knowledge production. Bacon quite simply loses interest when such transfer proves impossible: he would have no time for the sonnet, the genre at which James also tried his hand, for example. A form that to us appears as specifically and uniquely poetic, a form whose aesthetic function is not coupled with the production of knowledge, does not enter his vast enterprise of literature. Such forms as Bacon works with are those serviceable as a medium for transfer between distinct fields of learning: forms that are capable of being upheld by more than one kind of matter, and which therefore enable the analogical equivalence between two fields.

The Baconian mobility of forms that propels the work of discovery in seemingly distant fields is contrary to modern assumptions about the discipline-specific nature of methodologies derived from the object of study: Baconian forms cross boundaries and, rather than restricting them, extend the application of the political and the poetic to the study of nature. And not only are these forms – the aphorism and the monumental work – themselves crossing boundaries between, and formally joining, separate fields, but also, as our reading of Baconian forms has indicated, the understanding of their operation as portable technologies of knowledge production depends on the conjoined understanding of their textual as well as their material aspects. The work of the aphorism in creating Baconian science depends on its textual as well as on its material form, on its rhetorical and conceptual affordances, and on how it drives circulation, organization, and revision – demanding a reading that considers both.

In *Apophthegmes New and Old,* Bacon calls *sententiae* "pointed speeches." Our suggestion is that Bacon's own use of the pointed style – as exemplified in his rendering of James's political aphorism, itself pointed by Dorislaus for extraction – offers a resolution to the anxieties of contemporary literary scholarship that are symptomatically articulated in pointed aphoristic claims. Originating in the moment before the emergence of the formal boundaries that define modern disciplinarity, Baconian learning encourages us to cross rather than to nervously guard them. The convergence of formalism and book history may appear to be a sign of just such a happy overcoming of our anxieties about field-specific methodologies and about the choices that may determine the fate of the historicist study of writing.

But in conclusion we may note that in Bacon, the absence of boundaries is not the result of a suspension, or of a happy mingling, of distinct perspectives and methodologies, but rather the outcome of a push for the reformation of all branches of learning after the singular model of the instrumental study of the art of politics. Bacon was writing before the period of professionalization and specialization that have defined modern academic research. We are writing this essay at a time when for the humanities, that period may appear to be coming to a close. Calls for interdisciplinarity, and for "social," even instrumental utility, are being made even as academic departments are defunded and dismantled. The great Baconian instauration performed with the help of the "broken knowledge" of the political aphorism can steer clear of the worries we have about disciplinarity because it does not rely on methodological difference to establish the identity and distinction of various fields of study. It thus confirms the current anxieties surrounding the identity and distinction of literary scholarship as a historicist project operating in a disciplinary framework – it reveals "what men doe and not what they ought to do," something that recent efforts to link the study of literary form and the material text implicitly also invite us to consider.

NOTES

1 On the complexity and breadth of this problem, see, for example, Warren Boutcher, "Literature," in *Palgrave Advances in Renaissance Historiography,* ed. Jonathan Woolfson (Basingstoke: Palgrave, 2005), 210–40; Paul Zumthor, "Y a-t-il une 'littérature' médiévale?" *Poétique* 66 (1986): 131–39. The study of the notion of literature has tended to focus on the emergence of its modern concept. For a historical survey stopping short of the eighteenth century, see Adrian Marino, *The Biography of "The Idea of Literature" from Antiquity to the Baroque,* trans. Virgil Stanciu and Charles M. Carlton (Albany: State University of New York Press, 1996).

2 *The Twoo Bookes of Francis Bacon. Of the proficience and aduancement of Learning, diuine and humane* (London, 1605), 2G3r. We are quoting the text as presented in Michael Kiernan, ed., *The Advancement of Learning* (Oxford: Oxford University Press, 2000). Bacon is using the term "invention" in the sense of finding, discovery, rather than of creation.

3 See Ernst Robert Curtius, *Europäische Literatur und lateinisches Mittelalter,* 11th ed. (Tübingen: A. Francke Verlag, 1993), 323–29; Hans Blumenberg, *Die Lesbarkeit der Welt* (Frankfurt am Main: Suhrkamp, 1981), esp. 86–91.

4 On the alternatives and afterlives of the Baconian alphabetization of nature, see Joanna Picciotto, *Labors of Innocence in Early Modern England* (Cambridge: Harvard University Press, 2010): 211–25.

5 In the *Novum Organum,* however, Bacon calls forms "the laws and determinations… which govern any simple nature." For a brief overview of the various traditions Bacon was drawing on in his eclectic uses of the term "form," see Virgil K. Whitaker, "Bacon's Doctrine of Forms: A Study of Seventeenth-Century Eclecticism," *Huntington Library Quarterly* 33 (1970): 209–16; for an interpretaton of Bacon's use of the term, see Antonio Pérez-Ramos, "Bacon's Forms and the Maker's Knowledge Tradition," in *The Cambridge Companion to Bacon,* ed. Markku Peltonen (Cambridge: Cambridge University Press, 1996), 99–120.

6 Karl Marx, "The Holy Family," in *Selected Writings,* 2d ed., ed. David McLellan (Oxford: Oxford University Press, 2000), 166.

7 Marx talks about the entire, the whole man – "Die Materie lacht in poetisch-sinnlichem Glanze den ganzen Menschen an" – as if anticipating the idea of the dissociation of sensibility.

8 What enables poetry to do this is the fundamental unity of all forms of perception, and the power of the faculty of imagination, to which, as Bacon puts it, poesy has "reference" (2B3r).

9 Compare Pérez-Ramos, "Bacon's Forms," 108.

10 On the long history of the term "form" in literary and aesthetic theory, see Roman Ingarden, "The General Question of the Essence of Form and Content," *The Journal of Philosophy* 57 (1960): 222–33; Władysław Tatarkiewicz, "Form in the History of Aesthetics," in *Dictionary of the History of Ideas,* ed. Philip P. Wiener (New York: Charles Scribner's Sons, 1973), 2:216–25.

11 Katherine Duncan-Jones and Jan van Dorsten, eds., *Miscellaneous Prose of Sir Philip Sidney* (Oxford: Clarendon Press, 1973), 112. This use of the word is still familiar from such terms as "the matter of Britain" or "the matter of France" of medieval epic, as well as from the German concept of *Stoffgeschichte;* cf. Elisabeth Frenzel, *Stoffe der Weltliteratur: Ein Lexikon dichtungsgeschichtlicher Längsschnitte,* 10th ed. (Stuttgart: Alfred Kröner Verlag, 2005).

12 He continues: "It may refer to the language and conventions that give imagination form; it may mean the physical platforms on which writing is preserved and presented. It may mean the subject of the writing, or it may mean the object that enables it to be read. Perhaps this is to say nothing more interesting than that a word may have different meanings, though in this case the different meanings awkwardly extend to both sides of the familiar opposition of form and content. What's the matter?" (David Scott Kastan, "Afterword," in *Formal Matters: Reading the Materials of English Renaissance Literature,* ed. Allison K. Deutermann and András Kiséry [Manchester: Manchester University Press, 2013], 249–59 [249]).

13 Leah Price, *How to Do Things with Books in Victorian Britain* (Princeton: Princeton University Press, 2012), 5. Price's project is of course partly to demolish the binary abstraction from a monist perspective, dissolving it into a spectrum of uses.

14 Marjorie Levinson, "What Is New Formalism?" *PMLA* 122 (2007): 558–69 (558).

15 The essays collected in Mark David Rasmussen, ed., *Renaissance Literature and Its Formal Engagements* (Houndmills: Palgrave, 2002) all share a frustration with the (then) recent versions of "new historicism" and a sense that a return to form is necessary, but each offers a decidedly different model for correcting this problem.

16 Roland Barthes, "Myth Today," in *Mythologies,* trans. Annette Lavers (New York: Hill and Wang, 1972), 112. See, for example, Sasha Roberts, "Feminist Criticism and the New Formalism: Early Modern Women and Literary Engagement," in *The Impact of Feminism in English Renaissance Studies,* ed. Dympna Callaghan (Houndmills: Palgrave Macmillan, 2007), 67–92 (88); Susan J. Wolfson, "Introduction," in *Reading for Form,* ed. Susan J. Wolfson and Marshall Brown (Seattle: University of Washington Press, 2006), 3–24 (12). Wolfson continues, citing Barthes: "One might also add the reciprocal in the wake of new historicism: if a little history (say, the anecdote) turns one away from formalism, a lot of history brings one back to it. There is really no necessary standoff: not only is formalism a 'necessary principle' of analysis, but 'the more a system is specifically defined in its forms, the more amenable it is to historical criticism'" (ibid).

17 William Empson, *Argufying: Essays on Literature and Culture,* ed. John Haffenden (London: Chatto & Windus, 1987), 107, quoted by Richard Strier, "How Formalism Became a Dirty Word, and Why We Can't Do without It," in *Renaissance Literature and Its Formal Engagements,* 207–15 (212). The claim parallels Barthes's "there are said to be certain Buddhists whose ascetic practices enable them to see a whole landscape in a bean," but Barthes uses the anecdote to model narratological reduction, not historical capaciousness. Roland Barthes, *S/Z: An Essay,* trans. Richard Miller (New York: Hill and Wang, 1974), 3.

18 The passage from Theodor Wiesengrund Adorno, *Aesthetic Theory,* trans. Robert Hullot-Kentor (Minneapolis: University of Minnesota Press, 1997), 6, is quoted by Heather Dubrow, "Guess Who's Coming to Dinner? Reinterpreting Formalism and the Country House Poem," *Modern Language Quarterly* 61 (2000): 59–77 (63).

19 Geoffrey Hartman, "Beyond Formalism," *Modern Language Notes* 81 (1966): 542–56 (549–50).

20 Mark David Rasmussen, "Introduction: New Formalisms?" in *Renaissance Literature and Its Formal Engagements,* 1–14 (9).

21 Levinson, "What Is New Formalism?" 563.

22 The anxiety seems to extend beyond literary scholarship and is perhaps symptomatic of a concern that history has become the master discipline of humanities. As James Vernon observes, "the current resurgent fascination with form by scholars in the fields of literature, music, and visual culture sometimes appears as a return to disciplinarity that, intentionally or not, refuses history as a site of convergence across disciplines" (James Vernon, "The Social and Its Forms," *Representations* 104 [2008]: 154–58 [154]).

23 See Henry S. Turner, "Lessons from Literature for the Historian of Science (and Vice Versa): Reflections on 'Form,'" *Isis* 101 (2010): 578–89. Discussing gender-as-form, Caroline Levine argues that "Since hierarchies of social power are 'formal' in the sense that they, too, like artistic forms, are patterns that organize, subordinate, distinguish, and connect disparate materials, 'form' provides a language for bringing the two extremes – the single art object and the fact of power – into analytic relation with one another" ("Scaled Up, Writ Small: A Response to Carolyn Dever and Herbert F. Tucker," *Victorian Studies* 49 [2006]: 100–105 [104]).

24 Stephen Cohen, "Between Form and Culture: New Historicism and the Promise of a Historical Formalism," in *Renaissance Literature and Its Formal Engagements,* 17–41 (32).

25 David Kastan's first book, *Shakespeare and the Shapes of Time* (Hanover, N.H.: University Press of New England, 1982), is a compelling example of a historical

formalism that explores the temporality of human action as the shared focus of the historical world and of dramatic representation – but does so with a nod to George Kubler's *The Shape of Time,* whose focus – and subtitle, *Remarks on the History of Things* – seems, in retrospect, to anticipate Kastan's later interest in the materiality of (literary) history.

26 This reemergence was marked not only by conference panels from the late 1980s on, but also by such collections as Russ McDonald, ed., *Shakespeare Reread: The Texts in New Contexts* (Ithaca: Cornell University Press, 1994), and Stephen Cohen, ed., *Shakespeare and Historical Formalism* (Aldershot: Ashgate, 2007).

27 Paul de Man, *Allegories of Reading: Figural Language in Rousseau, Nietzsche, Rilke, and Proust* (New Haven: Yale University Press, 1979), 3.

28 Roger Chartier, *Forms and Meanings: Texts, Performances, and Audiences from Codex to Computer* (Philadelphia: University of Pennsylvania Press, 1995), 2; Leah Price, "Introduction: Reading Matter," PMLA 121 (2006): 9–16 (11–12).

29 D.F. McKenzie, *Bibliography and the Sociology of Texts* (Cambridge: Cambridge University Press, 1999), 18.

30 Chartier, *Forms and Meanings,* 4.

31 Roger Chartier, *The Order of Books: Readers, Authors, and Libraries in Europe between the Fourteenth and Eighteenth Centuries,* trans. Lydia G. Cochrane (Stanford: Stanford University Press, 1994), 3.

32 Chartier, *Forms and Meanings,* 4.

33 David Scott Kastan, *Shakespeare after Theory* (New York: Routledge, 1999), 55.

34 See Zachary Lesser's argument about the lessons a formalist New Historicism and book history hold for each other, in *Renaissance Drama and the Politics of Publication: Readings in the English Book Trade* (Cambridge: Cambridge University Press, 2004), 21–23.

35 Alexandra Gillespie, "The History of the Book," *New Medieval Literatures* 9 (2007): 245–86 (271–72).

36 Hartman, "Beyond Formalism," 548–50. For an excellent study of the social significance of the pointed style, which does not, however, consider its mediation through the material text, see James Biester, *Lyric Wonder: Rhetoric and Wit in Renaissance English Poetry* (Ithaca: Cornell University Press, 1997).

37 Gillespie, "The History of the Book," 274–75; McKenzie, *Bibliography and the Sociology of Texts,* 18–19.

38 Richard Helgerson, *Forms of Nationhood: The Elizabethan Writing of England* (Chicago: University of Chicago Press, 1992), 7.

39 Ibid., 1, 8.

40 This criticism was especially frequently leveled at New Historicism, attributing its failure as a form of historicism to its formalist tendencies. For a careful discussion of the issue, see Alan Liu, "The Power of Formalism: The New Historicism," ELH 56 (1989): 721–71.

41 See Julian Yates, *Error, Misuse, Failure: Object Lessons from the English Renaissance* (Minneapolis: University of Minnesota Press, 2003), 10–137; Alan Stewart, *Shakespeare's Letters* (Oxford: Oxford University Press, 2008); Leah Price, "From *The History of a Book* to a 'History of the Book,'" *Representations* 108 (2009): 120–38; Sarah Wall-Randell, *The Immaterial Book: Reading and Romance in Early Modern England* (Ann Arbor: University of Michigan Press, 2013).

42 On these issues, see the incisive remarks in Christina Lupton, *Knowing Books: The Consciousness of Mediation in*

Eighteenth-Century Britain (Philadelphia: University of Pennsylvania Press, 2012), 8–10, 16–17.

43 In addition to other examples cited, see Matthew Zarnowiecki's work, especially his *Fair Copies: Reproducing the English Lyric from Tottel to Shakespeare* (Toronto: University of Toronto Press, 2014), and his notion of "medium close reading" in "Reading Shakespeare Miscellaneously: Ben Jonson, Robert Chester, and the *Vatum Chorus* of *Loves Martyr*," in *Formal Matters: Reading the Materials of English Renaissance Literature*, 34–54.

44 See, for example, Benedict S. Robinson, *Islam and Early Modern English Literature: The Politics of Romance from Spenser to Milton* (New York: Palgrave Macmillan, 2007); and Adam Zucker, *The Places of Wit in Early Modern English Comedy* (Cambridge: Cambridge University Press, 2011).

45 See Alan B. Farmer's work on newsbooks and drama, e.g., his "Play-Reading, News-Reading, and Ben Jonson's *The Staple of News*," in *The Book of the Play: Playwrights, Stationers, and Readers in Early Modern England*, ed. Marta Straznicky (Amherst: University of Massachusetts Press, 2006), 127–58. For a literary reading of the form of news, see Joad Raymond, *The Invention of the Newspaper: English Newsbooks, 1641–1649* (Oxford: Clarendon Press, 1996), and the essays on the materiality of nonliterary genres in Joad Raymond, ed., *Cheap Print in Britain and Ireland to 1660*, The Oxford History of Popular Print Culture, vol. 1 (Oxford: Oxford University Press, 2011).

46 Lisa Jardine and Alan Stewart, *Hostage to Fortune: The Troubled Life of Francis Bacon* (London: Victor Gollancz, 1998), 265–74, 285–87.

47 The concepts of "literature" and "the literary" have been problematized and historicized by scholars from René Wellek to John Guillory: see Wellek, "What Is Literature?" in *What Is Literature?* ed. Paul Hernadi (Bloomington: Indiana University Press, 1978), 16–23; Raymond Williams, *Keywords: A Vocabulary of Culture and Society*, rev. ed. (New York: Oxford University Press, 1983); John Guillory, *Cultural Capital: The Problem of Literary Canon Formation* (Chicago: The University of Chicago Press, 1993). For "literature" as a term of privilege and demarcation, see Stephen Greenblatt, "What Is the History of Literature?" *Critical Inquiry* 23 (1997): 460–81; at 470–74, Greenblatt provides a reading of Bacon's argument about the writing and uses of literary history in the 1623 expanded Latin version of *Advancement of Learning, De Augmentis*. On the eighteenth-century transformation, see Trevor Ross, "The Emergence of 'Literature': Making and Reading the English Canon in the Eighteenth Century," *ELH* 63 (1996): 397–422; Jonathan Brody Kramnick, *Making the English Canon: Print-Capitalism and the Cultural Past, 1700–1770* (Cambridge: Cambridge University Press, 1998).

48 David Scott Kastan, "Humphrey Moseley and the Invention of English Literature," in *Agent of Change: Print Culture Studies after Elizabeth L. Eisenstein*, ed. Sabrina Alcorn Baron, Eric N. Lindquist, and Eleanor F. Shevlin (Amherst: University of Massachusetts Press, 2007), 105–24.

49 For discussions of the aphorism in Bacon, see especially Brian Vickers, *Francis Bacon and Renaissance Prose* (Cambridge: Cambridge University Press, 1968), 60–95; Lisa Jardine, *Francis Bacon: Discovery and the Art of Discourse* (London: Cambridge University Press, 1974) 176–78; Alvin Snider, "Francis Bacon and the Authority of Aphorism," *Prose Studies: History, Theory, Criticism* 11, no. 2 (1988), 60–71. Snider discusses how Bacon's aphorisms swerve from the ideal of sharp and pithy.

50 Motivated by James's cherished self-image as Great Britain's Solomon, Bacon provides a run of sentences from Proverbs and Ecclesiastes (2Z4v–3A3r).

51 James Spedding, ed., *The Letters and the Life of Francis Bacon Including All His Occasional Works* (London: Longmans, Green, Reader, and Dyer, 1868), 3:91.

52 Julian Martin, *Francis Bacon, the State, and the Reform of Natural Philosophy* (Cambridge: Cambridge University Press, 1992), 141–70.

53 John Michael Archer's important *Sovereignty and Intelligence: Spying and Court Culture in the English Renaissance* (Stanford: Stanford University Press, 1993) locates the rise of modern rationality and political intelligence in the sixteenth century, and the origins of Baconian science and of modern scientific observation in the methodologies of surveillance and political knowledge-production by and for the state.

54 Jardine and Stewart, *Hostage to Fortune*, 50.

55 Julianne Werlin has written brilliantly about Bacon's ideas of the mediated and error-prone nature of textual work that defines his enterprise and his vision of society structured and defined by communication. See her "Francis Bacon and the Art of Misinterpretation," *PMLA* 130 (2015): 236–51. We would like to thank Dr. Werlin for sharing her work with us before publication.

56 It might be taken as emblematic that while the first italicized sentence is a biblical quote referring to Solomon, the second is an observation from Tacitus: see A2v, A3r, respectively.

57 Sydney Anglo, *Machiavelli—The First Century: Studies in Enthusiasm, Hostility, and Irrelevance* (Oxford: Oxford University Press, 2005), 667–70.

58 F.J. Levy, "Francis Bacon and the Style of Politics," *English Literary Renaissance* 16 (1986): 101–22.

59 Vincent Luciani, "Bacon and Machiavelli," *Italica* 24 (1947): 26–40.

60 P. Alessandra Maccioni and Marco Mostert, "Isaac Dorislaus (1595–1649): The Career of a Dutch Scholar in England," *Transactions of the Cambridge Bibliographical Society* 8 (1984): 419–70; Ronald Mellor, "Tacitus, Academic Politics, and Regicide in the Reign of Charles I: The Tragedy of Dr. Isaac Dorislaus," *International Journal of the Classical Tradition* 11 (2004): 153–93.

61 His copy is now in the Cambridge University Library, Rare Books LE 7.45 (see also fig. 1). On gnomic pointing, see Arrigo Castellani, *Nuovi Saggi di Linguistica e Filologia Italiana e Romanza (1976–2004)*, ed. Valeria Della Valle et al., 2 vols. (Rome: Salerno Editrice, 2009), 1:71–85; G.K. Hunter, "The Marking of *Sententiae* in Elizabethan Printed Plays, Poems, and Romances," *The Library*, 5th ser., 6 (1951): 171–88; Zachary Lesser and Peter Stallybrass, "The First Literary *Hamlet* and the Commonplacing of Professional Plays," *Shakespeare Quarterly* 59 (2008): 371–420.

62 Until his full treatment of the social life of Montaigne's essays appears, the following articles by Warren Boutcher clarify the connections between the Bacons and Montaigne, and the use and importance of Montaigne's *Essais* in vernacular political education: "Montaigne et Anthony Bacon: la *Familia* et la Fonction des Lettres," *Montaigne Studies* 13 (2001): 241–76; "Marginal Commentaries: The Cultural Transmission of Montaigne's *Essais* in Shakespeare's England," in *Shakespeare et Montaigne: Vers un Nouvel Humanisme*, ed. Jean-Marie Maguin and Pierre Kapitaniak (Montpellier: Société Française Shakespeare, 2004), 13–27; "The Origins of Florio's Montaigne: 'Of the Institution and Education of Children,

to Madame Lucy Russell, Countess of Bedford,'" *Montaigne Studies* 24 (2012): 7–32. For an instance of an aphorism-oriented reading of Montaigne in England, see William M. Hamlin, "*Montagnes Moral Maxims:* A Collection of Seventeenth-Century English Aphorisms Derived from the *Essays* of Montaigne," *Montaigne Studies* 21 (2009): 209–24.

63 The phrase is Kastan's, in "The Body of the Text," *ELH* 81 (2014): 443–67 (443).

64 On the truth-utility connection, see Paolo Rossi, *Philosophy, Technology, and the Arts in the Early Modern Era,* trans. Salvator Attanasio (New York: Harper & Row, 1970), 157–60.

65 See the overview in the Introduction to Bacon's "Promus" in Alan Stewart, ed., *The Oxford Francis Bacon I: Early Writings, 1584–1596* (Oxford: Clarendon Press, 2012), 507–24.

66 For an interpretation that inserts Bacon's aphoristic practice in the context of contemporary scientific discourse, see Stephen Clucas, "'A Knowledge Broken': Francis Bacon's Aphoristic Style and the Crisis of Scholastic and Humanistic Knowledge Systems," in *English Renaissance Prose: History, Language, and Politics,* ed. Neil Rhodes (Tempe, Ariz.: Medieval and Renaissance Texts and Studies, 1997), 147–72.

67 See F.J. Levy, "Hayward, Daniel, and the Beginnings of Politic History in England," *Huntington Library Quarterly* 50 (1987): 1–34; Lisa Jardine and Anthony Grafton, "'Studied for Action': How Gabriel Harvey Read His Livy," *Past & Present* 129 (1990): 30–78; Lisa Jardine and William Sherman, "Pragmatic Readers: Knowledge Transactions and Scholarly Services in Late Elizabethan England," in *Religion, Culture, and Society in Early Modern Britain: Essays in Honour of Patrick Collinson,* ed. Anthony Fletcher and Peter Roberts (Cambridge: Cambridge University Press, 1994), 102–24; Alan Stewart, "Instigating Treason: The Life and Death of Henry Cuffe, Secretary," in *Literature, Politics and Law in Renaissance England,* ed. Erica Sheen and Lorna Hutson (Houndmills: Palgrave Macmillan, 2005), 50–70.

68 J.B. Leishman, *Themes and Variations in Shakespeare's Sonnets,* 2d ed. (London: Hutchinson & Co, 1963), 27–91; Marlin E. Blaine, "Milton and the Monument Topos: 'On Shakespeare,' '*Ad Joannem Roüsium,*' and *Poems* (1645)," *The Journal of English and Germanic Philology* 99 (2000): 215–34.

69 On the printed book as monument, see Richard C. Newton, "Jonson and the (Re-)Invention of the Book," in *Classic and Cavalier: Essays on Jonson and the Sons of Ben,* ed. Claude J. Summers and Ted-Larry Pebworth (Pittsburgh: University of Pittsburgh Press, 1982), 31–55; Timothy Murray, *Theatrical Legitimation: Allegories of Genius in Seventeenth-Century England and France* (New York: Oxford University Press, 1987), 21–104; John Pitcher, "Essays, Works and Small Poems: Divulging, Publishing and Augmenting the Elizabethan Poet, Samuel Daniel," in *The Renaissance Text: Theory, Editing, Textuality,* ed. Andrew Murphy (Manchester: Manchester University Press, 2000), 8–29; David Scott Kastan, "Humphrey Moseley and the Invention of English Literature." For surveys of the iconography of the title page, see Margery Corbett, "The Architectural Title-Page: An Attempt to Trace Its Development from Its Humanist Origins up to the Sixteenth and Seventeenth Centuries, the Heyday of the Complex Engraved Title-Page," *Motif* 12 (1964): 48–62; Margery Corbett and R.W. Lightbown, *The Comely Frontispiece: The Emblematic Title-Page in England, 1550–1660* (London: Routledge and Kegan Paul, 1979). About the significance of the folio

format, see David Scott Kastan, *Shakespeare and the Book* (Cambridge: Cambridge University Press, 2001), 50–78; Steven K. Galbraith, "English Literary Folios 1593–1623: Studying Shifts in Format," in *Tudor Books and Readers: Materiality and the Construction of Meaning*, ed. John N. King (Cambridge: Cambridge University Press, 2010), 46–67. Galbraith argues that the cultural connotations of the format had no material basis: publishing in folio rather than in quarto was often a matter of economy and necessity, and was not necessarily "expensive" *per se*. Furthermore, while "There is evidence that a connection between the quarto format and books of little worth was established in the Tudor period," there is no suggestion that quarto publishing is also actually cheap: see Joseph A. Dane and Alexandra Gillespie, "The Myth of the Cheap Quarto," in *Tudor Books and Readers*, 25–45 (43). These arguments about material value do not, however, challenge the notion that folios were a format *symbolically* appropriate for monumental enterprises.

A*Nthon*:
It wea
But ho
What
I am to
of me,
That I haue much ad-
Salarino. Your min
There where your A
Like Signiors and ri
Or as it were the Pag

Shakespeare after Queer Theory

MARIO DiGANGI

In recent years, a new presentism has been touted as a corrective to the alienating, objectivist premises of historicism. According to Hugh Grady and Terence Hawkes, editors of the collection *Presentist Shakespeares,* historicism obscures how early modern literary texts "continue to speak to us with urgency and insight"; unlike historicism, presentism "will deliberately begin with the material present and allow that to set its interrogative agenda."[1] Through the metaphor of old texts that continue to "speak to us" today, Grady and Hawkes appeal to an ideal of visceral communication between past and present cultures. Presentism thus promises an immediacy of cross-cultural identification and emotional response that is ostensibly foreclosed by historicist methods. Other contributors to *Presentist Shakespeares* develop this critique of historicism as an alienating methodology. Linda Charnes describes New Historicism and the "New Boredom" as projects aimed at "ever fine-tuning our estrangement from Shakespeare's era."[2] Michael Bristol asserts,

> Historicism is a tacit insistence on impersonal and intellectually detached forms of reading and in this sense it can be both arbitrary and quite alienating.... [P]resentism encourages readers to take things more personally, and to recognize their own feelings as the point of departure for the exploration of a complex, emotionally demanding text.[3]

For Charnes, historicism estranges through its commitment to things antiquated and unfamiliar; for Bristol, historicism alienates through its emotionally distanced reading practices.

Yet as histories of emotion by Gail Kern Paster and others have demonstrated, "emotion" and "history" are hardly antithetical categories. Moreover, queer historical scholarship has generated a great deal of self-conscious reflection on the presentist investments and desires that historicist critics bring to their engagements with the past.[4] In *Feeling Backward: Loss and the Politics of Queer History,* Heather Love writes that queer critics "have struggled to bring together traditionally polarized terms such as the psychic and the social, subject and structure, politics and loss, affect and law, and love and history."[5] Love cites the work of Ann Cvetkovich, Carolyn Dinshaw, Carla Freccero, David Halperin, Christopher Nealon, Valerie Traub, and others as representative practitioners of a "queer affective historiography" that has shifted the focus of queer history away from "epistemological questions" and toward "the vagaries of cross-historical desire and the queer impulse to forge communities between the living and the dead."[6] In early modern studies, Freccero has advocated a "queer historiography" that "registers the affective investments of the present in the past," including both "the complex pleasure-positivity of queer theory" as well as the "traumatic pain" of being haunted by the ghosts of history.[7] And Valerie Traub, in her conclusion to *The Renaissance of Lesbianism in Early Modern England,* holds that the critic's desire "is a resource for historical engagement and future imagining," because desire "takes us outside of ourselves, challenging us to meet and engage with an other."[8] Both Freccero and Traub acknowledge that historicism, *pace* Bristol, need not insist on "impersonal and intellectually detached forms of reading."[9]

My purpose in this essay is not to advocate "queer affective historiography" as a way of mediating between historicist and presentist readings of Shakespeare, but rather to demonstrate how historicism can illuminate queer affect in Shakespeare. A historicist analysis of queer affect in *The Merchant of Venice* can counter the misconception that historicism's purview is restricted to the impersonal facts and antiquarian reconstructions of a distant culture. Moreover, far from obscuring the ways in which *The Merchant of Venice* might "speak to us" today, a historicist analysis that accounts in sixteenth-century terms for Antonio's status as a desiring merchant can deepen our appreciation of the complex affects explored in the play. My approach reorients an understanding of Antonio's queer affects by arguing that the historical and dramatic significance of his representation lies not primarily in the sadness that attends his same-sex desire for Bassanio, but in his ability as a merchant to experience complex emotions at all.

In performing a historicist reading of queer affect in *The Merchant of Venice,* I do not intend to diminish presentist approaches that can illuminate the ways in which Antonio has signified in the critical, theatrical, and cinematic traditions as a figure of homosexual (or at least proto-homosexual) desire.[10] Yet presentism also runs the risk of reifying contemporary sexual identities and then projecting them back onto Shakespeare's characters – precisely the kind of projection that informs Eric S. Mallin's reading of *The Merchant of Venice* in his book *Godless Shakespeare,* a volume in the Shakespeare Now! series. According to series editors Simon Palfrey and Ewan Fernie, Shakespeare Now! bridges the gap between "scholarly thinking and a public audience" by moving away from "the supposed safety of historicism." Palfrey and Fernie complain that in historicist scholarship "too often there is little trace of any struggle; little sense that the writer is coming at the subject afresh, searching for the most appropriate language or method."[11] Accessible and innovative scholarship is a worthwhile goal. Yet Mallin's identification of the Antonios in *The Merchant of Venice* and *Twelfth Night* as "gay" according to a modern stereotype of sad "homosexuals whose love dooms them" fails to engage with the lesbian/gay scholarship that has debated the political and intellectual implications of such identifications.[12] Relying upon modern stereotypes, such a presentism falls short of opening up a "vast world of intellectual possibility" beyond the predictable "safety" of historicism.[13]

This is not to argue that any attempt to understand Antonio's sadness as a symptom of frustrated or marginalized same-sex desire is necessarily tainted by presentist stereotypes of gay men. For instance, in her analysis of melancholic characters in twentieth-century lesbian and gay literature, Heather Love explains negative emotions as a consequence of social trauma and exclusion. Eighteenth-century historian George Rousseau has coined the term "homodepressed" to describe a kind of melancholy "where the 'lowness' has arisen primarily as the result of a same-sex predicament and its social interdictions."[14] A diagnosis of queer melancholy does not, however, seem applicable to Antonio, whose friendship with Bassanio is socially recognized and validated, not excluded or interdicted.[15] Antonio's melancholy is a symptom, I will argue instead, of the pressures and risks of social *inclusion*, namely, of the public friendship between himself, a wealthy merchant, and Bassanio, a spendthrift aristocrat.

Antonio's generic status as a merchant is crucial to apprehending the significance of his mysterious sadness. Indeed the title page to the 1600 quarto of the play seems to define the play's subject matter, in the second line of text, as a "Historie of the *Merchant*": that the story concerns a particular merchant *of Venice* is specified only in the next line (fig. 7).[16] The title page also sharply distinguishes the unnamed "sayd Merchant" from his rival, "*Shylocke* the Iewe," who is identified by name and religion. Whereas Shylock is characterized by his "extreame crueltie," the Merchant's disposition remains mysterious, although one might be inclined to extrapolate the "most excellent" character of the Merchant from the "most excellent" character of the history in which he appears.

Although the quarto title page leaves the Merchant's character unspecified, in the late sixteenth century, the figure of the merchant would have raised certain expectations for a reader or playgoer. As Ceri Sullivan shows, sixteenth-century merchant manuals promoted an image of merchants as "manly risk-takers" who converted the constant hazards of trade into opportunities for profit.[17] While such texts tendentiously characterized merchants as courageous and vigilant adventurers, sixteenth-century moral and religious texts typically represented the merchant as a figure whose emotions could be easily identified and parsed into either joy (at financial success) or despair (at financial loss). The opening scene of *The Merchant of Venice,* in which Antonio, Solanio, and Salerio debate the cause of Antonio's melancholy, must therefore have been striking to its original audiences in its innovative suggestion that a merchant could be the subject of a play about the contradictory, tempestuous emotions that attend intimate relationships.[18] By connecting Antonio so intimately to Bassanio, Shakespeare enriches his merchant figure with the emotional burden of a friendship that cannot be affectively experienced in terms of simple gain or loss. The sixteenth-century type of the emotionally transparent merchant was still prevalent in the 1590s, despite changes in the cultural representation and social status of

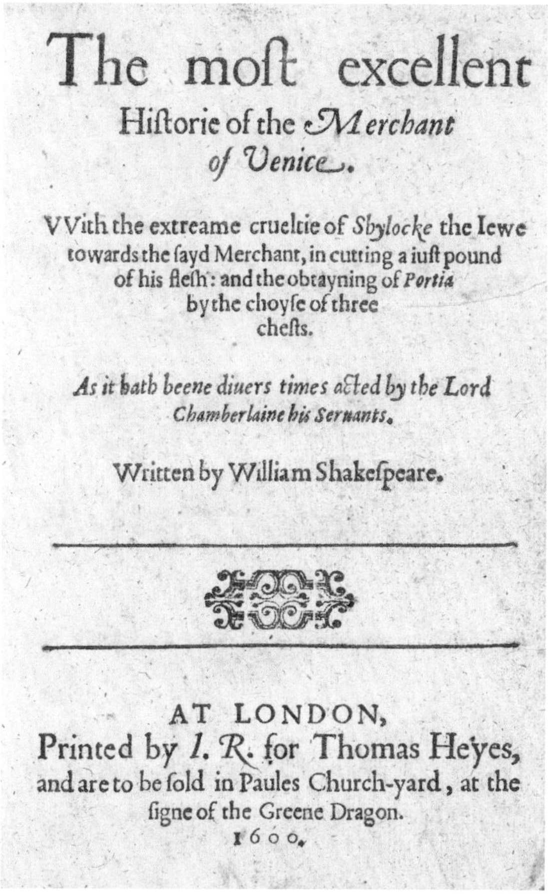

The moſt excellent
Hiſtorie of the *Merchant*
of Venice.

VVith the extreame crueltie of *Shylocke* the Iewe
towards the ſayd Merchant, in cutting a iuſt pound
of his fleſh: and the obtayning of *Portia*
by the choyſe of three
cheſts.

As it hath beene diuers times acted by the Lord
Chamberlaine his Seruants.

Written by William Shakeſpeare.

AT LONDON,
Printed by *I. R.* for Thomas Heyes,
and are to be ſold in Paules Church-yard, at the
ſigne of the Greene Dragon.
1600.

Fig. 7. William Shakespeare, *The most excellent Historie of the Merchant of Venice* (London, 1600), title page. Beinecke Rare Book and Manuscript Library, Yale University, Eliz 180

English merchants.[19] Before turning to a fuller analysis of Shakespeare's innovation with Antonio, I will consider how the emotionally transparent merchant appears as a stock figure in several texts published in close chronological proximity to *The Merchant of Venice* (1596).

In late-sixteenth-century moral and religious texts, merchants are typically defined in terms of the polarized emotions of hope and fear, joy and despair.[20] Considering the religious concerns of *The Merchant of Venice,* it is particularly noteworthy that English theologians proverbially use the merchant to illustrate the emotional suffering of those who, in Gratiano's words, "haue too much respect vpon the world" (A3r). In a sermon posthumously published in 1595, Richard Greenham, a popular and widely read Anglican preacher, describes the consequences of directing all one's hopes toward material gain:

> The more we seek outward pleasures to auoyde the inward trouble of minde, the more we hast and runne into it; and wee speedely plunge our selues in a wounded spirite [bef]or[e] wee be aware. Who posteth more to becom rich, than the merchant man? who hopeth lesse to become pore, than hee that aduentureth great treasures? who hazardeth his goods, who putteth in ieoperdie of his life; and yet suddenly he either rusheth vpon the rocke of hardnesse of heart, or else is swallowed vp of the gulphe of a despairing mind: from which happely he cannot be deliuered with a ship full of golde.[21]

Greenham allows of only two consequences for the merchant's "spirite": if his financial hopes are realized, wealth will harden his heart, shattering his peace like a ship propelled against the rocks; if his financial hopes are disappointed, the gulf of despair will devour him. To illustrate the sin of despair, Thomas Morton, in *The Diet of the Soule* (1597), offers an analogy based on the merchant's typically extreme affect:

> ...yea, as the Merchant venturer hauing receiued a great losse by sea, or the souldier a great wound in battaile, often become desperate, and carelesse of their owne estate: so, oftentimes a Christian by committing some grieuous sinne is brought to this passe, that hee laieth aside the care and studie of holinesse, and letteth all go at six and seuen.[22]

For Morton's one-dimensional merchant, emotional life is entirely wrapped up in trade: a "great losse" leads inevitably to a desperation that "letteth all go."

The devotional poet Henry Lok, in *Sundry Christian Passions Contained in Two Hundred Sonnets* (1593), uses the directness of the lyric persona and the regular structure of the sonnet form to convey the transparency of the merchant's search for happiness prior to the spiritual conversion that brings about a more complex subjectivity.

> SON. XXI.
> A Merchant I, full long abroad haue straide,
> By sea and land true happinesse to gaine,

The riches of the earth my eyes haue waide,
And see their profit to be light and vaine.
Such trifling trash my soule doth now disdaine,
And Iewels of more value I espye,
Among the rest, one doth all other staine,
Which with my wealth I wish that I might buye.
But this rare pearle is of a price so hie,
As all the earth cannot esteeme the same,
Much lesse to purchase it, can it come nie,
Yet doth the loue thereof my heart enflame.
Be thou the pledge (sweet Sauior) then for me,
That heauenly blisse shall so my riches be.[23]

In the first quatrain, the merchant serves as a figure of worldly desire for "light and vaine" riches, which offer false promises of happiness. The merchant comes to recognize true bliss in longing for the single pearl (heaven) that can be neither priced nor possessed, but only "pledge[d]." This new knowledge transforms his emotional disposition from one centered on transparent estimations of outward, perceptible value, to one based on a profound "wish" that cannot be fulfilled in this life, a promise that enflames but does not satisfy the heart.

Even in a secular text such as Richard Barnfield's "The Shepheard's Content" (1594), the merchant is readily available as a proverbial figure of transparent and antithetical affect. Running through the troubles typically faced by the monarch, courtier, scholar, soldier, merchant, and ploughman, Barnfield's shepherd elaborates on the emotional lives only of the monarch and the merchant. Whereas the careworn monarch is molested by a number of problems – foreign invaders and domestic traitors, rebellious subjects and envious aristocrats – the industrious merchant fears financial loss alone:

The wealthie Merchant that doth crosse the Seas,
To *Denmarke, Poland, Spaine,* and *Barbarie;*
For all his ritches, liues not still at ease;
Sometimes he feares ship-spoyling Pyracie,
Another while deceipt and treacherie
Of his owne Factors in a forren Land:
Thus doth he still in dread and danger stand.

Well is he tearmd a Merchant-Venturer,
Since he doth venter lands, and goods, and all:
When he doth trauell for his Traffique far,
Little he knowes what fortune may befall,
Or rather what mis-fortune happen shall:
Sometimes he splits his Ship against a rocke;
Loosing his men, his goods, his wealth, his stocke.

And if he so escape with life away,
He counts himselfe a man most fortunate,
Because the waues their rigorous rage did stay,
(When being within their cruell powers of late,
The Seas did seeme to pittie his estate)
But yet he never can recouer health,
Because his ioy was drowned with his wealth.[24]

Because the merchant's joy is so ruthlessly tied to his wealth, it is only after he loses everything that his constant anxiety can resolve itself into a settled sadness.

We can see the resilience of this discourse of merchant affect in a later text such as I.H.'s *The House of Correction: or, certayne satyricall epigrams* (1619). In the following epigram, the generically named merchant Venter goes mad upon learning that his ships have been destroyed:

Venter the Merchant is runne madde, they say,
On the report his Ships are cast away.
What, did he Venter with his goods his wits,
That he is falne into these franticke fits?
Then, peraduenture, it may well be found,
The Sea his goods, and he his wits hath drown'd.[25]

The texts from the 1590s I cited above simply assume that the merchant's happiness depends on the success of his ventures; I.H. questions the merchant's very sanity in investing his wits along with his goods. Whereas Barnfield concedes the aptness of the merchant's reputation as a universal "venturer" – "Well is he tearmd a Merchant-Venturer, / Since he doth venter lands, and goods, and all" – I.H. mocks Venter for venturing goods, and all, including his wits. By 1619, the link between the merchant's financial and emotional well-being is no longer taken as axiomatic;

Venter becomes frantic not because the sea has drowned his goods, but because he has drowned his own wits. I.H.'s satiric question – "What, did he venter with his goods his wits"? – is that of an observer who is unable to make sense of his subject's emotional disposition.

Mercantile emotion is rendered even more opaque in the opening scene of *The Merchant of Venice*. Exploring the causes of Antonio's sadness, Salerio and Solanio not only rehearse the familiar sixteenth-century account of the merchant venturer's emotional transparency; their dramatic function is to *embody* the familiarity of that account by behaving as if the cause of Antonio's sadness were fully self-evident.[26] We might say that Salerio and Solanio perform an inattentive historicist reading of their friend, interpreting him according to proverbial representations of merchant emotion that do not apply to his current situation. Evoking the trope of hope (of profit) and fear (of loss), Solanio confesses that, were he a merchant, the "better part" of his "affections would / Be with [his] hopes abroade" (A2r). On the one hand, his hope of profit would make him pluck the grass to determine the direction of the wind blowing his ships to safe harbor; on the other hand, "euery obiect that might make me feare / Mis-fortune to my ventures, out of doubt / Would make me sad" (A2r). Salerio, having already collapsed Antonio's mind into his merchandise – "Your minde is tossing on the Ocean" – elaborates on the all-consuming anxiety he attributes to his friend (A2r). When Antonio protests that his affections are not entirely tied to his fortunes, Solanio suggests that his melancholy derives from love, thereby recalling Benvolio's (accurate, in the event) diagnosis of Romeo's sadness in *Romeo and Juliet*. Again, Antonio quickly rejects his friend's diagnosis. Antonio is equally dismissive of Gratiano's later attempt to understand his sadness in terms of Christian wisdom: "You haue too much respect vpon the world: / They loose it that doe buy it with much care" (A3r). Antonio's exchanges with his friends thus reveal an emotional opacity within the very figure of the merchant who had proverbially stood for emotional transparency.[27]

Having suggested a mystery within his merchant, Shakespeare deepens that mystery by refusing us access to Antonio's interiority through a soliloquy or aside. This refusal is particularly remarkable at the end of the third scene, where an audience might expect Antonio to confess an anxiety about his bond with Shylock that he is unwilling to admit to

Bassanio. Instead, Antonio ends the scene with a rather hollow attempt to quell Bassanio's overt fears: "Come on, in this there can be no dismay, / My ships come home a month before the day" (B4v). In his affective opacity, Antonio's difference from the emotionally transparent merchants of sixteenth-century moral and theological discourse might be attributed in part to generic considerations, especially since the dramatic representation of merchants accrues greater psychological and sociological complexity during the 1590s.[28] But Antonio's affective opacity becomes harder to explain in generic terms alone when he is compared with the emotionally transparent merchants in late-sixteenth-century plays such as Robert Wilson's *The Three Ladies of London* (1584), Christopher Marlowe's *The Jew of Malta* (1589), and William Haughton's *Englishmen for My Money* (1598). Easily recognizable types of foreign merchants and usurers, Wilson's Mercadorus, Marlowe's Barabas, and Haughton's Pisaro are drawn with less psychological complexity than Antonio, and the avariciousness that fundamentally motivates them continues the legacy of the alternatively hopeful and fearful merchants of sixteenth-century texts. Barabas, for instance, is characterized by strong emotions regarding his financial successes (joy, pride), and losses (grief, rage). Already rather predictable, these dramatic merchants deliver soliloquies and asides that make evident to us the avaricious desires that they might choose to hide from their enemies and rivals.

Instead of referring Antonio's sadness to the proverbially antithetical poles of mercantile hope and fear, *The Merchant of Venice* offers it as a source of social and epistemological doubt. Like Salerio and Solanio, critics have proposed answers to the mystery of Antonio's sadness largely in terms of economics or sexuality. In the former camp are explanations that attribute Antonio's sadness to his financial anxieties,[29] his nostalgic wish to escape from credit relations,[30] or his "maladjustment to the material world";[31] in the latter camp are those who attribute Antonio's sadness to his impending loss of Bassanio,[32] or who see it as the sign of a passive solitude and attachment to the singular friend that prevents the full achievement of ethical virtue and political power.[33] My aim is to understand the mystery of Antonio's sadness as a dramatic technique for representing the affective dimensions of a friendship experienced as a public exchange of obligations involving risk, self-interest, and communal determinations of value. In a reading of the play that has informed my own understanding of the problem of worth within friendship, Henry Turner refers to friendship as "a relation that is difficult to calculate."[34] Alan Bray, too, demonstrates how the social and political dimensions of elite friendship in early modern England could lead to anxious scrutiny – both from within and without the friendship – of the motives, behavior, and aims of the friend: hence the import of writings such as Francis Bacon's "Of Followers and Friends."[35]

Through Antonio, Shakespeare represents friendship as an affective mystery in stark contradistinction to the radically parsed emotional life of the proverbial merchant. An idealizing strain of early modern friendship discourse presumes, in fact, that the affective experiences afforded to friendship would be sharply distinguished from those of merchandising.[36] Thus Portia, speaking of Bassanio and Antonio, affirms that when two "soules doe beare an egall yoke of loue, / there must be needes a like proportion / of lyniaments, of manners, and of spirit" (F4v).[37] Such celebrations of friendship as a relation of likeness and equality vigorously rejected the notion that friendship might involve a calculated exchange or "bargain." So explains Jeremy Taylor in his *Discourse of Friendship* (1657): "Others say that a friend is to value his friend as much as his friend values him; but neither is this well or safe, wise or sufficient; for it makes friendship a mere bargain,... It is not good to make a reckoning in friendship; that's merchandise, or it may be gratitude, but not noble friendship."[38] Yet *The Merchant of Venice* suggests that in practice even "noble friendship" cannot comprise an equal yoke of love, and consequently might be affectively experienced as "merchandise."[39] In a discussion of the spaces of mercantilism and romance in *The Merchant of Venice,* Russell West argues that in requiring Bassanio to return to Venice to see him "pay his debt" with his life (F4v), Antonio drags "friendship back into the commercial arena by placing it under the sign of a debt so great as to be unpayable."[40] I would argue, however, that the play represents friendship as always part of the "commercial arena," as always caught up in shifting, incommensurate, and socially negotiated values. Friendship is an affective mystery not because it *transcends* "mercantile" considerations of value and exchange, but precisely because it cannot escape such considerations, even though it is unable properly to calculate them.

This problem emerges most clearly when Bassanio first calls on Antonio to support his venture to Belmont. Admitting that he owes

Antonio most "in money and in loue," and "unburthen[ing]" his plot "to get cleere of all the debts" he owes, Bassanio implies that marrying Portia will allow him to pay back *both* debts to his friend (A3v). But how might one "get clear" of a debt of love? Does Bassanio mean that, should Antonio gratify his present desires, he will pay back Antonio's love by fully reciprocating it? And if so, how? Or, conversely, does Bassanio imply that once he has obtained Portia's love he will get clear of Antonio's love by releasing his friend of the need for any further emotional investment? At the core is the question of whether Bassanio will owe Antonio *more* or *less* once his friend's love and money have helped him secure a wife. William Cornwallis provides an apt gloss on the emotional peril Antonio faces in indebting his friend to his love: "It is daungerous if we enjoy a friend much our superiour to doo him offices not easily requited, such impossibilities make him desperate, and desirous to cancell that obligation with Some Action, that you shall not afterwards be able to complaine of his Ingratitude."[41] Lord Bassanio is in fact Antonio's social superior, and his "desperate" plan to win Portia might be understood in Cornwallis's terms as a daring action designed to cancel his emotional and financial obligations. Whereas Bassanio had simply spoken of getting clear of a debt, Cornwallis's stronger language of "cancell[ing]" an obligation suggests that the end result of such desperate repayment might be the cancellation altogether of the emotional bond of friendship.

What makes *The Merchant of Venice* so compelling in its exploration of the blurred boundaries of friendship and merchandise is the insistence that what is most at stake in the affective bonds of friendship is precisely what eludes capture by the specificities of calculation. One of the pleasures of Shakespearean comedy is the fantasy of being able to identify desire's precise causes and points of origin: the homosocial rivalry that sparks Proteus's immediate attraction to Silvia in *The Two Gentlemen of Verona;* the magic juice that compels Lysander to pursue Helena in *A Midsummer Night's Dream;* Rosalind's witnessing of Orlando's athletic prowess in *As You Like It;* or Antonio's rescue of the drowning Sebastian in *Twelfth Night*. In the *Merchant of Venice,* however, the origins of romantic desire – between Bassanio and Portia, Bassanio and Antonio, Lorenzo and Jessica – are almost entirely obscured in the past.

Furthermore, desire in the play is concealed within unusually dense networks of financial exchange, religious and civic affiliation, and contractual bonds.[42] This enmeshing of desire in voluntary and involuntary networks of socioeconomic obligation explains why, as Henry Turner observes, Shylock seems "compelled by an emotion larger than himself" in hating Antonio: Shylock is always already inserted into a structure of mutual enmity between Jews and Christians.[43] Justifying that hatred, Shylock speaks of an "affection" that is both arbitrary and involuntary:

> Some men there are loue not a gaping pigge?
> Some that are mad if they behold a Cat?
> And others when the bagpipe sings ith nose,
> cannot containe their vrine for affection.
> Maisters of passion swayes it to the moode
> of what it likes or loathes… (G3v)[44]

Shylock describes affection as a force that provokes distinctive emotional and physiological reactions in certain types of persons, whom he lists in order of their increasing subjection to the unavoidable – and outwardly legible – sway of their passions. The man who loves not a roasted pig could choose not to eat it, and might easily dissemble or conceal that distaste. The man who is unhinged by the sight of a cat, however, could hardly avoid seeing an occasional cat, and his consequent madness would likely manifest as wild behavior or speech. Finally, consider the difficulty of blocking out the sound of a bagpipe, and of concealing the "in euitable shame" of "force[d]" urination (G3v). Yet even when the signs of "affection" are abundantly evident, the origins and aims of affection might frustrate the logic of "firme reason" (G3v). Why, we might be provoked to ask, should anybody be unable to bear a harmless cat?[45]

Likewise, that the friendship between Antonio and Bassanio is so public does not diminish but instead intensifies others' scrutiny of their affection. Alan Bray asserts that in early modern England "friendship was *dangerous,* and it was so because friendship signified in the public sphere."[46] Through his link with Bassanio, we might say, Antonio "stand[s] within [the] danger" of his friend as well as his enemy (H1v). At a pragmatic level, the publicity of friendship carries potentially harmful consequences. We might wonder if Shylock has prior knowledge of Antonio's love for Bassanio, in that such knowledge might suggest to him the likelihood that Antonio would sign the "merry bond" (B4v). It is striking, too, that Shakespeare does not write a scene in which Bassanio privately takes leave of his distraught friend, but instead has Salerio report Antonio's emotional reaction to Bassanio's departure. Amidst other gossip, Salerio tells Solanio what he witnessed of Antonio:

> And euen there his eye being big with teares,
> turning his face, he put his hand behind him,
> and with affection wondrous sencible
> He wrung *Bassanios* hand, and so they parted. (D4r–v)

The word "wondrous" is particularly notable here, since it reveals the emotional state of *Salerio,* the observer of the scene. Salerio cannot claim to know how Bassanio perceived Antonio's wringing of his hand; rather, he must be saying that even a bystander could infer Antonio's extraordinary affection from the violence of his grasp. When Solanio opines, "*I* thinke hee onely loues the world for him" (D4v), is he admiring or disparaging Antonio's wondrous devotion to Bassanio? Antonio's public demonstration of affection might well be regarded as an "embraced heauines" (D4v), an excessive indulgence of unmanly passion.[47]

Solanio's observation returns us to the thorny issue evoked in the first scene of the play: the value of friendship. Antonio might value Bassanio above the world, but what is largely at stake in the play's representation of credit relations, competing loyalties, and the ethics of revenge is *Antonio's* worth. A notable feature of the play is the frequency with which characters praise Antonio, but even more remarkable is that the first to do so is Shylock: "*Anthonio* is a good man" (B2r). Bassanio's defensive response – "Haue you heard any imputation to the contrary" (B2r) – prompts the recognition that for a merchant, good financial credit might be a more apt measure of social worth than moral goodness.[48] Shylock's ability to define Antonio's value in financial terms, entirely apart from any consideration of moral virtue, points to the problem of a reputation that must be constantly asserted, maintained, and defended against "imputation to the contrary."[49] The Venetians' lavish praise of Antonio keeps open the question of a gap between reputation and merit, precisely the lesson of Portia's silver casket, with its material correlative in the coins that pass as "common drudge / tweene man and man" (F1r). Salerio asserts of Antonio that a "kinder gentleman treades not the earth" (D4r). For Gratiano, he is "that royall Merchant good *Anthonio*" (F2v); for Lorenzo, "how true a gentleman . . . / how deere a louer" of Bassanio (F4v). Bassanio extols Antonio to Portia as the "deerest friend to me, the kindest man, / the best conditiond and vnwearied spirit / in dooing curtesies: and one in whom / the auncient Romaine honour more appeares / then any that drawes breath in *I*talie" (F3v). Connoting an exemplary masculinity based on aristocratic status and heroic militarism, ancient Roman honor ill fits Antonio, no matter his reputation for generosity or self-sacrifice.

Ultimately, it is Portia who will be the arbiter of Antonio's value as her husband's "bosome louer" (F4v), and much has been written about her efforts in acts 4 and 5 to teach Bassanio the importance of valuing his wife (and her property) above his friend. To the degree that such lessons require Bassanio to recognize marriage as a locus of densely intertwined financial and emotional investments, marriage appropriates friendship's status in the play as an affective mystery open to public approbation and scrutiny. This is the conjugal theory at the heart of the "ring trick," which forces Bassanio publically to acknowledge not simply that in marriage affective value trumps material value – Nerissa's lesson to Gratiano – but that a husband must factor his wife into the equation when contemplating any course of action that might redistribute affective and material values within the marriage (or between the marital couple and the larger community). In addition to the claims that conjugal partnership makes on Bassanio's distribution of loyalties, Portia's orchestration of feelings and finances in the last moments of the play diminishes Antonio's affective hold on Bassanio by "resolving" Antonio's sadness in traditional mercantile terms that Salerio and Solanio would readily understand.[50] Revealing that three of Antonio's richly laden argosies have unexpectedly arrived to harbor, Portia provides Antonio with a reason to rejoice that has nothing to do with Bassanio's love, loyalty, or indebtedness to his friend.

Portia's mystifying revelation functions most clearly in the moment not to secure Antonio's financial well-being – already secured by his "use" of half of Shylock's estate – but to elicit his admission of indebtedness: "(Sweet Lady) you haue giuen me life and lyuing" (K1v).[51] Whatever its sincerity, Antonio's public admission that his life and living depend on the success of his ventures – not on the affective, social, or financial entanglements of his friendship with Bassanio – weakens any claim he might make on Bassanio's love as essential to his life.[52] Like the typical sixteenth-century merchant, Antonio rejoices because his ships have come to harbor. Through Portia's maneuvering, Antonio has allowed himself to be defined as the merchant whose emotional life can be reduced to the easily legible antipathies of joy and despair.[53] Antonio is thus emptied out, stripped of the emotional depth and opacity that had kept in public view the endlessly fascinating question of the value of his friendship with the aristocratic Lord Bassanio.

I hope to have demonstrated that in restoring to Antonio his historical significance as a desiring merchant, we deepen our understanding of the queer affects that inform friendship in the play. By contextualizing Antonio against a sixteenth-century figuration of the merchant as emotionally transparent, as moved by financial failure or success alone, a historicist reading unfolds the mysteries and risks involved in Antonio's incalculable affective bond with Bassanio. Historicism can thus deepen our empathy with Antonio (as a dramatic character) even as it situates him (as a literary artifact) in the discursive matrix of a particular time and place. In the terms of presentism, historicism allows the play to "speak to us" across boundaries of cultural difference.

With its exploration of religious intolerance as well as sexuality, *The Merchant of Venice* has continued to make Shakespeare relevant for twentieth- and twenty-first-century audiences. Aptly gritty and ironic for our times, the 2008–2009 production of *The Merchant of Venice* by Edward Hall's Propeller Theatre Company took place entirely in a prison. At the very start of the performance, the Duke, playing a prison warden, posed the central question of this production: "Which is the Christian here, and which the Jew?" In Shakespeare's play, when Portia enters the court for Antonio's trial, she famously asks, "which is the Merchant here? and which the *I*ew?" (H1r), a question that muddies the clarity of the distinction between the excellent "Merchant" and the cruel "Iewe" of the quarto title page. Propeller's substitution of "Christian" for "merchant" makes sense, in that modern audiences are much more likely to find emotional resonance in a conflict between a Christian and a Jew than between a merchant and a Jew. Nevertheless, we can better appreciate what is lost in this presentist erasure of the "merchant" when we understand the impression that the figure of a desiring merchant might have made on an audience in Shakespeare's time.

NOTES

1 Hugh Grady and Terence Hawkes, eds., *Presentist Shakespeares* (London: Routledge, 2007), 4. Ironically, Grady and Hawkes's presentist critique of historicism in their introduction to *Presentist Shakespeares* repeats passages verbatim from Hawkes's earlier book *Shakespeare in the Present* (London: Routledge, 2002), 1–4, 22. That this critique has remained essentially unchanged between 2002 and 2007 is particularly ironic considering Grady and Hawkes's call for "a heightened degree of critical self-awareness" and their celebration of presentism as "an open-ended and on-going project" (*Presentist Shakespeares,* 4, 5).

2 Linda Charnes, "Shakespeare, and Belief, in the Future," in *Presentist Shakespeares,* 65. The "New Boredom" is David Kastan's tongue-in-cheek moniker for his project to recover "the specific material and institutional conditions" through which early modern literary texts engaged the "world of lived history" (*Shakespeare after Theory* [New York: Routledge, 1999], 18). Charnes describes her own practice as a historicism that reveals the "contemporary implications" of Shakespearean texts (*Hamlet's Heirs: Shakespeare and the Politics of a New Millennium* [New York: Routledge, 2006], 10), and that dares to imagine "the importance of Shakespeare in the future" ("Shakespeare," 65).

3 Michael Bristol, "… And I'm the King of France," in *Presentist Shakespeares,* 54. Bristol's distinction between "impersonal" and "personal" forms of reading, however, is hardly self-evident, especially when one attempts to judge what counts as "personal" or "impersonal" for another reader.

4 Evelyn Gajowski remarks that "feminist and queer studies are *always already*… presentist" ("The Presence of the Past," in *Presentism, Gender, and Sexuality in Shakespeare,* ed. Evelyn Gajowski [New York: Palgrave Macmillan, 2009], 2). Gajowski presents an excellent overview of the development since the 1970s of historicist and presentist Shakespeare criticism focused on issues of gender and sexuality.

5 Heather Love, *Feeling Backward: Loss and the Politics of Queer History* (Cambridge: Harvard University Press, 2007), 10.

6 Ibid., 31. Also relevant here is recent work on queer temporalities by Lee Edelman (*No Future: Queer Theory and the Death Drive* [Durham: Duke University Press, 2004]) and Judith Halberstam (*In a Queer Time and Place: Transgender Bodies, Subcultural Lives* [New York: New York University Press, 2005]).

7 Carla Freccero, *Queer/Early/Modern* (Durham: Duke University Press, 2006), 79.

8 Valerie Traub, *The Renaissance of Lesbianism in Early Modern England* (Cambridge: Cambridge University Press, 2002), 353.

9 Bristol, "King of France," 54. For all his insistence on the historicist's accountability to the facts of the past, Kastan reads Shakespeare's tragedies in ways that are sharply attuned to social, physical, and psychic forms of suffering. For instance, in "Shakespeare and the Idea of Tragedy," Kastan argues that Shakespeare's tragic characters "struggle unsuccessfully to reconstruct a coherent worldview from the ruins of the old. And it is the emotional truth of the struggle rather than the metaphysical truth of the worldview that is at the center of these plays" (David Scott Kastan, "'A rarity most beloved': Shakespeare and the Idea of Tragedy," in *A Companion to Shakespeare's Works,* vol. 1, *The Tragedies,* ed. Richard Dutton and Jean E. Howard [Malden, Mass.: Blackwell Publishing, 2003], 8).

10 Alan Sinfield's historical reading of the play addresses how it resonates with gay readers in the present; see "How

to Read *The Merchant of Venice* without Being Heterosexist," in *Shakespeare, Authority, Sexuality: Unfinished Business in Cultural Materialism* (London: Routledge, 2006). See also Anthony Guy Patricia's presentist gay male reading of Michael Radford's 2004 film of *The Merchant of Venice:* "'Through the Eyes of the Present': Screening the Male Homoerotics of Shakespearean Drama," in *Presentism.*

11 Simon Palfrey and Ewan Fernie, preface to *Godless Shakespeare,* by Eric S. Mallin (London: Continuum, 2007), x, xi.

12 Mallin, *Godless Shakespeare,* 43.

13 Palfrey and Fernie, preface, *Godless Shakespeare,* x.

14 George Rousseau, "'Homoplatonic, Homodepressed, Homomorbid': Some Further Genealogies of Same-Sex Attraction in Western Civilization," in *Love, Sex, Intimacy, and Friendship between Men, 1550–1800,* ed. Katherine O'Donnell and Michael O'Rourke (New York: Palgrave Macmillan, 2003), 27.

15 Here I disagree with Steve Patterson, who argues that Antonio's sadness derives from his "marginal position" as an "amorous lover" – "sadly outmoded, himself a kind of anachronism" – in the mercantile society of Venice; see "The Bankruptcy of Homoerotic Amity in Shakespeare's *Merchant of Venice,*" *Shakespeare Quarterly* 50 (1999): 14.

16 William Shakespeare, *The most excellent Historie of the Merchant of Venice* (London, 1600). All citations from the play will come from the 1600 quarto text.

17 Ceri Sullivan, *The Rhetoric of Credit: Merchants in Early Modern Writing* (Madison, N.J.: Fairleigh Dickinson University Press, 2002), 57. Theodore B. Leinwand makes an important point about the inexact distinctions between such terms as "merchant," "tradesman," and "retailer" in late-sixteenth- and early seventeenth-century English discourse; see *The City Staged: Jacobean Comedy, 1603–1613* (Madison: University of Wisconsin Press, 1986), 21. Nonetheless, the texts I will discuss implicitly define the "merchant" as one involved in overseas trade. Leinwand identifies Antonio as the type of "gentleman who had turned to large-scale overseas trade," in distinction to the "merchant-citizens" whose place in early modern English society was hotly debated (22).

18 Merchants, of course, do appear in premodern English literature as subjects of romantic and sexual desire – e.g., the Merchant pilgrim and the merchant of *The Shipman's Tale* in Chaucer's *Canterbury Tales* (on which see Glenn Burger, "Queer Theory," in *Chaucer: An Oxford Guide,* ed. Steve Ellis [Oxford: Oxford University Press, 2005], 439–44). Moreover, the actual merchants whose adventures are recorded in Richard Hakluyt's *Voyages and Discoveries* experience a range of desires and passions. Nonetheless, Shakespeare's play seems uniquely to foreground the opacity of a merchant's emotional life around issues of love and desire.

19 Robert Brenner traces how economic and political power in early modern England gradually shifted from the Merchant Adventurers (exporters of English wool), who were the dominant merchant group in the earlier sixteenth century, to the Mediterranean and Near East merchants (importers of foreign goods) who emerged in the 1580s with the founding of the Turkey Company (1580–81) and the Venice Company (1583). In 1592, Turkey and Venice Company merchants combined to form the prosperous Levant Company, whose members later dominated the East India Company, founded in 1599; see *Merchants and Revolution: Commercial Change, Political Conflict, and London's Overseas Traders, 1550–1653* (London: Verso, 2003), 17–21. Along with Greek currants, the two most profitable imports of the Levant and East India companies were Eastern silk and spices, the very commodities that Salerio claims Antonio is trading

(ibid., 25). During the early decades of the seventeenth century, the once powerful Venetian trade in the Mediterranean suffered greatly (ibid., 45). As a successful merchant, then, Antonio resembles more the group of English merchants who had emerged at a time roughly contemporary to *The Merchant of Venice,* rather than the English Merchant Adventurers or Venetian traders whose long-standing dominance was already declining by the late 1590s. Theodore B. Leinwand makes a similar argument about Antonio in *Theatre, Finance and Society in Early Modern England* (Cambridge: Cambridge University Press, 1999), 113–14.

20 For example, Jacques Hurault's 1588 *Politicke, Moral, and Martial Discourses,* translated into English by Arthur Golding in 1595, presents a taxonomy of passions in which the merchant signifies hope (F5r). In *Acolastus his After-Witte* (London, 1600), poet and divine Samuel Nicholson writes that the merchant pursues his "weake-built hopes" of wealth, despite his "feare" of "[t]he waues, the winds, the rocks, the cruell foe" (C3r–v). In an essay on Antonio's failure to insure his ships, Luke Wilson addresses Antonio's sadness through Hume's analysis of hope and fear, joy and grief, in the *Treatise of Human Nature* (1739–40). According to the Humean model, Wilson argues, Antonio should experience fear, not sadness, at the probability of loss; his premature sadness suggests that he "can only grasp a possible negative outcome as already accomplished, never as a matter of probability" ("Drama and Marine Insurance in Shakespeare's London," in *The Law in Shakespeare,* ed. Constance Jordan and Karen Cunningham [New York: Palgrave Macmillan, 2007], 129–30).

21 Richard Greenham, *A most sweete and assured Comfort for all those that are afflicted in Consciscience* [sic], *or troubled in minde* (London, 1595), C6r–v. See Eric Josef Carlson, "Greenham, Richard," *Oxford Dictionary of National Biography,* online edition, doi: 10.1093/ref:odnb/11424.

22 Thomas Morton, *Two Treatises concerning Regeneration* (London, 1597), B3v.

23 Henry Lok, *Svndry Christian passions contained in two hundred Sonnets* (London, 1593), 12. The sonnet alludes to Matthew 13:45–46: "Again, the kingdom of heaven is like unto a merchant man, seeking goodly pearls: Who, when he had found one pearl of great price, went and sold all he had, and bought it."

24 In Richard Barnfield, *The Affectionate Shepheard. Containing the Complaint of Daphnis for the loue of Ganymede* (London, 1594), E3v–E4r.

25 I.H., *The House of Correction, or, Certain Satirical Epigrams* (London, 1619), B8r–v.

26 I disagree with Jeremy Lopez's argument that the dramatic function of Salerio and Solanio is to provide the "facts" on which we "judge the actions of other characters" since the accuracy of the "facts" they supply regarding Antonio's sadness is immediately called into question; see *Theatrical Convention and Audience Response in Early Modern Drama* (Cambridge: Cambridge University Press, 2003), 84. Notoriously, in the first scene of the play the 1600 Quarto identifies Antonio's interlocutors in the stage direction as "*Salaryno*" and "*Salanio*" and in some speech prefixes as "*Sola.*" and "*Sala.*" To avoid confusion, I refer to these characters as "Salerio" and "Solanio."

27 Douglas Trevor recognizes Shakespeare's innovation with Antonio, referring to his sadness as "part of Antonio's personality, potentially moored in his temperament, in ways that have not thus far been entertained in Shakespearean dramaturgy" (*The Poetics of Melancholy in Early Modern England* [Cambridge: Cambridge University Press, 2004], 70). He further observes that "Antonio's confusion about why and even *how* he feels sad signifies a shift away from the diagnostic tendencies evidenced in *Love's Labour's Lost* and *Romeo and Juliet*" (69–70). If *Shakespeare* is shifting away from the diagnostic tendencies of

earlier plays, however, Salerio and Solanio pointedly are not.

28 In an unpublished dissertation, Charlotte Coker Worley observes that merchants in early sixteenth-century drama "appeared simply as good or bad." In the 1590s, she argues, the stage merchant, reflecting the greater social prestige of merchants, becomes "glorified," and in the Jacobean period, during which crown and city overtly clashed, the stage merchant is presented satirically; see "The Character of the Merchant in English Drama from 1590 to 1612: His Metamorphosis after 1603 (Glorified, Satirized)," The University of Mississippi, 1984, ProQuest Dissertations & Theses Global (303298494). While Worley's distinction between "glorified" and "satirized" dramatic characters relies on too absolute and reductive a correspondence between theater and society, her overview does suggest the developing complexity of the merchant type. Leinwand argues that "in the plots and characterizations of Jacobean city comedies, the merchant-citizen has at once fewer faces (or roles) and greater complexity" than the merchant-citizens depicted in Tudor and Stuart pamphlets, which struggled "to bolster, suppress, or reformulate the traditional story, the time-honored derogation of the merchant" (*The City Staged,* 22–23).

29 Douglas Bruster, *Drama and the Market in the Age of Shakespeare* (Cambridge: Cambridge University Press, 1992), 56; Lars Engle, "'Thrift is Blessing': Exchange and Explanation in *The Merchant of Venice,*" *Shakespeare Quarterly* 37 (1986): 22–23.

30 Leinwand, *Theatre,* 16.

31 Cynthia Lewis, *Particular Saints: Shakespeare's Four Antonios, Their Contexts, and Their Plays* (Newark: University of Delaware Press, 1997), 59.

32 Sinfield, "How to Read," 54; Engle, "'Thrift,'" 23; Joseph Pequigney, "The Two Antonios and Same-Sex Love in *Twelfth Night* and *The Merchant of Venice,*" *English Literary Renaissance* 22 (1992): 210–11.

33 Henry S. Turner, "The Problem of the More-than-One: Friendship, Calculation, and Political Association in *The Merchant of Venice,*" *Shakespeare Quarterly* 57 (2006): 413–42.

34 Ibid., 425.

35 Alan Bray, *The Friend* (Chicago: University of Chicago Press, 2003). Kastan's interest in the "material realities" of the early modern theater might be pursued here by examining the intertwined relations of affective friendship, communal affiliation, and commercial obligation within Shakespeare's acting company. According to Jeffrey Masten, around the London theaters "there was a complicated culture of male relations...characterized by co(i)mplicated identifications and by (simultaneously) collaborative living and writing arrangements" ("Playwrighting: Authorship and Collaboration," in *A New History of Early English Drama,* ed. John D. Cox and David Scott Kastan [New York: Columbia University Press, 1997], 366).

36 Likewise, Turner describes two "prescientific modes of calculation" that were in effect at the end of the sixteenth century: "a system of reckoning with number and quantity typical of the merchant's account book" and "a method of reasoning about qualitative particulars fundamental to classical ethics" ("Problem," 429).

37 On the trope of likeness in male friendship discourse, and on Portia's manipulation of that trope to invent her own agency, see Laurie Shannon, "Likenings: Rhetorical Husbandries and Portia's 'True Conceit' of Friendship," *Renaissance Drama,* n.s., 31 (2002): 3–26.

38 Jeremy Taylor, A *Discourse of the Nature, Offices and Measures of Friendship* (London, 1657), 47–48.

39 Turner points out that in Cicero's *De officiis,* virtuous friendship in fact requires calculations of obligation to determine how much duty is owed to each individual ("Problem," 425).

40 Russell West, *Spatial Representations and the Jacobean Stage: From Shakespeare to Webster* (New York: Palgrave, 2002), 111.

41 William Cornwallis, quoted in Bray, *The Friend*, 61.

42 Walter Cohen similarly argues that *The Merchant of Venice* stands apart "from most other comedies of the period, both in the gravity of its subject and in its socio-economic emphasis" ("*The Merchant of Venice* and the Possibilities of Historical Criticism," in *Materialist Shakespeare: A History*, ed. Ivo Kamps [London: Verso, 1995], 85).

43 Turner, "Problem," 419.

44 The last few lines of this difficult passage are often amended. John Drakakis reads the quarto's "Maisters of passion" as "Maistrice of passion," a "hermaphroditic" term that connotes mastery but in its combination of "master" and "mistress" depicts lack of self-control as a feminine vice; see his "Present Text: Editing *The Merchant of Venice*," in *Presentist Shakespeares*, 88–89.

45 Gail Kern Paster argues that Shylock's strategy in this speech is to "ground behavioral difference in the undeniable variety and obduracy of the physical body's appetites and their resistance to reason" (*Humoring the Body: Emotions and the Shakespearean Stage* [Chicago: University of Chicago Press, 2004], 205).

46 Bray, *The Friend*, 59.

47 Lewis, *Particular Saints*, 57.

48 Leinwand similarly observes that Shylock provides a "prosaic market analyst's account" of Antonio's worth, which had just been elevated by Salerio's "aggrandizing verse" (*Theatre*, 15). Leinwand attributes Antonio's sadness to a futile desire to "extricat[e] himself from the *burgerlich* exchange function" (ibid.).

49 Drawing on Craig Muldrew's important study of the early modern "culture of credit," Alexandra Shepard observes, "Men of no worth were not dependable in a developing market economy which was founded upon myriad bonds of trust" (*Meanings of Manhood in Early Modern England* [Oxford: Oxford University Press, 2003], 192). She demonstrates that worth "needed constant defence and assertion in competitive bids for status" among men (188).

50 I would argue that Antonio's affective claim on Bassanio is diminished at the end of the play regardless of whether we imagine Antonio to be included in or excluded from Bassanio's future household. Julie Crawford (ed., *The Merchant of Venice*, by William Shakespeare [New York: Barnes & Noble, 2008], 9) and Joseph Pequigney counter the familiar argument that Antonio is excluded from the comic community at the end of the play, with Pequigney going so far as to affirm that Antonio is "incorporat[ed] into the marriage" of Portia and Bassanio ("The Two Antonios," 218). According to early modern friendship discourse, marriage does not necessarily signal the end of male friendship, although, as in Shakespeare's *The Winter's Tale*, physical separation or fear of infidelity might well threaten friendship. Alan Bray cites a story in William Painter's *Palace of Pleasure* about two gentlemen who "persevered in their usual amity" after one of them married (*The Friend*, 173): they all shared a bed, the husband sleeping between his wife and friend.

51 For a skeptical reading of the truth content of Portia's revelation, which offers an insightful account of the difference between marine insurance and "generic insurance," see Wilson, "Drama and Marine Insurance," 135–38.

52 See Harry Berger, Jr., "Marriage and Mercifixion in *The Merchant of Venice*: The Casket Scene Revisited," *Shakespeare Quarterly* 32 (1981): 161–62.

53 Leinwand makes the slightly different argument that "Portia jettisons the intrusive affective burden that is sad Antonio by restoring to him his ships and his Venetian mercantile calling" (*Theatre*, 127).

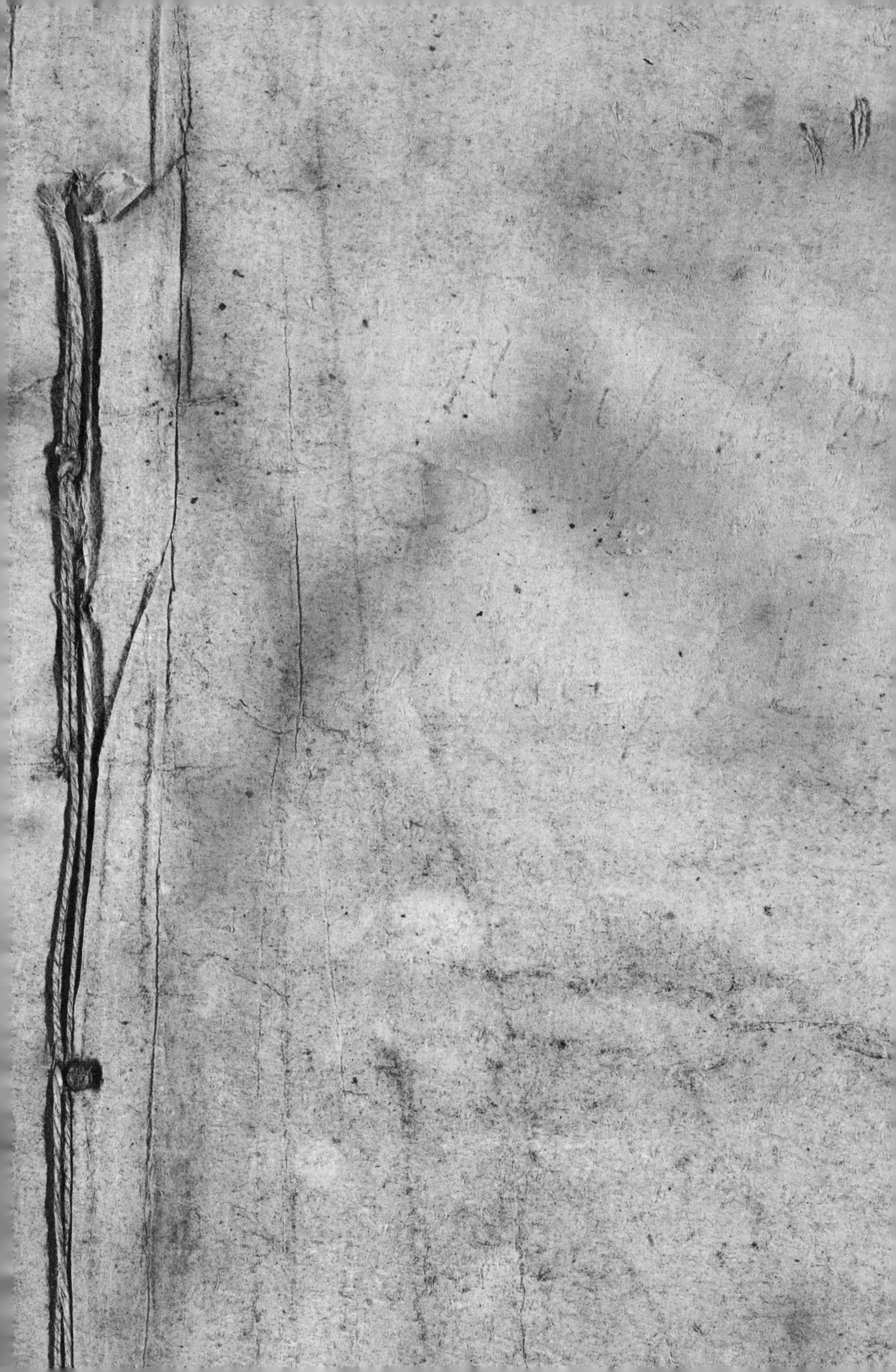

Playbooks and the Question of Ephemerality

ALAN B. FARMER

One of the increasingly common ways of studying the history of the book, the history of early modern literature, and indeed the history of literature more generally is to use quantitative methods of analysis. This approach, of course, is not new. Influential studies of printing history by D.F. McKenzie (1969) and Peter W.M. Blayney (1973), for instance, relied on quantitative methods for analyzing the output of particular early modern print shops, and foundational work on the history of the book in eighteenth-century France has likewise been informed by quantitative approaches to publishing history and the history of reading.[1] In recent years, however, the scope of this type of quantitative literary and book history has expanded to include larger-scale analyses of the printing, publishing, and reading of books. These analyses have looked at the output of all early modern printers during a specific period of time,[2] at all the editions published in the early modern English book trade over several decades,[3] at the linguistic features of large corpora of early modern texts,[4] and at the formal characteristics of various literary genres over entire centuries.[5] These data-driven studies, which might be called "Literary and Bibliographical Big Data," have enabled scholars to revisit familiar questions in these fields and ideally offer new understandings of literary and book history based on findings that would not have been possible using traditional methods that are narrower and more anecdotal in scope. This essay uses large-scale quantitative methods in order to revisit a central question about the cultural status of early modern playbooks, namely, whether these publications were treated as ephemera by early modern printers, publishers, booksellers, and readers.

In a classic article from 1950, Francis R. Johnson remarks that before plays were published in collections like the Jonson and Shakespeare folios, they were "treated as ephemeral literature," a straightforward statement more complex than it initially seems.[6] According to Johnson, the ephemerality of playbooks resulted from both how they were sold by stationers – "issued as popular pamphlets" – and how they were subsequently handled by readers: "the purchaser scarcely ever had them bound, unless he had several gathered into one volume." Johnson's claim is built on the idea that because early modern plays were perceived to be without lasting cultural or literary value, printed playbooks were treated neither by stationers nor by readers as publications worth preserving. The low cultural status of play texts, in other words, led to the low bibliographical value of playbooks.

In the ensuing decades, the bibliographical ephemerality of playbooks emerged as a foundational axiom in studies of early modern printed drama. Scholars stressed that plays were "ephemeral literature,"[7] and that playbooks "were all excluded almost as a matter of principle from most large libraries."[8] Since playbooks were not prestigious publications nor particularly valuable to stationers, printers churned out editions of substandard quality filled with careless errors: "Elizabethan printers could do meticulously scholarly work, but they rarely expended their best efforts on plays, which – at least in quarto format – they treated as ephemeral publications."[9] The ephemerality of playbooks soon became a truism of historical bibliography, according to one scholar, "and the truth of that truism ought not to be denied."[10]

For many critics and book historians, this truism was connected to the material features of playbooks. Plays from the professional theater were typically published in quartos of six to twelve edition-sheets (the number of sheets required to print one copy of an edition), or forty-eight to ninety-six pages. At this length, which has often struck scholars as intrinsically short, playbooks would have been sold to readers stab-stitched rather than in more sturdy and expensive sewn bindings, leading to the belief that playbooks were "cheap," "disposable," and "perishable."[11] In an influential essay, T.A. Birrell goes so far as to call the playbook a "self-destructing artefact": "it was issued unbound, probably not even stitched, but roughly stabbed with string or thread. After it was read it lay around, the top leaf and the bottom leaf got dirty and torn, then the string broke, and it disintegrated and was thrown away." These "vulnerable, throwaway quarto[s]," he continues, "had a low survival rate," another truism repeatedly voiced by other scholars.[12]

This view of the ephemerality of playbooks has begun to be challenged in the past decade on several fronts. Heidi Brayman Hackel, Lukas Erne, and Alan H. Nelson have demonstrated that many elite readers collected playbooks and included them in their libraries, while Erne has also provocatively argued that Shakespeare sought to write "literary drama" rather than "ephemeral entertainment."[13] Pointing to "the care taken over" the "typographic appearance" of printed plays, H.R. Woudhuysen has questioned whether playbooks were routinely printed in editions marked by shoddy workmanship.[14] And Joseph A. Dane and Alexandra Gillespie have disputed what they call "the myth of the cheap quarto," a myth grounded in the assumption that quartos in general were inherently shorter and less expensive than publications in other formats.[15] Each of these studies has productively reexamined evidence taken to indicate the ephemerality of playbooks, but the idea of playbooks as ephemeral remains entrenched. Two new important online resources, the British Library's *Shakespeare in Quarto* website and the *Shakespeare Quartos Archive* website, represent current scholarly views when they inform users, respectively, that printed plays "were considered to be ephemera"; "Sold unbound and often read to pieces, they are among the most ephemeral books of the age and survive in relatively low numbers."[16]

My goal in this essay is to challenge this view of the ephemerality of playbooks and to establish a more historically informed understanding of what it meant for publications to be ephemeral in early modern England. Were play quartos of six to twelve edition-sheets "cheap" and "perishable"? Is it true that "the life-expectancy of a play quarto was quite short"?[17] Compared to other types of publications, is there any reason to continue calling playbooks "ephemeral"? A central contention of the essay is that ephemerality should be thought of not as a strict binary between lasting and short-lived publications but as a continuum, with publications exhibiting varying degrees of ephemerality for a variety of reasons.

This approach allows for a reassessment of the presumed relationship between cultural and bibliographical ephemerality, in which texts of low cultural value are thought to have been printed poorly and subsequently treated by readers as disposable artifacts. In fact, there are good reasons to question this narrative. Cultural ephemerality is best seen as a discursive category shaped by ideological commitments and prejudices, whereas bibliographical ephemerality is a material category affected by a publication's physical characteristics; both of these could affect how readers subsequently handled publications, but neither absolutely determined whether a book would be destroyed or preserved. In the case of playbooks, whatever early modern readers may have thought about printed drama, these publications were not particularly ephemeral.[18]

THEORIZING BIBLIOGRAPHICAL EPHEMERALITY: COPIES AND LOST EDITIONS

The term "ephemeral" is derived from the Greek *ἐφήμερος ("ephemeros")*, meaning "lasting only for a day," and it was used in early modern England to describe fevers, flies, day lilies, herbs, and beasts that had brief, transitory existences.[19] Playbooks, however, were never described as ephemera in early modern England; in fact, no books were. The modern bibliographical category of "ephemera," defined in one influential study as "transient documents of everyday life," did not yet exist.[20] Nonetheless, some publications were of course seen as less valuable and less worthy of preservation in early modern England, and the idea that playbooks were among them has been remarkably persistent.

Two reasons for this persistence are that scholars often rely on anachronistic bibliographical categories or make erroneous assumptions about the survival of early modern books. An important criterion in judging the ephemerality of playbooks has been the number of copies that still exist: as H.S. Bennett has written, playbooks survive "in limited numbers – many in single and at times mutilated copies."[21] But in fact every early modern edition of every type of book now survives in limited numbers. Whether Bibles, religious treatises, poetry books, learned medical works, or Latin philosophical treatises, there is no genre of book for which the majority of copies printed in early modern England still exist. In the case of playbooks, this utterly normal bibliographical fact has led to the belief that these publications led an especially precarious existence.[22] Editions of playbooks survive in anywhere from one to around forty copies, with varying degrees of completeness, which may sound low for editions that were originally printed in press runs of 500 to 1,500 copies. These copy totals, however, do not themselves prove that playbooks were more susceptible to destruction than other types of books. To make that argument, scholars would need to know the number of extant copies for publications in other genres, which unfortunately have not been subject to similar systematic censuses of known copies.

Further, even if the numbers of extant copies of every early modern publication were accurately tallied, those figures would probably still not provide clear evidence of the ephemerality of playbooks. There are, for instance, more extant copies of playbooks than there are of some other popular genres, such as meditation and prayer books.[23] More generally, the number of extant copies in any genre is the product of a range of competing historical factors, as Oliver Willard detailed in a seminal 1942 essay about survival rates. A couple of his conclusions are straightforward and match the conventional scholarly wisdom, particularly that books from earlier years survive in fewer copies than those printed later in the early modern period, and that "small books" survive in fewer copies than "large books."[24] But his most significant claim is more counterintuitive. Copies of the most popular early modern works are scarcer, but not because fewer copies were originally printed; rather, he suggests, "the less there are, the more there were," that is, the fewer copies that now exist from a single edition, the more that were originally printed. Although Goran Proot and Leo Egghe have convincingly demonstrated that the size of an edition's print run would not greatly affect the odds of all the copies of an edition becoming lost, Willard's central insight – that economic popularity is inversely related to the survival of copies – is important and directly related to several other important observations he makes.[25] When a text has been reprinted in multiple editions, he notes, there are usually fewer copies of the early editions and more of the later ones. In addition, early editions of frequently reprinted texts usually survive in fewer copies than works that were printed only once. These twin phenomena, moreover, occur across genres. The fact that only two copies now exist of the first quarto of *Hamlet* and only one incomplete copy of the first quarto of *1 Henry IV* is, according to Willard, entirely typical for popular works printed in multiple editions from the 1590s through the 1630s, regardless of genre.

The logical endpoint for those books that proved *most* ephemeral is editions that have been entirely lost, for which zero copies now exist. Lost editions pose a significant problem for histories of the book trade, affecting, among other issues, estimates of the size of the retail market, the economic outlay for materials like paper, the popularity of different genres, the output of individual printers, the total economic investment of publishers, the publications sold by booksellers, and the works read by readers. Lost editions have the greatest potential to reshape our sense of the book trade as a whole, as well as the place and relative ephemerality of playbooks within it. One useful method for inferring lost editions often used by book historians is to compare extant editions of books in the *Short-Title Catalogue* (STC) with entries in the Stationers' Registers.[26] But this comparison also has several limitations. First, not all entries in the Stationers' Registers inevitably resulted in editions of those works; some titles were entered but never printed. Second, there are many works, both extant and lost, that were never entered; the loss of unentered titles can easily go undetected. Third, entries in the Stationers' Registers typically concern first editions and rarely reveal anything about reprints; matching up a Stationers' Register entry with a corresponding volume indicates that at least one edition was printed, but it does not tell us whether there were other earlier or later editions that are now lost.

Another method for estimating lost editions has been to use "zero-graphing," which seeks to derive the number of editions for which zero copies survive based on the number of editions for which one, two, or more copies are extant. In the most advanced of these studies, which focuses on lost editions of fifteenth-century publications, Jonathan Green, Frank McIntyre, and Paul Needham outline several justifications for using zero-graphing, key assumptions this method entails, and certain limitations in their bibliographical data.[27] Though not central to their analysis, one of their more suggestive theories is that "thick" and "slim" volumes printed either in Latin or in a vernacular language probably have different loss rates. In other words, some kinds of books are more likely to have become lost than others.[28] It is this aspect of bibliographical ephemerality that I want to consider further, though not by relying on necessarily incomplete censuses of known copies, but by analyzing a different group of books: the archive of numbered editions.

THE ARCHIVE OF NUMBERED EDITIONS

Three classic studies of early modern book collections have produced important estimates of lost editions. Oliver M. Willard investigated the 201 editions listed in William Jaggard's *Catalogve of such English Bookes, as lately haue bene, and now are in Printing for Publication* (1618; STC 14341); William A. Jackson examined the manuscript catalogue of 658 printed editions in the library of Humphrey Dyson, who died in 1632; and Franklin B. Williams, Jr., analyzed 1,832 editions of divinity and science listed in the bookseller Andrew Maunsell's *Catalogue of English printed Bookes* (1595; STC 17669). Each study computed a loss rate of around 14% to 16%, but each of these catalogues is limited in the kinds of books it includes.[29] None is representative of the book trade as a whole in the 1590s or the 1610s, much less in the entire sixteenth and seventeenth centuries. As useful as these articles are for establishing a starting point for thinking about bibliographical ephemerality, their analyses do not extend very far beyond reporting the loss rates for these three specific collections. As Williams himself observes, these catalogues do not tell us much about the relative ephemerality of different print genres, including of playbooks.[30]

Fortunately, there is a more comprehensive population of books that does take account of reprint editions and can be analyzed from a greater variety of perspectives. Originally alluded to by Willard in his 1942 article, this archive comprises "books whose editions were numbered by their printers." These are books that were identified on their title pages as the "second edition," "third impression," and so forth, as can be seen on the title page of the 1637 edition of John Ball's *A Short Treatise, Contayning all the Principall Grounds of Christian Religion* (STC 1318.3), which was sold to readers as "*The eleventh Impression*" (fig. 8). Willard does not indicate how many numbered editions he located, but he optimistically suggested that an "edition described on its title-page as the twenty-first is *prima facie* evidence that twenty other editions were printed, whether they all survive or not."[31] Though a tempting conclusion, this statement ignores the reality that sometimes the wrong edition number was printed on title pages, perhaps by mistake, because a compositor repeated the edition number from an earlier edition, or perhaps deliberately, because a printer wanted to make a work seem more popular by inflating its apparent

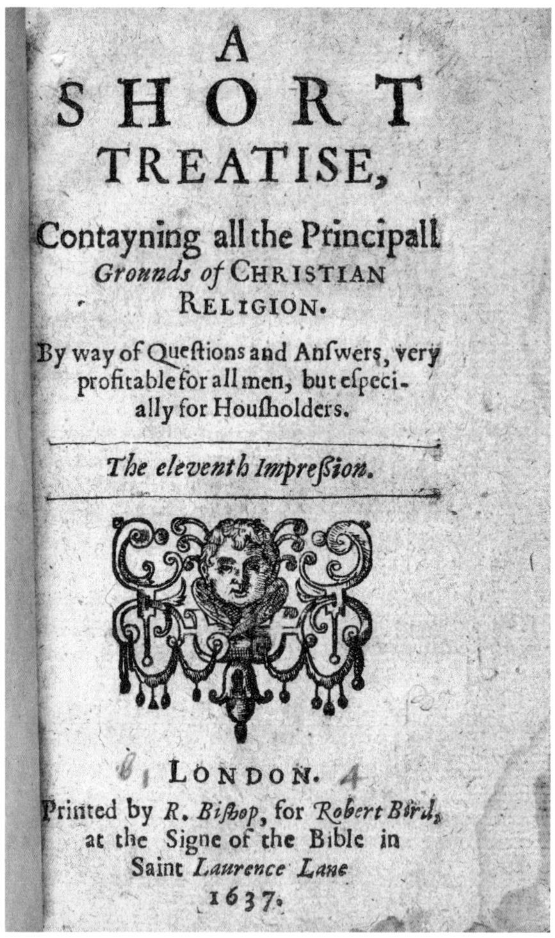

A
SHORT
TREATISE,
Contayning all the Principall
Grounds of CHRISTIAN
RELIGION.
By way of Queſtions and Anſwers, very
profitable for all men, but eſpeci-
ally for Houſholders.

The eleventh Impreſſion.

LONDON.
Printed by *R. Biſhop*, for *Robert Bird*,
at the Signe of the Bible in
Saint *Laurence Lane*
1637.

Fig. 8. John Ball, *A Short Treatise, Contayning all the Principall Grounds of Christian Religion* (London, 1637), title page. Beinecke Rare Book and Manuscript Library, Yale University, Mhc5 B210 Sh8 1637

edition total. And every edition number did in some sense advertise a text's popularity. Only about one in five speculative publications was reprinted within twenty years of its first edition, so the seemingly straightforward advertisement of any book as the second or third edition emphasized that the work had already proven popular with readers.[32] Rather than assume edition numbers are accurate, it is necessary to determine, first, whether they are reliable and can be used to infer the possibility of lost editions and, second, how representative those books with edition numbers are.

In order to find all the books with edition numbers on their title pages, I searched through the print *STC* while also consulting various online resources, particularly the *English Short Title Catalogue* (ESTC), *Universal Short Title Catalogue* (USTC), and *Early English Books Online* (EEBO).[33] I was able to locate 1,698 separate editions (of 742 distinct works) with edition numbers on their title pages, which then had to be checked for accuracy. Some edition numbers, for instance, might be accurate but at odds with the entries in the STC, a problem particularly associated with books in Latin that were also printed on the continent.[34] For example, the 1634 edition of Francis Bacon's *De Sapientia Veterum* (STC 1129) is called "*Editio quarta*" on its title page, but there are only two previous editions listed in the STC, both of which were printed in London. There was, however, an "Editio tertio" printed in Leiden in 1633, which the fourth edition's title page statement was almost certainly taking into account.[35] In contrast, the 1627 edition of *Sir Thomas Ouerbury His Wife* (STC 18915) was advertised as "The twelfth Impression," but it is actually the thirteenth edition listed in the STC. In this case, the edition number counts only London editions and excludes the 1626 edition printed in Dublin (STC 18914), which was likewise sold as "*The twelfth Impression*." These types of fine-grained distinctions obviously require the use of critical judgment, but in most cases the accuracy of edition numbers can be reasonably inferred.[36]

Of the 742 works printed with at least one numbered edition, I have excluded two single-leaf publications (STC 12473.5 and STC 16823) because of the problems posed by works in this format (an issue discussed further below). For another twenty-seven of these works, it is not possible to conclude with sufficient certainty whether their edition statements are accurate.[37] That leaves a remaining corpus of 713 titles printed in 2,496 editions; there are probably 501 editions of these works that are lost, which works out to a loss rate of 16.7%, very close to Willard's, Jackson's, and Williams's calculations.[38]

While D.F. McKenzie has warned that "[t]itle-page edition statements are notoriously unreliable," the archive of numbered editions suggests that this view is overstated.[39] Up through 1640, early modern printers seem to have been remarkably accurate in their numbering of editions: of the 1,698 editions with edition numbers, more than three-quarters are correct (76.0%). In contrast, obvious "counting errors" occur on relatively few. These errors are usually the result of an edition number being repeated from a prior edition in a subsequent reprint (6.4%) or an edition being reissued with a new title page that advertises the reissue with a higher edition number (1.4%).[40] Such errors, however, are dwarfed by the title pages with correct edition numbers. One reason for this accuracy is that printers usually began adding edition numbers on the second or third edition of a work; most edition statements did not have to take account of dozens of unnumbered prior editions.[41] Stationers also did not restrict edition numbers to unusually popular works that were printed again and again – although some exceptional bestsellers certainly did have them. Printers apparently did not find it difficult to number accurately works that had previously been printed only once or twice.[42] Perhaps most important, printers do not seem to have routinely inflated edition totals in order to make titles seem more popular; rather, stationers clearly preferred printing the correct edition number on title pages.

Given this accuracy, it is reasonable to consider discrepancies between extant edition totals and title-page edition numbers to be suggestive evidence of lost editions. There will always be other possibilities for these discrepancies besides lost editions, and inferences of lost editions can never establish with absolute certainty that a counting error or some other mistake was not made by an early modern stationer.[43] But in cases like the 1617 edition of Thomas Heywood's *A Woman Killed with Kindness* (*STC* 13372), which was advertised as "The third Edition," the logical conclusion is that there was another edition, now lost, probably printed after the first extant edition of 1607 (*STC* 13371) and before the 1617 edition.[44]

The practice of adding edition numbers is concentrated in those years when plays from the professional theater were being regularly published. Printers rarely added edition numbers to title pages during most of the sixteenth century, but around 1580 they started to use them with greater frequency. As fig. 9 shows, edition numbers became more and more common in the ensuing decades; by the 1630s they appear on a little over 30% of reprint (or second-plus) editions.[45] Numbered editions therefore provide solid evidence about lost editions after 1580, in the period when professional plays emerged as a significant part of the English book trade.[46] There are, moreover, enough works printed after 1580 with numbered editions to justify using these publications to make larger claims about the book trade as a whole.[47] Unlike the relatively narrow scope of books in Dyson's and Maunsell's catalogues, numbered editions are found in nearly all the major early modern genres. They therefore enable the type of comparative analysis of loss rates that is necessary for determining

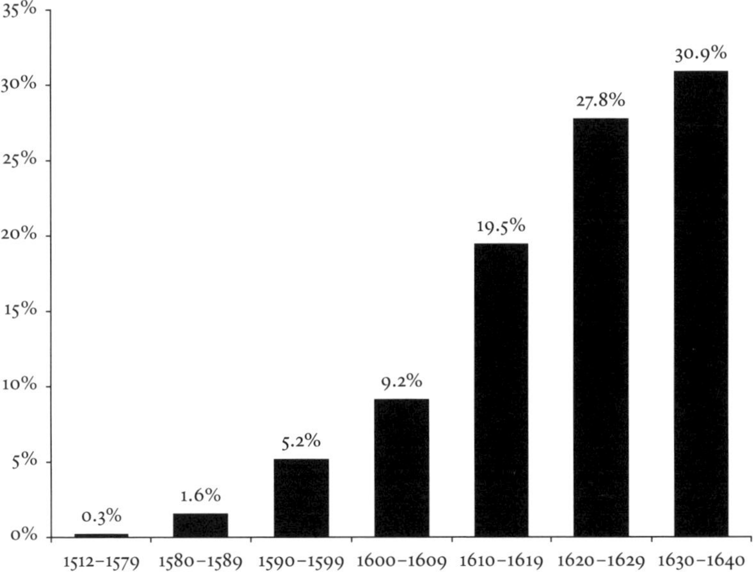

Fig. 9. The Rise of Numbered Editions. Percentage of Second-plus Editions with Title-Page Edition Numbers, 1512–1640

the relative ephemerality of different kinds of books and for constructing more general theories of bibliographical ephemerality in the sixteenth and seventeenth centuries.

ESTIMATING BIBLIOGRAPHICAL EPHEMERALITY: SIZE AND GENRE

Scholars have long posited that size and genre were likely to contribute to a book's ephemerality. But they have not agreed on which aspects of a book's size were most important nor which genres had higher loss rates. The archive of numbered editions can be used to begin constructing answers to these questions, suggesting new possibilities that sometimes run counter to prevailing beliefs about the ephemerality of different kinds of books in early modern England.

Among works with numbered editions, one of the most important factors affecting bibliographical ephemerality was a book's size; to quote David Scott Kastan, "size matters."[48] There are, however, several ways to conceptualize the size of a book. We can focus on the number of leaves (or pages) a book has – its bulk. Or we can focus on the dimensions of a book's pages – its height and width – which would mainly be the product of a book's format as well as the original dimensions of the sheets of paper on which it was printed.[49] The relationship between a book's bulk and the size of its pages, though, is not as straightforward as book historians have sometimes assumed, as Dane and Gillespie emphasize in their essay on "cheap quartos." Some folios were noticeably thin, whereas some quartos, octavos, and duodecimos could be thick and bulky.[50] These two ways of measuring a book's dimensions are obviously interconnected, but in ways that make it misleading to take either as an unambiguous marker of bibliographical size.

A third way to measure a book's size is to count the number of edition-sheets it has, the number of sheets of paper it would take to print one copy of a book in an edition. An important benefit of this method is that it captures a book's total volume – its height, width, and bulk – because what is lost in height and width when a sheet receives an additional fold (and so changes from a folio to a quarto) is offset by the extra leaves that correspondingly result. Edition-sheets also had a functional economic utility in the early modern book trade; they are what stationers across Europe used for valuing and exchanging books.[51] And as can be seen in fig. 10, edition-sheets matter: the loss rate of works with numbered editions decreases as the number of edition-sheets they contain increases.[52] The very shortest publications of less than two sheets have loss rates that rise above 60%, while those over forty sheets have loss rates that decline below 5%. This relationship is not mechanistic, of course, and there is a certain amount of variation in the loss rates of books with different edition-sheet lengths. The trend line in fig. 10, however, takes account of this variability and indicates the best fit among all the editions at different edition-sheet levels. A significant advantage in using edition-sheets is that this metric is better at predicting loss rates than are either total leaves or format alone.[53] An edition of ninety-six leaves could be a folio of forty-eight sheets, or a quarto of twenty-four, an octavo of twelve, a duodecimo of eight, or a sixteenmo of six edition-sheets. Because the dimensions of the pages in these formats would vary widely, it is understandable that there would be more variability in the loss rates of books with the same number of leaves but printed in different formats. Edition-sheets balance out, and ultimately incorporate, the competing effects of height, width, and bulk, so that books of ten edition-sheets end

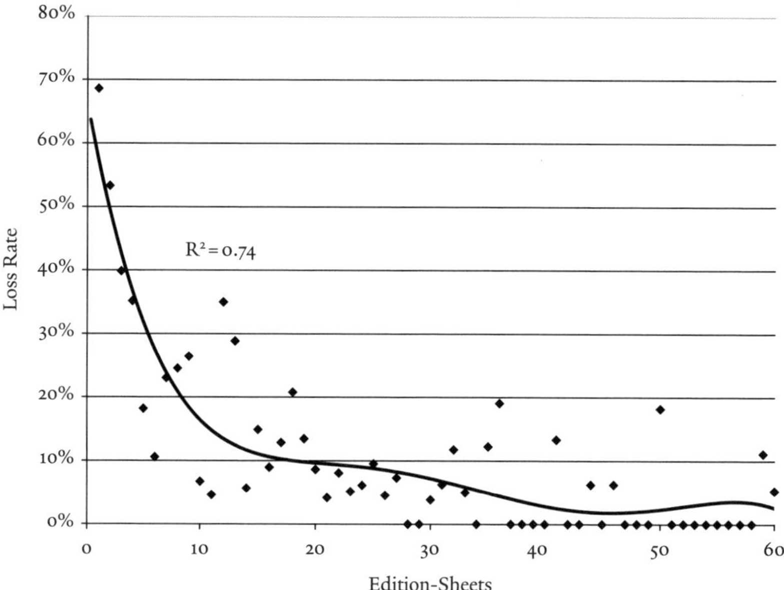

Fig. 10. Sheets Matter. Loss Rates and Lengths of Titles with Numbered Editions, 1580–1640 (through 60 sheets)

up being more similar in their loss rates than those with the same number of leaves or in the same format.

One exception to this theory of edition-sheets is single-leaf publications. There are only two extant single-leaf editions that were published with an edition number, both of which were advertised as "third" editions and neither of which has any earlier surviving editions. This loss rate is higher than that of other short publications, but there are good reasons to consider single-leaf publications separately. Only about one in ten single-leaf ballad titles from the second half of the sixteenth century survives, according to Tessa Watt, an estimate that does not even take into account reprint editions of these ballads; if reprints were included, their loss rate would be even higher.[54] Other single-leaf publications probably fared no better than ballads did. This extremely low survival rate means that single-leaf publications were much more prominent in the early modern book trade than they are in the archive of extant editions. Their share of extant publications is only 2.4% from the 1580s through the 1610s and then rises to 7.6% in the 1620s and 1630s. (It is possible that stationers tripled their output of single-leaf publications in these last two decades, but the more likely reason is that these works began to be preserved in the libraries of seventeenth-century collectors like Samuel Pepys.) If Watt's estimates are correct and apply equally well to genres other than ballads, then single-leaf publications may have composed up to half of the speculative publications in the period.[55] The problem with such a projection, however, is that there is almost no way to assess its accuracy. As a result, given how many single-leaf publications are lost, the uncertainty of their loss rate, and the uncertainty of their reprinting, it seems wiser simply to conclude that these are the most ephemeral publications in the early modern book trade. Trying to construct more precise estimates of their loss rates or lumping them together with codex publications would only lead to claims that are more speculative and less grounded in the bibliographical facts we do have.

Besides edition-sheets, the other crucial factor that seems to have led to lost editions is genre. Fig. 11 lists the titles that have the most lost editions among works with numbered editions, a list that includes Nicholas Themylthorpe's *The Posie of Godly Prayers*, the "thirtieth" edition of which was published in 1643 (*Wing* T847; fig. 12). None of the titles in fig. 11 is particularly lengthy: the longest is Sorocold's *Supplications of the Saints* (sixteen to nineteen sheets), whereas the shortest are one sheet (Andrewes's *The Golden Trumpet*) to one and a half sheets (Perkins's *Deaths Knell* and the anonymous *Heavens Happines*). But more striking is the recurrence of a few genres – catechisms, prayer books, and schoolbooks – suggesting that certain genres are more likely to have lost editions, even after their length is taken into account.[56] This is a crucial point. When the loss rates of genres are analyzed, it is important to keep in mind the effects of length. Works routinely published in short pamphlets, such as newsbooks, will normally have higher loss rates than those printed in large volumes, such as dictionaries. In order to assess the impact of genre on loss rates, it is therefore necessary to try to determine which genres have higher or lower loss rates *relative to other works of the same length.*

With that in mind, it is possible to divide numbered editions into high-loss and low-loss genres. The genres in the high-loss category include schoolbooks, handwriting manuals, works of moral philosophy containing advice for children, catechisms, prayer books, prose fiction, and books of needlepoint patterns (corantos are another high-loss genre,

Author, *Title*	First Extant Edition	Extant Editions	Lost Editions	Genre
Stephen Egerton, *A Briefe Methode of Catechising*	1597 (STC 7527.9)	15	28	Catechism
John Andrewes, *The Golden Trumpet*	1641 (*Wing* A3123)	0	24	Religious Treatise
Michael Sparke, *Crvmms of Comfort*	1627 (STC 23015.7)	8	20	Prayer Book
Nicholas Themylthorpe, *The Posie of Godly Prayers**	1611 (STC 23934.2)	9	20	Prayer Book
Edmund Coote, *The English Schoole-Maister*	1596 (STC 5711)	10	18	Reading Instruction
John Ball, *A Short Catechisme*	1628 (STC 1313.2)	4	14	Catechism
John Davies, *The Writing Schoolemaster*	[1620?] (STC 6344.3)	3	13	Handwriting Manual
William Perkins, *Deaths Knell: or, The sicke mans Passing-Bell*	1628 (STC 19684)	4	12	Religious Treatise
Thomas Sorocold, *Supplications of Saints*	1612 (STC 22932)	14	12	Prayer Book
Samuel Hieron, *The Doctrine of the Beginning of Christ*†	1606 (STC 13399.5)	7	10	Catechism
John Taylor, *The Needles Excellency*	1631 (STC 23775.5)	4	9	Needlework Patterns
Anon., *Lilies Rvles Constrved*‡	1603 (STC 15633.4)	1	8	Latin Grammar
Anon., *Heavens Happines*	[1628?] (STC 13018.5)	2	8	Religious Treatise
Thomas Deloney, *The Pleasant History of Iohn Winchcomb*	1619 (STC 6559)	5	8	Prose Fiction
John Norden, *A Poore Mans Rest*§	1620 (STC 18629)	6	8	Prayer Book

Fig. 11. Individual Works with the Greatest Number of Probable Lost Editions, 1580–1640

* The number of extant editions of Themylthorpe's prayer book does not include an unnumbered edition printed in Aberdeen in 1636 (STC 23935).

† The number of extant editions of Hieron's catechism includes three entries classified by the STC as "impressions" (STC 13402, 13402.2, 13403). It does not include three unnumbered impressions printed from 1632 to 1638 (STC 13404, 13405, 13405.5). Nor does it include "The sixth Edition" printed in the collection of Hieron's works, *All the Sermons of Samvel Hieron* (1614) (STC 13378). I have assumed that the publication history of *The Doctrine* is analogous to that of Hieron's prayer book, *A Helpe Vnto Devotion*, which was also printed in *All the Sermons* as "The sixth Edition." A separate edition of *A Helpe*, however, was published in that same year and likewise advertised as "The sixt Edition" (STC 13409). It therefore seems reasonable to conclude that *The Doctrine* was probably printed in an independent sixth edition as well.

‡ The number of extant editions of *Lilies Rvles Constrved* does not include two unnumbered editions printed in the 1630s (STC 15633.6, 15633.8).

§ The first extant edition of Norden's prayer book was advertised as "the eight time augmented," which means it was probably the ninth edition of the work to be published.

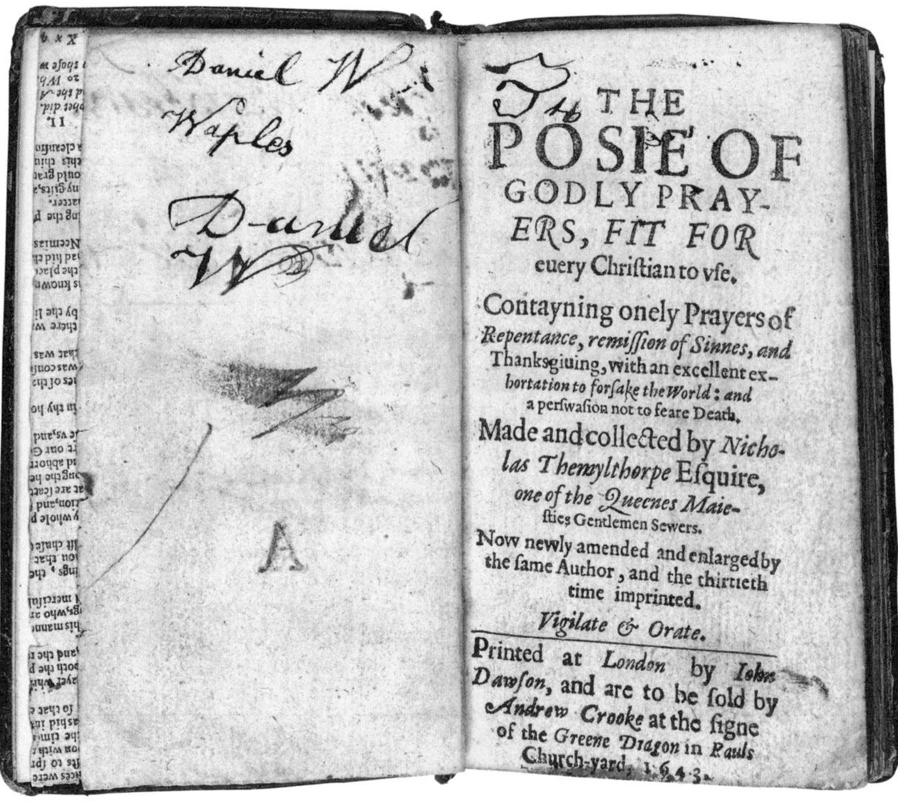

THE POSIE OF GODLY PRAY-ERS, FIT FOR euery Chriſtian to vſe.

Contayning onely Prayers of *Repentance, remiſſion of Sinnes, and* Thanksgiuing, with an excellent ex-*hortation to forſake the World: and* a perſwaſion not to feare Death.

Made and collected by *Nicholas Themylthorpe* Eſquire, *one of the Queenes Maie-*ſties Gentlemen Sewers.

Now newly amended and enlarged by the ſame Author, and the thirtieth time imprinted.

Vigilate & Orate.

Printed at *London* by *Iohn Dawſon*, and are to be ſold by *Andrew Crooke* at the ſigne of the *Greene Dragon* in *Pauls* Church-yard, 1.6.4.3.

Fig. 12. Nicholas Themylthorpe, *The Posie of Godly Prayers, Fit for euery Christian to vse* (London, 1643), title page spread. Beinecke Rare Book and Manuscript Library, Yale University, Mrx81 T34

as I discuss below). As figs. 13 and 14 show, works in high-loss and low-loss genres have strikingly different loss rates for editions between two and a half and fifty sheets.[57]

Overall, works in high-loss genres have a loss rate (37.3%) almost four times higher than those in low-loss genres (9.8%). Individual genres within these two categories obviously vary in their loss rates, but figs. 13 and 14 nonetheless capture how a work's genre could lead to a greater or lesser likelihood of lost editions.[58]

For each of the high-loss genres, fig. 15 lists the total number of works with numbered editions printed in that genre, the number of extant editions of those works, and their loss rate. The chart also includes the loss rate for books of the same length (i.e., with the same number of edition-sheets) in low-loss genres. As this chart makes clear, works in high-loss genres typically have loss rates two to seven times higher than those of the same length in low-loss genres. These comparisons help isolate the effects of genre from those of length.[59] For instance, there are surely more lost editions of poetry books than most other genres, but not because poetry books were inherently more ephemeral. They were among the most frequently printed types of books in early modern England – with the second-highest market share among speculative publications, behind only religious treatises – and they were also often short: there are almost eight hundred extant editions of poetry books that were printed from 1580 to 1640 that are four sheets or less, not to mention almost as many editions of single-leaf verse.[60] Among numbered editions, however, poetry books do not have an unusually high loss rate. There are forty-eight works of poetry with numbered editions; these have 135 extant editions and a loss rate of 11.8%. This is very close to the loss rate for other works in low-loss genres of the same length (16.0%), whereas those in high-loss genres of the same length have a much higher loss rate (45.0%). Poetry books clearly belong with other low-loss genres. The short length of many poetry books and the huge number of editions printed nevertheless would have led to a higher absolute number of total lost editions in this genre, especially compared to handwriting manuals or books of needlework and lace patterns, which were published much less frequently. Once edition-sheets are factored in, though, poetry books as a genre do not seem to have had an unusually high loss rate.

Although a range of causes surely led to different genres having different loss rates, one important factor seems to explain why high-loss genres ended up with more lost editions relative to other books of the same length. With the exception of works of prose fiction, the books in each of these genres were meant to be used, and not merely read, by owners. Handwriting manuals, books of language instruction, catechisms, and probably moral advice to children were generally intended to be used in educational settings; meditation and prayer books were used for contemplation and study during private and public devotion; and engraved needlework and lace patterns were cut out or pricked through when sewing. Such books were probably used more heavily than those in other genres and, as a result, were "used to death" more often.[61] The high loss

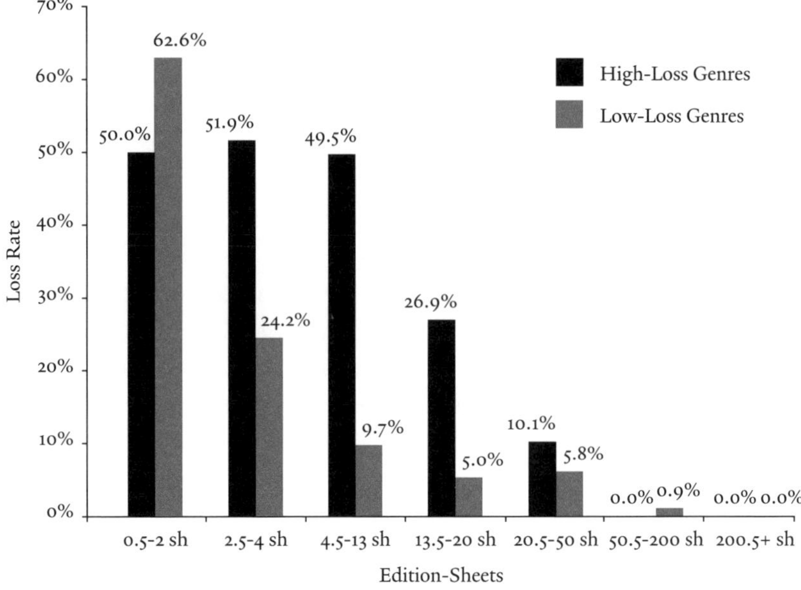

Fig. 13. Genre Matters. Loss Rates and Lengths of High-Loss and Low-Loss Genres, 1580–1640

rate for works of prose fiction probably had different causes underlying it. These books were not marked for particular uses beyond reading, so in their case it would seem their high loss rates came from their popularity with readers (being read to death) combined with readers' being less committed to the books' preservation.

These two ways of estimating lost editions – one based on the *absolute number* of lost editions, the other based on *rates* of lost editions – each tell us something important about bibliographical ephemerality. The genres with the most lost editions are mainly those that were printed most often, especially as short publications, information that is useful for predicting the overall composition of lost editions. Looking at the loss rates of specific genres, however, identifies which types of works were more likely to become lost due to their subject matter rather than merely their length. Fig. 16 shows those genres that probably have the greatest number of lost editions, while fig. 17 lists those genres with the highest estimated loss rates. The figures in these graphs are necessarily estimates and therefore include confidence intervals (these should be interpreted as suggestive

Genre Category	Edition-Sheets	Extant Editions	Probable Lost Editions	Probable Loss Rate	Confidence Interval
Both	0.5 to 2 sheets	44	67	60.4%	51.1% to 69.0%
High-Loss	2.5 to 4 sheets	74	80	51.9%	44.1% to 59.7%
Low-Loss	2.5 to 4 sheets	119	38	24.2%	18.1% to 31.5%
High-Loss	4.5 to 13 sheets	152	149	49.5%	43.9% to 55.1%
Low-Loss	4.5 to 13 sheets	604	65	9.7%	7.7% to 12.2%
High-Loss	13.5 to 20 sheets	106	39	26.9%	20.3% to 34.7%
Low-Loss	13.5 to 20 sheets	265	14	5.0%	2.9% to 8.3%
High-Loss	20.5 to 50 sheets	107	12	10.1%	5.7% to 16.9%
Low-Loss	20.5 to 50 sheets	519	32	5.8%	4.1% to 8.1%
Both	50.5 to 200 sheets	359	3	0.8%	0.2% to 2.5%
Both	200+ sheets	63	0	0.0%	0.0% to 6.9%
Total		2412	499	17.1%	15.8% to 18.6%

Fig. 14. Loss Rates of High-Loss and Low-Loss Genres with Numbered Editions, 1580–1640

Genre	Works	Extant Editions	Loss Rate	Loss Rate for Works of the Same Length in Low-Loss Genres
Needlework and Lace Patterns	1	4	69.2%	9.7%
Handwriting Manuals	6	18	51.4%	27.0%
Catechisms	31	151	42.6%	18.0%
Grammars and Reading Instruction	16	52	36.6%	9.5%
Meditation and Prayer Books	38	187	36.3%	6.7%
Moral Advice to Children	4	22	31.3%	17.7%
Prose Fiction	18	62	25.3%	5.5%

Fig. 15. Loss Rates of High-Loss Genres with Numbered Editions, 1580–1640

estimates, *not* as hard facts). As can be seen in fig. 16, the genres with the greatest number of probable lost editions are those that were generally printed most often, especially as short pamphlets. The genres in fig. 17, on the other hand, are primarily made up of the high-loss genres discussed above, in addition to a few other kinds of books that were frequently printed in short editions of only a few sheets (news pamphlets, almanacs, and verse).

The overall loss rate for the entire book trade (excluding single-leaf publications) from 1580 to 1640 can be estimated to be 23.3%.[62] For just over every four extant speculative publications in the *STC* during this period, there is therefore probably about one lost edition. (Remember that these figures concern only speculative books, i.e., books intended for retail sale, and hence exclude a great deal of job printing that has certainly been lost: advertisements, labels, tickets, posters, and so forth.[63]) The vast majority of these projected lost editions would have been thirteen sheets or less (91.7% of estimated lost editions) – in fact, almost two-thirds would have been four sheets or less (64.9% of estimated lost editions).

Another genre with an unusually high loss rate is corantos, which were serialized news pamphlets on the Thirty Years' War. Published from the 1620s through the early 1640s in numbered series of fifty to one hundred editions, corantos were never reprinted, but because they were published in numbered series, it is possible to deduce which editions are lost. From 1622 to 1640, numbered and dated corantos have an overall loss rate of 58.1% (281 extant editions, 390 lost editions), which is in line with other high-loss genres published in very short editions.[64] The serialized, weekly publication of corantos seems to have been a decisive factor in their increased loss rate. Other news pamphlets still had a relatively high loss rate because they were short, but they do not seem to have had the same type of bibliographical ephemerality as corantos.[65] One possible reason nonserialized news pamphlets did not have a higher loss rate is that, despite their topical subject matter, some readers collected them. For example, there are more news publications than any other genre among the books published from 1580 to 1630 that can be traced back to Humphrey Dyson's library.[66] For readers like Dyson, news pamphlets were not merely topical. Centered on issues of domestic and foreign politics, these works had a political, and eventually historical, value that made them worth preserving.

Many of the features that contributed to the ephemerality of corantos are shared by almanacs. Almanacs were short, often only two or three edition-sheets, with some printed as single-leaf publications. And although numbered editions cannot be used to estimate lost editions of almanacs, since only one was ever published with an edition number, the fact that they were published annually can. Almanacs remained useful only until the end of a particular calendar year, after which their material would become outdated. A good number were, in effect, published serially, with new editions written by the same compilers appearing year after year.[67] We can therefore infer that a gap in extant editions of almanacs by the same author within a sequence of years is probably evidence of a lost edition. For example, an almanac by Gregory Burton survives for every year from 1613 to 1621, except 1615, when one surely was published that is now lost. Overall, there are 622 editions of annual almanacs written by compilers like Burton, and another 126 "gap" years for which there is probably a lost edition, a loss rate of 16.8%.[68]

Of course, there is no way to know with absolute certainty that an almanac by Burton was published in 1615, nor is it possible to know if others by him were published before 1613 or after 1621. Despite these inevitable uncertainties, the number of years that do seem to have missing editions is instructive. The loss rate of annual almanacs (16.8%) is fairly close to that for books of the same length in low-loss genres (25.4%), but much lower than that for books of the same length in high-loss genres (52.1%). Given how many editions were printed and their short length, there are still probably over two hundred lost editions in this genre, in addition to an untold number of lost single-leaf almanacs. And it is true that almanacs often survive in fragmentary, incomplete copies. But, as with news pamphlets, the same features that contributed to their ephemerality seem to have led to their preservation by certain owners. People occasionally collected sequences of almanacs, or saved them because of the manuscript notes written in them, or bound together multiple almanacs from a single year.[69] The topicality of these works paradoxically helped to preserve them.

BINDINGS, "PAMPHLETS," AND EPHEMERALITY

The example of almanacs points to another factor in a book's preservation or destruction: its binding. When an almanac was sold to readers,

Fig. 16. Lost Editions of Genres. Genres with the Highest Totals of Probable Lost Editions, 1580–1640

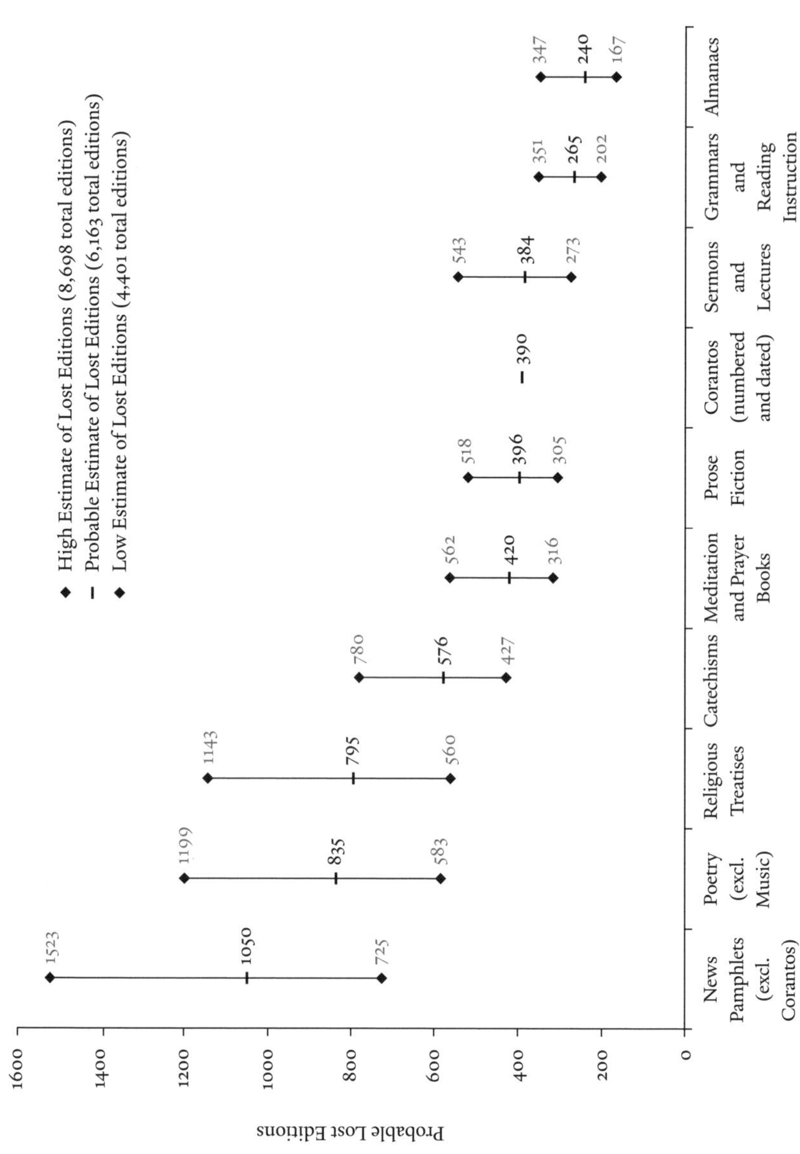

Fig. 17. Loss Rates of Genres. Genres with the Highest Probable Loss Rates, 1580–1640

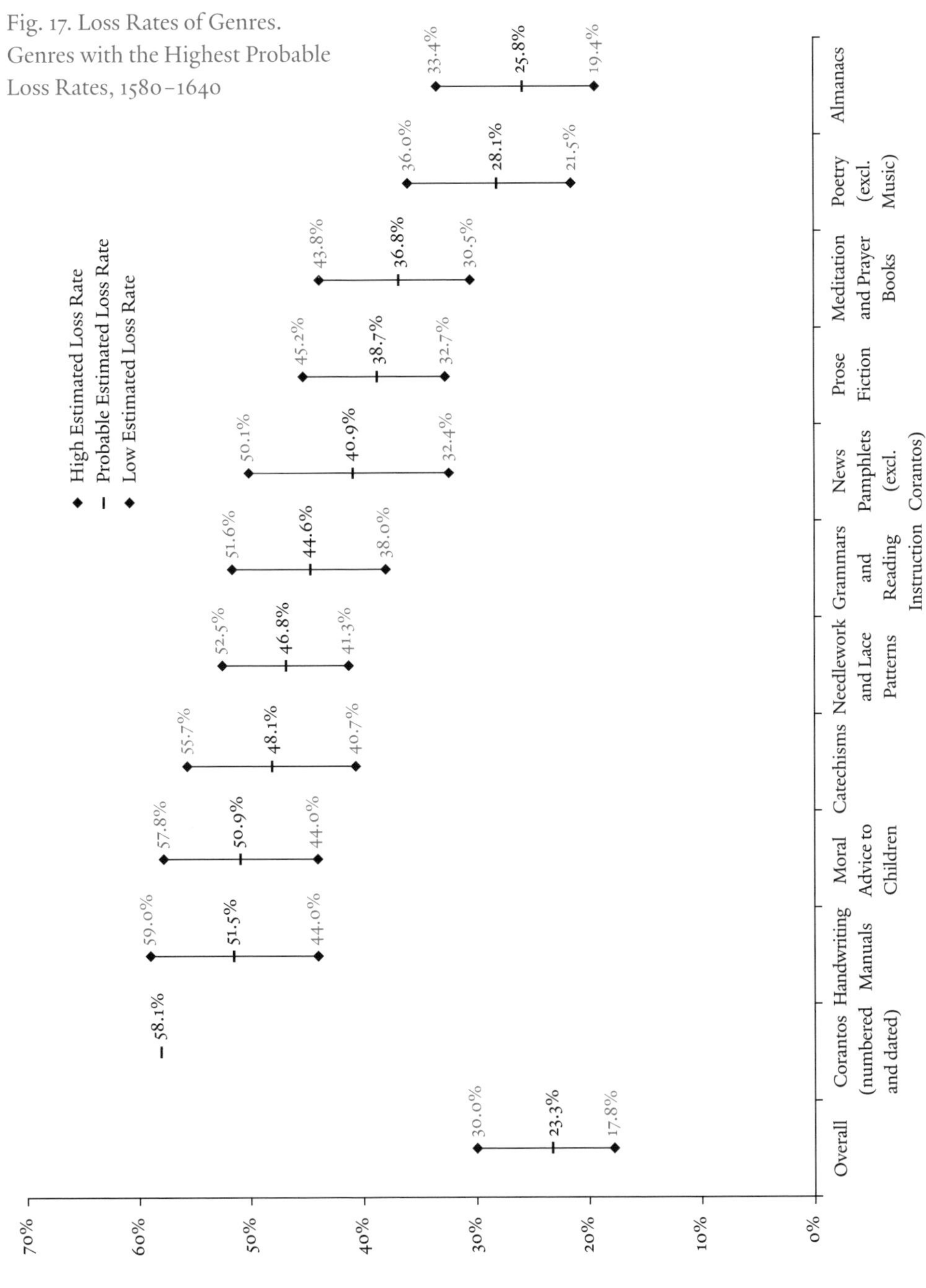

it would typically have been sold as a "stitched book"; a piece of string would be stabbed through a book two or three times near its spine to hold the volume together, with sometimes an inexpensive outer wrapper or cover attached as well. A longer book would have required a sturdier sewn binding; thread would be sewn through the book's folded quires in several places and attached to sewing supports that were laced into boards made of pasteboard, millboard, or wood.[70] If almanacs were collected, they usually would have been bound together with other short works in larger composite volumes (or *Sammelbände*) with boards and sewn bindings. The distinction between a publication that was stab-stitched and one that had a sewn binding has frequently been seen as a key factor separating an "ephemeral" from a "more lasting artifact."[71] Numerous scholars have stressed that stitched books led an especially precarious existence. It turns out, however, that there is good reason to doubt whether the method of binding with which a book was originally sold greatly affected the chances of its subsequent survival or destruction.

Such accounts of stitched books rest on two mistaken assumptions, one about their bibliographical ephemerality, the other about the length of books in early modern England. According to a 1586 Stationers' Company regulation concerning bookbinding practices, only books under certain lengths were allowed to be "stitched"; above those lengths, they were supposed to be sold to readers with more expensive sewn bindings. The lengths allowed for stab-stitching varied by format: forty sheets and less for folios, twelve sheets and less for octavos, five or six sheets and less for 16mos.[72] The reason for this variation is that the stitching or binding of a book depended on its bulk, from eighty leaves for a folio, to eighty to ninety-six leaves for a 16mo, to ninety-six for an octavo. Quartos are not mentioned in the regulation, but they probably had the same limit as octavos, ninety-six leaves, or twenty-four edition-sheets.[73] Since this regulation came about because of complaints by London bookbinders, many printers and booksellers before 1586 must have been selling books with stab-stitched bindings that exceeded these lengths. And even after the regulation went into effect, there were some books longer than these limits that were sold with stab-stitched bindings, which were cheaper to produce than sewn bindings. (Of course, there were also publications below these limits that were sometimes sold with sewn bindings.)[74]

According to many scholars, volumes that were stab-stitched would have been particularly prone to destruction.[75] On one level, it is undeniably true that longer publications were less likely to be destroyed. As fig. 10 demonstrates, the loss rates of all books went down as they increased in length, regardless of genre – but also regardless of binding style. Quartos of one hundred sheets, for instance, will usually have a lower loss rate than those of fifty sheets, even though both were almost always sold with sewn bindings. Conversely, the shortest pamphlets have the highest loss rates, but it is not clear that the method of binding is the reason for this greater ephemerality. If the 1586 Stationers' Company regulation provides a rough guide for dividing stab-stitched from sewn books, as various scholars have maintained, then there should be evidence pointing to the greater ephemerality of stitched books among the titles published with numbered editions. There isn't. Quartos, octavos, and duodecimos that are just under the prescribed limits for stab-stitching (twenty-four sheets for quartos, twelve for octavos, eight for duodecimos) have almost exactly the same loss rate as those just above these limits.[76] Quartos of 17.5 to 24 sheets in the archive of numbered editions have a loss rate of 8.4% (8 of 95 editions) while those of 24.5 to 32 sheets have a similar loss rate of 5.6% (4 of 71 editions). Octavos of 9.5 to 12 sheets have a loss rate of 6.5% (3 of 46 editions), compared to 8.7% (4 of 46 editions) for octavos of 12.5 to 15 sheets. Duodecimos of 6.5 to 8 sheets have a loss rate of 11.1% (6 of 54 editions) whereas duodecimos of 8.5 to 10 sheets have one that is only slightly lower, 7.6% (7 of 92 editions). For each of these formats, the dividing line roughly separating stab-stitched books from those with sewn bindings appears to have had almost no effect on loss rates.[77] This similarity in loss rates may have resulted from owners routinely binding short publications into *Sammelbände,* thereby transforming what had been stab-stitched books into ones with sewn bindings. If so, that practice would provide further evidence that readers often considered stitched books worth saving and that larger composite volumes with sewn bindings were considered a more effective method for storing multiple short works together. But what is most important here is that the type of binding in which books were *originally* sold seems to have had little or no effect on loss rates.

Implicit in claims about the ephemerality of stab-stitched books is a misconception about the length of most publications in early modern England. It has been repeatedly argued that stab-stitching was central to early modern conceptions of the pamphlet. As Joad Raymond writes, by the later seventeenth century the term "'stitched book' was used synonymously with 'pamphlet,'" a point echoed by Jason Peacey, who affirms that "it was this stitching that effectively defined the genre." Peacey, however, then goes on to claim that pamphlets represented a relatively small part of the book trade: "For much of the sixteenth and early seventeenth centuries it is possible merely to talk of 'pamphlet moments,' rather than a pervasive pamphlet culture." That started to change in the late 1630s, he continues, when pamphleteering "became truly pervasive."[78] Although certain types of political pamphlets did indeed become more plentiful in the late 1630s, it is also true that stitched books, which Raymond and Peacey claim were synonymous with pamphlets, were at the heart of the English book trade throughout the late sixteenth and early seventeenth centuries. If the binding limits specified by the Stationers' Company in 1586 generally separate stab-stitched editions from those with sewn bindings, then "pamphlets" constitute well over half (59.6%) of the extant publications printed from 1580 to 1640, even if all folios are excluded from the category of stitched books (because even when short enough to be stab-stitched, folios have traditionally been considered too tall and wide to warrant being called pamphlets).[79] Rather than stab-stitched books being thought of as a minor, disreputable, disposable segment of the early modern book trade, they should instead be viewed as its backbone. They outnumbered books that required sewn bindings by almost two to one, making long books the exception in the trade, not the default against which pamphlets should be judged. Stitched books are most prevalent among quartos and octavos (77.5% of extant quartos and 67.2% of extant octavos are under ninety-six leaves), less so among folios (26.7% are under eighty leaves), duodecimos (30.5% are under ninety-six leaves), and smaller formats (17.3% are under ninety-six leaves). But since quartos and octavos compose the vast majority of all extant codex publications (81.0%, again excluding single-leaf publications), most books would probably have been sold stab-stitched. Taking lost editions into account, moreover, would only serve to increase the proportion of stitched books. Indeed, there were very likely more stitched quartos and stitched octavos published in this period than all other books in all other formats combined.[80]

The number of stitched books in the early modern book trade leads to a broader point about the size of books in early modern England. Grouping together all stitched books into a single category of "short

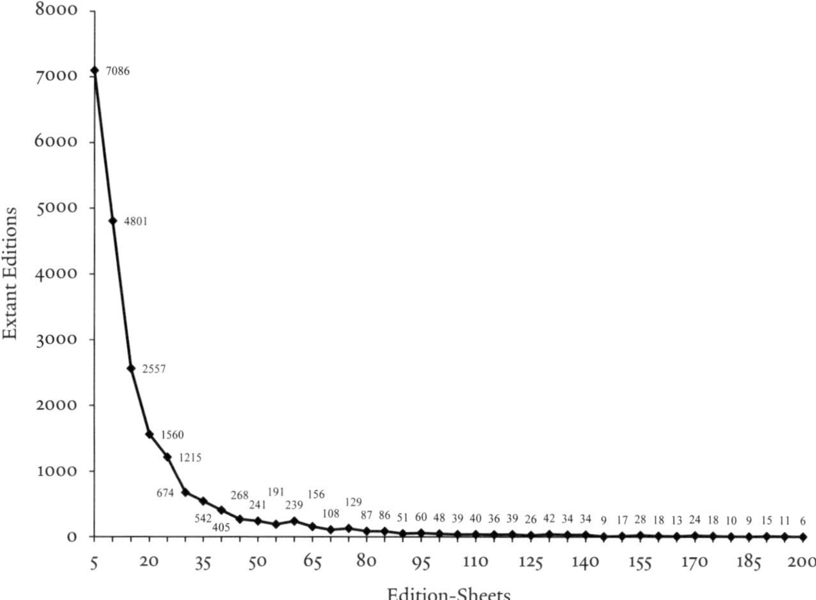

Fig. 18. Short Books. Extant Editions per Every Five Edition-Sheets, 1580–1640 (through 200 Sheets)

books" or "pamphlets" means treating as equivalent such disparate works as a two-sheet quarto of news about a domestic murder, a twelve-sheet octavo of a Latin scientific treatise on globes (STC 13906), and a twenty-four-sheet quarto of Francis Bacon's *The Elements of the Common Lawes of England* (STC 1136). Although each of these would have likely been sold as a stitched book, they would have noticeably differed in their size, not to mention their genre. A more precise and nuanced sense of short and long books is necessary than the catch-all term "pamphlet" allows. The median length of all *extant* speculative publications from 1580 to 1640 is nine sheets, a length much shorter than some scholars have believed could be true.[81] With lost editions factored in, the actual median length of speculative publications would be even shorter, perhaps around seven sheets. The book trade was awash in "short" books. Fig. 18 shows the distribution of extant publications in five-sheet intervals (that is, 0.5 to 5 sheets, 5.5 to 10 sheets, etc.); it vividly illustrates how many short books were being printed for the retail trade.[82] Stationers, as a group, were not routinely producing long folios, fat quartos, and thick octavos. They were concerned predominately with printing and publishing single-leaf publications and stitched books of only a few sheets.

THE BIBLIOGRAPHICAL EPHEMERALITY OF PLAYBOOKS

Noticeably missing from the genres with the highest loss rates or the most lost editions is printed drama from the professional London theater. Although the view of playbooks as ephemeral has long been entrenched in studies of early modern drama, there is little evidence to support it. In fact, they may have been among the less ephemeral genres in early modern England. Such a claim is sure to be met with skepticism, but printed plays from the professional stage do not possess those qualities that seem to have led to high loss rates.

There are thirteen works of professional plays that were sold with numbered editions; these have forty-five extant editions and only one probable lost edition (the missing edition of Heywood's *A Woman Killed with Kindness*).[83] Numbered editions of playbooks thus have a remarkably low loss rate of 2.2%. Books in high-loss genres that are the same length as numbered playbooks have an exponentially higher loss rate of 45.1%, and even books in low-loss genres the same length as numbered playbooks have a loss rate of 8.8%. This figure for numbered editions of professional plays, nevertheless, does not mean the genre as a whole had a loss rate of around 2%. For one thing, when the aggregate rates for low-loss genres at different sheet-lengths are applied to all 562 extant editions of professional playbooks printed from 1580 to 1640, the resulting projection would be for 59.6 lost editions, or an expected loss rate of 9.6% (including margins of error, a low estimate would be 7.5% and a high one 12.2%). A key reason this projected rate is not higher – and is well below the projected rates for works like meditation and prayer books (36.8%), catechisms (48.1%), and handwriting manuals (51.5%) – is that playbooks were not short. They have a median length of 9.5 sheets, almost exactly equal to that of the book trade as a whole. Playbooks were too long to be affected by the increased odds of destruction faced by the shortest publications in the book trade.

While the projected loss rate of 9.6% may be close to the real one for professional playbooks, there are good reasons to think it may have been even lower. Unlike almanacs and corantos, playbooks were never published in serialized editions, and so they never became obsolete or out of date after a week, a month, or a year. Nor do they appear to have been used by readers in ways that led to their destruction, as works in high-loss genres often were. Furthermore, since at least the eighteenth century, professional plays have been one of the most thoroughly collected and catalogued genres from the early modern book trade.[84] Fewer editions, as a result, have probably been lost due to the actions of later owners. But even in the seventeenth century, plays were being collected by readers with large and important libraries, readers who often bound together multiple copies in a single *Sammelband*.[85] As a result of these various factors, the loss rate for plays is probably closer to around 5% (with around twenty-eight lost editions), well below that for the genres with the highest loss rates.[86]

Nor were professional plays marked by limited topical appeal, as has sometimes been argued.[87] As Zachary Lesser and I have shown elsewhere, one of the distinguishing characteristics of playbooks is that they had an unusually long "shelf-life"; publishers were three times more likely to reprint a playbook for the first time more than a decade after its first edition compared to books in other genres.[88] The repertory system of London playing companies probably contributed to this long shelf life, as companies periodically produced revivals of their plays. But it also suggests that readers continued to purchase and read plays that had been printed and performed years, even decades, earlier. Plays did not automatically lose their appeal as they aged. In Caroline England, for instance, the publication of playbooks seems to have diverged into separate markets for new plays and "classic" plays, with some stationers seeking to bring out editions of "undiscovered classics," older plays that had never before been printed.[89] Older plays were therefore an unusually significant part of the market for printed drama. Performances of professional plays may have been transient and lasted only a few hours, but there apparently existed a real appetite to read plays even decades after they had originally been performed and printed.

Printed plays from the professional theater thus exhibit none of the features that typically led to high numbers of missing editions or high loss rates. They were never published in serialized editions, and there is only one missing edition among the playbooks published with numbered editions. They were published in editions that were neither short within the context of the overall book trade nor short enough to lead to many lost editions. Readers seem not to have "used" playbooks in ways that led to the destruction of entire editions. And rather than plays being treated as topical reading material that would interest readers only briefly, stationers invested in (and readers appear to have been interested in) editions of plays decades after their initial publication. Taken together, all of these features suggest that the bibliographical ephemerality of playbooks is an idea more grounded in assumptions than in facts. The weight of bibliographical evidence shows that they were not "self-destructing artefacts," destroyed by the negligence and disdain of early modern readers. There are genres that were ephemeral, such as catechisms, meditation and prayer books, schoolbook grammars, corantos, and pamphlets of two sheets or less. Playbooks, however, were not, and do not warrant being thought of as early modern ephemera.

NOTES

For helpful comments on earlier versions of this essay, I would like to thank Zachary Lesser, Aaron Pratt, Goran Proot, the members of Jonathan Sawday's Text Mining Initiative at St. Louis University, and the members of Jonathan Hope's Early Modern Digital Agendas seminar at the Folger Shakespeare Library. And especially, David Scott Kastan, whose influence and guidance permeate this entire project.

1 D.F. McKenzie, "Printers of the Mind: Some Notes on Bibliographical Theories and Printing-House Practices," *Studies in Bibliography* 22 (1969): 1–75; Peter W.M. Blayney, "The Prevalence of Shared Printing in the Early Seventeenth Century," *Papers of the Bibliographical Society of America* 67 (1973): 437–42; Robert Darnton, *The Business of Enlightenment: A Publishing History of the* Encyclopédie, *1775–1800* (Cambridge: The Belknap Press of Harvard University Press, 1979); Robert Darnton, *The Forbidden Best-Sellers of Pre-Revolutionary France* (New York: W.W. Norton & Co., 1995).

2 David L. Gants, "A Quantitative Analysis of the London Book Trade 1614–1618," *Studies in Bibliography* 55 (2002): 185–213; Mark Curran, "Beyond the Forbidden Best-Sellers of Pre-Revolutionary France," *The Historical Journal* 56 (2013): 89–112.

3 Alan B. Farmer and Zachary Lesser, "What Is Print Popularity? A Map of the Elizabethan Book Trade," in *The Elizabethan Top Ten: Defining Print Popularity in Early Modern England*, ed. Andy Kesson and Emma Smith (Farnham: Ashgate, 2013), 19–54; Michael F. Suarez, S.J., "Towards a Bibliometric Analysis of the Surviving Record, 1701–1800," in *The Cambridge History of the Book in Britain*, vol. 5, *1695–1830*, ed. Michael F. Suarez, S.J., and Michael L. Turner (Cambridge: Cambridge University Press, 2009), 37–65.

4 See *Visualizing English Print: Textual Analysis of the Printed Record* (University of

Wisconsin): http://graphics.cs.wisc.edu/VEPsite/projects.html.

5 Franco Moretti, *Distant Reading* (New York: Verso, 2013). See also the various projects published by the Stanford Literary Lab, dir. Franco Moretti and Mark Algee-Hewitt: http://litlab.stanford.edu.

6 Francis R. Johnson, "Notes on English Retail Book-prices, 1550–1640," *The Library,* 5th ser., 5 (1950): 83–112 (91).

7 Peter W.M. Blayney, *The Texts of* King Lear *and Their Origins,* vol. 1, *Nicholas Okes and the First Quarto* (Cambridge: Cambridge University Press, 1982), 27. See also Adrian Weiss, "Casting Compositors, Foul Cases, and Skeletons: Printing in Middleton's Age," in *Thomas Middleton and Early Modern Textual Culture: A Companion to the Collected Works,* gen. ed. Gary Taylor and John Lavagnino (Oxford: Clarendon Press, 2007), 195–225 (195).

8 Sears Jayne, *Library Catalogues of the English Renaissance* (Berkeley and Los Angeles: University of California Press, 1956), 54. See also David Bevington, *Shakespeare's Ideas: More Things in Heaven and Earth* (Oxford: Wiley-Blackwell, 2008), 5.

9 Stanley Wells and Gary Taylor, gen. eds., "General Introduction," *The Oxford Shakespeare: The Complete Works,* 2d ed. (Oxford: Clarendon Press, 2005), xxxix–xl. See also Valerie Hotchkiss and Fred C. Robinson, *English in Print from Caxton to Shakespeare to Milton* (Urbana-Champaign: University of Illinois Press, 2008), 33.

10 Joseph Loewenstein, *Ben Jonson and Possessive Authorship* (Cambridge: Cambridge University Press, 2002), 29.

11 Nigel Wheale, *Writing and Society: Literacy, Print and Politics in Britain 1590–1660* (London: Routledge, 1999), 58; Peter Stallybrass and Roger Chartier, "Reading and Authorship: The Circulation of Shakespeare 1590–1619," in *A Concise Companion to Shakespeare and the Text,* ed. Andrew Murphy (Oxford: Blackwell, 2007), 35–56 (42). See also Helen Hackett, *A Short History of English Renaissance Drama* (London: I.B. Tauris, 2013), 68–69.

12 T.A. Birrell, "The Influence of Seventeenth-Century Publishers on the Presentation of English Literature," *Historical and Editorial Studies in Medieval and Early Modern English,* ed. Mary-Jo Arn and Hanneke Wirtjes with Hans Jansen (Groningen: Wolters-Noordhoff, 1985): 163–73 (166). As I discuss below, Birrell here confuses the terminology of stab-stitching with that of sewn bindings; see David Pearson, *English Bookbinding Styles, 1450–1800: A Handbook* (London: The British Library; New Castle, Del.: Oak Knoll Press, 2005), 13–15, 148–50.

13 Heidi Brayman Hackel, "'Rowme' of Its Own: Printed Drama in Early Libraries," in *A New History of Early English Drama,* ed. John D. Cox and David Scott Kastan (New York: Columbia University Press, 1997), 113–30; Lukas Erne, *Shakespeare as Literary Dramatist* (Cambridge: Cambridge University Press, 2003), 11–14; Erne, *Shakespeare and the Book Trade* (Cambridge: Cambridge University Press, 2013), 186–232; Alan H. Nelson, "Shakespeare and the Bibliophiles: From the Earliest Years to 1616," in *Owners, Annotators and the Signs of Reading,* ed. Robin Myers, Michael Harris, and Giles Mandelbrote (New Castle, Del.: Oak Knoll Press; London: The British Library, 2005), 49–73.

14 H.R. Woudhuysen, "The Foundations of Shakespeare's Text," *Proceedings of the British Academy* 125 (2004): 69–100, esp. 88–92.

15 Joseph A. Dane and Alexandra Gillespie, "The Myth of the Cheap Quarto," in *Tudor Books and Readers: Materiality and the Construction of Meaning,* ed. John N. King (Cambridge: Cambridge University Press, 2010), 25–45.

16 *Shakespeare in Quarto* (The British Library), www.bl.uk/treasures/shakespeare/printedplays.html; *Shakespeare Quartos Archive,* www.quartos.org/info/about.html.

17 Margreta de Grazia, *Shakespeare Verbatim: The Reproduction of Authenticity and the 1790 Apparatus* (Oxford: Clarendon Press, 1991), 32. See also Eugene Giddens, *How to Read a Shakespearean Play Text* (Cambridge: Cambridge University Press, 2011), 47–48.

18 For similar claims about the category of ephemera in the eighteenth century, see the excellent essay by Paula McDowell, "Of Grubs and Other Insects: Constructing the Categories of 'Ephemera' and 'Literature' in Eighteenth-Century British Writing," *Book History* 15 (2012): 48–70.

19 "Ephemeron, *n.,*" OED *Online,* June 2013, Oxford University Press (accessed July 16, 2013).

20 Michael Twyman, "Editor's Introduction," in Maurice Rickards, *The Encyclopedia of Ephemera: A Guide to the Fragmentary Documents of Everyday Life for the Collector, Curator, and Historian,* ed. and completed by Michael Twyman with the assistance of Sally de Beaumont and Amoret Tanner (New York: Routledge, 2000), v–viii (v). See also Michael Harris, "Printed Ephemera," in *The Oxford Companion to the Book,* ed. Michael F. Suarez, S.J., and H.R. Woudhuysen, 2 vols. (Oxford: Oxford University Press, 2010), 1:120–29.

21 H.S. Bennett, *English Books and Readers 1558 to 1603* (Cambridge: Cambridge University Press, 1965), 255.

22 It has been repeatedly pointed out that the number of copies of play quartos is dwarfed by the hundreds of extant copies of the Shakespeare and Jonson folios; see, for instance, Birrell, "Influence," 166; de Grazia, *Shakespeare Verbatim,* 32. But as Peter W.M. Blayney has quipped, these folios "might well be the least rare seventeenth-century book[s] on the planet" ("Correspondence," *The Library,* 7th ser., 7 [2006]: 317–18 [318]). There are indeed many fewer copies of play quartos than of these two exceptionally large folios, and yet the same is true of every other early modern English publication. It is the Jonson and Shakespeare folios that are unusual, not play quartos.

23 See A.W. Pollard and G.R. Redgrave, eds., *A Short-Title Catalogue of Books Printed in England, Scotland, and Ireland and of English Books Printed Abroad, 1475–1640,* 2d ed., rev., ed. W.A. Jackson, F.S. Ferguson, and Katharine F. Pantzer, 3 vols. (London: Bibliographical Society, 1976–91) (hereafter referred to as STC). Among the entries in the STC for editions of professional plays, only 84 of 568 list three or fewer extant copies (14.8%). In contrast, most editions of meditation and prayer books printed from 1580 to 1640 (not including books of psalms) have three or fewer copies (468 of 711 editions, 65.9%). Although the STC's listings of extant copies are not a definitive census, the contrast points to the greater ephemerality of works of devotion, an issue discussed further below. Lukas Erne makes a similar point about the number of copies of Shakespeare quartos that still exist in comparison to "ballads, chapbooks, primers, almanacs, ABC, and books of popular piety," and to canonical works of poetry by Spenser, Sidney, Lanyer, and Milton: "The significant number of surviving copies does not suggest that Shakespeare's playbooks were considered discardable ephemera in his own time" (*Shakespeare and the Book Trade,* 192–93).

24 Oliver M. Willard, "The Survival of English Books Printed before 1640: A Theory and Some Illustrations," *The Library,* 4th ser., 23 (1942): 171–90, esp. 172–78.

25 Ibid., 173; Goran Proot and Leo Egghe, "Estimating Editions on the Basis of Survivals: Printed Programmes of Jesuit Plays in the *Provincia Flandro-Belgica* before 1773, with a Note on the 'Book Historical Law,'" *The Papers of the Bibliographical Society of America* 102 (2008): 149–74, esp. 165–66, 170–73.

26 On the STC, see n. 23. Edward Arber, ed., *A Transcript of the Registers of the Company of Stationers of London, 1554–1640 A.D.*, 5 vols. (London: n.p., 1875–94). See, for instance, Tessa Watt, *Cheap Print and Popular Piety, 1550–1640* (Cambridge: Cambridge University Press, 1991), 42–49; Alan B. Farmer and Zachary Lesser, "The Popularity of Playbooks Revisited," *Shakespeare Quarterly* 56 (2005): 1–32 (29–30).

27 Jonathan Green, Frank McIntyre, and Paul Needham, "The Shape of Incunable Survival and Statistical Estimation of Lost Editions," *Papers of the Bibliographical Society of America* 105 (2011): 141–75; see also Proot and Egghe, "Estimating."

28 Green, McIntrye, and Needham, "Shape," 170–71.

29 Oliver M. Willard, "Jaggard's *Catalogue of English Books*," in *Stanford Studies in Language and Literature*, ed. Hardin Craig (Stanford: Stanford University, 1941), 152–72; William A. Jackson, "Humphrey Dyson's Library, or, Some Observations on the Survival of Books," *The Papers of the Bibliographical Society of America* 43 (1949): 279–87; Franklin B. Williams, Jr., "Lost Books of Tudor England," *The Library*, 5th ser., 33 (1978): 1–14. Willard computed a probable loss rate of 15.9% (160), Jackson one of 16.3% (280–81), and Williams one of 13.7% (5). For the eighteenth century, Michael F. Suarez, S.J., reports that most studies estimate a somewhat lower overall loss rate of about 10% ("Towards a Bibliometric Analysis," 40–41).

30 Williams, "Lost Books," 7.

31 Willard, "Survival of English Books," 173.

32 On "speculative" publications and reprint rates, see Farmer and Lesser, "Popularity of Playbooks Revisited," esp. 13–14, 18–24; Farmer and Lesser, "What Is Print Popularity?" 26, 27–28.

33 *English Short Title Catalogue* (The British Library), http://estc.bl.uk; *Universal Short Title Catalogue* (University of Saint Andrews), www.ustc.ac.uk; *Early English Books Online* (Chadwyck Healy), http://eebo.chadwyck.com.

34 In checking for continental editions printed in Latin, USTC is particularly helpful, as is M.A. Shaaber, *Check-list of Works of British Authors Printed Abroad, in Languages Other than English, to 1641* (New York: The Bibliographical Society of America, 1975).

35 See Shaaber, *Check-list*, s.v. B45.

36 It is also necessary to count only editions printed prior to the final one containing an edition number. If the "third edition" of a work is followed by two more that were sold without edition numbers, I have counted only the first three editions, not the last two, because it is impossible to deduce whether there might have been lost editions published after the last with an edition number. I also have not included works first printed before 1640 but whose first extant numbered edition is from after 1640, with one exception. John Andrewes's *The Golden Trumpet*, a short religious treatise, was originally published some time before 1630 by Nicholas Okes, who on July 3 of that year transferred his right to the title to John Wright, Sr. (Arber 4:238). The first surviving edition of Andrewes's treatise, however, is from 1641, when it was sold as "The five and twentieth Impression" (*Wing* A3123). There were probably

twenty-four lost editions published up through 1640, and I have therefore included Andrewes's treatise among the works with lost editions analyzed in this essay.

37 In these cases, it is either unclear whether the edition number is meant to include editions that may (or may not) have been printed outside England, or what the number is meant to count for works with particularly knotty textual histories. I have also excluded John Norden's *The Pensive Man's Practice (Part One)* due to uncertainties about the precise number of lost editions it has. Norden's prayer book was first published in 1584 (STC 18616), and by 1620 an edition was advertised as "Newly corrected and amended by the *Author, after aboue forty* Impressions" (STC 18623). This was its twelfth extant London edition, suggesting there are probably more than twenty-eight lost editions of this work. In the next two decades, at least six more editions were published, but the number of editions advertised on the title page was increased only to "*aboue* 42. Impressions" (STC 18626.5 [1636] and STC 18626a [1640]). Although there are clearly many lost editions of Norden's prayer book, it is impossible to estimate exactly how many.

38 I have not counted editions printed abroad that early modern stationers factored into the edition statements they included in their STC volumes unless those continental editions are also listed in the STC. While there are justifiable reasons for including these continental editions in the figures for extant editions, it seems more prudent to restrict the essay's analysis to books listed in the STC. There are moreover relatively few such continental editions that would need to be included, so their exclusion does not affect the claims in this essay.

39 D.F. McKenzie, "Printing and Publishing 1557–1700: Constraints on the London Book Trades," in *The Cambridge History of the Book in Britain*, vol. 4, *1557–1695*, ed. John Barnard and D.F. McKenzie, with the assistance of Maureen Bell (Cambridge: Cambridge University Press, 2002), 551–67 (559).

40 Such instances of advertising a reissued first edition as a second edition, when few if any changes were introduced beyond adding a new title page, could at times have been an attempt by stationers to make works seem more popular than they were. On the other hand, when new material was added to a reissued edition, early modern stationers sometimes clearly felt justified calling the resulting volume "the second edition," whereas the STC considers it, bibliographically, to be another issue because the reissued old material composes the majority of the new volume.

41 For those works that would eventually have an edition number, printers almost always added an edition number by the third edition (87.0% of titles).

42 Most of the edition numbers on extant title pages are for the first through fifth edition (71.8%); many fewer are for the tenth or greater edition (13.5%).

43 Copies of some "lost" editions may, of course, still exist. They may have been discovered after the revised STC was published and not yet added to ESTC; they may still remain uncatalogued in an institutional library; or they may be held in a private collection and are currently unknown to scholars. For examples of recently located editions, see n. 56 below.

44 On the dating of this lost edition, see K.M. Sturgess, "The Early Quartos of Heywood's *A woman killed with kindness,*" *The Library*, 5th ser., 25 (1970): 93–104.

45 For the definition of "second-plus editions," see Farmer and Lesser, "Popularity of Playbooks Revisited," 6–7. These figures include the title-page edition

numbers for all 1,698 numbered editions; the graph is intended to establish how widespread the numbering of editions was, not how accurate that numbering was. Only six editions were identified specifically as "first" editions on their title pages, two of which were in fact reprints, though many more were advertised as "never before printed" (such title-page statements are not included in this study).

46 There seems to have been little change in the loss rates of numbered editions from 1580 to 1640, so this overall period does not need to be subdivided into smaller segments.

47 From 1580 to 1640, there are 1,671 extant numbered editions, which compose 8.2% of all extant speculative editions and 19.9% of all extant speculative second-plus editions in this period (these percentages exclude single-leaf publications and do not factor in those lost editions that probably were printed with edition numbers).

48 David Scott Kastan, *Shakespeare and the Book* (Cambridge: Cambridge University Press, 2001), 50–78.

49 For the height and width of books in different formats and with different sizes of paper, see Philip Gaskell, *A New Introduction to Bibliography* (1972; reprint, New Castle, Del.: Oak Knoll Press, 2000), 84–86.

50 Dane and Gillespie, "Myth of the Cheap Quarto," 27–29.

51 See Ian Maclean, *Learning and the Market Place: Essays in the History of the Early Modern Book* (Leiden: Brill, 2009), 13, 39–40, 65, 110, 120–21, 230, 317, 322; Blayney, *Texts of* King Lear *and Their Origins*, 39, 42–43.

52 All the statistical data in fig. 10 and in this section, unless otherwise indicated, are derived from the archive of numbered editions only for 1580 to 1640, excluding single-leaf publications, one nonspeculative publication, and works for which it is not possible to determine whether their edition statements are accurate. In this period, there are 696 works with 2,412 extant editions (1,602 of which are numbered) and 499 lost editions, which computes to a loss rate of 17.1%. Edition-sheets have been rounded up to the nearest whole sheet. Because the vast majority of extant reprints are in the same format as the preceding edition and usually contain the same number of edition-sheets, inferred lost editions are assumed to have had the same format and edition-sheets as the preceding and/or ensuing editions of the same work.

53 The R^2 number in fig. 10 measures how well the trend line matches the observed data. R^2 values range between 0, indicating no correlation among the data, and 1, indicating exact correlation. While obviously not perfectly matched, the R^2 value for edition-sheets (0.74) is much higher than the equivalent for edition-leaves (0.44). There is more variation, and less correlation, in the relationship between loss rates and edition-leaves.

54 Watt, *Cheap Print and Popular Piety*, 141.

55 For similar estimates of the market share of single-leaf publications in the Elizabethan book trade, see Farmer and Lesser, "What Is Print Popularity?" 31–32n30.

56 John Norden's *The Pensive Man's Practice, Part One* probably also had around thirty lost editions (see n. 37 above). Not included in fig. 11 are Henry Valentine's *Private Devotions* and William Hill's *The First Principles of a Christian*, each of which seems to have eight lost editions according to the STC. The first edition of Valentine's prayer book in the STC is called the "seventh edition" and dated 1635 (STC 24576.3), but ESTC contains records for two earlier editions: the "fifth edition," from 1633 (ESTC S126432), and

the "sixth edition," from 1634 (*ESTC* S470866). Similarly, the first extant edition of Hill's catechism in the *STC* is identified as the "third" edition and dated 1616 (*STC* 13503), but the Harvey Cushing/John Hay Whitney Medical Library at Yale University contains a copy of an earlier edition, probably the first, from 1611.

57 For the methodology used to categorize books by genre, see Farmer and Lesser, "What Is Print Popularity?" esp. 22–30. The percentages in these figures are based on the aggregate totals of high-loss and low-less genres in each edition-sheet range. I have subdivided editions into these sheet ranges because the ranges mark distinct changes in loss rates and better capture those changes than does computing the loss rates for smaller intervals, such as individual sheets (one sheet, two sheets, etc.). Editions within each range have fairly similar loss rates, and enough extant editions to justify making larger projections based on them. In order to apply these percentages to a specific genre or to use them to make projections for the book trade as a whole, it is necessary to calculate a 95% margin of error for each edition-sheet range. For publications that are very short (two sheets or less) or long (greater than fifty sheets), the differences in loss rates between high-loss and low-loss genres are not statistically significant, so it is best not to subdivide editions within those lengths.

58 For an analysis of the relationship between genre and loss rates for sixteenth-century French books, see Alexander S. Wilkinson, "Lost Books Printed in French before 1601," *The Library*, 7th ser., 10 (2009): 188–205.

59 Numbered editions in the smallest formats, 16mos, 18mos, and 24mos, have an overall loss rate much higher than those in any other format, a combined 50.7% (36 extant editions and 37 lost editions). The lost editions in these formats, however, are all meditation and prayer books. Although it would be tempting to attribute the high loss rates of these editions to their small formats, their loss rates are consistent with those of other high-loss genres of the same length (48.0%).

60 On the high market share of poetry books, see Farmer and Lesser, "What Is Print Popularity?" 36–37.

61 See William H. Sherman, *Used Books: Marking Readers in Renaissance England* (Philadelphia: University of Pennsylvania Press, 2008); Bradin Cormack and Carla Mazzio, *Book Use, Book Theory: 1500–1700* (Chicago: University of Chicago Library, 2005).

62 Calculating this estimate involves classifying all extant editions as either high-loss or low-less genres, and then counting how many editions were published in each category and within the edition-sheet ranges used in figs. 13 and 14.

63 See Peter Stallybrass, "'Little Jobs': Broadsides and the Printing Revolution," in *Agent of Change: Print Culture Studies after Elizabeth L. Eisenstein*, ed. Sabrina Alcorn Baron, Eric N. Lindquist, and Eleanor F. Shevlin (Amherst: University of Massachusetts Press, 2007), 315–41.

64 When they were printed as quartos of two sheets or less, corantos have a loss rate of 67.4% (170 extant, 351 lost), which is higher than that for other high-loss genres at that length. But their loss rate drops to 26.0% (111 extant, 39 lost) for editions longer than two sheets. All publication figures are derived from *STC* and Folke Dahl, *A Bibliography of English Corantos and Periodical Newsbooks, 1620–1642* (London: The Bibliographical Society, 1952). These figures mainly consist of the numbered corantos published by Nathaniel Butter and Nicholas Bourne, but they also include two brief series brought out by Thomas Archer

in 1624 (STC 18507.348–52) and 1628 (STC 18507.355–58). Corantos were suppressed between October 1632 and December 1638.

65 The fourteen works of nonserialized news printed with edition numbers have a cumulative loss rate of only 11.4% (31 extant editions and 4 probable lost editions), even though most of these are short (under nine edition-sheets).

66 About 30% of Dyson's books from this period are news publications (47 of 155 copies). These figures come out of the helpful lists compiled by Alan H. Nelson and published on his website: "Dyson Books Identified and Traced" (http://socrates.berkeley.edu/~ahnelson/PROVENANCE/dysonstc.html); "Dyson Books Identified and Not Traced" (http://socrates.berkeley.edu/~ahnelson/PROVENANCE/dysonlost.html).

67 Adam Smyth, "Almanacs and Ideas of Popularity," in *The Elizabethan Top Ten: Defining Print Popularity in Early Modern England*, ed. Andy Kesson and Emma Smith (Farnham: Ashgate, 2013), 125–33 (129).

68 I have excluded single-leaf almanacs from these calculations, as well as authors for whom there is only a single extant almanac because, for them, it is impossible to determine whether any other editions were ever printed. In order to ascertain if any almanacs are missing in 1640, I have checked ESTC for subsequent editions of yearly almanacs up through 1645.

69 Smyth, "Almanacs," 127, 130–31.

70 Pearson, *English Bookbinding Styles*, 13–15, 148–50.

71 Arthur F. Marotti, *Manuscript, Print, and The English Renaissance Lyric* (Ithaca: Cornell University Press, 1995), 286.

72 David Foxon, "Stitched Books," *The Book Collector* 24 (1975): 111–24, esp. 111–12.

73 In *Pamphlets and Pamphleteering in Early Modern Britain* (Cambridge: Cambridge University Press, 2003), Joad Raymond states that the maximum length for "a stitched quarto book or pamphlet was not more than twelve sheets" (82). This bibliographical definition of a pamphlet has since been frequently repeated in studies of the early modern book trade, for instance by Jason Peacey in his essay in *Cheap Print in Britain and Ireland to 1660,* The Oxford History of Popular Print Culture, vol. 1, ed. Joad Raymond (Oxford: Oxford University Press, 2011): "Technically, a pamphlet was conceived within the book trade as anything in size smaller than a folio (i.e., quarto, octavo, duodecimo), and in bulk consisting of fewer than twelve sheets" ("Pamphlets," 453–70 [454]). In fact, it was utterly normal for quartos longer than twelve sheets to be stab-stitched, including ones up to and above twenty-four sheets, and there is no reason to assume the Stationers' Company would require sewn bindings for quartos with only half the number of leaves as octavos; see Aaron T. Pratt's excellent essay, "Stab-Stitching and the Status of Early English Playbooks as Literature," *The Library,* 7th ser., 16 (2015): 304–28. Although there is no precise length that absolutely distinguishes publications sold with stitched and sewn bindings, it would be more accurate to describe stitched books up through 1640 as, generally, quartos and octavos of not more than ninety-six *leaves* (twice as long as Raymond claims) and duodecimos, 16mos, and other small formats of not more than eighty to ninety-six leaves. This redefinition has important implications for understanding the prevalence of "pamphlets" in the early modern English book trade, as I discuss below.

74 Pratt, "Stab-Stitching," 311–21. On the selling of books ready-bound in early modern England and the additional expense of sewn bindings, see Stuart

Bennett, *Trade Bookbinding in the British Isles, 1660–1800* (New Castle, Del.: Oak Knoll Press; London: The British Library, 2004), chap. 1–2.

75 See, for instance, Stallybrass and Chartier, "Reading and Authorship," 40–42.

76 There are not enough extant folios of forty sheets or less, nor enough 16mos of five to six sheets, to justify making claims about them.

77 None of the differences in these respective loss rates is statistically significant.

78 Raymond, *Pamphlets and Pamphleteering*, 10, 81; Peacey, "Pamphlets," 454, 459, 462.

79 In order to make these calculations, I computed the number of edition-sheets for every speculative publication printed from 1580 to 1640 and listed in the *STC*. I used standard bibliographies when possible and otherwise *ESTC* and *EEBO*. The above figure excludes single-leaf publications, which were sold without any bindings whatsoever.

80 See also Pratt, "Stab-Stitching," esp. 327–28. I would like to thank Aaron Pratt for many insightful discussions about stab-stitching and for sharing with me his work on this topic.

81 In "Popularity of Playbooks Revisited," Lesser and I calculated median length of speculative publications printed from 1609 to 1611 to be 10.5 sheets, which is a bit longer than the median length for these six decades. See also Suarez, "Towards a Bibliometric Analysis," in which he estimates that almost 80% of publications in the eighteenth century were ten sheets or less (60).

82 The graph is only of speculative publications, including ones of a single leaf. Not included are another 288 books longer than 200 sheets, which are a tiny fraction of extant publications (1.4%), nor seventy-four books for which the length cannot be plausibly estimated.

83 The edition numbers on these playbooks are all otherwise accurate, except for two: the sixth edition of *1 and 2 Edward the Fourth* (1626; *STC* 13346) was advertised as "The fourth Impression," and the fifth edition of *Philaster* (1639; *STC* 1685) was advertised as "*The fourth Impression*." The other plays with numbered editions include Francis Beaumont and John Fletcher's *Cupid's Revenge, A King and No King, The Maid's Tragedy, Philaster,* and *The Scornful Lady;* Thomas Heywood's *Love's Mistress* and *The Rape of Lucrece;* John Fletcher's *The Faithful Shepherdess;* William Cartwright's *The Royal Slave;* Thomas May's *The Heir;* and William Shakespeare's *Comedies, Histories, and Tragedies*. There are also seven editions of professional plays published from 1641 to 1660 with an edition number; these, too, are all correct, except for the 1655 edition of *Othello*, which is identified as "*The fourth Edition*," but which is in fact only the third extant quarto of the play. There may therefore be a lost edition of *Othello* printed between 1630 and 1655, or, because the second quarto of the play conflates the text of the first quarto and the 1623 Folio, the edition statement may be counting the 1623 Folio as a separate edition. Although my argument here concerns only plays from the professional London theater, seven nonprofessional plays were also published with numbered editions up through 1640; these too have a low loss rate of 5.3% (18 extant editions and 1 probable lost edition).

84 Richard Landon, "Collecting and the Antiquarian Book Trade," in *The Cambridge History of the Book in Britain*, vol. 5, *1695–1830*, 711–22, esp. 715–16.

85 See n. 13 above; Dane and Gillespie, "Myth of the Cheap Quarto," 42; Heidi Brayman Hackel, "The Countess of

Bridgewater's London Library," in *Books and Readers in Early Modern England: Material Studies,* ed. Jennifer Andersen and Elizabeth Sauer (Philadelphia: University of Pennsylvania Press, 2002), 138–59; Jeffrey Todd Knight, *Bound to Read: Compilations, Collections, and the Making of Renaissance Literature* (Philadelphia: University of Pennsylvania Press, 2013).

86 A loss rate of 3% to 7% would result in 17 to 39 lost editions of professional plays. See also Farmer and Lesser, "Popularity of Playbooks Revisited," 29–30, in which we arrive at a similar estimate of the number of lost editions of professional plays using a different methodology.

87 See, for example, Michael D. Bristol, *Big-time Shakespeare* (London: Routledge, 1996), 37.

88 Farmer and Lesser, "Popularity of Playbooks Revisited," 22–24.

89 Alan B. Farmer and Zachary Lesser, "Canons and Classics: Publishing Drama in Caroline England," in *Localizing Caroline Drama: Politics and Economics of the Early Modern English Stage, 1625–1642,* ed. Adam Zucker and Alan B. Farmer (New York: Palgrave Macmillan, 2006), 17–41.

COND

RT OF THE

AERIE QVEENE:

Containing

HE { FOVRTH, FIFT, & SIXT BOOKE.

By Ed. Spenser.

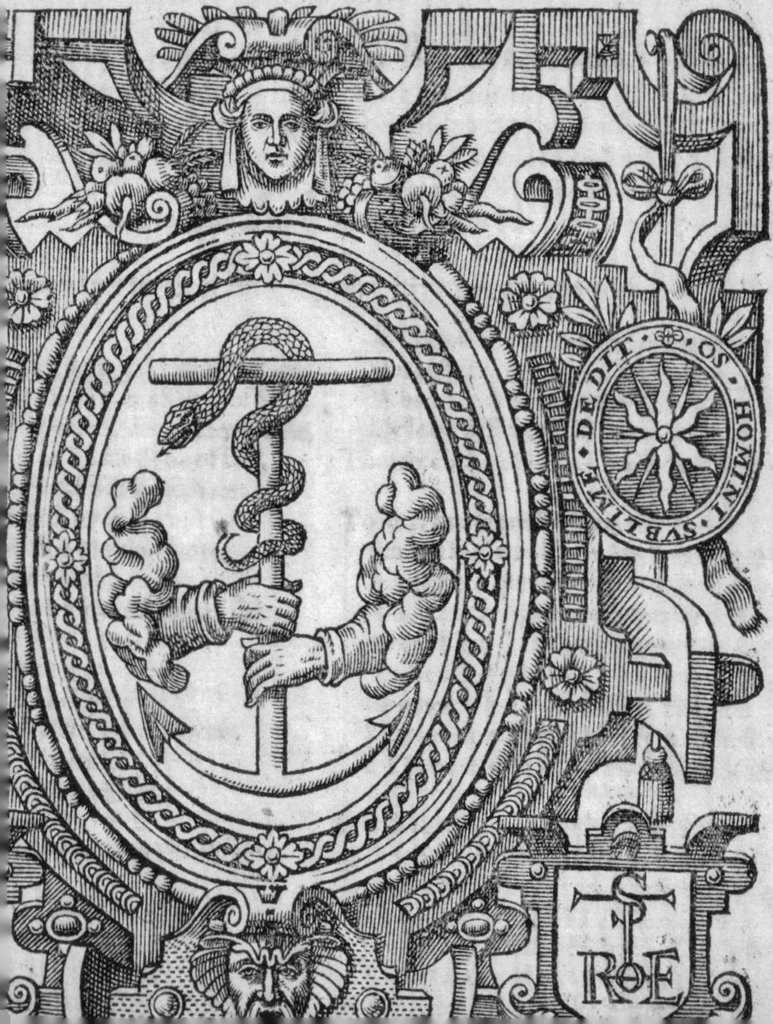

TEXTUAL INCARNATIONS

As nothing but
Thy powver doth cut.
Wherefore each part
Of my hard heart
Meets in this frame,
To praiſe thy name:
hat if I chance to hold my p
heſe ſtones to praiſe thee may not
thy bleſſed SACRIFIC
anctifie this ALTAR to

Book Fetishes

BENEDICT S. ROBINSON

In the narrative of his travels through the Ottoman Empire, George Sandys takes note of the reverence "the Turkes" display toward their holy book: "They neuer touch it with vnwasht hands: and a capitall crime it is, in the reading thereof to mistake a letter, or displace the accent. They kisse it, embrace it, and sweare by it."[1] Textual literalism, punishable by death, is accompanied by an affective, even erotic sensibility: Islamic devotion manifests itself as love for a thing, a book, imagined not just as the carrier of the divine word but also as an object to be touched in certain ways, embraced, kissed.[2] The anonymous *Policy of the Turkish Empire* – probably written by Giles Fletcher the Elder – devotes a full chapter to describing the bodily practices and movements of those who handle or hear the Qur'an. No one may touch it unless he "be first either cleane washed with fresh water,...or that he doe wrappe and couer his hands all ouer in some cleane and fine peece of lynen"; those who hear the text read to them "mooue and encline their bodies whilest they do intend to the reading of the same"; when the reader has finished, "hee kisseth the Booke with great reuerence."[3] A set of physical practices – postures, movements of the eyes and hands, kisses – regulates contact with the Qur'an.

This reverence for the book as sacred object extends even to its raw material. "If they find a paper in the streets," Sandys writes, "they will thrust it in some creuice of the adioyning wall; imagining that the name of God may be contained therein" (F4r). In Bartholomej Georgijevic's account of the Ottoman Empire we are told that

> if they but finde, a scroll, in what facion soeuer it be writen, lyinge on the earth, taking it vp, and often times kissed, they encloase the same, throuste into some chenke of the wal: for it is counted a synne, that the letters, wherwithe the name of God, and lawes of Mahomet are writen, shoulde be trode vnder their feete.[4]

When Ogier Ghiselin de Busbecq, imperial ambassador to the Ottoman Empire in the 1560s, stayed at an inn between Budapest and Istanbul, he noticed that the cracks of the walls were stuffed with paper. "The *Turks,*" he learned, "will not suffer the least bit of Paper to lye upon the Ground, but presently they take it up, and thrust it into some chink or hole or other, that so it may not be trampled under foot."[5] On the day of judgment, these pieces of paper will protect the feet of the faithful as they walk across the flames to salvation. "I remember that my *Turkish* Guides were once very angry with my servants," he recalls, "for making use of Paper to cleanse their *Posteriors*" (C9v–C10r).

One of the central elements of these accounts of the worship of the Qur'an is the act of kissing it. But if that gesture is presented as an exotic one, the embodiment of a misguided and alien devotion, it would also in the early modern period have been both familiar and contested. On the one hand, kissing the Bible was part of a long-established gestural lexicon of reverence for God's word; Thomas Heywood's dramatization of the early life of Queen Elizabeth ends with precisely this gesture: "this booke I kisse."[6] On the other hand, as both a liturgical act and a gesture that had long been part of the legal process of administering oaths, kissing the book became a center of controversy. For one thing, it was and remains an element of the Catholic Mass, and in this context Thomas Becon could seize upon it as evidence of a fetishistic relationship to the book that substitutes for the interpretive labor of preaching: Becon declaims against those Catholic priests who, instead of preaching, merely read "a few Latine sentences out of the Gospel" and then "kisse the booke."[7] To kiss the book is to turn it into a kind of mute idol. This was a claim Erasmus had already specifically refuted: "whan we do i[n] the chyrch kysse the gospel boke we do not worshyp the parchemente / or ye gold / or the yuery / but we do worshyp the doctrine of Christ."[8] Edmund Bonner argues along the same lines: "when we do kysse the booke of the Gospels," he writes,

> we haue not suche affection, and loue, to the parchement, paper or letters made with ynke, as for theyr sakes to kysse the boke, but hauynge onelye respect to those holsome comfortable and holy sayinges whych are in the boke conteyned.[9]

In Bonner's account, this is not idolatry but a full, physical and emotional pledge of the self: "with al our hole hartes & mindes," he writes, we "kysse and embrace, the booke." Erasmus similarly transfers the object of the kiss from the book to the words contained in that book – "Let vs kysse these swete wordes of Christ with a pure affection" – as part of a plea for the *reading* of scripture.[10] Not the book but the meaning is kissed.

Not all Protestants would find their consciences troubled by such a gesture. While the Book of Common Prayer says nothing about such kisses as part of Protestant liturgy, some Protestant ministers evidently continued the practice. In *A Rationale upon the Book of Common-Prayer,* Anthony Sparrow notes the custom of standing while scripture is read in church and the formulae for giving praise to God after the reading; he then adds, "In some places the fashion was, then to kiss the book." The gesture signifies a form of reverence, and as such Sparrow defends it, although he acknowledges that it is not enjoined.[11] The act of kissing the Bible could also be cited as a salutary alternative to uncertain or disputatious interpretations. In an often-quoted passage, William Pemble exhorts us to "a constant and serious study of the Scriptures" but warns, "Draw not all to reason, leave something for faith; where thou canst not sound the bottome, admire the depth, kisse the booke and lay it downe."[12] Kissing the book substitutes for reading at exactly the point where human comprehension – as the exercise of reason – fails. The substitution of gesture for interpretation seeks to block tendentious or interested appropriations of the text, putting in their place a simple, physical, intimate demonstration of devotion and submission: "Study to obey, not to dispute." This is precisely what worried Becon: gesture replaces speech, a potentially empty sign substitutes for communication. The meaning of this kiss depends entirely on how one interprets the significance and value of ritual gestures, and this was a matter that went to the heart of intra-Protestant controversy in the seventeenth century.

As the sign and seal of a certain kind of relationship, moreover, the gesture of kissing the book had a place in a whole series of legal rituals and ceremonies centering on the giving of oaths and the establishment of bonds. Various legal texts cite the gesture as part of a pledge of fealty; as recently as the coronation of Elizabeth II it has functioned as part of the coronation oath; it seems to have been part of the Oaths of Allegiance and Supremacy; it was used in swearing in jury members; it was part of the ceremonial of the Order of the Garter; and it appears generally in English courts to have functioned as the last step of the process of swearing an oath, the final seal on the promise to tell the whole truth and nothing but the truth.[13] This last practice remained a regular part of English jurisprudence until around 1900, when a campaign of opposition finally succeeding in removing it, not as irreligious but as unhygienic.[14] It is in this legal dimension of sealing an oath – and thereby also a bond, a relationship of allegiance and devotion – that "kissing the book" became idiomatic, surfacing several times in the drama as a way of describing an erotic kiss that is also a promise of love, as in John Day's *Humour out of Breath*.[15] In Aphra Behn's *The Rover* the scene is staged more thoroughly: at Hellena Barrer's command to "Kneel, – and swear," Willmore Smith promises not "to think – to see – to Love – nor Lye" with anyone but her. The lines play out the legal form, as the oath is then sealed with a gesture: "Kiss the Book," she commands, and the stage direction tells us that he "*Kisses her hand*."[16] In some plays – most famously *The Tempest* – the kiss that seals the bond could be transformed into a drink, while still preserving its function of oath-taking and the declaration of allegiance: when Caliban promises Stephano that he will "swear upon that bottle to be thy true subject," Stephano responds, "Here, kiss the book," and hands Caliban the bottle.[17]

In this legal and social dimension, the gesture was drawn into the wider radical Protestant attack on oath-taking.[18] In 1672 Richard Baxter dedicated an extensive section of his *Christian Directory* to enumerating and disproving the various objections that could be mounted against kissing the book, whether as part of the liturgy or as part of legal procedure. Among these we find the claims that "*It savoureth of the Romish superstition*," that it puts "*some adoration*" on the book itself, and that it is akin to other disputed ceremonies like "*Laying on the hand*" and "*the Cross in Baptism*." To the latter concerns Baxter argues, first, that the ceremony is only a sign of faith in the gospel, and, second and more generally, that "Significant words, gestures, or actions are not…evil" even if some have attacked them as "*Ceremonies*": for Baxter, gestures can be valid signs of true faith.[19] But as early as 1591 we find Henry Barrow asserting the idolatrous nature of the oaths taken by the High Commission and defending those who scruple to perform them. "The othe that is heere administred," he writes, "is, that laying their hand or 3 fingers vpon a booke, they sweare by God & by the contents of the booke, to answere truly vnto such things as shalbe demanded of them, and so kissing the booke their othe is accepted"; "But if anie make conscience, or denie to receaue this idolatrous wicked othe...yet wil these graceles Bishops inforce this othe." The ellipsis in this second sentence marks an astonishing, vituperative parenthesis in which Barrow piles up scriptural citations demonstrating that the oath-taking he has just described is "vnlawful," "contrarie to the commandement of God," "superstitious," "idolatrous, in ioyning any thing vnto or with God, in swearing by any thing besides or with God," and therefore subject to "the fearful curse of God."[20]

The gesture of kissing the book, in other words, resides at a center of controversy over worship, ritual, and oaths, and it at least potentially imports this instability of meaning into those accounts of Islam that put such weight on the gesture of kissing the Qur'an. If such accounts seem to give coherence to the issue by asserting its alien, Islamic affiliations, they nevertheless also risk activating intra-Protestant debate, generating a real indeterminacy of meaning precisely through their effort to fix the significance of Islamic practices with a kind of emblematic absoluteness. The material book – and even the material of the book – lies at the heart of early modern accounts of Islam. But the question of how we relate to the book in its materiality opens English discourses about Islam to a series of disputes within Christianity.

All of these accounts of Islam identify the Muslim treatment of the Qur'an as idolatrous: as Alexander Ross asserts in his translation of it, "never was there such an Idol as the *Alcoran*."[21] But an idol is properly an image of divinity; the veneration accorded to the book in these accounts suggests rather a kind of fetishism, a sacredness imputed to the material object in its materiality.[22] Thomas Herbert tells us that the Persians "interdict all superstitious worship of Images, Pictures, and such like, hated exceedingly, and therefore haue Popery in abomination" – a description that sounds oddly like Protestant iconoclasm – and then, at the end of the same paragraph, tells a now familiar story: "if they casually finde a piece of paper that has his [Muhammad's] name in it, they preserue it from all bad vses."[23] A thoroughgoing iconoclasm can do away with the worship of images, but it cannot prevent the fetishization of the sacred book itself. Descriptions of the handling of the Qur'an take place within a repository of related accounts – ritual washing, incantatory prayer, ceremonial practice – that imagine Islam as a legalistic and merely formal faith.[24] But these accounts also dissemble an issue central to Protestantism. The substitution of the book for the whole panoply of Catholic ceremonies, practices, orders, disciplines, foundations, and cults, faced the reformers with a problem: Protestant iconoclasm could dispense with every Catholic work, every Catholic ritual, every Catholic "idol," but how could it protect itself against the more insidious possibility of idolizing the book, of turning the word of God itself into a fetish?

That this *was* a problem can be seen in the strange handling of the Bible in Spenser's "Book of Holiness."[25] The whole first book of *The Faerie Queene* draws almost continually on Scripture, virtually turning itself into an epitome of both Old and New Testaments. But while the landscape of book 1 is also littered with actual books, only one of them is the Bible: rescued from Orgoglio, Redcrosse gives Arthur "A booke, wherein his Saueours testament / Was writ with golden letters rich and braue; / A worke of wondrous grace, and able soules to saue" (1.9.19). Redcrosse gives a "booke" on which the "letters" of the New Testament seem to be reduced to ornaments, beautiful and elaborate but nonsignifying patterns. When the Bible appears in Spenser's "Book of Holiness," it does so as a kind of fetish. Despite the assertion of the salvific power of this volume, Redcrosse himself is clearly not in possession of its "wondrous grace," and immediately after this scene succumbs to Despair. His spiritual rescue again involves a book, but a book whose description negotiates the threat of fetishization by turning it into an allegorical fiction that remains mysterious, inaccessible, unreadable. This is Fidelia's "sacred Booke, with bloud ywrit," which "none could read" except that Fidelia "did them teach" (1.10.19).[26] Even the New Testament is a dead letter without faith as its interpreter. In book 1 of *The Faerie Queene,* the Bible is everywhere, as quotation and allusion; but the book itself presents more of a problem.

While Catholics could rely on the church as a witness to and guarantor of the truth and meaning of scripture, Protestantism was left confronting its books without any obvious external guide for how to read them. Its first move was to assert the Bible's radical clarity. Luther writes that scripture is "most certain, most easy to understand, most clear, its own interpreter."[27] "If we look at it with clear eyes," Calvin asserts, we will "feel perfectly assured – as much so as if we beheld the divine image visibly impressed on it – that it came to us, by the instrumentality of men, from the very mouth of God."[28] We know the divinity of scripture in the same way that we know "light from darkness, white from black, sweet from bitter" (1.7.2). Scripture signifies in exactly the same way a light shines or a bitter taste tastes. It requires no interpretation. It simply is.

In Protestant polemics, the Qur'an appears as the perfect negation of this model. Alexander Ross describes it as "incongruous, . . . farced with contradictions, blasphemies, obscene speeches, and ridiculous fables," a "*Gallimaufry* of Errors," "mishapen and deformed," a "hodg-podge" of contradictions, a "Monster brought out of *Africa*" whose very deformity demonstrates God's truth (A2v; 2D7v; 2D8v; 2E5r; 2D7v). The Qur'an is a text that perfectly and immediately reveals its own falsehood. In both cases, interpretation disappears into a perfect obviousness, a perfect openness and availability of meaning. At the same time, the book disappears into a series of figures: the Qur'an becomes a monster or a deformed body, while Calvin's Bible becomes the image of God, as though we are dealing not with reading at all but with *seeing:* we "look at" the Bible, according to Calvin, and when we do so with clear eyes, it is "as if we beheld the divine image visibly impressed on it," or – in Thomas Norton's translation – "as if we beheld the maiesty of God himselfe there present."[29] We look at the book, but we see God.

For all of its insistence on the centrality of scripture to all true faith, Protestantism seems to evade the book itself, the book as a made thing.[30] If Spenser evades the book by allegorizing it, George Herbert does so through a series of figural displacements. His first sonnet on "The Holy Scriptures" begins with an apostrophe – "O Book!" – and a kind of literalist's desire for the text in its every smallest detail: "let my heart / Suck ev'ry letter." Even here, the act of reading shades into something else, a "sucking" of the letter in which the heart consumes the text like food or an erotic object; if the former, it opens up a very old image of reading as ingestion.[31] The rest of the poem is structured through repeated formulas of equivalence – "Thou art" and "this is" – which bury the book under a series of other figures: it is medicine, a mirror, a well, "joy's handsel," or "heav'n's lidger," the latter a phrase that equivocates between the sense of a written record and an ambassador, a textual message and a living messenger. The final lines sign and seal this disappearance of the book. "Heav'n lies flat in thee," Herbert writes; that is, in the flat pages of a reader's open Bible, heaven spreads itself open before us. In this phrase, there is an implicit scene of reading, a book that is not disappearing into another object but remains physically present in the image. But as the sentence continues into the next verse it rescinds that image and teaches us, further, that it is not enough merely to read, that salvation requires something else from us: "heav'n lies flat in thee, / Subject to ev'ry mounter's bended knee." From the reader's flat page we descend to the bended knee of someone praying. To read the text is a beginning, but to be a "mounter," to rise to the heaven that lies flat before us in the book, we must first enact our faith in a practiced devotion, in what Izaak Walton, in his *Life* of Herbert, twice calls "a practical piety."[32]

The second sonnet dwells on a hermeneutics of scripture driven by the work of comparing and collating passages: "This verse marks that, and both do make a motion / Unto a third, that ten leaves off doth lie." This looks like a method of reading that Carol Kaske associates with Philipp Melanchthon, centering on the notion that the Bible is structured by repeated returns to certain key images or terms, but that this repetition introduces real or apparent discrepancies, even contradictions, which the reader struggles to reconcile. In Kaske's account, the reader is led to make a series of corrections or qualifications to a first impression, and so is turned away from a dogmatic or absolutist affirmation of the meaning of a single passage toward a flexible understanding of the issues underlying the whole series, from a set of competing or balanced perspectives.[33] Renaissance readers produced books designed to assist this process, the *distinctiones,* which collected the scriptural references to a particular object or concept, or the appearances of a particular word, thereby enabling a mode of radically discontinuous reading, a way of leaping from passage to passage in order to trace connections and disjunctions between them, which Herbert imagines as constellations: "O that I knew how all thy lights combine, / And the configurations of their glory!" The second sonnet thus not only adds yet one more metaphorical displacement of the book to the list propounded by the first – the book becomes a constellation, its verses stars – but also adduces a mode of reading that fragments the book, construing it as a discontinuous series of points whose proper connections are created in the reader's mind.[34] In effect, the reader remakes the book through collational reading. In Little Gidding, as Patrick Collinson notes, this was a process literally enacted on the books themselves: "Bibles were cut to pieces, verse by verse, only to be reassembled into a continuous and harmonious textual confection."[35] The result, Adam Smyth writes, was the "harmonies," a set of "lavish folio books" constructed from cut-ups of the four Gospels, "glued into (usually) 150 chapters" depicting the life of Christ; despite the literal fragmentation on which the production of these books depended, the goal, Smyth argues, was to reconcile the gospel accounts in order to offer "a coherent, continuous, harmonized narrative" that foregrounded its own "totality and completeness."[36] Peter Stallybrass has argued that the codex form itself facilitates this kind of discontinuous access, a kind of reading that does not follow the text in sequence but intervenes into it through a series of disjunctive leaps. Printed Bibles were often bound with material designed to aid this process, including indexes, liturgical calendars, collations: "they incorporated a wide range of navigational aids – aids that showed one how to read the bible other than as continuous narrative."[37] For Herbert, this fragmentation of the book aims at creating a substitute, metaphorical book: from the totality of his theological reading – including scripture, patristic texts, scholastic commentaries, and "the later writers" – the country parson should compile "a book and body of Divinity."[38] The metaphor of the book, coupled with that of the body, evokes precisely that organic unity that Herbert's exegetical method is designed to destroy when it comes to the material book. The Protestant reader fragments the book, substituting an assemblage of verses for its apparently unitary objecthood. Ostensibly, to fragment the book in this way is also to perfect it, to recreate it – spiritually, metaphorically – as complete, whole, unified, rescuing it from mere textuality. But it is also to render the book inevitably plural – not "the Bible" but bibles, perhaps as many as there are readers.[39]

If the accounts of the Islamic worship of the book evoke a perverse parody of Protestant scripturalism, a preposterously literal display of love not for God's word but for the vehicle of its transmission, they perhaps also secretly testify to the truth of what a book-centered religion is. The encounter with the word of God becomes an embodied event, a matter of touch and gesture as well as of thought or feeling.[40] Such accounts fantasize an immediate, tangible contact with the divine. Their affective charge makes available a range of embodied sensations, of physical postures of worship and love, about which Protestantism seems divided: on the one hand, Calvin spiritualizes the book, turning it into "Dei numen"; on the other hand, he imagines it as a text that circumvents interpretation, reaching the Christian subject by a route analogized to immediate, sensory experience. Is it an accident that early modern descriptions of the Islamic relation to the Qur'an echo that anxiety about radical forms of Protestantism – Anabaptists to Quakers – that so continually concerns figures from Luther to the English bishops? Those hearing the Qur'an, in Sandys's description, stand with "such steadie postures of bodie, as if they were intranced"; others enumerate the names of God, "shaking their heads incessantly, vntill they turne giddie"; others still perform "dances that consist of continuall turnings, vntill at a certaine stroke they fall vpon the earth; and lying along like beasts, are thought to be rapt in spirit vnto celestiall conuersations" (F4r). Two things about this seem clear. First, Sandys focuses on a set of physical procedures for achieving rapture or ecstasy, an extra-bodily experience of the divine in which the whole being of the devotional subject is taken over. Second, this ecstatic experience of total immersion in God – so ardently desired in Herbert's poetry and throughout a whole seventeenth-century meditative poetics – is presented by Sandys as illusory, mad: the Muslims are "intranced," "giddie," "like beasts." There are clear echoes here of a wider seventeenth-century critique of "enthusiasm." The devotee's encounter with the sacred book becomes a physical event, but that event – far from testifying simply to Islamic fetishism – opens up areas that were being fiercely contested among Protestants.

Early modern polemics against the Qur'an also engage the issue of the book's materiality through the question of its textual history. The text embodied in the Qur'an was routinely dismissed as confused and corrupt, a claim associated above all with the Qur'an's alternate versions of stories familiar from Jewish and Christian scripture. Joshua Notstock writes that the Qur'an is a "strange miscellany" of "histories corruptly recited out of the Old Testament" and others "as fasly [falsely] quoted out of the New."[41] According to Samuel Purchas, it "corrupts, mingles, mangles, maimes" scripture, twisting and distorting its narratives.[42] These alternate versions were central to a controversy extending back at least to the tenth century, in which Christians accused Muhammad of having garbled God's word while Muslims claimed that the Jews and Christians had misunderstood or falsified their own sacred texts.[43] One of the speakers in the *Colloquium Heptaplomeres* – often attributed to Jean Bodin, though possibly assembled from a pastiche of his published writings sometime in the 1620s, and found circulating in manuscript throughout the seventeenth century – insists that, according to Muslims, the true gospel accounts have been lost: "the Ismaelites," he reports, "reject these books of the Gospels as completely corrupted by heretics.... [They] think the true Gospels, which, nevertheless they themselves do not have, have perished completely."[44] According to Humphrey Prideaux, Muhammad claimed that "the *Jews* and *Christians* had corrupted these holy Writings" – that is, the whole Bible – "and that he was sent to purge them from those Corruptions," and so "most of those Passages which he takes out of the *Old and New Testament* are related otherwise by him in his *Alcoran*."[45]

Christian attacks on the Qur'an serve to ward off Muslim counter-claims about the state of the Christian texts; thus religious controversy with Islam was conducted in significant measure over the territory of textual criticism. Purchas, Prideaux, and Lancelot Addison all spend time adducing the textual origins and history of the Qur'an. The source from which they draw their accounts seems to be – directly or indirectly – the *Confusion dela secta mahomatica y del alcoran* of Juan Andrés, by his own description a Muslim of the waning years of al-Andalus who converted to Christianity, took orders as a Dominican, and began proselytizing to the Muslims of Aragon and Granada. Andrés is a shadowy figure. He describes himself in the preface as the son of an "alfaqui" in Xàtiva – that is, a *Fakih,* a specialist in Islamic law and especially in that part of the law that concerns the elaboration of legal norms – who succeeded his father in "su oficio."[46] This scholar of Islamic law supposedly underwent a conversionary experience – a nineteenth-century book calls him a "segundo San Pablo"[47] – in the cathedral at Valencia in 1487 while listening to a sermon, and was baptized under the names of two of the presiding priests, which, if true, explains his peculiar name. We are not told why he was in the cathedral in the first place. Although the whole kingdom of Valencia had ceased to be under Muslim rule from the mid-thirteenth century, a substantial Muslim community remained, openly and legally practicing

Islam. The Mudejar community of Xàtiva was "the largest and most important" in the kingdom, and a *Fakih* there would have been a prominent figure, whose presence at the Christian cathedral seems difficult to explain.[48]

Nothing is known about Andrés except for what he tells us. There is no evidence of a Dominican by that name operating in Aragon or Granada. Gerard A. Wiegers has argued that there is no Juan Andrés, and that his book was written by a Christian with access to an unknown Muslim informant.[49] Others take the book's claims at face value, attributing to its author "a familiarity with Islamic sources seldom encountered in other Christian polemicists."[50] In any case, the *Confusion* became "one of the most-read tracts on Islam of the sixteenth and seventeenth centuries."[51] First published in Valencia in 1515, it was translated into Italian (1537), French (1574), Latin (1594), Dutch (1651), English (1652), and German (1664 and 1685). As late as 1705 Hadrian Reland could write that "when a young man who studies theology has a laudable desire to understand the Mohammedan religion, one gives him this [book]."[52] The *Confusion* itself seeks to confute Islam through two complementary procedures. On the one hand, Andrés argues that the Qur'an contradicts itself, descends into absurdities, and demonstrates no perceptible internal order (O7v–P1r). On the other hand, he pursues a textual-critical analysis designed to demonstrate its human origins and detailing its mode of composition and transmission, revealing it not as the word of God divinely given, not as "authentick," but as both fraudulent and preposterous (F4v). "O *Moore,*" Andrés apostrophizes his imagined reader, "what thinkest thou, of the Scripture which you so much reverence, that when ye take it in your hands ye kisse it, and swear by it, and keep it like a God?" (F7r).

Part of Andrés's argument lies in the assertion that, in writing the Qur'an, Muhammad sought out the help of two "sword-cutlers," Christian slaves in Mecca whom he "questioned…about many things of the Bible,…and as they answered so he set it down in *Arabick*." This seems plausible to Andrés "because in the *Alcoran* there are so many contrarieties, unnecessary stories, and fables"; the cutlers "told him what themselves did not certainly know, and as they said, so he wrote in his tablebooks and papers" (E3r–v). The cutlers are the pirates or rogue actors of Andrés's bibliographic narrative (I1v). Having traced the Qur'an's variant texts to this source, Andrés comfortably – and circularly – asserts the Qur'an's falsehood by noting that it contains alternate versions of scriptural history or stories not elsewhere attested: "if the things aforesayd were true," he insists of one story, "they would not have been forgotten to have been put into the old Testament" (I2v). The Qur'an can only be considered accurate when it faithfully copies Christian and Jewish scripture. But this also means that to read the Qur'an is to confront the possibility of errors or omissions in Jewish and Christian scripture.

Muhammad's "tablebooks and papers," rather than his interlocutors, are Andrés's main target. His central contention is that the Qur'an was never written as a *book* at all. Rather, over a period of twenty-three years Muhammad dictated various fragments to a series of secretaries, pronounced them to his followers – who were expected to commit them to memory – and finally interred them, written on loose "scrowls or papers," in a "shrine or box" (F4v, E8v). Because he continually generated new texts, some of which revised or revoked earlier ones, "*Muhamed* never commanded that his *Alcoran* should be collected or reduced into bookes and chapters, as now it is, but kept it in the said scrowles or papers in the aforesaid ark or shrine" (F4v–F5r). For the first quarter-century of its life the Qur'an was not a book at all but a collection of loose papers, and for this reason Andrés insists that the word "Qur'an" means a collection or compilation – a myth that persisted in European accounts for about a century.[53] Only after Muhammad's death did "*Hozman*" – 'Uthman, the third caliph – produce a uniform text: "he was the man who took the scrowles and papers out of the box or Shrine, and put them in order and entitled the Chapters" (F5r). In Prideaux's words, the Qur'an was "compiled in the same manner as *Homer's Rhapsodies* were out of the loose *Poems* of that *Poet*" (C3r–v).[54] But "*Hozman*" had set himself an impossible task. For one thing, in Muhammad's wife's house he found several sheets of paper so eaten by mice and rotted by damp that they were indecipherable (F6v). For another thing, some of the verses were never written down at all, and as he tried to track down everyone to whose memory such verses had been entrusted, Hozman found that "much" had been forgotten (F2v–F3r, F6v–F7r). And so the Qur'an that he produced did not include "all the *Alcoran*" from "*Muhamed's* time": in Sandys's words, the Qur'an is not "the same that was written by *Mahomet*."[55]

Andrés tries to anchor these claims to the text by concentrating on cases in which the Qur'an appears to him to contradict itself or to interrupt the linear unfolding of a historical narrative. All such instances become for him not interpretive problems – as they might be for Melanchthon, thinking about the Bible – but evidence of the book's troubled textual history. What Andrés seeks to do is to suture interpretation to a kind of history of the book, not in order to establish the text – as a humanist might do with "*Homer's Rhapsodies*" – but to demolish any claims for its divine origin. He insists on the materiality of the text, its vulnerability to mice or the damp, its real existence as a set of loose scrolls subject to loss and disorder, in order to divest it of any sacred aura. The history of the book seeks to annihilate the truth of the text. Andrés thus at once associates the idea of the book with a perfect textual integrity and wholeness – a true book is everything the Qur'an is not – and also troubles that notion, suggesting how the history of any book reveals its unity as the product of a forgetting.

Some information about the textual history of the Qur'an had long been part of medieval Christian polemics against it.[56] What is unusual about Andrés's book is the extent to which this textual account becomes the foundation of the argument. The weight Andrés places on the history of the text potentially opens up difficult questions about the composition, transmission, and canonization of the Bible itself.[57] In this, the *Confusion* is in many ways a work of its time, written at a moment when humanist philological procedures were starting to be applied to scripture with controversial effect. The most notorious case is that of the so-called Johannine comma, the passage at 1 John 5:7–8 in the King James version, left out of the first two editions of Erasmus's New Testament in 1516 and 1519 and then reincluded – after controversy – in 1522: according to one theory, the Johannine comma, which seems to reference the Trinity, was *added to* extant manuscripts of the Vulgate, or migrated into the text from marginal notes, at some point in the process of transmission, precisely in order to provide scriptural warrant for Trinitarianism.[58] The history of the "Higher Criticism" is usually treated as an Enlightenment phenomenon, and yet the seeds of a textual-critical approach to scripture lie in the soil of Renaissance philology and the deep, historical knowledge of the text that it seeks.[59]

Here too the history of the Qur'an as rehearsed by Andrés has the potential to rebound awkwardly onto some increasingly urgent questions within Christianity. In closing I want to look briefly at one of the texts often cited as a forerunner of the Higher Criticism, simply to note that here too the Qur'an makes its appearance as a kind of specter that haunts questions about the textual history of Christian and Jewish scripture. In the *Tractatus Theologico-Politicus,* Spinoza argues – along lines oddly parallel to those taken by Andrés – that the scriptural texts as we have them are belated compilations made from earlier, lost documents.[60] The Pentateuch, Joshua, Judges, Ruth, Samuel, and Kings are all "derivative works" (8.11, 125), not authored by those to whom they are traditionally attributed; Moses's original book of the law has been lost, although an amplified version was inserted into Deuteronomy (8.5, 122–23); all of these books were compiled by a "chronicler" (8.11, 125) who set out to compose a continuous history "many years after the event" (8.12, 126), but left the story unfinished, simply collecting a series of older stories "without examining them properly and setting them in due order" (9.1, 129); and none of the extant texts has been preserved without errors and variant readings (9.13, 135).[61] The only rule for interpreting scripture is "to claim nothing as a biblical doctrine that we have not derived, by the closest possible scrutiny, from its own history" (7.5, 99). This requires tremendous labor: we must understand the language and the opinions stated by each book on every subject; we must know "the life, character, and particular interests of the author of each book" (7.5.3, 101); and we must discover

> the fate of each book: namely how it was first received and whose hands it came into, how many variant readings there have been of its text, by whose decision it was received among the sacred books, and finally how all the books which are now accepted as sacred came to form a single corpus. (7.5.3, 101)

But this is impossible (7.12, 107). The method requires "a history of the vicissitudes of all the biblical books, and most of this is unknown to us"; "we have no knowledge whatever of the authors, or...the compilers of many of the books"; "we do not know under what circumstances these books...were composed or when" nor "into whose hands" they "subsequently came" nor "in whose copies so many variant readings occur" nor even whether there were "many additional readings in others" (7.15, 109).

Spinoza outlines the project that has obsessed textual study of the Bible ever since, even as he insists that that project will never reach its goals, because of "carelessness...in neglecting to construct the history of the Bible when it would have been possible to do so" (7.19, 112). This impossibility does not worry him because even as he demonstrates our ignorance about the history of the scriptural texts he also insists on the clarity of scripture on the most essential points. Scripture cannot be called "defective, distorted or truncated" because "the meaning, which alone entitles any text to be called divine, has come down to us uncorrupted, even though the words in which it was first expressed are deemed to have been frequently altered" (12.10, 164–65). Despite all textual losses and lacunae, the message is clear in its essentials: "[f]or we see from Scripture itself, and without any difficulty or ambiguity, that the essence of the Law is to love God above all things and one's neighbour as oneself" (12.10, 165). The moral content of scripture cannot be lost or falsified because it is based on a "universal foundation" of reason and ethics and above all on "the principle of charity which in both testaments is everywhere what is commended the most" (12.11, 165–66). What Spinoza outlines is a way of reading available to all humanity, and not only to those athletes of scholarship who can dedicate time and energy to seeking the lost history of the Bible. "Those who consider the Bible in its current state a letter from God, sent from heaven to men," he writes, "will undoubtedly protest that I have sinned 'against the Holy Ghost' by claiming the word of God is erroneous, mutilated, corrupt and inconsistent, that we have only fragments of it, and that the original text of the covenant which God made with the Jews has perished" (12.1, 158). What he has actually done is to show "on what grounds Scripture, or any inarticulate object, could be called sacred and divine" (12.4, 160):

> both reason and the beliefs of the prophets and Apostles evidently proclaim that God's eternal word and covenant and true religion are divinely inscribed upon the hearts of men, that is, upon the human mind. This is God's true original text, which he himself has sealed with his own seal, that is, with the idea of himself as the image of his divinity. (12.1, 158)

Those who fail to accept the facts about the textual condition of the Bible "verge…on adoring images and pictures, i.e. paper and ink, as the word of God" (12.3, 159). Spinoza's theory of scriptural reading in a strange way returns us to the immediacy and obviousness of scripture as articulated by Luther and Calvin. We turn aside from the darkness of a murky history of the book to encounter a truth that blazes out unobscured from a text that is no longer really a text but simply the directly apprehensible image of God. But the bearer of that text is no longer a book but the human heart and mind – a conclusion with which the poet who saw that the only true altar was cut from a living human heart could, perhaps, come to terms, even if he could clearly by no means accept Spinoza's attendant desacralization of the sacred book itself.

Spinoza continues to present the Qur'an, on the other hand, as the image of a merely human textuality: "if anyone reads the stories of holy Scripture and believes all of them without paying attention to the doctrine that the Bible uses them to teach, and without amending his life, he might just as well read the Koran or the dramatic plays of the poets, or at any rate the common chronicles" (5.19, 79). No amount of textual corruption can erase the message of scripture, written in the mind and heart; but plays, chronicles, and the Qur'an are all vulnerable to the stray forces and random damage that can affect any merely material thing. From the danger of a fetishization of the material book to the use of book history to provide new guidelines for reading scripture, the Qur'an was a contested site for thinking through issues central to the place of the material book in scriptural religion. In the early modern period, the materiality of the sacred text always potentially invited an encounter with the Qur'an, the sacred book that became the archetype of a fallen materiality, its worship evidence of textual fetishism.

NOTES

I owe my introduction to the various interests that come together in this essay to David Scott Kastan. My own book fetish began earlier, though David also helped me cultivate that. I'm sure he remembers a long drive through Long Island on a summer day in the late '90s with a few others also in this book, to a semi-abandoned warehouse where facsimiles of early modern books were being sold by the pound alongside piles of instruction manuals for long-dead computer languages.

1 George Sandys, *A Relation of a Iourney begun An: Dom: 1610* (London, 1615), F3v.

2 English readers might also have been aware of the place of the gesture in Jewish practice; see Alexander Ross, *ΠΑΝΣΕΒΕΙΑ: Or, A View of all Religions in the World* (London, 1655), C8v–D1r.

3 *The Policy of the Turkish Empire. The first Booke* (London, 1597), E1v–E2r. The passage is adumbrated by Samuel Purchas, *Pvrchas his Pilgrimage* (London, 1626), 297. Compare Lancelot Addison, *The First State of Mahuedism* (London, 1679), D8r–E1r. For a reading list of early modern sources about Islam, Muhammad, and the Qur'an, see the bibliography appended

to Humphrey Prideaux, *The True Nature of Imposture Fully Display'd in the Life of Mahomet* (London, 1697), K5r–M2v.

4 Hugh Gough, trans., *The Ofspring of the House of Ottomanno* (London, [1568?]), D4v.

5 *The Four Epistles of A.G. Busbequius, Concerning his Embassy into Turkey* (London, 1694), C9v. Compare Addison, E2v.

6 Thomas Heywood, *If You Know Not Me, You Know No Bodie* (London, 1605), G4r.

7 Thomas Becon, *The Displaying of the Popish Masse* (London, 1637), C3r–C4r. On the Catholic liturgy, see *The Catholic Encyclopedia*, "Gospel," section IV, "Present Ceremony of the Gospel," which the entry traces back to "the seventh or eighth centuries."

8 Desiderius Erasmus, *A playne and godly exposytion or declaratio[n] of the com[m]une Crede* ([London, 1534]), T8r.

9 Edmund Bonner, *A profitable and necessarye doctrine* (London, 1555), 2I3r.

10 Desiderius Erasmus, *An exhortation to the diligent studye of scripture* ([Antwerp], 1529), A5v.

11 Anthony Sparrow, *A Rationale upon the Book of Common-Prayer of the Church of England* (London, 1672), K11v.

12 William Pemble, *Vindiciae Gratiae. A Plea for Grace* (London, 1627), D2v–D3r. The passage is quoted by Richard Baxter in *The Saints Everlasting Rest* (London, 1649), 4Q2r (marginal note), and in shortened form by Samuel Clarke, *The Saints Nose-gay* (London, 1642), H9v–H10r.

13 For oaths of fealty, see the anonymous *Institutions in the lawes of Englande* (n.p., 1538), E3r, and John Fitzherbert, *[T]he boke of surueyinge and improume[n]tes* (n.p., 1523); for the coronation oath, see Gilbert Burnet, *A Collection of Papers Relating to the Present Juncture of Affairs in England* ([London], 1688), F4r, and Edward Wolley, *Loyalty amongst Rebels* (London, 1662), E6v; for the swearing-in of jurors, see Jonas Adames, *The Order of keeping a court leete* (London, 1593), A3r; for the Oaths of Allegiance and Supremacy, see *The Examination and Tryall of Margaret Fell and George Fox* ([London], 1664), D4v; for the Order of the Garter, see Elias Ashmole, *The Institutions, Laws & Ceremonies of the most noble Order of the Garter* (London, 1672), 2X2r, 3A2r, 3K1r. More generally, see Honoré de Mareville, "Oaths," *Notes and Queries*, no. 211 (November 1853): 471–72.

14 "Need Not Kiss the Book," *The New York Times*, June 20, 1886; "English to Abandon Kissing the Book," *The New York Times*, January 17, 1909. The latter quotes one justice observing, "To meet the case of those who desire to kiss the Book…I have given directions to have Books with washable bindings." The *British Medical Journal* in 1901 printed a notice announcing, "We are glad to see that some progress is being made towards the abolition of the uncleanly and dangerous English practice of administering the oath by requiring a witness to 'kiss the Book'" (*BMJ* 1 [1901]: 726).

15 John Day, *Humour out of breath* (London, 1608), E4v.

16 Aphra Behn, *The Rover* (London, 1677), F1v.

17 *The Complete Works of Shakespeare*, ed. David Bevington (New York: HarperCollins, 1992), 2.1.124–25, 129. See also Thomas Randolph, *Aristippus* (London, 1630), B2v.

18 On judicial oaths, see Keith Thomas, *Religion and the Decline of Magic* (New York: Charles Scribner's Sons, 1971), 67–78.

19 Richard Baxter, *A Christian Directory: Or, A Summ of Practical Theologie, and Cases of Conscience* (London, 1673), 3H2r–v.

20 Henry Barrow, *A Brief Discoverie of the False Chvrch* ([n.p.], 1590), 2K1r–v. Compare Francis Howgill, *The Dawnings of the Gospel-Day* ([n.p.], 1676), 3H2v.

21 Alexander Ross, *The Alcoran of Mahomet* (London, 1649), 2F1v.

22 See William Pietz, "The Problem of the Fetish, I," *RES: Anthropology and Aesthetics*, no. 9 (1985): 5–17, and "The Problem of the Fetish, II," *RES: Anthropology and Aesthetics*, no. 13 (1987): 23–45.

23 *A Relation of Some Yeares Travaile, Begvnne Anno 1626* (London, 1634), X1r–v.

24 In this, it was always possible to imagine Islam as *the same* as other religions: in his commentaries on Galatians, Luther conflates Islam, Catholicism, Judaism, and radical Protestant sectarianism as having "the same heart, opinion, and cogitation." See *A Commentarie of M. Doctor Martin Lvther vpon the Epistle of S. Paul to the Galatians* (London, 1575), 2A4v.

25 Compare Kenneth Gross, *Spenserian Poetics: Idolatry, Iconoclasm, and Magic* (Ithaca: Cornell University Press, 1985).

26 As David Lee Miller notes, the letter of the text "is associated…with blood, death, and blindness" (*The Poem's Two Bodies: The Poetics of the 1590* Faerie Queene [Princeton: Princeton University Press, 1988], 89).

27 Quoted from Mickey L. Mattox, "Martin Luther," in *Christian Theologies of Scripture: A Comparative Introduction*, ed. Justin S. Holcomb (New York: New York University Press, 2006), 105.

28 *Institutes of the Christian Religion*, trans. Henry Beveridge, 3 vols. (Edinburgh: Calvin Translation Society, 1845–46), 1.7.4, 1.7.5.

29 Jean Calvin, *The Institvtion of Christian Religion*, trans. Thomas Norton (London, 1578), C2v. John Allen turns the act of seeing into "an intuitive perception," but the point is the same: perception and sensation, rather than interpretation, are the model for how scripture impresses itself upon us. See *Institutes of the Christian Religion*, 2 vols., trans. John Allen (Grand Rapids: W.B. Eerdmans, 1949), 1:90–91.

30 On Protestant anxiety about the private reading of scripture, see David Scott Kastan, "'The noyse of the new Bible': Reform and Reaction in Henrician England," in *Religion and Culture in Renaissance England*, ed. Claire McEachern and Debora Shuger (Cambridge: Cambridge University Press, 1997), 46–68 (62).

31 Michael Schoenfeldt, "Reading bodies," in *Reading, Society and Politics in Early Modern England*, ed. Kevin Sharpe and Steven N. Zwicker (Cambridge: Cambridge University Press, 2003), 215–43.

32 "Izaak Walton's *The Life of Mr George Herbert*," in George Herbert, *The Complete English Poems*, ed. John Tobin (New York: Penguin Books, 1991), 301 and 302. The word "practical" echoes through Walton's account of Herbert's religion: see also 295, 303, and 308.

33 Carol V. Kaske, *Spenser and Biblical Poetics* (Ithaca: Cornell University Press, 1999).

34 Compare Herbert, *A Priest to the Temple*, in *The Complete English Poems*, 205, on what he calls "a diligent collation of Scripture with Scripture": "For all Truth being consonant to itself, and all being penned by one hand and the selfsame Spirit, it cannot be but that an industrious and judicious comparing of place with place must be a singular help for the right understanding of the Scriptures."

35 Patrick Collinson, "The Coherence of the Text: How it Hangeth Together: The Bible in Reformation England," in *The Bible, the Reformation and the Church: Essays in Honour of James Atkinson*, ed. W.P. Stephens (Sheffield: Sheffield Academic Press, 1995), 84–108 (105).

36 Adam Smyth, "Little Clippings: Cutting and Pasting Bibles in the 1630s," *Journal of Medieval and Early Modern Studies* 45 (2015): 595–613 (596, 598).

37 Peter Stallybrass, "Books and Scrolls: Navigating the Bible," in *Books and Readers*

in *Early Modern England: Material Studies,* ed. Jennifer Andersen and Elizabeth Sauer (Philadelphia: University of Pennsylvania Press, 2002), 42–79 (51).

38 Herbert, *A Priest to the Temple,* 206.

39 Kastan, "'The noyse of the new Bible.'"

40 A number of scholars have emphasized the embodiedness of reading: Roger Chartier, *The Order of Books: Readers, Authors, and Libraries in Europe between the Fourteenth and Eighteenth Centuries,* trans. Lydia G. Cochrane (Stanford: Stanford University Press, 1994), 16–17; Adrian Johns, *The Nature of the Book: Print and Knowledge in the Making* (Chicago: University of Chicago Press, 1998), 380–443; and Schoenfeldt, "Reading bodies."

41 Juan Andrés, *The Confusion of Muhamed's Sect,* trans. Joshua Notstock (London, 1652), B7r. Notstock took his translation from the French (B8v).

42 Samuel Purchas, *Purchas his pilgrimage* (London, 1626), Y6v.

43 *Encyclopedia of Islam,* 2d ed., ed. P. Bearman et al. (Leiden: Brill, 2010), s.v. "Tahrif," "Indjil."

44 *Colloquium of the Seven about Secrets of the Sublime: Colloquium Heptaplomeres de Rerum Sublimium Arcanis Abditis,* trans. Marion Leathers Kuntz (Princeton: Princeton University Press, 1975), 252.

45 Humphrey Prideaux, *The True Nature of Imposture Fully Displayed in the Life of Mahomet* (London, 1697), C2r.

46 See the autobiographical narrative reproduced from the first Spanish edition in Hartmut Bobzin, "Bemerkungen zu Juan Andrés und zu seinem Buch *Confusión de la secta mahomatica* (Valencia 1515)," in *Festgabe für Hans-Rudolf Singer,* 2 vols., ed. Martin Forstner (Frankfurt am Main: Peter Lang, 1991), 529–48 (536–37). On the *Fakih,* see D.B. MacDonald, "Fakih," and N. Calder, "Usulal-Fikh," *Encyclopedia of Islam.* See also Mark D. Meyerson, *The Muslims of Valencia in the Age of Fernando and Isabel: Between Coexistence and Crusade* (Berkeley: University of California Press, 1991), 104, describing the functions of the *Fakih* in the Valenica of Andrés's time.

47 D. Vicente Boix, *Xátiva. Memorias, Recuerdos y Tradiciones de esta Antiqua Ciudad* (Xátiva: Blas Bellver, 1857), 212.

48 Isabel A. O'Connor, *A Forgotten Community: The Mudejar Aljama of Xàtiva 1240–1327* (Leiden: Brill, 2003), 1. The unstable but long-established *convivencia* between the city's Muslim, Jewish, and Christian inhabitants seems only to have been destroyed in the 1520s, though it became increasingly difficult after about 1499: Meyerson, 272.

49 Gerard A. Wiegers, review of *Confusión o confutación de la secta Mahomética y del Alcorán,* ed. Elisa Ruiz García and María García-Monge, *Aljamía* 16 (2004): 254–61.

50 Bobzin, 539: "eine Kenntnis islamischer Quellen, die bei anderen christlichen Polemikern gegen den Islam nicht anzutreffen ist."

51 Ibid., 534: "einer der meistgelesenen Traktate über den Islam im 16. und 17. Jahrhundert."

52 Quoted in Bobzin, 534, from *Zwey Bücher von der Türckischen oder Mohammedanischen Religion* (Hannover, 1716), a book first published in Latin as *De religione Mohammedica libri duo* in 1705: "Wann ein junger Mensch die Theologie studiret, und eine löbliche Begierde hat, die Mohammedische Religion zu verstehen, dem gibt man."

53 Andrés, E6v. See the discussion in William Bedwell's "The Arabian Trudgman" and "Index Assvratarum Muhammedici Alkorani," in *Mohammedis Imposturae* (London, 1615), L3v–L4r and O3r; in Purchas, 2B4r–v; and in George Sale, *The Koran, commonly called The Alcoran of Mohammed* (London, 1734), 56.

54 The Qur'an was frequently condemned for being in verse; see Purchas, 2B4v. On the question of scriptural verse, see Targoff, *Common Prayer*, 57–84.

55 Andrés, F6r; Sandys, F3v. Compare also Fletcher, D4v. For the history of the "collection" of the Qur'an, see especially *Encyclopedia of Islam*, s.v. "al-Kur'an," sec. 3, "History of the Kur'an after 632."

56 The ultimate source of textual knowledge about the Qur'an in medieval polemics seems to be the *Risálah* attributed to 'Abd al-Masíh ibn Isháq al Kindi, dated probably to before the eleventh century: see Norman Daniel, *Islam and the West: The Making of an Image* (1960; Oxford: Oneworld, 1993), 54–55; also 22, 30, and 80–81.

57 See Bernhard Lohse, "Die Entscheidung der lutherischen Reformation über den Umfang des alttestamentlichen Kanons," in *Evangelium in der Geschichte: Studien zu Luther und der Reformation*, ed. Leif Grane et al. (Göttingen: Vandenhoeck and Ruprecht, 1988), 211–36 (214), on the "im späten 15. Jahrhundert einsetzende Diskussion über den Umfang des Kanons sowie über die Verfasserschaft mancher biblischer Schriften."

58 The literature here is enormous, but see especially H.J. de Jonge, "Erasmus and the *Comma Johanneum*," *Ephemerides Theologicae Lovanienses* 56 (1980): 381–89, available online from Leiden University at https://openaccess.leidenuniv.nl/bitstream/handle/1887/1023/279_050.pdf?sequence=1. For the later seventeenth-century history, see Rob Iliffe, "Friendly Criticism: Richard Simon, John Locke, Isaac Newton and the *Johannine Comma*," in *Scripture and Scholarship in Early Modern England*, ed. Ariel Hessayon and Nicholas Keene (Burlington: Ashgate, 2006), 137–57. Thanks to Tom Festa for drawing my attention to the issue, in a talk about Milton and the Johannine Comma in Fall 2015.

59 See, for instance, Debora Shuger, *The Renaissance Bible: Scholarship, Sacrifice, and Subjectivity* (Berkeley: University of California Press, 1998), 11, which puts the "first stirrings" of the Higher Criticism in the late seventeenth century.

60 Spinoza develops his argument about the textual status of scripture primarily by a reading of Jewish commentaries on the Torah, although he claims it can be extended to the gospels. My thinking about Spinoza and religion has been guided by Nancy K. Levene, *Spinoza's Revelation: Religion, Democracy, and Reason* (Cambridge: Cambridge University Press, 2004); Steven Nadler, *Spinoza's Heresy: Immortality and the Jewish Mind* (Oxford: Oxford University Press, 2001); J. Samuel Preus, *Spinoza and the Irrelevance of Biblical Authority* (Cambridge: Cambridge University Press, 2001); and Yirmiyahu Yovel, *Spinoza and Other Heretics*, 2 vols. (Princeton: Princeton University Press, 1989).

61 See, generally, Benedict de Spinoza, *Theological-Political Treatise*, ed. Jonathan Israel, trans. Michael Silverthorne and Jonathan Israel (Cambridge: Cambridge University Press, 2007), chapters 8 and 9. All citations are by chapter and paragraph according to the Akkerman division as followed by Israel and Silverthorne; see *Tractatus Theologico-Politicus*, ed. Fokke Akkerman, trans. Jacqueline Lagrée and Pierre-François Moreau (Paris: Presses Universitaires de France, 1999). I also provide page numbers for the Gebhardt edition (Spinoza, *Opera*, 4 vols., ed. Carl Gebhardt [Heidelberg: Carl Winters, 1925], 3:3–267).

Iuine *Plat*
of many w
and the con
pithy persw
num, and *E*
Academie, s
his ordinary
of a certaine
by the nobl
the great c
profound an
But when su
harkening t
the drift of
out, to conc
num, and *En*
nite, Æterna

Nothyng beyng alledged or expressed, How, worldly goods
tie: how, health, Strẽgth or lustines of body: nor yet the mea
sensible and bodyly blysse and felicitie hereafter, might be a
the fantasies of those hearers, were dampt: their opinion of
ged: yea his doctrine was by them despised: and his schole,
ted. Which thing, his Scholer, *Aristotle*, narrowly cõsidering,
of, to be, For that they had no forwarnyng and information
his doctrine tended. For, so, might they haue had occasion, e
his schole hauntyng: (if they, then, had misliked his Scope
stantly to haue continued therin: to their full satisfaction: if
intent, had ben to their desire. Wherfore, *Aristotle*, euer, aft
forewarne his owne Scholers and hearers, both of what m
ende, he tooke in hand to speake, or teach. While I conside
these two excellent Philosophers (and am most sure, both,

Spenser's Thaumaturgy: "Mental Space" and the Material Forms of The Faerie Queene *(1590)*

THOMAS FESTA

Sometimes there is both less and more to reading a book than meets the eye. In recent years, paratextual, "accidental," or ephemeral materials that scholars once thought unworthy of serious attention have received careful study, and most scholars today own that the monumental modern editions in which the vast majority of readers still encounter early modern works, valuable as they are, do not accurately represent the historical documents for which they stand. Strictly speaking, if texts exist only in the material forms in and as which they appear, then it is critical to ask whether each book is, as David Scott Kastan puts it, "a unique textual incarnation whose materiality itself crucially shapes meaning, altering in some way the significance of the linguistic organization of the work."[1] Kastan makes a radical claim about the power of materiality to alter literary meaning at the dual sites of a book's production: first, in its making, whether in print or manuscript, published or unpublished; and second, in the event of its reception by readers. By shaping the presentation of the received text, and thereby altering our perception of "the linguistic organization of the work," every "unique textual incarnation" arguably has the power to transform the meaning of a work altogether.

As Kastan's figurative language so acutely suggests, a danger inheres in taking this argument too far, a kind of fundamentalism of the material book that shades over into an unaccountable idolatry backed by metaphysical conviction.[2] From this veneration of the material object arises a counterbalancing "crisis of the book," originally "occasioned by the

Reformation" and centered on distrust "of all human media, of the fallen material dimension of all representation."[3] Even before the advent of the Reformation, readers comprehended the dangerous allure of the book as an object and suspected bibliophilia as a form of pathology, "not nourishing the mind with literature," in the words of the inveterate collector Petrarch, "but killing it and burying it with the weight of things."[4] To give one famous Elizabethan example, fear of just such fetishism informs Thomas Harriot's description of the Algonquians responding to his "declaration of the contentes of the Bible" to them:

> And although I told them the booke materially & of it self was not of anie such vertue, as I thought they did conceiue, but onely the doctrine therein co[n]tained; yet would many be glad to touch it, to embrace it, to kisse it, to hold it to their brests and heades, and stroke ouer all their bodie with it; to shewe their hungrie desire of that knowledge which was spoken of.[5]

For Harriot, this idolatry, much like the worship of Una's donkey by members of the "saluage nation" in *The Faerie Queene,* suggests the susceptibility of a people to Catholic conversion.[6] One form of idol worship leads on to another, as the carnality of the practice gives way to a literalizing adherence to ritual. For modern scholars, in the zeal of its application, fundamentalism of the book runs the risk of replacing ignorance of textual history with antiquarian pedantry, a fetishism of obscure details, and a resistance to contemporary critical pursuits. As Leah Price observes, "to the disciplines represented in the MLA, 'book history' has come to stand for a materialist resistance to theory, to idealism, even to ideas."[7]

Given what we know of the history of the production and reception of *The Faerie Queene,* this opposition itself presents a rich paradox: an idealizing allegory in material form. The book was printed by John Wolfe for William Ponsonby and published in 1590, and its physical production notoriously included a series of authorial interventions and modifications that in all likelihood disrupted what would otherwise have been an efficient job carried out by a professional shop with four operating presses. To note that the first edition of Spenser's poem took many different forms in its initial print run may seem akin to saying what is merely axiomatic: stop-press corrections were a commonplace aspect of early modern authorship, as well as a predictable feature of the first centuries of print publication. Milton memorably dramatizes this part of the process as an ordinary occurrence: "And what if the author shall be one so copious of fancie, as to have many things well worth the adding, come into his mind after licencing, while the book is yet under the Presse, which not seldom happ'ns to the best and diligentest writers; and that perhaps a dozen times in one book."[8] The interruptions to this particular print job – the 1590 *Faerie Queene* – indicate a special authorial sensitivity to moments in the poem in which Queen Elizabeth I is addressed, such as Britomart's vision of Artegall, and Merlin's prophecy of their progeny. Moreover, some extant copies lack the dedication to the queen on the verso of the title page; the dedication itself, remarkably, was a stop-press correction to the inner forme of the outer sheet of gathering A. This detail leaves a strong impression that, as Andrew Zurcher has shown, the poet's politics, not least his attitude toward the queen, were marked by anxiety, hesitation, and revision.[9]

With these material circumstances in mind, my aim is to extend Kastan's claim – that the physical form in which the book appears has a critical influence on the literary significance of the work – in order to read the text aesthetically, thematically, and conceptually. In other words, I want to try to understand how the "linguistic organization" of *The Faerie Queene* means something different when we attend to its earliest incarnations, how the physical book produced in 1590 directs our attention to the specific question of incarnation and idolatry, and how the conjuration of meaning at both sites of production – from author to printer, and from printer to reader – may be challenged and reconfigured by a supposedly extra-textual and almost certainly nonauthorial inclusion.

MIMESIS VERSUS THAUMATURGY

In his lecture on Spenser from 1819, Coleridge famously deems "The exceeding *vividness* of his descriptions not picturesque; but a wondrous *series* as in certain Dreams." *The Faerie Queene*'s narrative proceeds according to an order of cognition instead of visual sense, the episodes creating not scenic tableaux of "picturesque" physical space, but rather a process of mental illumination. The images' "*exceeding* vividness" heightens their intelligibility while diminishing their painterly verisimilitude. The setting of *The Faerie Queene* is, for Coleridge, liberated from the constraints of imitation required "in the domains of History or Geography"; it seems to exist only as an ideal, "ignorant of all artificial boundary – truly in the Land of Faery – i.e. in mental space."[10] To be, as Coleridge says, "truly in the Land of Faery" would seem to require letting mimesis go and embracing the mental image as if it exhibited reality to at least the same extent as an object that could be imitated. According to readers in the transcendental idealist or Romantic traditions, Spenser is "an iconoclastic iconographer" whose writing, as Kenneth Gross says, "inevitably develops a highly figured, *wholly nonmimetic* surface, as if the allegorical argument depended on images with an almost magical power to elevate and entrance the mind."[11]

To emphasize the "nonmimetic" quality of the work is to insist on a decidedly modern, or post-Kantian, understanding of perception, but this does not negate the utility of Coleridge's observation, even for historically minded critics. Although such perceptual processes may be central to any conception of mimesis, we should expect Spenser's own vocabulary to derive or deviate from the debates raging in the sixteenth century over Aristotelian prescriptions for epic action.[12] Still, there comes a point when one must acknowledge the idiosyncrasy of Spenser's creative claims, the paradox posed by his rhetorical contempt for imagination and his evident "systematic violation of all probability" so well described by Michael Murrin.[13] "We speak of imitation flowers and fake flamingos," Paul Woodruff writes in an essay on Aristotle, "but not of imitation goblins or fake fairies."[14] Spenser challenges his readers to confront both, to tell "fake faeries" and "imitation goblins" from real ones – in E.K.'s terms, "Elfes and Goblins" from "Guelfes and Gibelines" – or, to paraphrase Marianne Moore, to know the difference between imaginary gardens and the real toads in them.[15]

In this beguiling way, *The Faerie Queene* presents us with a species of conjuration through allegory, what I am calling Spenser's poetic "thaumaturgy." The relation between thaumaturgical magic and poetry has a long history, since it is at the root of the critical term used in the Platonic tradition to dismiss the "wonderworking" of the imitative arts. Plato employs versions of this word repeatedly in his attacks on mimetic art (*thaumatopoiois* appears in the Allegory of the Cave, at *Republic* 514B;

the Sophist is called "a kind of *thaumatopoios*" at *Sophist* 235B and 268D). According to Liddell and Scott, *thaumastos* means "wondrous, wonderful, marvelous"; *thaumato-poios* means "wonder-working; as substantive, a conjuror, juggler."[16] Especially in the substantive, the noun is cognate with *poiesis*, or poetic composition as "making." Thus, to appear to do wonders by means of conjuration in thaumaturgy is likened by Plato to the concept of the poet as a maker of images of things, an imitator in words. According to F.M. Cornford, who translates *thaumatopoion* as "the class of illusionists," the term means specifically "the puppet-showman" used "to cover all species of 'imitators'—artists and poets as well as Sophists.... They are all 'creators of *eidola*.'"[17] In this, the thaumaturge is a figure combining the worst of sophists' and painters' violations of truth, since the conjuror, like the painter, merely creates images (*eidola*) to imitate a semblance or appearance (*phantasma*). Rhetorical semblance-making (*phantastiké*), therefore, is even lower in Plato's estimation than creation of a pictorial likeness (*eikastiké*), for which Socrates had pummeled the sophists at least since the early dialogue the *Protagoras*. Seth Benardete refers to the sophist's "apparitional omniscience" or "opinionative knowledge" and shows that the Eleatic Stranger "likens the painter's duplication of reality to the sophist's replacement of reality. The painter images the beings the sophist makes."[18]

In the early modern English lexicon, the term also carried aesthetic and moral senses that render thaumaturgy even more applicable to the production of Spenser's art, particularly given the "generall end" in the Letter to Raleigh "to fashion a gentleman or noble person" (714). But the arts of the thaumaturge were considered to be technical as well. Throughout the sixteenth century and well into the seventeenth, thaumaturgy was understood as a derivative mathematical art and was particularly associated with the production of automata and simulacra by Cornelius Agrippa and Giordano Bruno, and in Elizabethan England by mages such as John Dee, Thomas Harriot, and Thomas Hood. As apologists for the mathematical arts, practitioners conjured rhetorical images in their prefaces that misled the uneducated public hungry for knowledge of the esoteric to suppose that their art was magical.[19] In the most famous example, Dee introduced the word "Thaumaturgike" and its cognate forms into the English language. Dee writes of all manner of

Iohn Dee his Mathematicall Præface.

opportunitatesq; temporum presentire, non minus rei militari, quàm Agriculturæ, Nauigationiq; conuenit. To foresee the alterations and opportunities of tymes, is conuenient, no lesse to the Art of Warre, then to Husbandry and Nauigation. And besides such cunnyng meanes, more euident tokens in Sonne and Mone, ought of hym to be knowen: such as (the Philosophicall Poëte) *Virgilius* teacheth, in hys *Georgikes*. Where he sayth,

Sol quoq; & exoriens & quum se condet in vndas,
Signa dabit, Solem certißima signa sequuntur. &c.

———— Nam sæpe videmus,
Ipsius in vultu varios errare colores. Georgic. I.
Cæruleus, pluuiam denunciat, igneus Euros.
Sin maculæ incipient rutilo immiscerier igni,
Omnia tum pariter vento, nimbisq; videbis
Feruere: non illa quisquam me nocte per altum
Ire, neq; a terra moueat conuellere funem. &c.
Sol tibi signa dabit. Solem quis dicere falsum
Audeat? ———— &c.

And so of Mone, Sterres, Water, Ayre, Fire, Wood, Stones, Birdes, and Beastes, and of many thynges els, a certaine Sympathicall forewarnyng may be had: sometymes to great pleasure and proffit, both on Sea and Land. Sufficiently, for my present purpose, it doth appeare, by the premisses, how *Mathematicall*, the *Arte* of *Nauigation*, is: and how it nedeth and also vseth other *Mathematicall Artes*: And now, if I would go about to speake of the manifold Commodities, commyng to this Land, and others, by Shypps and *Nauigation*, you might thinke, that I catch at occasions, to vse many wordes, where no nede is.

Yet, this one thyng may I, (iustly) say. In *Nauigation*, none ought to haue greater care, to be skillfull, then our English Pylotes. And perchaunce, Some, would more attempt: And other Some, more willingly would be aydyng, if they wist certainely, What Priuiledge, God had endued this Iland with, by reason of Situation, most commodious for *Nauigation*, to Places most Famous & Riche. And though, (of* Late) a young Gentleman, a Courragious Capitaine, was in a great readynes, with good hope, and great causes of persuasion, to haue ventured, for a Discouerye, (either *Westerly*, by *Cape de Paramantia*: or *Esterly*, aboue *Noua Zemla*, and the *Cyremisses*) and was, at the very nere tyme of Attemptyng, called and employed otherwise (both then, and since,) in great good seruice to his Countrey, as the Irish Rebels haue* tasted: Yet, I say, (though the same Gentleman, doo not hereafter, deale therewith) Some one, or other, should listen to the Matter: and by good aduise, and discrete Circumspection, by little, and little, wynne to the sufficient knowledge of that Trade and Voyage: Which, now, I would be sory, (through Carelesnesse, want of Skill, and Courrage,) should remayne Vnknowne and vnheard of. Seyng, also, we are herein, halfe Challenged, by the learned, by halfe request, published. Therof, verely, might grow Commoditye, to this Land chiefly, and to the rest of the Christen Common wealth, farre passing all riches and worldly Threasure.

**Anno.1567 S. H. G.*

**Anno.1569*

Thaumaturgike, is that Art Mathematicall, which giueth certaine order to make straunge workes, of the sense to be perceiued, and of men greatly to be wondred at. By sundry meanes, this *Wonderworke* is wrought. Some, by *Pneumatithmie*. As the workes of *Ctesibius* and *Hero*,

A.j. Some

wondrous simulacra and automata in his "Mathematicall Praeface" to the first printed English translation of Euclid: "Thaumaturgike, is that Art Mathematicall, which giueth certaine order to make straunge workes… of men greatly to be wondred at" (fig. 19). As that great compiler of commonplaces, Robert Burton, explained, "thaumaturgical works" were thought to include self-moving machines, the ability "to make a chariot to move *sine animali* [without animal traction], diving-boats, to walk on the water by art and to fly in the air, to make several cranes and pulleys" that would "lift up and remove great weights" and allow "mills to move themselves."[20]

Given the equation of thaumaturgy and the miraculous – discernible, for instance, in the honorific epithet applied to St. Gregorius Thaumaturgus – a moral suspicion of "wonderworking" naturally accrued to the poetic craft in the early modern period, with particularly acute and contradictory implications for Protestant writers. Nonetheless, in a way that made possible the recuperation of the idea for sixteenth-century poets, Aristotle backhandedly defended the deviation from strict mimesis as proper to epic in *Poetics* 24: "In tragedy one needs to create a sense of wonder [*to thaumaston*], but epic has more scope for the irrational [*to alogon*], the chief cause of wonder, because we do not actually see the agent."[21] In this formulation, seeing countermands believing, and the scope of narrative beggars performance. On the stage, of course, one cannot deny the palpable absurdity of certain actions that would be permissible in epic and romance, such as Achilles' pursuit of Hector "Thrice fugitive about Troy wall" while the Greek army looks on.[22] This representational problem set theorists of the early modern stage, such as Sir Philip Sidney and John Lyly, at odds with the practice of depicting implausible travel and expansive time periods in popular stage romances.[23] Following continental poets' reacquaintance with Aristotle's strictures in the early sixteenth century – via Giorgio Valla's 1498 Latin translation, Manutius's 1508 Greek *editio princeps,* and Alessandro de' Pazzi's 1536 bilingual Greek-Latin text – something of this mimetic problem carries over into mid-sixteenth-century debates about the limits and license of the epic genre as well.[24]

Fig. 19. Euclid, *The Elements of Geometrie* (London, 1570), A1r.
Beinecke Rare Book and Manuscript Library, Yale University, Z90 013

Suspicious therefore of his own powers of conjuring and their theological implication, Spenser may have adapted from Tasso a representational strategy for challenging mimesis, an irony worth considering for a moment when one thinks of the premier poet of the Counter-Reformation inspiring the sage and serious Protestant. In the *Gerusalemme liberata,* similes often mark an unfortunate deception or misperception – neither an elevation of poetic tone, nor a likening of something abstruse to something homely, so much as a dimming of a character's awareness, almost a fugue state of similitude:

As the sick man that in his sleep doth see
Some ugly dragon or some chimere new,
Though he suspect or half-persuaded be
It is an idle dream, no monster new,
Yet still he fears, he quakes, and strives to flee,
So fearful is that wond'rous form to view:
So fear'd the knight, yet he both knew and thought
All were illusions false by witchcraft wrought.[25]

The movement away from mimesis in some key similes, rather than toward concrete expression of things hard to imagine or things remote as one often finds in Homer or Virgil or Dante, exposes Tasso's Inquisition-fueled anxiety about the poetic sorcery of likening things that are unlike.[26]

Neither imitation nor allegory, similitude introduces a sophisticated third term into the representational scheme that both poets found productively ambiguous for thematic, theological reasons. As the most fully realized recent example of both the theory and practice of epic narration, the *Liberata* would have presented a complex model of negotiation with the classical theory from within a Christian framework. Indeed, there is some intriguing early evidence that Spenser's mastery of the simile held a particular fascination for readers acutely aware of classical poetics. In his copy of the 1617 folio edition of Spenser's *Works,* Ben Jonson's most frequent marginal annotation to *The Faerie Queene* focuses attention on the similes. Jonson identified fifteen of particular interest, all of which were from the books included in the 1590 version of the poem, and labeled them "Simile" or "Excellent Simile."[27]

Of course, the aesthetic complexities of similitude extend beyond the formal device of the epic simile, but it is worth thinking through how Spenser's use of the poetic device reflects upon the larger representational schemes of the poem and, ultimately, the material book in which we encounter it. Spenser presents readers not only with a false Una and a false Florimell, but also with a protean enchanter whose illusion is so exact that the text repeats the knight's epithet verbatim: "Full iolly knight he seemde" (1.2.11; 1.1.1). Seeming and deeming are inextricably linked. We have just been told the actual identity of "The true *Saint George*" for the first time, when presented with Archimago's illusory "semblaunt" (1.2.12).[28] Even the figure of forsaken Truth, questing after Holiness "With paines far passing that long wandring *Greeke*, / That for his loue refused deitye," is deceived by the same play of shadows (1.3.21). Persuaded by the enchanter's sophistical rhetoric ("His louely words" [1.3.30]), Una thinks she sees Redcrosse, and at this precise moment, Spenser introduces a simile to depict her false homecoming. The simile analogizes the reunion to a scenario fraught with the potential for misrecognition and self-deception. Moreover, Spenser draws upon a device that is formally charged with introducing a resemblance or a simular, so that the very fact of a simile's appearance at this juncture in the action becomes as important as its specific content. The device allows the poet to appropriate a feigned likeness in an act of dissimulation for which he, with a nice and characteristic irony, coined the term "counterfesaunce" (1.8.49). Spenser's coinage is itself an imitation of a French word, *contrefaisance,* which is cognate with *contrefaire* and *contrefaict,* defined by Cotgrave as "*Counterfeit, adulterate, fained, forged, false; also, deformed, disfigured, mishapen, ill fauoured; crooked, hulchbacked; or (as we say) a changeling.*"[29] From Una's vantage, "Before her stands the knight, for whom she toyld so sore" (1.3.30), and Spenser introduces a simile (one of those labeled by Jonson in his folio copy):

> Much like, as when the beaten marinere,
> That long hath wandred in the *Ocean* wide,
> Ofte soust in swelling *Tethys* saltish teare,
> And long time hauing tand his tawney hide,
> With blustring breath of Heauen, that none can bide,
> And scorching flames of fierce *Orions* hound,
> Soone as the port from far he has espide,
> His chearfull whistle merily doth sound,
> And *Nereus* crownes with cups; his mates him pledg around.
> (1.3.31)[30]

Having endured hardships "that none can bide," "the beaten marinere" strains to overcome distance, intoxication, and wishful thinking, and in so doing creates a false sense of security that ultimately leads to collective delusion. Spenser emphasizes that Una fabricates what she sees, that her vision is of her own making, so that the likeness adduced in the simile is as false a likeness as the figure she rejoices to behold: "Such ioy made *Vna,* when her knight she found" (1.3.32). Further implying the Odyssean intertext, the arrival at port then occasions a reversal of perspective, where Archimago, in the guise of Redcrosse, becomes "the glad marchant, that does vew from ground / His ship far come from watrie wildernesse" (1.3.32).[31] The ironies multiply as she prevents Sansloy from killing the disguised Archimago, whom she calls "one the truest knight aliue," when in fact he is neither "true" nor "one," as her name indicates that she is, but rather, like Duessa, by nature two (1.3.37). The extension of the simile from the other side shows both characters to be momentarily suspended in a facsimile within the fiction, the alternate or virtual reality of Truth's fantasy.

HOLINESSE AND THE DREAM OF BELIEF

Within the allegorical realm of "mental space," then, both characters *and* readers must work out a credible relationship between perception and belief—between what is in the words of the Letter to Raleigh "delightfull and pleasing to the commune sence" and the "good discipline" which such allegorical devices ought to exemplify (716). "[W]hether dreams delude, or true it were," we, like Arthur dreaming of Gloriana, may never know, since the faery queen appears only as the imprint her absent body has left, the "pressed grass, where she had lyen" (1.9.15)—as an ideal, we might say, that is visible merely in its bare outline. Likewise, the seeming arbitrariness of the knights' movement through "mental space" indicates the internal or allegorical rather than plot-based or exterior logic of the narrative. Episodes are linked through their allegorical unity and structural significance rather than their external probability as fictions, and in fact the two (narrative plausibility and allegorical cogency) may be in direct opposition.[32] For instance, in his second fall in the battle with the dragon, as he writhes in pain from the dragon's "scorching fire," the guiding force of Redcrosse's story appears on the outside to be random, but internally (suggestively placed in parentheses) confirms providence: "It chaunst (eternall God that chaunce did guide) / As he recoiled backeward, in the mire / His nigh foreweried feeble feet did slide, / And downe he fell…" (1.11.45).

Although the "dread of shame" terrifies the knight, his physical fall proves to be the means of his spiritual elevation in a type of *felix culpa,* since he lands, by the grace of God, in the resurrecting balm of the Tree of Life, as Una witnesses:

> …gentle *Vna* saw the second fall
> Of her deare knight, who weary of long fight,
> And faint through losse of blood, moou'd not at all,
> But lay as in a dreame of deepe delight,
> Besmeard with pretious Balme, whose vertuous might
> Did heale his woundes, and scorching heat alay… (1.11.50)

This "pretious Balme" recalls the gift Arthur gives Redcrosse when they part: the box of diamond containing "a few drops of liquor pure, / Of wondrous worth, and vertue excellent, / That any wownd could heale incontinent" (1.9.19). As commentators often note, the two healing balms may both signify the sacrament of communion (or, alternatively, of baptism and communion). Again, more crucial than the symbol, however, is its spiritual meaning, since the two falls of Redcrosse, and indeed his backing into salvation, principally illustrate the precept of humility before grace and the disavowal of works in Spenser's theology: "Ne let the man ascribe it to his skill, / That thorough grace hath gained victory," instructs the poet just before Redcrosse's arrival at the House of Holiness. "If any strength we haue, it is to ill, / But all the good is God's, both power and eke will" (1.10.1). Puffed up with Una's misleading interpretation of the events after the fact, Redcrosse's self-regard at having defeated the monster Errour thus may be read as an encoded critique of the doctrine of works, so that even his proud victory in this instance (1.1.27–28), like his victory over Sansjoy and subsequent swearing of fealty to the "mayden Queene" Lucifera in the tourney in the House of Pride (1.4.8; 1.5.16), bespeaks psychological degradation and spiritual degeneracy.[33] The concept is uncontroversial enough within the mainstream of Protestant theology. Martin Luther's comment on Galatians 4:1–2 may serve as exemplary: "A sonne and a seruaunt are so contrary one to an other, that the same man can not be both a sonne and a seruaunt. A sonne is free and willing, a seruaunt is compelled and vnwilling: a sonne liueth, and resteth in faith: a seruaunt in works."[34] However, the implications of this Reformed doctrine for heroism in epic romance threaten to render the action almost static in the hero's passivity. In an attempt to personify this doctrine, Spenser makes St. George's slaying of the dragon seem almost like an afterthought, a reflex conditioned and enabled entirely by his own will's defeat and by prevenient grace, that is, divine grace anticipating or preceding willed human action.

St. George, who, in Northrop Frye's arrestingly simple phrase, stands for "the English people trying to be Christian," finally attains through passivity the strength to slay the dragon of false faith.[35] At this climactic moment of spiritual regeneration, Spenser suggests a structural analogue to Arthur's vision of the faery queen. As Una looks on, praying, Redcrosse lies "as in a dreame of deepe delight" (1.11.50). Surely James Nohrnberg is right to conjecture that "it is possible to know what he is dreaming about." If indeed, as Nohrnberg argues, the relevant typological antecedent for Redcrosse's dream is Adam's ecstatic dream of Eve during her creation, then it stands to reason that Redcrosse's dream of Una, herself like the church a "second Eve," is the dream of the English people to wed the nation to the true church. The traditional association of Eve with the ecclesiastical body prefigures the prophecy of the church being taken out of Christ's side, which is concretely typified by the blood and water that flow from Christ's pierced side in the Gospel of John, commonly understood in the exegetical tradition as the anticipation of baptism.[36]

The typological interpretation of the stanza is persuasive at the level of historical-religious allegory, which strongly suggests the relevance of Dantesque allegory to the passage. Yet the anagogical level, called by Dante *sovrasenso* ("above the senses"), cannot be accessed so easily as it "points through the things signified to the supernal things of eternal glory."[37] If we think for a moment of this crucial stanza in fourfold fashion, then, we recall that our starting point, the literal or historical level of the narrative, is enclosed within a specific perspective. After all, we do not see Redcrosse from a neutral or omniscient perspective, but rather, from the vantage of Una, who looks on, worried: "When gentle *Vna* saw the second fall,"

> Againe she stricken was with sore affright,
> And for his safetie gan deuoutly pray;
> And watch the noyous night, and wait for ioyous day. (1.11.50)

Una devoutly prays for her beloved champion, afraid that his earthly strength, his nerve, his faith, might fail, for which she has ample precedent in the action up to that point. Another, more tendentious way of putting the matter would be to say that, for a moment, while holiness dreams of truth, truth doubts the fortitude of holiness to rise to the occasion of spiritual combat. Isn't it odd, moreover, that Redcrosse presumably dreams of Una while she stands over him, thereby embedding an idealizing dream within a reality that would, could he only snap out of it, render the dream an actuality? Just as Arthur's "dream or vision" of the faery queen manifests the material trace of the "pressed gras," Redcrosse's "dreame of deepe delight" ironically engages in a fantasy that must remain fantastical, just out of reach, an elusive token of belief. The poet seems in this way to be telling us what *we* see by describing merely what Una sees, not what we might see from some unavailable omniscient perspective. The limited purview of Una's perspective is, in narrative context, the crucial fact. In this way, Spenser emblematically represents the dream of belief: a faith enfolded within the protean field of appearances, whose reality remains a troubling and unbridgeable parallel to a dream that can only hypothetically be known – even to a figure held throughout the poem to represent Truth.

It is as if the two allegorical registers cannot simply be bridged, which may signify a cautionary note sounded by the author, an oblique comment on the difficulty if not impossibility of uniting ideal with actual even when the two seem to be identical. Perhaps the knight lies under the overlapping penumbras of both the Tree of Life and the Tree of Knowledge, a symbolic warning of the seeming impossibility of uniting intention with meaning, action with signification, in an unproblematic way after the Fall. The scenario's interpretive predicament therefore directs our attention to Spenser's nuanced pessimism about the interaction of his poem with the world outside of it. As a counterexample that warns against Redcrosse's dream, Spenser depicts Cymochles languishing in the Bower of Bliss, pouring out "his ydle mynd / In daintee delices, and lauish ioyes" (2.5.28). Idle becomes idol in Cymochles' solipsistic fantasy. Against the poem's pronounced, idealizing intention "to fashion a gentleman or noble person in vertuous and gentle discipline" – in effect to impose ideological form on material conduct – we must measure the "historicall fiction" Spenser pointedly tells us that he has also "fashioned" to that end (714–15).[38]

Two further notions seem to be conveyed in this moment. First, given the apparent identifications of the dragon in the historical allegory with ships – "His flaggy winges when forth he did display, / Were like two sayles," etc. (1.11.10) – and thus with Philip II of Spain and the Spanish Armada, the ensuing defeat of the Roman Catholic dragon would seem to figure a post-Armada exhilaration at the possibility (however fleeting) of the English Protestant state attaining its true identity as the elect nation. In this way, the analogical linkage of Arthur's dream, also representing Spenser's libidinal quest for wholeness in the subject of his poem, with the Redcrosse knight's dream of Truth, evokes both knight's and nation's holiness before victory has in fact been obtained. The oft-noted glance in this episode back at Redcrosse's enraging erotic dream of the false Una as spawned by Archimago (1.2.5–6), which parts the pair until they are reunited through Arthur's intervention, seems designed to remedy that earlier failing, even as it looks forward to their betrothal in canto 12 and prepares the knight for his final battle with the dragon. So Redcrosse's "dreame of deepe delight" prefigures the "deare delights" of his union with Una (1.12.41), the marriage of Holiness with Truth symbolic of the ultimate union of England with the true church historically, and believers with Christ apocalyptically.

Yet this union's very incompleteness at the time of the dream does not merely look forward to a consummation devoutly to be wished, but also looks awry at that consummation's grotesque double in the spectacle of Duessa's "neather partes misshapen, monstruous" (1.2.41). Exposed and released as the horrific bride of Antichrist, "Fidessa" confronts readers' and characters' desire to experience the unity, closure, and stability of England's patron saint's betrothal to true faith with the shattering parodic multiplicity of her animal parts (1.8.46–48).[39] The dismantling of negative fantasy produces palpable discomfort in the narrator's voice, of course, during her perverse blazon, but her release signifies the resilience of enmity and falsity and the concomitant unreality of any final defeat of the false church – as the disruptive intrusion in the marriage ceremony by Duessa's "letters" reveals, her bad news delivered by Archimago disguised as the messenger of "Fidessa" and thus a kind of satanic evangelist (1.12.23–36). By virtue of their undeniable materiality, the "letters" interrupt the wedding and serve as a reminder, like the "bookes and papers" in Errour's vomit (1.1.20), of the stubborn and threatening persistence of

Catholic propaganda in Reformed lands. Even as the knee-jerk misogyny during Duessa's stripping registers disgust at the disfiguration of belief when faith manifests itself in too literal a way, Spenser casts the withering light of skepticism on the benighted simplicity of any belief not rigorously scrutinized and therefore taken for granted. Perhaps this is why the marriage is deferred indefinitely within the fiction of the poem, and why the King of Eden must, after dispensing with Archimago, "renew the late forbidden" banns of marriage. To suggest otherwise would be to fall prey to delusion, as Redcrosse does when he falls into despair at the nadir of his tale, "As he were charmed with inchaunted rimes" (1.9.48).

A second point, however, urges further qualification. This dream of belief, as I have just argued, must remain a figment, an illusion, a desire unfulfilled, veiled as Una's beauty under her stole. Our perspective, moreover, does not merge with Redcrosse's: his "dreame of deepe delight" in canto 11 is never described, and so we must surmise its content hypothetically. No proof is on offer, and thus we, as readers, must rest content with evidence of things unseen. What we can see, in the stanza, we see through Una's long-suffering gaze. Her piety, as she prays on behalf of Redcrosse, who seems to her to be yet once more in the midst of a moral, constitutional failure, is lonely, isolate, mournful. And this is precisely how Spenser leaves her at the end of the book. Betrothed to her seeming savior, she must await her true savior for consummation. As Redcrosse leaves her to return at the behest of the faery queen, to do battle for six years with the pagan king, Una is "left to mourne" (1.12.41) – and she had been from the first depicted "As one that inly mournd" (1.1.4) – her dream ultimately left unrealized, half-accomplished as the English Reformation in the so-called Elizabethan settlement of the church. Within the narrative, then, the knight departs from actuality in pursuit of a heroic ideal. Spenser draws our attention to the pathos of Una's plight and her longing, which remain, like Arthur's dream of Gloriana, unanswered and irremediable for the remainder of his unfinished poem, as imperfect as the state of human experience in this fallen world.

SIMULACRUM AND BELIEF IN *THE FAERIE QUEENE*

Thus with a mature theological wit Spenser turns our attention to the irreducible paradox of materialism in Faeryland. In the insistence on the ocular proof of Gloriana's presence in "the pressed grass," and in the emblem of Una standing over a knight dreaming of her, Spenser lends an ironic comment on desire a nuanced moral shading by embedding the material within the imaginary. Like Titania's "vot'ress," who we are told in *A Midsummer Night's Dream* would imitate the traders embarked for India "and sail upon the land / To fetch me trifles, and return again / As from a voyage, rich with merchandise," so the knights inhabit a Faeryland dense with material artifacts, objects that seem to shuttle between realms and as a result signify more complexly in each.[40] In one sense, this inclusion of the material in the ideational serves as a reminder of the very real consequences of belief.

The 1590 text conveys a further irony, perhaps even at the expense of what, by reconstructing the textual history, we might deduce as the author's intent. In the exchange of gifts at the parting of Redcrosse and Arthur, "the *Redcrosse* knight him gaue / A booke, wherein this Saueours testament / Was writt..." (1.9.19; fig. 20).[41] With the text worded so, "this Saueours testament" suggests some odd possibilities: (1) that *Arthur* is the savior in question, and thus "heauenly grace," as Arthur is designated on the explicit register of the personification allegory (1.8.1), here receives a material record of his own deeds; (2) that the nearest antecedent for "this" savior is *Redcrosse,* who therefore offers written testimony of his own actions to Arthur; (3) that "this...testament" is *The Faerie Queene* itself, and Redcrosse therefore hands Arthur a copy of the book we are reading, in which they are both characters. Regardless of whether we follow the list of "Faults escaped in the Print[ing]" from the 1590 text and emend "this" to "his Saueours"—as the 1596 and 1609 texts print it, thus making the reference to Redcrosse's savior more directly Christ—the supposedly unintended error causes us to sense a further interpretive strangeness suggested by the episode.[42] What, allegorically, can it mean for Redcrosse to hand the New Testament to Arthur, as if he had never owned a copy and perhaps never before read it?[43]

Spenser extends the challenge of self-reference outside the poem, too, as when he remarks of Arthur's armament that "when he dyde, the Faery Queen it brought / To Faerie lond, where yet it may be seene, if sought" (1.7.36). The wit of this provocation places skeptical readers in the awkward position of having to set aside their own doubts about Spenser's fictional world, lest they should send themselves off on the fool's errand of finding empirical confirmation of an object in "Faerie lond." In a similar

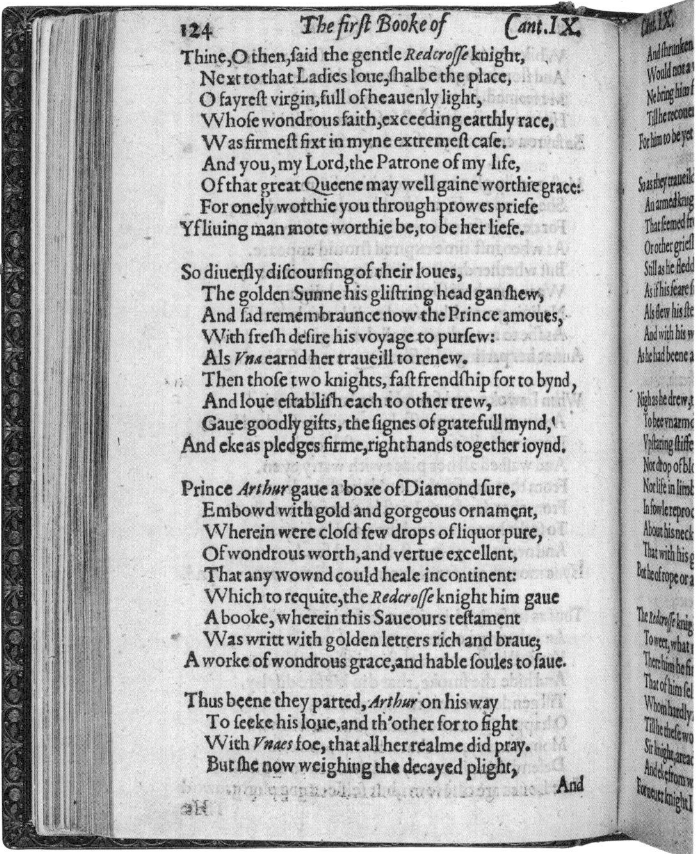

124 *The firſt Booke of* *Cant.IX.*

Thine, O then, ſaid the gentle *Redcroſſe* knight,
Next to that Ladies loue, ſhalbe the place,
O fayreſt virgin, full of heauenly light,
Whoſe wondrous faith, exceeding earthly race,
Was firmeſt fixt in myne extremeſt caſe.
And you, my Lord, the Patrone of my life,
Of that great Queene may well gaine worthie grace:
For onely worthie you through prowes prieſe
Yf liuing man mote worthie be, to be her liefe.

So diuerſly diſcourſing of their loues,
The golden Sunne his gliſtring head gan ſhew,
And ſad remembraunce now the Prince amoues,
With freſh deſire his voyage to purſew:
Als *Vna* earnd her traueill to renew.
Then thoſe two knights, faſt frendſhip for to bynd,
And loue eſtabliſh each to other trew,
Gaue goodly gifts, the ſignes of gratefull mynd,
And eke as pledges firme, right hands together ioynd.

Prince *Arthur* gaue a boxe of Diamond ſure,
Embowd with gold and gorgeous ornament,
Wherein were cloſd few drops of liquor pure,
Of wondrous worth, and vertue excellent,
That any wownd could heale incontinent:
Which to requite, the *Redcroſſe* knight him gaue
A booke, wherein this Saueours teſtament
Was writt with golden letters rich and braue;
A worke of wondrous grace, and hable ſoules to ſaue.

Thus beene they parted, *Arthur* on his way
To ſeeke his loue, and th'other for to fight
With *Vnaes* foe, that all her realme did pray.
But ſhe now weighing the decayed plight,
And

Fig. 20. Edmund Spenser, *The Faerie Queene* (London, 1590), H7v. Beinecke Rare Book and Manuscript Library, Yale University, 1976 1671

vein, Thomas More writes in a familiar letter to Peter Giles of his fictional character from the *Utopia*, Raphael Hythloday, that if incredulous people will not take the word of the respectable and upstanding men who have also heard his tale, then "they can visit Hythloday himself.... I just heard from some persons who recently returned from Portugal that on the first day of last March he was healthy and vigorous as ever."[44]

On the plane of the poem's action, the knights exercise their virtue through disciplined behavior; ideally, in a mimetic parallel of their actions, readers would practice their "gentle discipline" through the aesthetic discernment of veracity (Letter to Raleigh, 714). In this sense, the poet of *The Faerie Queene* posits a relationship to his poem that demystifies and works rigorously to exclude the mere facsimile of creation promulgated by the illusionists Archimago, Acrasia, and Busirane. In another sense, however, Spenser troubles the distinction by calling attention to it and owning his poetic thaumaturgy, as when the chamber of the melancholy figure Phatanstes is said to swarm with "all that fained is, as leasings, *tales,* and lies" (2.9.51; italics mine).

Belief, therefore, impacts the experience of the poem in twofold fashion: the believability of fiction, on the one hand, and the credibility of religious commitment, on the other. Each kind inspires its own form of suspicion. In the Aristotelian mimetic tradition, the danger of falling into a contemplative regress of ersatz objects can be avoided only by our grasping what Sidney calls a poem's "*Idea* or fore-conceit."[45] This is the guarantor of meaning that mimesis follows and gives the appearance of plausibility. Spenser at times inverts the relationship of material and ideal in Sidney's formulation. In place of the schematic of representation suggested by Sidney's "fore-conceit," then, Spenser calls attention to the "fore-material" that needs accommodation in and by the fiction. In the parade of the Seven Deadly Sins in the House of Pride, for example, Idlenesse bears in his hand a "Portesse," or a portable breviary, which exudes the physical traits of a well studied copy, even though, the poet comments, the book "much was worne, but therein little redd" (1.4.19). The material object, like so many props of a performed faith, outwardly signifies piety, when in fact the apparent symbolic and idealized meaning a spectator is likely to project onto it belies the actual conduct of its bearer. Abundance of materiality deceives just as the profusion of ideas can.

When the authenticity of the "fore-conceit," that to which one might remain faithful, is itself in doubt, Spenser asks, what is left to hold onto? How does one recognize something within "mental space" as an exact replica instead of a cheap fake when there exists (as yet) no material referent against which to compare it? For such an eidolon may serve as a provocation to virtue, as when Britomart confides to Glauce that in her desire for Artegall she pursues not a "liuing wight" but "th'only shade and semblant of a knight, / Whose shape or person yet I neuer saw" (3.2.38); or it might conversely cause "dreadfull visions," as when Arthur longs for the self-delusion that would allow him to take Florimell for Gloriana: "And thousand fancies bett his ydle brayne / With their light wings, the sights of semblants vaine" (3.4.57, 54). Then there are instances that seem indeterminately in between, as when Guyon praises the faery queen at Medina's request in loaded terms: "men beholding so great excellence /... / Doe her adore with sacred reuerence, / As th'Idole of her makers great magnificence" (2.2.41). How, in other words, to differentiate true belief from its shadow, Spenser's eikastic wonderworking, his likeness-generating thaumaturgy, from that figured for example in Archimago's phantastic semblance-making, his "true-seeming lyes" (1.1.38)? How can inward belief authenticate itself when performance of conviction is always greeted with the suspicion that it will turn into its own parodic double, a mere simulacrum of belief?

Suggestively, even Archimago fears loss of credibility after Redcrosse's victory: "His credit now in doubtfull ballaunce hong" (2.1.3). In the first canto of *The Legend of Temperuance,* Guyon is "amoued from his sober mood" by Archimago's stage-managed spectacle of Duessa's plight (2.1.12). The encounter occasions a duplicate of "Fidessa's" disrobing—only this time the illusion is despoiled not by Arthur but by the author, who informs us that "vnder simple shew and semblant plaine / Lurkt false *Duessa* secretly vnseene" (2.1.21). Spenser thereby places the passage connecting the stories of the books in an anamorphic relation to Arthur's exposure of Duessa, cast for a second time, we might say, in the dubious light of Fradubio's ill-fated discovery of her while she was bathing (1.8.46–68; 1.2.41). Allegorical interpretation "undresses" the rhetoric of textual ornament, figured in the poem as the stripping of an apparently attractive woman to reveal underlying deformity. Ariosto makes the motif explicit in the *Orlando Furioso* when Ruggiero learns to "read the cards aright and see the truth which for so many years had been kept hidden" by viewing Alcina's body while wearing a magic ring that allows him to see through her dress.[46] Donne wittily inverts the figure of allegoresis as revelation in his early elegy "To his Mistress going to Bed":

> Like pictures, or like bookes gay coverings, made
> For lay men, are all women thus arayd,
> Themselues are mistique bookes, which only wee
> Whom their imputed grace will dignify
> Must see reuealed.[47]

Thus, amid the figural revelation of Duessa's identity, Guyon's pageant begins with a cautionary reminder of the enduring power of the simulacrum to overwhelm reason, temperance, and (almost) holiness by instilling "errour" and "haynous violence" in both knights (2.1.28) – and ends with "the tempest of his wrathfulnesse" in his destruction of the "goodly workmanship" of the Bower of Bliss (2.12.83). The unveiling of the "semblant plaine" by the narrator discloses Spenser's anxiety about the duplicity of his allegorical technique, its dangerous reliance upon eidola such as the evil Genius produces at the threshold of the Bower: "That secretly doth vs procure to fall, / Through guilefull semblants, which he makes vs see" (2.12.48). Likewise, Dante goads readers of the *Inferno* to "mark the doctrine hidden under the veil of the strange verses" at the precise moment when Virgil's hands cover the pilgrim's inquisitive eyes and they begin their descent into the realm of heresy; then, unable to stay silent, Dante swears to the reader *per le note* ("by the verses") of the *Commedia* when faced with a truth that has the face of a lie (in the figure of Geryon) just before entering the realm of the fraudulent.[48] Indeed, as George Puttenham explained in *The Art of English Poesy* (1589), allegory itself was commonly regarded as a figure, "which for his duplicity, we call the Figure of False Semblant or Dissimulation," a "courtly figure" that allows one to "speak one thing and think another."[49] This is precisely the rhetorical tradition's way of treating allegory as a figure of diction, called *permutatio* in the *Rhetorica ad Herennium* and *illusio* in Quintilian's *Institutio Oratoria,* both of which Spenser was almost certain to have known well as they were two of the most common texts on the University of Cambridge booklists of the Elizabethan era.[50] The idolater is tempted by "semblants," yet the iconoclast too comes dangerously close to transforming into an automaton of an opposite sort as the reflex to tear down images provokes a fetishistic response to their threat, a psychological response akin to the metallic giant Disdayne who threatens Guyon in the Cave of Mammon (2.7.40–42). Spenser's thaumaturgy conjures such automata and simulacra in us. Spenser shuns the easy absolutes of iconoclasm by revealing the idolatry that invests images with such power.

Contrary to the confidence in a mimetic educational process set forth in the "Letter to Raleigh," then, the poem seems to insist that we have no alternative set of symbols to which we might turn without running the risk of falling prey to idolatry or its attendant reactionary complexes. In the proem to book 2, Spenser demands that we regard his poem as "matter of iust memory" and not judge it as mere "painted forgery" (2.Pr.1). But Spenser ironically warns against the credulity required to grant "that happy land of Faery" the same reality as "Indian *Peru*" and "fruitfullest *Virginia,*" which could of course have existed only as imagined locations for the author, as for most readers in his time (2.Pr.2). The logic of the second proem depends upon our granting the poet his speculative hypothesis; as he puts it: "What if within the Moones fayre shining spheare, / What if in euery other starre vnseene / Of other worldes he happily should heare?" (2.Pr.3). The "antique history" is at risk of seeming the eidolon of an "ydle brain" and therefore a "painted forgery." This is because no living person knows the *location* of Faeryland, yet, we are assured, "such [possible worlds] to some appeare" (2.Pr.3). The second proem again purports to the objective reality of an illusion, a fabricated world, and sets it in parallel to ethical recollection of the historical past as well as the imagined reality of the New World in readers' minds. The second proem, concerned as it is to inoculate the poem against "th'aboundance of an yldle braine" (2.Pr.1), evokes a monstrous shadow poem that may overtake the poet's design.[51] The effect is that, as A. Bartlett Giamatti put it, "The poet's powers of formation and re-formation, in an aesthetic and moral sense, seem to draw strength from what the poem abhors, the images and sources of deformation."[52]

The questions I have been raising – about *The Faerie Queene,* mimesis, and the propagation of virtue – become especially pressing when we consider the relationship of book 2 to *The Legend of Holinesse*. At risk of asking too naive a question, but one that I think Spenser actively encourages: what does holiness look like? The woodcut illustration of St. George slaying the dragon, on the verso of the leaf that ends *The Legend of Holinesse,* or the page facing the proem to book 2 in the 1590 and 1596 editions (fig. 21), seems to have been placed there to provide an answer to just this question. This feature, reproduced in facsimile in some readily available modern texts such as A.C. Hamilton's admirable scholarly edition for the Longman Annotated Poets series, is omitted from Thomas Roche's edition for Penguin and both Carol Kaske's and Erik Gray's editions of books 1 and 2 for Hackett – in other words, the current student editions

Fig. 21. Edmund Spenser, *The Faerie Queene* (London, 1590), M5v–M6r. Beinecke Rare Book and Manuscript Library, Yale University, 1976 1671

The second Booke of the Faerie Queene.

Contayning

The Legend of Sir Guyon.

OR

Of Temperaunce.

RIght well I wote most mighty Soueraine,
That all this famous antique history,
Of some th'aboundance of an ydle braine
Will iudged be, and painted forgery,
Rather then matter of iust memory,
Sith none, that breatheth liuing aire, does know,
Where is that happy land of Faery,
Which I so much doe vaunt, yet no where show,
ut vouch antiquities, which no body can know.

ut let that man with better sence aduize,
That of the world least part to vs is red:
And daily how through hardy enterprize,
Many great Regions are discouered,

Which

To the honorable minded Souldier.

THese late frostie mornings (pleasing my humor) rousedme sooner (then of custome) from my drowsie bedde, and with desire (presing me) I went abroad to walke.

Where all alone, betrampling frosned ground,
Me thought to heare, some fierce and warlike sound:
For *Phœbus* then began his course in skies,
On rolling wheeles, his fierie wagon flies,
Most swift, to send blacke *Pluto* to his bed:
Who giuing place, left skie like blood as red.

This made me conceiue some discourse within my selfe, and wondering much, there came vnto mind, how God had pleased to blesse, and keepe our Queene, and land from the thundering and tempestious stormes of all our mortall, and furious enimies: with this conceit my ioy was much augmented, and did amase me greatlie to consider, how far from common expectation, the late rumors of wars, and the rage of those which wrought to destroy vs, were blowne ouer and gone from vs (with their owne confusion:) and we in rest still liuing (in all felicitie) ruled, and gouerned by Elizabeth *our most blessed, and redoubted Princes. This seemed to my wonder most maruellous, and more moued me to muse, when stepping on a peece of broken Ice, I spurned forth a paper (rolled vp,) wherein when I had opened and read, appeared matter fitting my present deuise: which noting, by what chance and fortune, and in what season it came to my hands, sodenly resolued to haue it printed: yet not willing to be ouer rash in presenting vnto your viewes, what I knew not assuredly true, found after occasion of cenference, with sundrie of good iudgement, who I knew had long frequented the Low countries (from whence they lately came) By whom vnderstanding all*

A 2 *was*

3

Newes latelie come on the last day of February 1591. From diuers parts of France, Sauoy, and Tripoly in Soria. Truelie translated out of the French and Italian coppies, as they were sent to right Honorable persons.

HE King accompanied with his own forces, and the Marshall Birons hauing a long time laine about Chartres, hoping in the end to reduce the Citty to his deuotion, and perceiuing it a very harde thing to obtaine the same by main force, vnles it were by surprise, by reasō of the strength of the same both by Art and nature, though there were very fewe Souldiers or none in it, except the Cittizens and Townes-men thereof.

About the fourteenth of February last, hee diuided himselfe from the Marshall Biron, and faigned to giue ouer the siedge, and to goe towards Dreux, hauing first giuen out that hee would goe to besiege that towne, and went but two or thrée miles from Chartres. The Marshall Biron, séeming the next day to leaue the siege, and to followe the King, as if he dispaired to doe any good there, which those of Chartres perceiuing, they presently with such Souldiers as they had, resolued themselues to make a saly, and to sette vppon the rearewarde of the Marshall as hee was marching towards Dreux, which accordingly they did, and issuing out of the Town most

A 2 bravely

of choice. If book 1 has concluded by presenting readers with a knight who has achieved holiness, or a process of attaining holiness worthy of emulation – and this is for recent critics a big if – then the image ought to represent the culmination of that process.[53]

The material book, however, pulls against the ease of this conclusion in a variety of ways. First, what, if anything, can the fact that the printer John Wolfe (then, in 1596, Richard Field) recycled this facsimile of virtue over and over in his printing jobs tell us about the poem, or about Spenser's attitude to Redcrosse? Surrounded by the text of *The Faerie Queene,* much more than the propagandistic pamphlets celebrating Baron Willoughby or Henri of Navarre for which the printer Wolfe originally used the illustration of St. George (figs. 22 and 23), the woodcut becomes an image that is *idolized* – or a simulacrum devoid of object reference, held up to be interrogated, with no truth located "behind" it (figuratively or spatially – not even Una as personified Truth, that is, or the analogous maiden princess of the myriad visual representations of the saint's tale that draw upon *The Golden Legend*).[54]

The blank page accommodating the woodcut in 1590 implies either that the inclusion was foreseen when the printing was undertaken, or, more likely, the blank space suggested to the printer an opportunity to reuse an illustration that was ready to hand.[55] Regardless, neither Spenser, who oversaw the printing in 1590, nor William Ponsonby, the publisher, had this – the only woodcut to adorn the poem in the early editions – removed when the six-book version appeared in 1596. Because the inclusion of the image cannot be proven to express a specific intention on Spenser's part, it brings the cluster of issues surrounding image making and worship into focus and intensifies an interpretive issue that certainly concerned Spenser deeply. Concentrating on the formatting of a book in this way, as Randall McLeod provocatively claims, will force us to see our own interpretive practices in a different and perhaps less flattering light: "The reward of intense scrutiny of the anomalies and mistransmissions of editorial history at this point will be not merely to resolve our

Fig. 22. I.B., *A Mirrour to all that loue to follow the warres* (London, 1589), A1v–A2r. ©The British Library Board, C.132.h.21

Fig. 23. Anon., *News Lately come* (London, 1591) A1v–A2r. ©The British Library Board, C.132.h.25(26)

blurred image of the *objective* textual evidence…, but also ultimately to bring into sharp focus the *subjective* image – the image of *ourselves* – the image of ourselves *reading* – the image of ourselves reading *badly*."[56] Close reading the object presented as *The Faerie Queene* in 1590, our attention to the artifact's embodiment of conflicting intentions, even of contradiction between word and image in the "ensample," causes us to represent what Kastan calls "the linguistic significance of the work" with different emphasis.[57] Why conjure an authorial phantom – the dispositive ghost of authorial intention – to disqualify what is materially *there,* in the book, affecting our experience of the text?

Spenser's text shows up the inauthenticity of the woodcut of St. George in a way that John Wolfe would not in all likelihood have intended either. T.S. Eliot expressed a kindred matter of perception thus: "the roses / Had the look of flowers that are looked at."[58] The first edition renders in visual form Spenser's complex status as both iconoclast and thaumaturge, a conjuror of an icon of virtue that "had the look of an image that is looked at." If the real is, as Baudrillard claims, "that of which it is possible to give an equivalent reproduction," then the facsimile of St. George radiates this aura of inauthenticity, to be not what is capable of being reproduced, but rather to be – like the changeling or "base Elfin brood," swapped for Redcrosse at his birth, who became the false St. George idolatrously worshipped in Catholicism (1.10.65) – "that which is always already reproduced."[59] The printer uses the image as an allegorical personification of Henri of Navarre in his pamphlets, and thus as an *ideological* betrayal of the signifier through a motivated realignment of its signified; whereas *The Faerie Queene* places *simulacrum* beside the authorial plea for belief, "matter of iust memory" on one page staring down the "painted forgery" on the leaf facing it.[60] The image seems to stand for the character of Holinesse, just as the enchanter's conjuration of Redcrosse's semblance seems to Una to represent "The true *Saint George.*" This is what it means to be "truly in the Land of Faery," as Coleridge suggested long ago. The material text allows us to understand more fully what is at stake in the rival claims that "mental space" can make through rhetorical means when it opposes the ready-made image. The physical artifact of the 1590 *Faerie Queene* illustrates the difference.

NOTES

1 David Scott Kastan, *Shakespeare and the Book* (Cambridge: Cambridge University Press, 2001), 117.

2 Margreta de Grazia, "The Essential Shakespeare and the Material Book," *Textual Practice* 2 (1988): 69–86, esp. 71–72, 82, brings similar language to bear on the history of editing Shakespearean texts in the production of some of the most influential examples of modern scholarly editing. Showing how the proponents of the New Bibliography – most notably R.B. McKerrow, W.W. Greg, A.W. Pollard, and J. Dover Wilson – relied upon the "immaterial" abstractions of idealized texts and hypothetical documents to reconstruct inferred authorial intentions, de Grazia explains that "'Incarnational' proves an apt term for the birth of New Bibliography," since, according to its basic tenets, as "letter needs spirit, so too the book as material object needs its essential spirit" (71).

3 James Kearney, *The Incarnate Text: Imagining the Book in Reformation England* (Philadelphia: University of Pennsylvania Press, 2009), 2, 3.

4 Petrarch, *De liborum copia* ("On the Abundance of Books"), in *Four Dialogues for Scholars,* ed. and trans. Conrad H. Rawski (Cleveland: The Press of Western Reserve University, 1967), 35.

5 Thomas Harriot, *A briefe and true report of the new found land of Virginia* (1588; Frankfurt-am-Main: Ioannis Wecheli for Theodore de Bry, 1590), 27. See further Andrew Hadfield, "The Revelation and Early English Colonial Ventures," in *The Bible as Book: The Reformation,* ed. Orlaith O'Sullivan (London: The British Library; Newcastle, Del: Oak Knoll Press, 2000), 145–56, esp. 151–52 on this passage. For more on this topic of kissing the book, see Benedict S. Robinson's chapter above.

6 Quotations of Spenser's poem and his Letter to Raleigh throughout are taken from the edited version of the 1590 text as presented in *The Faerie Queene,* ed. A.C. Hamilton, Hiroshi Yamashita, and Toshiyuki Suzuki, 2d ed. (Harlow: Longman, 2001) except where otherwise noted. The quotation appears at 1.6.11, the episode with Una's donkey at 1.6.19.

7 Leah Price, "Introduction: Reading Matter," *PMLA* 121 (2006): 10. This, of course, is not Price's position; she goes on to argue the reverse: "Far from replacing hermeneutics by pedantry, book history insists that every aspect of a literary work bears interpretation – even, or especially, those that look contingent" (11). The opposition itself is clearly overdetermined: witness Anthony Grafton, "The History of Ideas: Precept and Practice, 1950–2000 and Beyond," *Journal of the History of Ideas* 67 (2006): 1–32, esp. 26–32, who, in an essay written to inaugurate the new editorial agenda of the journal, extends its purview so as to "be open to the investigation of books and other material objects," with a special emphasis "on practices and material texts" (30 and 29).

8 John Milton, *Areopagitica* (1644), in *Complete Prose Works of John Milton,* ed. Don M. Wolfe et al., 8 vols. (New Haven: Yale University Press, 1953–82), 2:532.

9 See Andrew Zurcher, "Printing *The Faerie Queene* in 1590," *Studies in Bibliography* 57 (2005–2006): 115–50, for these and other detailed findings about the first edition, 135 for commentary on the printing of book 3, cantos 2–3, and 117 on the dedication. Jean R. Brink, "Materialist History of the Publication of Spenser's *Faerie Queene,*" *The Review of English Studies* 54 (2003): 1–26, carefully reconstructs the problems that surrounded the printing of the dedicatory sonnets and concludes that

"the 1590 *Faerie Queene* was not a printing success" (15), though she does not analyze the text of the poem itself. Brink notes (4) that the first issue of the first edition lacks the dedication to Elizabeth and gives as an example the Harmsworth copy (now at the Folger Shakespeare Library).

10 S.T. Coleridge, *Lectures 1808–1819: On Literature*, ed. R.A. Foakes, vol. 5 (in 2 parts) of the *Collected Works* (Princeton: Princeton University Press, 1987), 2:409, 1:289, 2:409–10.

11 Kenneth Gross, *Spenserian Poetics: Idolatry, Iconoclasm, and Magic* (Ithaca: Cornell University Press, 1985), 16 (italics mine).

12 Bernard Weinberg, *A History of Literary Criticism in the Italian Renaissance*, 2 vols. (Chicago: University of Chicago Press, 1961), remains the standard account of these debates. For a concise overview, see the two contributions by Daniel Javitch to *The Cambridge History of Literary Criticism*, vol. 3, *The Renaissance*, ed. Glyn P. Norton (Cambridge: Cambridge University Press, 1999): "The Assimilation of Aristotle's *Poetics* in Sixteenth-Century Italy," 53–65; and "Italian Epic Theory," 205–15.

13 Michael Murrin, "Spenser's Fairyland," in *The Allegorical Epic: Essays in Its Rise and Decline* (Chicago: University of Chicago Press, 1980), 131–52, esp. 134, 145.

14 Paul Woodruff, "Aristotle on *Mimēsis*," in *Essays on Aristotle's Poetics*, ed. Amélie Oksenberg Rorty (Princeton: Princeton University Press, 1992), 81. For a discussion of the potential objects of imitation in mimesis including concepts, ideas, abstractions, types, and sense data or physical phenomena, see S.K. Heninger, Jr., *Sidney and Spenser: The Poet as Maker* (University Park: Pennsylvania State University Press, 1989), 33–38, 508–10.

15 See E.K.'s gloss to line 25 of the June Eclogue of *The Shepheardes Calender*, in *The Yale Edition of the Shorter Poems of Edmund Spenser*, ed. William A. Oram et al. (New Haven: Yale University Press, 1989), 115; compare *FQ* 2.10.73. For the persistent problem of recognizing what is allegorical from what is not, Plato in the *Republic* (378D–E) employs the term *hyponoia*, literally "under-thought," with which our word "hypnosis" shares a root, to signify the true meaning at the bottom of the allegorical. See the salient comments of Jonathan Lear, "Allegory and Myth in Plato's *Republic*," in *The Blackwell Guide to Plato's "Republic,"* ed. Gerasimos Santas (Oxford: Blackwell Publishing, 2006), 27.

16 H.G. Liddell and R. Scott, *Greek-English Lexicon*, 9th ed. (Oxford: Clarendon Press, 1996), *svv.*

17 *Plato's Theory of Knowledge: The "Theaetetus" and the "Sophist,"* trans. with commentary by Francis M. Cornford (1934; reprint: Mineola, N.Y.: Dover Publications, 2003), 196n.

18 Plato, *Protagoras*, in *Platonis Opera: Volume 3*, ed. John Burnet, Oxford Classical Texts (Oxford: Clarendon Press, 1903), 312C–D; *Plato's Sophist: Part II of "The Being of the Beautiful,"* trans. with commentary by Seth Benardete (Chicago: University of Chicago Press, 1986), 101, 103, 106.

19 J. Peter Zetterberg, "The Mistaking of 'the Mathematicks' for Magic in Tudor and Stuart England," *The Sixteenth Century Journal* 11 (1980): 83–97, esp. 87–88, 91, 93–96. But see William H. Sherman, *John Dee: The Politics of Reading and Writing in the English Renaissance* (Amherst: University of Massachusetts Press, 1995), 12–23, 95–96, 233n42. Sherman argues for the appeal of Dee "to the mercantile and mechanical classes as much as to academics or adepts" (22) and lays out how the mid-twentieth-century myth of the magus in the writings of Frances Yates and her students has led subsequent scholars to misrepresent Dee's "Mathematicall Praeface," which is in fact far more traditional in its approach to the genre than is usually assumed.

20 John Dee, "A præface specifying the chiefe sciences," in Euclid, *The Elements of geometrie,* trans. H. Billingsly (London, 1570), sig. A1; OED, s.v. "Thaumaturgy": "The working of wonders; miracle-working; magic." OED, s.v. "Thaumaturgic," sense 2.B.a. "The art of constructing marvellous or apparently magical devices"; Robert Burton, *The Anatomy of Melancholy* (1621), 2.2.4, ed. Holbrook Jackson, 3 vols. in 1 (reprint: New York: New York Review Books, 2001), 2:96.

21 Aristotle, *Poetics,* 1460A11–14, ed. and trans. Stephen Halliwell, 2d ed., Loeb edition (Cambridge: Harvard University Press, 1996), 122–23. I have modified Halliwell's translation slightly. Rachel Falconer, "Epic," in *A Companion to English Renaissance Literature and Culture,* ed. Michael Hattaway (Oxford: Blackwell, 2000), 334–35, provides a succinct summary of recent scholarship on the application of this moment in the *Poetics* to early modern epic theory and practice.

22 Homer describes this episode, Aristotle's exemplar at *Poetics* 1460A14–17, in the *Iliad* (22.131–207). The quotation is from John Milton, *Paradise Lost,* ed. David Scott Kastan (Indianapolis: Hackett, 2005), 9.16.

23 For more on these aspects of dramatic representation during this period of English global expansion, see Cyrus Mulready, "'Asia of the One Side, and Afric of the Other': Sidney's Unities and the Staging of Romance," in *Staging Early Modern Romance: Prose Fiction, Dramatic Romance, and Shakespeare,* ed. Mary Ellen Lamb and Valerie Wayne (New York: Routledge, 2009), 47–71.

24 For the history of the early modern recovery, publication, and reception of the *Poetics,* see Stephen Halliwell, "Influence and Status: the *Nachleben* of the *Poetics,*" in *Aristotle's Poetics* (1986; reprint, Chicago: University of Chicago Press, 1998), esp. 291–301.

25 Torquato Tasso, *Jerusalem Delivered,* 13.44, trans. Edward Fairfax (1600; reprint, New York: Capricorn Books, 1963), 275. See further, e.g., *Jerusalem Delivered,* ed. and trans. Anthony M. Esolen (Baltimore: Johns Hopkins University Press, 2000), which is in many respects closer to the Italian original: 5.28, 7.46, 8.74, 9.26, 12.51, 12.90, 13.18, 13.21, 15.14, 15.60, 16.28–29, 16.31, 16.43, 16.70, 18.27, 20.105. We know from extensive borrowings from the *Liberata* in book 2 that Spenser read Tasso with great care, sometime between 24 June 1581 and 1 December 1589, according to David Scott Wilson-Okamura, "When Did Spenser Read Tasso?" *Spenser Studies* 23 (2008): 277–82.

26 On Tasso's psychic conflict as mapped onto the similes' interruptions to epic narration, see Sergio Zatti, *The Quest for Epic: From Ariosto to Tasso,* ed. Dennis Looney, trans. Sally Hill with Dennis Looney (Toronto: University of Toronto Press, 2006), 163–64. Furthermore, the anxiety visible in Tasso's insistence on separating imitation of action from spiritual allegory in his "Allegory of the Poem" gives some context for this aspect of the similes, and it is evident from the Letter to Raleigh, which imitates Tasso's "Allegory" in several places, that Spenser had Tasso in mind when he set down his theory of his own poem, regardless of the Letter's deviations from *The Faerie Queene* itself.

27 Fourteen of the fifteen instances occur in books 1 and 2, the fifteenth in book 3. See the transcription of Jonson's marginalia in James A. Riddell and Stanley Stewart, *Jonson's Spenser: Evidence and Historical Criticism* (Pittsburgh: Duquesne University Press, 1995), 162–86. Jonson's copy is now in the Wormsley Library, Buckinghamshire, England, shelfmark RH54.

28 Though, of course, there is something doubly ironic about speaking of the cultic myth as true or actual. See Jonathan Bengtson, "Saint George and the

Formation of English Nationalism," *Journal of Medieval and Early Modern Studies* 27 (1997): 317–40, for an account of the way "The Roman soldier of Nobatia" came to be "firmly and utterly established as a most English of saints," so much so that "England was caught up in a kind of George-mania" by the time Caxton produced his version of Voragine's *Legenda Aurea* in the mid-fifteenth century (327–28).

29 Randle Cotgrave, *A Dictionarie of the French and English Tongues* (London, 1611), s.v.

30 Riddell and Stewart, *Jonson's Spenser*, 165.

31 Wonderfully, the Odyssean intertext is doubly present, since Spenser not only alludes to Homer, but in comparing Una to Odysseus, also imitates the gendered reversals recovered for modern scholarship by Helene P. Foley, "'Reverse Similes' and Sex Roles in the *Odyssey*," *Arethusa* 11 (1978): 7–26.

32 Jeff Dolven, *Scenes of Instruction in Renaissance Romance* (Chicago: University of Chicago Press, 2007), 140–44, vividly describes this tension in the somewhat different terms of "paradigmatic and narrative modes of understanding" (140).

33 See Paul Suttie, *Self-Interpretation in "The Faerie Queene"* (Cambridge, UK: D.S. Brewer, 2006), 61–73.

34 Martin Luther, "A Sermon…concerning them that be vnder the Law, and them that be vnder Grace," *Special and Chosen Sermons*, trans. W.G. (London, 1578), 315. Students of Spenser will find a useful conspectus of the issues that surround Reformed doctrine in the action of the first two books of *The Faerie Queene* in Darryl J. Gless, "Nature and Grace," in *The Spenser Encyclopaedia*, ed. A.C. Hamilton et al. (Toronto: University of Toronto Press, 1990), 505–7.

35 Northrop Frye, "The Structure of Imagery in *The Faerie Queene*," *University of Toronto Quarterly* 30 (1961): 109–27, reprinted in *Edmund Spenser's Poetry*, ed. Hugh Maclean and Anne Lake Prescott, 3d ed. (New York: W.W. Norton, 1993), 713.

36 James Nohrnberg, *The Analogy of "The Faerie Queene"* (Princeton: Princeton University Press, 1976), 196–98. For the gloss on John 19:34 and its interpretation as a miracle by Origen, Aquinas, Cornelius à Lapide, and others, see the commentary in Raymond E. Brown, *The Gospel According to John*, 2 vols. (New York: Anchor/Doubleday, 1966), 2:946–52. The English Protestant tradition follows suit; see the marginal glosses in the Geneva Bible (John 19:31–34), which liken the dead body of Christ to "his mysticall body," so that readers may "witnesseth by a double signe, that he onely is the true satisfaction, and the true washing for the beleeuers." I quote from the London edition of 1599.

37 Dante, *Il Convivio*, tract 2, chap. 1, trans. David Wallace, in *Medieval Literary Theory and Criticism, c. 1100–c. 1375: The Commentary Tradition*, rev. ed., ed. A.J. Minnis and A.B. Scott, with David Wallace (Oxford: Clarendon Press, 1991), 396. See further the extract from the *Epistle to Can Grande* in the same volume, 460.

38 In his now classic chapter, "To Fashion a Gentleman: Spenser and the Destruction of the Bower of Bliss," Stephen Greenblatt, *Renaissance Self-Fashioning: From More to Shakespeare* (Chicago: University of Chicago Press, 1980), chap. 4, makes valuable and influential remarks on this passage, albeit without questioning the mechanics of the mimetic principle at work (what Greenblatt calls the "mirroring – the conscious purpose of the work seeming to enact the larger cultural movement" [169–79, at 175]). On the complex ideological resonances of pleasurable violence associated with subordinating the material in allegory, see Gordon Teskey, *Allegory and Violence* (Ithaca: Cornell University Press, 1996), 23–55 and *passim*.

39 For a useful survey of the poetics of this device in the period, with some commentary on Spenser's poetic practice, see Hannah Betts, "'The Image of this Queene so quaynt': The Pornographic Blazon 1588–1603," in *Dissing Elizabeth: Negative Representations of Gloriana*, ed. Julia M. Walker (Durham: Duke University Press, 1998), 153–84.

40 William Shakespeare, *A Midsummer Night's Dream*, ed. Peter Holland (Oxford: Clarendon Press, 1994), 2.1.132–34.

41 *The Faerie Queene* (London: John Wolfe for William Ponsonby, 1590), 124.

42 Ibid., 606.

43 Analyzing the episode from the perspective of Redcrosse, Kearney, *The Incarnate Text*, 122–24, suggests that the knight misconstrues the significance of having given the New Testament away by supposing he has given away a *text* instead of a *book*, an interpretive mistake that leads him to follow the decoupled Old Testament directly to Despair.

44 More, *Utopia*, trans. Clarence H. Miller (New Haven: Yale University Press, 2001), 139. This is from the second letter to Peter Giles, which was included only in the second edition published in Paris in 1517 (see Miller's introduction, xx).

45 Sir Philip Sidney, *An Apology for Poetry*, ed. Geoffrey Shepherd (London: Thomas Nelson, 1965), 101.

46 Ludovico Ariosto, *Orlando Furioso*, 7.74, trans. Guido Waldman (1974; reprint: Oxford: Oxford University Press, 1998), 69. Melinda J. Gough, "Tasso's Enchantress, Tasso's Captive Woman," *Renaissance Quarterly* 54 (2001): 525, quotes the key passages from Ariosto in a much looser translation that reads "interpret the pages" instead of "read the cards aright" and analyzes the traditional motif in order to contrast Tasso's relation to it.

47 "Elegy 8," ll. 39–43, in *The Variorum Edition of the Poetry of John Donne*, vol. 2, ed. Gary A. Stringer et al. (Bloomington: Indiana University Press, 2000), 164 and 666 for date. And see further "The Exstasie," ll. 79–82, in *The Elegies and Songs and Sonnets*, ed. Helen Gardner (Oxford: Clarendon Press, 1965), 61: "To our bodies turne we then, that so / Weake men on love reveal'd may looke; / Loves mysteries in soules doe grow, / But yet the body is his booke."

48 *Inferno*, 9.61–63 and 16.124–28, ed. and trans. Charles S. Singleton, *The Divine Comedy*, vol. 1 (Princeton: Princeton University Press, 1970), 92–93, 170–71. For an excellent inquiry into the semiotic, semantic, and narrative strategy in Dante's realm of fraudulence, which has exerted a general but powerful influence over my thinking about the poetic stakes of this kind of self-reflexivity, see Teodolinda Barolini, *The Undivine "Comedy": Detheologizing Dante* (Princeton: Princeton University Press, 1992), 74–98.

49 George Puttenham, *The Art of English Poesy: A Critical Edition*, 3.18, ed. Frank Whigham and Wayne A. Rebhorn (Ithaca: Cornell University Press, 2007), 270–71.

50 *Ad Herennium*, ed. and trans. H. Caplan, Loeb edition (Cambridge: Harvard University Press, 1954), 4.34.46; Quintilian, *Institutio Oratoria: Volume 3*, ed. and trans. Donald A. Russell, Loeb edition (Cambridge: Harvard University Press, 2002), 8.6.54. On Spenser's rhetorical education, see Peter Mack, "Spenser and Rhetoric," in *The Oxford Handbook of Edmund Spenser*, ed. Richard A. McCabe (Oxford: Oxford University Press, 2010), 420–36, esp. 425–28.

51 This notion of the existence, within the poem, of what I am calling a "monstrous shadow poem" has been explored in different terms, especially as a "counterpoem" (Gilman) or "countertext" (Berger), in studies concerned to trace

Archimago as the poet's double. See Ernest B. Gilman, *Iconoclasm and Poetry in the English Reformation: Down Went Dagon* (Chicago: University of Chicago Press, 1986), 75; Harry Berger, Jr., "Archimago: Between Text and Countertext," *Studies in English Literature 1500–1900* 43 (2003): 19–64; and David Quint, "Archimago and Amoret: The Poem and Its Doubles," in *Worldmaking Spenser: Explorations in the Early Modern Age*, ed. Patrick Cheney and Lauren Sillberman (Lexington: University Press of Kentucky, 2000), 32–42.

52 A. Bartlett Giamatti, *Play of Double Senses: Spenser's* Faerie Queene (New York: W.W. Norton, 1975), 69–70. More specifically, Ernest Gilman details "the agonistic mode of [*The Faerie Queene*'s] pictorialism," or "the urge to depict and the complementary urge to deface" (*Iconoclasm and Poetry*, 80). For a powerful argument that this contradictory impulse derives from the post-Reformation effort to recuperate an uncorrupted memory of the past out of the traumatic ruins of the monastic libraries, see Jennifer Summit, "Monuments and Ruins: Spenser and the Problem of the English Library," *ELH* 70 (2003): 16–20.

53 The woodcut is reproduced in *The Faerie Queene*, ed. A.C. Hamilton et al., 2d ed. (2001), 156, and as a frontispiece to the older student edition (still in print) *The Faerie Queene Book I*, ed. P.C. Bayley (Oxford: Oxford University Press, 1966); but it is not reproduced in: *The Faerie Queene*, ed. A.C. Hamilton (London: Longman, 1977); *The Faerie Queene*, ed. Thomas P. Roche, Jr. (Harmondsworth: Penguin, 1978); *Edmund Spenser's Poetry*, ed. Maclean and Prescott, 3d ed. (1993); *The Faerie Queene: Book One*, ed. Carol V. Kaske (Indianapolis: Hackett, 2006); *The Faerie Queene: Book Two*, ed. Erik Gray (Indianapolis: Hackett, 2006). For the skeptical reading of Redcrosse's achievement of holiness, see esp. Suttie, *Self-Interpretation*, 57–145.

54 The woodcut first appeared as a frontispiece in a quarto news pamphlet by "G.D.," *A Briefe Discoverie of Doctor Allens seditious drifts, contriued in a Pamphlet written by him, Concerning the yeelding vp of the towne of Deuenter, (in Ouerrissel) unto the King of Spain, by Sir William Stanley* (London: I. W[olfe] for Francis Coldock, 1588), STC 6166. Reused by Wolfe: STC 1041.7 (1588), 3127 (1589), 23080 (1590), 11283 (1591), 11260 (1592); by Wolfe and E. White: STC 13130 (1592); by R. Field: 23082 (1596). See Ruth Samson Luborsky and Elizabeth Morely Ingram, *A Guide to English Illustrated Books, 1536–1603*, 2 vols. (Tempe: Medieval and Renaissance Texts and Studies, 1998), 1:311. Paul J. Voss, "The Faerie Queene, 1590–1596: The Case of Saint George," *Ben Jonson Journal* 3 (1996): 59–73, usefully traces the history of the woodcut through John Wolfe's catalogue, arguing that the image, at least through 1592, would have resonated with many readers as an image associated principally with the French Huguenot King Henri of Navarre, Henri IV, who remained a major ally of the English government until his reconversion to Catholicism in 1594. Voss believes that the image would have held this association through 1596, but with a very different valence of disappointment instead of hope; he concludes that Field, inheriting the stock of Wolfe, lazily included the image in 1596 and that "Field and other compositors, in their haste, failed to understand or recognize the resonances" (73n29). The principal difficulty with Voss's interpretation is that it relies upon the idea that the same book buyers from the late 1580s to the mid-1590s were not only paying attention to the allegorical significance of the repeated use of a stock image, but also that these readers were recalling both this image and its previous significance by the time they reached the end of the first book of Spenser's poem. The more natural implication would certainly be to associate the image of St. George directly with the poem in hand.

55 Zurcher, "Printing *The Faerie Queene*," 121, notes the accommodation of the woodcut and the similar but unillustrated blank page between books 2 and 3, though he does not speculate about the inclusion.

56 Randall McLeod, writing as Random Cloud, "Enter Reader," in *The Editorial Gaze: Mediating Texts in Literature and the Arts*, ed. Paul Eggert and Margaret Sankey (New York: Garland, 1998), 3–50 (46).

57 Kastan, *Shakespeare and the Book*, 117.

58 T.S. Eliot, "Burnt Norton," *Collected Poems* (New York: Harcourt Brace, 1988), 176.

59 Jean Baudrillard, *Simulations*, trans. Paul Foss, Paul Patton, and Philip Beitchman (New York: Semiotext[e], 1983), 146. On the "countergeneric" strategy of Spenser's assimilation of an iconoclastic attack upon the conventions of saints' lives that it also appropriates, and for speculations that Archimago himself is to be identified with the "base Elfin brood," and that the changeling "became the mythic subject of the discredited saint's legend," see John N. King, *Spenser's Poetry and the Reformation Tradition* (Princeton: Princeton University Press, 1990), 190. Nohrnberg, *Analogy*, 158, followed by King, 189, suggests that Archimago reads to Una and Redcrosse from *The Golden Legend* at 1.1.35.

60 This distinction between ideology and simulacrum is that of Baudrillard, *Simulations*, 48–49.

C
K
E
G
F

Indicating Commodities in Early English Discovery Narratives

DANIEL VITKUS

Like maps of foreign lands and seas, early modern travel narratives offer the reader a representation of faraway places that is partial, biased, and distorted. There is, of course, no way to map, write, or perform that would provide a transparent or complete image or description of a foreign place or people. This is the iron law of representation. So the question becomes this: *how* did early modern English texts organize and represent the data gathered by travelers? What were the usual modes of representation, and how do those modes reinforce or alter the cognitive habits of the writers and readers who produced and consumed travel texts? Why were certain kinds of information included while others were left out? These are large questions, and they cannot be answered fully or adequately in this essay, but I do want to raise some particular questions about how the flood of information about foreign cultures and landscapes that poured into early modern England was channeled. And I will argue that the labor of traveling, data-gathering, and writing was largely hidden by the fetishization of the text as commodity, and driven by a rising tendency to define "discovery" in terms of the commodities and exchange values produced by English transactions taking place at specific locations within the expanding global trade network. Just as purely abstract lines on a map come to dictate the terms of subsequent history, so the cultural definition and conventional modes of ethnographic and geographic description came to dictate the terms of England's self-definition as a commercial, expansionist nation reaching out to the rest of the world to obtain and vent commodities. In what sense did early modern travel narratives work to fetishize commodities?

William Pietz has argued that "the fetish, as an idea and a problem, and as a novel object not proper to any prior discrete society, originated in the cross-cultural spaces of the coast of West Africa during the sixteenth and seventeenth centuries."[1] In the intercultural commercial environment of coastal West Africa, where the Portuguese initiated the European trade in African slaves, the prosecutors of an emergent maritime capitalism probed the African coast for commodities, including gold and human beings, as they pursued the quest for an oceanic route to the Indies. According to Pietz, between the fifteenth and the eighteenth centuries "a fundamental change occurred in the conception of the natural powers of the material object."[2] Pietz claims that this shift is crucially exemplified in sixteenth- and seventeenth-century collections of voyage narratives that were compiled by authors like Giovanni Battista Ramusio in Venice, Theodor de Bry in Frankfort, and in England Richard Hakluyt and then Samuel Purchas.[3] In these texts, argues Pietz, "the truth of material objects came to be viewed in terms of technological and commodifiable use-value, whose 'reality' was proved by their silent 'translatability' across alien cultures. All other meanings and values attributed to material objects were understood to be the culture-specific delusions of peoples lacking 'reason.'"[4] What Pietz is describing here is the emergence of a modern materialist discourse, one that privileged the allegedly objective logic of the secular-rational marketplace over any precapitalist, traditional value system.[5] While it began on the West African coast as a pidgin word, "fetisso," used to describe material objects of exchange that held a high personal and social value, the word "fetish" went on to be used by Marx in *Capital* in a sense that, with typical Marxian irony, pointed to the barbaric cruelty, primitive object-worshipping, and tyrannical exploitation practiced by the capitalists themselves, who fetishized and revered the commodity, giving it "magical" powers to produce exchange value while masking and concealing the coarse material realities of capitalist exploitation and the expropriated labor-power that formed the basis of that value.[6] And it was in the expansion of long-distance, overseas trade that the merchant class in England gained a tremendous boost in its power to accumulate and reinvest capital. At the same time, we should keep in mind that when long-distance trade became more prevalent for the English, the distance between the commodity as a local, demystified product of labor, and the commodity as a mysterious and aura-bearing fetish, became greater. We have an entirely different feeling about the apples we pick at a local orchard and bring home to eat, as compared to the Nike shoes made far away by underpaid workers in Asia that we purchase in a fetishization framework like that of Niketown. Similarly, in Elizabethan England a woolen cap purchased from a local artisan would not convey the transgressive thrill or the fetishized prestige of a Turkey carpet or a garment made of imported silk. Imported luxury goods had been available to English elites for centuries, of course, but the outward expansion that began to accelerate during the late sixteenth century was unprecedented, as was the incoming flood of foreign goods that resulted.[7] This was the beginning of the globalized commodity fetishism that has triumphed today.

But if we return to Pietz's thesis that early modern discovery narratives were indicators and embodiments of capitalist fetishization, we will find Pietz suggesting that early colonial texts, including early voyage accounts, can be studied "as novel productions resulting from the abrupt encounter of radically heterogeneous worlds; as descriptive records they are often phantasmal, but because of this it is possible to view them as remnants of the creative enactment of new forms of social consciousness."[8] What Pietz does not observe, however, is that the phantasmic projections that are found in discovery texts are increasingly accompanied by empirical data-fetishes in the form of quantified lists of commodities, often with their exchange values specified. Early modern discovery narratives functioned as indices, signs, or maps pointing out a potential path for commercial or colonial venturers to follow. Sometimes, they include actual maps, charts, and ordered lists of data for merchants and colonizers to use in their plans and in their actual ventures. According to early modern usage, the "index" accompanies the main body of a text, indicating (or pointing the way) toward the rest of the book. Such indications mediate between the reader and the main bulk of the data offered by the book, when a reader comes to the index looking for a guide to its full contents. I am concerned in this essay with the way that travel texts *indicate*, with how they point the way, like the manicule – that little hand in the margin with its index finger directing the reader to pay attention to certain statements in the body of the text.[9] One function of the early modern discovery narrative is to point the way toward future activity, especially commercial and colonial activity. While guiding the reader's understanding of foreign places and people, the travel narrative arranges its data, not only by charting journeys or by plotting events and observations along the course of a linear narrative, but also by laying out information in ordered maps, charts, diagrams, and lists.

The index that appears in the opening or closing pages of the early modern discovery narrative is, in a sense, an index to an index: the bulk of the text already summarizes and organizes a long and complex process, choosing the most significant and useful details to form its narrative and leaving much untold. There were many early modern books that carried on the tradition of the compendium, the epitome, a practice carried on from an older scribal culture into print culture. By the late sixteenth century in England, this practice was still an important element in the pedagogical system in which educated elites were trained. And of course, it was carried over into the culture of courtiers, councillors, bureaucrats, merchants, and economic experts. From Gabriel Harvey to Francis Bacon and after, English writers and readers both produced and consumed "abstracts" that attempted to encapsulate the essence of an argument, a narrative, or even a whole body of knowledge.[10] These distillations functioned as a bureaucratic procedure by which the secretary or proto-functionary could provide quick and easy information, reduced from an extensive mass of particularities to a brief survey or convenient gist. Such procedures derive from two information-gathering and synthesizing modes of operation: first, the scholastic tradition that compiles authoritative knowledge in the form of the compendium, and second, the beginnings of the modern enterprise of the encyclopedia—a collective, scientific project of specializing experts whose work contributed to the Enlightenment project of universal knowledge. This kind of intellectual labor became increasingly important during an age in which information about other parts of the world proliferated, and in which printed books proliferated as commodities that were accessible to readers outside monastic or courtly manuscript cultures. For early modern culture, this synoptic procedure was so familiar that it could serve as a figure for representation itself, as it does, for example, in the dedicatory epistle that introduces the printed edition of *The Travels of the Three English Brothers,* a play written in 1607 by John Day, William Rowley, and George Wilkins.[11] This drama represented on stage the exploits of the three traveling Sherley brothers, Thomas, Anthony, and Robert, whose adventures are set mostly in Turkey and Persia. The text's dedicatory letter offers this excuse for being unable to represent the Sherley brothers exactly or fully: "Being unable to present the substances, we have epitomised their large volume in a compendious abstract, which we wish all to peruse."[12]

The word "Travel" in the title *The Travels of the Three English Brothers* refers to the sufferings, trials, and difficulties experienced by the three wandering brothers. In the sixteenth century and early seventeenth century, "travel" was considered a form of "travail" or arduous labor. Later, the word "travel" came to be associated with leisure and pleasure, while a separate signifier, "travail," continued to bear the signification of labor and suffering. And so today we have two separate words and meanings, distinguished by an orthographic difference that indicates two different pronunciations – "travel" and "travail." In the sixteenth and seventeenth centuries the two words were one, and there was no orthographical separation of terms: "travel" *was* "travail" – it was associated with hard work, pain, and suffering. Early modern "travel" was something to be endured, not enjoyed (think about the cramped and smelly conditions on board a ship, or the bumpy ride on early modern roads). Here is the OED definition of early modern "travel/travail": "bodily or mental labour or toil, especially of a painful or oppressive nature; exertion; trouble; hardship; suffering."[13] Travel as travail was linked to the difficult work of commerce: you did not want to undertake it, risk it, or take the time required to cover long distances using early modern technology – but you did it, or hired others to do it, so that you could make a profit. For Columbus, the purpose of long-distance travel was to get from Europe to the Indies by the fastest possible overseas route, and in doing so he had to manage the laborers on his vessels, tricking them into thinking that they had traveled a shorter distance than they really had by altering and falsifying the log of the voyage. When Columbus and subsequent navigators and adventurers came to record their voyages in a form designed for broad dissemination, they often repressed or concealed the cost of their travel in order to serve promotional and profit-seeking purposes – for the sake of encouraging overseas ventures, and in order to sell books. The messy process of carrying out an overseas venture, including the cost in victuals, labor, and lives, was often hidden by texts that offered a condensed narrative account and delivered packets of practical information – news that readers could use – without dwelling on all of the material challenges that had to be met.[14] Furthermore, sixteenth- and early seventeenth-century travel narrators do not dwell on the aesthetics of the journey as much as later travelers do: instead, they gather nuggets of information, which are then retailed, imported, objectified, and offered to those readers who value these packets of information.

Early modern travel was rough, but reading about *other* peoples' travels while sitting at home could be a source of pleasure. In his 1531 work, *The Boke named the Gouernour,* Sir Thomas Elyot describes the delight experienced by readers of maps and other geographical texts:

> For what pleasure is it, in one houre to beholde those realmes… that vneth[15] in an old mannes life can not be iournaide and pursued: what incredible delite is take in beholding the diuersities of people, beastis, foules, fisshes, trees, frutes, and herbes: to knowe the sondry maners & conditions of people, and the varietie of their natures, and that in a warme studie or perler, without perill of the see, or daunger of longe and paynfull iournayes: I can nat tell, what more pleasure shulde happen to a gentil witte, than to beholde in his owne house euery thynge that with in all the worlde is contained.[16]

For Elyot, the pleasure of comfortable armchair travel, experienced through reading, is enhanced by the knowledge that others have suffered the "perill of the see, or daunger of longe and paynfull iournayes." And that pleasure is intensified further by the almost magical effects of the book's condensation and abstraction of information – it incorporates all the variety of the world while contracting travel's labor in time and space into a single hour in the cozy parlor of one's own home. Elyot would clearly prefer to stay at home and leave the travel to others.

The idea that travel was a positive educational or aesthetic experience remained controversial throughout the sixteenth century and into the seventeenth. In fact, the desire to travel for travel's sake was considered a form of folly or madness – literally, an error (this is the case, for example, of Sir Politic Would-Be in *Volpone* or Peregrine in Brome's *The Antipodes*). But people did travel to make money through trade, to conduct diplomacy, and eventually to plant colonies (and the latter was an arduous task indeed). It was the commercial function of travel that would eventually make travel fully normative for the bourgeoisie, and it was the new commercial elites who would enjoy the emergent culture of tourism. But in sixteenth- and seventeenth-century England, that kind of freedom to travel for pleasure was not available for the vast majority of people, who were tied to their localities and needed a passport just to leave their own parish.

* * *

Having described the labor of travel, let me now turn to the labor of writing about travel, and to a notion of the travel book as a distillation of travel-labor, in the form of an index of information that was made possible by an intensive knowledge-gathering effort and by the manual and navigational seagoing labor that made such knowledge-gathering possible. A typical discovery narrative offers a condensed account of a long and complex enterprise that was made possible by the travail, the suffering, and (in frequent cases) the death of many maritime laborers. This collective effort is indicated by the pronoun "we" employed by the first-person narrators describing the events of the voyage. While the writerly perspective of the narrator suggests the individual body, moving through time and space, observing, questioning, gathering, and reporting, the "we" reveals the necessarily collective enterprise of travel and the constant requirement that mariners, porters, servants, and other workers perform the labor of travel. The discovery narrators represent themselves as the eyes and ears of a laboring body that toils and sweats but is only occasionally mentioned or acknowledged.

When the early English discovery narrators packaged and delivered their information in the form of the printed book, this form was inflected by a new ideology of social space. In the early modern age of the "new geography" or "new cartography," the world became available to the literate imagination in a newly mediated way, sometimes still packaged in microcosmic texts that claimed to deliver the whole world; and sometimes organized around a narrative that traced a linear journey through a particular foreign time and space. From the cosmographic compendium, to the atlas, to the limited location of the travel narrative or "relation," a new kind of information packaging and consumption arose in early modern Europe. These innovative forms of data delivery accompanied a shift in mentality from analogical thinking to hierarchical thinking, from a metaphysical worldview toward a commercial conception of the world as a storehouse of circulating commodities. The age of the *mappa mundi* passed away and began to be replaced by the age of the scientific or commercial inventory. The system of magical, occult analogies that structured the medieval and early modern understanding of the material world was losing ideological force, after the Reformation and before the Enlightenment. The neat synecdochic symmetries of the concentric cosmos gradually gave way to ordered catalogues, full of precise measurements. The whole was replaced by a more specialized list of commodified parts. During the early modern period, this lack of wholeness was particularly acute because the Ptolomaic framework was no longer capable of incorporating the known world, and no complete, confident description of the world could take its place until all of the blank spots in the world map were filled in. *Terra incognita* stubbornly resisted incorporation in a global or cosmological whole with a fully articulated form. According to Frank Lestringant, this "cosmographic revolution," beginning in the early sixteenth century, comprised a "sudden rupture of scales that changed people's way of viewing the world, and consequently the world itself."[17] This is what Bernhard Klein has called "the cartographic transaction," "a shift from a dominant spatial model in which the Mediterranean centre of the world was poised against a liminal, uncivilized and possibly non-human periphery, to a model which translated the earthly globe into a vast pictorial frame circumscribing a space ready for European inscription."[18] It is an epistemological shift that took place in all sorts of texts and forms, not just maps. This new epistemology produced new organizational principles and discursive regimes, new ways of classifying what was being "discovered," and new ways of valuing things, places, and people. We can see this novel approach in the writings of Francis Bacon, for example, whose scientific projects and writings on "discovery" sustain a parallel between the generation of new empirical data and the imperial mission to journey beyond Europe and the Mediterranean. This dual project is clearly indicated by the frontispiece to Bacon's *Novum Organum* (1620), which depicts a ship sailing through the Pillars of Hercules, an analogy for the pursuit of scientific "discoveries" that Bacon advocates and predicts will be the result of his new method (fig. 24).[19] By focusing on the close

Fig. 24. Francisci de Verulamio [Francis Bacon], *Summi Angliae Cancellarii, Instauratio magna* (London, 1620), title page. Beinecke Rare Book and Manuscript Library, Yale University, 1988 +163

and systematic observation of material things, Bacon hoped to reduce the variety of objective phenomena to their essential principles. To do so, Bacon called for philosophers to produce ordered lists of observations, and in his Utopian narrative, *The New Atlantis,* he imagines a society of data gatherers, the Brethren of Salomon's House, who systematically import and hoard useful knowledge. Toward the end of that unfinished text, Bacon's mock discovery narrator provides a catalogue of powerful technologies and manufactured objects (including food, medicines, and textiles) made and possessed by these Brethren. The "governor" explains to the narrator that the Bensalemites "maintain a trade, not for gold, silver, or jewels; nor for silks; nor for spices; nor any other commodity of matter; but only...to have *light*...of the growth of all parts of the world."[20] But the narrator remains dazzled as much by rich commodities as he is by the light of this knowledge: like the real-world discovery narrators, he obsessively describes in detail the valuable clothing and other rich carpets, cushions, and objects worn and used by the high officials of Bensalem and Salomon's House. When the "Father of Salomon's House" tells the narrator about the technologies and experiments that are the result of this knowledge-gathering, he explains that the "End" of the House of Salomon is "the enlarging of the bounds of Human Empire,"[21] and the first project he mentions is an artificial mine that can produce metals. The technologies controlled by the House of Salomon produce perfumes, precious stones, and "instruments of war,"[22] among other things. In the end, the purpose of all this science is to manufacture valuable commodities through domestic industries (though there are no accompanying descriptions of the labor required to run these "motions"). After describing these industries and their products, the Father declares, "These are (my son) the riches of Salomon's House"[23] and leaves the narrator and his crew with a gift of two thousand ducats. Bacon's New Atlantis is a place where only knowledge need be imported because that knowledge is used to produce all of the commodities that would otherwise need to be obtained through trade. And yet, the narrator brings with him a commodifying gaze that dominates the text.

The new scientific, cartographic, and spatial consciousness encouraged a vast inventory of places, people, and objects. In fits and starts, early modern writers contributed to a grand but unsystematic project of cataloguing the world, and in doing so these writers facilitated the notion of the commodity, and of the world as a giant collection of potential commodities. Data was accumulated, packaged, mass-produced, and disseminated in various printed texts, and these were, in turn, accumulated, repackaged, and circulated in lengthy, multivolume collections like those of Hakluyt and Purchas. In fact, this commodified vision of the world is succinctly expressed by Hakluyt himself on the second page of the 1589 edition of *The Principal Navigations* in Hakluyt's "Epistle Dedicatorie," in which he recalls a visit paid to his cousin's chamber, where the youthful Hakluyt "found lying open vpon his boord certeine bookes of Cosmographie, with an vniuersall Mappe."[24] His cousin then "pointed with his wand to all the knowen Seas, Gulfs, Bayes, Straights, Capes, Riuers, Empires, Kingdomes, Dukedomes, and Territories of ech part, with declaration also of their speciall commodities, & particular wants. . . ."[25] This globalized understanding of geography was to be the structuring principle for Hakluyt's systematic gathering and arrangement of texts in *The Principal Navigations,* which took on a large-scale, incorporating form that could contain and arrange a variety of more specific data sets describing each part of the known world and its commodities and wants, its potential exports and imports.

In what follows, I will discuss three specific examples of the discovery narrative genre, beginning with Humphrey Gilbert's *Discourse of a Discoverie*. The early English discovery narratives function to point the way for empire, conquest, and profitable commerce, but Gilbert's *Discourse* gestures toward a navigational dead end. Printed in 1576, Gilbert's text promotes the English effort to find a Northwest Passage to the Indies. It is a text that attempts to point the way, literally "indicating" a quick route from England to India, via the Northwest Passage. "A General Map, Made Onelye for the Particvler Declaration of This Discovery" (fig. 25) is a projection that makes the passage from Europe to the Indies appear to be an easy journey through the "zona temperata." On the page facing the map is the beginning of chapter 10, titled, "What commodities woulde ensue, this passage once discouered."

OVERLEAF
Fig. 25. Humphrey Gilbert, *A Discovrse of a Discouerie for a new Passage to Cataia* (London, 1576), "A General Map." Beinecke Rare Book and Manuscript Library, Yale University, Taylor 138

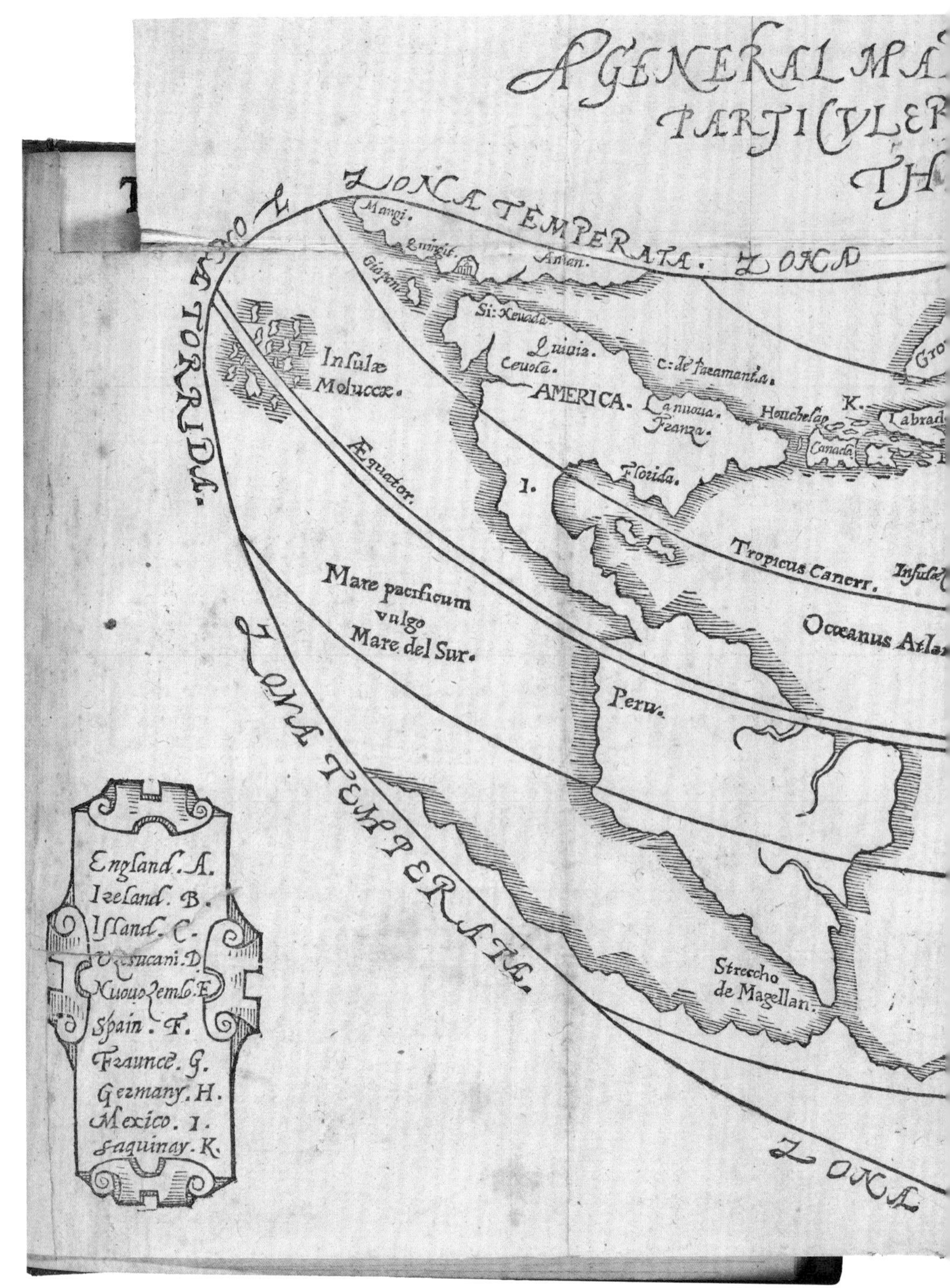
A GENERAL MA
PARTICULER
TH
ZONA TEMPERATA. ZONA
ZONA TORRIDA.
Mangi.
Amian.
Si: Nevada
Quivira.
Ceuola.
Insulæ Moluccæ.
AMERICA.
La nuoua Franza.
K.
Canada.
Florida.
Æquator.
I.
Tropicus Cancri.
Mare pacificum vulgo Mare del Sur.
Oceanus Atla
Peru.
ZONA TEMPERATA.
Strecho de Magellan.
ZONA
England. A.
Izeland. B.
Island. C.
Nuouo Zemlo. E.
Spain. F.
Fraunce. G.
Germany. H.
Mexico. I.
Saguinay. K.

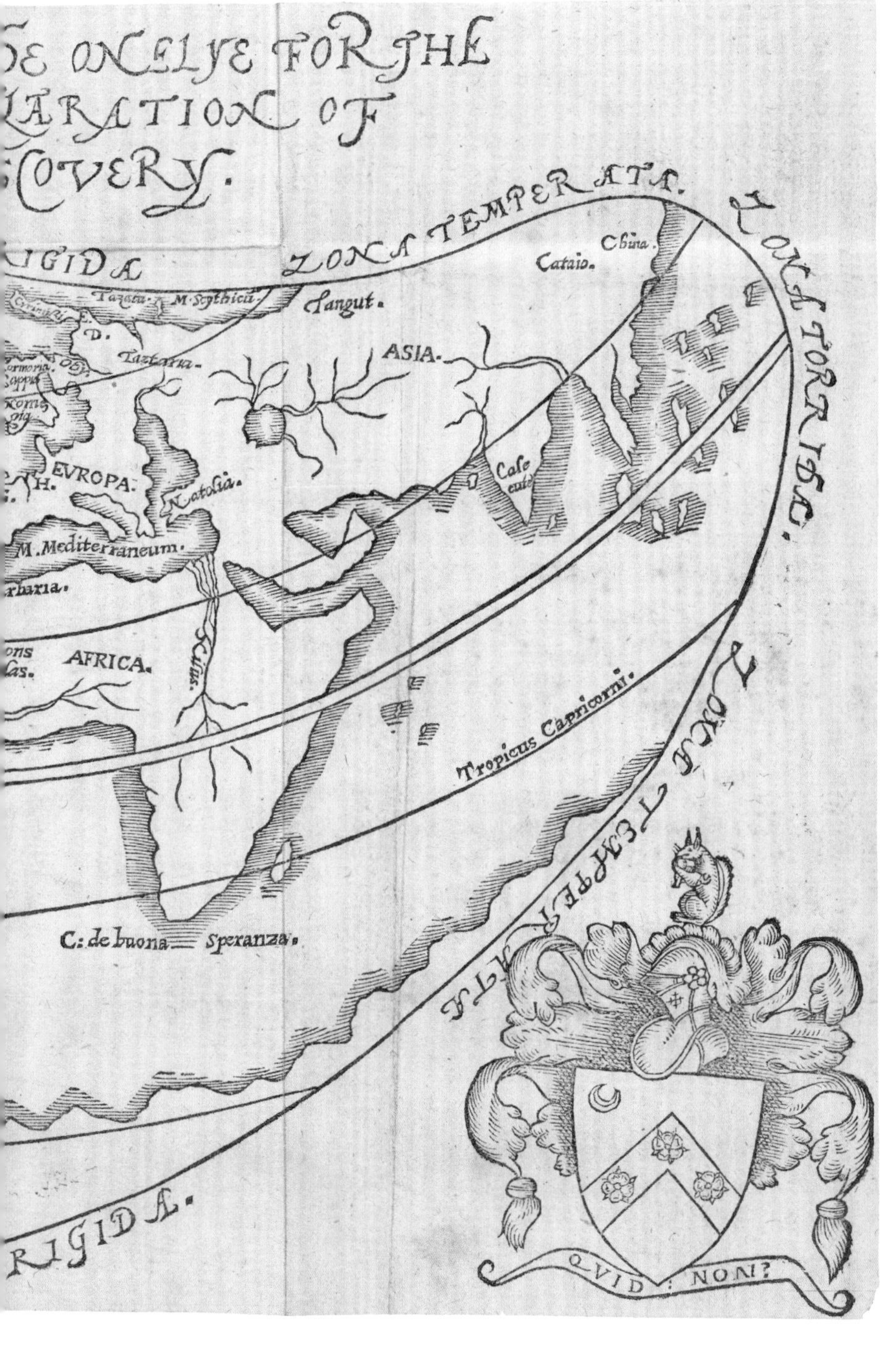

E ONELYE FOR THE
LARATION OF
SCOVERY.

RIGIDA ZONA TEMPERATA. ZONA TORRIDA.

China. Cataio. Tangut. M. Scythicu. Tartaria. ASIA. EVROPA. Natolia. Cale cute. M. Mediterraneum. rbaria. AFRICA. Nilus. Tropicus Capricorni. C: de buona Speranza.

ZONA TEMPERATA

RIGIDA.

QVID NON?

In this section of the text, the term "commodity" takes on a magical quality combining the sense of "commodity" as a valuable imported object with the early modern definition of the word as "ease" or "convenience." Gilbert declares that the Northwest Passage is "the onely way for our princes, to possesse the welth of all the East partes...of the worlde, which is infinite...which would be a great aduauncement to our Countrie, wonderfull inriching to our Prince, and unspeakeable commodities to all the inhabitants of Europe."[26] Gilbert also sees the Passage as a way to found new colonies that will provide an outlet for the "needie people of our Countrie, which now trouble the common welth," and establish a trade with "the Indians" that would help to employ "poore mens children" and "idle persons" in manufacturing "trifles."[27] Gilbert argues that the discovery of the Northwest Passage will help to transform idleness and poverty into productive labor, and he seizes the occasion of the cosmographic revolution in order to imagine yet another possible spatial breakthrough. The irony is that Gilbert's *Discourse of a Discoverie* is a discovery narrative that predicts discovery without having accomplished it, and before any labor or travel/travail is undertaken. In a dedicatory epistle addressed to his brother Sir John Gilbert, Humphrey Gilbert admits, "you might iustly haue charged mee with an vnsetled head if I had at any time taken in hand, to discouer *Utopia,* or any countrey fained by imagination: But *Cataia* [i.e., China] is none such, it is a countrey, well knowen to be described and set foorth by all moderne *Geographers....*"[28] In hindsight, we might well view Gilbert's proposal as a Utopian fantasy, backed by a raft of authorities from classical and contemporary texts, but doomed to failure. In its usage of the optative mood, Gilbert's text differs from those discovery narratives that not only point the way, but have the authority of firsthand experience when they report an actual arrival, "discovery," and return. Thus Gilbert's promotional *Discourse* can only speculate about the "welth" and "commodity" to be gained by the Northwest Passage, and its references to "Cataia" assume that a profitable trade in specific commodities will naturally ensue once the route to the East is discovered.

My second example of geographic indexing and indication is Lawrence Keymis's *A Relation of the second Voyage to Guiana* (1596), an account of Sir Walter Raleigh's 1595 voyage to seek gold in the region near the estuary of the Orinoco River. At one end of the text we find a porno-tropic dedicatory poem that employs the conventional colonizing analogy of the potential colony embodied as Virgin Land:

> *Riches* with honour, *Conquest* without bloud,
> Enough to seat the Monarchie of earth,
> Like to *Ioues* Eagle, on *Elizas* hand.
> *Guiana,* whose rich feet are mines of golde,
> Whose forehead knockes against the roofe of Starres,
> Stands on her tip-toes at faire *England* looking,
> Kissing her hand, bowing her mightie breast,
> And euery signe of all submission making…[29]

Keymis's narrative is an indication of imperial ambition, pointing the way toward Guiana, calling upon the English queen and her followers to imitate the model of Spanish conquest and empire in Peru. The text ends with a table that offers an orderly, regimented presentation of data (fig. 26), a mode of organizing and displaying information that is non-narrative and nonfigurative. The text employs poetry, storytelling, and finally this empirical catalogue, in order to communicate and justify the same call to build an empire in Guiana.

My third example is a text that was produced and transmitted, not only through the labor of travel, writing, and printing, but also by means of translation. It is a translation of Jan Huygen van Linschoten's *Voyages into ye Easte & West Indies,* which was written in 1596 and then printed in English in 1598.[30] This book is a compilation of travel texts, describing Linschoten's own journey in the East along with various other accounts of travels in other regions. His book brings together ethnographic, navigational, and commercial data, and includes page after page describing in great detail the kinds of valuable commodities that are available abroad and how they may be obtained or extracted – from cinnamon and pepper to rubies and emeralds. Sections of Linschoten's book were adopted by Hakluyt and Purchas in their travel compilations. This distribution, rendering, and reordering of information, traveling from author to book to translation to yet another book and so on, forms a process of fragmentation, recombination, and dissemination that demonstrates quite clearly how each geographic and ethnographic text is merely, as Foucault says, "a node within a network," not a stable, autonomous "work" that could stand on its own.[31]

to Guiana.

bliſh our Countrey in a ſtate flouriſhing and peaceable. O lett not then ſuch an indignitie reſt on vs, as to depraue ſo notable an enterpriſe with falſe rumors, and vaine ſuppoſitions, to ſleepe in ſo ſerious a matter, and renouncing the honour, ſtrength, wealth, and ſoueraingtie of ſo famous conqueſt, to leaue all vnto the Spaniard.

A Table of the names of the Riuers, and Townes that in this ſecond Voyage were diſcouered. Together *with the Nations, and Caſſiques or Captaines* that doe inhabite them.

	Riuers.	Nations.	Townes	Captain.	
1	*Arrowari* great.	Arwaos Pararweas. *Charibes.*			1 Theſe are enemies to the Iaos, their money is of white and greene ſtones. They ſpeak the Tiuitiuas language: ſo likewiſe doe the nation of the Arricarri, who haue greater ſtore of thoſe moneyes then any others.
2	*Iwaripoco.* very great	Mapurwanas. Iaos.			2 Here it was, as it ſemeth, that Vincent Pinzon, the Spaniard, had his Emeralds. In one of theſe two riuers, certain French mē that ſuffered ſhipwrack ſome two or three yeares ſince, do liue.
3	*Maipari. g.*	Arricarri.			3.4.5. Theſe with the other 2 ſeem to be branches of the great riuer of Amazones. When wee firſt
4	*Caipurogh. g.*	Arricurri.			
5	*Arcooa. g*	Marowannas. *Cha.*			
6	*Wiapoco. g*	Coonoracki Wacacoia. Wariſeaco. *Charib.*			
7	*Wanari.*				

Fig. 26. Lawrence Keymis, *A Relation of the second Voyage to Guiana* (London, 1596), F4r. Beinecke Rare Book and Manuscript Library, Yale University, Taylor 206

The final, appendix-like section of Linschoten's text includes "A most true and certain extract & summarie of all the Rents, Demaines, Tolles, Taxes, Impostes, Tributes, Tenthes, third-pennies, and incommings of the King of *Spaine*" (fig. 27). He presents this information to the reader, "Hoping that it will be accepted in as courteous sort, as it will be dilectable to all those that are desirous of nouelties."[32] Linschoten had once served in the Portuguese colonial system, which had given him privileged access to this information, and now, like a kind of industrial spy, he passes this economic data along to others who can make commercial use of it.

The formal organization of books like those of Gilbert, Keymis, and Linschoten both encourages and manifests the new behaviors and identities that accompanied the deterritorialized anxieties and desires of overseas expansionism. These texts indicate the way toward a more robust English participation in the global trade matrix, and in doing so they offer forms of data organization that compensate for the instability, unbelievability, and disorderliness that marked the raw information brought home by European traders and travelers. As time went on, and as the overabundance of geographic information increased further, more authors and compilers provided indexes and charts to organize that information and make it accessible to readers who were searching for particular kinds of data without wanting to read entire texts. For those who wanted to know about the value and availability of commodities in particular locations, the labor of reading was made easier by means of indexes.

What we see in all three of these travel narratives is exemplary of a broad tendency. The production of discovery narratives and travel books (with their lists, charts, and maps) comprises a double commodity fetishization: it obscures much of the labor of traveling and data collection by offering an account of faraway places, events, and people that conceals the process of information extraction and selection. We see through the eyes of the traveler, and we can trace their journey across the map, but we are only allowed rare glimpses of the labor that makes the traveler's journey possible.[33] And secondly, the book itself is a commodity fetish, an object that offers information for sale, purporting to bestow, almost magically, the possession of global reach and measurement on the book owner or reader. The travel book becomes a fetish that fetishizes: in its account of people and places, it divides and distinguishes by assigning a value to social, geographic, or economic units that become sites for the

440 A Discourse of the heights of the riuers & Hauens

The degrees of the south side of the Equinoctial lyne.

CAbo, or the point of Lopo Gonsalues vnder deg. 1
Cabo, or the point of Catharina vnder 2.
Angra da Iudia, or the hauen of the Iewe, vnder 5.
Praya de San Domingos, or the strād of S. Dominico vnder 6.
Rio or the riuer of Congo vnder. 7
A Ilha d'Ascention, or the ascention vnd. 8.
Rio or the riuer of Angola, and the Iland of Loanda vnder 9
Cabo Ledo vnder 10.
Rio, or the riuer of S. Lazaro vnder 11.
Cabo de Loubos, or ye riuer of wolues vn. 12
Monte Negro, or the black hill vnder 14
Serra Parda or the gray hill vnder 15
Angra das Aldeas, or the open hauen of the villages, & the Iland of S. Helena vnd. 16.
Manga das Areas, or the sandy sleue vn. 17.
Cabo Negro, or the blacke point vnder 18.
Os Mendoins vnder 19
A Serra de S. Lazaro or Hill S. of Lazaro vnder 20.
Praya or the straight of Ruy Pires vnd. 21.
Cabo do Padrao or the point of Colosso or Colume vnder 22.
Praia Fria, or the cold strand vnder 23.

The lyne or Tropicus Cancri.

Ponta da concepsao, or the conceptiō vn. 24
Praya das Ala-goas vnder 25.
Feiaco da Boca, or the māner of the mouth vnder 26.
Angra, or the hauen of S. Anthony vnd. 27
Angra, or hauen of S. Thomas vnder 28.
Angra or the hauē of S. Christopher vn. 29
Rio do Infante, or the Riuer of the Kinges sonne vnder 32.
Angra, or hauen of S. Helena vnder 33.
As Ilhas, or Ilād of Tristan de Cūha v. 34.
Cabo de Bona Speranza, or poynt of good hope vnder 34.$\frac{1}{2}$.

From the cape de Bona Speranza northwards, along the coast to Soffala, Mosambique and Melinde, to the Equinoctial lyne, all being on the south side of the same lyne.

CAbo das Agulhas, or the poynt of the Compas full vnder 35.
Cabo de Infante, or point of the kings sonne vnder 34.$\frac{1}{2}$.
Cabo Talhado, or the clouen point vnd. 34.
Cabo das Vaccas, or point of cowes, & Baya Fermosa, or the faire bay vnder 34.
Cabo de Arecisse, or the point of the Cliffe vnder 33.
Rio de infante or point of ye kings son v. 32.
Ponta Primeira, or the first point vnder. 32.
Terra do Natal vnder 31.
Ponta or the point of S. Lucia vnder 28.
Terra dos fumos or the lād of smok v. 27.$\frac{1}{2}$.
Rio d'Alagoa or riuer of the lake, and the Iland of Ioan de Lisboa, & vttermost south point of the Iland of S. Laurence vnd. 26.
Agoa de Boa Pas or ye riuer of peace vnd. 25
Cabo das correntes, or point of the streame vnder 24.$\frac{1}{2}$.
Rio, or riuer of Mataca or monument, & the Iland A Ilha do Mascharenhas vn. 21.$\frac{1}{2}$.
Os Baixos da Iudia, or ye Iewes sands vn. 22
Cabo, or the point of S. Sebastian vnd. 21.
Rio, or the Riuer of Quiloan or Quiloane, vnder 20.$\frac{1}{2}$.
Soffala and the Iland of Diego Rodrigues vnder 20.
Porto, or the hauen of Bango vnder 19.$\frac{1}{2}$.
Rio, or the riuer of Cuama vnder 18.$\frac{1}{4}$.
Os Baixas dos Garaiaus or sands of Seamewes vnder 18.
Rio dos bons finais, or of good tokens v. 17$\frac{3}{4}$
A Ilha, or Iland of Brandao vnder 17.
The Iland A Ilha Primeira, or the first Iland vnder 17.$\frac{1}{2}$.
A Ilha or Iland of Iohn de Noua vnd. 16.$\frac{1}{2}$.
Rio or riuer of Angoxa vnder 16.
Mosambique vnder 15.
Rio de S. Antonio vnder 14.
Rio dereito, or the straight line vnder 12.
Ilha do Comoro vnder 11.
Cabo del Gado, or thinne point vnder 10.
The towne of Quiloa vnder 9.
A Ilha de Monfia vnder 7.
Ilha de Sansibar vnder 6.
Ilha de Pemba vnder 5.
A Ilha dos tres Irmaos, or Iland of three brethren vnder 4.
A Ilha do Almirante, or the Iland of the Admirall vnder 3.$\frac{1}{2}$.
Mombassa, or riuer of Tacharigo vnder 3.
The towne and hauen of Melinde vnder 2.
The towne and hauen of Pate vnder 1.

The Equinoctial lyne.

The heigth and degrees of the Hauens, points, and riuers, of the Equinoctiall lyne, to the straights of Mecca, otherwise called the red sea, on the North side of the Equinoctiall.

The degrees on the north side.

BArra Boa, or the good hauen vnder 1.
The town and hauen of Braba vnder 2
The town & hauē of Magadoxa vnder 2.$\frac{1}{2}$.
Zarzella vnder 6.
Cabo, or poynt of Guardafu, and the Iland a Ilha de Sacotora vnder 12.

From the point of Guardafu, inwardes to the red sea, on the south coast.

MIte or Barbora vnder 11.
Zeila vnder 12.
Ilha Dalaca vnder 15.

The 3. Booke. Ilha

production and extraction of commodities. While cosmographic compendia like Sebastian Münster's *Cosmographia* continued to be printed in the seventeenth century, the proliferation of more site-specific travel accounts or "relations" altered the meaning of even those texts that attempted to survey the world.[34] The shift from divine order to empirical process had begun, and what, ultimately, is indicated by this shift is the beginning of what, today, we call globalization. In other words, the early modern era commenced a process that would culminate in our present dilemma, that of a Google world without *terra incognita,* ruled by a globalized capitalism that penetrates to every corner of the earth, destroying the very cultural diversity and difference that struck early modern voyagers with wonder.

NOTES

1 William Pietz,"The Problem of the Fetish, I," *RES: Anthropology and Aesthetics,* no. 9 (1985): 5–17 (5). On the concept of the fetish, see also his "Fetishism and Materialism: The Limits of Theory in Marx," in *Fetishism as Cultural Discourse,* ed. Emily Apter and William Pietz (Ithaca: Cornell University Press, 1993), 119–51; "The Problem of the Fetish, II," *RES: Anthropology and Aesthetics,* no. 13 (1987): 23–45; "The Problem of the Fetish, IIIa: Bosman's Guinea and the Enlightenment Theory of Fetishism," *RES: Anthropology and Aesthetics,* no. 16 (1988): 105–23; and the very useful adaptation and application of Pietz in Ann Rosalind Jones and Peter Stallybrass, "Fetishisms and Renaissances," in *Historicism, Psychoanalysis, and Early Modern Culture,* ed. Carla Mazzio and Douglas Trevor (New York: Routledge, 2000), 20–35.

2 Pietz, "Problem of the Fetish, II," 36.

3 Giovanni Battista Ramusio, *Viaggi e Navigazioni* (Venice, 1550); Theodor De Bry, *India Orientalis* (Frankfort, 1597); Richard Hakluyt, *The Principal Navigations, Voyages, Traffiqves and Discoveries of the English Nation* (London, 1599–1600); Samuel Purchas, *Haklvytvs Posthumus or Purchas His Pilgrimes* (London, 1625).

4 Pietz, "Problem of the Fetish, II," 36.

5 See James Kearney, "The Book and the Fetish: The Materiality of Prospero's Text," *Journal of Medieval and Early Modern Studies* 32 (2002): 433–68, who sees this shift in relation to the rise of Protestantism and its iconoclastic rejection of sacred objects.

6 See Karl Marx, *Capital: A Critique of Political Economy,* vol. 1 (Moscow: Progress Publishers, 1963), chap. 1.

7 On the rapid expansion of English overseas commerce during the sixteenth and seventeenth centuries, see Kenneth

Fig. 27. Jan Huygen van Linschoten, *Iohn Hvighen van Linschoten. his Discours of Voyages into ye Easte & West Indies* (London, 1598), 2P2v. Beinecke Rare Book and Manuscript Library, Yale University, Taylor 216A

R. Andrews, *Trade, Plunder and Settlement: Maritime Enterprise and the Genesis of the British Empire, 1480–1630* (Cambridge: Cambridge University Press, 1984) and Robert Brenner, *Merchants and Revolution: Commercial Change, Political Conflict, and London's Overseas Traders, 1550–1653* (Princeton: Princeton University Press, 1993).

8 Pietz, "Problem of the Fetish, I," 6.

9 On the manicule in early modern texts, see William H. Sherman, "Toward a History of the Manicule," in *Owners, Annotators and the Signs of Reading*, ed. Robin Myers, Michael Harris, and Giles Mandelbrote (Newcastle, Del.: Oak Knoll Press; London: The British Library, 2005), 19–48.

10 On early modern methods for handling information overload, see the work of Ann M. Blair: "Organizations of Knowledge," in *The Cambridge Companion to Renaissance Philosophy*, ed. James Hankins (Cambridge: Cambridge University Press, 2007), 287–303; "Reading Strategies for Coping with Information Overload, ca. 1550–1700," *Journal of the History of Ideas* 64 (2003): 11–28; "The Rise of Note-Taking in Early Modern Europe," *Intellectual History Review* 20 (2010): 303–16; "Student Manuscripts and the Textbook," in *Scholarly Knowledge: Textbooks in Early Modern Europe*, ed. Emidio Campi, Simone De Angelis, Anja-Silvia Goeing, and Anthony T. Grafton (Geneva: Droz, 2008), 39–73; and *Too Much to Know: Managing Scholarly Information before the Modern Age* (New Haven: Yale University Press, 2010).

11 John Day, William Rowley, and George Wilkins, *The Travels of the Three English Brothers*, in *Three Renaissance Travel Plays*, ed. Anthony Parr (Manchester: Manchester University Press, 1995).

12 Ibid., 54.

13 "Travail, *n.1*," OED *Online*, May 2010, Oxford University Press (accessed May 30, 2010).

14 Richmond Barbour describes the exploitation of maritime labor by the East India Company, including the need to replace mariners along the way because of high mortality rates, in "A Multinational Corporation: Foreign Labor in the London East India Company," in *A Companion to the Global Renaissance: English Literature and Culture in the Era of Expansion*, ed. Jyotsna G. Singh (Oxford: Wiley-Blackwell, 2009), 129–48.

15 For a discussion of this word, see Sarah Kelen's essay in this volume.

16 Sir Thomas Elyot, *The boke named the Gouernour* (London, 1531), 37v.

17 Frank Lestringant, *Mapping the Renaisance World: The Geographical Imagination in the Age of Discovery*, trans. David Fausett (Berkeley: University of California Press, 1994), 4.

18 Bernhard Klein, *Maps and the Writing of Space in Early Modern England and Ireland* (New York: Palgrave, 2001), 6.

19 Francis Bacon, *Novum Organum* (London, 1620).

20 Francis Bacon, *New Atlantis*, in *Three Early Modern Utopias:* Utopia, New Atlantis, *and* The Isle of Pines, ed. Susan Bruce (Oxford: Oxford University Press, 1999), 168.

21 Ibid., 177.

22 Ibid., 183.

23 Ibid.

24 Richard Hakluyt, *The Principall Navigations, Voiages and Discoveries of the English Nation* (London, 1589), 2r.

25 Ibid.

26 Sir Humphrey Gilbert, *A Discovrse of a Discouerie for a new Passage to Cataia* (London, 1576), H1r.

27 Ibid., H1v and H2r.

28 Ibid., 3P3r.

29 Lawrence Keymis, *A Relation of the second Voyage to Guiana* (London, 1596), A1v.

30 Jan Huygen van Linschoten, *His Discours of Voyages into ye Easte & West Indies* (London, 1598).

31 See Michel Foucault's discussion of the "author-function" in "*What Is an Author?*" trans. Donald F. Bouchard and Sherry Simon, in *Language, Counter-Memory, Practice,* ed. Donald F. Bouchard (Ithaca: Cornell University Press, 1977), 124–27.

32 Linschoten, 2Q2r.

33 This is more clearly the case for successful voyages. It is in cases of failed voyages, when the passengers and crew suffer deprivation together, that the reliance on the crew's labor is revealed more clearly. See, for example, David B. Quinn, ed., *The Last Voyage of Thomas Cavendish, 1591–1592* (Chicago: University of Chicago Press, 1975).

34 Sebastian Münster, *Cosmographia* (Basil, 1544). Münster's *Cosmographia* was first published at Basel in 1544 in German. It was translated into many languages and appeared in twenty-four editions over the course of the next century. It was never printed in a full English translation but did appear in 1572 as *A Briefe Collection and compendious extract of strau[n]ge and memorable thinges, gathered oute of the Cosmographye of Sebastian Munster,* a shortened version that exemplifies the tendency toward synopsis and extraction that I have discussed above.

2	11	e	2	Purification of our Ladye.	
0	19	f	3	John Claydō martyr.	1413
	8	g	4	Richard Turmine. martyr.	1413
1		A	5	Ziſca a confeſſour.	1416
3	16	b	6	Syr Iohn Ould Caſtell, Lord Cobham Martyr.	1418
3	5	c	7	Richarde Honeden martyr.	1430
3		d	8	Thomas Bageley Prieſt, martyr.	1431
1	13	e	9	Paule Craws, martyr.	1431
5	2	f	10	Thomas Rhedon. martyr.	1436
5		g	11	Raynolde Pecocke Biſ. confeſſour.	1457
6	10	A	12	Sir Roger Onley knight, martyr.	1441
5		b	13	Elenor Cobham gētlewoman confeſſor.	
6	18	c	14	Mother of the Lady Yong, martyr.	1490
6	7	d	15	Thomas Norrice martyr.	1507

"His Idoliz'd Book": Milton, Blood, and Rubrication

BIANCA F.-C. CALABRESI

"For books are not absolutely dead things..."
John Milton, *Areopagitica*

The sixth volume of Samuel Purchas's early seventeenth-century *Pilgrimage* provides the first reference to "fetish" noted in English. Describing the "Marriages, Manners, Religion, Funerals, Gouernment, and other Rites of the Guineans, collected out of a late Dutch Author," Purchas addresses the subject of Adultery, claiming that, "[i]f the husband suspects his wife, hee makes tryall of her honesty, by causing her to eate salt with diuers Fetisso ceremonies hereafter mentioned, the feare whereof makes her confesse."[1] A marginal note explains that "Fetisso is the name of their Idols, &c," thus eliding what comes to be a significant distinction in later anthropological discourse between an "idol" – the image of a divine being – and a "fetish" – an object consecrated as such.[2]

What concerns Purchas most, however, and what is most relevant for this discussion of Milton's own flirtation with fetishism, is the Guineans' ability "with their ceremonious Art" to "make them *Fetissos,* or Gods, at pleasure" (719): this ability to create idols at will Purchas associates particularly with "Funerall" rites, occasioned by and conducted in the presence of the dead body before its interment. Not until the new Fetisso is complete can the burial take place:

> Then they sprinkle the same with the bloud of the Henne, and hang a chaine or Garland of herbes about their neckes. After

> this, the women set the Hen, now sodden, in the middest of the *Fetisso's* and the *Fetissero* takes water in his mouth, which amidst his Exorcismes and Charmes he spoutes on those *Fetisso's* and taking two or three herbes from his necke, he rols the same in forme of a ball, which after certaine ceremonies he layeth downe, and so doth, till all his Herb-garland bee spent; and then makes them all into one great ball, and therewith besmeareth his face, and thus is it made a *Fetisso;* and the partie deceased is now at rest. (720)

Purchas's lengthy description makes overt the derivation of "fetisso" or "fetish" from the Latin *facticius*. As in the Old French *faitis,* Italian *fattizio,* Spanish *hechizo,* and Purchas's direct source, the Portuguese *feitiço,* "fetisso" indicates an object that is specifically handmade and manmade – "made by art, artificial, skillfully contrived."

This notion of the fetish as produced manually by human motivation (in contrast to the idol's origins in the Greek *eidolon,* "image, phantom, idea, fancy, likeness" [OED *Online*]), animates Milton's textual response to the 1649 *Eikon Basilike* of Charles I, although like Purchas Milton blurs the distinction between the two objects of worship.[3] Milton's *Eikonoklastes,* published in October 1649 as a counter to the *Eikon Basilike,* is deeply interested in the process of how to make and unmake a sacred object, in this case a book, as if it were a sacred body itself. The Guineans "haue no Leters, nor Bookes" writes Purchas (719), and their Fetisso takes no textual form. But earlier in his sixth book, in his chapter on the Library at Alexandria, Purchas discusses at great length the vivid and revivifying nature of books and the cult of somatic textuality. On the one hand, "these [books] indeed are the best mens best Images, in which their *Immortall Soules* speake Immortally, yea, Immortality to themselues and others; they *being dead, yet speaking*" (649). On the other hand, "what else is store of Bookes...without Students, but carkasses without soule? and what They without Bookes and mayntenance, but walking Shadowes and wandring Ghosts?" Without readers, books are dumb, dead flesh; without books, readers are phantasms – ghostly immaterial form; the first resembles a fetish in its mistaken manmade veneration, the second an idol – "an image, phantom, likeness" – in its transient and insubstantial effects.

Allegedly written by the imprisoned Charles I in the days leading up to his death, the *Eikon Basilike* was a notoriously fetishized text and as such an extremely successful publication. Milton himself attacks it as an "Idoliz'd Booke" and responds pointedly to a number of its man-made features that contribute to its revivifying function.[4] From the start (well before Milton's response), however, the "Kings booke" (3.339) was associated with the king's dead body, serving as a substitute for his corpse whole or in parts. First issued the day of the execution, bound and wrapped in mourning weeds, or "in a Cover coloured with His Blood," *Eikon Basilike* reached well over thirty English editions within the year, offering "a *Living Memoriall* of Princely piety, and devotion" to its readers.[5] The small text quickly became an integral part of what Elizabeth Skerpan Wheeler terms "the King Charles experience": Elizabeth Sauer writes "[t]he king's book had become one of the relics," while Thomas Corns notes "[j]ust owning it, having it, meant that in a sense you hadn't sold out" to anti-Royalist forces.[6]

In comparison, Milton's *Eikonoklastes,* his "Answer" to the *Eikon Basilike,* was by most reports a publishing failure, at least as a challenge to the *Eikon Basilike* as the vestiges of the king's body. Almost univocally, critics have argued that the *Eikonoklastes* failed to provide an adequate counter-image to the visual and verbal "Pourtraicture of his Sacred Majestie in his Solitudes and Sufferings."[7] Despite its public burning in 1660, writes Sauer, "the inefficacy of the text [*Eikonoklastes*] had already been established; it proved to be no match for *Eikon Basilike.*"[8] Kevin Sharpe writes, even more pointedly, "There was almost no visual response to these images.... If Milton's contempt for images expressed a broader reluctance to engage on these terms, it was a polemical disaster."[9]

This essay argues, however, that Milton's *Eikonoklastes* not only acknowledges the powerful visual strategies of *Eikon Basilike* but also appropriates them, at times dangerously, for its own use. As a result, the *Eikonoklastes,* despite its title, reveals a Parliamentarian response that is more iconographic and textually material than critics have acknowledged thus far and possibly more rhetorically successful than has been recognized. Substituting Word *as* Image for Word *and* Image, Milton's text seems at first to refute 1649 readings of books as bleeding bodies, only to return the reader to a more sanguine but equally sanguineous corpus by its end.

As critics have come to realize, the *Eikonoklastes* in fact takes as its target not simply the *Eikon Basilike* as a whole but a very specific embodied version of that text: the twenty-second edition printed in March 1649 by William Dugard for Francis Eglesfeld.[10] All the 1649 editions of the *Eikon Basilike* sought to establish the king as "The Martyr of the People," as he had termed himself in his execution speech, and to serve as an immediate stand-in for the king's body itself. However, Dugard's publication is remarkable in several ways. Like earlier editions, it includes the famous frontispiece engraving of a praying Charles I that critics have judged the most effective piece of visual propaganda to come out of the January 1649 spectacle. But it adds to this image an exposition in verse, a poem which begins by emphasizing the importance of the portrait but which, in its continuation, presents the *text* itself as a material instantiation of the king. Addressing the dead monarch as "Blest Soul!...now mounted up on High / Beyond our *Reach,* yet not above our *Eie,*" it directs the king, as First Reader, to find "Lo here thy *other*-Self: thus Thou canst bee / In Heav'n and Earth, without *Ubiquitie*."[11] Like the volumes in Purchas's Alexandrian library, the book allows the king immortality – the paradox of "being dead, yet speaking": indeed, both texts cite the lines from Hebrews 11.4 prominently (the *Eikon Basilike* places the phrase on the title page surrounding the royal arms; fig. 28). Faced with the prospect of outright idol worship that the portrait and its gloss offer, Dugard attempts to nullify the threat of idolatry by *embracing* it: he claims that this "*other*-Self" has achieved a godlike stature, arguing "So Divine, / Might anie *Image* bee ador'd, 't were *Thine*" (A1r–v).

The lines that follow shift the focus even more explicitly from portrait to print, moving from graphic arts as the way to revivify the corpse to metaphors of reading and writing as dominant embalming media: "They that would know thy Parts, must read *Thee:* Look / You'l find each *Line* a *Page,* each *Page* a *Book*." The poem ends,

Our *Bodley's* shelves will now bee full; No man
Will want more Books; This one's a *Vatican.*
Yet 'tis but CHARLS contracted: Since His fall,
Heav'n hath the *Volume,* Earth the *Manual.* (A1v)

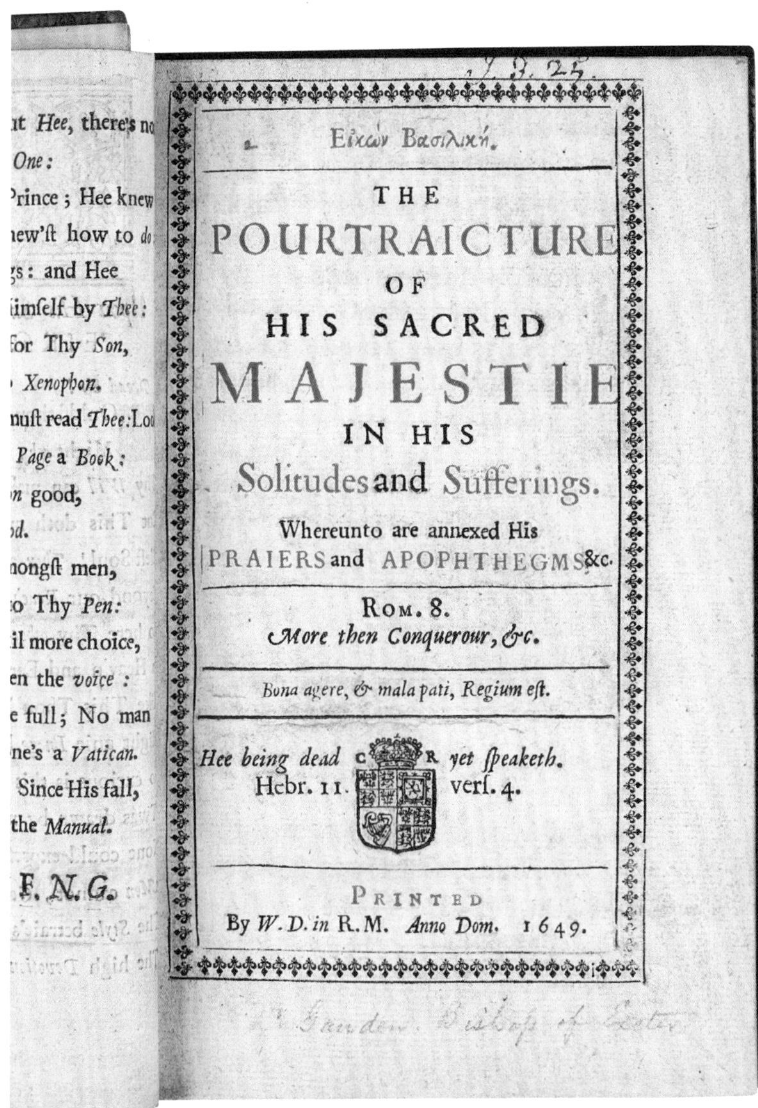

Εἰκὼν Βασιλική.

THE
POURTRAICTURE
OF
HIS SACRED
MAJESTIE
IN HIS
Solitudes and Sufferings.

Whereunto are annexed His
PRAIERS and APOPHTHEGMS &c.

ROM. 8.
More then Conquerour, &c.

Bona agere, & mala pati, Regium est.

Hee being dead C R *yet speaketh.*
Hebr. 11. vers. 4.

PRINTED
By *W. D. in* R. M. *Anno Dom.* 1649.

Fig. 28. *Eikon Basilike* (London, 1649), title page. Princeton University Library, Ex.14432.32.14

The text becomes Charles in epitomized form, a kind of binding testament, requiring its readers to make good on their part of the exchange: Charles contracted, it turns out, will demand a particular type of readerly response to this embodied text.

Like Purchas's Alexandrian library, Charles as "Vatican" will allow the dead to live, and speak again, now immortal. Here "Vatican" refers specifically to the famous galleries and library of the pope's palace, rather than the seat of power itself. Nonetheless, the effect is startling, all the more so when followed by the claim that Charles's presence on earth as a "Practick *Pattern*" should be understood as taking the form of a "*Manual*" a term specifically linked to Roman Catholic practice. At its most capacious, a "manual" in the early modern period could be said to be any "handbook or textbook, *esp* a small or compendious one;..." (OED *Online*) that could be held in the hand and could serve as a guide to behavior or action. Practically, however, the word was still associated strongly with the guides provided for priests to aid in the administration of the sacraments, including those of communion, and as such with illicit, if not illegal, texts in the period. Acts 3 and 4 of the 1549 Edwardian Statute, one hundred years earlier, commanded "That all Bookes called...Processionalles, Manuelles,...shalbe...abolished." Likewise, Act 3 of the 1605/6 Statute under James I stated that "No person...shall bring from beyond the Seas, nor shall print, sell, or buy any Popish Prymers, Ladies Psalters, Manuells, Rosaries, Popishe Catechismes."

Dugard's edition did become a manual of sorts for both readers and printers in the weeks and months following its publication. As Skerpan Wheeler writes, by the addition of a separately titled section, "the Apophthegms Theological Moral and Political derived from the Incomparable Eikon Basilike" usually bound with the source text, "Dugard's edition...provides readers with their own commonplace book for ready reference."[12] A number of other extradiagetical features that Dugard first introduces became models for inclusion in subsequent editions, most significantly the four prayers used by the king, especially the so-called "Pamela prayer" to which Milton devotes so much attention in *Eikonoklastes*. Less frequently discussed, but equally a preoccupation for Milton's text, rubrication – the use of red ink – emerges as another influential feature of Dugard's version, employed in at least three variant editions with which Dugard was involved, and then taken up by several other publishers of the "Kings booke." By rendering "Eikon Basilike" in red, Dugard transformed the by then conventional title of the work—and its description, "The POURTRAICTURE of His Sacred MAJESTIE"—into something new.

At its most basic, Dugard's use of red ink on the title page calls the reader's attention to a relatively late entry in the biggest publishing phenomenon of the year, three months and twenty-one editions after the event. But Dugard's rubrication also accords with the text's newly explicit function as a "Manual" for readers, that is as a guide to reading, particularly to the ordering and enacting of sacred rituals around a holy body. Primers, Psalters, Manuals, and Books of Common Prayer all contained "Calendars" in which "saints' days," or the festivals of the saints, were, in the sardonic words of one early commentator, "garnished with glorious titles and with red letters, promising much grace and pardon," features which the same Reformation critic attacks as having "sore deceived the unlearned multitude."[13]

As this 1530s citation suggests, the rubricated calendar created difficulties for religious hard-liners from the earliest days of England's engagement with reform. Notoriously, the writer John Foxe came under attack for the act of sanctifying associated with employing rubrication, specifically for including in his *Actes and Monumentes* a section in which he listed the names of the "Martyrs" to the Protestant cause highlighted with red ink. When charged with "thrustyng and shouldryng out the old and auncient holy sanctes aforenamed out of this Calendare, & placing other new come sanctes in their rowmes," Foxe argues for a distinction between a "Calendare…of…sanctes" and "a Table of good and godly men that suffered for the truth, to shewe the day and moneth of their sufferyng."[14] At issue, Foxe recognizes, is the power to make and unmake sacred bodies for worship: Foxe counters that this is rather Catholic malpractice: "If the Pope had not abused his arrogant iurisdiction in Canonising and deifyeng his sanctes, more thē I haue done: the yeare should not be cōbred with so many idle holy dayes, nor the Calendares with so many raskall sanctes" (693).

Thus, Foxe attacks the Catholic use of rubrication in the calendar as proof of the pope's "idolatrous makyng and worshyppyng of sanctes," but defends his own textual practice, summarizing,

> And what so euer the pope doth or hath done in his Calendare, my purpose in my Calendare was neither to deface any old sancte, or to solemnise any newe. In my booke of Actes and Monumentes, entreatyng of matters passed in the churche, these latter v. hundreth yeares, I did regulate out a Calēdare, not for any Canon to constitute sanctes, but onely for a table of them, whiche within the same tyme dyd suffer for the testimonie of the woorde, whom I did and do take to be good and Godly mē. If any haue other iudgement of them, I binde no man to my opiniō, as the Pope doth to his. (694)

Foxe recognizes that the creation of a calendar is a means "to constitute sanctes" – a way to direct not only a reader's attention in the text but more importantly to command the reader's ritual acts through an engagement *with* the text, to "binde...man to...opinion, as the Pope doth." Thus he argues for the distinction between rubrication as a directed reading and rubrication as simulated blood: the one can indicate figuratively the presence of sanctity, the other creates it. In that vein, unwittingly, the pope himself has composed the calendar of Protestant saints that his defenders attack:

> he maketh moe Martyrs & sanctes of these foresaid poore laymen, & laywomen, then euer he did of any other. For he burneth them, he hangeth them, he drowneth them, inprisoneth & famisheth them, and so maketh them truer Martyrs of Christ, then any other of his new shrined sanctes, whom he hath so dignified in his Calēdare. For the one he doth rubricate, onely with his read letters, the other hee doth rubricate with their owne bloud. (693)

At the end of this section of book 5, devoted to the attacks on the Calendar, Foxe again emphasizes a distinction between the pope's rubrication – "the greate sancte maker of Rome, who hath redded them [Protestant martyrs] much more then euer did I...with their own bloud" – and his own text which "did but onely colour them with red letters." However, Foxe contends that the application of red ink in a text depends wholly on the maker of the physical book, "which was as pleased the painter or printer" (695).[15]

In his own accounts of the specific sufferings of the faithful, as well, Foxe minimizes the authorizing and sanctifying effects of blood, particularly when blood is linked to textuality. For example, according to Foxe, Rafe Allerton preserved his examination by writing it in "his owne hand with bloud for lacke of other incke": the heading reiterates that these documents were "wrytten by hym selfe, with hys owne bloud" (2208). While blood would seem to be a sign of authenticity, the source of the blood in the account undermines any kind of transcendent sanguineous effect. When asked where he obtained the blood used to compose letters, Allerton recounts that he got it from another Protestant accused, Richard Roth, whose own letter Foxe also introduces in the text as written "with his bloud" (2215). Rothe can bleed at will, according to Allerton: his controlled bloodletting counters Roth's status as victim, all the more so when Allerton recounts that "Richard Roth, sometime his prison fellow did make his nose bleede, and thereby he got the bloud wherwith he did then write" (2213). By having sacrificial blood turn out to be the product of self-induced epistaxis, Foxe's text deflates any "glorious" associations of rubrication with martyrdom. Indeed, the sheer materiality and mundanity of the source of the blood – not from torture or execution but self-generated from the nose – suggests that such sanguineous markers are both overly literal and profoundly suspect for Foxe, whether in their origin or in their significance.[16]

MEN OF BLOOD

In Samuel Daniel's letter "To the Friendly Reader," introducing his 1585 translation of Paolo Giovio's *Discourse of rare inuentions, . . . called Imprese*, Daniel writes of color's powerful ability to express passions, emotional and moral, as well as psychological or physical states not immediately visible to the eye: "besides the figuring of things corporall and of visible forme, men haue also represented things incorporal, which they could not doe more fitly then by colours, as representing sorowe by blacke, desire to shed bloud by red, puritie by white, &c."[17] According to Daniel, his own era has raised that system of signification to its apogee: "And now sith time hath brought to perfection many notable deuises, which rude antiquitie could not discerne: Let vs consider by howe many Wayes we may discouer our secret intentions by colours and figures . . ." (A3r–v)."[18]

Like Dugard's edition of the *Eikon Basilike,* a number of Royalist works published in the days and weeks following the execution of Charles I apply the symbolic use of color on title pages or within texts. In these cases, however, there is nothing covert or "secret" in the use of red ink to highlight the cold-blooded murder of the king, or make manifest Charles's own Christological willingness to bleed for his country. The rubricated title page of *Veritas inconcussa* asserts openly the sanguineous context in which its own frontispiece coloration means to be seen, declaring "that King Charles the First, was no man of blood, but a martyr for his people" – that its red ink affirms the king's sacrificial bleeding rather than bloody royal deeds.[19]

Likewise, Henry Leslie makes use of rubrics as signs of martyrdom in his sermon preached in the Netherlands in 1649 when he speaks of a directed textual reading that helped his own understanding of Charles I's execution and its subsequent meaning:

> This is a parricide so heinous, so horrible, that it cannot be *parralelld* by all the *murthers* that ever were committed since the world began, but onely in the murther of Christ. And indeed the providence of God gave me first occasion to institute this paralell: for that day that our gracious Soveraigne was murthered, being the 30. *Jan.* a day for ever to be noted with a black coale, as his Majesty was at divine service, before he was led forth into the scaffold, the Chapter that was read unto him, was the 27. *Mat.* Gospel, which containes the *passion of Christ;* and that Chapter was read not by choise, but by the direction of the Rubrick, it being the Lesson appointed for that day, so that we could not but conceive, that the murther then to be acted, was like unto that which in the Chapter is described.[20]

Leslie's linking of "the passion of Christ" to "the murther to be acted" stems directly, he claims, from "the direction of the Rubrick," the rubricated chapter heading which indicates "the lesson appointed for that day." The rubric ("a heading of a chapter, section, or other division of a book, written or printed in red" and often, as in this case, serving as "a direction for the conduct of divine service inserted in liturgical books, and properly written or printed in red") thus not only provides a guide to understanding the text but also a key to its larger significance – "so that we could not but conceive, that the murther then to be acted, was like unto that which in the Chapter is described." But it serves as a guide to conduct in another, equally significant, way, Leslie implies. For Leslie begins his recollection with his own imagined appropriation of word as image, suggesting that the "day that our gracious Soveraigne was murthered, being the 30. *Jan.*" should be "a day for ever to be noted with a black coale." In other words, the association of the red rubric with both Christ's and Charles's passion leads Leslie himself to begin imagining a proper writing of the event that would use color as a means of signification.

A number of other Royalist texts from 1649 show similar directed readings occasioned by the inclusion of anomalous or excessive coloration. The "Elegy upon King Charles" published in the early months of 1649 follows earlier mourning devices by including a fully blackened page opposite the text: in this case matching each page of verse with its own tomblike rectangle on the verso. The text also invites the reader to reflect on the symbolism of color in relation to the execution: "what rubicundious light / Is this? that bloodyes my amazed sight? / What Reformation's this that's newly bred, / And turns my white, into so deep a Red."[21] The 1649 rubricated edition of Sophocles' *Electra* would seem to be an anomaly, until one notes that it contains two appended poems to Charles's daughter Princess Elizabeth "shewing the parallel in THE RETURN and THE RESTORATION" between the tragic Mycenean and English royal families."

In contrast, Theodore Verax, aka Clement Walker, uses rubrication in his *Anarchia Anglicana: The History of Independency* to expose the specific members of the "bloudy, cheating, tyrannicall faction" who called for and oversaw Charles's execution; here red ink functions as a mark of their involvement in that "Arbitrary bloudy Inquisition."[22] Facing Walker's account of the trial and the sentencing of the king, the text lists in red "the Names of such Persons as did actually sit as Judges upon the Tryall of His Majesty, with the Councel and Attendants of the Court" (O4r/103). Proper names appear in red ink while titles remain in black, thus distinguishing significantly between the person and the office, especially in the case of the participating peers.

Chief among those listed in red, not surprisingly, is Oliver Cromwell, whose name heads the roster. However, the text assiduously includes everyone implicated in this bloody act, including the names of all those

"Councellours assistant to this Court," and even the "Messengers, and Dorekeepers" who were present, down to "M. King Cryer" (O4r/103). Likewise, the errata sheet is rubricated: realizing, upon completion of the main body of the book, that the record is still not complete, Walker adds a Postscript explaining that "[i]n the 103 . Page in the Catalogue of those Persons who did actually sit vpon Tryall of King CHARLES the First. These Following Names are omitted, who ought to haue been inserted" (A1r), each rubricated accordingly.

The visual juxtaposition on pages 102 and 103 of the king's sentence and the "guilty" parties is strikingly effective, save for one moment of potential confusion as both "Mr. King Cryer" and "the KING" appear in red. In fact, this conflation of lowest and highest, guilty and innocent, suggests more generally the difficulty of using red ink as a system of signification, one which Walker particularly invites with his talk of, on the one hand, "Cromwell and Ireton and their Canniball Counsell of Officers" and, on the other, Charles as "Civil Martyr" (O4v/104).

In effect, rubrication collapses the differences that Walker hopes to establish between the two sides through his methodical rendering of trials and events, for example the identification of the Independents with the bloodiest deeds of the civil war and their specific comeuppance, the "Bloudy flux" (2L3r/261) that befalls Cromwell's troops. Ultimately, in Walker's text, red ink comes to stand as much for the war and its general aftermath, the "Oceans of English Blood spilt" (2H4r/239) and, more generally, "that stage of Bloud" (P1r/105) on which History takes place, as it does for the individual participants. England itself has been bloodied, as the title page emphasizes: not only "PARLIAMENT" but also "Anarchia Anglicana" appear in red. The largest word on the page, the rubricated "HISTORY," is only secondarily qualified by "INDEPENDENCY": below, the author's pseudonym, "THEODORVS VERAX," and the citation from Psalm 88 equally appear in red, as messenger and message of how to interpret these bloody events.

In short, there seems to be more than enough blood to go around: the identification of the "*Virum sanginum & dolosum*" with "K. *Oliver*" rather than K. Charles (2Br/185 and 2Dv/202 and *passim*) seems at best optimistic given the overdetermined associations already in play of Charles as the preeminent Man of Blood. Indeed, as the rubricated "THEODORVS

VERAX," Walker seems to wish to prefigure himself as a similarly bloodied martyr: he writes to "The Reader" that he

> ...thought it as easie & more honourable to die waking and working for my God, my King, and Country, than to die sleeping, and have my throat cut in a Lethargy. I know these Schismaticks thirst as much after bloud, as they hnnger [*sic*] after money: and I am sure to be involved in the common and inevitable ruine of my Country, why should I not rather perish for it now, them [*sic*] with it hereafter?... it is a mixt cause, and he that dies for it is a Martyr... (B1v–B2r/2–3)

For the most part, Royalists best exploit the association of red ink with blood when they use it to further their cause of rehabilitating and sanctifying Charles rather than to attack the opposing side. John Cleveland's *Monumentum Regale,* appearing in a 1649 collection of elegies, epitaphs, and memorials for Charles, far more successfully deploys red ink in its text than does Walker's, using it as a sign of both murdered and sacrificial bodies that specifically alternates with mourning black to elegize the King and intimate his potential rebirth. Subtitled "A TOMBE, Erected for that incomparable and Glorious Monarch, / *CHARLES* THE FIRST," the work strategically plays with the possibilities of simultaneous readings enabled by dual color printing.[23] The opening pages build the case for the bloody crime against Charles, word by word and stanza by stanza, by repeating and amplifying, while clarifying, the setting of the king's name in sanguineous ink: CHARLES... / CHARLES our Dread-Soveraign!... / CHARLES our Dread-Sveraign's murther'd!... / CHARLES our Dread-Soveraign's murther'd at His Gate!" (A2v/2). Charles's body, and indeed his self, are so fully identified as bleeding that the "catch word" of A2v – CHARLES – (set to indicate the page to follow in the signature), is likewise printed in red (fig. 29). While the text warns from the start that we should "forbear, forbear ! lest / Mortals prize / His name too dearly; and Idolatrize. / His Name ! Our Losse !," such selective rubrication, here as well as in the examples above, invites the readers, rather, to do just that, instructing them to "Idolatrize...Our Losse," if not his name.

Cleveland's poem not only uses red ink cumulatively to generate increasing outrage for the shedding of royal blood made ever more

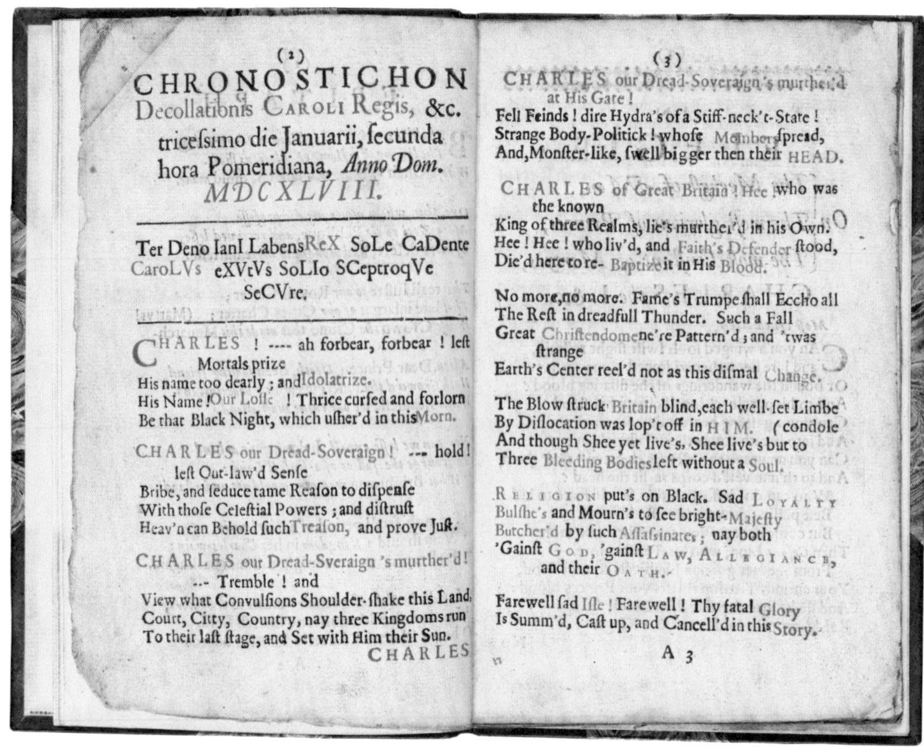

(2)

CHRONOSTICHON
Decollationis CAROLI Regis, &c.
tricesſimo die Januarii, ſecunda
hora Pomeridiana, *Anno Dom.*
MDCXLVIII.

Ter Deno IanI LabensReX SoLe CaDente
CaroLVs eXVtVs SoLIo SCeptroqVe
SeCVre.

CHARLES ! ---- ah forbear, forbear ! leſt
Mortals prize
His name too dearly ; andIdolatrize.
His Name !Our Loſſe ! Thrice curſed and forlorn
Be that Black Night, which uſher'd in thisMorn.

CHARLES our Dread-Soveraign ! --- hold !
leſt Out-law'd Senſe
Bribe, and ſeduce tame Reaſon to diſpenſe
With thoſe Celeſtial Powers ; and diſtruſt
Heav'n can Behold ſuchTreaſon, and prove Juſt.

CHARLES our Dread-Sveraign 's murther'd !
--- Tremble ! and
View what Convulſions Shoulder-ſhake this Land,
Court, Citty, Country, nay three Kingdoms run
To their laſt ſtage, and Set with Him their Sun.
CHARLES

(3)

CHARLES our Dread-Soveraign 's murther'd
at His Gate !
Fell Feinds ! dire Hydra's of a Stiff-neck't-State !
Strange Body-Politick ! whoſe Members ſpread,
And, Monſter-like, ſwell bigger then their HEAD.

CHARLES of Great Britain ! Hee ! who was
the known
King of three Realms, lie's murther'd in his Own.
Hee ! Hee ! who liv'd, and Faith's Defender ſtood,
Die'd here to re- Baptize it in His Blood.

No more, no more. Fame's Trumpe ſhall Eccho all
The Reſt in dreadfull Thunder. Such a Fall
Great Chriſtendome ne're Pattern'd ; and 'twas
ſtrange
Earth's Center reel'd not as this diſmal Change.

The Blow ſtruck Britain blind, each well-ſet Limbe
By Diſlocation was lop't off in HIM. (condole
And though Shee yet live's, Shee live's but to
Three Bleeding Bodies left without a Soul.

RELIGION put's on Black. Sad LOYALTY
Bulſhe's and Mourn's to ſee bright-Majeſty
Butcher'd by ſuch Aſſaſsinates ; nay both
'Gainſt GOD, 'gainſt LAW, ALLEGIANCE,
and their OATH.

Farewell ſad Iſle ! Farewell ! Thy fatal Glory
Is Summ'd, Caſt up, and Cancell'd in this Story.

A 3

Fig. 29. John Cleveland, *Monumentum Regale or A Tombe* (London, 1649), A2v–A3r. Beinecke Rare Book and Manuscript Library, Yale University, Ij C599 649M

manifest on the page. It also strategically uses the alternation of red and black ink, sometimes within the same compound verb, to suggest the possibility of transformation – indeed redemption – enabled by this bleeding idol. The first stanza ends with an invocation of that "Thrice cursed and forlorn / . . . Black Night, which usher'd in this Morn": "Black Night" giving way to an ominous Red Dawn whose meaning will be revealed as the "Chronostichon Decollationis CAROLI Regis, &c." unfolds. The second stanza likewise contrasts bloody "Treason" with Heaven's Justice, whose balance is now questionable if still marked in truth's colors of black and white. Nonetheless, in one important case, Cleveland's text cannily suggests the *ameliorative* effects of such transformations, that is, when speaking of Charles's sacrifice alone:

CHARLES of Great Britain ! Hee ! who was
the known
King of three Realms, lie's murther'd in his Own.
Hee ! Hee ! who liv'd, and Faith's Defender stood,
Die'd here to re-Baptize it in His Blood. (A3r/3)

Here murder, death, even the title of king, remain unrubricated, as if to mark a shift in signification from treacherous to redemptive sanguinity. The text truncates the anticipated line ending – "lie's murther'd in his Own [Blood]" – to repay that expectation with the resurrected Blood of the final line. The transformation from mortal life, to death, to eternal life is shrewdly depicted as a shift from black to red, from "liv'd" of the third line to "Die'd here," via the intervention of "Faith's Defender," understood first as Charles but also anagogically as Christ. That movement, from death to resurrection, is epitomized again in the final line by the single word "re-Baptize": where the secondary nature of Charles's sacrifice – "re" – becomes transformed into Christological power – "re-Baptize it in His Blood" – and the referent, "His," no longer clearly distinguishes between Divine and Mortal King as their blood and powers of salvation become one.

"FALSE COLOURS . . . WASHED OFF"

It is within this horizon of reception, both the heightened associations for rubrication in 1649 and an earlier tradition of "Imprese" associated with "Justs, Maskes, or other solemne festiuall sportinges,"[24] that Dugard's edition of *Eikon Basilike* and Milton's *Answer* appear. Notoriously, Milton's attack on *Eikon Basilike* focuses on what he calls the text's "quaint emblems and devices begged from the old pageantry of some Twelfth-Night's entertainment," which he argues "will do but ill to make a saint or a martyr" (3.343). Commentary on this passage concentrates almost exclusively on the reference to the masque as a critique of Charles's theatricality and deceit. But the passage in full equally suggests Milton's interest in how the making of a material book can "Martyr [Charles] and Saint him to befoole the people" (3.343).

Milton first attacks "those who took upon them to adorn the setting out of this Booke" (3.343), in other words the printers and publishers who, as Foxe remarked a century before, are primarily responsible for the visual dimensions of the text, specifically the choice of color for the title page. But he includes as culpable the Royalist followers whom he also implicates for their textual misuse and gullibility: "if the People resolve to take him [the king] Sainted at the rate of such a Canonizing, I shall suspect their Calendar more than the *Gregorian*" (3.343). This reference to the Calendar and to its papist implications casts the attacks on "quaint Emblems and devices" in more visual terms, allowing readers to recognize *Eikon Basilike* as "the common grounds of tyranny and popery, drest up...in a new Protestant guise, and trimly garnish'd over" (3.339) and casting his critique as part of a long history of Protestant attacks on the garish coloration of suspect papist texts and the setting up and "canonizing" of idols for adoration. Indeed, Milton attacks the book precisely for its attempt to do what belongs only to divine creation – as "the boldest of all Forgery" (3.564) and a "counterfeit [of] the hand of God" (3.564). By emphasizing the work of the hand in this critique, Milton sharpens his accusation that "sure it was the hand of Godd that let them [Royalist readers] fall & be tak'n in such a foolish Trapp...if for nothing els, to throw contempt and disgrace in the sight of all Men upon this, his Idoliz'd Booke, and the whole rosarie of his prayers" (3.364). Through such references, *Eikonoklastes* reminds the reader of the *Eikon Basilike*'s dubious status as a manual, associated with other ostensibly papist rituals of the hand, like the telling of the rosary. Elsewhere, *Eikonoklastes* accuses the "Kings booke" directly of being a manual, "model'd into the form of a private Psalter. which they who so much admire either for the matter or the manner, may as well admire the Arch-Bishops late Breviary, and many other as good *Manuels*, and *Handmaids of Devotion*..." (3.360). The reference to "good *Manuels*" suggests that *Eikonoklastes* attacks Dugard's self-proclaimed "Manual" specifically, seeing it as a particularly egregious form of the book's "Psalmistry" (3.360; another Miltonic pun on false handiwork). For, in its attention to the *Eikon Basilike* as "a Writt'n and publish'd prayer" (3.432/74), the *Eikonoklastes* shows an express concern with the role of rubrication in the inscribing of martyrdom. The text decries, for example, the *Eikon Basilike*'s "pious flourishes and colours" (3.552) which when "examin'd thoroughly, are like the Apples of *Asphaltis*, appearing goodly to the sudden eye, but looke well upon them, or at least but touch them, and they turne into Cinders" (3.552). Here a false piety marked in red turns to sooty black, not, as in Cleveland's poem or Leslie's sermon, as a sign of grief, but rather as the ephemeral marks of mortal ash.

Eikonoklastes accuses Charles and his followers of creating "a fals copy" (3.564) in contrast to "God, [who] hath writ'n his impartial Sentence in Characters legible to all Christ'ndome" (3.368). It is not simply the text but Charles himself who falls subject to the accusations of creating false objects of veneration associated with false coloring: "Hee who writes himself *Martyr* by his own inscription, is like an ill Painter, who, by writing on the shapeless Picture, which he hath drawn, is fain to tell passengers what shape it is; which els no man could imagin" (3.575). Just as the pope claims the spurious ability to rubricate, yet unwittingly does so authentically through bloodshed rather than by textual production, so too Charles sheds blood "whether of Subjects or of Rebels with an indifferent eye, *as exhausted out of his own veines;* without distinguishing as hee outght, which was good blood and which corrupt; the not letting out wherof endangers the whole body" (3.485). Charles's bloodshed fails to work as a signifying system, then, because it fails to perform the most basic functions of rubrication – "to distinguish . . . which was good blood and which corrupt." Indeed, he comes close to writing in blood himself: "by dipping voluntarily his fingers end . . . in the blood of *Strafford* . . . he thinks to scape that Sea of innocent blood wherein his own guilt inevitably hath plung'd him all over" (3.376). The *Eikonoklastes* thus provides an alternate reading of the rubrication of Majesty, a false social phlebotomy that ostentatiously displays healthy blood as if diseased: "we may well perceive to what easie satisfactions and purgations he had inur'd his secret conscience, who thinks, by such weak policies and ostentations as these, to gaine beliefe and absolution from understanding Men" (3.376).

But if *Eikonoklastes* is so hostile not just to the text but to its rubrication of "ostentations such as these," why then does its own title page use red ink as one of its visual strategies? For, while Dugard's rubrication was influential, the majority of editions of the *Eikon Basilike* circulated solely in black and white: given those dominant variants, it might well have seemed sufficient to attack the book's contents and form verbally and not visually, as Thomas and others claim the Parliamentarians were forced to do by their professed iconoclasm. In fact, other printed responses by Parliamentarians eschew rubrication not to avoid an iconographic engagement but to counter explicitly in visual form red ink's deceptive associations. The *Eikon Alethine* [the True Image] "Published to undeceive the World" a few months before *Eikonoklastes,* claims to be *The Povrtraitvre of Truths most sacred Majesty truly suffering, though not solely. Wherein the false colours are washed off, wherewith the Painter-steiner had bedawbed Truth, the late King and the Parliament, in his counterfeit Pieces entituled* Eikon Basilike" (London: Printed by Thomas Paine, 1649). The title makes clear that the text seeks to counter the "Kings booke" not only through its inclusion of a satirical version of the famous portrait but also by its coloration, returning Truth to its true colors, "blacke and white," as Protestant polemic had long maintained.[25] Given these alternatives, why then does Milton's *Eikonoklastes* take on the very aspect that the text seems to find so troubling about its precedent? To answer, one needs to look explicitly at the title page to see how and where red ink appears in comparison with its source.

"THE TITLE TO THIS BOOK...THAT IS TO SAY, THE KINGS IMAGE"

Unlike its fellow Parliamentarian text the *Eikon Alethine,* the *Eikonoklastes* offers an "Answer" that includes rather than erases color. Rubrication forms a dominant part of the text's self-conscious response to Dugard's book and to its visual influence. If Dugard's title page emphasizes the martyrological associations of red ink, Milton's title page initially eschews blood for an alternative textual authority, changing the size and focus of the rubricated lines in order to redirect the reader's attention to a seemingly less problematic tradition of rubricated word as image.

Given that the *Eikon Basilike* has long been best known by its Greek title, the king's Greek words appear surprisingly small compared with the rest of its title page. Rather, "THE POURTRAICTURE OF HIS SACRED MAJESTIE" dominates, linked by color with the "Solitudes and Sufferings" and the "PRAIERS and APOPHTHEGMS" that become the rubricated models for readers' own devotional practice. These pairings require considerable care and attention in printing, necessitating not simply a second run, with blanks placed in the black printing to leave space for the rubricated lines, but a double setting or resetting of the particular lines to allow for the alternation of red and black in each case.

Milton's title page shows an equal care, although for a different effect. Here too, rubricated words are paired around the fulcrum of a black

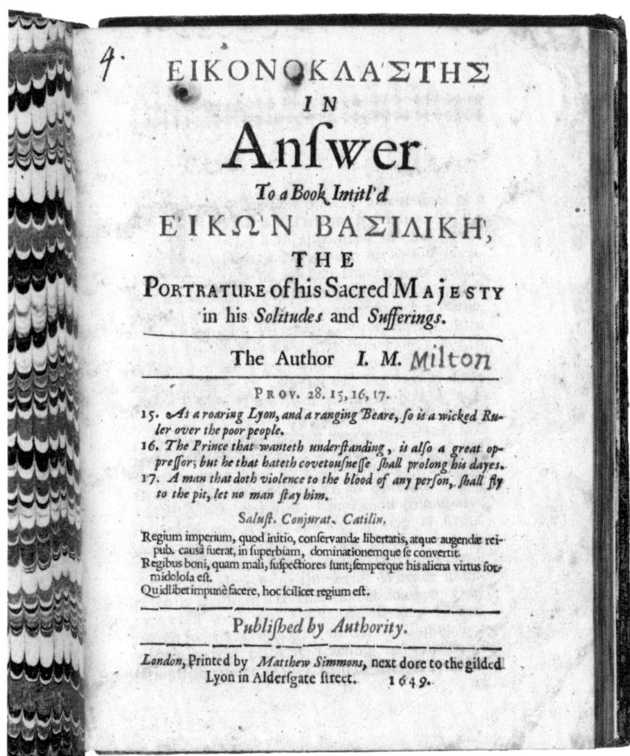

ΕΙΚΟΝΟΚΛΑ'ΣΤΗΣ
IN
Anſwer
To a Book Intitl'd
Ε'ΙΚΩ'Ν ΒΑΣΙΛΙΚΗ',
THE
PORTRATURE of his Sacred MAJESTY
in his *Solitudes* and *Sufferings.*

The Author I. M. Milton

PROV. 28. 15, 16, 17.
15. *As a roaring Lyon, and a ranging Beare, ſo is a wicked Ruler over the poor people.*
16. *The Prince that wanteth underſtanding, is alſo a great oppreſſor; but he that hateth covetouſneſſe ſhall prolong his dayes.*
17. *A man that doth violence to the blood of any perſon, ſhall fly to the pit, let no man ſtay him.*

Saluſt. Conjurat. Catilin.
Regium imperium, quod initio, conſervandæ libertatis, atque augendæ reipub. cauſa fuerat, in ſuperbiam, dominationemque ſe convertit.
Regibus boni, quam mali, ſuſpectiores ſunt; ſemperque his aliena virtus formidoloſa eſt.
Quidlibet impunè facere, hoc ſcilicet regium eſt.

Publiſhed by Authority.

London, Printed by *Matthew Simmons,* next dore to the gilded Lyon in Alderſgate ſtreet. 1649.

Fig. 30. John Milton, *Eikonoklastes in Answer to a Book Intitl'd Eikon Basilike* (London, 1649), title page. Beinecke Rare Book and Manuscript Library, Yale University, Ij M642 C641 3

center (fig. 30). In this case, however, the Greek title EIKON BASILIKE has been enlarged to match the exact size and face of EIKONOKLASTES. Each flanks the dominant "Answer" placed in black in the title page's top half, where it visually towers over the newly darkened "PORTRATURE of his Sacred MAJESTY in his *Solitudes* and *Sufferings*" below. Now set in smaller type and monochrome ink, the king's portrait and majesty – the "gaudy name of Majesty" (3.338) as *Eikonoklastes* calls it – has literally been blackened and reduced, as have the magnitude and significance of the king's "*Solitudes* and *Sufferings.*"

This restructured title page thus accords with the best-known citation from the *Eikonoklastes,* which suggests Milton's particular attention to titles in this text. Directly following his criticism of the *Eikon Basilike* as a so-called "Calendar," Milton writes

> In one thing I must commend his open'ness who gave the Title to this Book,. . . , that is to say, The Kings Image;. . . For this reason

> the Answer also is intitl'd *Iconoclastes,* the famous Surname of many Greek Emperors, who in thir zeal to the command of God, after long tradition of Idolatry in the Church, tooke courage and broke all superstitious Images to peeces. (3.343)

To title is a powerful act in Milton's lexicon, closely correlated with one of the earliest meanings of *titulus* – the term for the charge hung on the crucifixion, "from Latin *titulus,* the inscription on the Cross" (*OED Online*).[26] Milton faults Charles not only for titling himself as Martyr (see above) but also for disregarding this original more legitimate title: "The rest of his discours quite forgets the Title...imitating therein, not our Saviour, but his Grand-mother *Mary* Queen of Scots" (3.597).

As an "Answer *To a Book Intitl'd,*" *Eikonoklastes* focuses attention on the role the title plays in *creating* an image as well as in destroying it, asking the reader to consider the title as a visual phenomenon that contributes to the fabrication of an "Idoliz'd Booke." To break that "superstitious Image...to peeces," then, is to deconstruct it in some sense, substituting alternative titles and traditions of print authority for the king's own. Thus, *Eikonoklastes*'s title page replaces one rubricated title with others. Whereas textual authority is typically not rubricated on the front of *Eikon Basilike* (e.g., Rom. 8, Hebr. 11) the rubricated words printed on *Eikonoklastes*'s title page are, with one exception ("*Published by Authority*"), *all* titles: "PROV. 28. 15, 16, 17."; "*Salust. Conjurat. Catilin.*"; as well as the two Greek titles of the competing texts.[27] *Eikonoklastes* reclaims the rubric through and for a tradition of textual authority removed from the realm of the Psalter or Calendar where it had troubled Reformation readers, redirecting the reader to an equally powerful tradition of printing Greek editions of and commentaries on the Bible in red.

By the 1640s, editions of the New Testament printed in England regularly use rubrication to set off the Greek text on the title page and for textual explication on the four books of the Gospel, in particular. For example, biblical works containing Greek titles and text produced by the Cambridge University printer Roger Daniels in the decades up to 1649 frequently rubricate the Greek content. Daniels employs red ink for the 1640 publication of Daniel Heinsius's *Sacrarum exercitationum Ad Novum Testamentum Libri XX* as well as for Eustachius's *Summa Philosophiae Quadripartita* a few years earlier. In this Daniels follows a convention of rubrication that began in 1570s England to denote texts linked to the Septuagint. The 1577 publication of the Church of England's *Leitourgia Brettanike egoun Biblos* rubricates parts of its Greek title on the front page but also words like "Sacrementorum," "Rituum," and "Caeremoniam," a coloration which emphasizes their authority as sources for contemporary ritual. Thomas Vautrollier's 1587 edition of Henri Estienne's New Testament—H KAINH DIAOHKH—places the Greek title in red letters and uses rubrication to denote alternate anagogical and allegorical readings of the text throughout, directing the reader to consider literal and figurative text in tandem or to proceed through the work scanning just the red or the black, privileging for the moment one reading over another.

By evoking this alternate tradition of printing in red, through its own Greek rubrication, the title page of *Eikonoklastes* attempts to rewrite the visual associations of red ink as royal blood emphasized in the prior months of 1649, counting on its readers' familiarity with the Christological association of titulus and the humanist tradition of published authority that it legitimizes. Indeed, this greater authority is emphasized in the only instance of rubrication the *Eikonoklastes* employs that is not a title itself. Where Dugard's title page sets "PRINTED" in the face and color of textual appropriation, Milton's title page substitutes "*Published by Authority*": the difference lies precisely in the question of who or what hands are legitimized to create a rubricated text.[28] Like Foxe's preface, Milton's title page attempts to separate justifiable rubrication "with red letters" from unacceptable rubrication "in blood," a form of writing in red that Milton links explicitly with Royalists when he castigates Archbishop Laud, who, during the "common-Prayer-Book Warrs" (3.479), "with his Sword went about to score a bloody *Rubric* on thir [the Scots'] backs"(3.488–89). Charles becomes Laud's textual counterpart, like the Whore of Babylon with her mysterious letters in Revelation 17.5, "dipt from head to foot and staind over with the blood of thousands that were his faithfull subjects...covering the ignominious and horrid purple-robe of innocent blood that sate so close about him, with the glorious purple of Royaltie and Supreme Rule" (3.595).[29]

But does Milton's *Eikonoklastes* ultimately succeed in rewriting the associations for rubrication with its title page? Clement Walker's *Anarchia Anglicana* has already revealed the pitfalls of using a broad system of coloration to indicate value and culpability. And Daniel has suggested that secret intentions might lurk in the emblematic use of color, immaterial passions and desires "to shed blood" not easily expressed in another form. So what of Milton's red ink?

> But the people,..., prone ofttimes not to a religious onely, but to a civil kind of Idolatry in Idolizing thir Kings; though never more mistaken in the object of thir worship;...now...are ready to fall flatt and give adoration to the Image and memory of this Man, who hath offer'd at more cunning fetches to undermine our Liberties and putt Tyranny into an Art, then any Brittish King before him. (3.343–44)

Even as Milton repudiates "a civil kind of Idolatry," attributing it to the "cunning fetches" of the late king, his text seeks to persuade using the same visual techniques, ostensibly counting on the reader of 1649 to be able to distinguish rubrication when it appears as scholarly, not sanguineous, intertextuality. Yet, blood often threatens to reappear at the site of vengeance, as Milton himself notes in his criticism of the king, who, like the tyrant Ahab, was destined to bleed where he caused "the blood of Naboth" to be shed. Speaking of Charles, Milton writes in the *Eikonoklastes*,

> Neither is it slightly to be pass'd over, that in the very place where blood was first drawn in this cause, as the beginning of all that follow'd, there was his own blood shed by the Executioner. According to that sentence of Divine Justice, *In the place where Dogs lick'd the blood of Naboth, shall Dogs lick thy blood eev'n thine*. (3.393)

Accordingly, Milton's text, as it reaches its end, grows increasingly bloody, and blood-thirsty, claiming

> And by that most ancient and universal Law, *whosoever sheddeth mans blood, by man shall his blood be shed;* we find heer no exception. If a king therefore doe this, to a King, and that by men also, the same shall be don. This is in the Law of *Moses*, which came next, several times is repeated, and in one place remarkably, *Numb. 35. Ye shall take no satisfaction for the life of*

> *a murderer, but he shall surely be put to death: the Land cannot be cleansed of the blood that is shedd therein,* but by the blood of him that shed it. (3.586)

If, in his last hours, the king's "discours quite forgets the Title," by contrast, Milton's text never does. As God has "testifi'd by all propitious, & evident signes" historically, *Eikonoklastes* seeks to demonstrate, textually, that the execution "was no *mockery of Justice,* but a most gratefull and well-pleasing Sacrifice" (3.356). At such moments, *Eikonoklastes* itself seems to come closest to acknowledging Thomas Corns's claim that "[t]he most violent element of Milton's tract is its title," asking, on behalf of its own rubrication, "...what satisfaction could be giv'n for so much blood, but Justice upon him that spilt it?"[30]

NOTES

1 Samuel Purchas, *Purchas his Pilgrimage or Relations of The World and the Religions Observed in All Ages and Places Discovered, From the Creation Unto the Present...* (London, 1626), 719.

2 On the early modern fetish see, in particular, William Pietz , The Problem of the Fetish, I," *RES: Anthropology and Aesthetics,* no. 9 (1985): 5–17; William Pietz, "The Problem of the Fetish, II: The Origin of the Fetish," *RES: Anthropology and Aesthetics,* no. 13 (1987): 23–45; Peter Stallybrass and Ann Rosalind Jones, "Fetishizing the Glove in Renaissance Europe," *Critical Inquiry* 28 (2001): 114–32; Peter Stallybrass, "The Value of Culture and the Disavowal of Things," *Early Modern Culture: An Electronic Seminar,* no. 1 (2000), http://emc.eserver.org/1-1/issue1.html; and Crystal Bartolovich, "Response," *Early Modern Culture: An Electronic Seminar,* no. 1 (2000), http://emc.eserver.org/1-1/issue1.html.

3 See *OED Online* entry for "fetish": "A *fetish* (in sense 1b) differs from an *idol* in that it is worshipped in its own character, not as the image, symbol, or occasional residence of a deity"; and Pietz, "The Problem of the Fetish, 1."

4 John Milton, *Eikonoklastes* (London, 1649), in John Milton, *Complete Prose Works of John Milton,* vol. 3, *1648–1649,* ed. Merritt Y. Hughes (New Haven: Yale University Press, 1962), 3.364.

5 Abraham Wright, *Parnissus Biceps. Or several choice pieces of poetry* (London, 1656), cited in Elizabeth Sauer, *"Paper-contestations" and Textual Communities in England, 1640–1675* (Toronto: University of Toronto Press, 2005), 72. *The Princely Pellican. Royall Resolves....Extracted from His Majesties Divine Meditations* (n.p., 1649), cited in ibid., 74.

6 Elizabeth Skerpan Wheeler, "*Eikon Basilike* and the Rhetoric of Self-Representation," in *The Royal Image: Representations of Charles I,* ed. Thomas N. Corns (Cambridge: Cambridge University Press, 1999), 122; Sauer, *"Paper-contestations,"* 72; Thomas N. Corns, *John Milton: The Prose Works* (New York: Twayne Publishers, 1998), 83.

7 John Gauden and Charles I, *Eikon Basilike. The Pourtraicture of His Sacred Majestie in His Solitudes and Sufferings…* (London: W[illiam] D[ugard] for Francis Eglesfield, 1649), title page.

8 Sauer, *"Paper-contestations,"* 76.

9 Kevin Sharpe, "'An Image Doting Rabble': The Failure of Republican Culture in Seventeenth-Century England," in *Refiguring Revolutions: Aesthetics and Politics from the English Revolution to the Romantic Revolution,* ed. Kevin Sharpe and Steven N. Zwicker (Berkeley: University of California Press, 1998), 35. See also Steven N. Zwicker, *Lines of Authority: Politics and English Literary Culture, 1649–1689* (Ithaca: Cornell University Press, 1996), 37: "it [the *Eikonoklastes*] was no match for the *Eikon Basilike*."

10 See n. 7 above. William Dugard was well known to Milton, serving as the Council of State's Latin Printer during Milton's tenure as Secretary for Foreign Tongues. See Joad Raymond, "Milton," in *The Cambridge History of the Book In Britain*, vol. 4, *1557–1695,* ed. John Barnard and D.F. McKenzie, with the assistance of Maureen Bell (Cambridge: Cambridge University Press, 2002), 381–82.

11 *Eikon Basilike,* A1r–v.

12 Skerpan Wheeler, "*Eikon Basilike,*" 133.

13 William Marshall, *A Prymer in Englyshe, with certeyn prayers & godly meditations* (London, 1534), preface, cited in Eamon Duffy, *The Stripping of the Altars: Traditional Religion in England c. 1400–c. 1580* (New Haven: Yale University Press, 1992), 382.

14 John Foxe, *Actes and Monumentes of the church* (London, 1570), 692.

15 On Foxe's use of rubrication and his self-defense, see John N. King, *Foxe's* Book of Martyrs *and Early Modern Print Culture* (Cambridge: Cambridge University Press, 2006), 252–53, 257, 261: "The use of red lettering designates the importance of readings, rather than a degree of sanctity" (257). See also King (268) where he cites Andrew Lacey, *The Cult of King Charles the Martyr* (Woodbridge: Boydell Press, 2003), 52, that "Charles I read the *Book of Martyrs* during his imprisonment." Skerpan Wheeler argues that in its construction the *Eikon Basilike* in fact "mirrors the great work of Protestant martyrology" (130).

16 A similar antiheroism colors Bardolph's account of how Falstaff staged the bloodletting meant to prove his valor in the highway robbery scene of *1 Henry IV:* interestingly, the Royalist side attempts to use just such associations with nosebleeds to discredit Cromwell during the months leading up to and following Charles's execution.

17 Samuel Daniell [*sic*], *The Worthy tract of Paulus Iouius, contayning a Discourse of rare inuentions, both Militarie and Amorous called Imprese. Whereunto is added a Preface contayning the Arte of composing them, with many other notable deuises* (London: for Simon Waterson, 1585), A3r.

18 As Daniel suggests, color plays a prominent role in revealing hidden meaning—or "secret intentions"—in early combinations of word and image. However, he cautions: "colours alone, are now seldom vsed but of Mourners, or such like" (ibid). Moreover, Daniel associates such signification by "colour alone" with aristocratic ephemera, with the need for an uncomplicated and rapid reading: "*Liurees* of onely colours, and also with colours and figures are wont to serue in effect, but for the shewe of one day, either at Justs, Maskes, or other solemne festiuall sportinges."

19 Fabian Philipps, *Veritas inconcussa or a most certain truth asserted, that King Charles the First, was no man of blood, but a martyr for his people* (London: Richard Hodgkinson, 1649).

20 Henry Leslie, *The Martyrdome of King Charles, or, His Conformity with Christ in his Sufferings* (The Hague, and re-printed at London, 1649), B2v. See also Zwicker, *Lines of Authority*, 41.

21 John Quarles, "Elegy upon King Charles," in *Regale Lectum Miseriae: Or a Kingly Bed of Miserie* (n.p., 1649), D4r/46.

22 Clement Walker, *Anarchia Anglicana: Or, The History of Independency. The Second Part. Being A Continuation of Relations and Observations Historicall and Politique upon this present Parliament, Begun Anno 16 Caroli Primi*, Theodorvs Verax [Clement Walker] (n.p., 1649), O4v/104. See Sabrina Alcorn Baron, "Red Ink and Black Letter: Reading Early Modern Authority," in *The Reader Revealed*, ed. Sabrina Alcorn Baron, Elizabeth Walsh, and Susan Scola (Washington, D.C.: Folger Shakespeare Library, 2001), 23 and 101.

23 John Cleveland, *Monumentum Regale or A Tombe, Erected for that incomparable and Glorious Monarch, Charles the First…* (n.p., 1649), title page.

24 Daniell, *Worthy tract*, A4v.

25 Thomas Dekker, *The Whore of Babylon* (London: Nathanial Butter, 1607), H1v.

26 For example, the Wyclyffe Bible's translation of Mark 15:26 has this description of the inscription on the cross: "And the title of his cause was writun, Jhesus of Nazareth, kyng of Jewis."

27 As do many copies of the 1649 *Eikonoklastes*, the Beinecke example reproduced here contains a handwritten attribution to "Milton"; in this particular case, interestingly, the unknown annotator has attempted to match the coloration as well as the typeface of the printed title page. On Milton's rhetorical use of title-page epigrams, see Joad Raymond, "Milton," 379–80.

28 Unlike Milton's *Articles of Peace* (May 1649), by its inclusion of Milton's initials, the title page of *Eikonoklastes* implies his role in the construction of the pamphlet. See Corns, *John Milton: The Prose Works*, 76 and 81–82.

29 For parallels with earlier Anti-papist discourse that presents red ink as at times murderous, at times salutary, blood, see Bianca F.-C. Calabresi, "'Red Incke': Reading the Bleeding on the Early Modern Page," in *Printing and Parenting in Early Modern England*, ed. Douglas A. Brooks (Aldershot: Ashgate, 2005). Like Dekker, Milton mistrusts a deceitful "excremental whiteness," claiming Charles "washes over with a court-fucus the worst and foulest of his actions…." (*Eikonoklastes* [1649]: preface to 2d ed., B2v).

30 Thomas N. Corns, *Uncloistered Virtue: English Political Literature, 1640–1660* (Oxford: Oxford University Press, 1992), 208. Milton, *Eikonoklastes*, 3.596.

Magister David Carnegius.

Anagramma

Grandis JESV dux mea gratia

Dum dego in terris et specto tandem gaudia cæli,
Me ducat semper tua gratia grandis JESV.

Excute torporem qui cæli quæris honorem
Non dabitur segni cœlestis gloria regni.

Scrutemur patefacta. Discamus necessaria. Faciamus mandata. Laetantes præsenti gratia et futura gloria.	Bucholcerus parte. 1. ad finem.	In quibus Scriptura nihil certi de moribus populi Dei et instituta majorum Lege habenda sunt.

Carne, est quasi Sol in nube, mel in cera, lumen in testa, corvus in Lucerna. Berna

Master David Carnegye

Anagrams

Dear JESV tym and grace

Sinne dayly against the Lord
Dear JESV tym and grace
Grant to thy servant to repent
And then enjoy thy face.

Sit meus introitus felix, meus exitus unum
Perpetuo curæ sit, maneatque Deo.

The age off my Children who ar yet alyve

My sone Master David Carnegie was borne upon Wednesday the 23. day off November 163
and was baptized upon Sunday nixt the 27. day of November
My daughter Mary was borne upon Sunday the 20 day off March 1636. and was
baptized upon Munday nixt the 21. of March
My sone James was borne upon Saturnday the 6. day off April 1639. and was baptized upon Tuesday nixt the 9. day off April
My Sone Robert was borne upon Saturnday the 24. day off October 1646. and
was baptized upon Fridday nixt the 30 day off October.
My daughter Agnes was borne upon Wednesday the 4. day off August 1652
and was baptized upon Thursday the 5. day off August.
Deo duce

My wyf Euna Gardyne & I wa maryed at the kirk of Guthrie on
[illegible]

GLOSSING THE TEXT AND THE SELF

The old and obscure words of Chaucer, explaned.

ed, abashed, dāted.
d, arose, recouered.
yd, breake off.
bertie.
m below.
leth.
ered.
epe place, a promi-
anging hill.
; on.
de.
te.
iued.
ed.
le.
ne.
age.
npred.
rie.
oashed.
waked.
, coate armour.
se.
ult.
e, stirre.
dines.
rust.
.
carreth.
ended.
nitted.
t full of pleights.

aledgement, release.
all a bone, made request.
algates, notwithstanding.
algates, euer.
alestake, a maypole, or alebush.
aldrian, (*vide annot.*)
als, aswell.
als, also.
alswa, also.
algate, altogither.
algates, for all that.
algates, euen now.
alcalt, Nightshade.
almagist, a worke of Astronomie, written by *Ptolomie.*
alixer, Quintessence of golde.
alures, walkes.
allaunds, grayhounds.
ally, kinne.
Amadriades, Nymphes that die and liue with the trees.
Amalgaminge, (*mixtura ex hydrargyro cum metallis.*)
amenused, diminished.
ametised, quenched.
anney, annoy.
anoy, forethink.
annueler, seculer.
any gate, occasion.
apparell, prepare.
appall, decay.
appeteth, desireth.

arite, arest, or sta
argolle, clay.
arsenecke, ratsb
arten, constrain
arke, compasse
ascaunces, as w as though.
askaunce, if per
askaunce, aside
askes, ashes, (c
ashate, buying
asure, blew.
aswith, forthw
assiced, sure, fir
assoyle, answer
assoylen, decla
asseth, assent.
assise, order.
astert, passed.
astert, let passe.
asterlagour, A
attaint, tried.
attaint, found
atamed, set on
atterly, extreme
attenes, at one
at erst, in earne
atcheked, chok
attoure, towar
attoure, attire f
athamant, ada
athroted, cloie

New Poet, Old Words: Glossing the Shepheardes Calender

SARAH A. KELEN

Notoriously, Spenser "writ no language." As everyone knows, Spenser affected a pseudo-Chaucerian diction to invoke the cultural authority of his poetic predecessor as well as of the national past.[1] Such retrospection may seem curious, given that Spenser wrote from within an early modern literary culture now recognized as much more influential in the later history of English letters than that of the Middle Ages. Spenser's embrace of archaic English is, in fact, part of a greater sixteenth-century tension between old and new language and literary culture. Developmental narratives of linguistic and literary history do not fully account for the extent to which past forms of the language were still present as written texts. Linguistically, Middle English had indeed been supplanted by Early Modern English by 1579; however, Spenser's anachronistic usages undermine the commonsense notion of unidirectional linguistic change.[2]

The anonymous poet of the *Shepheardes Calender* (who signs himself Immeritô) preserves an outmoded poetic diction. The poem's glossator, E.K., concedes that this is a counterintuitive, if justifiable, compositional choice: "of the wordes to speake, I graunt they be something hard, and of most men vnused, yet both English, and also vsed of most excellent Authors and most famous Poetes."[3] Indeed, E.K. introduces the possibility that Immeritô's anachronistic language is merely accidental, the unintentional result of his diligent reading of his poetic predecessors: "hauing the sound of those auncient Poetes still ringing in his eares, he mought needes in singing hit out some of theyr tunes" (2r).[4] E.K. quickly reverses this implausible explanation, however, establishing the pseudo-medieval diction of the *Shepheardes Calender* as a virtue, and even as a generous act of linguistic restoration:

> In my opinion it is one special prayse, of many whych are dew to this Poete, that he hath laboured to restore, as to theyr rightfull heritage such good and naturall English words, as haue ben long time out of vse & almost cleare disherited. (2v)

English, E.K. continues, has been erroneously considered too "bare & barrein" for literary composition, which has led some to "[patch] vp the holes with peces & rags of other languages, borrowing here of the french, there of the Italian, euery where of the Latine," making English "a gallimaufray or hodgepodge of al other speches" (2v).

The early modern vocabulary did include a number of newly borrowed words, but it was hardly recently that English had become such a "gallimaufray or hodgepodge" of other tongues. E.K.'s disparagement of contemporary borrowings conveniently ignores the fact that English had been absorbing words from Latin and French, if not Italian, for centuries; Chaucer's poetic diction was already French as much as Anglo-Saxon. Ironically, as the noun duplication in the phrase implies, E.K. is himself guilty of using borrowed words where a native term would do. The word "gallimaufray" derives from the French *galimafrée*, itself of obscure origin. E.K. had no particular need to use this foreign term; he pairs it with a perfectly reasonable Anglo-Saxon alternative, "hodgepodge." Both gallimaufray and hodgepodge describe a heterogeneous combination, a usage transferred from each word's primary denotation: a stew or other dish made from odds and ends.[5] The *OED* entry for each word includes the other word as a synonym: a gallimaufray is glossed as a hodgepodge, and a hodgepodge is glossed as a gallimaufray. E.K.'s use of the foreign term gallimaufray therefore adds little (beyond irony) to his description of English as a hodgepodge.

E.K. praises Immeritô's incorporation of archaic diction rather than "borrowing here of the french, there of the Italian, [and] euery where of the Latine," but conveniently ignores the extent to which the *Shepheardes Calender* is a multilingual text. Of the shepherds' eighteen emblems appearing at the end of the eclogues, one is in French, two are in English, two are in Greek, six are in Italian, and seven are in Latin. This seems a remarkably polyglot community of shepherds.[6] The emblems, although short, are visually significant on their pages; their italic type is

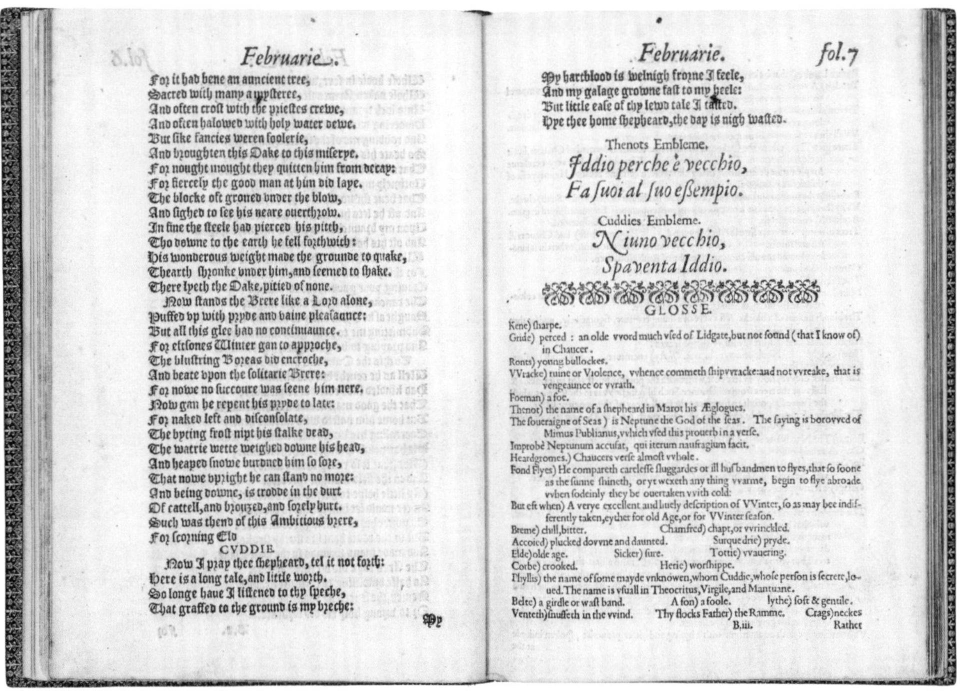

Februarie.

For it had bene an auncient tree,
Sacred with many a mysteree,
And often crost with the priestes crewe,
And often halowed with holy water dewe.
But like fancies weren foolerie,
And broughten this Oake to this miserye.
For nought mought they quitten him from decay:
For fiercely the good man at him did laye.
The blocke oft groned vnder the blow,
And sighed to see his neare ouerthrow.
In fine the steele had pierced his pitth,
Tho downe to the earth he fell forthwith:
His wonderous weight made the grounde to quake,
Thearth shronke vnder him, and seemed to shake.
There lyeth the Oake, pitied of none.
Now stands the Brere like a Lord alone,
Puffed vp with pryde and vaine pleasaunce:
But all this glee had no continuaunce.
For eftsones Winter gan to approche,
The blustring Boreas did encroche,
And beate vpon the solitarie Brere:
For nowe no succoure was seene him nere.
Now gan he repent his pryde to late:
For naked left and disconsolate,
The byting frost nipt his stalke dead,
The watrie wette weighed downe his head,
And heaped snowe burdned him so sore,
That nowe vpright he can stand no more:
And being downe, is trodde in the durt
Of cattell, and brouzed, and sorely hurt.
Such was thend of this Ambitious brere,
For scorning Eld

CVDDIE.

Now I pray thee shepheard, tel it not forth:
Here is a long tale, and little worth.
So longe haue I listened to thy speche,
That graffed to the ground is my breche:

My

Februarie. fol. 7

My hartblood is welnigh frorne I feele,
And my galage growne fast to my heele:
But little ease of thy lewd tale I tasted.
Hye thee home shepheard, the day is nigh wasted.

Thenots Embleme.

Iddio perche è vecchio,
Fa suoi al suo essempio.

Cuddies Embleme.

Niuno vecchio,
Spaventa Iddio.

GLOSSE.

Kene) sharpe.
Gride) perced: an olde vvord much vsed of Lidgate, but not found (that I know of) in Chaucer.
Ronts) young bullockes.
VVracke) ruine or Violence, vvhence commeth shipvvracke: and not vvreake, that is vengeaunce or vvrath.
Foeman) a foe.
Thenot) the name of a shepheard in Marot his Æglogues.
The soueraigne of Seas) is Neptune the God of the seas. The saying is borovved of Mimus Publianus, vvhich vsed this prouerb in a verse.
Improbè Neptunum accusat, qui iterum naufragium facit.
Heardgromes.) Chaucers verse almost vvhole.
Fond Flyes) He compareth carelesse sluggardes or ill husbandmen to flyes, that so soone as the sunne shineth, or yt wexeth any thing vvarme, begin to flye abroade vvhen sodeinly they be ouertaken vvith cold:
But eft when) A verye excellent and liuely description of VVinter, so as may bee indifferently taken, eyther for old Age, or for VVinter season.
Breme) chill, bitter. Chamfred) chapt, or vvrinckled.
Accoied) plucked dovvne and daunted. Surquedrie) pryde.
Elde) olde age. Sicker) sure. Tottie) vvauering.
Corbe) crooked. Herie) worshippe.
Phyllis) the name of some mayde vnknowen, whom Cuddie, whose person is secrete, loued. The name is vsuall in Theocritus, Virgile, and Mantuane.
Belte) a girdle or wast band. A fon) a foole. lythe) soft & gentile.
Venteth) snuffeth in the vvind. Thy flocks Father) the Ramme. Crags) neckes

B.iii. Rather

Fig. 31. Edmund Spenser, *The Shepheardes Calender* (London, 1579), B2v–B3r. Folger Shakespeare Library, STC 23089

significantly larger than either the blackletter of the verse that precedes them or the roman type of the Glosse that follows (fig. 31). The emblems are typographically marked through both typeface and type size, calling attention to their linguistic otherness. E.K. praises the poet of the *Shepheardes Calender* for embracing the English literary tradition, yet foreign elements appear throughout the volume. Moreover, significant elements of Immeritô's verse, from its vocabulary to the eclogue genre itself, are nonnative. E.K. may be correct to deny that English is "bare & barrein," but he also overstates the extent to which the *Shepheardes Calender* "hit[s]" the "tunes" of its English predecessors.

In his praise of Immeritô's linguistic nationalism, E.K. uses a legal metaphor: Immeritô "restore[s], as to theyr rightfull heritage such good and naturall English words, as haue ben long time out of vse & almost cleare disherited" (2v); in this image, the English language is both heir and estate. The obsolete words are restored to their heritage (entering back into the holdings of the language) rather than being "disherited" (removed from the line of succession). The shifting metaphor may attest to E.K.'s uncertainty whether Immeritô's pseudo-medieval language is outdated or still current. E.K. concludes his chastisement of the reader who decries Immeritô's unfamiliar, anachronistic vocabulary by deploring those who:

> of their owne country and natural speach, which together with their Nources milk they sucked, they haue so base regard and bastard iudgement, that they will not onely themselues not labor to garnish & beautifie it, but also repine, that of other it shold be embellished. (2v)

By casting the "good and naturall English words" (2r) that Immeritô revives in the *Shepheardes Calender* as an embellishment and beautification of contemporary poetic language, E.K. in some sense concedes the claims of his opponents: "that we speak no English" (2v). Despite the repetitions of the word "naturall" and of natural imagery (like the nursing infant absorbing the mother tongue), E.K. implicitly presents Immeritô's medieval English diction as unnatural, an embellishment of the language, to "garnish & beautifie" it, not contemporary English.

E.K.'s shifting descriptions of the status of Immeritô's archaisms are emblematic of a larger instability in the valuations E.K. gives to the old and the new, two terms that echo throughout his commentary on the poem. In the February eclogue, Cuddie and Thenot debate the relative merits of young and old men. The eclogue concludes with their contrasting emblems:

> Thenots Embleme.
> *Iddio perche e vecchio,*
> *Fa suoi al suo eſsempio.*
>
> Cuddies Embleme.
> *Niuno vecchio,*
> *Spaventa Iddio.*

Thenot's emblem can be translated: God, because he is old, makes what is his according to his own example. E.K. notes that "the blessing of age is not giuen to all, but vnto those, whome God will so blesse" (7v). Cuddie's emblem (no one old fears God) is directed against old men who have come to feel invincible; E.K. compares them to Aesop's fable of an Ape who becomes so familiar with a Lion that he foolishly loses his natural fear of the predator.

E.K. cites Erasmus's more favorable construction of the proverb "Nemo Senex metuit Iouem" as meaning "[old men] be furre from superstition and Idolatrous regard of false Gods, as is Iupiter," but concludes: "[Erasmus's] greate learning notwithstanding, it is to plaine, to be gainsayd, that olde men are muche more enclined to such fond fooleries, then younger heades" (8r). As E.K. notes, Erasmus is a "good old father," and therefore "more fatherly and fauourablye... construe[s] it in his Adages for his own behoofe" (8r). E.K. sides with Cuddie in the debate between youth and age, even though he disparages Cuddie's emblem as "byting and bitter" (7v). E.K. could be seen as the advocate for the young, beginning with the Dedicatory Epistle's header, commending "the new Poete" to Harvey. However, immediately following that address, E.K. introduces an allusion to poetic history: "Vncovthe vnkiste, Sayde the olde famous Poete Chaucer."[7] Chaucer's fame as the "olde" poet is explicitly contrasted with the anonymity of "this our new Poete," who is "vnknown to most me[n]" (¶2r). Old men may be categorically foolish, as the gloss to the February emblems implies, but the old poet is a source of gnomic wisdom.

Ironically, although E.K.'s reference comes from Pandarus's advice that Troilus reveal his love to Criseyde, E.K. uses the expression in order to praise the work of a poet who (rather like E.K.) refuses to reveal his name, signing his own prefatory verse "To His Booke" only as "Immeritô" (undeserving, unworthy).[8] E.K.'s praise of the "vncovthe" poet belies the modesty topos of a poet who calls himself unworthy, even as he puts into circulation a work that flaunts its own learnedness and virtuosity in a range of poetic forms.[9] Pandarus uses the aphorism hortatively, to urge that Troilus approach Criseyde; E.K. uses it descriptively, opining that:

> I dout not, so soone as his name shall come into the knowledg of men, and his worthines be sounded in the tromp of fame, but that he shall be not onely kiste, but also beloued of all, embraced of the most, and wondred at of the best. (¶2r)

E.K. implies that the new poet's future reputation will reiterate that of the old poet. For two centuries, Chaucer's readers from "his scholler Lidgate" to "our Colin clout in his Aeglogue" have praised Chaucer, "for his excellencie and wonderfull skil in making." In E.K.'s vision, Immeritô will gain similar renown for his "wittinesse in deuising, his pithinesse in vttering, . . . and generally in al seemely simplycitie of handeling his matter, and framing his words" (¶2r). E.K. constructs the anonymous poet of the *Shepheardes Calender* as becoming a latter-day Chaucer (a new old poet), once his name is revealed. Lynn Staley Johnson notes that E.K.'s description of the unknown poetry by the anonymous poet of the *Shepheardes Calender* echoes Chaucer's own descriptions of his poetic oeuvre, another way in which Spenser is cast as reproducing Chaucer.[10] If the new poet, Immeritô, is a poetic successor of the old poet, Chaucer, the opposition between poetic tradition and poetic innovation, and between the literary past and present, is not as clear-cut as the Epistle's epithets for the two poets would suggest.

The Epistle's ambivalence on the question of Immeritô's novelty is in keeping with a more consistent Tudor ambivalence about novelty itself. The derogatory adjective "newfangle" was in use by the fifteenth century, and the stereotype that the English were infatuated with novelty was already commonplace in the fourteenth; however, in the sixteenth century, the significance of that newfangledness became more explicitly political. Given the repeated sixteenth-century reversals of religion, and the concomitant royal anxiety about sedition, a populace fickle by nature risked treason, not simply absurd fashions.[11] On the other hand, early modern European exploration of the Western Hemisphere imbued "the new" with a sense of both jingoism and adventure.[12] Meanwhile, the medieval respect for the authority of the old or traditional, while still in place, was beginning to wane; the first OED citation for definition 1c of the adjective "old," the use of the term disparagingly rather than descriptively, is from 1508.

The sixteenth-century cultural ambivalence about the relative values of old and new demonstrated by the Epistle differentiates the *Shepheardes Calender* from its antecedent, the *Kalender of Sheepehards,* which E.K. cites as the model for the work's title, "for that [the eclogues] be proportioned to the state of the xij monethes" (¶3r).[13] The *Kalender of Sheepehards* repeatedly invokes the antiquity of its medical, zodiacal, religious, and meteorological lore in order to authorize its validity. In the *Kalender*'s Prologue, one shepherd asks how many stars are within each sign of the zodiac; when his fellow answers, the questioner then asks for proof. The star-counting shepherd rebukes his inquisitive colleague by reminding him of the inherent authority of traditional lore: "it ought to suffice for

Sheepheards and touching this matter to beleeue simply, without to enquire ouer much, of that their predicessours Sheepheards haue sayd afore."[14]

The premise that old knowledge is validated by its very age is reiterated by the publishing tradition of the *Kalender of Sheepehards*. The work went through many editions, but the editorial history was extremely conservative: the *Kalender of Sheepehards* was printed with nearly identical content and format through editions spanning a century and a half.[15] Given the wide circulation of the book, readers would likely have seen multiple editions and would thus be aware of this conservatism. Purchasers of the *Kalender* were not looking for the latest scientific or religious teachings; they were seeking to reiterate what, to some extent, they already knew from past editions of this very work. E.K. highlights the ideological and epistemological difference between the two works' respective valuations of innovation by remarking that Immeritô "apply[ed] an olde name to a new worke" (¶3r).

E.K. presents his own contribution to this "new worke" in terms of old knowledge and old language; "I added a certain Glosse or scholion for thexposition of old wordes & harder phrases," E.K. says (¶3r). The Epistle extols Immeritô's recuperation of medieval English diction and disparages the practice of borrowing English vocabulary from Romance languages, but E.K.'s gloss of the harder phrases in the *Shepheardes Calender* looks beyond the native tradition to highlight Immeritô's extensive invocations of classical texts and of Greek or Latin etymology. Indeed, the word "scholion" itself calls attention to Immeritô's classicizing. The late Latin *scholium* was already in use in the sixteenth century to designate an exegetical note upon a text, but Immeritô may have been the first to incorporate into English the Greek word "scholion" from which that Latin word was derived.[16] The heavily annotated format of the *Shepheardes Calender* makes it "a fictional imitation of a humanist edition of classical texts."[17] Thus, even as E.K. praises Immeritô for his adherence to a native vocabulary, he also highlights the poet's participation in an older, more authoritative, non-English literary tradition.

The Shepheardes Calender demonstrates E.K.'s and Immeritô's simultaneous valuation of the native and the classical literary in the presence of the "scholion" and also in its typography. The eclogues that make up the *Calender* are printed in black letter, "the sole instance [of black letter publication] in the Spenser canon," as Richard A. McCabe notes.[18] The black letter type visually situates the eclogues within the native English literary tradition. Unlike Immeritô's pastoral verse, E.K.'s framing texts (the Epistle to the Reader, the Glosse following every month's eclogue) are printed in a Roman face, the typographical hallmark of humanism. In terms of the volume's visual rhetoric, if E.K. is a pseudo-humanist glossator, Immeritô is (implicitly) a pseudo-classical author, and, indeed, E.K.'s glossarial apparatus for the *Shepheardes Calender* presents the poetry (and its poet) as deeply learned, despite the rustic fiction of the pastoral genre.

In the gloss for January, for example, E.K. glosses Colin's reference to Hobbinol and "his clownish gyfts" by explaining that Immeritô here "imitateth Virgils verse, Rusticus es Corydon, nec munera curat Alexis" (A2v). Even a reader who was well-versed in Virgil and actively looking for parallels between the English and Latin eclogues might be excused for missing the allusion that E.K. sees here. The quotation E.K. has in mind is from Virgil's second eclogue, "Alexis." Corydon, in an apostrophe to an absent Alexis, promises him gifts of fruits, herbs, and flowers, then, in the line quoted by E.K., chastises himself for proposing such a homely gift: "You are a rustic fool, Corydon! Alexis does not care for gifts" (line 56). E.K.'s explanation has Immeritô transferring the speech from the mouth of the pining, lower-status lover to that of the higher-status beloved who scorns the lover's pastoral gifts. Immeritô's rewriting of Virgil also transfers the epithet clownish/*rusticus* from the speaker ("rustic fool") to the gifts ("clownish gyfts"). Given the obliqueness of this alleged imitation, a reader might well need E.K. to flag the reference.

Several of E.K.'s glosses are of this type, claiming echoes of classical antecedents in quite short phrases that may parallel antique texts without, in fact, being allusions. In April, for example, Hobbinol sings Colin's lay of Queen Elisa, in which the song's persona exhorts the nymphs: "Of fayre *Elisa* be your siluer song" (C4v). By way of explaing the expression "your siluer song," E.K. observes that it "seemeth to imitate the lyke in Hesiodus [ἀ]ργύρέον μέλος" (D2v). Perhaps the conjunction of "silver" and "song" is an imitation of Hesiod, as E.K. claims, but there is no reason to grant this supposed allusion much weight. The association of silver with melodious sounds is cited by the OED as early as 1526.[19] Whether or not a reader is convinced that Immeritô means to invoke Hesiod in this phrase, the gloss links the *Shepheardes Calender*'s "new poet" to a poet even older than the "olde famous Poete," Chaucer. The Greek and Latin allusions that E.K. claims for Immeritô may, at times, be spurious.

Nevertheless, they reinforce the idea that Immeritô, the unnamed author of the eclogues, synthesizes two poetic lineages, classical and English, in the *Shepheardes Calender*.

The detailed apparatus, or "scholion," that E.K. appends to the *Shepheardes Calender* may authorize the poem, granting it the status of a pseudo-classic, a text fit for scholars. By extension, E.K.'s glosses posit the authority of the poet who, far from being the unworthy one that he names himself, is the "new [English] Poete": the Chaucer of his age, soon to gain the appreciation of his reading public. The glosses also stake out an authoritative role for E.K. as a learned glossator and intimate friend of Immeritô. Less obviously, but significantly, the apparatus positions the reader, too, as a source of authority, not least insofar as E.K. presumes a reader sufficiently conversant in the classical tradition to read phrases printed in the Greek alphabet. The value of the poem and of the poet is granted through the audience's expertise and admiration. In the Epistle to Harvey, E.K. prophesies that the New Poet shall be "beloued of all, embraced of the most, and wondred at of the best" (2r). The hierarchy of connoisseurship invites the reader to inhabit the position of "the best" audience, those who wonder at the New Poet. The difficulties of the *Shepheardes Calender* thus stand as a test of the reader's merit and proof of Immeritô's.

The extensive (perhaps exaggerated) glossing of the *Shepheardes Calender* pulls in two directions, however. The presence of the apparatus simultaneously invites the reader into the role of the erudite scholar and puts the reader in the position of the schoolboy who needs E.K.'s explication. E.K.'s overglossing, claiming classical allusions where there may be none, authorizes the poem by making it seem more learned, but the glosses also allow the reader a sense of superiority insofar as E.K. sometimes egregiously overexplains Spenser's basic poetics. In the eclogue for September, for example, Diggon Davie laments his attempts to make his fortune in another land where shepherds "bene false, and full of couetise, / And casten to compasse many wrong emprise" (I4v). E.K.'s gloss explains that Spenser uses "emprise" "for enterprise. Per syncopen" (K3r). These four words are the complete gloss for the word "emprise," and while the reader may stumble over the variant form, it is unlikely that any late-sixteenth-century reader would need the elementary rhetorical explanation that the shorter form was a syncope. Furthermore, the form "emprise" was in current circulation as a variant of "enterprise" and may not have required any annotation, whether poetic or semantic.[20]

This pedantic explication of a fairly obvious rhetorical device is not unique. At the end of the March eclogue, Willye observes that "the Welkin thicks apace, / And stouping *Phebus* steepes his face" (C2r), which, as E.K. notes in his gloss, "Is a Periphrasis of the sunne setting" (C3r). A reader with any formal education would likely recognize this periphrasis without the rhetorical glosses. As Steinberg points out about E.K.'s translation of the January eclogue's phrase "neighbor towne," as analogous to the Latin use of *vicina* as an adjective, "This is an explanation which any sixteenth-century schoolboy could have given."[21] The "hard phrases" that E.K. claims to explicate are often anything but.

Turning to E.K.'s glossing of the Middle English terminology, one can see an identical phenomenon: glosses to phrases that needed none. The second gloss for the January eclogue is to a single word: "vnnethes) scarcely." The gloss is correct but unnecessary. The OED cites "uneath" (or unneathes) as "In very common use from *c* 1300 to *c* 1600."[22] This first translation of a Middle English word establishes a pattern for E.K.'s glosses of Immeritô's Middle English vocabulary: they frequently translate words that most readers would be likely to understand on their own. In the third line of the February eclogue, Cuddie refers to "The kene cold" (A3v). E.K.'s gloss for February begins with the simple translation: "Kene) sharpe" (B3r). The literal sense of the adjective "keen" meaning "sharp" (as a weapon) is attested in the OED from the thirteenth through the nineteenth century; moreover, the transferred use of the adjective to refer to sharpness beyond that of weapons, for example sharpness of scent or taste, is attested in the OED from the fourteenth century to the nineteenth century, as is the more particular transferred use of the adjective "keen" to refer to an intensity of weather.[23] Indeed, all of these uses of "keen" to mean "sharp" are still current today, four and a half centuries after E.K. translated the word for readers of the *Shepheardes Calender*.

E.K.'s overly generous glossing of Middle English forms and vocabulary already comprehensible to an early modern reader belies the fact that elsewhere his apparatus presumes his reader's familiarity with medieval verse, particularly that of Chaucer. Chaucer's name appears frequently in the glosses, often as an explanatory function, manifesting (and thus justifying) particular usages. In the March gloss, for example, E.K. seeks to explain Thomalin's use of the word "spell" in discussing a ewe who has injured herself: "Mought her necke bene ioynted attones, / She shoulde haue neede no more spell" (C1r). The gloss begins by defining a spell as "a kinde of verse or charme," a definition appropriate to Thomalin's point that breaking her neck, rather than a leg, would have put the ewe beyond help. From there, E.K. offers an etymology of the "spell" morpheme in the word "gospel": "as it were Gods spell or worde. And so sayth Chaucer, Listeneth Lordings to my spell" (C2v).

It is not clear what specific verse E.K. alludes to; this is not an exact citation of any line in Chaucer's works. The Host makes similar pleas twice in the General Prologue of the *Canterbury Tales,* though without using the word "spell": "'Lordynges,' quod he, 'now herkneth for the beste'" (GP, I, 788); and "Lordynges, herkneth, if yow leste" (GP, I, 828). The *Canterbury Tales* narrator uses the word "spelle" in the Tale of Sir Thopas ("herkenyth to my spelle" [VII, 897]), but not in conjunction with "lordynges."[24] The allegedly Chaucerian usage that E.K. cites fits the gloss only indirectly. The exhortation "listen to my spell" uses the word "spell" to mean story, a somewhat different denotation than simply "word" (as in E.K.'s etymology of gospel) or charm (E.K.'s original definition of "spell"). E.K. refers to Chaucer as though a Chaucerian usage could explain an archaic word, but Chaucer is only partially relevant here.

The logic of this gloss is dubious; E.K cites a moderately garbled Chaucer allusion to explicate a denotation that Chaucer himself does not use. In this instance, Chaucer's name seems to serve an iconic more than an explanatory purpose. Chaucer represents an English poetry that is both authoritative and antique. It is thus valuable for E.K. to represent Chaucer in the notes even when the Chaucerian reference is less than illuminating. The fact that Chaucer used a word means that Immeritô may credibly use that word, even if slightly differently. Chaucer's name is totemic, even if some of E.K.'s Chaucerian references are vague. Chaucer is repeatedly invoked elsewhere in the glossaries to justify particular usages. In the May glossary, Chaucer's name is used that way three times: to explain the range of meanings of "Cheuisaunce"; to prove that the pronoun "her" could also mean "their"; and to support the gloss "key hole" for "Clincke" (F1v–F2r).

Chaucer is not the only medieval author cited by E.K. In the August gloss, E.K. refers to John Lydgate: "Welked) shortned or empayred. As the Moone being in the waine is sayde of Lidgate to welk" (47v). In the February gloss, E.K. differentiates Lydgate's Middle English from Chaucer's: "Gride) perced: an olde word much vsed of Lidgate, but not found (that I know of) in Chaucer" (7r). Similarly, in the July gloss, E.K.

explains the "-and" form of the present participle, still widely used in Later Middle English, although Chaucer's London English favored the newer "-ing" form : "Glitterand) Glittering. a Participle vsed sometime in Chaucer, but altogether in I. Goore [i.e., John Gower]" (20v). E.K. may not recognize the different dialects of Middle English, but he can differentiate the vocabulary and morphology used by different medieval authors, and he is happy to demonstrate that knowledge for his readers.

In differentiating Chaucer's Middle English from that of Gower and Lydgate, E.K. acknowledges that Chaucer may be better known to his readers, and he does assume that his readers already possess some level of familiarity with Chaucer's works. Immeritô, too, certainly imagined a reader conversant with Chaucer. His valedictory poem "To His Booke" begins: "Goe little booke: thy selfe present, / As child whose parent is vnkent" (¶1v). In fact, this poem has two parents, one unknown (Immeritô) and one known: Chaucer, whose "go litel book" apostrophe appears near the conclusion of *Troilus and Criseyde*.[25] The "go litel book" allusion is repeated in the Epilogue to the *Shepheardes Calender,* when the poet instructs his book:

> Goe lyttle Calender, thou hast a free passeporte,
> Goe but a lowly gate emongste the meaner sorte.
> Dare not to match thy pype with Tityrus hys style,
> Nor with the Pilgrim that the Ploughman playde a whyle. (52r)[26]

Immeritô takes on a Chaucerian form in this address to his work, a rhetorical gesture he uses twice in the *Shepheardes Calender,* once at the beginning and once at the end. In effect, the double allusion frames the *Shepheardes Calender,* wrapping Immeritô's work in the merit of his poetic antecedent. The initial verse ("Goe little booke") is visually prominent on its spread: its eighteen lines fill their page in italic type roughly double the size of the roman type used for the Epistle on the facing page (fig. 32). Given the Chaucerian frame of the *Shepheardes Calender,* it can only be ironically that, in the concluding verse, "Loe I haue made," Immeritô warns his departing work: "Dare not to match thy pype with Tityrus hys style" (N4r), not to presume to match the style of Tityrus (who is consistently glossed by E.K. as Chaucer).[27]

Immeritô engages in some misdirection in this Epilogue verse, making reference to one of Chaucer's lines but marking a different allusion.[28] The glosse that in this case precedes the text (fig. 33) identifies a different

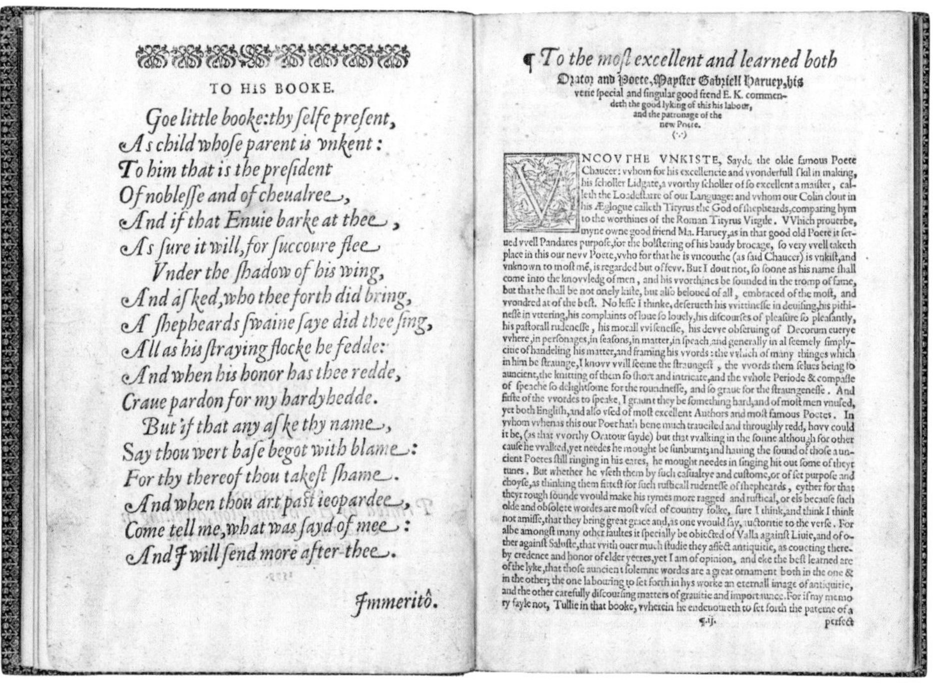

TO HIS BOOKE.

Goe little booke: thy selfe present,
As child whose parent is vnkent:
To him that is the president
Of noblesse and of cheualree,
And if that Enuie barke at thee,
As sure it will, for succoure flee
Vnder the shadow of his wing,
And asked, who thee forth did bring,
A shepheards swaine saye did thee sing,
All as his straying flocke he fedde:
And when his honor has thee redde,
Craue pardon for my hardyhedde.
But if that any aske thy name,
Say thou wert base begot with blame:
For thy thereof thou takest shame.
And when thou art past ieopardee,
Come tell me, what was sayd of mee:
And I will send more after thee.

Immeritô.

¶ *To the most excellent and learned both*
Orator and Poete, Mayster Gabriell Haruey, his
verie special and singular good frend E. K. commen-
deth the good lyking of this his labour,
and the patronage of the
new Poete.
(∴)

VNCOVTHE VNKISTE, Sayde the olde famous Poete Chaucer: vvhom for his excellencie and vvonderfull skil in making, his scholler Lidgate, a vvorthy scholler of so excellent a maister, calleth the Loadestarre of our Language: and vvhom our Colin clout in his Æglogue calleth Tityrus the God of shepheards, comparing hym to the worthines of the Roman Tityrus Virgile. VVhich prouerbe, myne owne good friend Ma. Haruey, as in that good old Poete it serued vvell Pandares purpose, for the bolstering of his baudy brocage, so very vvell taketh place in this our nevv Poete, vvho for that he is vncouthe (as said Chaucer) is vnkist, and vnknown to most mé, is regarded but of fevv. But I dout not, so soone as his name shall come into the knovvledg of men, and his vvorthines be sounded in the tromp of fame, but that he shall be not onely kiste, but also beloued of all, embraced of the most, and vvondred at of the best. No lesse I thinke, deserueth his vvittinesse in deuising, his pithinesse in vttering, his complaints of loue so louely, his discourses of pleasure so pleasantly, his pastorall rudenesse, his morall vvisenesse, his devve obseruing of Decorum euerye vvhere, in personages, in seasons, in matter, in speach, and generally in al seemely simplycitie of handeling his matter, and framing his vvords: the vvhich of many thinges which in him be straunge, I knovv vvill seeme the straungest, the vvords them selues being so auncient, the knitting of them so short and intricate, and the vvhole Periode & compasse of speache so delightsome for the roundnesse, and so graue for the straungenesse. And firste of the vvordes to speake, I graunt they be something hard, and of most men vnused, yet both English, and also vsed of most excellent Authors and most famous Poetes. In vvhom vvhenas this our Poet hath bene much traueiled and throughly redd, hovv could it be, (as that vvorthy Oratour sayde) but that vvalking in the sonne although for other cause he vvalked, yet needes he mought be sunburnt; and hauing the sound of those auncient Poetes still ringing in his eares, he mought needes in singing hit out some of theyr tunes. But whether he vseth them by such casualtye and custome, or of set purpose and choyse, as thinking them fittest for such rusticall rudenesse of shepheards, eyther for that theyr rough sounde vvould make his rymes more ragged and rustical, or els because such olde and obsolete wordes are most vsed of country folke, sure I think, and think I think not amisse, that they bring great grace and, as one vvould say, auctoritie to the verse. For albe amongst many other faultes it specially be obiected of Valla against Liuie, and of other against Saluste, that vvith ouer much studie they affect antiquitie, as coueting thereby credence and honor of elder yeeres, yet I am of opinion, and eke the best learned are of the lyke, that those auncient solemne wordes are a great ornament both in the one & in the other; the one labouring to set forth in hys worke an eternall image of antiquitie, and the other carefully discoursing matters of grauitie and importaunce. For if my memory fayle not, Tullie in that booke, vvherein he endeuoureth to set forth the paterne of a

¶.ij. perfect

Fig. 32. Edmund Spenser, *The Shepheardes Calender* (London, 1579), ¶1v–¶2r. Folger Shakespeare Library, STC 23089

allusion. The Epilogue promises that the *Shepheardes Calender* will outlast "steele in strength, and time in durance" (Epilogue, line 2), a boast that E.K. identifies as "folowing the ensample of Horace and Ouid an the like" (N4r). Although the Chaucer allusions of the framing verses are unmarked and to some extent obscured, Immeritô clearly presumes his audience's ability to read Chaucerian English and to recognize allusions to Chaucer's works. On its surface, E.K.'s glossing of Immeritô's Middle English vocabulary could be explained by his disagreement with the poet over the audience's familiarity with Chaucerian English, but for the fact that E.K. too seems to presume a reader who already has a deep familiarity with Chaucer (and perhaps also with Middle English more generally). E.K.'s uses of Chaucer in the apparatus, like his classical allusions, seem to presuppose a learned reader, one familiar with Middle English verse as well as Greek and Latin verse. E.K. does not, however, argue that Immeritô's uses of Middle English are direct allusions to particular Chaucerian works, although he identifies in the *Shepheardes Calender*

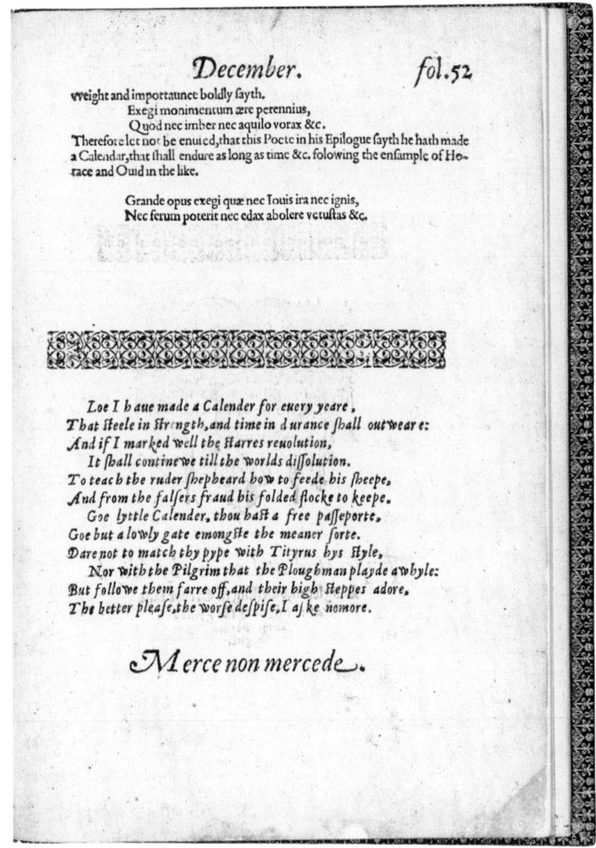

December. fol.52

vveight and importaunce boldly ſayth.

Exegi monimentum ære perennius,
Quod nec imber nec aquilo vorax &c.

Therefore let not be enuied, that this Poete in his Epilogue ſayth he hath made a Calendar, that ſhall endure as long as time &c. folowing the enſample of Horace and Ouid in the like.

Grande opus exegi quæ nec Iouis ira nec ignis,
Nec ferum poterit nec edax abolere vetuſtas &c.

Loe I haue made a Calender for euery yeare,
That ſteele in ſtrength, and time in durance ſhall outweare:
And if I marked well the ſtarres reuolution,
It ſhall continewe till the worlds diſſolution.
To teach the ruder ſhepheard how to feede his ſheepe,
And from the falſers fraud his folded flocke to keepe.
Goe lyttle Calender, thou haſt a free paſſeporte,
Goe but a lowly gate emongſte the meaner ſorte.
Dare not to match thy pype with Tityrus hys ſtyle,
Nor with the Pilgrim that the Ploughman playde awhyle:
But followe them farre off, and their high ſteppes adore,
The better pleaſe, the worſe deſpiſe, I aſke nomore.

Merce non mercede.

Fig. 33. Edmund Spenser, *The Shepheardes Calender* (London, 1579), N4r. Folger Shakespeare Library, STC 23089

various direct allusions to classical poetry. The obvious Chaucerian allusions in the poet's apostrophes to his book are, significantly, unglossed. They are there for the reader to recognize without guidance from E.K.

Interestingly, E.K. himself may engage in a covert Chaucerian allusion of his own. The April eclogue begins with Hobbinol distraught because Colin's love for a woman has diminished his attention to Hobbinol, who loves him. Thenot wonders why Hobbinol is crying, asking, "bene thine eyes attempred to the yeare?" (11v). In E.K.'s gloss, he explains Thenot's meteorological joke:

> Attempred to the yeare] agreeable to the season of the yeare, that is Aprill, which moneth is most bent to shoures and seasonable rayne: to quench, that is, to delaye the drought caused through drynesse of March wyndes. (14r)

England is no doubt rainy in the spring, and E.K.'s weather report can stand on its own as a reasonable gloss. However, the reference to April rains quenching a March drought may well contain an uncited allusion to the opening lines of the *Canterbury Tales*, which situate the pilgrimage in early spring, when April's "shoures soote, / The droghte of March hath perced to the roote"(GP, I, 1–2). In this covert echo of Chaucerian imagery, as in the case of the "go litel booke" allusion, the reader can still make sense of the passage in question, even without thinking back to Chaucer. However, for the reader who hears the echoes, this is one more link E.K. makes between the *Shepheardes Calender* and its Chaucerian antecedents.

In his Epistle to Harvey, E.K. explains that the New Poet, Immeritô, may use some of his archaisms inadvertently. Immeritô is "much traueiled and throughly redd" in earlier English poetry, and thus, "hauing the sound of those auncient Poetes still ringing in his eares, he mought needes in singing hit out some of theyr tunes" (2r). E.K.'s ability to gloss the poem's archaisms marks him, too, as a scholar "much traueiled and throughly redd," and his unmarked allusions to the *Canterbury Tales* are a rhetorical device to position the reader within this company as well. Even as E.K. explicates Immeritô's highly allusive and anachronistic poetic diction for the readers, he seems to presume readers who have some familiarity with the literary forms, works, and authors of later medieval England.[29] In considering how to read these glosses, as helpful or comic, necessary or arch, it is worth keeping in mind that the Middle English glosses in *Shepheardes Calender* had no precedent in the printing of Middle English poetry.

Editions of Chaucer's works were published in 1532, 1542, 1561, 1598, and 1602 by three different editors. The 1598 edition of Chaucer's works by Thomas Speght was the first to include a separate glossary, "The old and obscure words of Chaucer, explaned." Speght's title for the glossary could suggest either that he thought late-sixteenth-century readers would find Chaucer's language "obscure" because it was "old," or that Speght intended to explain both old words and obscure words (that is, the two categories overlapped but were not identical). In either case, the glossary's presence seems to demonstrate Chaucer's linguistic opacity for at least some Elizabethan readers. Speght's description of Chaucer in his prefatory letter "To the Readers" takes a contrasting position, however.

Like E.K. in the Dedicatory Epistle to the *Shepheardes Calender*, Speght presents it as shameful to undervalue Chaucer, whom he calls "our English Poet himselfe." Given how much Chaucer was esteemed "in most vnlearned times and greatest ignorance," Speght concludes that he "cannot in these our daies, wherein Learning and riper iudgement so much flourisheth, but be had in great reuerence, vnlesse it bee of such as for want of wit and learning, were neuer yet able to iudge what wit or Learning meaneth" (A2r). Reversing the logic of linguistic change, which would diminish later readers' appreciation for Chaucer, Speght claims that the growth of learning in his day should lead later sixteenth-century readers to value Chaucer at least as much as Chaucer's contemporaries did. Belying the stereotype that the Renaissance rejected medieval darkness, Speght argues that the "rebirth" of learning that characterized his own century should make his contemporaries all the more interested in Chaucer's medieval poetry. Those who do not love Chaucer clearly lack the wit and learning of "these our daies."

If Chaucer is a chronologically transcendent poet, and if only those who "were neuer yet able to iudge what wit or Learning meaneth" question Chaucer's preeminence, why then do Chaucer's "old and obscure words" need to be explained, or rather to whom? Speght, like E.K., presents Middle English as simultaneously alien and familiar. Their ambivalence echoes the puzzling linguistic history described by George Puttenham in his 1589 *Art of English Poesy*. In explaining why he starts his history where he does, Puttenham announces:

> I will not reach above the time of King Edward III and Richard II for any that wrote in English meter, because before their times by reason of the late Norman conquest, which had brought into this realm much alteration both of our language and laws, and therewithal a certain martial barbarousness, whereby the study of all good learning was so much decayed, as long time after no man or very few intended to write in any laudable science, so as beyond that time there is little or nothing worth commendation to be found written in this art.[30]

Puttenham describes the "late Norman conquest" as affecting the language until the time of Edward III and Richard II. Even allowing the tendentious assertion that the "martial barbarousness" of early Middle English, and the decayed state of learning in twelfth- and thirteenth-century English culture, meant that little worth reading was written until the reign of

Edward III, the adjective "late" hardly describes the temporal relationship between the Norman Conquest and the mid-fourteenth century.

Puttenham groups later Middle English with early modern English. His list of English poets begins: "Those of the first age were Chaucer and Gower, both of them, as I suppose, knights. After whom followed John Lydgate, the monk of Bury, and that nameless who wrote the satire called *Piers Plowman;* next him followed Hardyng the chronicler; then in King Henry VIII's time Skelton (I wot not for what great worthiness surnamed the Poet Laureate)" (148). The chronology is accurate, but the temporal compression is interesting. Skelton and Chaucer were both poets of the "first age," although they lived a century apart, while poets who wrote within a generation of Skelton are sorted into a later category: "In the latter end of the same king's [Henry VIII's] reign sprung up a new company of courtly makers, of whom Sir Thomas Wyatt the elder and Henry, Earl of Surrey, were the two chieftans" (148). For Puttenham, early Middle English language and literature were distant and barbarous, while later Middle English literary culture was continuous with early sixteenth-century literature.

When E.K. makes paradoxical statements about the relationship between the old and the new, about Immeritô's relationship to Chaucer, and about the legibility of Middle English for an early modern reader, he anticipates the similar ambivalence toward Middle English language and poetry shown by Speght and Puttenham. Late-fourteenth-century English was undoubtedly different from that of the late sixteenth century.[31] Nevertheless, despite those linguistic differences, early modern speakers could also be (belated) readers of Middle English.[32] A history of the language that does not attend to the history of the reading is necessarily incomplete. English vocabulary and morphology did change from 1400 to 1600, yet earlier works retained an audience, keeping archaic forms poetically present.[33]

The *Shepheardes Calender*'s use of Middle English is an egregious example of the phenomenon of Middle English literature influencing early modern readers, but it is not altogether unique. The glossaries of Middle English that appear in early modern works indicate a complex relationship between early modern readers and the *idea* of Middle English. The pseudonymous Immeritô may be "vncovthe" and thus "vnkiste," according to E.K., but Chaucer is neither. In calling the "new

Poete" to the reader's attention, E.K. puts Immeritô into the role of his medieval predecessor, undermining chronology. In the future, when the new poet comes to be known by name, he will not only become one more "olde famous Poete," he will antiquate himself through his own novelty.

NOTES

1 On Spenser's use of obsolete language, see B.R. McElderry, Jr., "Archaism and Innovation in Spenser's Poetic Diction," *PMLA* 47 (1932): 144–70; David A. Richardson, "Duality in Spenser's Archaisms," *Studies in the Literary Imagination* 11 (1978): 81–98; and Nathan A. Gans, "Archaism and Neologism in Spenser's Diction," *Modern Philology* 76 (1979): 377–79. The claim that Spenser "writ no language" is Ben Jonson's; it occurs in *Timber,* where he also warns of "letting [young readers] taste Gower or Chaucer at first, lest, falling too much in love with antiquity...they grow rough and barren in language" (Ben Jonson, *Timber, or Discoveries Made Upon Men and Matter,* ed. Felix E. Schelling [Boston: Ginn & Company, 1892], 57).

2 As with most diachronic changes, the chronological boundaries between the Middle English and Early Modern English periods are subject to debate, not least because the changes to phonology and morphology that define Early Modern English happened at different times in different places. Matthew Giancarlo explores the artificial yet persistent narrative of when, how, and where the Great Vowel Shift took place in "The Rise and Fall of the Great Vowel Shift? The Changing Ideological Intersections of Philology, Historical Linguistics, and Literary History," *Representations* 76 (2001): 27–60. In a study of the fifteenth-century English printing industry, William Kuskin argues against the notion of a decisive break between the literary cultures of the medieval and early modern periods: "Introduction: Following Caxton's Trace," in *Caxton's Trace: Studies in the History of English Printing,* ed. William Kuskin (Notre Dame: University of Notre Dame Press, 2006), 1–31.

3 The quotation is from the Dedicatory Epistle, "To the most excellent and learned both Orator and Poete, Mayster Gabriell Haruey" (¶2r); Immeritô [Edmund Spenser], *The Shepheardes Calender: Conteyning twelue Æglogues proportionable to the twelue monethes* (London, Hugh Singleton, 1579). Some have argued that E.K.'s glosses and commentary were written by Spenser himself. For a discussion of E.K.'s identity (by a scholar who argues that E.K. is Spenser's fiction), see Lynn Staley Johnson, *The Shepheardes Calender: An Introduction* (University Park: Pennsylvania State University Press, 1990), 7 and 26. Arguments for an identity between the glossator and the poet include Agnes Duncan Kuersteiner "E.K. is Spenser," *PMLA* 50 (1935): 140–55; Theodore L. Steinberg, "E.K.'s *Shepheardes Calender* and Spenser's," *Modern Language Studies* 3 (1973): 46–58. David R. Shore dismisses the claim that Spenser invented E.K., lending his support to the argument that E.K. is most likely Spenser's Cambridge colleague Edmund Kirke; see his "E.K.," in *The Spenser Encyclopaedia,* ed. A.C. Hamilton et al. (Toronto: University of Toronto Press, 1990), 231. Analyses of the poem that presume a difference between E.K. and Spenser but set aside the question of E.K.'s true identity include those in Evelyn B. Tribble, *Margins and Marginality: The Printed Page in Early Modern England*

(Charlottesville: University Press of Virginia, 1993), and William W.E. Slights, *Managing Readers: Printed Marginalia in English Renaissance Books* (Ann Arbor: University of Michigan Press, 2001). E.K. may or may not have been Spenser, but he was also not likely to have been working independently of Spenser. The elaborate formatting of the work suggests Spenser's close control of the text, and E.K. presents himself as a close colleague of the poet, not a completely independent commentator. I would therefore argue that the question of E.K.'s true identity is not tremendously urgent. Throughout this essay, I use the names the *Shepheardes Calender* itself uses for its poet and the glossator (Immeritô and E.K., respectively).

4 Again, although E.K. may indeed be Spenser himself, as some critics have argued, the second persona of the glossator does exist in the poem as distinct from Immeritô, the putative poet. This seems sufficient reason to claim for Immeritô and E.K. different identities and intentions, even if we conclude that those identities are both literary disguises for the same author.

5 For both gallimaufray and hodgepodge, the OED has earlier citations for the transferred definition than the literal (culinary) definition. Surely this is a function of the available sources rather than an indication of when the different meanings of the words came into use.

6 E.K., at least, takes the emblems to be spoken by the shepherds themselves, rather than being the poet's more learned moralizing of the shepherds' stated opinions. In his gloss of the two February emblems (discussed below), E.K. describes the first "spoken of Thenot," "Whom Cuddye doth counterbuff with a byting and bitter prouerbe" (7v).

7 William Kuskin discusses E.K.'s misquotation of Pandarus. Pandarus uses the adjective "unknowe" (*TC*, I, 809) rather than E.K.'s "vncouth." Kuskin notes that "uncouth" is "a word similar [to "unknowe"] in meaning, but emphasizing strangeness and leaning – almost – toward 'indecorous,' which the *Oxford English Dictionary* first records in 1589" ("'The loadstarre of the English language': Spenser's *Shepheardes Calender* and the Construction of Modernity," *Textual Cultures: Text, Contexts, Interpretations* 2, no. 2 [2007]: 9–33 [16]). To that extent, the substitution of "vncovth" for "unknowe" echoes E.K.'s ambivalence about Spenserian archaism as both natural and unnatural.

8 Geoffrey Chaucer, *Troilus and Criseyde*, in *The Riverside Chaucer*, 3d ed., ed. Larry D. Benson (Boston: Houghton Mifflin Company, 1987), 1:799–819.

9 In "reco[m]mending the Author vnto" Harvey, E.K. presents himself as the agent behind the *Calender*'s publication, yet the presence of the poet's prefatory verse "To His Booke" suggests that the poet was involved in the publication of the *Calender*, notwithstanding his reticence about "promulgat[ing]" his other works (¶3r).

10 Johnson, *The Shepheardes Calender*, 34–35. One of Chaucer's descriptions of his works and their genres is in the so-called Retraction at the end of the *Canterbury Tales*, and is in the voice of (a fictionalized version of) the poet (*CT*, X, 1085–88); the other is in the voice of Alceste in the Prologue of the Legend of Good Women (*LGW*, G, 405–20).

11 *OED*, s.v., "newfangle" and "newfangled." For several examples of sixteenth-century texts linking newfangledness to treason or social disorder, see Sara Warneke, *Images of the Educational Traveller in Early Modern England* (Leiden: E. J. Brill, 1994), 90–93; as well as Sara Warnecke, "A Taste for Newfangledness: The Destructive Potential of Novelty in Early Modern England," *The Sixteenth Century Journal* 26 (1995): 881–96.

12 Thomas Harriot's *A Briefe and True Report of the New Found Land of Virginia* was published a year after the *Shepheardes*

Calender, in 1589, but Richard Hakluyt's *Divers Voyages Touching the Discoverie of America* (1582) was already in circulation, as was Richard Eden's *The Decades of the Newe Worlde or West India* (1550).

13 The *Kalender of Sheepehards* is not unified, as the *Shepheardes Calender* is, but it contains several sections organized by calendars: zodiacal information, feast day calendars, analogies between the calendar year and the human lifespan, and information about medical treatment appropriate to different seasons. Thus, the *Shepheardes Calender* resembles its antecedent less in format than in title. Lynn Staley Johnson notes further that: "In choosing that particular old name for a new work, Spenser had implicitly chosen to ally himself with the spirit of the Reformation... [Since] The *Kalendrier des Bergers,* or its English edition, *The Kalender of Shepherdes* (1506), had from the beginning been associated with Lollardy" and thus with the principle of church reform (*The Shepheardes Calender,* 34).

14 S.K. Heninger, Jr., ed., *The Kalender of Sheepehards (c. 1585), a Facsimile Reproduction* (Delmar, N.Y.: Scholars' Facsimilies & Reprints, 1979), 8 (A4v of the *Kalender*).

15 Heninger, vi–vii.

16 *OED,* s.v. "scholium" and "scholion." "Scholion" and "glosse" were both theologically loaded words insofar as they figured in the debates over biblical translation. In his *Apology,* George Joye rebukes Tyndale for advocating that a translator "shulde make scholias / notis / and gloses in the mergent," saying: "I had as lief put the trwthe in the text as in the margent... I wolde the scripture were so puerly and plyanly translated that it neded nether note / glose nor scholia / so that the reder might once swimme without a corke" (*An Apology made by George Joy to satisfy, if it may be, W. Tindale [1535],* ed. Edward Arber [Birmingham: The English Scholar's Library, 1882], 23). "Gloss" and its Middle English form "glose" had for centuries simultaneously denoted both explication and untruth – a rare example of a simultaneous oxymoron and tautology.

17 Michael McCanles, "The *Shepheardes Calender* as Document and Monument," *Studies in English Literature, 1500–1900* 22 (1982): 5–19 (6–7).

18 Richard A. McCabe, "Annotating Anonymity, or Putting a Gloss on The Sheperdes Calender" in *Ma(r)king the Text: The Presentation of Meaning on the Literary Page,* ed. Joe Bray, Miriam Handley, and Anne C. Henry, 35–54 (Aldershot: Ashgate, 2000), 37. McCabe argues that the black letter verse "mak[es] the verse look, as well as sound, 'Chaucerian,' visually endowing the 'new Poete' with the charisma of tradition" (37). As I indicate, it is more accurate to identify the black letter as visually English more than visually Chaucerian; in 1579, black letter type was not yet uncommon, but its use was limited to texts in English.

19 The *OED* cites the expression "swete syluer sounde" from the *Pilgrimage of Perfection;* closer to Spenser's time is a citation from Nicholas Breton's *The Countess of Pembroke's Love* (1592): "Some brought in musicke of most siluer sounde" (*OED,* s.v. "silver," 13a). Moreover, the phrase "siluer song" (*argureon melos*) that E.K. cites here does not appear in Hesiod's works. Robert Lamberton, *Hesiod* (New Haven: Yale University Press, 1988), 154.

20 *OED,* s.v. "emprise."

21 Steinberg, "E.K.'s *Shepheardes Calender* and Spenser's," 54.

22 *OED,* s.v. "uneath."

23 *OED,* s.v., "keen" (adj.), definitions 3a, 4, and 4b, respectively.

24 In the Stow edition that Spenser would have used, these passages occur on fols. A4r, A4v, and N4v, respectively. Stow's texts of these lines are not substantially different from those of the Riverside edition. None matches the line cited by E.K.

25 *TC*, V, 1086–98.

26 There is some disagreement as to whether "the Pilgrim that the Ploughman playde awhyle" is Langland, author of *Piers Plowman*, or Chaucer, to whom the Plowman's Tale was attributed in the sixteenth century.

27 On the Epilogue's imitation of Chaucer's "go litel book" apostrophe, see Glenn A. Steinberg, "Spenser's *Shepheardes Calender* and the Elizabethan Reception of Chaucer," *English Literary Renaissance* 35 (2005): 31–51 (50). Steinberg argues that Spenser's understanding of Chaucer is nuanced and deep, quite unlike the stereotype of an early modern misreading of Chaucer. As should by now be clear, I agree with Steinberg that Spenser knew Chaucer well and expected an audience who did likewise.

28 Immeritô was not the first to make such an allusion to the "Go litel boke" epilogue to *Troilus and Criseyde*. Similar addresses to the written work appear in John Lydgate's *Churl and the Bird* (published 1477), the anonymous *Unto my Lady the Flower of Womanhood* (1450–60?), and Henry Bradsaw's *The Holy Lyfe and History of Saynt Werburge* (1513). For these allusions, see Caroline F.E. Spurgeon, *Five Hundred Years of Chaucer Criticism and Allusion (1357–1900), Part I* (London: Chaucer Society, 1914), 15, 53, 71.

29 Steinberg argues that E.K.'s explanation of terms his audience already understood marks his social, not to mention scholarly, ineptitude. Steinberg considers E.K. to be Spenser's fiction, and argues that Spenser uses E.K.'s explicatory overkill to parody the Pléiade, whose aesthetic theories E.K. shares ("E.K.'s *Shepheardes Calender,*" 48).

30 George Puttenham, *The Art of English Poesy: A Critical Edition,* ed. Frank Whigham and Wayne A. Rebhorn (Ithaca: Cornell University Press, 2007), 147.

31 As David Matthews points out, however, the language of the twelfth through fourteenth century was not yet called "Middle English." David Matthews, *The Making of Middle English, 1765–1910* (Minneapolis: University of Minnesota Press, 1999).

32 Tim William Machan correctly observes that fifteenth-century English printing, unlike that of the sixteenth century, largely featured works in Middle English. While a handful of Middle English works were printed in the fifteenth century, then reprinted in the sixteenth, many more of those published in the fifteenth century were not republished in the next century. Machan's analysis of the "short-lived genre" that he calls "early modern Middle English" (the corpus of fifteenth-century editions of Middle English texts) calls attention to the narrowing of the Middle English canon in the transition from the fifteenth to sixteenth century. Tim William Machan, "Early Modern Middle English," in *Caxton's Trace,* 299–322 (301). Machan's interpretation of the fifteenth-century history of the book is valuable, although I see a less decisive boundary between the fifteenth- and sixteenth-century awareness of medieval literature. Books are durable; they can continue to have readers long after their publication date. The sharp drop in new editions of medieval texts is worth noting, but it might not tell the whole story of sixteenth-century readership of Middle English.

33 As Paula Blank has pointed out, after Spenser, early modern poetic diction was shaped not only by the inherited medieval literary inheritance but also by the Spenserian precedent for archaism, so the poetic language of the sixteenth and seventeenth centuries intentionally reversed some of the language changes that differentiated early modern from Middle English. Paula Blank, "Languages of Early Modern Literature in Britain," in *The Cambridge History of Early Modern Literature,* ed. David Loewenstein and Janel Mueller, 141–65 (Cambridge: Cambridge University Press, 2002), 165.

Faults escap't in Printing are here corr

ine 10. for *tender*, reade it *render*. p.30.

ants a *Comma*, p.34.l.11. reade it *tre.*

. reade it *subscribe*. p.58.l.34.reade *arc*

Glossing the Margins in Milton's The Reason of Church-governement

CHLOE WHEATLEY

King Charles I, following the advice of his bishops, pressed in the 1630s for a return to the sacerdotal ceremonialism of an earlier era, with an emphasis upon the divinely conferred right of English bishops to restore the jurisdiction and properties that they had lost in the processes of reform begun in the previous century. By the early 1640s, however, crises in Scotland and Ireland had intensified concerns about such policies and impelled an outpouring of pamphlets debating who actually had the authority to decide the direction of religious reform and hence the shape of the Church of England. Between 1641 and 1642, John Milton published five powerfully polemical treatises, known collectively as his antiprelatical tracts, thereby lending his considerable learning to this debate. In these tracts, Milton used a variety of rhetorical strategies – vivid imagery, satire, direct address, historical argument, and, not least, creative manipulation of the conventions of marginal citation – to undercut the authority of the bishops and their supporters. *The Reason of Church-governement* (1642) was written in part to advocate for the replacement of the bishops by a Presbyterian ministry (fig. 34). As Milton puts it at the conclusion of the treatise, "I shal move yee Lords in the behalf I dare say of many thousand good Christians, to let your justice and speedy sentence passe against this great malefactor Prelaty" (*CPW* 1:861).[1] Yet, while *The Reason of Church-governement* is framed in its conclusion as a direct, deliberative address to Parliament, it also aims, in broader terms, to transform some basic habits of reading, a shift that Milton clearly considered crucial to a broader process of reform.[2] This essay will focus on Milton's efforts to sharpen

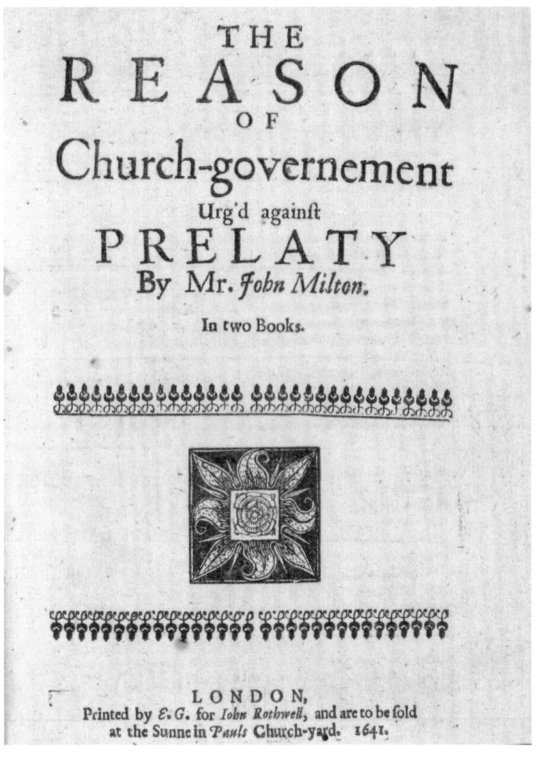
THE
REASON
OF
Church-governement
Urg'd againſt
PRELATY
By Mr. *John Milton.*

In two Books.

LONDON,
Printed by *E. G.* for *John Rothwell*, and are to be ſold
at the Sunne in *Pauls* Church-yard. 1641.

Fig. 34. John Milton, *The Reason of Church-governement* (London, 1641 [1642]), title page. Beinecke Rare Book and Manuscript Library, Yale University, 1977 2507

awareness of the various modes of citation that could be used to incite readers to belief and ultimately to action.

The practice of marginal citation was common enough in printed prose works of the early modern period. Marginal notes, often printed in a distinct typeface and style, enabled writers to stage conversations or invoke external authorities to support claims made in the body of a text. While the actual "practical value" of such citations might seem questionable (one might wonder, along with Stephen Dobranski, just how many readers actually did work to track down sources or hack their way through especially deep thickets of marginal citation), writers tended to use the marginal citation to advertise their credibility.[3] Certainly, many writers debating issues of religious reform in the mid-seventeenth century treated the marginal citation as an indispensable necessity, a way to claim scriptural authority and patristic precedent for their particular visions of church governance. Yet, as Evelyn Tribble so astutely puts it in her groundbreaking study of the meanings that could be embedded in the

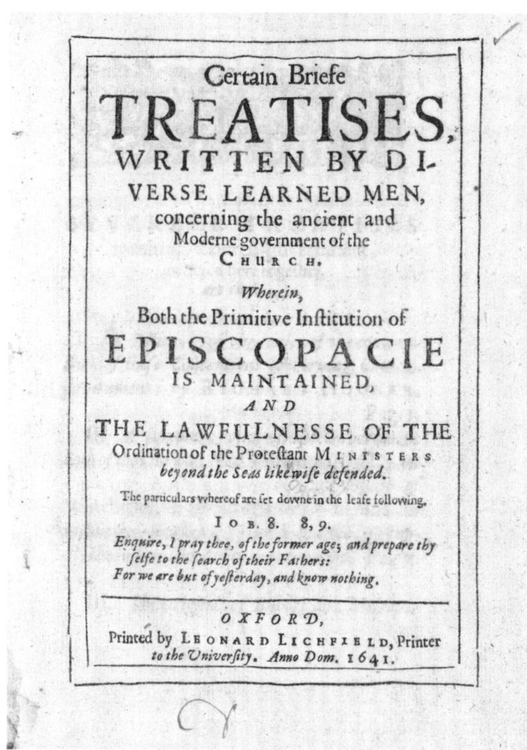

Certain Briefe
TREATISES,
WRITTEN BY DI-
VERSE LEARNED MEN,
concerning the ancient and
Moderne government of the
CHURCH.
Wherein,
Both the Primitive Inſtitution of
EPISCOPACIE
IS MAINTAINED,
AND
THE LAWFULNESSE OF THE
Ordination of the Proteſtant MINISTERS
beyond the Seas likewiſe defended.
The particulars whereof are ſet downe in the leafe following.
IOB. 8. 8, 9.
Enquire, I pray thee, of the former age; and prepare thy ſelfe to the ſearch of their Fathers:
For we are but of yeſterday, and know nothing.

OXFORD,
Printed by LEONARD LICHFIELD, Printer
to the Univerſity. Anno Dom. 1641.

Fig. 35. *Certain Briefe Treatises* (Oxford, 1641), title page. Beinecke Rare Book and Manuscript Library, Yale University, Mra35 C33

printed page, "the margins and the text proper" of the early modern book were in "shifting relationships" – a fact certainly not lost on a writer like Milton.[4] His prose tracts, *The Reason of Church-governement* in particular, reflect Milton's sustained interest in glossing – and hence transforming – the way in which a citation could be used to emblematize the writer and reader's relationship to sacred text and sacred authority.[5]

It becomes clear early on in *The Reason of Church-governement* that Milton has chosen to frame his tract as a response to a "little treatise lately printed among others of like sort at *Oxford*" (1:768), namely, *Certain Briefe Treatises* (fig. 35).[6] This collection's probable compiler, James Ussher, Archbishop of Armagh, was by 1641 in exile in England, and solicited by both Parliament and the king to lend his learning to their respective causes. *Certain Briefe Treatises* reflects a deep learnedness rivaling Milton's own (Ussher had spent many years studying church history) and also Ussher's support of a middle position, situated against Laudian high-church innovations, but also drawing upon ancient precedent to claim the legitimacy – and practicality – of church hierarchy.[7] Comprised of works by Ussher and also by well-respected divines (many from an earlier generation), this collection includes no authorial preface. Instead, the compilation opens with an excerpt from the writings of Richard Hooker, who comments on the function of teaching as the cure for religious controversy born of ignorant misapprehension. Overviews of "The Forme of Government in the Old Testament" and "the Forme of Church-Government in the New Testament" follow. Ussher's work (accompanied by works by Martin Bucer and John Rainolds) engages with both biblical sources and early records of the Christian church as a way to trace the proliferation of ranked distinctions among early church officials. Ussher's contributions to this volume are followed by examples of how the form of controversial debate could be reduced and hence wholly domesticated within the parameters of the printed question-and-answer session. Edward Brerewood's assessment of "The Patriarchicall Government of the Ancient Church,'" for example, is "declared" by way of a series of interchanges in which the reader is first prompted to ask the right questions and then is provided with the answers to those questions. Finally, the reader following "the progression of *Certain Briefe Treatises*...from Biblical times to contemporary" finds evidence of the hierarchical nature of other continental churches.[8]

The Reason of Church-governement critiques the basic presuppositions about Scripture and church history that have shaped Ussher's compilation. In fact, when one looks at the structure of his tract, it becomes clear that Milton has ordered his critique as a gloss that opens up for extensive reinterpretation three key terms – commanding, correcting, ordaining – foundational to the argument of *Certain Briefe Treatises*. Chapter 2 of *The Reason of Church-governement*, for example, in its emphasis on exactly what sort of "commanding" can be derived from I Timothy, functions as an extended elaboration of the first of the three actions Andrewes has identified as integral to "the *Apostolick* function."[9] Milton's chapter addresses the question of *who* is authorized to command, and predictably the list is quite limited: God appoints church government and sets its pattern and direction. Chapter 3 of *The Reason of Church-governement* ("That it is dangerous and unworthy the Gospell to hold that Church-government is to be pattern'd by the Law, as B. Andrews and the Primat of Armagh maintaine"), in turn follows with a meditation upon what we might learn from the New Testament more broadly not only about

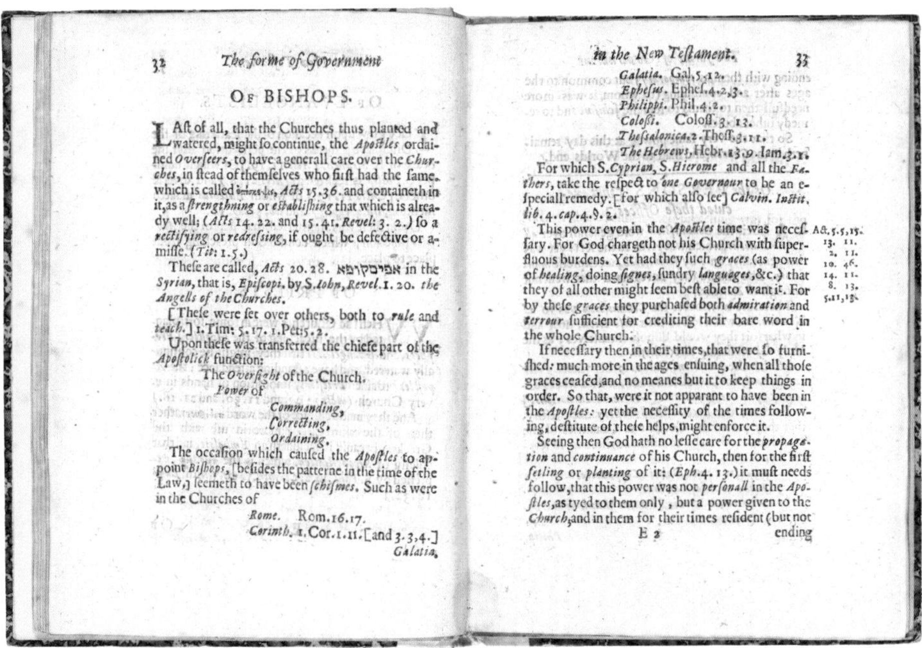

32 *The forme of Government*

OF BISHOPS.

LAst of all, that the Churches thus planted and watered, might so continue, the *Apostles* ordained *Overseers*, to have a generall care over the *Churches*, in stead of themselves who first had the same. which is called [illegible], *Acts* 15.36. and containeth in it, as a *strengthning* or *establishing* that which is already well; (*Acts* 14.22. and 15.41. *Revel*: 3. 2.) so a *rectifying* or *redressing*, if ought be defective or amisse. (*Tit*: 1.5.)

These are called, *Acts* 20.28. אפיסקופא in the *Syrian*, that is, *Episcopi*. by *S.Iohn*, *Revel*.1.20. *the Angells of the Churches*.

[These were set over others, both to *rule* and *teach*.] 1.Tim: 5.17. 1.Pet:5.2.

Upon these was transferred the chiefe part of the *Apostolick* function:

The *Oversight* of the Church.
Power of
Commanding,
Correcting,
Ordaining.

The occasion which caused the *Apostles* to appoint *Bishops*, [besides the patterne in the time of the Law,] seemeth to have been *schismes*. Such as were in the Churches of

Rome. Rom.16.17.
Corinth. 1.Cor.1.11.[and 3.3,4.]
Galatia.

in the New Testament. 33

Galatia. Gal.5.12.
Ephesus. Ephes.4.2,3.
Philippi. Phil.4.2.
Colossi. Coloss.3.13.
Thessalonica.2.Thess.3.11.
The Hebrews, Hebr.13.9. Iam.3.1.

For which S.*Cyprian*, S.*Hierome* and all the *Fathers*, take the respect to *one Governour* to be an especiall remedy. [for which also see] *Calvin. Instit. lib*.4.*cap*.4.§.2.

This power even in the *Apostles* time was neces- Act.5.5,15.
sary. For God chargeth not his Church with super- 13. 11.
fluous burdens. Yet had they such *graces* (as power 2. 11.
of *healing*, doing *signes*, sundry *languages*, &c.) that 10. 46.
they of all other might seem best able to want it. For 14. 11.
by these *graces* they purchased both *admiration* and 8. 13.
terrour sufficient for crediting their bare word in 5.11,13.
the whole Church.

If necessary then in their times, that were so furnished: much more in the ages ensuing, when all those graces ceased, and no meanes but it to keep things in order. So that, were it not apparant to have been in the *Apostles*: yet the necessity of the times following, destitute of these helps, might enforce it.

Seeing then God hath no lesse care for the *propagation* and *continuance* of his Church, then for the first *setling* or *planting* of it: (*Eph*.4.13.) it must needs follow, that this power was not *personall* in the *Apostles*, as tyed to them only, but a power given to the *Church*, and in them for their times resident (but not

E 2 ending

Fig. 36. *Certain Briefe Treatises* (Oxford, 1641), E1v–E2r. Beinecke Rare Book and Manuscript Library, Yale University, Mra35 C33

"commanding" but also "correcting." Milton invites readers to rethink both what and who needs correcting: in his reading, the New Testament corrects the Old Testament with its "imperfect and obscure institution of the Law" (1:762). Finally, chapter 4 takes up the question of "ordaining." The chapter most centrally inspires the reader, through the example of Timothy who "receav'd ordination by the hands of the Presbytery," to meditate upon what exactly ordination implies (1:767). Milton questions the episcopal assumption that historical evidence, such as Timothy's ordination by "the hands of the Presbytery" (I Timothy 4:14), implies a hierarchy of power. Having first enjoined the reader to "pass over" certain aspects of Andrewes' argument in order to devote serious attention to the three key components of discipline (commanding, correcting, and ordaining), Milton returns in chapter 5 to more direct and polemical engagement with "the Arguments of B. Andrews and the Primat" (1:768). Finally, the last two chapters of book 1 take up the argument raised at the very bottom of page 32 (E1v) of *Certain Briefe Treatises* (fig. 36). Corinthians and Romans, cited by Andrewes as evidence that schism impelled the appointment of bishops, in Milton's rereading becomes the source of a counterargument. "If Prelaty had beene then esteem'd a remedy against schism, where was it more needfull then in the great variance among the Corinthians which S. Paul so labour'd to reconcile?" (1:780).

Posing substantive objections to the arguments found in *Certain Briefe Treatises* as a whole and in the works by Andrewes and Ussher in particular, Milton makes a bold claim, basically, that very little of *Certain Briefe Treatises* actually needs to be read. He supports this claim by drawing attention not simply to the arguments made by these supporters of episcopacy, but also to their very methods of gathering and displaying their supporting evidence. In the famously autobiographical digression included at the opening of book 2, Milton draws a sharp contrast between his own citational strategies and those of his opponents, expressing a particular disdain for what writers like Ussher presume about the places – scriptural and historical – from which they rightfully might derive their authority. Milton writes of how he felt compelled to leave the peace of retired study to

> come into the dim reflexion of hollow antiquities sold by the seeming bulk, and there be fain to club quotations with men whose learning and beleif lies in marginal stuffings, who when they have like good sumpters laid ye down their hors load of citations and fathers at your dore, with a rapsody of who and who were Bishops here or there, ye may take off their packsaddles, their days work is don, and episcopacy, as they think, stoutly vindicated.[10] (1:822)

Milton speaks elsewhere in this tract of his opponents' "tedious muster of citations, Sees, and successions" (1:778) and of those who "fly to supportment" of the "unweildy volumes of tradition" (1:827). This precisely vivid characterization, which casts writers who defend episcopacy as beasts of burden, links Milton's critique of standard practices of citation with his broader critique of how the episcopacy as a whole carries a tottering church along on "unlawfull waggonry" (1:755) of its own devising:

> But no profane insolence can paralell that which our Prelates dare avouch, to drive outragiously, and shatter the holy arke of the Church, not born upon their shoulders with pains and labour in the word, but drawne with rude oxen their officials,

> and their owne brute inventions. Let them make shewes of reforming while they will, so long as the Church is mounted upon the Prelaticall Cart, and not as it ought betweene the hands of the Ministers, it will but shake and totter.... (1:754–55)

In fact, Milton makes it quite a habit to sneer at others' citations. In *Of Reformation,* for example, he proclaims his unwillingness to "run into a paroxysm of citations" (1:566). One might characterize his work as filled to capacity with "the imagery of excess."[11]

It is hard, after reading Milton's powerfully imagistic characterizations, not to look askance upon the visual rhetoric of Ussher's tracts. Ussher not only surrounds his texts with works by his esteemed predecessors; his own words are framed within an elaborate and extensive system of citational reference. As Ussher explains how episcopacy was "deduced" from "Apostolical times,"[12] the margins fill up with Latin and Greek excerpts out of a formidable array of texts and authorities, ranging from Timothy to Ignatius, Polycrates, Tertullian, Eusebius, and other histories and commentaries (fig. 37). Ussher's "A Geographicall and Historical Disquisition, Touching the Lydian or Proconsular Asia" with no less citational rigor lays out evidence of his extensive reading in the annals and geographies that provided him evidence of how a hierarchical structure of governance developed in the church's earliest years. Ussher's margins are filled with notes that add an extra layer of citational sanction to his "brief" defense of the episcopacy. Likewise, Andrewes' "A Summarie View" redistributes the matter of both the Old and New Testaments in the form of a diagrammatic summary, replete with Ramist brackets, in which various authorities are organized into hierarchically ordered subcategories. In discussion of the form of government in the time of the Apostles, a diagrammatic layout is used not only to delineate a succession of authority from Christ to Apostles to Bishops, but also to codify the various functions properly performed by this succession of authorities, and to pull together various supporting citations from Acts, Corinthians, and other scriptural sources (figs. 38 and 39).

Clearly such bibliographic choices were meant to provide, in as economical a way as possible, proof that a writer's conclusions reflect his labor of learning. But Milton manages to suggest as well that a rather frenetic if facile energy helped to fill those pages with an overload of citational references. Milton puts the bibliographic code of Ussher's

the death of *Domitian*, hee applyed himſelfe to the government of the Churches of *Aſia*, is confirmed likewiſe both by [s] *Euſebius*, and by [t] *Hierom:* who further addeth, that [u] at the earneſt intreaty of the *Biſhops of Aſia* he wrote there his *Goſpell*.

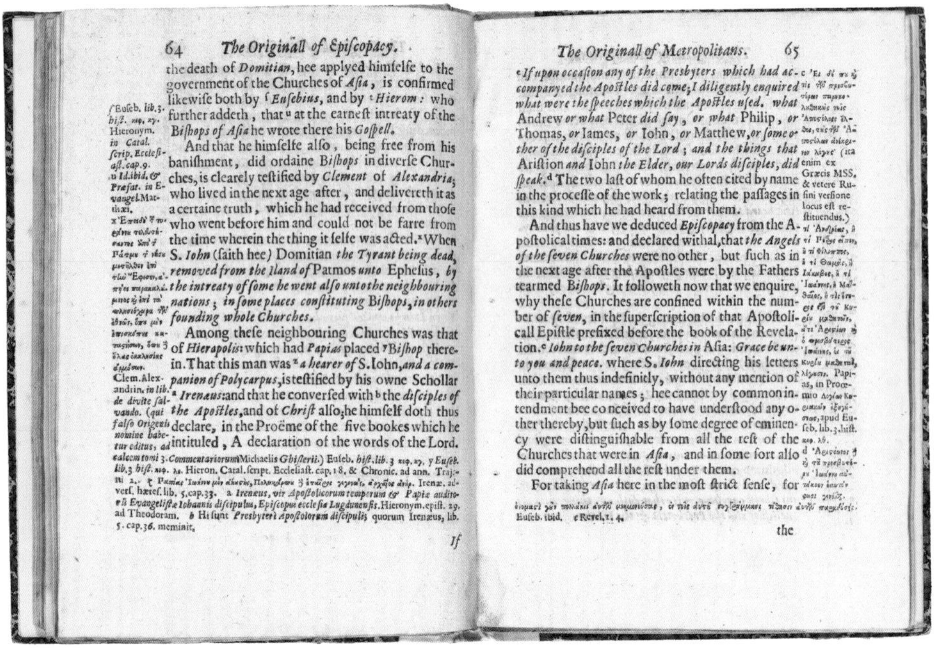

And that he himſelfe alſo, being free from his baniſhment, did ordaine *Biſhops* in diverſe Churches, is clearely teſtified by *Clement* of *Alexandria*; who lived in the next age after, and delivereth it as a certaine truth, which he had received from thoſe who went before him and could not be farre from the time wherein the thing it ſelfe was acted. [x] When S. *Iohn* (ſaith hee) Domitian *the Tyrant being dead, removed from the Iland of* Patmos *unto* Epheſus, *by the intreaty of ſome he went alſo unto the neighbouring nations; in ſome places conſtituting* Biſhops, *in others founding whole Churches.*

Among theſe neighbouring Churches was that of *Hierapolis*: which had *Papias* placed [y] *Biſhop* therein. That this man was [z] *a hearer of* S. Iohn, *and a companion of Polycarpus*, is teſtified by his owne Schollar [a] *Irenæus*: and that he converſed with [b] the *diſciples of the Apoſtles*, and of *Chriſt* alſo; he himſelf doth thus declare, in the Proëme of the five bookes which he intituled, A declaration of the words of the Lord.

[s] Euſeb. lib. 3. *hiſt.* [illegible]. Hieronym. *in Catal. ſcrip. Eccleſiaſt. cap.* 9. [u] Id. ibid. & *Præfat. in Evangel.* Matthæi. [x] [illegible Greek] Clem. Alexandrin. *in lib. de divite ſalvando.* (*qui falſo Origenis nomine habetur editus, ad calcem tomi* 3. *Commentariorum* Michaelis *Ghiſlerii.*) Euſeb. *hiſt. lib.* 3 [illegible]. y *Euſeb. lib.* 3 *hiſt.* [illegible]. Hieron. Catal. ſcript. Eccleſiaſt. cap. 18. & Chronic. ad ann. Trajani 2. z [illegible Greek] Irenæ. advers. hæreſ. lib. 5. cap. 33. a *Irenæus, vir Apoſtolicorum temporum & Papiæ auditoris Evangeliſtæ Iohannis diſcipulus, Epiſcopus eccleſiæ Lugdunenſis.* Hieronym. epiſt. 29. ad Theodoram. b Hi ſunt *Presbyteri Apoſtolorum diſcipuli;* quorum Irenæus, lib. 5. cap. 36. meminit.

If

[c] *If upon occaſion any of the Presbyters which had accompanyed the Apoſtles did come; I diligently enquired what were the ſpeeches which the Apoſtles uſed. what* Andrew *or what* Peter *did ſay, or what* Philip, *or* Thomas, *or* Iames, *or* Iohn, *or* Matthew, *or ſome other of the diſciples of the Lord; and the things that* Ariſtion *and* Iohn *the Elder, our Lords diſciples, did ſpeak.* [d] The two laſt of whom he often cited by name in the proceſſe of the work; relating the paſſages in this kind which he had heard from them.

And thus have we deduced *Epiſcopacy* from the Apoſtolical times: and declared withal, that *the Angels of the ſeven Churches* were no other, but ſuch as in the next age after the Apoſtles were by the Fathers tearmed *Biſhops*. It followeth now that we enquire, why theſe Churches are confined within the number of *ſeven*, in the ſuperſcription of that Apoſtolicall Epiſtle prefixed before the book of the Revelation. [e] *Iohn to the ſeven Churches in* Aſia: *Grace be unto you and peace.* where S. *Iohn* directing his letters unto them thus indefinitly, without any mention of their particular names; hee cannot by common intendment bee conceived to have underſtood any other thereby, but ſuch as by ſome degree of eminency were diſtinguiſhable from all the reſt of the Churches that were in *Aſia*, and in ſome ſort alſo did comprehend all the reſt under them.

For taking *Aſia* here in the moſt ſtrict ſenſe, for

c [illegible Greek] (ita enim ex Græcis MSS. & vetere Rufini verſione locus eſt reſtituendus.) [illegible Greek] Papias, in Proœmio [illegible Greek], apud Euſeb. lib. 3. hiſt. [illegible]. d [illegible Greek] [illegible Greek] Euſeb. ibid. e Revel. 1. 4.

the

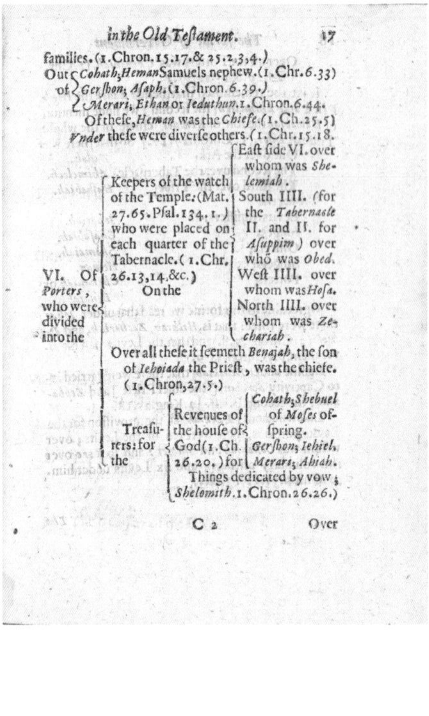

families. (1. Chron. 15. 17. & 25. 2, 3, 4.)

Out of
- *Cohath*; *Heman* Samuels nephew. (1. Chr. 6. 33)
- *Gerſhon*; *Aſaph*. (1. Chron. 6. 39.)
- *Merari*; *Ethan* or *Ieduthun*. 1. Chron. 6. 44.

Of theſe, *Heman* was the *Chiefe*. (1. Ch. 25. 5)

Vnder theſe were diverſe others. (1. Chr. 15. 18.

VI. Of *Porters*, who were divided into the

Keepers of the watch of the Temple: (Mat. 27. 65. Pſal. 134. 1.) who were placed on each quarter of the Tabernacle. (1. Chr. 26. 13, 14, &c.) On the
- Eaſt ſide VI. over whom was *Shelemiah*.
- South IIII. (for the *Tabernacle* II. and II. for *Aſuppim*) over whō was *Obed*.
- Weſt IIII. over whom was *Hoſa*.
- North IIII. over whom was *Zechariah*.

Over all theſe it ſeemeth *Benajah*, the ſon of *Iehoiada* the Prieſt, was the chiefe. (1. Chron, 27. 5.)

Treaſurers: for the
- Revenues of the houſe of God (1. Ch. 26. 20.) for
  - *Cohath*; *Shebuel* of *Moſes* ofſpring.
  - *Gerſhon*; *Iehiel*.
  - *Merari*; *Ahiah*.
- Things dedicated by vow; *Shelomith*. 1. Chron. 26. 26.)

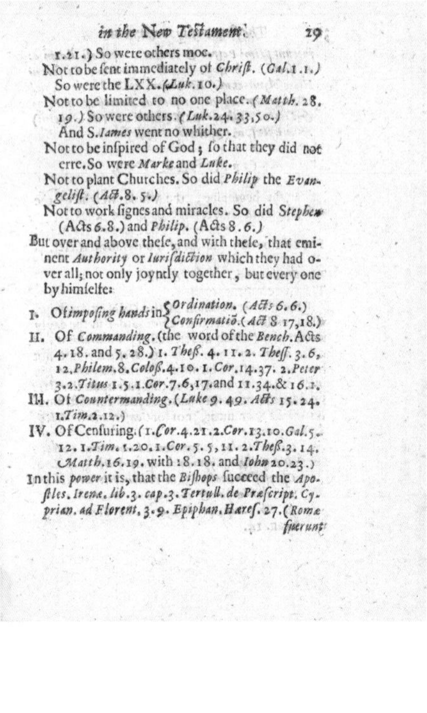

Over

1. 21.) So were others moe.

Not to be ſent immediately of *Chriſt*. (*Gal.* 1. 1.) So were the LXX. (*Luk.* 10.)

Not to be limited to no one place. (*Matth.* 28. 19.) So were others. (*Luk.* 24. 33, 50.) And S. *Iames* went no whither.

Not to be inſpired of God; ſo that they did not erre. So were *Marke* and *Luke*.

Not to plant Churches. So did *Philip* the *Evangeliſt*. (*Act.* 8. 5.)

Not to work ſignes and miracles. So did *Stephen* (Acts 6. 8.) and *Philip*. (Acts 8. 6.)

But over and above theſe, and with theſe, that eminent *Authority* or *Iuriſdiction* which they had over all; not only joyntly together, but every one by himſelfe:

I. Of *impoſing hands* in
- *Ordination*. (*Acts* 6. 6.)
- *Confirmatiō*. (*Act* 8 17, 18.)

II. Of *Commanding*. (the word of the *Bench*. Acts 4. 18. and 5. 28.) 1. *Theſ*. 4. 11. 2. *Theſſ*. 3. 6, 12. *Philem*. 8. *Coloſ*. 4. 10. 1. *Cor*. 14. 37. 2. *Peter* 3. 2. *Titus* 1. 5. 1. *Cor*. 7. 6, 17. and 11. 34. & 16. 1.

III. Of *Countermanding*. (*Luke* 9. 49. *Acts* 15. 24. 1. *Tim*. 2. 12.)

IV. Of Cenſuring. (1. *Cor*. 4. 21. 2. *Cor*. 13. 10. *Gal*. 5. 12. 1. *Tim*. 1. 20. 1. *Cor*. 5. 5, 11. 2. *Theſ*. 3. 14. *Matth*. 16. 19. with 18. 18. and *Iohn* 20. 23.)

In this *power* it is, that the *Biſhops* ſucceed the *Apoſtles*. *Irene. lib.* 3. *cap.* 3. *Tertull. de Præſcript. Cyprian. ad Florent.* 3. 9. *Epiphan. Hæreſ.* 27. (*Romæ*

fuerunt

compilation under scrutiny. In so doing, he undercuts the awe – and a palpably felt distance between reader and author – that Ussher's book, on the simple level of page layout, was clearly designed to provoke.

Milton's tract, in contrast, models for readers how to reform the very act of citation itself. Rejecting out of hand the legitimacy of arguments that would ground their vision of church government in patterns established in the Old Testament, for example, Milton counters that such arguments are "repugnant to the plaine dictat of Scripture" and that "we rather are to *cite* all those ages to an arraignment before the word of God" (1:778; italics mine). In other words, one type of citation – the act of arraying references to a variety of sources along the margins of one's argument – is replaced by another sort of citation – the bringing of the accused (in this case the writings of Ussher and others) into a court of judgment. It is no mistake that a vocabulary of guilt and justice creeps into the tract as this process of citation gets under way: "[T]hat the Prelates have no sure foundation in the Gospell, their own guiltinesse doth manifest: they would not else run questing up as high as Adam to fetch their originall, as tis said one of them lately did in publick" (1:762).

One of the reasons why Milton's argument seems to jump up and down in one place (to paraphrase Huntley) is that he takes such care to model for readers the crucial skill of textual arraignment.[13] If one accepts Milton's claim that the writings of the New Testament – specifically the Epistles of Paul to Timothy and Titus – are the sole source of authoritative information about the nature of church government (1:758), then critiquing a work like *Certain Briefe Treatises* becomes an exuberantly simplified and energizing task. As Milton writes, "let them chaunt while they will of prerogatives, we shall tell them of Scripture, of custom, we of Scripture, of Acts and Statutes, stil of Scripture, til the quick and pearcing word enter to the dividing of their soules, & the mighty weaknes of the Gospel throw down the weak mightines of mans reasoning" (1:827). We might add to this "let them provide citations, we shall provide anti-citations."

Fig. 37. *Certain Briefe Treatises* (Oxford, 1641), I3v–I4r. Beinecke Rare Book and Manuscript Library, Yale University, Mra35 C33

Fig. 38. *Certain Briefe Treatises* (Oxford, 1641), C2r. Beinecke Rare Book and Manuscript Library, Yale University, Mra35 C33

Fig. 39. *Certain Briefe Treatises* (Oxford, 1641), D4r. Beinecke Rare Book and Manuscript Library, Yale University, Mra35 C33

In the end, what sort of reformed understanding can be produced through this process of textual arraignment? A learned search for analogues and precedents proving the "superiority of Bishopship" (1:765) is replaced by an assessment of how little evidence is actually found in Paul's epistles regarding the "worldly degrees of autority, honour, temporall jurisdiction" (1:766). Defining citation as an active process of textual arraignment proves particularly productive as Milton turns from questioning the origins of ecclesiastical authority to refuting the claim that the process of religious reform introduces "schism" that a hierarchical church government counteracts. Here Milton proves a careful reader of apostolic writings not only for their prescriptive powers but also for their historical resonance: "it was well knowne what a bold lurker schisme was even in the houshold of Christ betweene his owne Disciples and those of John the Baptist about fasting: and early in the Acts of the Apostles the noise of schisme had almost drown'd the proclaiming of the Gospell: yet we reade not in Scripture that any thought was had of making Prelates, no not in those places where dissention was most rife" (1:779–80).

Even if one were to allow writers like Ussher to avail themselves of authority from the Old Testament, Milton claims, a close look at their highly selective exploitation of texts like Isaiah would prove them inconsistent in their own treatment of the Old Testament as a source from which one should draw "punctual correspondence" (1:774). We read much about the establishment of forms of superiority as it is expressed in Isaiah; we hear nothing about how that same source calls for "monthly solemnity answerable to the new moons" (1:774).

Thus far I have emphasized how Milton recasts citation as a method to discipline the arguments of others; he also explores how a reformed ministry might be built upon the very same reading habits that have been used to demolish the arguments of his opponents. Milton promises great rewards to readers who follow to the best of their own capacities the prime dictate of I Timothy 5 and "labour in the word and doctrine" (1:765). As we have seen, the removal of disorder involves first and foremost teaching readers to be highly sceptical about the power of the Old Testament to prescribe the shape of contemporary church government. But this is not to say that Milton finds the Old Testament wholly irrelevant. The issue, rather, is finding an alternative to the episcopal tendency to treat the "law" as a prescriptive rather than historical body of evidence.

12 *The Reaſon of Church-government.*

Sabbath, ſhe does not therefore imitate the law her underling, but perfect her. All that was morally deliver'd from the law to the Goſpell in the office of the Prieſts and Levites, was that there ſhould be a miniſtery ſet a part to teach and diſcipline the Church, both which duties the Apoſtles thought good to commit to the Presbyters. And if any diſtinction of honour were to be made among them, they directed it ſhould be to thoſe not that only rule well, but eſpecially to thoſe that labour in the word and doctrine.
1 Tim. 5. By which we are taught that laborious teaching is the moſt honourable Prelaty that one Miniſter can have above another in the Goſpell: if therefore the ſuperiority of Biſhopſhip be grounded on the Prieſthood as a part of the morall law, it cannot be ſaid to be an imitation; for it were ridiculous that morality ſhould imitate morality, which ever was the ſame thing. This very word of patterning or imitating excludes Epiſcopacy from the ſolid and grave Ethicall law, and betraies it to be a meere childe of ceremony, or likelier ſome misbegotten thing, that having pluckt the gay feathers of her obſolet bravery to hide her own deformed bareneſſe, now vaunts and glories in her ſtolne plumes. In the meane while what danger there is againſt the very life of the Goſpell to make in any thing the typical law her pattern, and how impoſſible in that which touches the Prieſtly government, I ſhall uſe ſuch light as I have receav'd, to lay open. It cannot be unknowne by what expreſſions the holy Apoſtle S. *Paul* ſpares not to explane to us the nature and condition of the law, calling thoſe ordinances which were the chiefe and eſſentiall offices of the Prieſts, the elements and rudiments of the world both weake and beggarly. Now to breed, and bring up the children of the promiſe, the heirs of liberty and grace under ſuch a kinde of government as is profeſt to be but an imitation of that miniſtery which engender'd to bondage the ſons of *Agar*, how can this be but a foul injury and derogation, if not a cancelling of that birth-right and immunity which Chriſt hath purchas'd for us with his blood. For the miniſtration of the law conſiſting of carnall things, drew to it ſuch a miniſtery as conſiſted of carnall reſpects, dignity, precedence, and the like. And ſuch a miniſtery eſtabliſh't in the Goſpell, as is founded upon the points and termes of ſuperiority, and neſts it ſelfe in worldly honours, will draw to it, and we ſee it doth, ſuch a religion as runnes back againe to the old pompe and glory of the fleſh. For doubtleſſe there is a certaine attraction and magnetick force betwixt the religion and the miniſteriall forme thereof. If the religion be pure, ſpirituall, ſimple, and lowly

Fig. 40. John Milton, *The Reason of Church-governement* (London, 1641 [1642]), B2v. Beinecke Rare Book and Manuscript Library, Yale University, 1977 2507

In Milton's vision, real points of historical continuity link the places of Old Testament, New Testament, and early modern England – and, importantly, as we shall see, these are points of connection and resonance that he expects readers, with a little help, to discover for themselves.

Having made so much of the "marginal stuffings" of his opponents, how does Milton treat citations in his own text? Barbara Lewalski has termed the margins of Milton's prose tracts "defiantly bare."[14] Just as the "Prelates" adore excess trappings in their church, one can imagine Milton saying, so too they love the excess trappings of a heavily cited page. The simplicity of Milton's imagined church would be best reflected, one would assume, by an unadorned margin. Yet the margins of *The Reason of Church-governement* are not as bare as one might expect: Milton's text contains marginal citations that point to I Timothy 5, Zechariah 8, and Haggai 2, as well as II Corinthians 10 (figs. 40–42).[15]

The Reaſon of Church-government, &c. 31

and loyall deeds have now bought themſelves an honourable name to poſterity, whatſoever malice by ſlander could invent, rage in hoſtility attempt, they greedily attempted, toward theſe murdrous Iriſh the enemies of God and mankind, a curſed off-ſpring of their own connivence, no man takes notice but that they ſeeme to be very calmely and indifferently affected. Where then ſhould we begin to extinguiſh a rebellion that hath his cauſe from the miſgovernment of the Church, where? but at the Churches reformation, and the removall of that government which purſues and warres with all good Chriſtians under the name of ſchiſmaticks, but maintains and foſters all Papiſts and Idolaters as tolerable Chriſtians. And if the ſacred Bible may be our light, we are neither without example, nor the witneſſe of God himſelfe, that the corrupted eſtate of the Church is both the cauſe of tumult, and civill warres, and that to ſtint them, the peace of the Church muſt firſt be ſetl'd. *Now for a long ſeaſon*, ſaith *Azariah* to King *Aſa*, *Iſrael hath beene without the true God, and without a teaching Prieſt, and without Law; and in thoſe times there was no peace to him that went out, nor to him that came in, but great vexations were upon all the inhabitants of the countries. And nation was deſtroy'd of nation, and City of City, for God did vex them with all adverſity. Be ye ſtroug therefore*, ſaith he to the reformers of that age, *and let not your hands be weake, for your worke ſhall bee rewarded.* And in thoſe Prophets that liv'd in the times of reformation after the Captivity often doth God ſtirre up the people to conſider that while eſtabliſhment of Church matters was neglected, and put off, there was *no peace to him that went out or came in, for I*, ſaith God, *had ſet all men every one againſt his neigbour.* Zechar.8.
But from the very day forward that they went ſeriouſly, and effectually about the welfare of the Church, he tels them that they Haggai 2.
themſelves might perceave the ſudden change of things into a proſperous and peacefull condition. But it will here be ſaid that the reformation is a long work, and the miſeries of *Ireland* are urgent of a ſpeedy redreſſe. They be indeed; and how ſpeedy we are, the poore afflicted remnant of our martyr'd countrymen that ſit there on the Sea-ſhore, counting the houres of our delay with their ſighs, and the minuts with their falling teares, perhaps with the deſtilling of their bloody wounds, if they have not quite by this time caſt off, and almoſt curſt the vain hope of our founder'd ſhips, and aids, can beſt judge how ſpeedy we are to their reliefe. But let their ſuccors be haſted, as all need and reaſon is, and let not therefore the re-

formation

Fig. 41. John Milton, *The Reason of Church-governement* (London, 1641 [1642]), D4r. Beinecke Rare Book and Manuscript Library, Yale University, 1977 2507

The citation to I Timothy 5 seems easiest to explain, as Milton insists throughout *The Reason of Church-governement* that one can use 1 Timothy 5's injunction that one "labour in the word" as a starting point in a progressively involved engagement with divine truth. It is a dictate that stands at the foundation of Milton's vision of a ministry "free and open to any Christian man though never so laick, if his capacity, his faith, and prudent demeanor commend him" (1:844). He emphasizes a church discipline that, in the importance it accords "laborious teaching" (1:765), is able to privilege as well a "reverence of our elders, our brethren, and friends," and thereby provide "the greatest incitement to vertuous deeds" (1:840).

The marginal citations to Haggai and Zechariah are perhaps more difficult to explain but, I will argue, no less significant. They are included in a chapter filled with examples of Milton's standard rhetorical procedure of not relegating his citations to the margins, but rather deftly folding the reference to a particular passage into the body of his argument. And

58 *The Reaſon of Church-government.*

his humble remorſe, till he regain his firſt health and felicity. This is the approved way which the Goſpell preſcribes, theſe are the *ſpirituall weapons of holy cenſure*, and miniſteriall *warfare, not carnall,*
Cor. 2. 10. *but mighty through God to the pulling downe of ſtrong holds, caſting down imaginations, and every high thing that exalteth it ſelfe againſt the knowledge of God, and bringing into captivity every thought to the obedience of Chriſt.* What could be done more for the healing and reclaming that divine particle of Gods breathing, the ſoul, and what could be done leſſe? he that would hide his faults from ſuch a wholſome curing as this, and count it a two-fold puniſhment, as ſome do, is like a man that having foul diſeaſes about him, periſhes for ſhame, and the fear he has of a rigorous inciſion to come upon his fleſh. We ſhall be able by this time to diſcern whether Prelaticall juriſdiction be contrary to the Goſpell or no. Firſt therefore the government of the Goſpell being economicall and paternall, that is, of ſuch a family where there be no ſervants, but all ſons in obedience, not in ſervility, as cannot be deny'd by him that lives but within the ſound of Scripture, how can the Prelates juſtifie to have turn'd the fatherly orders of Chriſts houſhold, the bleſſed meekneſſe of his lowly roof, thoſe ever open and inviting dores of his dwelling houſe which delight to be frequented with only filiall acceſſes, how can they juſtifie to have turn'd theſe domeſtick priviledges into the barre of a proud judiciall court where fees and clamours keep ſhop and drive a trade, where bribery and corruption ſolicits, paltring the free and monileſſe power of diſcipline with a carnall ſatisfaction by the purſe. Contrition, humiliation, confeſſion, the very ſighs of a repentant ſpirit are there ſold by the penny. That undeflour'd and unblemiſhable ſimplicity of the Goſpell, not ſhe her ſelfe, for that could never be, but a falſe-whited, a lawnie reſemblance of her, like that aire-born *Helena* in the fables, made by the ſorcery of Prelats, inſtead of calling her Diſciples from the receit of cuſtome, is now turn'd Publican her ſelf; and gives up her body to a mercenary whordome under thoſe fornicated ches which ſhe cals Gods houſe, and in the ſight of thoſe her altars which ſhe hath ſet up to be ador'd makes merchandize of the bodies and ſouls of men. Rejecting purgatory for no other reaſon, as it ſeems, then becauſe her greedines cannot deferre but had rather uſe the utmoſt extortion of redeemed penances in this life. But becauſe theſe matters could not be thus carri'd without a begg'd and borrow'd force from worldly autority, therefore prelaty ſlighting the

Fig. 42. John Milton, *The Reason of Church-governement* (London, 1641 [1642]), H1v. Beinecke Rare Book and Manuscript Library, Yale University, 1977 2507

the citational reference to these "Prophets that liv'd in the times of reformation after the Captivity" (1:799) seems at first glance to mark out, simply, yet more evidence of how God marks his displeasure at human "misgovernment" as a way to "stir up" reform (1:798–99). But the reader who has attended to Milton's critique of his opponents' modes of citation might very well feel impelled to meditate with more care upon Milton's choice to adorn his margins at this particular place in his text.

The question becomes, why do these particular passages have marginal citations? In order to answer this question, we must remember that throughout *The Reason of Church-governement* Milton emphasizes how a margin filled with citations may be designed to lend weight to an argument, but a skeptical glance, especially at citations of church fathers and Old Testament writings, can test this function. Milton has modeled a process of "arraignment" for readers: most daringly he has called into question the relevance of the places cited; and he has called writers' bluffs by returning to the fuller source that stands behind the quotation. The reader interested in Milton's marking out of Zechariah and Haggai might well note Milton's special interest in pointing the reader to a set of prophetic voices that *Certain Briefe Treatises,* in its emphasis on *forms* of government, passes over. In contrast, Milton's readers are invited to dwell upon the resonances that can be traced between seventeenth-century England and post-exilic Jerusalem. Haggai and Zechariah actively inspired the rebuilding of the Temple after work, "barely begun, ground to a halt."[16] These prophets figure forth the pivotal function of the committed faithful who work continuously even in times (especially in times) of uncertainty to inspire others to continue along the path of reform. Through the carefully placed marginal citation, Milton celebrates his own integrity as a careful reader of the Bible and invites readers, likewise, to use the Old Testament as source that can renew their sense of urgency, even in the midst of division, disappointment, and grim awareness of how "reformation is a long work" (1:799).

The final marginal citation found in *The Reason of Church-governement,* at the end of book 2, is to II Corinthians 10. The passage so marked functions as a culminating exhortation in which the voice of Paul is melded with Milton's and yet marked off in italics as a voice apart.[17] Having provided his vision of the efficacy of reformed church discipline, Milton concludes that "this is the approved way which the Gospell prescribes, these are the *spirituall weapons of holy censure,* and ministeriall *warfare, not carnall, but mighty through God to the pulling downe of strong holds, casting down imaginations, and every high thing that exalteth it selfe against the knowledge of God, and bringing into captivity every thought to the obedience of Christ*" (1:848). As with the citations to Haggai and Zechariah, here the marginal citation marks out a passage that rewards further study. Paul's challenges in his relationship to the Corinthians resonate in particular with Milton's felt need to incite rather than let stagnate a process of reform that had begun yet faltered.[18]

Milton in this tract does not provide glosses of Scripture. He in fact argues quite explicitly for the clarity of the Gospel: "Let others…dread and shun the Scriptures for their darknesse; I shall wish I may deserve to be reckon'd among those who admire and dwell upon them for their clearnesse" (1:750). Instead, he creates a careful gloss of the act of citation. What is more, all of Milton's printed marginal citations point to places in

Scripture that speak to his concerns on many more levels than are explicitly enumerated. Each time period thus cited has experienced turmoil, but also the resumption or pursuit against difficult odds of a project of building or rebuilding. Each historical time and place is shaped by the actions of those who incite others to help ensure forward progress. There is an eloquent resonance, perhaps even a kind of harmony, to be created out of the jarring conflicts and failures that constitute human history. Importantly, this is a resonance most fully activated by the inquiring reader.

NOTES

1 All quotations from Milton's prose works are cited with reference to *The Complete Prose Works of John Milton*, ed. Don M. Wolfe et al., 8 vols. (New Haven: Yale University Press, 1953–82). Parenthetical citations refer to *The Complete Prose Works* (CPW) by volume and page number.

2 For a useful overview of the immediate historical context in which Milton published this, his fourth antiprelatical tract, and for a wry assessment of the "theatricality" with which Milton invokes the power of Bishops who in fact had had their institutional power effectively dismantled a year earlier, see Paul Stevens, "Discontinuities in Milton's Early Public Self-Representation," *Huntington Library Quarterly* 51 (1988): 260–80, doi: 10.2307/3817476.

3 Stephen B. Dobranski, *Milton, Authorship, and the Book Trade* (Cambridge: Cambridge University Press, 2009), 28. Dobranski is particularly interested in how the place of the page becomes a place of collaboration – between author and cited authority, as well as between writer and compositor, who through his careful typesetting enables the distinction between text and margin to be made manifestly present on the page. For another exemplary study of the collaborative relationship of author, printer, and literary text, see David Scott Kastan, *Shakespeare and the Book* (Cambridge: Cambridge University Press, 2001). Milton's tract was published by the London bookseller John Rothwell, who had a stall at the Sun in St. Paul's and who "dealt almost wholly in theological works" (Henry R. Plomer, *A Dictionary* [1907], 157; cited in CPW 1:744).

4 Evelyn B. Tribble, *Margins and Marginality: The Printed Page in Early Modern England* (Charlottesville: University Press of Virginia, 1993), 6. Devoted to the study of early modern Bibles, Spenser, the Marprelate Tracts, and Jonson, Tribble's study draws upon the immensely important insights of Elizabeth Eisenstein, Roger Chartier, Jerome McGann, and D.F. McKenzie regarding the social impact of the material book.

5 For in-depth analysis of how Milton was "always artful in the adaptation of written material to his reading public" and "never more so than in the way in which he fitted Biblical passages into his various prose writings," see Harris Fletcher, "Milton's Use of Biblical Quotations," *The Journal of English and Germanic Philology* 26, no. 2 (1927): 145–65 (146), http://www.jstor.org/stable/27703025. Fletcher observes that Milton tends to reserve "specific citation with accompanying quotation" to "technical works" like *De Doctrina Christiana* (147). Thomas Roebuck, in "Milton and the Confessionalization of Antiquarianism,"

in *Young Milton: The Emerging Author, 1620–1642*, ed. Edward Jones (Oxford: Oxford University Press, 2013), 48–71, argues that the antiprelatical tracts reflect a diminishing interest in "engaging with primary historical sources" (64).

6 *Certain Briefe Treatises, Written by Diverse Learned Men, concerning the ancient and Moderne government of the Church* (Oxford, 1641), http://gateway.proquest.com/openurl?ctx_ver=Z39.88-2003&res_id=xri:eebo&rft_id=xri:eebo:citation:12326060. This compilation is invoked obliquely by Milton several times throughout *The Reason of Church-governement*. Elizabeth Skerpan, in *The Rhetoric of Politics in the English Revolution, 1642–1660* (Columbia: University of Missouri Press, 1992), makes the important point that the pressures of political and religious crisis inspired rhetorical improvisation. See also Nigel Smith, *Literature and Revolution in England, 1640–1660* (New Haven: Yale University Press, 1994), for analysis of generic innovations of the time period.

7 For a more extensive summary of this treatise and its "pacific and moderate" appeal to public opinion, see CPW 1:193–99. See also Alan Ford, *James Ussher: Theology, History, and Politics in Early-Modern Ireland and England* (Oxford: Oxford University Press, 2007), and Hugh Trevor-Roper, "James Ussher," in *Catholics, Anglicans, and Puritans: Seventeenth Century Essays* (Chicago: University of Chicago Press, 1987).

8 CPW 1:197.

9 Lancelot Andrewes, "A Summarie View of the Government both of the Old and New Testament," in *Certain Briefe Treatises*, 32.

10 Thomas N. Corns, in *Uncloistered Virtue: English Political Literature, 1640–1660* (Oxford: Clarendon Press, 1992), emphasizes Milton's use of the language of the marketplace, and his ambivalent relationship to the concept of the writer as merchant vending his wares (33).

11 Thomas Kranidas, "'Decorum' and the Style of Milton's Antiprelatical Tracts," *Studies in Philology* 62 (1965): 176–87 (180), http://www.jstor.org/stable/4173488. Kranidas diagnoses Milton's attitude as a "disdain for excess in language" that gets "mingled with contempt for pedantry in general" (179n), and emphasizes how images of textual excess feed into a "master image of excess and disharmony" (181). See Sharon Achinstein, *Milton and the Revolutionary Reader* (Princeton: Princeton University Press, 1994), for analysis of how civil war writers based their writings upon a system of symbolic opposition. Keith W. Staveley, in *The Politics of Milton's Prose Style* (New Haven: Yale University Press, 1975), provides close analysis of how the syntax of *The Reason of Church-governement* works in complex ways to enrich and enliven concepts under discussion with an emphasis on "the disciplined freedom of his moral imagination" (34–46). Critical assessment of *The Reason of Church-governement* has focused upon why this tract seems to fail so profoundly at making good on its promise to produce the "reason of church-government." The titular evocation of "reason" seems to some a bit of a joke, as the tract's argument seems to progress most powerfully through the force rather of "resonance" (as Stanley Fish puts it) or "rhetoric" (Sylvia Brown's term). See Stanley E. Fish, *Self-Consuming Artifacts: The Experience of Seventeenth-Century Literature* (Berkeley: University of California Press, 1972); and Sylvia Brown, "Household Words and Rhetorical Seductions in Milton's *The Reason of Church-government*," *Prose Studies: History, Theory, Criticism* 23, no. 1 (2000): 63–80, doi: 10.1080/01440350008586695. For a more recent discussion of this tract and its place in Milton's "transition from an arguably conservative scholar to an increasingly unorthodox politico-religious thinker," see Elizabeth Sauer, "Milton and Caroline Church Government," *The Yearbook of English Studies* 44 (2014): 196–214, doi: 10.5699/yearenglstud.44.2014.0196.

12 "The Original of Bishops and Metropolitans, Set down by James Arch-Bishop of Armagh," in *Certain Briefe Treatises*, 51–75 (65).

13 John F. Huntley, "The Images of Poet and Poetry in Milton's *The Reason of Church-Government*," in *Achievements of the Left Hand: Essays on the Prose of John Milton*, ed. Michael Lieb and John T. Shawcross (Amherst: University of Massachusetts Press, 1974), 83–120 (101).

14 Barbara K. Lewalski, *The Life of John Milton: A Critical Biography*, rev. ed. (Oxford: Blackwell Publishing, 2003), 122.

15 Consideration of how faithfully a modern edition records such typographic details is an interesting question. The Yale University Press edition, clearly highly authoritative (it glosses and annotates Milton's text quite thoroughly), is also the one that gives us the least clear sense of the rhetoric of the original page. (To be fair, it does indicate in the footnotes which citations are by "M" and which are by the editors.)

16 John Bright, *A History of Israel* (Philadelphia: Westminster Press, 1981), 366.

17 See Stevens, "Discontinuities in Milton's Early Public Self-Representation," on how Milton's stance is at once self-asserting and self-dissolving in the face of the Christian imperative that he prove he has internalized the word of God.

18 For an important analysis of how Milton's works place the dynamics of cyclical and linear history in tension with each other, see David Loewenstein, *Milton and the Drama of History: Historical Vision, Iconoclasm, and the Literary Imagination* (Cambridge: Cambridge University Press, 1990). On Milton's desire to foster environments that permit innovation, see Thomas N. Corns, "Milton's Antiprelatical Tracts and the Marginality of Doctrine," in *Milton and Heresy*, ed. Stephen B. Dobranski and John P. Rumrich (Cambridge: Cambridge University Press, 1998), 39–48.

[t]hen consider the preciousnesse of tyme
[l]et us learne to distinguishe tyme according to the occasion.

[R]ectos corrumpunt mores colloquia prava
[B]etter it is to abyde at a resolution,
[al]though there be some defect in it, than
daily changing to effectuate nothing.

Noxa caput sequitur.

[E]xperience is the schoolemaister of fooles

There follow certaine sentences written
out of a book made by Mr Perkins: which book
teacheth how to liue well & dye well.

[1] Pet. 5.7. he careth for you. And Psalm: 34.9. Nothing
shall be wanting to them that feare god.

A man upon good securitie lendeth to an other an hundr[ed]
pounde, hoping for the principall with the increase at the
yeares end: yet dare he not scarce deliver an hundr[ed]
pence to the poore members of Christ upon the promise
& bond of god himselfe, who saith He that giues to th[e]
poore, lends to the lord, and he will returne the
said gift with a blessing.

Faith in Christ & repentance is so farre forth possible
to all that will & desire it, that whosoever doth seriousl[y]
but will to beleeve & to be converted doth indeed beleeve

Hot Protestant Shakespeare

CLAIRE McEACHERN

The antipathy of Tudor-Stuart religious reformers toward the Tudor-Stuart theater has long been held to be fierce and probably mutual. Malvolio, Angelo, and Zeal-of-the-Land Busy don't help matters. Critics occasionally essay qualifications: Margot Heinemann has argued for a more nuanced consideration of religiously motivated anti-theatricalists, and Jeff Knapp for the self-styling of Reformation dramatists as religious thinkers.[1] Yet with the exception of the consideration of soliloquies as sites of Protestant interiority, literary history rarely considers the cross-pollination of committed reformist writing and Tudor-Stuart theater.[2] No doubt the standoff of drama and dogma owes something to our understanding of their respective affective functions: plays as pleasure-producing, whereas religious thought – at least that of a "Puritan" stripe – as anxiety-provoking. Studies of religion and Shakespeare's drama almost exclusively focus on the nature of his confessional allegiance, and in this priest-hunt, Puritan is the only label that remains beyond the pale.

Drama's cultural function has in recent decades acquired gravitas through accounts of its social instrumentality. But our image of post-Reformation religious thought has remained a dour one. Indeed, the contiguities we do grudgingly allow between literature and Reformed religion depend on the latter's no-more-cakes-and-ale aspect, its conscience-wracked contribution to, say, a character like Hamlet. This essay seeks to characterize an affiliation between reformist thought and

Shakespeare's dramaturgy that is primarily technological, but also temperamental. What happens if we think about William Shakespeare and William Perkins as soul mates?

Such an association requires rethinking the place of "Puritan" thought in the later Elizabethan religious palette. Tudor-Stuart theater and committed reformist thought occupied equally liminal positions in Elizabethan culture. However, whereas Shakespeare's subsequent cultural centrality has served to retrospectively bolster the Tudor-Stuart theater's contemporary social presence and impact, the antecedents of the Mayflower's self-exiling sailors continue to be understood as socially marginal. This despite the work of historians such as Peter Lake who have emphasized that the term "Puritan" applied to the first decades of reformist thought is itself anachronistic.[3] The cultural centrality of committed reformist thought is attested to by its predominance in the publication record as well as its support in the highest reaches of government. By "committed" I mean thought that addressed head-on and unflinchingly the core question of Calvinist thought: how do we know we are saved?

Characterizations of what was new or different about Reformation English Protestantism can tend to the anodyne, but historians are quite firm about the fact that, even if matters of predestination, grace, and the ethics and efficacies of human action were hardly new under the sixteenth-century sun, the practical syllogism by which one's salvific status could be inquired into was invented in the Reformation moment: "all who have the effects have faith; but I have the effects, therefore...I have faith." Scholars typically credit Theodore Beza for this formulation, sourcing it to his effort to address the question raised by Calvin's distinction between saving faith and the merely temporary: how do I know my faith is the real deal? R.T. Kendall argues that Beza asserts that one can (and must) persuade oneself of one's belief, and that in order to do so one must turn inward. The self thus becomes an evidentiary site that manifests God's decree: "We do not begin with Him but with the effects, which points us back, as it were, to the decree of election.... For the *knowledge* of faith is the 'conclusion' deduced by the effects."[4] A person's experience is where the divine decree makes itself felt and, ideally, known.

The ripples of Calvin's rock spread throughout Reformation culture in multiple domains, as thinkers sought to determine how and whether and how far it was ethical, possible, prudent, or pleasurable to undertake to approach a God's-eye view of the world. English elaborations of the practical syllogism ultimately result in William Perkins's works on conscience and the vast publishing industry of self-detection they spawned, and to whose protocols I will shortly turn. But these protocols were a response to a question that we can see emerging quite early on in the history of English absorption of the implications of predestination for the state and for the self. For the former, the most disturbing was the prospect of passivity or libertinism: why should anyone constrain him- or herself within the bounds of civil order if hellfire was not a disincentive for failing to do so? For individuals, what gave pause were the questions of whether one was saved and how to tell. Twenty years prior to the arrival of Perkins's works, with his flowcharts, checklists, and self-help manuals, we find not an insignificant body of sermons, letters, and other writings intended to reassure anxious souls who were beginning to digest the fact that the downside of gratuitous grace was its selective distribution. The elaboration of a method of assurance was a response to the question of "comfort."[5]

In 1590, for instance, there appeared a collection of fourteen *Certaine Godly and Verie comfortable Letters, full of Christian consolation. Written by M. Ed. Dering unto sundry of his friends*. Dering, a star at Cambridge in the 1560s, was the up-and-coming preacher of the Protestant urban elite in the early 1570s, which is from when most of the letters date (he died of tuberculosis in 1576). A darling of well-born and well-positioned Protestant women, himself of gentry stock, in 1572 Dering married Anne Locke, a widow of substance ten years his senior with impressive reformist credentials: a poet, translator of Calvin, and intimate of Knox, on whose advice she had joined other Marian exiles in Geneva, leaving her first husband behind in London. Dering was deprived of his preaching license by Elizabeth I owing to the pointedness of his scriptural application (to her), in the most-reprinted (1570) sermon of the Elizabethan period. In response, his wife along with the four learned Cooke sisters – Mildred, Lady Burghley; Anne Bacon, widow of the Lord Keeper of the Seal Nicholas Bacon (and mother of Francis); Lady Elizabeth Russell, widow of Thomas Hoby; and Katherine, wife of the illustrious diplomat Henry Killigrew – undertook to rehabilitate his reputation with the queen by joining in the preparation of an illustrated manuscript of *Giardino cosmografico coltivato* by Bartholo Sylva, "a compendium of received scientific thinking" that Louise Schleiner argues "was to stress without explicit statement that Dering and the reformist party supporting him are learned, cultivated, internationally respected, and loyal to the queen."[6] Dering was one of many "hot" Protestant preachers patronized by the Cooke sisters throughout their long lives (ca. 1526–1609), and while in later ages such a fan club of "spiritual patients" surrounding an esteemed spiritual guide in delicate health would sound like something out of Trollope, what we have in the Cooke sisters is not a group of females doting on a curate, but a group of curates under the protection of fierce standard-bearers of Calvinism, whose own publications were among the first to introduce Calvinist thought into England.[7]

As "comfortable letters," Dering's words attempt to address the most pressing concern of Protestant thought, and they ring with an urgency underwritten by the increasing imminence of his own death.[8] He wrote to Katherine Killigrew that he knew that her own "weake and sicklie body" causes her to "grieueth . . . that you cannot eyther haue care ouer your house, as you wishe, or attende on your children as you desire, or reioyce with your husbande, as otherwise you might." But, he argues, a silver lining exists: "this is the lot of Gods saintes, to enjoye his blessinges with afflictions, so that the more that you bee sorrowfull, the more you be sure that the liuing God hath giuen you your portion: And so your sorrowe is ioye vnto you."[9] What appears a foreboding harbinger of her eternal prospects is in fact a confirmation. Plus, he goes on, sorrows will "tempringe" [temper] her for heaven, preventing her from growing too fond of the world, just as conversely, in times of affliction, faith should comfort.

This contraindicative reading of the value of an experience would become central to the epistemology of assurance: the more you doubt, the more certain you should be; the hallmark of a sincere faith is the fear that one might not be sincere. It is the reflex of the reflex act, the willingness to read one's own doubt as the chief sign of hope, and we find it voiced across a wide range of locations. Thomas Sparke is another rising leftish clergyman in the 1580s: along with Walter Travers, we find him a delegate to the anticlimactic 1584 Lambeth conference about the Prayer Book, where they confined themselves to the matter of readings from the Apocrypha rather than a direct assault on the liturgy. Twenty years later, despite attending the Hampton Court conference pointedly not in clerical costume but "such that Turkey merchants wear," he would again pull his punches, choosing not to speak on the first day and on the second, having had a private audience with James I, abandoning the Puritan position.[10] Apparently no stranger to the art of self-rationalization, in his 1580 "A short Treatise, very comfortable for all those Christians that be troubled and disquieted in theyr consciences with the sight of their owne infirmities," Sparke displays rhetorical moves that would become institutionalized. "Doest thou not greatly mislike this thy doubting?" he asks his reader, "art thou not greeued with thy selfe for it? findest thou not in thy selfe an earnest desire to be ridde of it?" Not to worry: "so farre off is it that you should be perswaded that God hath forgotten you or left you off, bycause of the trouble and vexation which you feele in your soule, that euen therein you haue matter of comfort, assuring you that you are one whome most tenderly he looketh vpon and regardeth."[11] To doubt your own doubt is the double negative that produces the positive evidence of faith. So too in 1586 John Deacon preached at Ridlington a sermon "full of singular comfort" which argued that not only were afflictions, for the godly, "properly no punishments for sinne, but argumentes rather of the vnspeakable loue of God," and not only would sin persist in the elect, but anguish itself is encouraging: "Be glad then my soule, rouse up thy selfe and reioyce, yea, and in the verie anguish it self doe take a good courage, return to thy Christ, get a sweet nap in his louing affections."[12]

One can get the sense from reading such tracts that a nap might well be in order, as the inversions they propose are taxing in their counterintuitive imperatives. It is a funny kind of evidence that needs to be read as warrant for its opposite: sorrow as cause for joy, doubt as certainty, a broken heart as an encouraging sign, the moment of conversion as both the lowest and the starting point; God's apparent unresponsiveness to you as a spur to increase your desire for Him. Reading perversely, against the grain of worldly values, is of course a Christian tic, the hermeneutic that requires one to always stand slightly apart from the evidence on offer, to imagine otherwise. But it must be acknowledged that the comfort on offer bears little resemblance to that of an old shoe. The gymnastic challenge of the inverse hermeneutic in soteriological self-study is compounded by the abstract quality of many of its indices. For instance, while the seeker was provided with the helpful rubric of the *ordo salutis* – election, calling, justification, adoption, sanctification, and glorification – intended to measure and plot progression toward assurance of one's elect status, most of its stages are highly esoteric in formulation: justification, for instance, is "the imputation of righteousness,...whereby such as believe, having the guilt of their sins covered, are accounted just in the sight of God through Christ's righteousness."[13] Perhaps because they recognized it was easy to lose one's bearings in such a landscape, writers attempted to provide practical measuring sticks of salvation.

The tokens of salvation are often termed its "fruits," or the actions of a person in the world that demonstrate his or her salvific status. These included garden-variety practices of frequent prayer, meditation, sermon attendance, and consultation with learned ministers; and more specifically, adherence to the commandments, which provided both a goad to search out sin and a conduct book for godly living. Lest the ten seem to consider instances of behavior too extreme for most purposes, writers such as John "Decalogue" Dod provided dilations upon them that expanded their reach to include the most mundane practices. "Thou shalt not kill" is no doubt sound advice, but not for most people an injunction of daily utility. But in Dod's handling it expands into a discussion of patience, anger, remedies against envy, forgiveness, swaggerers, almsgiving, and covetousness.[14] As Perkins assured, "Gods word ministers sufficient direction for all actions whatsoever."[15]

The task of expounding if not expanding the reach of the Ten Commandments was a major engine of the early modern publishing industry. The 1612 edition of Dod's book is 378 quarto pages long, and as these things go, a modest effort. The standard guide, Lewis Bayley's *Practice of Piety* (1601), was 813 pages long and went through thirty-six editions in fifteen years. Not only was it possible to describe marks of salvation, it was profitable; as far as market-share of the early modern publishing industry goes, "Puritanism" was anything but eccentric. In fact, the earliest and one of the best-selling devotional how-to manuals of this period, *A Christian Directory guiding men to eternall salvation* (1584), was a Protestantized edition, by a minister "conventionally classified as a moderate Puritan," of a text authored by a Spanish Jesuit and midwifed for an English audience by an English one.[16] Such recycling could mean that the market for such texts anticipated the texts themselves, or equally, that Edmund Bunny – the moderate Puritan – did not conceive of such emendation as an especially difficult fix. In other words, inter-Protestant confessional divisions at this moment are not as strident as we usually conceive them to be.

The need for uniquely Protestant pietistic texts soon found an ample respondent in William Perkins (1558–1602). Perkins's works were an industry unto themselves and prompted numerous redactions, imitations, and spin-offs. His first soteriological text, *A Treatise Tending unto A Declaration whether a man be in the estate of damnation or in the estate of grace,* appeared in 1589 and was followed in rapid succession throughout the 1590s by elaborations on this theme.[17] Perkins's thought founds itself in an entrenched theoretical and theological working-through of the possibility and necessity of the search for assurance. He readily anchors the evidence for salvation in demonstrable physiological signs. These are considered to be involuntary and hence presumably (in advance of method acting) untheatrical. Sorrow for sin, for example, "hath certaine Symptomes in the bodie, as burning heate, rowling of the intrals, a pining and fainting of the solide parts."[18] "The effect of the accusing and condemning conscience," he writes, "is to stirre up sundrie passions and motions in the heart, but specially these five": shame, which "sheweth it selfe by the rising of the blood from the heart to the face"; sadness and sorrow, often but not to be confused with melancholy, in that they do not respond to medical treatment; fear, which is characterized by the tendency of the subject to startle at small objects, "if he see but a worme peepe out of the ground." In its more extreme form, "terrours of conscience" can "cause other passions in the body as exceeding heate, like that which is in the fitte of an ague, the rising of the entrals towards the mouth; and souning [swooning]" (*DC,* 39–40). While a person may well find it difficult to judge the adequacy of his own self-judgment, presumably vomiting is less open to question.

This drive toward a positive forensics of salvation does not mean these writers were unaware of the hermeneutic challenges posed by a search for assurance. It was bedeviled by questions of motive, of sincerity, and the fact that even reprobates can possess a faith virtually indistinguishable from that of the elect. Perkins, for instance, readily acknowledges that blushes are notoriously fickle: not only do the shameless not blush, but the elect may continue to do so. Ideally, repentance will be accompanied by "a bodily mooving of the heart, which causeth crying and teares," but if one is not the crying type, "the latter is not simply necessarie, though it be commendable in whomsoever it is."[19] In fact, in some cases, the more authentic and heartfelt the affect, the more likely it is to be beyond visible expression. For instance, the difference between "true" and "presumptuous" testimony is that the former "stirs up the heart, to praier and invocation…it causeth a man to crie and call earnestly unto God, in the time of distresse, with a sense and felling [*sic*] of his owne miseries: and with deepe sighes and groanes, *which cannot be uttered*" (*DC*, 113, italics mine). In fact, to be picky about it, in a predestinarian scheme, action, let alone intention, is never one's own, in that a person is not a cause, but an effect, "because every action comes from God, who is the first cause of all things and actions" (*CC*, 92).

As the rise of Arminianism attests, of all the counterintuitive demands put by thinking soteriologically, the sense of ownership over one's own actions was the hardest to put aside. Always dogging the question of salvation is the role of an individual's participation, and haunting the thousands of pages of practical piety printed in this period is the question of how to measure the sincere performance of an act. No affect is mentioned in these texts unaccompanied by its authenticating modifier: truly, properly, heartfelt. Yet the regard urged for the self is, on the face of it, an estranged one: alien and alienated, wearingly meta-. These texts direct the seeking soul not merely to feel, but to consider one's feelings as a sign, at a distance and as a spectacle. Thus while they urge sincerity everywhere, their procedures legislate against it. Nicholas Byfield warns, for instance, that those most likely to be hypocrites are those who appear most resolute, they "that are swift to speake, and full of words, and forward to expresse their masterlike conceits."[20] Ideally, then, assurance should never be too assured, and always self-effacing: "presumption is peremptorie without doubting: whereas the testimonie of the conscience is mingled with manifold doubtings" (*DC*, 63).

No doubt if human character were more readily apparent we would have less need of practical piety books, but what is self-perpetuating as a publishing strategy appears self-defeating as personal inquiry. (In fact, it is precisely because it is self-defeating that it is self-perpetuating.) Such, at least, has been the critical estimate, in which such descriptions of the subject are understood as contributing to an early modern increase in skepticism, epistemological crisis, and anxiety about the possibility of self-knowledge. Nor is it just to we alienated postmoderns that it seems this way; as David Como writes, a major impulse for early modern antinomian thought was the charge "that the 'mixed' faith of puritanism (a faith that incorporated doubt) was nothing but a subtle trap whereby mainstream puritan ministers snared unsuspecting listeners, delivering them into a state of bondage, insecurity, and fear."[21]

Certainly the selfhood many of these texts enjoin can present as an exhausting prospect, one that is perpetually second-guessing, agonistic, disassociated, ever-attenuating, and interminably self-conscious, never simply *being*. Given the cultural prominence of this identity it is no surprise that the hallmark of literary personhood from this moment is an overweening self-doubt, nor that the dream and dramatization of passionate action were at once so charismatic and so reductive (see *Hamlet*). But post-panopticon emphases on the discouraging and deconstructive aspects of a doubt-driven faith miss the way in which, for its practitioners, not only was it possible to ascertain salvation, but it was also precisely doubt that served as the mark of sincerity—ambivalence of authenticity. The motto of assurance was "do worry, be happy." The fact that sincerity is always subject to skepticism becomes the measure of correct action: rather than expect ourselves to be sincerely sin-free, we need to take (with apologies to *The Music Man*) the sincere out of the sin: "A wicked man, when hee sinneth in his heart hee giueth full consent to the sinne: but the godly though they fall into the same sinnes with the wicked, yet they neuer giue full consent" (*TT*, 47). Writers such as Perkins stated unequivocally that it was indeed possible to discern the elect from the reprobate, chiefly by means of the presence of self-examination, as instructed by 2 Peter 1:10: "Give all diligence to make your calling and election sure: for if ye do these things ye shall never fail."

Of course, strictly speaking, self-examination is not necessary to election, just as a deathbed conversion is still in bounds. God can save whomever he wants whether they ever know it or not. But according to Perkins a deathbed conversion is not statistically the most certain: "late repentance is seldome true repentance," presumably because even when one's entire life is flashing before one's eyes, the effort of self-examination takes time (*TT*, 16). The reprobate could indeed pray, even preach, hear sermons, observe the commandments, "thi[n]k it enough to make a common protestation of the faith" (*TT*, A2v), and all sincerely enough, but what distinguished him from the elect is that he did not examine himself doing so, was not skeptical of his own motives. He lacked self-reflection. "It is a grace peculiar to the man Elect to trie himselfe whether hee be in the estate of grace or not" (*TT*, A2v). Of course, self-reflection in the privacy of one's own mind is usually (absent the groans) indetectable; it was hence best performed not by oneself, but in godly company, in concert with learned ministers.[22] But however self-examination was conducted, it was generally agreed that the unexamined life was not worth heaven.

Signally, the fear of tendentiousness or subjectivity, of finding what you look for, which for us would be a real concern, is not a problem, or at least less of one than not looking at all. It is only *because* you look for signs of salvation that you find them; looking is not only the condition of finding, *but the sign itself.* The distortions of selfhood don't enter into it. This is not because the self is not distorting; original sin makes sure of that. But for Perkins, being moved to search for assurance means that God will refurbish one's senses so as to make them extra capable of accurate discernment: "he *openeth their senses, hearts, eares, understandings*… the holie Ghost is their anoyntment, and their eyesalve, to cleare the eyes of their minde" (*TT,* 23). Once a person undertakes to self-examine, not only the perceptive faculties but also signs themselves become dependable, Plato's flickering shadows no more; again and again we find the language of "clear evidence," "infallible signs and tokens," "infallible marks"; "Sure mark."[23]

Crucially, unlike many notions of invigilation, and despite the fact that it bore no small resemblance to the one institution of early modern statehood that *was* relatively established – the informer – soteriological self-examination was not primarily understood as prosecutorial. It was instead a comfort; it gave purchase and perspective. For Perkins, the conscience is a kind of personal archivist, who "observes & takes notice of all things that we do…inwardly & secretly whithin the heart, tell us of them all. In this respect it may fitly bee compared to a Notarie, or a Register that hath alwaies the penne in his hand, to note & record whatsoever is said or done: who also because he keepes the rolles and records of the court can tell what hath beene said or done many hundred yeares past" (*DC,* 8). Conscience makes every "Christian man…not onely a Priest and a Prophet, but also a spirituall king, even in this life:…renewed within him shall bee his solliciter to put him in mind of all his affaires and duties which he is to performe to God" (*DC,* 65). Or better yet, a friend: "when none can comfort us, it will be an amiable comforter, and a friend speaking sweetely unto us, in the verie agonie and pang of death"

(*DC,* 77). Conscience did not represent internal division but society: "*Scire,* to know, is of one man alone by himselfe: and *conscire* is, when two at the least knowe some one secret thing; either of them knowing it togither with the other" (*DC,* 7). In a metaphysics where action was not strictly own's own, self-spectatorship, or the observation of God's work in oneself, was one kind of participation that was available to the person. The genius of Perkins is to convert the disconcerting import of predestination – the supreme dramatic irony that God alone knows our fate, and we can only hope to discover it – into a kind of spectator sport, in which merely to watch is to win.

Put as a matter of mere self-consciousness, the bar for election seems set rather low, especially considering it is meant to be an elite condition. (Are there really people who act without watching themselves act? How nice for them.) This may be an anachronistic observation; perhaps self-reflection was a rare as well as novel condition in the late sixteenth century, requiring literacy and Ramus-trained memory. A rap sheet requires record-keeping. Perkins describes conscience almost as a kind of sense; but arguably, the real players in self-examination were longing, memory, and literacy. For Richard Rogers, author of *Seven Treatises,* underlying the resistance to self-examination are "many infirmities, much dulnesse, slipperie memories, and sundriey other pulbackes" (29). The many safety nets built into the process support the sense of a low bar. Perkins acknowledges that it is indeed highly unlikely that self-examination can unearth all of one's sins, "as the heart of man is a vast gulfe of sinne, without either bottome or bancke" (*TT,* 23). For that reason, he recommends a kind of blanket self-suspicion, or "godly iealousie," that translates, in turn, to a general amnesty: "when God pardons the knowne sinnes of men whereof they do in particular repent, he doth withall pardon the rest that are unknowne" (*DC,* 60). In similar fashion, ideally one will have processed through the entirety of the *ordo salutis,* but not necessarily so – nor, necessarily, in any given order. In *A Grain of Mustard Seed* Perkins sets out to establish "The least measure of grace that can befall the true child of God, lesser than which there is no grace effectual to salvation." The measurement is infinitesimal: "a man that doth but begin to be converted is even at that instant the very child of God."[24]

In fact, one gets the sense in many of these first-generation soteriological treatises that despite the fear of impostors, false faith, and self-deceit, the only persons that need not apply are those who give themselves over to "Hunting, Hawking, Dicing, Carding, or any such vaine practiles," and "giue themselues wholly" at that (that is, ambivalent hunters, hawkers, and gamers are not beyond hope).[25] Just as all actions whatsoever are comprehended by the Decalogue, sometimes it seems like all doubts short of actual suicide are recuperable. Locating salvation in the mere act of self-examination begs the further question of what might count as sincere self-skepticism (or is it skeptical sincerity?) of whether one is "examining [oneself] soundly and throughly";[26] to be of service, doubt about your own salvation must be both a source of genuine anguish and yet something to be shrugged off. But in general Perkins's rubric seems as forgiving as his God.

This is not, admittedly, the attitude we associate with "Puritanism," and it may well be only Perkins who is able to present the prospect in a welcoming light. Even in his writing there can be a careening quality, as he moves from trying to assuage doubt to inculcating it; apparently when preaching he could "pronounce the word *Damne* with such an emphasis as left a dolefull Echo in his auditours ears a good while after."[27] As later critics of this posture seized upon, to read self-doubt as the hallmark of belief risks the charge of sophistry and probably requires an unusually self-congratulatory personality. But at least in the 1580s and '90s, the temper of these writings is encouraging, even coaxing, pitched less to exhort or to scourge than to invite and to comfort. This is feel-good literature. True, somewhere around the turn of the century the tone of practical piety shades toward the more hectoring and exclusionary. The shift may have to do with the dawning realization on the part of practical pietists that book sales were driven by the doubtful: people don't buy a self-help book unless they can be made to feel in need of help. Perkins dies in 1602, and, as of the 1604 Hampton Court Conference, those agitating for further reform began to realize that their desire for changes to public and official liturgical practices might not have the same traction as their recommendations for interiority, whereas in 1595 Whitgift had reiterated the official centrality of predestinarian principles in the Lambeth Articles. But the first generation of soteriological discourse is on the whole rather optimistic in conception and in tone, intended to ward off despair rather than browbeat. All the things that would become hallmarks of working out your salvation with "fear and trembling" were yet understood as good and exciting things: meta is good, agon is good, even attenuation and the consequent need for persistence were good. What makes the suspense of perpetual self-doubt a form of certainty is that it beats the alternative of a definitive "no." Even the protracted nature of the ever-anticipatory experimental trial is imagined as enjoyable as well as exhausting: the flirtatious dilations of doubt a kind of foreplay to salvation. Total assurance, as Calvin insisted, might be presumptuous, but it was also boring, a rush to the revelation that only death provides for sure. Suspense is necessary to salvation-seeking; belief is compelled by the feeling that something hangs in the balance.

None of these forms of self-alienation preclude the certainty of salvation – on the contrary, they are the preconditions for it. On rhetorical grounds alone, Perkins's style of argumentation, a kind of power point *avant la lettre,* conveys a confidence that the very soul itself can be diagrammed (fig. 43). Diagnostic protocols helped the believer substantiate the degree of his faith. Fact-gathering within reason and memory and community was possible. The *ordo salutis* provided a plot and a *telos* of sorts. And despite the premium on doubt, there is at this moment great confidence in the axiomatic status of intense feeling. One's memory may be faulty, but longing is not: "A naked and bare desire of saluation" can become "feruent and constant" (Rogers, 38). Perkins's riposte to the papist charge that assurance is "given onely by an experiment or feeling of an inward delight or peace, which breedes in us not an infallible, but a conjectural certentie," is an exposition of Romans 8:15–16. He writes: "Ye have received the spirit of adoption, whereby we crie *Abba, father.*" "Crying to God as to a father argues courage, confidence, and boldnesse. . . . & therefore it must needes be a spirit giving assurance of libertie" (*DC,* 50). Doubt and fear may be subject to suspicion, sorrow might in the end prove to be melancholy, but joy is unmistakable.

Above all, Protestant soteriology at this juncture urges not only the link between knowledge and power, but also knowledge and feeling. The idea that a supreme being knows our true worth is a profoundly appealing promise of recognition and individual value, less a vision of hostile scrutiny than a reassurance that someone is paying attention. "God knows perfectly all the doings of man, though they be never so hid and concealed: and man by a gift given him of God; knowes togither with God, the same things of himselfe" (*DC,* 7). Salvation might be unearned,

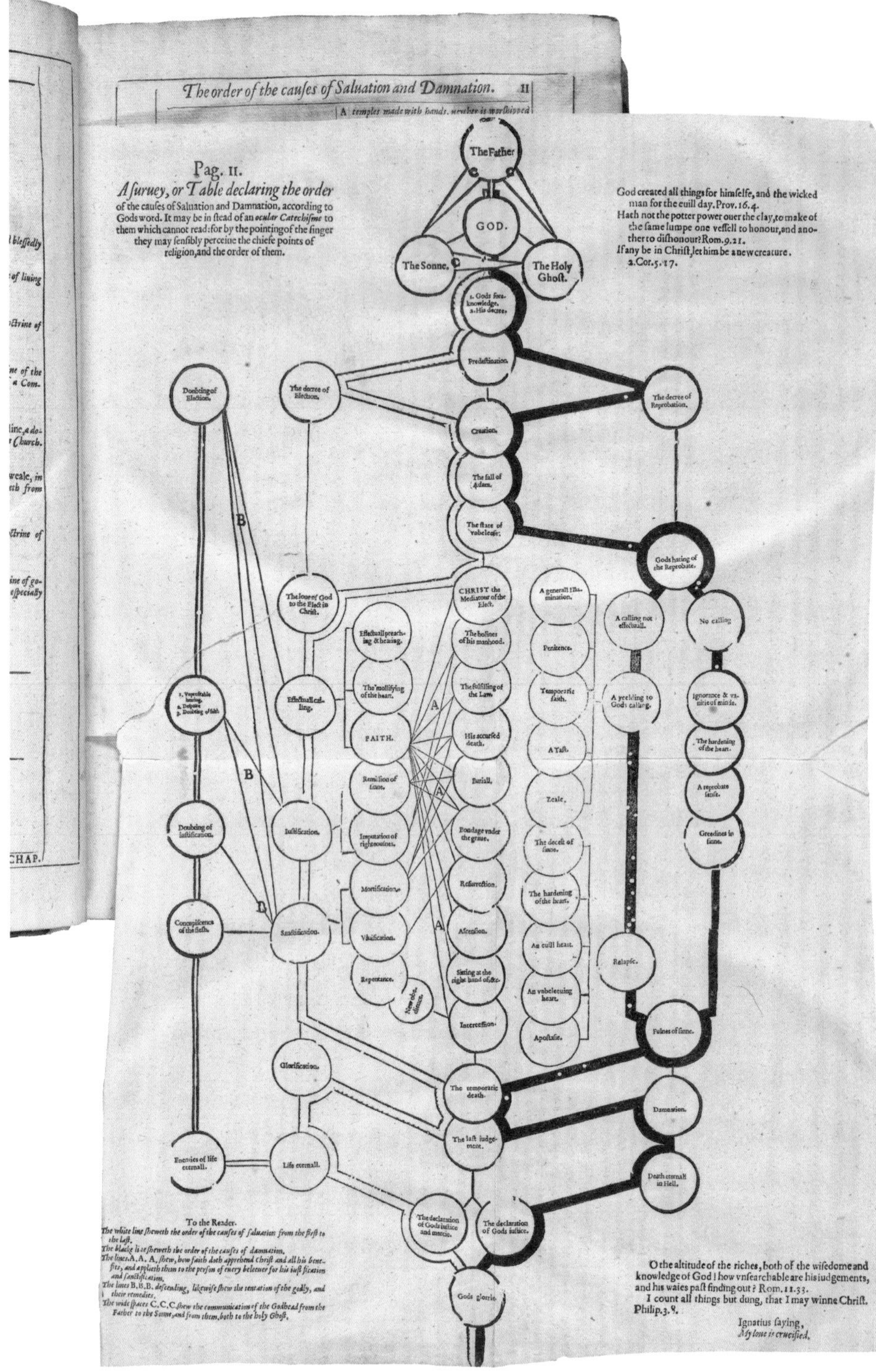
The order of the causes of Saluation and Damnation. II
Pag. II.
A Suruey, or Table declaring the order of the causes of Saluation and Damnation, according to Gods word. It may be in stead of an ocular Catechisme to them which cannot read: for by the pointing of the finger they may sensibly perceiue the chiefe points of religion, and the order of them.
God created all things for himselfe, and the wicked man for the euill day. Prov. 16.4.
Hath not the potter power ouer the clay, to make of the same lumpe one vessell to honour, and another to dishonour? Rom. 9.21.
If any be in Christ, let him be a new creature. 2.Cor.5.17.
The Father
GOD.
The Sonne.
The Holy Ghost.
1. Gods foreknowledge. 2. His decree.
Predestination.
The decree of Election.
The decree of Reprobation.
Doubting of Election.
Creation.
The fall of Adam.
The state of vnbeleefe.
Gods hating of the Reprobate.
The loue of God to the Elect in Christ.
CHRIST the Mediatour of the Elect.
A generall illumination.
A calling not effectuall.
No calling.
Effectuall preaching & hearing.
The holines of his manhood.
Penitence.
The mollifying of the heart.
The fulfilling of the Law.
Temporarie faith.
A yeelding to Gods calling.
Ignorance & vanitie of minde.
Effectuall calling.
FAITH.
His accursed death.
A Tast.
The hardening of the heart.
Remission of sinne.
Buriall.
Zeale.
A reprobate sense.
Iustification.
Imputation of righteousnes.
Bondage vnder the graue.
The deceit of sinne.
Greedines in sinne.
Doubting of Iustification.
Mortification.
Resurrection.
The hardening of the heart.
Concupiscence of the flesh.
Sanctification.
Viuification.
Ascension.
An euill heart.
Relapse.
Repentance.
Sitting at the right hand of God.
An vnbeleeuing heart.
New obedience.
Intercession.
Apostasie.
Fulnes of sinne.
Glorification.
The temporarie death.
Damnation.
The last iudgement.
Enemies of life eternall.
Life eternall.
Death eternall in Hell.
The declaration of Gods iustice and mercie.
The declaration of Gods iustice.
Gods glorie.
A
B
C
To the Reader.
The white line sheweth the order of the causes of saluation from the first to the last.
The blacke line sheweth the order of the causes of damnation.
The lines A. A. A. shew, how faith doth apprehend Christ and all his benefits, and applieth them to the person of euery beleeuer for his iustification and sanctification.
The lines B. B. B. descending, likewise shew the tentation of the godly, and their remedies.
The wide spaces C. C. C. shew the communication of the Godhead from the Father to the Sonne, and from them, both to the holy Ghost.
O the altitude of the riches, both of the wisedome and knowledge of God! how vnsearchable are his iudgements, and his waies past finding out? Rom. 11.33.
I count all things but dung, that I may winne Christ. Philip. 3.8.
Ignatius saying,
My loue is crucified.

but knowledge of it wasn't. And central to this knowledge was the act of self-spectatorship. A self-examining subject not only sees God at work in himself, but he also sees himself as God sees him. While in a human being this God's-eye view can never be omniscient, it is a sight closer to it.

* * *

I have discussed soteriological thought at some length not only because I believe the temperament of early Puritanism needs revisiting but also because, of our two Williams, Perkins is the least familiar and most caricatured. I would like now to turn briefly to the other, in order to examine the relations between the cognitive conditions imposed upon the audience by Shakespeare's plays and their affective impact.

There are several possible models of connection between Shakespeare and Perkins. Take first the atmospheric one. From the 1570s on and beginning with special intensity in the 1590s – the years when Shakespeare begins to write and produce plays – the question of comfort and the answer of conscience resounded in both print and pulpit. Their proponents considered themselves to be spelling out the practical implications of established theology, and their own positions as comprehended within the established church. While separatist factions existed, they did not include Cambridge-based chairs of divinity. Malvolio's self-banishment in 1600 may be prophecy, but it is not at that moment history; besides, he is only a "kind of Puritan," as if Shakespeare is only groping toward the notion. (In other words, Shakespeare is no puritan, but puritans weren't puritans either.) The writers and readers of comfort and conscience constituted what we might call an intellectual elite; perhaps even an avant-garde. Their patrons were themselves learned, gentle, well-placed persons of power and fashion. As for more raffish circles, several Cambridge products – just to stay with Perkins's intellectual home – who did not follow the dictates of their university preparation but still chose to make their way in the world with words found their way to the world of the London literati. There was a kind of Cambridge-Southwark pipeline for ministers manqué. Conscience was not only comfortable; it was a highly visible cultural concern, something to conjure with.

Fig. 43. William Perkins, *A Golden Chaine* (Cambridge, 1597), "A suruey, or Table declaring the order of the causes of Saluation and Damnation." Beinecke Rare Book and Manuscript Library, Yale University, Mhc5 P419 Ar55

Of course, while zeitgeists are nice, when it comes to studies of literary influence, smoking guns, otherwise known as verbal parallels, are nicer. The term "conscience" appears in many places in Shakespeare's writings.[28] Yet the name "Perkins" appears nowhere in the indexes to Geoffrey Bullough's numerous volumes of Shakespeare's known sources. Perkins's works were not part of Shakespeare's grammar school curriculum (though they were both in grammar school at the same time). Discussions of the contribution of Protestant thought to Shakespeare's plays tend to emphasize the skeptical nature of conscience, which is found to be manifest either in the self-effacing meta-theatrical gestures in the plays, or in the agonized subjectivity of those tragic protagonists, both of which scholars consider indexes of Shakespeare's dramatization of the epistemic instability presaging the advent of Cartesian thought and, ultimately, secularism.[29]

I wish instead to proceed toward the goal of subjectivity by thinking about the self-conscious spectator: how does Shakespeare use our own awareness of our own knowledge to shape our feelings about his characters? What would count as the dramatic equivalent of self-conscious self-examination, and what might the contribution of such knowledge be to our belief in the plays?

As in studies of Protestant affect, or histories of the impact of the Reformation upon the secular cultural turn, the tendency in Shakespeare studies has been to consider the result of self-consciousness to be an alienating one. Kent Cartwright describes "the spectator's heightened self-consciousness" as constituted in and by "our interpretations aroused from moment to moment, our sense of removal from the point of view of any single character, our contrasting of events and attitudes, our awareness of illusion, our moral or intellectual judgments as invited by the dramatic context, and even our hypotheses about "facts."[30] This judgment tallies with the conventional equation of dramatic irony with a skeptical relation to a spectacle and its characters. The theory of self-consciousness and estrangement overlooks, however, what I consider to be a fundamental paradox of Shakespearean theater, one that is not unlike the contra-indicative hermeneutic of soteriological thought: namely, we tend to believe the most in characters who have most trouble believing in things (usually each other).

Obviously, states of audience knowledge are highly genre-specific. In a comedy, knowledge is often pleasure ("Lord what fools these mortals be").[31] In a tragedy, our vantage point can produce a nearly physical pain ("Iago is a liar!"). In a history play, dramatic irony seems especially unavoidable. Klaus Peter Jochum has argued that "Shakespeare's histories are deliberately built on the audience's foreknowledge of a long historical sequence from Richard II to Henry VII."[32] This advantage applies even if one's grasp of the particulars of medieval history is a tenuous one: one needn't be a devotee of Holinshed in order to know more than the characters ever can – at the very least, we know we inhabit a future our ancestors can only intuit. They are dead, and we are not. The challenge for the dramatist, as it is for the experimentalist, is to cultivate suspense, either by making us forget what we know, or by giving us the impression that the course of represented events needn't have taken the path it did, to counterpoise necessity with possibility.

That said, most of Shakespeare's history plays conjure not with our omniscience but the opposite. Some of them even thematize this confusion: in *Richard III,* the duet of Queens Margaret and Elizabeth caricatures the difficulty of tracking events and persons ("I had an Edward, till a Richard killed him.... Thou hadst an Edward, till a Richard killed him..." (4.4.40–42).[33] The first scene of *Richard II* is an instance where Shakespeare seems particularly bent on disorienting his audience. For instance, while it is clear enough that Bolingbroke and Mowbray are accusing each other of high treason, Bolingbroke's charges seem too comprehensive ("all the treasons for these eighteen years" (1.1.95) and Mowbray's too coy ("For Gloucester's death, / I slew him not, but to my own disgrace, / Neglected my sworn duty in that case" (1.1.122–24).[34] If we are prescient enough to sense there might an ulterior charge present, we probably don't know which of the several voiced is the one at issue. It is only as of scene 2, when the Duchess of Gloucester upbraids Gaunt with failing to avenge her husband Woodstock's murder, and Gaunt replies "God's substitute...Hath caused his death" (1.2.39), that the penny begins to drop. We may then realize that the reason the content of the first scene eludes us is because the participants were being evasive. However, the fact that 1.2 begins with Gaunt and an unidentified woman discussing the death of someone named "Woodstock," who is then called "Thomas," before being named "my dear lord" and then "Gloucester" by the Duchess (who thereby identifies herself), means that we only gradually discern what is under discussion. The additional mention of an Edward, his seven sons, seven vials, and seven fair branches, like the rhyme about the man traveling to St. Ives, causes more confusion than it eliminates. This is an instance where we can be tempted to imagine that the confusion is due to our not being Elizabethans, but I think this both overestimates Elizabethans and underestimates Shakespeare's calculated assault on our bearings and viewerly good will. Thus while what transpires in this scene comes close to, as it were, naming names, the indirection of Gaunt's expression (e.g., "God's substitute" for Richard, "hath caused" for "had killed") reinforces the sense that characters are failing to disclose, whether their reasons be prudent circumspection or just not needing to explain their referents to each other. Names may have been named, but, as in the case of Bolingbroke's charges, perhaps too many to be of much use.

Shakespeare's nomenclature in the history plays makes few concessions to the novice, but this play may be especially challenging in this regard. The first opening lines of the play introduce "Old John of Gaunt, time-honoured Lancaster"; "Henry Hereford, thy bold son"; and the "Duke of Norfolk, Thomas Mowbray" (1.1.1–4). Gaunt has three names – his Christian name, a nickname, and a place name – ; his son is called by none of them; and Mowbray also three. Some might object that the array-per-person is only bewildering to an auditor unfamiliar with the titular habits of British nobility, but even the fan of Burke's peerage might be hard-pressed to absorb this information (the existence of such a book supports my point). There is more at stake here, both politically and cognitively. Henry Hereford will go on to acquire many more names throughout the play: "Cousin of Hereford" (1.1.28); "Bolingbroke" (1.1.124); "Harry Hereford" (1.3.1); "Duke of Hereford" (1.3.20); "Harry of Hereford, Lancaster, and Derby" (1.3.35; 99; 113); "high Hereford" (1.4.2); "Harry Duke of Hereford" (2.1.144); "Hereford" (2.1.145); "Harry" (2.1.191); the banished Duke" (2.1.260); "my lord of Hereford" (2.3.69); "Lancaster" (2.3.70); "Duke of Lancaster" (2.3.124); "Harry Bolingbroke" (3.3.105); "King Bolingbroke" (3.3.173); "Henry Bolingbroke" (4.1.182) – and, of course, "King Henry" (4.1.220). To the ear, this is a barrage of name-dropping, a display of familiarity and supremacy, insider knowledge wielded like a truncheon. The variety speaks to this figure's breadth of political possessions and the reach of his ambitions (cf. the hobbit-like monikers of Bushy, Bagot, and Green), as well as the changing demands of the iambic line. But the many-handled

Henry Hereford also expresses the way in which the ironically "silent king" is an elusive and mutating one, aware of the politically advantageous mobility of multiple representations as opposed to claiming to be the thing itself. For Bolingbroke, as the times change, so does his name: "As I was banished, I was banished Hereford; But as I come, I come for Lancaster" (2.3.113). Richard has only one.

While any play demands an initial information-gathering stint of its audience, during which we assimilate personnel and situation, *Richard II*'s is a particularly protracted one. There are movements toward clarification, and occasional concessions to our need to know; Gaunt, for instance, defends "this England's" national chastity (a point any passerby can grasp) and is comfortingly present in four out of the first five scenes. But for every step forward, there are two back. For instance, Richard's opening lines in the first scene indicate that he has in the past deferred attending to the "late appeal" (1.1.4), but at the close of the scene he again defers a resolution; history seems to be repeating itself, but the fact that it is deferral and evasion that are being repeated means that reiteration reinforces nothing but the sense that we are making no headway. At the beginning of scene 3, we find ourselves in a reprise of the first scene, which is promising, especially given what looks like, in Richard's ritualized performance of ignorance, another opportunity to clarify the specifics of the charges in question: "Marshal, demand of yonder champion / The cause of his arrival here in arms" (1.3.9–10). However, when the challengers are finally at the point of enacting the judicial and theological denouement that is a duel—presumably at the conclusion of which we might at least be able to find out which of the insinuators is correct, if not necessarily the content of their insinuations—Richard summarily cancels it.

Throughout the opening scenes, Richard's actions are opaque and preemptory. As Wilbur Sanders has noted, Shakespeare's staging of York as a figure who struggles to sort out loyalties amidst the swift course of events comfortingly echoes our own cognitive condition.[35] Like the duet of the queens in *Richard III,* this is an implicit acknowledgment that what passes before us is difficult to grasp and keep pace with. Along with our beleaguered state of knowledge goes a state of feeling and relation to character. Tracking this experience of cognitive disorientation is Shakespeare's presentation of Richard as remote, arbitrary, formal of speech, careless of the rights of his nobility and of our own ability to comprehend his actions; both Richard and Shakespeare are unwilling to explain. Refusal of the expository mode gives the sense that we are witnesses to characters wholly – and "realistically" – immersed in their universe, unconscious of an audience to whom they need explain anything, and who have no need or desire to spell matters out to each other. It is also an accurate representation of persons who by virtue of their station don't generally feel the need to explain themselves. However, for Shakespeare to pivot this play so that Richard becomes a figure of our compassion will require that both of these elements shift: we will need to gain some purchase on the course of events, and perhaps also some feeling for the king.

Legibility of events comes first. Once Richard leaves for his Irish wars, we begin, through the "meanwhile" technique, to know things that he cannot, primarily concerning Bolingbroke's fortunes. The dire premonitions of the queen or York in 2.2 and 2.3 signal, reassuringly, to our knowledge of Richard's eventual fate (or absent that, at least to the play's title of "Tragedy"). We also receive expository news, such as "The nobles they are fled, the commons they are cold" (2.2.88) and witness the departure of the Welsh forces (2.4). Bolingbroke begins to exercise authority with the dispatching of Bushy and Green in 3.1. When Richard returns from Ireland, it is not only to a country but to an audience newly fortified against him by having been witness to events of which he is as yet ignorant. Now, instead of working to orient ourselves and keep pace with a mysterious king, we get to sit back and watch him catch up to us.

The question then becomes for us: when will he know what we do? Act 3, scene 2 marks the beginning of Richard's poetic flights: the first his apostrophe to the earth, the second his analogy of himself to the sun, the third his paean to deposed kings, all of them responses to recent developments. Critics often term these "excessive," and an indulgence of a man more poet than king, but what we know and he does not is in the first two instances what his rhetoric most exceeds is the number of his soldiers. The last outburst, where Richard resolves to think about the "death of kings," exceeds even Bolingbroke's cognizance of his own military advantage (which the latter only discovers in 3.3). In one respect Richard is prescient, but we might also feel him, as Aumerle does, to be outrunning the facts. While his plight is pitiable, there is also the sense that pity for Richard here would be a matter of coals to Barkeley Castle. But at least instead of our trying, as in the opening scenes, to decipher and order information being flung at us, we now find ourselves in the relatively comfortable position of watching Richard react "by small and small" to various disclosures. This scene presents a pivot in at least the first category, of our own competence. By the end of the scene, we are allied with Richard – or he with us – at least as regards knowledge of the political landscape.

True, our sympathies may still lag, but in ways that are now cued to our new knowledge. Richard out of hand condemns Bushy, Bagot, and Green as "vipers" and "Judases," because he "warrant[s] they have made peace with Bolingbroke" (3.2.127–32) – whereas we know from the prior scene that two have died loyal to Richard. His poetry may be arresting, and give us more with respect to his character to go on than has been previously the case, but it repeatedly overshoots the information we possess; it is histrionic in the degree to which it outpaces history. Incidentally, as far as concerns the political realities of the transfer of power from Richard to Henry IV, the action of the play is now complete. In that sense, at least, there is nothing further to be known.

What, then, remains? For Henry IV, it is to make Richard's resignation official, to "surrender" "in common view" "So we shall proceed / Without suspicion" (4.1.156–57). For Shakespeare, perhaps, it is to shape our response so as to make of it something other than "ding dong the king is dead" – in other words, to complete the work of shared knowledge with that of shared feeling, to replace the high-handed and alienating figure of the play's opening or the histrionic and embarrassing figure of the play's middle, with a person whose loss we mourn. As David Scott Kastan has written, the political resonances of the Elizabethan theater stem from the fact that "on stage the king became a subject – the subject of the author's imaginings and the subject of the attention and judgment of an audience of subjects."[36]

How does Shakespeare engineer this shift? The traditional answer to the question of how Shakespeare engineers Richard's pull on our sympathies points to the prison scene and the way in which, shed of his royal office, Richard comes into his own as a philosopher-poet, offering us a window into his interior.[37] It is indeed true that as the play moves toward its end, the "person" revealed by the poetry is one in a state of ambivalence that borders on the soteriological. But I would locate the work of engagement elsewhere. For the question that generates suspense in this play is whether and when Richard is or is not a king. Shakespeare manufactures our contact with the character of Richard not through a representation of *his* inward doubt, but by soliciting our own through the construction of a teetering narrative pattern by which a matter of fact is called into question.

Beginning in 3.2, over the course of four lengthy scenes (approximately 200; 200; 100; and 335 lines), the question of Richard's un-kinging is raised, seemingly answered, revisited, and re-revisited. On several occasions we are asked to accept his fall as complete, and then the question is reopened. Again and again we are offered moments where it feels as if the balance could be tipped against what we know will be the case. In 3.2 Richard seemingly capitulates; in 3.3 at line 72 he recovers ("We are amazed, and thus long have we stood / To watch the fearful bending of thy knee"); at line 143 he capitulates again (although not in the hearing of his opponent); Bolingbroke calls him "Majesty" and claims "I come but for my own"; but then at 206 Richard tells Bolingbroke "What you will have, I'll give, and willing too." In the following scene the gardener still anticipates "depressed he is already and depos'd / 'Tis doubt he will be" (3.4.68–69). (The enjambment in that sentence enacts in its very prosody the process of advance and retreat we have been experiencing. The first six words, nearly perfect iambic pentameter, form a complete declarative statement. As we travel down the verse column, "'Tis doubt he will be" modifies "depos'd," eroding the previous sense of a complete action.) In 4.1 York tells Bolingbroke "plume-plucked Richard...with willing soul / Adopts thee heir, and his high sceptre yields / To the possession of thy royal hand (4.1.109–110). Yet by the end of the scene Richard has upstaged Bolingbroke, compelled him to fetch a mirror, and does not in fact read the confession of his sins meant to ratify his resignation. As we watch this performance, we can almost wonder whether Richard might choose to brave it out, and cause Bolingbroke to flinch.

The deposition scene of *Richard II* was notoriously subject to Elizabethan censorship, but given the taxing sequence of events from 3.2 onwards, the Master of Revels might well have been hard-pressed to name which scene it was, precisely, that he was meant to excise. The aporia, such as it is, may have to do with the fact that Shakespeare himself did not wish or did not know how to expose the specifics of and moment when a king stops being king – is it when he reads a confession, hands over the physical crown, names an heir, loses his Welsh forces, seizes a subject's lands, farms his lands, or orders the death of Woodstock? Never? Whereas in the play's opening we feel ourselves behind the action, and in the middle we wait for Richard to catch up to us, in the tortuous and teetering process of deposition (I do not say the moment, for there is none), we see a monarch that we seem to accompany in real time, as if we were moving forward into an unknown future with him, whom we know not less than, or more than, but with, *con-scientia*. This allows us to hope even against our own knowledge that he will brazenly outface history. Unlike the play's opening moves, what makes the process of deposition so taxing is not our bewilderment, but that we know too much, and wish we could unknow it.

He doesn't, of course. But the double-thinking tension between what we know of Richard's end and the imaginative possibility that he might avoid it, animates this history; it is what makes us hold our breath despite ourselves. This is not to say that we forget how it turns out, but we may well feel the need to reassure ourselves that we do know how it turns out. Of course we know well in one part of our minds that the uncertainties generated by Richard's prevarications are, if not implausible, at least beside the ultimate point and facts of history, "just" Shakespeare's imagination of what might have happened. We are merely flirting with their possibility. But much as a soul might keep the possibility of salvation in play by means of doubts, it is that very sense of uncertainty that makes this play feel so "real," as if we were witnessing it as if for the first time, allowing us to relive what is behind us as if it had yet to happen.

NOTES

1 Margot Heinemann, *Puritanism and Theatre: Thomas Middleton and Opposition Drama under the Early Stuarts* (Cambridge: Cambridge University Press, 1980); Jeffrey Knapp, *Shakespeare's Tribe: Church, Nation and Theater in Renaissance England* (Chicago: University of Chicago Press, 2002).

2 As in Barbara Kiefer Lewalski, *Protestant Poetics and the Seventeenth-Century Religious Lyric* (Princeton: Princeton University Press, 1979).

3 Peter Lake, *Anglicans and Puritans? Presbyterianism and English Conformist Thought from Whitgift to Hooker* (London: Unwin Hyman, 1988).

4 See R.T. Kendall, *Calvin and English Calvinism to 1649* (Oxford: Oxford University Press, 1979), 33; and Richard A. Muller, *Christ and the Decree: Christology and Predestination in Reformed Theology from Calvin to Perkins* (Durham, N.C.: Labyrinth Press, 1986), 25.

5 See, for instance, John Freeman, *The Comforter: or a comfortable Treatise, wherein are contained many reasons...to assure the forgiveness of sins* (London, 1600); or William Fulke, *A Comfortable Sermon of Faith, in temptations and Afflictions* (London, 1586).

6 See Louise Schleiner, *Tudor and Stuart Women Writers* (Bloomington: Indiana University Press, 1994), 40–45 (40, 41).

7 Anne Cooke, for instance, translated the sermons of Italian Calvinist Barnadine Ochino: *Sermons of Barnardine Ochine of S[i]ena godlye, frutefull, and uery necessarye for all true Christians* (London, 1548).

8 See Patrick Collinson, "A Mirror of Elizabethan Protestantism: The Life and Letters of 'Godly Master Dering,'" in *Godly People: Essays on English Protestantism and Puritanism* (London: Hambledon Press, 1983).

9 Edward Dering, *Certaine Godly and Verie comfortable Letters* (London, 1590), C5r–v.

10 *Dictionary of National Biography* 53, ed. Sidney Lee (New York: The Macmillan Co., 1898), 313.

11 Thomas Sparke, *A short Treatise* (London, 1580), C1r–C2r.

12 John Deacon, *A verie godly and most necessarie Sermon, full of singuler comfort for so many as see their sundry sinnes: and are inwardly afflicted with a conscience and a feeling thereof* (London, 1586), A2r, A4r, B2v.

13 William Perkins, *A Golden Chain*, in *The Work of William Perkins*, ed. Ian Breward (London: Appleford, 1970), 233.

14 John Dod, *A Plain and Familiar Exposition of the Ten Commandments* (London, 1612), 255–83.

15 William Perkins, *A Discourse of Conscience*, in *William Perkins, 1558–1602, English Puritanist*, ed. Thomas F. Merrill (Nieuwkoop: B. De Graaf, 1966), 42; hereafter cited as *DC*.

16 Respectively, Edmund Bunny, Gaspar Loarte, and Robert Persons; Bunny's version retains 90 percent of the Loarte/Persons text, cutting references to purgatory, works, and free will. See Patrick Collinson, "Literature and Religion," in *The Cambridge History of Early Modern English Literature*, ed. David Loewenstein and Janel Mueller (Cambridge: Cambridge University Press, 2002), 397.

17 See Louis B. Wright, "William Perkins: Elizabethan Apostle of 'Practical Divinity,'" *Huntington Library Quarterly* 3 (1940): 171–96.

18 William Perkins, *A Treatise Tending Vnto A Declaration, whether a Man be in the estate of damnation, or in the estate of grace* (London, 1595), D4v; hereafter cited as *TT*.

19 William Perkins, *The Whole Treatise of the Cases of Conscience* (1606), in Merrill, 105; hereafter *CC*.

20 Nicholas Byfield, *The Signes of the Wicked Man* (London, 1619), 43.

21 David R. Como, *Blown by the Spirit: Puritanism and the Emergence of an Antinomian Underground in Pre-Civil-War England* (Stanford: Stanford University Press, 2004), 121–22.

22 Writers such as Steven Shapin (*A Social History of Truth: Civility and Science in Seventeenth-Century England* [Chicago: University of Chicago Press, 1994]) and Barbara J. Shapiro (*A Culture of Fact: England, 1550–1720* [Ithaca: Cornell University Press, 2004]) concur that collective witness is a component of facticity in this moment, although neither cites religious contexts.

23 Respectively, Richard Rogers, *Seaven Treatises* (London, 1605), 25, 49; Dod, *Ten Commandments*, 48.

24 William Perkins, *A Grain of Mustard Seed*, in Breward, 392.

25 Dod, *Ten Commandments*, 28.

26 Rogers, *Seaven Treatises,* 25.

27 Thomas Fuller, *The Holy and the Profane State* (1642), quoted in Wright, "William Perkins," 173.

28 In descending order of greatest frequency, *Henry VIII* (24), *Henry V* and *Richard III* (13), *Merchant* (10), *Cymbeline* (9), *Hamlet* (8). See Abraham Stoll, "Thus Conscience: *Synderesis* and the Destructuring of Conscience in Reformation England," *Exemplaria* 24 (2012): 62–77.

29 E.g., Stanley Cavell, *Disowning Knowledge in Six Plays of Shakespeare* (Cambridge: Cambridge University Press, 1987). For Protestant interiority and poetic subjectivity, see Barbara Kiefer Lewalski's *Protestant Poetics and the Seventeenth-Century Religious Lyric* (Princeton: Princeton University Press, 1979).

30 Kent Cartwright, *Tragedy and Its Double: The Rhythms of Audience Response* (University Park: Pennsylvania State University Press, 1991), 14.

31 That the knowledge advantage of a Shakespearean audience frequently engenders a degree of equanimity if not outright dispassion is borne out by the fact that the chief scholarly study we have of dramatic irony in Shakespeare's plays concerns the comedies: Bertrand Evans's *Shakespeare's Comedies* (Oxford: Clarendon Press, 1960).

32 Klaus Peter Jochum, *Discrepant Awareness: Studies in English Renaissance Drama* (Frankfurt: Peter Lang, 1979), 15.

33 *Richard III,* ed. James Siemon, Arden 3d series (London: Bloomsbury, 2009).

34 All references are to the Arden 3d series: *King Richard II,* ed. Charles R. Forker (London: Bloomsbury, 2002).

35 Wilbur Sanders, "Shakespeare's Political Agnosticism: *Richard II,*" in *The Dramatist and the Received Idea: Studies in the Plays of Marlowe and Shakespeare* (Cambridge: Cambridge University Press, 1968).

36 David Scott Kastan, "'Proud Majesty Made a Subject': Representing Authority on the Early Modern Stage," in *Shakespeare after Theory* (New York: Routledge, 1999), 101.

37 Irving Ribner, *The English History Play in the Age of Shakespeare* (New York: Barnes and Noble, 1957), 151–68.

HE

Thomas Sedgewick
it is not his Book

GEDY

F

OTAS.

DANIEL.

RECOMPOSING SHAKESPEARE

nts awake caruing the faſhion
ont to ſpeake plaine, & to the
n & a ſouldier) and now is he
vords are a very fantaſticall ba
diſhes: may I be ſo conuerte
I cannot tell, I thinke not:
oue may transforme me to an
on it, till he haue made an oy
ake me ſuch a foole: one wom
other is wiſe, yet I am well: a
well: but till all graces be in
hall not come in my grace: n
aine: wiſe, or Ile none: vertu
ier: faire, or Ile neuer looke o
neere me: Noble, or not for a
ſe: an excellent Muſitian, and

Early Modern Punctuation and Modern Editions: Shakespeare's Serial Colon

WILLIAM H. SHERMAN

When Jonathan Finegold opened his New Albion Press in 2009, the first book he produced was the Quatercentenary Edition of *Shakespeare's Sonnets*.[1] An act, at once, of inauguration and commemoration, it marks not one but two milestones in the textual life of Shakespeare. As the title suggests, it celebrates the four hundredth anniversary of the first printing of the *Sonnets,* issued by George Eld in 1609 (fig. 44).[2] And the title page, colophon, typeface, and layout also invoke the Tercentenary Edition, published in 1909 by T.J. Cobden-Sanderson at the Doves Press (successor to the Kelmscott Press and producer of some of the twentieth century's most beautiful books).[3] In form and function, then, this is as much a centenary as a quatercentenary volume.

A quick glance at the opening sonnet in the Doves Press and New Albion editions reveals that the latter is, in effect, a type facsimile of the former – no mean feat since the entire Doves font (with the original punches and matrices) was thrown into the River Thames by Cobden-Sanderson in 1917 (figs. 45 and 46).[4] Using Torbjörn Olsson's reconstructed type, Finegold carefully follows every aspect of Cobden-Sanderson's distinctive design, seen at its most striking in Sonnet 1. In a major departure from Eld's original presentation, the first two poems are given their own pages and set in all caps, with the final word or phrase in every line wrapped around and indented to the middle of the page. The tapered crossbar (which now literally bears the "memory" in

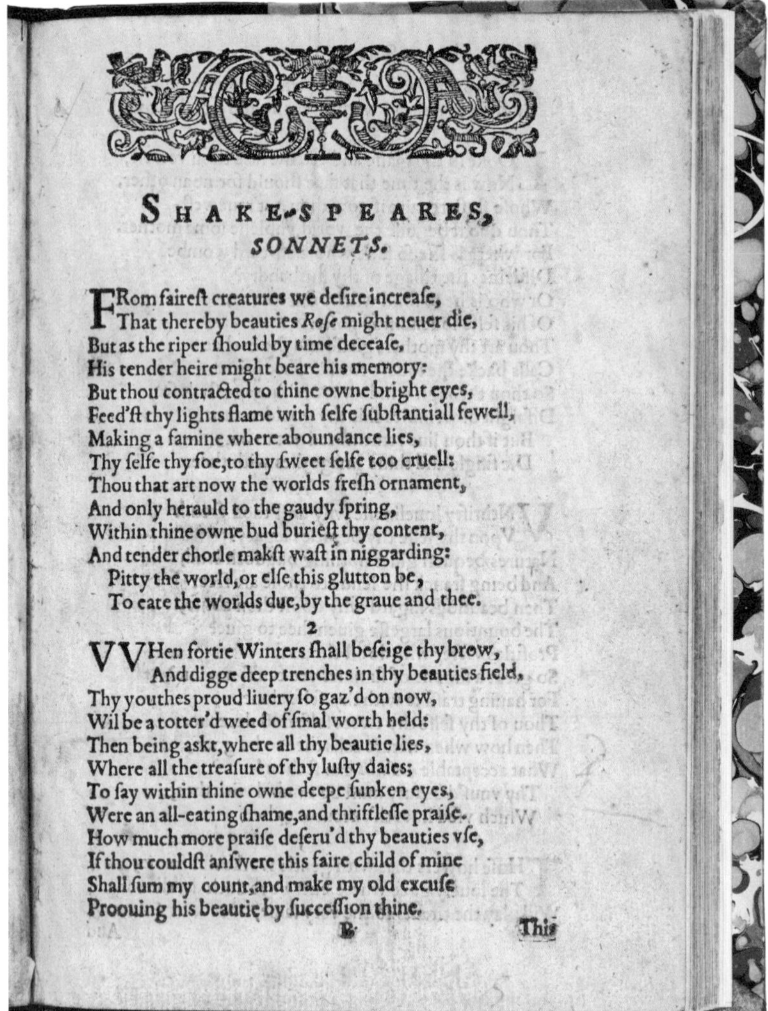

SHAKE-SPEARES,
SONNETS.

FRom faireſt creatures we deſire increaſe,
That thereby beauties *Roſe* might neuer die,
But as the riper ſhould by time deceaſe,
His tender heire might beare his memory:
But thou contracted to thine owne bright eyes,
Feed'ſt thy lights flame with ſelfe ſubſtantiall fewell,
Making a famine where aboundance lies,
Thy ſelfe thy foe,to thy ſweet ſelfe too cruell:
Thou that art now the worlds freſh ornament,
And only herauld to the gaudy ſpring,
Within thine owne bud burieſt thy content,
And tender chorle makſt waſt in niggarding:
Pitty the world,or elſe this glutton be,
To eate the worlds due,by the graue and thee.

2

VVHen fortie Winters ſhall beſeige thy brow,
And digge deep trenches in thy beauties field,
Thy youthes proud liuery ſo gaz'd on now,
Wil be a totter'd weed of ſmal worth held:
Then being askt,where all thy beautie lies,
Where all the treaſure of thy luſty daies;
To ſay within thine owne deepe ſunken eyes,
Were an all-eating ſhame,and thriftleſſe praiſe.
How much more praiſe deſeru'd thy beauties vſe,
If thou couldſt anſwere this faire child of mine
Shall ſum my count,and make my old excuſe
Proouing his beautie by ſucceſſion thine.

B This

Fig. 44. William Shakespeare, *Shake-speares Sonnets* (London, 1609), B1r. Folger Shakespeare Library, STC 22353

Fig. 45. William Shakespeare, *Shake-speares Sonnets: Tercentenary Edition* (London: Doves Press, 1909), 6. Huntington Library, RB 607694, the copy given by Cobden-Sanderson to Furnival

Fig. 46. William Shakespeare, *Shakespeare's Sonnets: Quatercentenary Edition* (San Francisco: New Albion Press, 2009), 6. Folger Shakespeare Library, PR2848.A1 2009

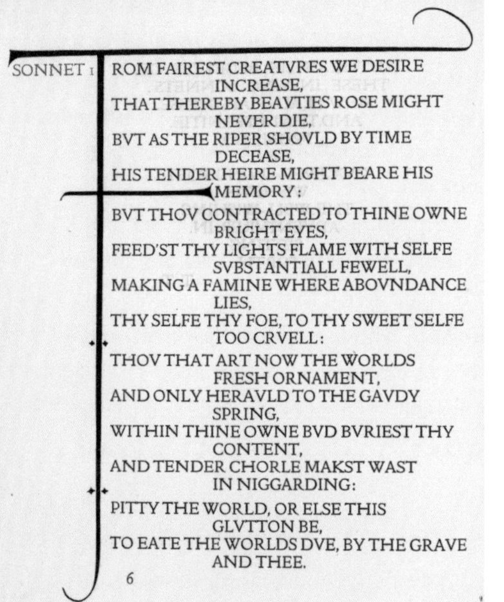

SONNET 1

FROM FAIREST CREATVRES WE DESIRE INCREASE,
THAT THEREBY BEAVTIES ROSE MIGHT NEVER DIE,
BVT AS THE RIPER SHOVLD BY TIME DECEASE,
HIS TENDER HEIRE MIGHT BEARE HIS MEMORY:
BVT THOV CONTRACTED TO THINE OWNE BRIGHT EYES,
FEED'ST THY LIGHTS FLAME WITH SELFE SVBSTANTIALL FEWELL,
MAKING A FAMINE WHERE ABOVNDANCE LIES,
THY SELFE THY FOE, TO THY SWEET SELFE TOO CRVELL:
THOV THAT ART NOW THE WORLDS FRESH ORNAMENT,
AND ONLY HERAVLD TO THE GAVDY SPRING,
WITHIN THINE OWNE BVD BVRIEST THY CONTENT,
AND TENDER CHORLE MAKST WAST IN NIGGARDING:
PITTY THE WORLD, OR ELSE THIS GLVTTON BE,
TO EATE THE WORLDS DVE, BY THE GRAVE AND THEE.

6

SONNET 1

FROM FAIREST CREATURES WE DESIRE INCREASE,
THAT THEREBY BEAUTY'S ROSE MIGHT NEVER DIE,
BUT AS THE RIPER SHOULD BY TIME DECEASE,
HIS TENDER HEIR MIGHT BEAR HIS MEMORY.
BUT THOU, CONTRACTED TO THINE OWN BRIGHT EYES,
FEED'ST THY LIGHT'S FLAME WITH SELF-SUBSTANTIAL FUEL,
MAKING A FAMINE WHERE ABUNDANCE LIES,
THYSELF THY FOE, TO THY SWEET SELF TOO CRUEL.
THOU THAT ART NOW THE WORLD'S FRESH ORNAMENT
AND ONLY HERALD TO THE GAUDY SPRING,
WITHIN THINE OWN BUD BURIEST THY CONTENT,
AND, TENDER CHURL, MAK'ST WASTE IN NIGGARDING.
PITY THE WORLD, OR ELSE THIS GLUTTON BE,
TO EAT THE WORLD'S DUE, BY THE GRAVE AND THEE.

6

line 4) and two pairs of diamonds (like colons turned on their side) divide the three quatrains that lead, in the typical Shakespearean sonnet, to a final rhyming couplet.

While Finegold follows his typographical model with exceptional fidelity, he makes some changes that ought to give us pause for thought. All spelling is modernized, and the punctuation is brought into line with current conventions. In the process, Finegold edits out of the sonnet what we might call the "serial colon" (that is, a series of two or more colons within a single sentence), a pattern that breaks modern rules but turns out to be a pervasive feature of premodern punctuation – particularly in passages where the speaker is pausing for thought. Eld ends all three quatrains with a colon, making the entire sonnet one complex sentence with three linked segments leading to the couplet's closing exhortation. Finegold changes all three colons to full stops, transforming the sonnet into a sequence of four more or less discrete sentences.

Cobden-Sanderson would no doubt be delighted to see his design revived by Finegold, but his protégé's pointing (as punctuation was generally known in Shakespeare's day) must have him rolling in his grave. When the Doves Press started work on the Tercentenary Edition in the summer of 1909, Cobden-Sanderson found the work of repunctuating the *Sonnets* "an engrossing and captivating occupation," as he had done when printing his modernized *Hamlet* earlier that year. But halfway through the job, with many pages of paper and vellum already printed, he began to lose faith. He paid a visit to the great philologist and Shakespeare editor F.J. Furnivall, who lived down the street, and—against his stern advice—resolved to start again from scratch.[5]

In a letter to *The Times,* published on October 26, 1911, and issued separately as a Doves Press chapbook a year later, Cobden-Sanderson explained his change of heart:

> When I undertook the reprint of Shakespeare's Sonnets, thinking that for so exquisite a form of poetry the punctuation should be as exquisite, I decided to make an exception to my rule of following the text and to revise what had superficially seemed to me arbitrary and haphazard in the punctuation of the original. I accordingly revised the punctuation of the 1609 edition, sonnet by sonnet; & a fascinating & alluring balancing of nice probabilities I found it to be: but as I proceeded I found two other & more important things, first, that slowly, like the coming on of night, I was changing the whole aspect of the Sonnets, and, secondly, that the original punctuation had a method in its seeming madness.... I therefore cancelled all the sheets I had already printed, both vellum and paper, and began the edition over again, keeping, with few exceptions, punctiliously to the punctuation, and to all other characteristics, of the original.[6]

For Cobden-Sanderson, modernization brings darkness rather than light to the Shakespearean text, obscuring instead of illuminating its essential structure and style. For Finegold, the opposite is true: enlisting the support of "the best recent scholarship," he suggests that the original punctuation creates an unnecessary obstacle to the modern readers who will use his book, one that gets in the way of "the flow of the poetry."[7] Every major current edition—from private, trade, and academic presses—would seem to agree since not one of them keeps a serial colon in Sonnet 1.[8] Helen

Vendler (Harvard), Colin Burrow (Oxford), and G. Blakemore Evans (Cambridge) opt for alternating colons and periods, which retains much of the rhetorical complexity of the original while conforming to modern conventions. Furthermore, their version makes the first eight lines a single grammatical unit while also linking the final six. Readers familiar with the history of the sonnet will realize that more is at stake in these numbers than the relative strength of the links between independent clauses: the Italian (or Petrarchan) sonnet adapted by Shakespeare and his English contemporaries is distinguished by a two-part structure of eight-line *octave* and six-line *sestet*. And while the "primary structure" of Sonnet 1, according to Vendler, signals a change of register after the first quatrain, she observes that "the ghost of the Italian sonnet can be said to underlie all the sonnets in [Shakespeare's] sequence," and suggests that in cases like this one there is a "'shadow sonnet'…behind the sonnet we are reading."[9] The 1609 punctuation keeps both sonnet forms open, though it requires hard work by readers to make their way through them; the pattern chosen by Finegold and others makes the reader's job easier, but banishes the ghost of the Italian sonnet to the shadows.[10]

There are, in other words, various argumentative, rhetorical, and generic structures at work in Shakespeare's sonnets, which can be enhanced or effaced by changes in punctuation. This does not necessarily mean that Eld and Cobden-Sanderson got it right and Finegold et al. got it wrong, but it does suggest that colons, commas, and full-stops are more complex and consequential than we might imagine, and prompts us to ask a series of questions: What kind of punctuation does the best job of giving modern readers access to early modern texts? Whose punctuation is preserved in early texts like Eld's 1609 Sonnets? What was the function of a colon in Shakespeare's day and what, for that matter, was a sentence?

II

The problem of punctuation is by no means exclusive to the Sonnets, and there is hardly a line in any text to which it does not apply; but, despite the obvious importance of these questions for the sense we make of Shakespeare, they have rarely been asked. "It is a common practice at the present day," Percy Simpson observed early in the twentieth century, "to treat the punctuation of seventeenth-century books as beneath serious notice; editors rarely allude to it, and if they do, they describe it as chaotic and warn the reader that they have been driven to abandon it."[11] Almost a century later, Jonathan Crewe argued that we still have not moved beyond the attitudes of one of Shakespeare's eighteenth-century editors, Samuel Johnson, who explained that, "In restoring the authour's works to their integrity, I have considered the punctuation as wholly in my power; for what could be their care of colons and commas, who corrupted words and sentences? Whatever could be done by adjusting points is therefore silently performed. . . ." As we enter the twenty-first century, Crewe observed, "repunctuation, often silent, remains a prerogative assumed by those editing Shakespeare's texts for the mass market and even for fairly restricted academic circulation."[12]

Almost every other issue involved in presenting early modern texts in modern forms – including the question of modern vs. old spelling, the problem of inconsistent speech prefixes and absent stage directions, the challenge of multiple texts, and the presence of other authors and agents in the line of transmission – has been thoroughly debated, with visible and sometimes radical implications for our editorial and interpretative practices. But when it comes to punctuation, editors are now given minimal guidance and almost total power, while readers and viewers are for the most part unaware of the silent performances that profoundly shape the Shakespeare they see and hear.

Having edited plays by Shakespeare, Jonson, and Marlowe for both the mass market and a more restricted academic readership, I have been required in every case to repunctuate, mostly silently and generally in conformity with modern conventions. Like Cobden-Sanderson, I initially found the process of updating the pointing in the early printings of these texts satisfying, solving their syntactical puzzles and delivering the clarity and speed that effective modern punctuation is capable of providing. But the more editing I do, the more unsettling I find the license I have been given and the liberties I have taken with it, and the closer I come to the position articulated by Theodor Adorno in his little-known essay on punctuation:

> The writer is in a permanent predicament when it comes to punctuation marks; if one were fully aware while writing, one would sense the impossibility of ever using a mark of punctuation correctly and would give up writing altogether. . . . The writer cannot trust in the rules, which are often rigid and crude; nor can he ignore them without indulging in a kind of

> eccentricity. . . . The conflict must be endured each time, and one needs either a lot of strength or a lot of stupidity not to lose heart.[13]

What Adorno says of writing applies – with less irony – to editing. As those of us who have been strong or stupid enough to take it on can testify, the conflict must be endured not just each time we edit but each time we encounter a punctuation mark – particularly when they appear where we think they shouldn't, when they don't appear where we think they should, or (worst of all) when they appear in a form for which there is no obvious modern equivalent. In fact, it may not be going too far to suggest that every piece of punctuation poses something of a textual crux.

In the face of this struggle, Cobden-Sanderson was by no means the only twentieth-century editor to have misgivings about modernization. When R.B. McKerrow wrote his *Prolegomena for the Oxford Shakespeare* (1939), he argued strongly for retaining the spelling and the punctuation of his copy texts, except in cases of obvious error:

> As regards punctuation my rule has been to allow this to remain unaltered whenever, though perhaps insufficient or careless, it is not clearly *mistaken*.
>
> By "mistaken," however, I do not mean at all what we should now call incorrect. There are innumerable cases in which the punctuation is, from a syntactic point of view, quite wrong, at least according to modern ideas.

These differences should be tolerated, he suggests, first because they might point us toward different patterns of written or spoken language and, second, because we need to do far more research on punctuation "before it will be possible to say what usages would have been regarded, by an educated Elizabethan, as allowable and what would have been regarded as definitely wrong."[14] When the *Oxford Shakespeare* finally appeared in 1986, however, its editors were far more comfortable with modernization: indeed, they had literally written the book on updating Shakespeare's spelling for modern readers.[15]

Silent repunctuation is now the order of the day in all of the major series – for both complete works and single-text volumes. The practical results are variable – more so, perhaps, than with any other aspect of the editorial presentation of Shakespeare's texts. If we compare more than one modern edition of any of these texts, we will find that different editors provide very different interpretations of the punctuation.[16] Where almost all modern editions of Shakespeare and his contemporaries have the same spellings (since they all now use the *Oxford English Dictionary* as the arbiter for current usage), and even share the same basic layout (allowing for variations in house style), no two editions will offer the same punctuation unless one is directly copied from another.

Having said that, since the eighteenth century, some general conventions have emerged in the updating of punctuation – some of which we have already seen in the modernization of Sonnet 1. First, they tend to simplify the syntax, breaking longer sentences into shorter ones, and removing those marks that are most essential for sustaining the early modern preference for long strings of balanced clauses. Second, they tend to remove capitalizations unless they are proper nouns or personifications. Third, they tend to add exclamation points. Michael Warren cites an extraordinary passage in the Ribner-Kittredge edition of *Cymbeline,* where the editors add five exclamation marks to four and a half lines of a Folio text that do not have any, resulting in a reading that Warren calls "grossly histrionic."[17] Even when editions profess their adherence to the original pointing in an early printing, their editors can still be found substantially repunctuating the text. Consider M.R. Ridley's Arden 2 edition of *Antony and Cleopatra* (1954). In his preface, Ridley claims that "no modern editor can neglect the Q[uarto] and F[olio] punctuation…[indeed] no editor can desert it without very careful consideration" – but in just over 3,000 lines of text, Ridley makes just under 1,500 silent changes in punctuation, including the addition of no fewer than 217 exclamation points.[18]

Modern editors are traditionally forced to justify all departures from their early modern copy texts, and they are supposed to have a good reason if they change some feature in the most authoritative source text. But this burden is largely lifted when it comes to punctuation. How, then, did this position come to win out, and on which arguments and/or assumptions does it rest? The best place to start is with W.W. Greg's comments on the relationship between punctuation and meaning in what would become the twentieth century's most influential essay on editing, "The Rationale of Copy-Text" (1950). Greg divided the features of any text into what he called *substantives* and *accidentals:* he put punctuation in the latter category alongside spelling and layout, describing them as surface features that shape and inflect but do not usually contain the verbal meaning found in the words themselves.[19] His primary concern in this essay was with the relative authority of each category rather than with their linguistic nature and function, and his conclusion was that editors of a particular text might need to take their substantives from one version or witness and their accidentals from another. Greg himself was careful to acknowledge that, in practice, punctuation "*could* have an effect on the substantive meaning of a sentence," and he even granted punctuation variants that affect meaning the status of "semi-substantives."[20] But the effect of Greg's argument was to set in editorial stone the general tendency to see punctuation as an adjunct to rather than component of meaning: Vivian Salmon has explained that the term "accidental," as it became hardened in editorial ideology, implies that the marks between words are *contingent* rather than *constitutive,* the product of happenstance rather than control.[21] The Latin etymology suggests that they simply fall onto the page and might just as well have fallen elsewhere; and the relevant entry for "accidental" in the *Oxford English Dictionary* defines them (citing Greg) as "any feature that is non-essential to the author's meaning."

For Eric Partridge, however, punctuation is an integral part not just of what a text says but of what it is: "It is not something that one applies as an ornament, for it is part of the structure; so much a part that, without it, the structure would be meaningless."[22] While Shakespeare and his contemporaries did not always depend on punctuation to structure their texts, they had fully grasped its power to transform meaning. Thomas Wilson's 1553 logic textbook, *The Rule of Reason,* cites an extended example from the schoolmaster and playwright Nicholas Udall where changes in punctuation give the same words "double sense, and contrarie meaning." The page-long passage begins:

> Swete maistresse, whereas I loue you nothing at al,
> Regarding your richesse and substau*n*ce chief of al,
> For your personage, beautie, demeanoure, & witte,
> I commende me vnto you neuer a whitte.
> Sorie to heare reporte of your good welfare.

On the facing page we find "The contrarie sense of the same in the same woordes":

> Swete maistresse, whereas I loue you, nothing at al
> Regarding your richesse and substau*n*ce, chief of al
> For your personage, beautie, demeanoure, & witte,

> I commende me vnto you, neuer a whitte
> Sorie to hear reporte of your good welfare.[23]

This is precisely the game played by Shakespeare in Peter Quince's botched prologue from the rude mechanicals' play in *A Midsummer Night's Dream* (and may well have been a source for it). As in Udall's interlude, Quince's prologue shows what can happen to meaning when we get the words right but the punctuation wrong:

> If wee offend, it is with our good will.
> That you should thinke, we come not to offend,
> But with good will. To shew our simple skill,
> That is the true beginning of our end.
> Consider then, we come but in despight.
> We doe not come, as minding to content you,
> Our true intent is. All for your delight,
> Wee are not here. That you should here repent you,
> The Actors are at hand: and, by their showe,
> You shall know all, that you are like to knowe.

"This fellow," replies Theseus, "doth not stand vpon points."[24] But this is of course a case where the garbled punctuation is the very point, and it is therefore one of the very few passages in Shakespeare where modern editors have felt compelled to let the original punctuation stand.

It is also one of the few passages where, we imagine, Shakespeare must have given a clear indication to the printer of the kind of punctuation he wanted.[25] From what we know of the process by which authors' papers became printed books in Elizabethan and Jacobean England, manuscripts submitted to printing houses tended to be much more lightly pointed than the books that were published from them, and it was part of the printer's job to (re)punctuate the text: "Joseph Moxon, author of the first English manual on printing-house practices, observed, in an often quoted passage, that it was the compositor's '*task and duty…to discern and amend the bad* Spelling *and* Pointing *of his Copy.*'"[26] It is therefore difficult to say with any confidence which specific marks or general habits derive from the author himself and which from the person or people responsible for preparing the texts for printing; and in cases like Shakespeare, where we have almost nothing in the way of authorial manuscripts for comparison, the task may be impossible.[27]

The loss of faith in the purity and singularity of Shakespeare's accidentals leads naturally to the modernizing imperative. The mediating obligations of Shakespeare's early scribes and compositors are shifted to his modern editors: in cases where the editor lacks faith in the authority of his control text's punctuation, Wells argues, "The aim...should be to give the reader and the actor such pointing as is essential to intelligibility without attempting to impose on the text interpretative nuances and directions for emphasis which restrict the reader's or actor's range of response."[28] Some intervention is almost always necessary, however, because the practices of Shakespeare's early printers are bound to be confusing to modern readers, to whom they will seem either less systematic or *differently* systematic.

Everyone who writes about punctuation in the sixteenth and seventeenth centuries spends some time explaining two things. First, that until the sixteenth century there were only four punctuation marks in general use (comma, colon, period, and question mark), and that the great European printers introduced new ones that were adopted by writers in a slow and irregular fashion over the ensuing centuries.[29] And second, that these marks served two different systems that were both in play during Shakespeare's day. We now see the function of punctuation as primarily *grammatical*, intended to guide us through the structure of a sentence by clarifying the relationship between the separate syntactic units within it. But in the Renaissance there was a second (and, to some extent, dominant) approach that can be described as *rhetorical*, indicating pauses for breath and changes of pitch and volume – a form of marking that becomes increasingly subordinate as we move toward the present.[30]

This latter system was clearly articulated in the sixteenth century's leading texts for the teaching of reading and writing. In Frances Clement's paraphrase of William Lily's widely used Latin grammar, the "points" are described as "pauses": the comma or "underpause" is the "point of the shortest rest in reading, so bearing the voyce at the stay of silence, that ye sentence may appeare to remaine vnfinished," while the period or "perfect pause" is set down "when the sent*en*ce is fully & perfectly finished."[31] Richard Mulcaster's *Elementarie* (1582) described the system in more explicitly musical terms, describing the art of pointing as conducive "to the right and tunable vttering of our words and sentences." The comma "is a small crooked point, which in writing followeth some small branch of the sentence, & in reading warneth vs to rest there, and to help our breth a litle"; the period "followeth a perfit sentence, and in reading warneth vs to rest there, and to help our breth at full"; and parentheses are used to "enclose som perfit branch…not fullie co[i]ncident to the sentence, which it breaketh, and in reading warneth vs, that the words inclosed by them, ar to be pronounced with a lower & quikker voice…."[32] George Puttenham's *Arte of English Poesie* (1589) seems to put more emphasis on syntactical relationships, describing the three main marks as "a treble distinction of sentences or parts of speach, as they happened to be more or lesse perfect in sense"; but he then defines their functions purely in terms of the length of pause they indicate, prescribing the (soon to be standard) series of values whereby the colon is twice as long as the comma and the period three times as long.[33]

"To a person accustomed to…modern syntactical pointing," Fredson Bowers observed, "the Elizabethan rhetorical system with its quite different values attached to the marks in the weighting of pause through commas, semi-colons, and colons is at least as confusing as would be the presentation of the words in their original spelling." While Bowers remained as committed as anyone to the recovery of Shakespeare's intended texts, he argued that modern readers deserve modern texts and had no misgivings at all about updating punctuation that was careless, obsolete, or both. This position grew out of the distrust he shared with Greg of both the work of early printers and the significance of early punctuation. But it ultimately rested on a widespread conviction that there are no meaningful aspects of Elizabethan punctuation that cannot be adequately translated into modern conventions: "it is absurd to argue that Elizabethan flexibility and rapidity," for instance, "cannot be indicated by…modern pointing."[34] When it comes to punctuation, there is much to be gained from translation and little, if anything, lost.

III

Enter Lance, with dog, to deliver a speech that not only provides a useful test case for Bowers's claim but also takes us back to the questions I posed in the opening section of this essay. It may be the most elaborate piece of punctuation in the entire Shakespearean canon, and it provides the most egregious case of repunctuation I have yet encountered. As with Quince's prologue, it features a comic figure who does not stand upon points, the clown from *Two Gentlemen of Verona*. At the beginning of act 2, scene 3, in the company of the long-suffering Crab, Lance describes his emotional departure from home in a remarkable display of controlled disorder. Here is his entire speech as printed in the earliest surviving text, the First Folio of 1623 (where it forms two very long sentences), alongside the same passage as it appears in the Norton/Oxford edition (where it forms thirty-five very short ones):

Nay, 'twill bee this howre ere I haue done weeping: all the kinde of the *Launces,* haue this very fault: I haue receiu'd my proportion, like the prodigious Sonne, and am going with Sir *Protheus* to the Imperialls Court: I thinke *Crab* my dog, be the sowrest natured dogge that liues: My Mother weeping: my Father wayling: my Sister crying: our Maid howling: our Catte wringing her hands, and all our house in a great perplexitie, yet did not this cruell-hearted Curre shedde one teare: he is a stone, a very pibble stone, and has no more pitty in him then a dogge: a Iew would haue wept to haue seene our parting: why my Grandam hauing no eyes, looke you, wept her selfe blinde at my parting: nay, Ile shew you the manner of it. This shooe is my father: no, this left shooe is my father; no, no, this left shooe is my mother: nay, that cannot bee so neyther: yes; it is so, it is so: it hath the worser sole: this shooe with the hole in it, is my mother: and this my father: a veng'ance on't, there 'tis: Now sir, this staffe is my sister: for, looke you, she is as white as a lilly, and as small as a wand: this hat is *Nan* our maid: I am the dogge: no, the dogge is himselfe, and I am the dogge: oh, the dogge is me, and I am my selfe: I; so, so: now come I to my Father; Father, your blessing: now should not the shooe speake a word for weeping: now should I kisse my Father; well, hee weepes on: Now come I to my Mother: Oh that she could speake now, like a would-woman: well, I kisse her: why there 'tis; heere's my mothers breath vp and downe: Now come I to my sister; marke the moane she makes: now the dogge all this while sheds not a teare: nor speakes a word: but see how I lay the dust with my teares.

Nay, 'twill be this hour ere I have done weeping. All the kind of Lances have this very fault. I have received my proportion, like the prodigious son, and am going with Sir Proteus to the Imperial's court. I think Crab, my dog, be the sourest-natured dog that lives. My mother weeping, my father wailing, my sister crying, our maid howling, our cat wringing her hands, and all our house in a great perplexity, yet did not this cruel-hearted cur shed one tear. He is a stone, a very pebble-stone, and has no more pity in him than a dog. A Jew would have wept to have seen our parting. Why my grandam, having no eyes, look you, wept herself blind at my parting. Nay, I'll show you the manner of it. This shoe is my father. No, this left shoe is my father. No, no, this left shoe is my mother. Nay, that cannot be so, neither. Yes, it is so, it is so, it hath the worser sole. This shoe with the hole in it is my mother, and this my father. A vengeance on't, there 'tis. Now, sir, this staff is my sister, for, look you, she is as white as a lily and as small as a wand. This hat is Nan our maid. I am the dog. No, the dog is himself, and I am the dog. O, the dog is me, and I am myself. Ay, so, so. Now come I to my father. 'Father, your blessing.' Now should not the shoe speak a word for weeping. Now should I kiss my father. Well, he weeps on. Now come I to my mother. O that she could speak now, like a moved woman. Well, I kiss her. Why, there 'tis. Here's my mother's breath up and down. Now come I to my sister. Mark the moan she makes. —Now the dog all this while sheds not a tear nor speaks a word. But see how I lay the dust with my tears.

It is technically possible to reduce Lance's almost unstopped stream of colons, semicolons, and commas into something approaching grammatically correct modern pointing – and, indeed, every modern edition does exactly this. The Norton/Oxford text is not particularly extreme in the extent to which it reins in Lance's rambling clauses: the same passage is turned into thirty-one sentences in the Folger edition and thirty in the Cambridge. And while the Norton/Oxford text is unique in removing all of the Folio's thirty-seven colons, the Folger only retains two and the Cambridge one. No modern edition contains a single instance of the serial colon; and more surprisingly, perhaps, none of the editors makes any reference to the Folio's unusual pointing in their collations, commentary notes, or textual introductions.

Unlike Udall's interlude or Quince's prologue, this is not a case where the changes of punctuation produce major changes in sense (or nonsense). The text remains funny in its thoroughly modernized form, and actors performing the speech in the different versions will all find ways to convey its comic energy. But can we be as confident as Bowers that the modern punctuation has captured the complex effects conveyed by the Folio's pointing? What work, in particular, might the colons be doing, and can the same work be done by replacing them with other marks?

Were this an isolated example that could be clearly chalked up to the carelessness of Compositor C (who set the type for this page in the First Folio) or the idiosyncrasy of the scribe Ralph Crane (who prepared the script for the printers), we need not be troubled by the silent removal of so many colons. But the phenomenon appears throughout the Folio, in texts prepared by other scribes and compositors and in speeches delivered by characters who have more control over their words.[35] Percy Simpson cited several examples in his chapter on the colon:

> But sure he is starke mad:
> When I desir'd him to come home to dinner,
> He ask'd me for a hundred markes in gold:
> 'Tis dinner time, quoth I: my gold, quoth he:
> Your meat doth burne, quoth I: my gold, quoth he:
> Will you come, quoth I: my gold, quoth he;
> Where is the thousand markes I gaue thee villaine?
> The Pigge quoth I, is burn'd: my gold, quoth he:

My mistresse, sir, quoth I: hang vp thy Mistresse:
I know not thy mistresse, out on thy mistresse.
The Comedy of Errors, II.i

Val. No (Madam) so it steed you, I will write
(Please you command) a thousand times as much:
And yet–
Sil. A pretty period: well: I ghesse the sequell;
And yet I will not name it: and yet I care not.
And yet, take this againe: and yet I thanke you:
Meaning henceforth to trouble you no more.
Speed. And yet you will: and yet, another yet.
. . .
Val. Please you, Ile write your Ladiship another.
Sil. And when it's writ: for my sake read it ouer,
And if it please you, so: if not: why so:
. . .
Speed. Oh Iest vnseene: inscrutible: inuisible,
As a nose on a mans face, or a Wethercocke on a steeple:
My Master sues to her: and she hath taught her Sutor,
He being her Pupill, to become her Tutor.
Two Gentlemen of Verona, II.i[36]

There are other passages that take us closer to Lance's speech, suggesting that the serial colon may be connected with clowning and/or soliloquizing:

He sir, that must marrie this woman: Therefore you Clowne, abandon: which is in the vulgar, leaue the societie: which in the boorish, is companie, of this female: which in the common, is woman: which together, is, abandon the society of this Female, or Clowne thou perishest: or to thy better vnderstanding, dyest; or (to wit) I kill thee, make thee away, translate thy life into death, thy libertie into bondage: I will deale in poyson with thee, or in bastinado, or in steele: I will bandy with thee in faction, I will ore-run thee with police: I will kill thee a hundred and fifty wayes, therefore tremble and depart.
As You Like It, V.i

> I will not bee sworne, but loue may transforme me to an oyster, but Ile take my oath on it, till he haue made an oyster of me, he shall neuer make me such a foole: one woman is faire, yet I am well: another is wise, yet I am well: another vertuous, yet I am well: but till all graces be in one woman, one woman shall not come in my grace: rich shee shall be, that's certaine: wise, or Ile none: vertuous, or Ile neuer cheapen her: faire, or Ile neuer looke on her: milde, or come not neere me: Noble, or not for an Angell: of good discourse: an excellent Musitian, and her haire shal be of what colour it please God...
>
> *Much Ado About Nothing*, II.iii[37]

These examples are sufficient to suggest that the colon could do a wide range of jobs in Renaissance texts, some of which were different from those it performs today. Is it possible that a string of colons signaled a particular set of speech-acts or -genres in the sixteenth and seventeenth centuries (associated, perhaps, with the turning of phrases, the unfolding of ideas, or the weighing of options)? In scripting "a speaker who seems to think his way to his conclusions before our very eyes," as Vendler described the effect of Shakespeare's sonnets, the serial colon may have been the pointing of choice.[38]

In Lance's speech, some of the colons clearly serve as loose stitching for his motley cloth, catch-all connectors like Dickinson's dashes or Beckett's ellipses. But in both the logical and the rhetorical system deployed by Shakespeare's contemporaries, colons are a sign (first and foremost) that the sense is not yet complete: in Charles Butler's *English Grammar* of 1633, the colon is described as "a point of perfect sens[e], but not of perfect sentenc[e]."[39] Butler echoes the definition of "colon" found in several contemporary dictionaries, including John Bullokar's *An English Expositor* (1616), where it is simply described as "A marke of a sentence not fully ended."[40] And the formulation may derive from Quintilian's *Institutio Oratoria,* the Renaissance period's most influential classical handbook on the art of rhetoric. In the section on punctuation in book 9, chapter 4, Quintilian explains that the colon is "the expression of a thought which is rhythmically complete, but is meaningless if detached from the whole body of the sentence...as the hand, foot or head if separated from the body." In early Greek and Latin usage, the colon refers not to the punctuation mark but rather to the clause (or, literally, *member*) which it accompanies; and since rhetorically effective sentences often need multiple clauses before they bring their sense to an end, classical authorities accepted that there could be many *cola* in a sentence. Quintilian says that Cicero advocates an average of four, and finds them especially useful when we want to "relax the texture of our periods by considerable pauses and looser connexions."[41]

This description points us toward a fundamentally different understanding of the nature and function of sentences and the use of colons within them, one poised between written and spoken speech and capable of a length and complexity that we are no longer trained to tolerate. When Quintilian's guidance was revived by Renaissance humanists, they inherited his taste for multiple colons – not just clauses, that is, but actual marks of punctuation. In 1566, Aldus Manutius Jr. published a short treatise on the rules of punctuation – the *Interpungendi Ratio* – and he devoted unusual space to the mark he called "the double point" which "takes rank between the point used in conjunction with the comma [i.e., the semicolon] and the point standing alone [i.e., the period]." In some cases, he suggests, "the sentence continues to such a length, that a break has to be made by the double point not simply once, but a second time, and even oftener." Indeed, in cases where short words end or begin a sentence, Aldus finds himself using "the double point more freely, than the single, As for instance: *Make ready a lodging for me: for I shall arrive to-morrow:* and so [on]."[42]

For English readers, the most explicit statement along these lines was found in the chapter on "distinction or pointing" in John Hart's 1551 treatise, *The opening of the unreasonable writing of our Inglish Toung*. He begins with the comma (which he compares to the crotchet in music) before moving on to the mark

> the Grekes cal colon...which is in inglish the iointes, or that which is betuixt the iointes...for that yt devideth the membres of a sentence, as our ioints doo the membres of our bodies: whose quantitie is dooble, of that of the foresaid rest, which we may compare to the minem yn music.... The same membre may containe 1. 2. 3. or more of the said restes: and his use is; as you see in everi periode...in this boke written: that is to sundre...membres of sentences...as, I am veri glad of your prosperite: for I herd say you were in trouble: which now appeareth otherwise: and so of others.[43]

By the time Ben Jonson wrote not only his plays but his own textbook on *English Grammar,* he joined Aldus and Hart in combining the different functions of punctuation: in the organic body of the text, logical punctuation marks its skeletal structure and rhetorical punctuation marks its breath or music.[44] Faced with an author working with such a different understanding of language, Stephen Orgel suggested in his Yale edition of Jonson's *Complete Masques,* "no method of modernizing can be wholly satisfactory" since "Elizabethan syntax was vastly different from ours, and included devices for which there is no modern equivalent."[45] Like many other editors of early modern texts, he has tried to help his readers by lightening Jonson's heavy marking and clarifying his tangled syntax, but unlike most of them he does so with a full awareness of what is lost as well as gained in translation.

When we modernize the punctuation in Renaissance plays or poems, we are not so much replacing one system with another as taking texts from a culture where two (or more) different systems are in open and often ambiguous play into a culture where one has won out. This problem led Orgel to acknowledge that "attempt[ing] to reduce Jonson's practice to ours is as impossible as it is misguided," and Michael Warren to argue that editors should be much more cautious in removing non-modern pointing and much more generous in telling readers what exactly is being removed.[46] The serial colons in Shakespeare's plays and poems are, I would suggest, a particularly interesting case in point.

NOTES

This essay, like the *Sonnets* edition with which it begins, is a double tribute. It started its life as a contribution to the symposium marking Barbara Mowat's retirement from the Folger Shakespeare Library and has been developed for this celebration of David Scott Kastan. It is a pleasure to acknowledge here the teaching of the two people who have taught me most about the theory and practice of editing.

1 For a full description see http://newalbionpress.com.

2 William Shakespeare, *Sonnets* (London: G[eorge] Eld for T[homas] T[horpe], 1609).

3 *Shakespeare's Sonnets: Tercentenary Edition* (London: Doves Press, 1909). The best source of information on the Doves Press and its books is Marianne Tidcombe, *The Doves Press* (London: The British Library; Newcastle, Del.: Oak Knoll Press, 2002).

4 The classic account of this remarkable story is Carole Cable, "The Printing Types of the Doves Press: Their History and Destruction," *The Library Quarterly* 44

(1974): 219–30; see also Simon Garfield's lively chapter on "drowned type" in *Just My Type: A Book about Fonts* (London: Profile Books, 2010).

5 In his journal, Cobden-Sanderson recorded Furnivall's response: "I am sorry that you are not going to repunctuate the Sonnets. They want it badly.... Your *Hamlet* practice was the right one: edit, and give notice of change. Let facsimilists reproduce old blunders, uncorrected" (Tidcombe, 166). Cobden-Sanderson stuck to his guns in future printings of Shakespeare: in his *Anthony and Cleopatra* and *Venus and Adonis* of 1912, he corrected obvious errors but otherwise offered "the unchanged punctuation of the original."

6 T.J. Cobden-Sanderson, "Shakespearian Punctuation: A Letter Addressed to the Editor of *The Times,* October 26, 1911" (London: Doves Press, 1912).

7 Unpaginated prospectus for the Quatercentenary Edition. James Thorpe's description of the punctuation as an "opaque curtain" is typical of this later view ("Watching the Ps & Qs: Editorial Treatment of Accidentals," 16th Annual Public Lecture on Books and Bibliography, University of Kansas, April 30, 1971, 20–21), and echoes Fredson Bowers's famous claim that the goal of bibliography should be to "strip the veil of print from a text" (see Gabriel Egan, *The Struggle for Shakespeare's Text: Twentieth-Century Editorial Theory and Practice* [Cambridge: Cambridge University Press, 2010], 47).

8 Except, of course, for old-spelling editions, which seem to be coming back in style (for poetry at least): see Carl D. Atkins, ed., *Shakespeare's Sonnets* (Madison: Fairleigh Dickinson University Press, 2007), and Paul Hammond, ed., *Shakespeare's Sonnets: An Original-Spelling Text* (Oxford: Oxford University Press, 2012).

9 Helen Vendler, *The Art of Shakespeare's Sonnets* (Cambridge: Harvard University Press, 1997), 49–50.

10 For a fuller discussion of the problem of Sonnet 1, see William H. Sherman, "Punctuation as Configuration; or, How Many Sentences Are There in Sonnet 1?" in *Shakespearean Configurations,* ed. Jean-Christophe Mayer, William H. Sherman, Stuart Sillars, and Margaret Vasileiou, *Early Modern Literary Studies,* Special Issue 21 (2013), http://extra.shu.ac.uk/emls/si-21/00-Contents.htm.

11 Percy Simpson, *Shakespearian Punctuation* (Oxford: Clarendon Press, 1911), 7.

12 Jonathan Crewe, "Punctuating Shakespeare," in *Shakespeare Studies* 28, ed. Leeds Barroll (Madison: Fairleigh Dickinson University Press, 2000), 23–40 (23), citing Johnson's *Preface to Shakespeare* (1765).

13 Theodor W. Adorno, "Punctuation Marks," trans. Shierry Weber Nicholsen, *Antioch Review* 48 (1990): 300–305 (305). The essay first appeared in Adorno's *Notes to Literature,* vol. 1 (New York: Columbia University Press, 1958).

14 Ronald B. McKerrow, *Prolegomena for the Oxford Shakespeare: A Study in Editorial Method* (Oxford: Clarendon Press, 1939), 40–41. This represented a hardening of the position he had adopted in his great edition of the works of Thomas Nashe (London: Sidgwick & Jackson Ltd., 1904–10): "On the one hand, much Elizabethan prose, especially that with a Euphuistic tendency, can hardly be punctuated at all according to modern rules, and even when this is possible, such treatment tends greatly to obscure the antithesis of phrase, often unreal, which is one of its chief characteristics. On the other hand, the old punctuation, more especially the superfluity of commas, is very irritating to a reader. My principle has therefore been to keep the old punctuation wherever it is neither misleading nor actually disturbing to a reader, but to alter it without scruple where it is so" (1:xiii).

15 Stanley W. Wells, *Modernizing Shakespeare's Spelling*, with *Three Studies in the Text of Henry V* by Gary Taylor (Oxford: Clarendon Press, 1979); cf. Wells's brief comments on punctuation in his *Re-editing Shakespeare for the Modern Reader* (Oxford: Clarendon Press, 1984).

16 We may even find this with the same editor: I recently reedited the same play (*The Tempest*) for the same publisher (Norton) and found myself making many minor changes to the punctuation.

17 Michael J. Warren, "Repunctuation as Interpretation in Editions of Shakespeare," *English Literary Renaissance* 7 (1977): 155–69 (160–61).

18 Patrick Turner, *Secrets of Acting Shakespeare* (New York: Routledge, 2002), 240–49.

19 W.W. Greg, "The Rationale of Copy-Text," *Studies in Bibliography* 3 (1950–51): 19–36.

20 Antony Hammond, "The Noisy Comma: Searching for the Signal in Renaissance Dramatic Texts," in *Crisis in Editing: Texts of the English Renaissance,* ed. Randall McLeod (New York: AMS Press, 1994), 203–49 (203) (italics mine).

21 Vivian Salmon, "English Punctuation Theory 1500–1800," *Anglia* 106 (1988): 285–314.

22 Eric Partridge, *You Have a Point There: A Guide to Punctuation and Its Allies* (1953; London: Routledge, 1977), 8.

23 Thomas Wilson, *The Rule of Reason, conteinyng the Arte of Logique* (London: Richard Grafton, 1553), S2v–S3r.

24 William Shakespeare, *A Midsommer nights dreame* (London: [Richard Bradock] for Thomas Fisher, 1600), G4r–v.

25 I owe this point to Peter Stallybrass.

26 Michael Cordner, "'To Show Our Simple Skill': Scripts and Performances in Shakespearian Comedy," *Shakespeare Survey* 56 (2003): 167–83 (170).

27 As Thorpe explains, "the probability is all on the side of the writer being indifferent about accidentals and of the printer changing, with considerable freedom, the accidentals in his copy-text: it seems reasonable for the editor to assume that such are the source and authority of the accidentals when other evidence is lacking" ("Watching the Ps & Qs," 20).

28 Wells, *Modernizing Shakespeare's Spelling,* 33.

29 M.B. Parkes, *Pause and Effect: An Introduction to the History of Punctuation in the West* (Aldershot: Scolar Press, 1993), 41–61.

30 Ibid., 87–96; Walter Ong, "Historical Backgrounds of Elizabethan and Jacobean Punctuation Theory," *PMLA* 59 (1944): 349–60; Salmon, "English Punctuation Theory 1500–1800"; and Anthony Graham-White, *Punctuation and Its Dramatic Value in Shakespearean Drama* (Newark: University of Delaware Press, 1995).

31 Frances Clement, *The Petie Schole* (London: Thomas Vautrollier, 1587), B5r–v.

32 Richard Mulcaster, *The First Part of the Elementarie* (London: Thomas Vautroullier, 1582), T3r.

33 Cited in Graham-White, *Punctuation and Its Dramatic Value,* 40.

34 Fredson Bowers, *Textual and Literary Criticism* (Cambridge: Cambridge University Press, 1966), 138–39. This seems to contradict his position in "Today's Shakespeare Texts, and Tomorrow's," also published in 1966: by assessing the accidentals of early printings, "the informed reader will be freed from the strait-jacket of inappropriate and arbitrary modern punctuation contrived for a different kind of syntax, and will be able to read the texts with the indication of pauses…that seemed appropriate at

the time. No one is so foolish any more as to argue that the punctuation...is Shakespeare's own or that it represents in any way the authority of the playhouse. But such as it is, it is the most authentic that we have, and it is usually well suited to clarify the casual Elizabethan syntax" (*On Editing Shakespeare* [Charlottesville: University Press of Virginia, 1966], 177–78).

35 Ralph Crane's marked preference for colons may go some way toward accounting for the peculiar pointing of Lance's speech: the frequency of colons, hyphens, and parentheses in the five Folio texts prepared by Crane is roughly twice that found in the rest of the volume (T.H. Howard-Hill, *Ralph Crane and Some Shakespeare First Folio Comedies* [Charlottesville: University Press of Virginia, 1972], 32 and 82). But similar examples can be found in non-Crane texts, and they do not fall neatly within the assignments of individual compositors as determined by Charlton Hinman and reported in his *The Printing and Proof-Reading of the First Folio of Shakespeare*, 2 vols. (Oxford: Clarendon Press, 1963).

36 Simpson, *Shakespearian Punctuation*, 75.

37 The Norton/Oxford text once again translates almost all of Benedick's colons into full-stops, turning the Folio's single sentence into twelve. Other editions, however, stay closer to the original punctuation: the Folger makes this passage three sentences and the Cambridge keeps it as one.

38 See Vendler's unpaginated introduction to the Arion Press edition of the *Sonnets* (San Francisco: Arion Press, 1997).

39 Charles Butler, *The English Grammar* (Oxford: William Turner, 1633), H1v.

40 See *Lexicons of Early Modern English* [http://leme.library.utoronto.ca] using a keyword search for "colon."

41 Quintilian, *Institutio Oratoria*, trans. H.E. Butler (London: William Heinemann, 1921), 3:577–79.

42 I cite the English translation found in Appendix B to T.F. and M.F.A. Husband, *Punctuation: Its Principles and Practice* (London: George Routledge, 1905), 133–34.

43 Bror Danielsson, ed., *John Hart's Works on English Orthography and Pronunciation*, 2 vols. (Stockholm: Almqvist & Wiksell, 1955), 1:159–60.

44 See especially Sara van den Berg, "Marking his Place: Ben Jonson's Punctuation," *Early Modern Literary Studies* 1, no. 3 (1995); Bruce R. Smith, "Prickly Characters," in David M. Bergeron, ed., *Reading and Writing in Shakespeare* (Newark: University of Delaware Press, 1996); A.C. Partridge, 'The Punctuation of Shakespeare and Ben Jonson,' in *Orthography in Shakespeare and Elizabethan Drama* (London: Edward Arnold, 1964); and Ros King, "Seeing the Rhythm: An Interpretation of Sixteenth-Century Punctuation and Metrical Practice," in *Ma(r)king the Text: The Presentation of Meaning on the Literary Page*, ed. Joe Bray, Miriam Handley, and Anne C. Henry (Aldershot: Ashgate, 2000). Milton's punctuation, too, has repaid research into its distinctive workings and led at least some scholars to resist the drift toward modernization: see Stephen B. Dobranski, "Editing Milton: The Case against Modernisation," *The Review of English Studies*, n.s., 59 (2008): 392–408.

45 Stephen Orgel, ed., *Ben Jonson: The Complete Masques* (New Haven: Yale University Press, 1969), 44.

46 Warren, "Repunctuation as Interpretation," 155–69.

Ist Shakespear

Jst Shakespeare ein Problem? Jst de
ichter nicht nur menschlicher Leidenschaft
tränkter Spiele und weltweiser Symbole
- Deuter englischer Gärung und Entfaltu
e Intendanten, die ihn spielen, und die
ı Jahre des neu angebrochenen Kriege
r, sicherlich mit vollem nationalen St
Kleinod in die Silbersee gefaßt“ prägte,
e weltumspannende Sendung des engli
Wir Deutsche sind durch Goethe nicht
eratur geworden, sondern haben der
eltliteratur heißt. Allein die Geschichte
gen Beweis für die Grenzenlosigkeit d
lem Brauchbaren (und leider oft auch a
ng geleistet haben. Mehr als e i n fremd
st eigentlich geboren worden und dann
ner eigenen Nation zurückgekehrt. Frei
ıs in den letzten Jahren eine geklärte, n
cht Allerweltsliteratur, sondern we
enn wir daher entgegen geschäftigen Ei
ı statt der überall gleichgängigen Litera
ugenden Dichtern Heimstatt boten, so e
tterer Konsequenz, auch den Dichter der
ıchten, wie seine geistigen Waffen mit

Unser Shakespeare *in 1940*

ZOLTÁN MÁRKUS

Both materially and imaginatively the text is, of course, a product of collaborative energies and exchanges. If its circumstantial materiality obviously involves effective agencies other than the author's, its seemingly essential symbolic dimension is no more a realm of authorial autonomy and freedom.... Indeed if authorship is to retain a significant, rather than a merely normal position in our accounts of literary meaning, it must be restored to its enabling and inhibiting circumstances.

David Scott Kastan, *Shakespeare after Theory*[1]

More than four decades after Roland Barthes's programmatic essay on the death of the author, Shakespeare as author is alive and well. In popular culture, following a Romantic tradition rooted in the late eighteenth and early nineteenth centuries, he is frequently conjured up as the sui generis "genius" author. In current academic discourse, on the other hand, he is more often imagined as a special function of the texts attributed to him: he is seen as a relatively convenient and historically determined category under which the "collaborative energies and exchanges" that produced his texts are gathered and assimilated. In this sense, Shakespeare ceases to be the sole creator of his texts; as an author, he becomes the effect of his texts. Since early modern plays were the results of a network of collaborations in which the author did not have a particularly distinguished role, Shakespeare as an author is understood as an effect of the process of producing, disseminating, and appropriating his plays.

Author Shakespeare, therefore, has always been a protean concept that has adjusted to the demands of various times and regions in Britain and beyond.

Shakespeare and his plays have been imagined in vastly different ways since the early seventeenth century, and these imaginings have created their own cultural hierarchies. In this chapter, I focus on a historical moment in which nationalistic British and German constructions of Shakespeare competed and clashed during World War II. In addition to trying to understand the conflicting ways in which Shakespeare was appropriated in these two cultural contexts, I discuss the cultural processes accumulated around appropriating Shakespeare. Although the subject matter and comparative methodology of my chapter might seem somewhat different from the other studies in this volume, my work also develops from the theoretical framework of *Shakespeare after Theory*. Like several other essays in this book, it strives to move beyond the increasingly exhausted (and exhausting) presentist-historicist debate by emphasizing the significance of the *history* of our interventions over Shakespeare's texts from his time to the present.

APPROPRIATING SHAKESPEARE

The differences between the German and the English appropriations of Shakespeare lie mainly in their different histories. But if we look at their ideological investments and priorities, these engagements with Shakespeare appear analogous. We will be able to account for this duality with a concept of appropriation ("Aneignung") as a simultaneously reciprocal process of interpreting Shakespeare's works. On the one hand, every interpretation is embedded in, and determined by, the cultural context in which it takes place. Every interpretation, therefore, is the projection of this cultural context onto the interpreted work. On the other hand, the changing materiality and past significance of Shakespeare and his plays determine their present uses: the local history and the changing actualizations of a text influence and modify its interpretations. Like any other works of art, Shakespeare's plays are also simultaneously subjects and objects of appropriation.

Author Shakespeare is a historically and contextually determined product of these reciprocal activities. As a function or myth of the text,

Shakespeare is continuously conjured up in the process of dealing with his plays. The expression "appropriating Shakespeare," therefore, is a synecdochical reference to author Shakespeare as it emerges while his plays are appropriating and appropriated at the same time. Both inscribing and being inscribed by its cultural context, "Shakespeare" is a manifestation of the Janus-faced nature of cultural appropriations.

This deployment of the concept of appropriation aims to raise a double consciousness of transcendence and historicity while exploring Shakespeare in any given historical moment and culture. In addition, conceiving of appropriation as a culturally and temporally determined event for generating meanings in which Shakespeare's plays are simultaneously objects and subjects helps augment the static model of appropriation referring to interpreting subjects' (ab)using of Shakespearean texts for their (frequently extraliterary) purposes. In this sense, appropriation is a reciprocal process in which Shakespeare's plays are appropriating and appropriated at the same time. On the one hand, these plays are appropriated whenever they are interpreted, evoked, or otherwise used in discursive or nondiscursive events. Whenever *Hamlet, Othello,* or *The Merchant of Venice,* or any other Shakespeare play is interpreted or staged, it is always adjusted to the given cultural context.

On the other hand, how and what can Shakespeare's plays appropriate? In opposition to all of this, Terence Hawkes provocatively claims, "Shakespeare doesn't mean: *we* mean *by* Shakespeare," by which (presumably) he *means* that, "the plays have the same function as, and work like, the words of which they are made. We *use* them in order to generate meaning."[2] For Hawkes, "meaning" is necessarily relative, plural, and exclusively dependent on the interpreting person rather than the interpreted work, let alone the author. For him, therefore, every text is always only an object of appropriation. There is no European, or German, or English Shakespeare; there are only local *Hamlets, Othellos,* and *Merchants.*

Hawkes might be right in shifting the emphasis from the author (or the author's intentions) to the reader/viewer in the process of generating meaning: the meaning intended by an author is always secondary and necessarily subordinated to the meaning that a reader or viewer assigns to Shakespeare's texts. But meaning is never completely arbitrary. There is very little intellectual purchase in the "anything goes" view claiming that any given text can mean absolutely anything. Even if it is true that "Shakespeare doesn't mean," "Shakespeare" (understood as an effect or tradition) does affect (and even effect) the meaning of any Shakespearean text. In other words, whatever we mean by Shakespeare at a given time is strongly influenced by the history of Shakespeare reception leading up to that point. "Generating meaning" is not only a private affair between a reader or a viewer and a text but is also a social activity: meanings exist side-by-side and necessarily influence one another. Shakespeare in 1940 was, therefore, both an object and a subject in the nationalistic struggle between Germany and England.

UNSER SHAKESPEARE IN ENGLAND

In addition to relevant book reviews, theater notices, and other Shakespeare-related stories, a great number of articles in the wartime London press were devoted to the remarkably popular and yet sensitive subject of German appropriations of Shakespeare. Elderly readers must have felt a strong sense of déjà vu: this same topic had been popular during World War I. During this new war, it returned with a vengeance. Its reappearance was usually triggered by news (and anxiety) about Shakespeare's academic and theatrical popularity in Germany or by reports of German intellectuals' preposterous claims that the Bard was actually (spiritually or even ethnically) German.

The nineteenth-century idea of a German Shakespeare was vigorously revived at the beginning of the twentieth century, and it became particularly prevalent again after Hitler came to power in 1933. The English press regularly and somewhat apprehensively followed the Germans' expropriating efforts. On Shakespeare's birthday in 1934, for instance, the German Shakespeare-Gesellschaft celebrated its seventieth anniversary in Weimar with lectures on this subject. Several English dailies reported on the renewed German claims: *The Morning Post,* for example, made the point that, "[i]t is characteristic of our times that the German Shakespeare Society...is interesting itself anew in the 'German-ness' of Shakespeare," whereas *The Evening Standard* in a brief article titled "Wilhelm Shakespeare" also observed, "Not for the first time, Germany has acclaimed Shakespeare as 'a true German.' He appears to be, if anything, rather truer than before."[3] It is interesting (but not surprising) that these articles only reported on the absurdity that some Germans thought Shakespeare had actually been German and not English, and did not take the trouble to explain what these Germans might have meant by making such a provocative claim.

The general attitude of the English press regarding German claims to Shakespeare was disdainful and unsympathetic. As a response to the news that Shakespeare's plays were "booming" in the theaters of Nazi Germany,[4] *The Times,* for instance, had the following to say in November 1935: "Every one, even the Devil, can find something in Scripture for his purpose; every one, even a Germany at war with England or a Russia at war with society, can find something in Shakespeare for his purpose."[5] Drawing parallels between the Devil and England's political enemies in 1935 (Germany and Russia), on the one hand, and between the Bible and Shakespeare's works on the other, the metaphor drives home its didactic point. In this metaphysical image of jingoism (perhaps inspired by Bardolph's reference to the "three German devils, three Doctor Faustuses" in *The Merry Wives of Windsor*), Shakespeare is metaphorically identified as the "ultimate author," the author of the "Scripture."

By 1940, however, the neat formula of an evil Germany violating the immaculate Shakespeare of holy England had become problematic. At the end of March 1940, *The Times* published a brief article outlining a debate on Shakespeare in the latest issue of the Hitler Youth monthly, *Wille und Macht*. A few anti-Shakespearean Nazi voices argued, "Shakespeare may no longer be indispensable because 'the Germans' day has arrived'" and "the Nazis should be thinking of 'carrying on without Shakespeare.'"[6] The main point of the argument, reports *The Times,* was that young German National Socialist playwrights should take over the privileged position of the old German(ic)/English Bard. This sudden doubting of Shakespeare's semisacred value challenges the English jingoistic formula above: is the Devil still evil if he does not want to lay hands on the holy Scripture of the Bard? Is the Scripture of the Bard still holy if the Devil ceases to want to violate it?

On Shakespeare's birthday in 1940, *The Times* published an article titled "Germany and Shakespeare," which depicts a more balanced picture of the German Shakespeare. Although, at first, the article discusses the cultural "debt" to Shakespeare incurred by the Germans in the eighteenth century ("When Germany discovered Shakespeare anew in the middle of the eighteenth century, his plays were of incalculable value in liberating the German spirit from self-distrust and from the bondage of pedantry"), later on it also mentions some of the positive contributions of the German Shakespeare reception:

> Germany has certainly repaid that debt, German Shakespearians, from Lessing and Goethe in the eighteenth century to Creizenach and Schücking in the twentieth, have helped to make plain the greatness of Shakespeare before the whole civilized world; and in the German theatre, from Schroeder at Hamburg in the eighteenth century to Reinhardt in Berlin and many another in the twentieth, Shakespeare has been played with a frequency unknown in the English theatre till very recent years.[7]

All these positive developments are only mentioned here, however, to underscore the folly of some Germans' injunction to replace the legacy of Shakespeare with a new dramatic tradition created by young and loyal National Socialist playwrights. We learn from the article that, "according to the organ of the Hitler Youth, there was now some danger that Germany might drop Shakespeare"; when a new and genuinely "heroic" Nazi playwright appears, "there will not be room in Germany for both him and the poet who was at once universal and intensely English." Whereas the other articles discussed above sarcastically criticized the Germans for claiming Shakespeare – partly or exclusively – as "theirs," this one chides them for "disowning" the Bard. The other articles wanted Shakespeare "back" from Germany; this one scoffs at the Germans for not wanting Shakespeare any longer.

A contemporary reader of these articles, therefore, could conclude that whatever the Germans did to Shakespeare was clearly absurd. As for Shakespeare, his defining qualities originate from the dichotomy that was repeatedly emphasized: he "was at once universal and intensely English." "Universal" probably indicates that Shakespeare's works articulate the human types and conflicts in ways that rise above cultural and historical differences. The "intensely English," on the other hand, secures his place in the national pantheon as a token of national pride and glory. Any

English accolade to Shakespeare's universality is simultaneously a praise of his Englishness. In this classic example of nationalistic appropriation, we see clearly that "nationalistic" and "universal" are not exclusive features; on the contrary, they mutually complement one another. Shakespeare is valuable because his works are worth appropriating outside England as well. The ostensible corollary that the German efforts at appropriating Shakespeare were ridiculous can be sharply reversed by pointing out the contradictions within and between the arguments of these very same articles. If Shakespeare is truly universal, he should be available to the Germans as well. If the Germans cannot (or do not want to) claim Shakespeare, because he is "intensely English," then he may not be worth claiming, since he is not universal.

UNSER SHAKESPEARE IN GERMANY

The nationalistic fluctuation between particularity as universality and universality as particularity was a main characteristic of imagining Shakespeare in National Socialist Germany as well. Those who argued against Shakespeare did so not because he was English, but because they could not imagine him as German enough. These initial attacks during the first few months of the war, however, were quickly countered in various walks of German cultural life. As a decisive blow to the doubters and detractors of Shakespeare, *Wille und Macht* devoted its February 1, 1940, issue to the Bard (fig. 47). Its title page offered a brief editorial on "Shakespeare 1940," followed by journalist, translator, and theater researcher Herbert A. Frenzel's article "Ist Shakespeare ein Problem?" Frenzel and his fellow authors, such as writer, playwright, and painter Hermann Burte, actor and director Gustaf Gründgens, and Reichsdramaturg Rainer Schlösser (he contributed both a brief poem and a brief article on "The 'German' Shakespeare"), all did their best to demonstrate that Shakespeare was not a problem at all. On the contrary, the German Shakespeare offered great inspiration and guidance in those momentous days of war against Shakespeare's unworthy homeland, England.

But what exactly was at stake behind these anxious defenses of Shakespeare in *Wille und Macht*? Although the articles do not address any concrete detractor of Shakespeare, one does not have to be a particularly

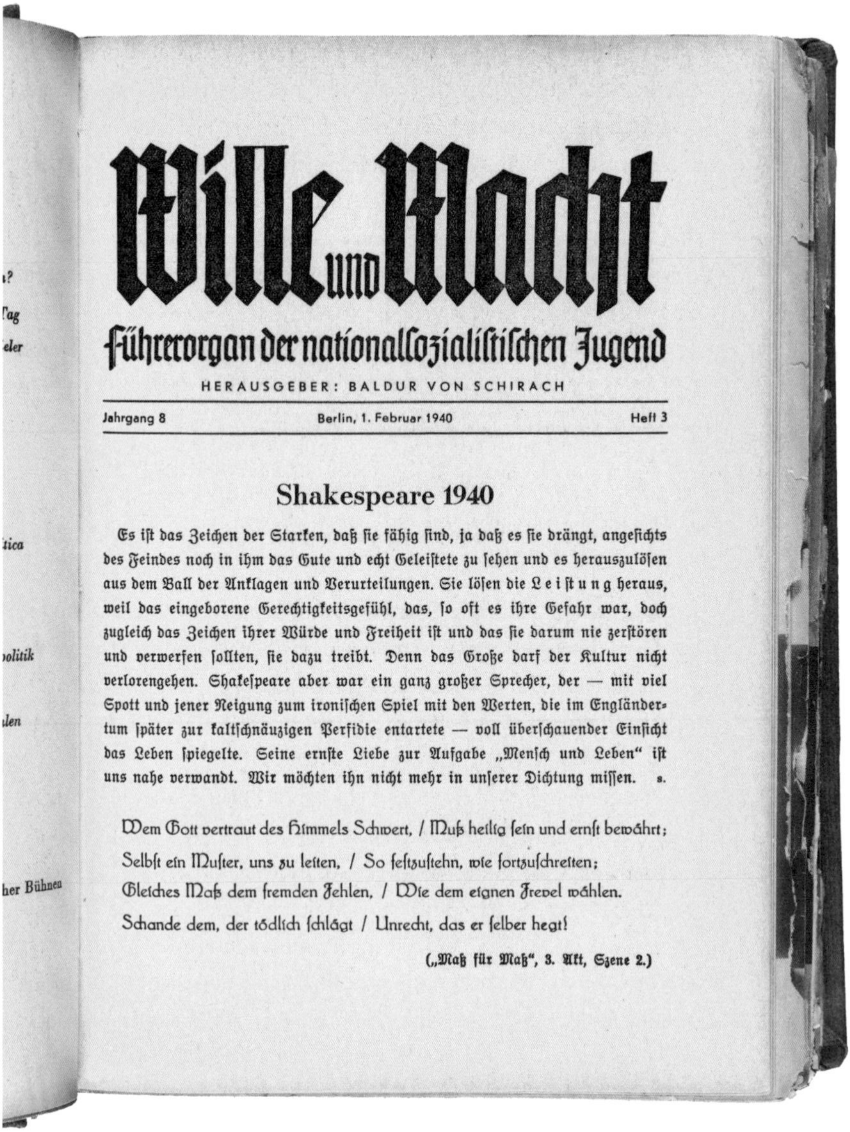

Wille und Macht

Führerorgan der nationalsozialistischen Jugend

HERAUSGEBER: BALDUR VON SCHIRACH

Jahrgang 8 | Berlin, 1. Februar 1940 | Heft 3

Shakespeare 1940

Es ist das Zeichen der Starken, daß sie fähig sind, ja daß es sie drängt, angesichts des Feindes noch in ihm das Gute und echt Geleistete zu sehen und es herauszulösen aus dem Ball der Anklagen und Verurteilungen. Sie lösen die L e i s t u n g heraus, weil das eingeborene Gerechtigkeitsgefühl, das, so oft es ihre Gefahr war, doch zugleich das Zeichen ihrer Würde und Freiheit ist und das sie darum nie zerstören und verwerfen sollten, sie dazu treibt. Denn das Große darf der Kultur nicht verlorengehen. Shakespeare aber war ein ganz großer Sprecher, der — mit viel Spott und jener Neigung zum ironischen Spiel mit den Werten, die im Engländertum später zur kaltschnäuzigen Perfidie entartete — voll überschauender Einsicht das Leben spiegelte. Seine ernste Liebe zur Aufgabe „Mensch und Leben" ist uns nahe verwandt. Wir möchten ihn nicht mehr in unserer Dichtung missen. s.

Wem Gott vertraut des Himmels Schwert, / Muß heilig sein und ernst bewährt;
Selbst ein Muster, uns zu leiten, / So festzustehn, wie fortzuschreiten;
Gleiches Maß dem fremden Fehlen, / Wie dem eignen Frevel wählen.
Schande dem, der tödlich schlägt / Unrecht, das er selber hegt!

(„Maß für Maß", 3. Akt, Szene 2.)

Fig. 47. *Wille und Macht* (Berlin: Baldur von Schirach, 1940), 3. Sterling Memorial Library, Yale University, A85 151

shrewd (or paranoid) reader to wonder: if such great National Socialist luminaries take the trouble to address the youth of the Third Reich to assure them that Shakespeare was acceptable, even commendable, is it not reasonable to assume that there are people in Germany who do not necessarily think so? The question "is Shakespeare a problem?" and even the negation, "Shakespeare is not a problem," both make it possible to entertain the idea that, for some, Shakespeare was indeed problematic. Some of the potential apprehensions are addressed immediately in the eleven-line editorial, "Shakespeare 1940," on the title page:

> It is a sign of the strong that, facing the enemy, they are able, obligated even, to see the good in him and his true achievements, and to distinguish these from the bulk of accusations and condemnations. They separate the accomplishments, because their native sense of justice, which so often both endangered them and revealed their honor and freedom at the same time, and which they, therefore, should never destroy or condemn, drives them to do so. For culture cannot give up greatness. Shakespeare, however, was a great storyteller, who – with a lot of mockery and an inclination to ironical playing with values that later degenerated into a callous perfidy in the English – reflected life with a sharp insight. His intense love of the business of "Man and Life" is closely related to us. We would not like to do without him in our literature.[8]

In this article (signed with a tiny type "s.," which probably refers to editor-in-chief Baldur von Schirach), we encounter a relatively mild form of "nostrification": although Shakespeare belongs to the enemy, we need him, because he is also related to us – plus, he is great. A German translation of the following lines from *Measure for Measure* follows the passage quoted above:

> He who the sword of heaven will bear / Should be as holy as severe:
> Pattern in himself to know, / Grace to stand, and virtue, go:
> More nor less to others paying / Than by self-offences weighing.
> Shame to him whose cruel striking / Kills for faults of his own liking![9]

The Duke's lines from the end of act 3 – much like other Shakespeare quotes yanked out of a play without proper contextualization – offer a dubious message about the responsibility of the powerful and the dangers of hypocrisy. In relation to Shakespeare, whose "cruel striking / Kills for faults of his own liking"? In the process of appropriating Shakespeare, who are the ones who commit the faults they reprimand in others?

In his article "Ist Shakespeare ein Problem?" Herbert A. Frenzel imagines Shakespeare as a "foster son" of the German nation: "So the Englishman Shakespeare found a foster nation in us, which made the foster son through its long love so much its own that it does not find him a stranger anymore." Frenzel, however, warns the English that "the greatness of this love" should not be misinterpreted by assuming that "Shakespeare was indispensable for the foster nation." Continuing the parent-child metaphor, he argues, "There are cultural rights that one can forfeit in the same way in which there are parental rights that, due to deliberate renunciation or simple carelessness, exist only biologically, but no longer morally."[10] Following an old topos of German Shakespeare appropriations, Frenzel argues that Germany has more rights to Shakespeare than the playwright's native land.

On the other hand, Frenzel is also eager to emphasize that Shakespeare is not indispensable to his foster nation: "The German theater would not suffer any serious damage if it decided to prove, for the sake of an experiment, that it can exist without Shakespeare." In his conclusion, he attempts to draw a balanced picture: "For us Germans, the English Shakespeare is a special case of a writer who is not affected by the state of war with England.... Even reasonable English people must admit, however, that the German trusteeship of Shakespeare has been such a blessing that it would be irresponsible to break this trusteeship."[11] Frenzel presents German culture as a guardian of and the true home to Shakespeare.

Professor Wolfgang Keller, the President of the German Shakespeare-Gesellschaft, followed a similar line of argument in his address to the Shakespeare Society in Weimar in April 1940. He posed the question of whether the German Shakespeare Society should celebrate Shakespeare, "a son of the English soil," while Germany was at war with England. To support his answer in the affirmative, first he quoted the German poet laureate Gerhart Hauptmann's famous lines from World War I: "There is not a people, not even the English, that would have as much right to claim Shakespeare as the Germans. Shakespeare's characters are part of our world; his soul became one with ours; and if it is in England where he was born and buried, Germany is the country where he truly lives."[12] In times of international conflicts, this German, even Nordic, Shakespeare was deployed as a token of German genius and cultural superiority. After this quotation, Professor Keller followed the tack of drawing parallels between Nazi Germany and Elizabethan England:

> Well, Shakespeare is neither a contemporary of, nor of the same mind as, the British politicians and rich stockholders who are fighting against our German Empire. 350 years ago he emerged feeling sacred pride and passionate love for his country and people – for a heroic England ruled by Queen Elizabeth, led in an authoritarian way and happy in this state-form: *Merry Old England*. But this England is dead. It had much more similarity with our present-day Germany than with the democratic, or rather, plutocratic, trading power that the British World Empire governs today. The Elizabethans' "life feeling" [*Lebensgefühl*] was heroic, military, young, and ambitious; hungry for action and adventures. And it was William Shakespeare who articulated this genuinely Germanic "life feeling" in the most beautiful way and kept it alive for all times. He provides our youth and our people with the most gripping and most thrilling examples of manliness and womanliness, of courage and stamina, veracity and honor, of human kindness and interdenominational piety.[13]

Here Keller combined elements of old-fashioned "Shakespeare lives in Germany" nationalism with a more philosophical, Gundolfian sort of chauvinism, as well as direct references to Nazi ideology. Following this section in his report, he reiterated some of the greatest achievements of the German Shakespeare reception (including the Schlegel-Tieck translations and the foundation of the German Shakespeare-Gesellschaft seventy-six years before), after which – with great pride – he compared the theatrical dearth of, and the audience's lack of interest in, Shakespeare productions in London with Shakespeare's great popularity in the Third Reich.

If Shakespeare was more often played and published in Germany than in England, Professor Keller wondered in his address to the German

Shakespeare-Gesellschaft in 1940, was it not fully reasonable to conclude that, at that historical moment, Shakespeare was more alive in Germany than in England? Keller argued that the story was more complicated than the simple truism "Shakespeare was born in England, thus he is English" would permit. Shakespeare, at least at a symbolic level,[14] was also considered a German classic author in the German national pantheon next to Goethe and Schiller.

"Shakespeare" is a geographically and historically determined cultural phenomenon: the product of local Shakespeare appropriations over the course of centuries. As such, Shakespeare is never immediately or directly present or presentable but continuously produced and mediated in various cultural contexts. From this point of view, the German Shakespeare tradition is significantly different from the English. This difference is also hinted at in *The Times* article from April 1940, which refers to "German Shakespearians" from Lessing and Goethe to Creizenach and Schücking and German theater producers from Schröder to Reinhardt. A telltale sentence even admits, "in the German theatre,...Shakespeare has been played with a frequency unknown in the English theatre till very recent years." This statement reveals a frequently reoccurring concern: is Shakespeare more popular in Europe in general and in Germany in particular than in England? The anxiety that the answer to these questions might well be "yes" incessantly haunts the discourse of Shakespeare appropriations in wartime London.

WHOSE SHAKESPEARE?

We often use the phrase *unser Shakespeare* as shorthand for a conservative, even nationalistic, manifestation of the "Shakespeare myth." Marjorie Garber, for instance, employs the term as a reference to Shakespeare as "fetish" and "ideology": "He is – whoever he is, or was – the fantasy of originary cultural wholeness, the last vestige of universalism: *unser Shakespeare*."[15] For her, Shakespeare is a last "tug of nostalgia," the last bulwark of a humanistic tradition, and *unser Shakespeare* conjures up universal(izing) appropriations of Shakespeare. As we have seen in this chapter, however, it is significant that the expression *unser Shakespeare* should not refer to "our Shakespeare" – meaning a global and universal "Bard" – but specifically to the Germans' own tradition or

"Shakespeare-Kultus." In its function as the title of Theodor Eichhoff's publication series at the beginning of the twentieth century, and as emphasized by the journalist and playwright Ludwig Fulda around the same time, *unser Shakespeare* is first and foremost a reference to German Shakespeare. As such, it highlights the fact that Shakespeare had a significant role in German culture and, ultimately even if indirectly, in forging German identity and nationalism.

When we use *unser Shakespeare* for a general type of Shakespeare appropriations, we disregard differences that, in fact, work to question further the possibility of a universal Shakespeare. While Garber underscores the detrimental naturalizing and universalizing effects of the Shakespeare fetish in relation to class, gender, and race within the current context of the United States, she also places her argument against a non-distinct Shakespeare tradition and (like the majority of other contemporary cultural critics) thus evokes an "originary wholeness" that implies an equally universal and general Shakespearean essence.

The manifestations of *unser Shakespeare* in England and Germany show that Shakespeare is always what he is imagined to be in a cultural and historical context: there is no singular "Shakespeare," only local and national Shakespeares. The various local appropriations and the universality of the cultural icon clash in the daily practice of interpreting, performing, and teaching Shakespeare's plays. An amusing and edifying example of this conflict between *unser Shakespeare* and "our Shakespeare" is a story about the Hungarian theater director Arthur Bárdos, who was invited to direct *Hamlet* in England in 1949. When interviewed by the BBC about his experience, Bárdos joked, "Of course, it is a great honour and a challenge, but to tell you the truth, it's strange to hear the text in English because I am used to the original version, translated by Janos [*sic*] Arany."[16] Calling Arany's translation an "original version," Bárdos points out that both Shakespeare and his plays mean something different in the various national contexts. Rooted in a different history, language, and tradition, the English Shakespeare distinctly differs from the (translated) German and Hungarian Shakespeares.

The Platonic model, according to which we assume the existence of an ideal, authentic Shakespearean text – and the surviving late-sixteenth- and early seventeenth-century editions are, to a varying degree, corrupt representations of this ideal original – has been intensely contested by most of the authors in this volume. We agree that the desire of New Bibliographers to establish an ideal, authentic, authorial text by Shakespeare and to "strip the veil of print from a text"[17] is misconceived. As David Kastan has pointed out, the "desire for innocence and authenticity, however understandable, is possibly misplaced" and "may be a longing for an inappropriate object."[18] Shakespeare exists in, and through, the material manifestations of his plays; his plays exist in their variants, in the diverse forms of various editions and productions as well as translations. *Unser Shakespeare* – in 1940 as much as today – is both ours and theirs; it is a historically and geographically determined "product of collaborative energies and exchanges."[19]

NOTES

I thank the editors of and contributors to this volume for their help shaping not just this essay but, directly or indirectly, my work in general as well. Of course, my profoundest thanks go to the dedicatee of the volume. I would also like to acknowledge Collegium Budapest's residential fellowship that I much enjoyed while I was working on this article.

1 David Scott Kastan, *Shakespeare after Theory* (New York: Routledge, 1999), 38–39.

2 Terence Hawkes, *Meaning by Shakespeare* (London: Routledge, 1992), 3.

3 "Claiming Shakespeare for Germany," *The Morning Post,* April 27, 1934; and "Wilhelm Shakespeare," *The Evening Standard,* April 26, 1934. Also, "Our Universal Poet," *The Daily Telegraph,* April 27, 1934.

4 See *The Daily Express,* September 23 and 28, 1935.

5 *The Times,* November 27, 1935.

6 "In Germany To-day: Waiting for Their Shakespeare," *The Times,* March 30, 1940.

7 "Germany and Shakespeare," *The Times,* April 25, 1940.

8 "Shakespeare 1940," *Wille und Macht: Führerorgan der nazionalsozialistischen Jugend* 8, no. 3 (February 1, 1940): 1. All translations from the German are mine.

9 *Measure for Measure,* The Arden Shakespeare, 2d series, ed. J.W. Lever (1965; New York: Routledge, 1988), 93–94 (3.ii.254–61).

10 Herbert A. Frenzel, "Ist Shakespeare ein Problem?" *Wille und Macht* 8, no. 3 (February 1, 1940): 2.

11 Ibid., 3.

12 Gerhart Hauptmann, "Deutschland und Shakespeare," *Shakespeare Jahrbuch* 51 (1915): xii.

13 Wolgang Keller, "Die 76. Hauptversammlung der Deutschen Shakespeare-Gesellschaft zu Weimar am 22. und 23. April 1940: Ansprache und Jahresbericht

des Präsidenten Professor Wolfgang Keller," *Shakespeare Jahrbuch* 76 (1940): 1–2.

14 Werner Habicht points out that, despite repeated arguments that Shakespeare was a German classic along the lines of Goethe and Schiller, German literary histories tended to discuss Shakespeare as a foreign author and "permitted no more than marginal references to his 'influence,' summary recapitulations of his eighteenth century 'discovery,' and the occasional dropping of his name to confer distinction on some German dramatist considered less than inferior" (Werner Habicht, "Shakespeare and the German Imagination: Cult, Controversy, and Performance," in *Shakespeare: World Views,* ed. Heather Kerr, Robin Eaden, and Madge Mitton [Newark: University of Delaware Press, 1996], 97–98).

15 Marjorie Garber, "Shakespeare as Fetish," in *Symptoms of Culture* (New York: Routledge, 1998), 168.

16 John Elsom, ed., *Is Shakespeare Still Our Contemporary?* (London: Routledge, 1989), 94. See also Dennis Kennedy, ed., *Foreign Shakespeare: Contemporary Performance* (Cambridge: Cambridge University Press, 1993), 1.

17 Fredson Bowers, *On Editing Shakespeare* (Charlottesville: University Press of Virginia, 1966), 87.

18 Kastan, *Shakespeare after Theory,* 62–63.

19 Ibid., 38.

aux vieilles tours fi- dè - le, oh, vo le! et monte à tire d'ai-le, de

du haut clocher du haut clocher au grand don-jon. vieux aigle

montagne sente nai - re, que blanchit l'hiver éter - nel!

e jamais l'aube ne vit - mu - et te, monte, monte, oi

te, monte au ciel

et maintenant, du haut de l'arbre, des flèches de l

l'enflamme, à l'horizon parmi la brume, voyez-vous flotter une plume,

Making Histories; or, Shakespeare's Ring

ADAM G. HOOKS

Triumph, my Britaine, *thou hast one to showe,*
To whom all scenes of Europe *homage owe.*
Ben Jonson[1]

Shakespeare translated the dry but honest historic Chronicle into the living speech of Drama. This Chronicle outlined with exact fidelity, and step by step, the march of historical events and the deeds of those engaged therein: it went about its task without any criticism or individual views, and thus gave a daguerreotype of historic facts. Shakespeare had only to vivify this daguerreotype into a luminous oil-painting; he necessarily had to unriddle from the group of facts their underlying motives, and to imprint these on the flesh and blood of their transactors.
Richard Wagner[2]

Jonson's commanding praise, directed at mythical Britain itself, raises Shakespeare above all other dramatists, past, present, and future: as the following line of his memorial poem famously exclaims, "*He was not of an age, but for all time!*" With characteristic pomp, Jonson calls forth, and even resurrects, the great classical tragedians – Aeschylus, Euripides, and Sophocles, along with Pacuvius, Accius, and Seneca – to "*heare thy Buskin tread, / And shake a stage,*" while banishing the comedians of "*insolent* Greece" and "*haughtie* Rome," who do not deserve comparison with the comic style of Shakespeare "*when thy Sockes were on.*" For all its insistent acclamation, Jonson's imperious imperative retains an ironic ambivalence, and not simply because the entity he addresses had yet to make the difficult transformation from myth to political reality, nor because his praise was both necessitated and tempered by Shakespeare's own "*small* Latine, *and lesse* Greeke." By defining (and indeed, attiring) Shakespeare in the conventional terms of comedy and tragedy, Jonson bestows the authority of the classical tradition on Shakespeare.

In doing so, however, Jonson neglects the genre in which Shakespeare had detailed the bloody battles and occasional triumphs of the nation's recent past – a genre prominently displayed on the title page of *Mr. William Shakespeares Comedies, Histories, & Tragedies*. When Shakespeare's friends and fellow King's Men John Heminge and Henry Condell assembled their commemorative folio volume – the format explains why the book is now called the "First Folio" – they chose to organize the plays by genre, gathering the ten plays based on the chronicles of English history under the rubric of the "Histories," where they appear in the chronological order of the events depicted.[3] The chronology stretches from King John to Henry VIII, but is principally focused on the eight plays which cover the consecutive reigns from Richard II to Richard III. Their classification was a convenient way to make sense of Shakespeare's diverse and often generically resistant work. The category of "Histories" in particular offered the opportunity to consolidate a characteristically Shakespearean form, since he had written more plays based on the chronicles than any other dramatist. The generic classification has been strikingly successful, both within and beyond Shakespeare's corpus, for the history play is now defined by the implicit terms of the First Folio's arrangement, excluding plays based on mythical or foreign history (no *King Lear* or *Macbeth*) or classical history (no *Julius Caesar,* either). Jonson's neglect of the genre is thus all the more surprising, considering his persistent identification of Shakespeare's "*Booke,*" the First Folio itself, and his "*Fame,*" an identification most visibly manifested in the short poem "To the Reader" opposite the frontispiece portrait. By failing to acknowledge the "Histories," Jonson would seem to be at cross-purposes with the commemorative and canonizing aims of Heminge and Condell.

Jonson's omission of the histories can be explained by the need to make a classicizing gesture, claiming and conferring an ancient authority on behalf of Shakespeare's drama. But it may also be a result of his professed disdain for the noisome and noisy genre of the history play. In the prologue to *Every Man In His Humour,* as published in his own folio volume seven years prior, Jonson sets himself apart from the "customes of the age," including plays which, "with three rustie swords, / And helpe of some few foot-and-halfe-foote words, / Fight ouer *Yorke,* and *Lancasters* long iarres."[4] The objection to the clamor and commotion of history plays was common enough, but Jonson here refers to Shakespeare's exceptionally popular plays of the 1590s depicting the Wars of the Roses. For Jonson, Shakespeare's histories, lacking an Aristotelian warrant and violating the principles of classical comedy and tragedy, need to be expunged in order for him to transcend his age. Shakespeare must be remade in Jonson's own image, even if it means losing the most distinctively Shakespearean genre.

Jonson's assertion that "*all the* Muses *still were in their prime*" when Shakespeare came forth may be strategically disingenuous, but Clio would eventually get her due, in an anonymous prefatory poem added to the Second Folio nine years later.[5] Here, "*the buskind Muse*" and "*the Commicke Queene*" are superseded by "*the graund / And lowder tone of* Clio," who is joined by the "*Silver voyced Lady*" Calliope, the "*melodious paire*" who "*joyntly woo'd*" Shakespeare. When added to his own "*cunning braine,*" the favor of the muses granted Shakespeare extraordinary control over history, and hence over death itself: making "*Time past*" a "*pastime,*" he was able to "*raise our auncient Soveraignes from their herse,*" enlivening their "*pale trunkes*" on stage and evoking such potent emotions that audience members were "*Stolne from our selves.*" Shakespeare's authority and achievement derive from his power to "*Make Kings his subjects,*" subduing past monarchs and present audiences alike. As a more famous addition to the Second Folio attests, such is the "*lasting Monument*" of Shakespeare's book – and such is its effect on the imaginations of readers – "*That Kings for such a Tombe would wish to die.*"[6] The young John Milton could not have known it then, but his prophetic line would soon be realized, as his king – an avid reader of Shakespeare's Second Folio, his "Closet Companion" according to Milton himself – would soon be made to suffer the fate of rebellious subjects.[7]

Shakespeare is praised by his anonymous admirer for giving life to "*auncient Soveraignes*" by granting "*voyce*" and "*action*" and representing them in "*their lively colours just extent*." Centuries later Richard Wagner would make a similar claim on behalf of Shakespeare, if in a radically different context, claiming that he had "translated the dry but honest historic Chronicle into the living speech of Drama." In Wagner's vivid account, he describes the chronicle sources as a "daguerreotype," an exact, industrial reproduction, which Shakespeare vivified into a "luminous oil-painting," impressionistically exercising the artist's prerogative to shape and transform the stark facts of history. Engaged in his own creative struggle, Wagner extols (and perhaps envies) Shakespeare's expansive scope, even while lamenting the impossibility, in the modern age, of "dressing History" with the "chronicler's fidelity" of a distinctly premodern Shakespeare, "heedless as to brevity or length."[8] Wagner inherited this view of Shakespeare from the German Romantics, who had recruited the histories in order to cultivate a national unity they conspicuously lacked. The ten history plays were considered as a coherent sequence, a single, organic work, thereby confirming Shakespeare's singular status as the genius responsible for authoring a secular epic. For Wagner, Shakespeare's sprawling series of plays provided one model for his own ambitious epic – a model to be surpassed by the *Gesamtkunstwerk*, which would create, rather than chronicle, a mythical history intended to unify both the arts and the *Volk*. Once Wagner's masterpiece was completed and performed as a marathon cycle of four dramas, *Der Ring des Nibelungen* itself influenced the subsequent perception and performance of Shakespeare's histories as two linked "tetralogies." Reclaimed by their native land in the twentieth century, the histories were (and continue to be) performed as a triumphant theatrical extravaganza, displaying – and even displacing – the nation's actual history.

The prevailing view of the histories as a single cycle would have a profound impact on the criticism of the plays, providing the implicit and unquestioned condition of possibility for the idea, advanced most influentially by E.M.W. Tillyard, that the histories were designed by Shakespeare (and Shakespeare alone) as a national epic, and further, as a manifestation of the providential Tudor myth.[9] Tillyard's central thesis has been largely discredited; it was criticized early and often, especially by those who considered the plays as separate and even collaboratively written works, or who balked at the idea of Shakespeare as an apologist for the Tudor state, and, by extension, for wartime nationalist politics. But Tillyard's fundamental assumption that the histories form a unified whole – an "organism," rather than a mere "compilation" – remains a powerful idea, and in many ways it continues to structure the discussion of the plays.[10]

Tillyard commenced his analysis of the histories by noting that in the First Folio, the ten plays were "distributed in a curious regularity."[11] This "regularity" brought order to a diverse group of plays of seemingly disparate structures, making visible a similarity in form, not just content, and thereby consolidating the genre of the history play. By foregrounding the chronological connections among the plays, the Folio effectively defined the genre as a serialized form in which the structural principle of the larger work transcends its individual parts.[12] As Jonson predicted of Shakespeare himself, this view of the histories would eventually transcend its age – but it did so only eventually. This generic genealogy cannot be traced back to a solitary, originary source, either to Shakespeare, or to the First Folio. The histories have always been subject to different modes of interpretation and appropriation which have been conditioned by the different material forms in which the plays circulated. The Folio inaugurated an important and influential way of interpreting the histories, yet one that was neither immediately nor inexorably accepted.

MAKING "HISTORIES"

The First Folio is a self-consciously monumental object, constructing and representing the integrity of Shakespeare and his corpus. The generic divisions that constitute its title are so resolutely and materially distinct, though, that they call into question the integrity of the volume itself. The plays that make up the sections of comedies, histories, and tragedies were printed in separate signature sequences, making them bibliographically independent entities. The separate sections may have been a result of the vagaries of the printing process, the course of which did not always run smooth, but it may also have been the result of an economic exigency, allowing the sections to be sold separately, and thus more cheaply and quickly.[13] Although the sections are materially discrete, the generic divisions are not as resolute as they may at first appear to be. The table of contents is called "A Catalogve of the seuerall Comedies, Histories, and

A CATALOGVE

of the ſeuerall Comedies, Hiſtories, and Tragedies contained in this Volume.

COMEDIES.

HISTORIES.

TRAGEDIES.

Tragedies contained in this Volume," the adjective "seuerall" here meaning "separate" or "distinct," as Shakespeare would have understood the term, rather than simply "numerous" (fig. 48).[14] The term does as much to distinguish the individual plays from each other as separate works as it does to differentiate the generic categories themselves. The titles of the "Histories" are nevertheless the most consistent and formulaic on the page, taking one of only two forms, ending with the name of each play's eponymous monarch: either "*The Life and Death of King John*," for example, or, for plays with multiple installments, "*The First part of King Henry the fourth*."[15] The "Tragedies," in contrast, are either explicitly labeled as such ("*The Tragedy of Macbeth*") or simply take the name of the central protagonist—with the significant exceptions, however, of "*The Life and death of Julius Cæsar*" and "*Cymbeline King of Britaine*," which share part of the nominal formulation of the histories, thereby providing at least an implicit recognition of the historical sources for those plays.

Inside the volume the generic instability is more obvious: labeled as a history play in the catalogue, where *Richard III* is called "*The Life & Death of Richard the Third*," on the first page of the play it is instead titled "The Tragedy of Richard the Third: with the Landing of Earle Richmond, and the Battell at Bosworth Field." While no other history play switches its genre altogether, the protagonists of other plays do change: "The First Part of Henry the Fourth" is subtitled "with the Life and Death of Henry Sirnamed Hot-Spvrre," while the second and third parts of "Henry the Sixt" feature "the death of the Good Duke Hvmfrey" and "the death of the Duke of Yorke," respectively. And while *Julius Caesar* is labeled on its first page as "The Tragedie of Ivlivs Caesar," another of the tragedies takes on the formulation of a history: "The Life of Tymon of Athens," on a par with "The Life of Henry the Fift" and "The Famous History of the Life of King Henry the Eight." The variable titles disrupt, at least partially, the strict division between the two genres that the catalogue presents; put more positively, the titles demonstrate the deep affinities between the histories and the tragedies, especially considering that some of the latter ultimately derive from the same historical sources as the former. The two genres are

Fig. 48. William Shakespeare, *Mr. William Shakespeares Comedies, Histories, & Tragedies* (London, 1623), B2r. Beinecke Rare Book and Manuscript Library, Yale University, 1978 +83

also united in their difference from the comedies, which make no claim to be historical, and which do not feature a proper name in any of the titles, favoring instead emblematic descriptions of the plot of each play.

The Folio standardizes the titles of all the plays, a logical extension of the generic scheme chosen by Heminge and Condell, but this standardization is particularly noticeable in the histories and tragedies. The previously published quarto editions of several of the plays exhibit a significant variability in genre and title. The Folio did not immediately supersede these earlier quartos, since they continued to be published and remained in circulation long after the Folio appeared. Both *Richard II* and *Richard III* – two of the most frequently reprinted of Shakespeare's plays – were titled as tragedies in quarto, while *3 Henry VI* was first published in 1595 as "The true Tragedie of Richard *Duke of Yorke, and the death of* good King Henrie the Sixt." In this case, the standardization imposed by the Folio incorporated the play into a larger, tripartite work, but in doing so it obscured the link already evident between the play and its companion piece. *2 Henry VI* was first published in 1594 as "The First part of the Contention betwixt the two famous Houses of Yorke and Lancaster," and the next year "The True Tragedie" was explicitly connected to its predecessor, advertised on its title page as including "the whole contention betweene the two houses Lancaster and Yorke." The two plays were later rebranded as a single work that had been "Diuided into two Parts," "The Whole Contention betweene the two Famous Houses, Lancaster and Yorke," published as the initial stage in a collection of ten Shakespeare plays by Thomas Pavier and William Jaggard in 1619. Before the Folio, only one other set of plays were explicitly coupled together, "The History of Henrie the Fovrth" (first published in 1598, and eventually published nine times in quarto through the seventeenth century) and its sequel, "The Second part of Henrie the fourth," published in an individual quarto for the first (and only) time in 1600. Integrating the history plays into a larger, chronological sequence emphasized the connections among all the plays, but it also denied the distinctiveness of the plays which had initially been designed and marketed as an interconnected pair. This denial has been especially harsh to the *Henry VI* plays, which have been overshadowed by the massive popularity of Falstaff and the *Henry IV* plays – although this popularity has rested almost exclusively on the first part of that play, which far outpaced its sequel. Indeed, before the Folio appeared, the "Whole Contention" was the most successful and visible two-part Shakespearean play – popular enough (in all the senses of that term) to provoke the ire of Jonson, who sneered at "*Yorke,* and *Lancasters* long iarres."

The undeniable popularity and profitability of Shakespeare's history plays in individual quartos helped to guarantee the success of the First Folio. The three most popular of Shakespeare's plays in print were *1 Henry IV, Richard III,* and *Richard II,* and, remarkably, all three plays had first been published by the same stationer, Andrew Wise.[16] When Wise left the business in 1603, he transferred the rights to his most dependable titles to his partner Matthew Law – including his three blockbuster Shakespeare plays.[17] Law would continue to republish Shakespeare's three best-sellers until the end of his career, and they would prove to be some of his most profitable titles, going through a combined ten editions.[18] As the owner of the most popular Shakespeare plays already in print, Law was in a position to drive a hard bargain with the Folio syndicate, and sometime in late 1622, the Jaggards stopped printing *Richard II,* about halfway through the play; they proceeded by working around the three titles owned by Law, resuming work on *Richard II* after an interruption that may have lasted weeks, or even months.[19] The most likely explanation is that Law caused the interruption and used the time to force the Folio publishers to meet his terms. The Folio could hardly appear without Law's consent, since he had essentially cornered the market on Shakespeare's most popular printed plays – and plays that, no less, formed a crucial part of what was to become a chronological sequence of "Histories." Law saw his advantage and capitalized on what was for him a fortuitous business opportunity. Law's bid to maximize the value of his Shakespeare properties was not limited to driving a trade with the Folio syndicate, for at some point in 1622, he republished both *Richard III* and *1 Henry IV*. Textual scholars have often characterized Law's behavior as an underhanded attempt to undercut the Folio in some way, but there is no reason to believe he was engaging in sharp practice, since he rightfully owned the titles and was more than justified in selling them in a more accessible format. (We might call this the Barnes & Noble strategy, which is not uncommon today: bookstores usually stock only a few copies of Shakespeare's complete works, along with a much larger number of copies of individual plays, typically only the few which have proven to be bestsellers).

The different formats provided different ways of acquiring, reading, and interpreting Shakespeare's plays. In quarto, they could be approached as the self-sufficient stories of sensational central characters. The title page of *Richard III* lists a series of Richard's actions – his "treacherous Plots," a "pittiefull murther," and his "tyrannicall vsurpation" – while the two *Henry IV* plays prominently advertised the "*humorous conceits*" of Falstaff and his companion, "*swaggering* Pistoll," who was even given equal billing with the battle of Agincourt on the title page of *Henry V* (1600). Contemporaries certainly perceived, and even exploited, the connections between plays, particularly those, like the "Whole Contention" and the *Henry IV* plays, which had been designed and marketed as continuations. Indeed, *The Merry Wives of Windsor,* published in 1602 as "A Most pleasaunt and excellent conceited Comedie, of Syr *Iohn Falstaffe,*" owes its existence to Shakespeare's willingness to make the most of his famously fat knight. There was also an attempt to adapt the two *Henry IV* plays as a single work. Edward Dering prepared a conflation of the two plays firmly focused on the relationship between Henry and Prince Hal, relegating Falstaff and his companions to the margins. The conflation survives only in manuscript and was intended to serve as the script for a private performance.[20] Other than this isolated instance, there is no evidence that the history plays were ever publicly performed together, or even as a two-part play on consecutive days. The two parts of *Henry IV* were performed during the same winter season at Whitehall, in 1612–1613, but not at the same time, and the titles of the plays given in the accounts argue against the perception of the plays as parts of a coherent whole.[21]

By organizing Shakespeare's oeuvre into three distinct generic categories, and by ordering the "Histories" as a sequence of interdependent historical events, Heminge and Condell altered the way the plays could be approached, effectively encouraging readers to make connections among successive plays that now seemed to constitute an orderly dramatic progression. The requisite reclassification and renaming of the plays certainly brought order to the Folio's contents, but it also shifted the focus away from what customers had long found attractive about the plays – the exploits so exhaustively enumerated on the quarto title pages. (Like the newly crowned Henry V, Heminge and Condell banished Falstaff, at least from his place as the titular star of the show). Shakespeare's set of character-driven plays was transformed into a systematic account of the nation's political past, the names of the monarchs now serving more as demarcations of historical epochs than indications of dramatic interest. The Folio emphasizes the narrative continuity of the histories, but this emphasis was only an enabling condition. The model of Shakespeare's histories it presented did not displace other, alternative models. The Folio may have defined and consolidated the genre of the Shakespearean history play, but the status of this genre was far from secure.

"A RUDE, HISTORICK PLAN"

Two years before the first appearance of the Third Folio of Shakespeare's plays (published in 1663), Francis Kirkman, a bookseller and inveterate dramatic enthusiast, created a catalogue of extant printed plays, ordering them alphabetically by the name of the play, and including author and genre attributions.[22] For Shakespeare's plays, Kirkman followed the generic organization of the Folio: so, for example, both "Richard the second" and "Richard the 3d" are labeled histories, rather than tragedies. Most of Kirkman's inventory was, of course, made up of individual play quartos, and he relies on these to determine the genres of plays that did not appear in the Folio, and, more importantly, to determine his concept of the history play itself. Kirkman's attributions show that his definition of the genre was far more expansive than that of Heminge and Condell, at least for non-Shakespearean plays, for he included plays based on both foreign and classical history. Kirkman also listed several plays not in the First or Second Folio that were ascribed to Shakespeare in quarto. Of those labeled a history, some are predictable, such as those based on historical events – "Old Castles life and death" and "Cromwels History"[23] – while others are more surprising, such as "Pericles Prince of Tyre."[24] "Leir & his three daughters" is ascribed to Shakespeare and labeled a tragedy, as it is in the First Folio (where it is simply called "*King Lear*"), whereas the anonymous play on the same story is listed as "Leir and his three daughters" and labeled a history – as both plays had been called when initially published in quarto.[25]

When Kirkman revised his catalogue a decade later, he included a page of commentary where he remarked, with some novelty, that "by Playes alone you may very well know the Chronicle History of *England*, and many other Histories," thereby anticipating the Duke of Marlborough's famous acknowledgment of Shakespeare's plays as his favorite source for English history.[26] Kirkman continues by saying that "I could enlarge much on this account, having for my own fancy written down all the Historical Playes in a succinct orderly method, as you may do the like." Kirkman presumably means that he had created a list of all the history plays (and not just Shakespeare's) in the chronological order of the events they depict, much as Heminge and Condell had done in the First Folio – but only for "my own fancy." In the printed catalogue, though, the histories appear scattered throughout the list, which again is alphabetized by the title of the play. Kirkman's comment reveals an awareness of the connections among history plays – both chronological and generic – even as it demonstrates that these connections were not as important as other, competing forms of organization, namely authorship and alphabetization.

Kirkman may have found history plays edifying and informative, but the earliest formal critics of English drama disparaged the genre for its refusal to conform to the neoclassical unities. The most salient characteristics of the history plays – their open-ended, episodic structure, and their basis in the chronicles – therefore had to be detached from Shakespeare in order to protect his authorial status. The first proper critical essay written about Shakespeare, by Margaret Cavendish, defended his "Wit and Eloquence" upon "all Subjects" – so much so that Shakespeare "wanted Subjects for his Wit and Eloquence to Work on, for which he was Forced to take some of his Plots out of History, where he only took the Bare Designs, the Wit and Language being all his Own."[27] The anxiety Cavendish articulates here (which would persist in some form for centuries) reveals a tension between the derivative origins of Shakespeare's dramatic plots and the creative talents that would transform them into transcendent works of art. For Cavendish, the "Bare Designs" of the plot are far less important than the characters, for "there is not any person he hath Described in his Book [i.e., one of the Folio editions], but his Readers might think they were Well acquainted with them," to the extent that "one would think he [Shakespeare] had been Transformed into every one of those Persons he hath Described." Shakespeare can be forgiven the use of his historical sources because he was a "Natural Poet" who created, and indeed inhabited, naturalistic characters, from clown to king, Falstaff to Henry V. By doing so, Shakespeare not only uses historical figures, but improves on them, for "certainly *Julius Cæsar, Augustus Cæsar,* and *Antonius,* did never Really Act their parts Better" – a remark that shows Cavendish's willingness to expand the definition of a historical play beyond what is "Described in his Book."

The conflicted attitudes toward Shakespeare's natural talents, and their failure to conform to the regular rules of neoclassical drama, were most memorably expressed by John Dryden. In his critical dialogue *Of Dramatick Poesie* (1668), Dryden criticized the history plays in the voice of Lisideius: enamored of French drama, he complains that "the Historical Playes of *Shakespeare*" are "rather so many Chronicles of Kings, or the business many times of thirty or forty years, crampt into a representation of two hours and a half, which is not to imitate or paint Nature, but rather to draw her in miniature."[28] Dryden answers this accusation in the voice of his proxy Neander, who defends the honor of the nation by declaring that "in most of the irregular Playes of *Shakespeare* or *Fletcher*" there is "a more masculine fancy and greater spirit in all the writing, then there is in any of the French."[29] (Jonson needed no defense, since his plays "are for the most part regular.") Neander continues by confirming Shakespeare's status as the poet of nature, thus putting him beyond the kind of critique offered by Lisideius: those who indict his lack of learning thereby "give him the greater commendation" for he was "naturally learne'd; he needed not the spectacles of Books to read Nature; he look'd inwards, and found her there." The irregularities of Shakespeare's plays could be conveniently forgiven, or even held up as proof of his natural genius, but they could not be forgotten. Just as Cavendish had felt the need to justify Shakespeare's recourse to historical sources by minimizing the importance of doing so, Dryden refused to completely excuse Shakespeare's violation of the unities. A few years later, Dryden derided the episodic *Pericles* as "some ridiculous, incoherent story," grouping it with the "Historical Plays of *Shakespear*" as prime examples of the playwright's lapses.[30]

For Dryden and his contemporaries, Shakespeare's shortcomings were as undeniable as his accomplishments, which were all the more remarkable for having been produced in a comparably primitive age. Shakespeare's defects were a result of the times in which he lived, and were thus no fault of his own; Shakespeare transcended not only his age, but his own imperfections. If the sprawling plots of the history plays, constrained by the unrelenting chronology of the chronicles, remained a critical liability, they could at least be isolated from Shakespeare's true genius – which meant that they could either be rationalized, or simply improved upon.

Shakespeare's faithfully episodic plots were also convenient for those who adapted his history plays for the Restoration stage, particularly those with a distinct, if necessarily covert, political or ideological agenda. Nahum Tate unwisely adapted *Richard II* during the Exclusion Crisis in 1680, and the play was banned almost immediately – twice – despite Tate's decision to set the play on foreign soil and rename it *The Sicilian Usurper*. Tate defended himself and his play by pointing to his predecessor's fidelity to the chronicles, claiming that Shakespeare "*bated none of his Characters an Ace of the Chronicle; he took care to shew 'em no worse Men than They were, but represents them never a jot better*." Acknowledging "*how dissolute then the Age, and how corrupt the Court*" was in the age of the historical Richard II allowed Tate to disclaim any "*design of Satyr on present Transactions*."[31] He could thus proclaim his own fidelity to Shakespeare's play even while claiming to reform the objectionable behavior of the protagonist. Forty years later, Shakespeare's *Richard II* was adapted again, this time by Lewis Theobald.[32] Like Tate, Theobald wanted to enhance the dignity of Shakespeare's Richard – not by reforming his character, though, but by taking the "*scatter'd Beauties*" of the play and weaving them together "*in a regular Fable*," and for this purpose Theobald justified his "*Innovations upon History and* Shakespear." Theobald discards the "*rude, Historick Plan*" in order to maintain the unity of action, which in turn supports "*the* Dignity *of the* Characters."[33] Theobald is less concerned with the dignity of Richard, however, than he is with that of Shakespeare: as he explains, he adapted the play so that, "*in confessing my Obligations to* Shakespear," he might do "*some Justice upon the Points of his* Learning, *and* Acquaintance with the Antients." What had been a significant liability is again recuperated, as Theobald seizes the opportunity to demonstrate the ways in which Shakespeare's reliance on source material (especially the classics) complemented and enabled, rather than contradicted and inhibited, his natural artistic talents.

"ONE WORK, UPON ONE PLAN"

Adapting Shakespeare on stage was one way of restoring and demonstrating his superiority as a dramatist; altering and emending the plays on the page, though, proved to be more influential in the following century. The succession of scholarly editions produced in the eighteenth century supplanted the single-volume format of the folio collections by providing smaller, more convenient multivolume editions. Nevertheless, they still depended, in part, on the original organizational scheme of Heminge and Condell, even if the influence of the original generic classifications was necessarily diminished: the Folio genres were often viewed as inadequate, and the plays were at any rate spread out over several volumes, disrupting the strict equivalence between the canon and the material book. The chronological sequence of the English history plays remained securely intact, though, the only aspect of the Folio catalogue that would survive the century.

The first of these, edited by Nicholas Rowe and published in six volumes in 1709, followed the order of the plays in the Folios, even preserving the titles of the plays as they appeared on the first page of each play. So, for example, *1 Henry IV* retained its Folio title of "The First Part of Henry IV. with the Life *and* Death of *Henry* Sirnam'd *Hot-Spur*." Although Rowe retained the Folio order of plays, he rejected its generic scheme, arguing in his preface that Shakespeare's plays "are properly to be distinguish'd only into Comedies and Tragedies," since those plays "which are called Histories, and even some of his Comedies, are really Tragedies, with a run or mixture of Comedy amongst 'em." Echoing earlier laments for the lack of dramatic decorum, Rowe redefined the mixed form of the history play as "Trage-Comedy," labeling it the "common Mistake of that Age." Rowe also condemned the history plays for their failure to adhere to the principles of "exact Tragedy," since "all his Historical Plays comprehend a great length of Time," citing as evidence the very titles of the plays (which "very often tells you, 'tis *The Life of King* John, *King* Richard, &c."). By refusing to choose judiciously and shape historical events, Shakespeare neglected his duty as a poet, instead depicting characters in the manner of a historian. Rowe does acknowledge that Shakespeare should not be judged by "a Law he knew nothing of," but rather than serving as the precondition for a vindication of his natural genius, this only demonstrates the "State of almost universal License and Ignorance" in which he lived and worked."[34]

Several of Rowe's key critical judgments influenced the next major edition of Shakespeare, published in 1725 and edited by Alexander Pope. Shakespeare's unsophisticated audience is once again offered as an explanation for the plays' defects: in Pope's words, the "Historical Plays strictly follow the common *Old Stories* or *Vulgar Traditions* of that kind of people."[35] Until Jonson brought "critical learning" to the stage, the prejudices of "that kind" of people dictated dramatic forms which were indebted to history, to their detriment. Pope does not altogether condemn Shakespeare's learning, though, for it in fact provides Pope with the organizational scheme for his six-volume edition, which he divides according to the source material for the plays. While Pope generally follows the Folio order for the comedies, which make up the first two volumes, he begins the third volume, "consisting of Historical Plays," with *King Lear,* thereby reclaiming it as a history. The remainder of volumes four and five include the ten Folio histories in chronological order, but the final two volumes of tragedies abandon the Folio order altogether: the fifth consists of "Tragedies from History" (the Roman histories, plus *Macbeth*), and the sixth "Tragedies from Fable" (including *Cymbeline,* which, although set in ancient Britain like *King Lear,* is excluded from the realm of proper history).

Pope's more expansive, and at least implicitly laudatory, view of Shakespeare's history plays was unsurprisingly rejected by Theobald, Pope's successor as editor of Shakespeare (and the object of his ridicule in *The Dunciad*). Theobald's objection to the "*rude, Historick Plan*" of *Richard II,* in his adaptation of 1720, has already been noted, and he expanded on this objection when he published his edition of Shakespeare in 1733, stating with characteristic confidence that "almost in every Scene of his historical Plays" Shakespeare "commits the grossest Offences against Chronology, History, and Antient Politicks."[36] Concerned as he was to demonstrate the degree of Shakespeare's learning (not to mention his own editorial labor), Theobald stresses that Shakespeare "was a close and accurate Copier where-ever his *Fable* was founded on *History,*" and concludes that any offenses were not the result of "Ignorance, as is generally supposed," but rather "thro' the too powerful Blaze of his Imagination; which, when once raised, made all acquired Knowledge vanish and disappear before it."[37] Like Pope, his awareness of generic affinities influenced the organization of the edition, so that the tragedies are reordered in a way that displays the differences in their sources. The fifth volume begins with the final play in the sequence of English histories, *Henry VIII,* which is followed by *King Lear* and *Macbeth,* which similarly derive from the chronicles. *Timon of Athens* and *Titus Andronicus* come next, beginning the series of Roman histories that continues in the sixth volume. Theobald's next and last section is identical to Pope's "Tragedies from Fable," beginning with *Cymbeline* at the end of the sixth volume, and continuing into the seventh and final volume with *Troilus and Cressida, Romeo and Juliet, Hamlet,* and *Othello.*

Theobald found the history plays valuable because they so clearly confirmed Shakespeare's study of textual sources – his "Knowledge of *History* and *Books*"[38] – even as this very indebtedness had to be denounced as a failure of dramaturgy. They were an unfortunate but necessary embarrassment in the Shakespeare canon, at once guaranteeing his erudition while freeing him from its constraints. This prevailing opinion of the histories began to shift with Samuel Johnson's edition of 1765. Johnson struggled with the generic incongruities of Shakespeare's "mingled drama," which could not be contained in convenient or conventional categories. He criticizes the generic arrangement of the Folio, contending that Heminge and Condell "seem not to have distinguished the three kinds, by any very exact or definite ideas." Johnson sets out to provide such a definition for the history play, which "is not always very nicely distinguished from tragedy." Nevertheless, as neither proper tragedies, nor comedies, the history plays "are not subject to any of their laws": history was "a series of actions, with no other than chronological succession, independent of each other, and without any tendency to introduce or to regulate the conclusion." The genre of history requires only that the action be understood, the incidents affecting, and the characters consistent; "no other unity is intended, and therefore none is to be sought."[39]

Johnson's validation of the "chronological succession" of the history plays transformed their vice into a virtue, and as such would have a profound impact on the critical perception of Shakespeare's purpose and development as a dramatic author. If history was simply "a series of actions," then it "might be continued through many plays; as it had no plan, it had no limits." What began here, in the preface, as merely a defense of the history plays from the tyranny of the unities, became, in Johnson's notes to the individual plays, a crucial indication of Shakespeare's method of composition, and thus a revelation of his artistic objective. Johnson was the first to suggest that the history plays that depict consecutive reigns were not only conceived as a linked sequence of events, but were deliberately intended by Shakespeare to constitute a single work. Noting the continuation of action at the beginning of *1 Henry IV,* carried over from the end of *Richard II,* Johnson states that "Shakespeare has apparently designed a regular connection of these dramatick histories from Richard the Second to Henry the Fifth." Johnson elaborates on this theory at the end of *2 Henry IV,* declaring that "when these plays were represented, I believe they ended as they are now ended in the books; but Shakespeare seems to have designed that the whole series of action from the beginning of *Richard the Second,* to the end of *Henry the Fifth,* should be considered by the reader as one work, upon one plan, only broken into parts by the necessity of exhibition."[40] What had previously been characterized as Shakespeare's tedious adherence to the chronology of the chronicles, which could only be justified and overcome by the exercise of his natural genius, is here reclaimed as evidence of that genius – of Shakespeare's artistic ambition and authorial intention. Although Johnson's sense of early modern performance has been called "extremely shaky," he nevertheless recognized the important differences between watching and reading a play.[41] The "necessity of exhibition" may have dictated the form and length of the individual parts, in both performance and in print, but when published together, they could be considered as one work by a reader who could fully appreciate Shakespeare's artistic accomplishment.

This is not to say that Shakespeare intended to privilege his readers; rather, his readers occupied a privileged position, recognizing (and criticizing) Shakespeare's achievement in the fullness of time. It was Johnson, after all, who accused Shakespeare of forsaking posterity, thinking only of "present popularity and present profit" in the theater, so careless of his "future fame" that he failed to collect and publish his works. For Johnson, a "dramatick exhibition is a book recited with concomitants that encrease or diminish its effect," and he makes it clear that the latter often outweighs the former, for what delights on the stage often suffers on the page. While Johnson praises Shakespeare's ambition, he does not think that Shakespeare was always, or even very often, capable of fulfilling it, for he constantly reveals his frustration at Shakespeare's inattention to details, or even worse, his outright artistic disappointments. Although *Richard II* is an integral part of a historical sequence, it is nevertheless "desultory and erratick" in and of itself, and, in a significant slippage of generic terms, Johnson determines that "it is not finished at last with the happy force of some other of his tragedies." In contrast, the two parts of *Henry IV* and *Henry V* are "among the happiest of our authour's compositions." However, the "second class" of history plays consists only of those which are not part of a coherent sequence: *King John* and *Henry VIII* are joined here by *Richard III,* which Johnson is hesitant to connect to the less successful *Henry VI* plays.[42]

Johnson's hesitation over the *Henry VI* plays reveals an anxiety at their problematic place in the Shakespeare canon. Johnson refutes the arguments of previous editors – Theobald, for one – that the *Henry VI* plays are "supposititious," that is, not written entirely by Shakespeare (Johnson had used this adjective to explain the word "bastard" in his dictionary). He is willing to admit that Shakespeare composed haphazardly, and that he revised plays; he is not willing, however, to exclude the *Henry VI* plays simply because they are artistically inferior, in part because of his belief that Shakespeare exploited the open-ended form of the history play to his advantage. Still, his lack of enthusiasm is striking: he cautiously states that the three *Henry VI* plays "seem to be declared genuine by the voice of Shakespeare himself," since they are mentioned in the epilogue to *Henry V,* and there are some apparent connections among the three plays and *Richard III*. However, he refrains from explicitly defining the four plays as "one work, upon one plan."

The "supposititious" status of the *Henry VI* plays persisted, in part because they had been written *before* the plays that depicted earlier historical events. The two questions – which of the plays traditionally attributed to Shakespeare he had actually written, and in what order – were necessarily and closely related, and the *Henry VI* plays would prove to be the crucial test case. Edmond Malone was the first to take up the two matters in earnest, bringing a remarkable range of textual and historical evidence to bear on the chronology and composition of the Shakespeare canon. Malone's goal was to establish a reliable timeline by which to assess Shakespeare's artistic development as a writer, thereby combining the concerns of the biographer with those of the literary critic. His first major contribution to Shakespeare scholarship was *An Attempt to Ascertain the Order in which the Plays attributed to Shakspeare were Written* (1778), a work which he kept revising throughout his lifetime.[43] Malone dated the *Henry VI* plays to the very beginning of Shakespeare's theatrical career, and the rest of the history plays (correctly, with one exception) to the mid- to late 1590s.[44] Unlike Johnson, then, Malone was not concerned to identify the history plays as a coherent sequence; indeed, his research had shown that they had been written over a number of years, alongside several other unrelated plays.

A decade later, Malone published a densely argued treatise on the *Henry VI* plays, arguing that they were not initially written by Shakespeare, but only revised by him.[45] The texts of *2* and *3 Henry VI* as they appeared in the First Folio represented versions of the earlier (and textually defective) quartos that had been reworked and improved by Shakespeare; *1 Henry VI,* on the other hand, was a collaborative play with only the most minimal contribution by Shakespeare. By attempting to determine which plays Shakespeare had written alone, Malone aimed to recover, and hence to preserve, the integrity of Shakespeare's authorial corpus; in doing so, however, Malone had challenged the authority of the book that was responsible for creating the idea of that integrity in the first place: the First Folio. Confronted with this problem, Malone explained the presence of *1 Henry VI* in the Folio by citing its connection to the subsequent plays in the historical sequence: after suggesting that Heminge and Condell may simply have forgotten Shakespeare's insignificant involvement with the play, he proposes that "they imagined the insertion of this historical drama was necessary to understanding the two pieces that follow it."[46]

The order of the plays in Malone's edition of 1790 followed the editions published over the previous decade by Johnson, George Steevens, and Isaac Reed, which had made only slight alterations from Johnson's first edition in 1765.[47] Malone's goal of organizing the plays in the order in which Shakespeare had written them was finally fulfilled, though, in the massive variorum edition of 1821, prepared by James Boswell the younger in the decade following Malone's death. In Boswell's words, he had carried out Malone's plan to organize the plays in chronological order so that "the reader might be thus enabled to trace the progress of the author's powers, from his first and imperfect essays, to those more finished performances which he afterwards produced."[48] At least he had done so "as far as his miscellaneous plays are concerned," for as Boswell went on to state, he had "found it universally objected to by all whom I had an opportunity to consult, if it were made to comprehend the plays which were founded on English history." The chronological succession of events in the ten Folio histories was deemed indispensable – so essential to the idea of Shakespeare that it trumped any insight to be gained from putting the plays in their proper place in Shakespeare's professional life. The ten plays were thus consigned to volumes fifteen through nineteen, and were followed only by the two volumes which included Shakespeare's poetry, and the doubtful plays *Pericles* and *Titus Andronicus*. The importance and integrity of the sequence of English history plays had prevailed; indeed, in the case of the *Henry VI* plays, the existence of such a sequence both superseded and guaranteed their status as authentic Shakespearean compositions. Boswell's decision ultimately produced exactly the opposite effect of what Malone intended, as the order in which Shakespeare worked was disrupted by the order of the historical events on which he worked. Shakespeare once again became a mere chronicler of history, rather than the artist responsible for shaping it.

SHAKESPEARE'S *RING*

Malone's conclusions regarding the authorship and chronology of Shakespeare's plays would prove to be fundamental for subsequent scholarship, even if the form this influence took was unintended by Malone. Even though he had shown that the Folio could not be considered coterminous with the Shakespearean corpus, the Folio's arrangement of the history plays became ever more firmly established. Boswell was not exaggerating when he characterized the objection to disrupting the continuity of the English histories as universal, for the plays were increasingly considered as a single, national epic. It was not in England in which this belief first took hold, though, but across the channel in Germany. Just a few years after Malone's 1790 edition was published, A.W. Schlegel began translating several of Shakespeare's plays into German. His translations started to appear in 1797, and in short order Schlegel would publish seventeen plays – including the entire series of

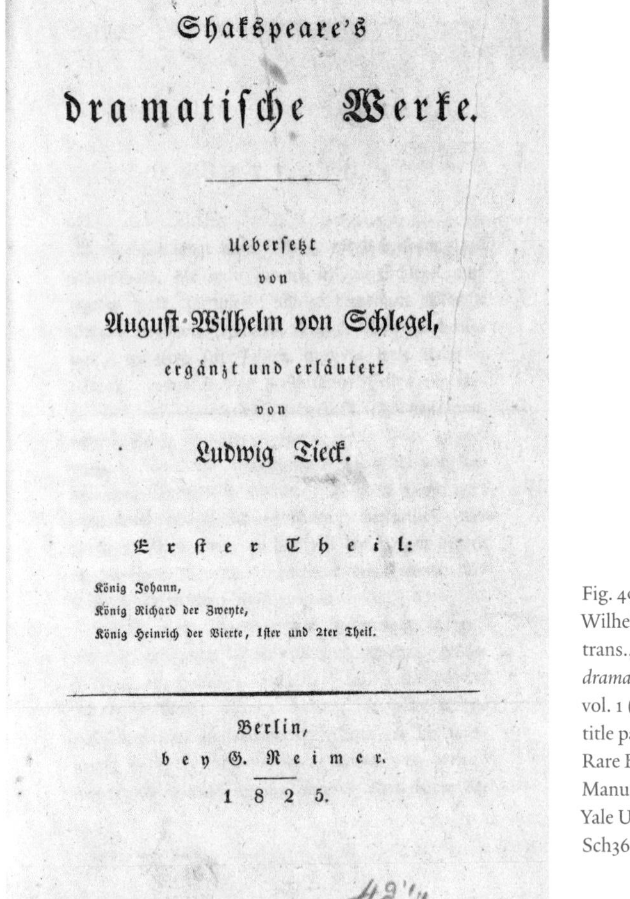
Shakspeare's

dramatische Werke.

Uebersetzt

von

August Wilhelm von Schlegel,

ergänzt und erläutert

von

Ludwig Tieck.

Erster Theil:

König Johann,
König Richard der Zweyte,
König Heinrich der Vierte, 1ster und 2ter Theil.

Berlin,

bey G. Reimer.

1825.

Fig. 49. August Wilhelm Schlegel, trans., *Shakspeare's dramatische Werke*, vol. 1 (Berlin, 1825), title page. Beinecke Rare Book and Manuscript Library, Yale University, Zg19 Sch363 797sf

ten history plays.[49] When Schlegel's translations were reissued as part of the influential Schlegel-Tieck edition, the ten history plays were given pride of place, appearing in the Folio order in the first three volumes (fig. 49).[50]

For Schlegel, and for many of his Romantic compatriots, Shakespeare's history plays provided a crucial model of and inspiration for the renewal of a specifically German national literary tradition.[51] In the prologue to his sensational lectures on the dramatic arts, delivered in the shadow of Napoleon, in Vienna in 1808, Schlegel explicitly invoked the idea of national reunification.[52] Schlegel's nationalistic impulse mirrored his critical emphasis on the organic unity of dramatic works, and in the

Shakespeare canon this unity was nowhere more evident than in the history plays. Schlegel radically extended the idea first put forth by Johnson that the history plays could be considered "one work, upon one plan." This had not stopped Johnson from objecting to what he saw as the erratic structure of the individual plays, and Schlegel rigorously criticized Johnson for failing to consider the plays as a unified work.[53] According to Schlegel, in the histories, Shakespeare gave "unity and rounding" to a series of events that were "detached from the immeasurable extent of history," yet without "in any degree changing them."[54] The difficulty of historical drama is that it must simultaneously be a "crowded extract" and "a living development of history,"[55] a difficulty Shakespeare overcame by dividing the events into multiple parts. The English histories may be "ten in number," but they "form one of the most valuable of Shakspeare's works," and Schlegel stresses that "I say advisedly *one* of his works, for the poet evidently intended them to form one great whole," "an historical heroic poem in the dramatic form, of which the separate plays constitute the rhapsodies."[56] Shakespeare's fidelity to the chronology and causality of events, as depicted in the "living picture" of his drama, "furnishes examples of the political course of the world," serving as a vital mirror for kings, not only to learn the "intrinsic dignity" of their vocation, but also, pointedly, the "ruinous consequences" of their crimes – the latter being of the utmost urgency in Vienna, on the cusp of a renewed resistance to the emperor.[57]

The ten English histories constituted a single "historical heroic poem" not only because they depicted a chronological succession of events (with the outliers *King John* and *Henry VIII* serving as the prologue and epilogue, respectively), but because "the poet evidently intended them to form one great whole." The unity of the work depended on the intended design of Shakespeare; formal, dramatic integrity – and hence national integrity – demanded authorial integrity. Schlegel thus needed to refute the claims of scholars like Malone who had dared to dispute Shakespeare's authorship. Schlegel defended the *Henry VI* plays by pointing to their manifest connections to each other, and to *Richard III:* the four plays were "undoubtedly composed in succession, as is proved by the style and the spirit in the handling of the subject."[58] Malone would surely have cringed at the imprecise criteria used here, but Schlegel did not depend entirely on the style and spirit of Shakespeare to make his point: he also directly criticized "diligent Malone" for his attempt at determining the Shakespearean chronology, which "could not possibly be attended with complete success."[59] Schlegel instead relied on the authority of the First Folio. The inclusion of a play in the Folio was not to be questioned, and was cited as irrefutable evidence of Shakespeare's authorship. To challenge the authority of the volume was to challenge the personal integrity of Shakespeare's "fri[e]nds and fellow-managers," Heminge and Condell, and thus of Shakespeare himself. Taking *Titus Andronicus* as his test case – a play which Malone had relegated to the fringes of his own editions – Schlegel argues that the play was "to be found in the first folio edition," asking if it was therefore possible to "lay to the charge of these honourable men an intentional fraud," when "we know that they did not show themselves so very desirous of scraping everything together which went by the name of Shakspeare."[60] Rather than attempting to explain away the inclusion of plays in the Folio, Schlegel valorizes the Folio and its compilers, and by extension the version of Shakespeare they presented.

Schlegel's view of the histories as a single work was not only a result of his valorization of and dependence on the First Folio. His ambitious course of thirty lectures set out to tell the entire history of drama, and fully half the lectures concerned the dramatic traditions of the ancient Greeks and Romans. Schlegel was not shy about drawing parallels between the ancients and the moderns, and the form of the classical trilogy proved particularly useful in explaining the unity he found so evident in Shakespeare's histories. Performed at the festival of Dionysus in Athens, the Greek trilogy consisted of three tragedies (which could be accompanied by a fourth, satiric play) which, in Schlegel's words, were "connected together in one great cycle by means of a common destiny running through the actions of all."[61] Schlegel used this classical precedent to justify the unity of the *Henry VI* plays, and, just as importantly, to explain the fact that Shakespeare had written the plays of his great cycle out of order: "the trilogies of the ancients have already given us an example of the possibility of forming a perfect dramatic whole, which shall yet contain allusions to something which goes before, and follows it."[62] Schlegel does not push the analogy much further than this, and he does not claim that Shakespeare modeled his own epic after the Greeks, only that the idea of the trilogy provided a model for thinking about Shakespeare's plays as a unified and designed totality.

In the century following, the term "trilogy" was often applied to the histories, especially the three *Henry VI* plays, but this is not the term that would come to define Shakespeare's cycle. As Schlegel recognized, the eight plays which cover consecutive reigns can be neatly divided into two sets of four, and these two sets of plays have come to be known as "tetralogies." The term originally named the entire series of four plays (the three tragedies plus the satiric drama) performed at the Greek festivals. The use of both "trilogy" and "tetralogy" to describe classical drama dates back to the mid-seventeenth century, and neither term was applied to Shakespeare's histories before the nineteenth century.[63] In the years following Schlegel's lectures, "trilogy" was used to describe various combinations of Shakespeare's histories: usually the three *Henry VI* plays, but the two *Henry IV* plays and *Henry V* as well.[64] "Tetralogy" was used to describe one of the sets of four plays as early as the 1830s, although it was not common until much later in the nineteenth century (for reasons that are outlined below).[65] The idea of the histories as constituting two tetralogies would be immensely influential; indeed, we still think of the history plays in this way, implicitly and often pedagogically.

Schlegel's assessment of Shakespeare's histories was imported back into England, most famously by Coleridge, who had read the Vienna lectures in the original German. Coleridge echoed Schlegel's concern with the unity of the historical plays, ascribing this quality to Shakespeare's infusion of "a principle of life and organization into the naked facts," thereby making an "animated whole."[66] In a decidedly romantic reverie, Coleridge mused that it would be "a fine national custom" to act a series of history plays like Shakespeare's during the Christmas holidays every year, as a way to inculcate patriotic virtue.[67] England would have to wait nearly a century to see just such a performance of Shakespeare's history plays, but Germany did not. A similar desire to stage the series had been expressed as Schlegel's translations first began to appear. In a letter sent to Goethe late in 1797, just months after reading *Julius Caesar* with Schlegel, Friedrich Schiller wrote that he had been reading "those of Shakespeare's plays which treat of the Wars of the Roses," and continued by suggesting that it would "truly be worth the trouble to adapt this whole series of eight plays for the German stage," since it might "introduce a new epoch." Schiller would never witness a performance like this – he was in any case focused on the more immediate completion of his own multipart historical drama, *Wallenstein* – but his prediction of a "new epoch" would indeed come to pass.[68]

Schiller's letter to Goethe partly inspired the first performance of the complete cycle of Shakespeare's history plays. When Franz Dingelstedt, a theater manager and director, came across Schiller's characterization of the eight plays covering the Wars of the Roses, he agreed wholeheartedly. Dingelstedt started adapting Shakespeare's plays in Weimar in the 1850s with the goal of staging all eight plays of the history sequence as a single, grand cycle. In the final week of April 1864 – during the celebration of the Shakespearean tercentenary – Dingelstedt succeeded in staging the entire series, a landmark event in German theater and the director's most enduring accomplishment.[69] As Schlegel had done, Dingelstedt invoked the relevance of the plays to the present lack of national unity, interpolating a prologue that compared the Wars of the Roses to the ongoing conflict within Germany. Shakespeare's importance to German scholarship and culture – and vice versa, of course – was also confirmed in a more uplifting manner, as the tercentenary week in Weimar ended with the founding of the Shakespeare-Gesellschaft.

Dingelstedt's stunning success provided a template for the serial performance of Shakespeare's histories as a national epic, but it also connects Shakespeare to the other reigning artistic figure of nineteenth-century Germany: Richard Wagner. Dingelstedt utilized all of the theatrical resources available to him and aimed to give Shakespeare the full operatic treatment, equal to the dazzling productions of Wagner's operas that he had designed in Munich in the decade before moving to Weimar.[70] Wagner in turn had based his own theory of dramatic art in part on his understanding of Shakespeare, and in particular of the histories. Shakespeare showed how history could be transformed and shaped into art; Schiller provided another, more advanced model in his *Wallenstein*, but the latter still suffered in comparison to the former. While admiring Shakespeare's ability to borrow "the stuff for Drama" from history, his reliance on and appeal to "Phantasy" is impossible in the modern age, "for *us*, who demand a sense-convincing exhibition of the Scene as well."[71] The total sensory environment of the *Gesamtkunstwerk* was intended to provide just such an "exhibition," thereby surpassing both Shakespeare and Wagner's principal model, the trilogies of the Greek tragedians.[72]

Wagner's epic *Der Ring des Nibelungen*, composed over nearly thirty years and consisting of four separate dramas, has often been seen as a work analogous to Shakespeare's series of national histories. But it was in fact the *Ring* that was largely responsible for propagating the view of Shakespeare's histories as a similarly coherent, epic cycle. The *Ring* was widely referred to as a "tetralogy" long before the debut of the entire series at Bayreuth in 1876, after which references to Shakespeare's histories as a similar "tetralogy" increase dramatically. By the end of the century, Shakespeare's English epic could be neatly tied together to both its Greek model and its German parallel: as John Bell Henneman remarked in 1897, "The three parts of 'Henry VI.' and 'Richard III.' constitute a sort of tetralogy after the manner of the Greek play-wrights and are brought together as parts of one concerted movement very much as Wagner joined together his four operas of the 'Nibelungen Ring.'"[73] The implied agency and uncertain tenses evident here – who is, or was, responsible for constituting and bringing together Shakespeare's histories? – demonstrate how easily chronology can be confused, how critical suppositions harden into historical fact, how collaboration can be reduced to and redefined as authorial virtuosity.

If the histories were Shakespeare's *Ring,* then his nation deserved a performance of the epic on its own soil – and so the full cycle was first staged in Stratford-upon-Avon, Shakespeare's very own Bayreuth, in 1906.[74] The cycle was repeated in Stratford a half-century later by the Royal Shakespeare Company, whose very name embodies the theatrical expression of national identity. The cycle has been performed regularly ever since, including the exhaustingly Wagnerian "Glorious Moment," a weekend marathon performance in 2008, and "King and Country: Shakespeare's Great Cycle of Kings," which marks the quatercentenary in 2016.[75] Heminge and Condell might have been pleased at the irony: the decision of two theater men to feature the "Histories" in a book would ultimately gain its fullest expression in performance. The First Folio may have established the genre of the history play as distinctly Shakespearean, but the history of this book – and indeed, the history of the book, as a methodology – is not sufficient to explain the history of the "Histories." Book history must be combined with other approaches in order to attend to the material intersections of textual and theatrical history. We need to listen to the ways that different disciplines and different media speak to each other, as they transform and translate historical narratives in both print and performance – or, in Wagner's terms, as the "daguerreotype of historic facts" is brought to life in a "luminous oil-painting." Only then can we understand how history is made.

NOTES

1 "To the memory of my beloued, The Avthor Mr. William Shakespeare," in *Mr. William Shakespeares Comedies, Histories, & Tragedies* (London, 1623).

2 Wagner's manifesto *Oper und Drama* was first published in 1851; I quote here from *Richard Wagner's Prose Works,* vol. 2, *Opera and Drama,* trans. William Ashton Ellis (London: Kegan Paul, Trench, Trübner, 1893), 143.

3 It is generally assumed that Heminge and Condell were the compilers of the folio collection, since they signed the two dedicatory epistles. (They also held prominent roles in the theater company and were remembered by name in Shakespeare's will). However, we cannot know with any certainty that Heminge and Condell were solely or primarily responsible for the compilation and organization of the collection, or for the decision to separate the plays into generic categories. Throughout this essay, then, "Heminge and Condell" is used as a convenient designation of the multiple agencies involved in the production and organization of the volume.

4 "Every Man in His Hvmovr," in *The Works of Beniamin Jonson* (London, 1616), A3r. For a reading of this prologue as a neoclassical manifesto, see Richard Dutton, *Ben Jonson: To the First Folio* (Cambridge: Cambridge University Press, 1983), 24–25.

5 "On Worthy Master Shakespeare and his Poems," in *Mr. William Shakespeares Comedies, Histories, and Tragedies* (London, 1632). The poem is signed "I.M.S.," initials which have never been convincingly explained.

6 "An Epitaph on the admirable Dramaticke Poet, W. Shakespeare," in ibid.

7 John Milton, *Eikonoklastes* (1649), D3r. On the subjection of Charles I, see David Scott Kastan, "Proud Majesty Made a Subject: Shakespeare and the Spectacle of Rule," *Shakespeare Quarterly* 37 (1986): 459–75. On Milton's references to Shakespeare and to Charles I, see Charles Whitney, *Early Responses to Renaissance Drama* (Cambridge: Cambridge University Press, 2006), 256–70; and Nicholas McDowell, "Milton's Regicide Tracts and the Uses of Shakespeare," in *The Oxford Handbook of Milton,* ed. Nicholas McDowell and Nigel Smith (Oxford: Oxford University Press, 2009), 252–71.

8 Wagner, *Opera and Drama,* 143.

9 E.M.W. Tillyard, *Shakespeare's History Plays* (London: Chatto & Windus, 1944).

10 The phrase is taken from Tillyard's defense of his influential book, "Shakespeare's Historical Cycle: Organism or Compilation?" (1954), republished in *Essays Literary and Educational* (London: Chatto & Windus, 1967), 39–46. For a recent reassertion of the organic unity of the histories, see Nicholas Grene, *Shakespeare's Serial History Plays* (Cambridge: Cambridge University Press, 2002).

11 Tillyard, *Shakespeare's History Plays,* 147.

12 David Scott Kastan has argued that the history play is "an episodic and open-ended structure…that emphasizes the contingency of human action and the artificiality of the dramatic field of vision," and therefore "can only be defined on the basis of dramatic form" (*Shakespeare and the Shapes of Time* [Hanover, N.H.: University Press of New England, 1982], 23, 41).

13 Charlton Hinman, *The Printing and Proof-Reading of the First Folio of Shakespeare,* 2 vols. (Oxford: Clarendon Press, 1963), 1:31n1. Hinman considers the possibility of printing-house accidents, but prefers the explanation that the independent series of signatures was "a kind of precautionary *economic* measure; for thus the three

major sections of the book could be sold separately – as parts of other books sometimes were – if it proved that they could not all be sold together ('all in one [very expensive] volume') within a reasonable time." William St. Clair makes a similar proposal from a different perspective, suggesting that the Folio may have been sold in "numbers," or installments, since the generic sections were paginated separately. See *The Reading Nation in the Romantic Period* (Cambridge: Cambridge University Press, 2004), 145–46.

14 "Several, *adj.*, *adv.*, and *n.*," OED *Online*, 2015, Oxford University Press (accessed August 20, 2015).

15 Edward Burns notes that the formula "the life and death of..." functions as a compromise between the generic and interpretive demands of history and tragedy. See "Shakespeare's Histories in Cycles," in *Shakespeare's History Plays: Performance, Translation, and Adaptation in Britain and Abroad,* ed. Ton Hoenselaars (Cambridge: Cambridge University Press, 2004), 151–68 (167n2).

16 *1 Henry IV* was published nine times in quarto through the seventeenth century; *Richard III* eight times; and *Richard II* six times; Wise published all three plays three times, from 1597 to 1602.

17 The argument in this paragraph is adapted from the second chapter of my own *Selling Shakespeare: Biography, Bibliography, and the Book Trade* (Cambridge: Cambridge University Press, 2016).

18 Law published *Richard II* twice, and both *1 Henry IV* and *Richard III* four times.

19 Hinman, *Printing and Proof-Reading,* 1:351–58; see also W.W. Greg, *The Shakespeare First Folio: Its Bibliographical and Textual History* (Oxford: Clarendon Press, 1955), 443–44.

20 The manuscript has been dated ca. 1622–24. Dering used a copy of Q5 (1613) of *1 Henry IV,* and the second issue of the 1600 quarto of *2 Henry IV,* as the copy-texts for his conflation; Dering thus did not use the First Folio in producing his adaptation. See *The History of King Henry the Fourth, as revised by Sir Edward Dering, Bart,* ed. George Walton Williams and Gwynne Blakemore Evans (Charlottesville: University Press of Virginia, for the Folger Shakespeare Library, 1974).

21 "The two plays were performed at Whitehall during the festive season of 1612/13, the first part titled *The Hotspur* and the second, *Sir John Falstaffe;* but they were not staged as one continuous play, and even the titles given them suggest dramatic foci at odds with a unitary focus on the royal narrative" (James C. Bulman, "Performing the Conflated Text of *Henry IV:* The Fortunes of *Part Two,*" *Shakespeare Survey* 63 [2010]: 89–101 [90n6]).

22 Francis Kirkman, "A True, perfect, and exact Catalogue of all the Comedies, Tragedies, Tragi-Comedies, Pastorals, Masques and Interludes, that were ever yet printed and published, till this present year 1661." The title of the catalogue, worthy of Polonius, notably excludes histories.

23 "The first part Of the true & honorable history, of the Life of *Sir Iohn Old-castle, the good* Lord Cobham" (one of the quartos published in 1619) was advertised as "Written by William Shakespeare." "The True Chronicle Historie of the whole life and death of *Thomas* Lord *Cromwell*" (London, 1602) was advertised as "Written by W.S.," an ambiguous, and therefore attractive, authorial designation that could easily be interpreted as the initials of the famous playwright. When the second issue of the Third Folio was published in 1664, it included both plays among the additional "seven Playes, never before Printed in Folio," all of which had previously been ascribed to Shakespeare in quarto (or at least ascribed to the initials "W.S.").

24 When first published in 1609, the title page of the play called it "The Late, and

much admired Play, Called Pericles, Prince of Tyre. With the true Relation of the whole Historie, aduentures, and fortunes of the said Prince." The anonymous prose pamphlet based on the play prepared by George Wilkins, Shakespeare's collaborator, was published in 1608 as "The Painfull Aduentures of *Pericles* Prince of Tyre. *Being* The true History of the Play of *Pericles*." The recurrence of the term "History" (or "Historie") on the title pages may have influenced Kirkman's designation as much as the classical name of the eponymous character.

25 The first quarto edition of Shakespeare's play was called "M. William Shak-speare: *His* True Chronicle Historie of the life and death of King Lear and his three Daughters" (1608). The anonymous play, published only once, was titled "The True Chronicle History of King Leir, and his three *daughters*" (1605).

26 For Kirkman's comment, see "A True, perfect, and exact Catalogue, of all the Comedies, Tragedies, Tragi-Comedies, Pastorals, Masques and Interludes, that were ever yet Printed and Published, till this present year 1671," B4v. Coleridge reported that "Marlborough, we know, was not ashamed to confess that his principal acquaintance with English history" derived from Shakespeare's plays. See *The Literary Remains of Samuel Taylor Coleridge*, ed. Henry Nelson Coleridge (London: William Pickering, 1836), 2:166.

27 Margaret Cavendish, *CCXI Sociable Letters* (London, 1664), 2H2v–2H4v.

28 John Dryden, *Of Dramatick Poesie, An Essay* (London, 1668), E3r.

29 Ibid., G3v–G4r.

30 John Dryden, "Defense of the Epilogue. Or, *An Essay on the* Dramatique Poetry *of the last Age*," appended to *The Conquest of Granada* (London, 1672), X2r.

31 Nahum Tate, *The History of King Richard The Second Acted at the Theatre Royal, Under the Name of the Sicilian Usurper* (London, 1681), A1v, A1r.

32 Lewis Theobald, *The Tragedy of King Richard the II* (London, 1720). For an analysis of this adaptation in the context of Theobald's career as an editor of Shakespeare, see David Scott Kastan, *Shakespeare and the Book* (Cambridge: Cambridge University Press, 2001), 91–95.

33 Theobald, *The Tragedy of King Richard the II*, 2A1r, 2B3r.

34 Nicholas Rowe, *The Works of Mr. William Shakespear*, 6 vols. (London, 1709), 1:xvi–viii.

35 *The Works of Shakespear in Six Volumes. Collated and Corrected by the former Editions, By Mr. Pope* (London, 1725), 1:v.

36 *The Works of Shakespeare: in Seven Volumes. Collated with the Oldest Copies, and Corrected; With Notes, Explanatory and Critical: By Mr. Theobald* (London, 1733), 1:xxx.

37 Ibid., 1:xlii and xxx. In the section that outlines "*The Editor's particular Pains taken*," Theobald modestly notes that "to clear up several Errors in the Historical Plays, I purposely read over *Hall* and *Holingshead*'s Chronicles in the Reigns concern'd" (1:lxvii).

38 Ibid., 1:xxx.

39 Johnson's edition was published in eight volumes as *The Plays of William Shakespeare* (London, 1765). Quotations from Johnson's Preface, and from the notes to individual plays, are taken from *The Yale Edition of the Works of Samuel Johnson*, vols. 7–8, *Johnson on Shakespeare*, ed. Arthur Sherbo (New Haven: Yale University Press, 1968), quoted here at 7:66–67, 68, 75.

40 *Johnson on Shakespeare*, 7:68, 453; 8:522.

41 See Peter Holland, "Playing Johnson's Shakespeare," in *Comparative Excellence: New Essays on Shakespeare and Johnson*, ed. Eric Rasmussen and Aaron Santesso (New York: AMS Press, 2007), 1–24 (14).

42 *Johnson on Shakespeare,* 7:91–92, 79, 438, 452; 8:658.

43 Malone's *Attempt* was first published in the second Johnson-Steevens edition of Shakespeare in 1778; subsequent revisions appeared in Malone's 1790 edition of Shakespeare, and the (posthumously published) 1821 variorum edition. See Peter Martin, *Edmond Malone: Shakespearean Scholar* (Cambridge: Cambridge University Press, 1995), 30–35; cf. Margreta de Grazia, *Shakespeare Verbatim: The Reproduction of Authenticity and the 1790 Apparatus* (Oxford: Clarendon Press, 1991), 141–51.

44 The exception was the outlier *Henry VIII,* which Malone incorrectly dated to the middle, rather than the end, of Shakespeare's career; see Martin, *Edmond Malone,* 34n40.

45 *A Dissertation on the Three Parts of King Henry VI, tending to shew that those plays were not written by Shakspeare* (London, 1787). Malone's *Dissertation* was incorporated into the sixth volume of his 1790 edition and the eighteenth volume of the 1821 edition.

46 Malone is quoted here from the 1790 edition, *The Plays and Poems of William Shakspeare,* 6 vols. (London), 6:424.

47 The so-called first Johnson-Steevens edition was published in 1773, and the second in 1778; Reed's edition appeared in 1785. The only significant changes in the order were that *Macbeth* now preceded *King John;* after the English histories and Roman histories, *King Lear* and *Cymbeline* appeared together.

48 *The Plays and Poems of William Shakspeare,* 21 vols. (1821), 1:xvii.

49 *Shakspeare's dramatische Werke,* Übersetzt von August Wilhelm Schlegel, 9 vols. (Berlin: Unger, 1797–1810). For an account of Schlegel's translation, see Roger Paulin, *The Critical Reception of Shakespeare in Germany 1682–1914: Native Literature and Foreign Genius* (Hildesheim: Olms, 2003), 304–29. Nine of the ten histories appeared in a two-year span from 1799 to 1801; the outlier was *Richard III,* which appeared in 1810.

50 *Shakspeare's dramatische Werke,* Uebersetzt von August Wilhelm von Schlegel, ergänzt und erläutert von Ludwig Tieck, 9 vols. (Berlin: Reimer, 1825–33). See Kenneth E. Larson, "The Origins of the 'Schlegel-Tieck' Shakespeare in the 1820s," *The German Quarterly* 60 (1987): 19–37; and Paulin, *Critical Reception,* 344–48.

51 Paulin notes that Schlegel's "particular insistence" in translating the histories, "indeed his willful decision to translate the whole cycle in preference to *Macbeth* or *Lear,*" was a key instance of his use of "the Shakespearean paradigm as a stimulus for a renewed national literary production" (*Critical Reception,* 267).

52 "In the mental dominion of thought and poetry, inaccessible to worldly power, the Germans, who are separated in so many ways from each other, still feel their unity: and in this feeling, whose interpreter the writer and orator must be, amidst our clouded prospects we may still cherish the elevating presage of the great and immortal calling of our people, who from time immemorial have remained unmixed in their present habitations." The lectures were first published in German as *Über dramatische Kunst und Litteratur,* 3 vols. (Heidelberg: Mohr und Zimmer, 1809–11). They were first translated into English in 1815 by John Black as *A Course of Lectures on Dramatic Art and Literature;* I quote here from the edition revised by A.J.W. Morrison (London: Henry G. Bohn, 1846), 6.

53 Even while praising Johnson for condemning the "superficial and cheap" mode of criticism which concentrates on the beauty of isolated passages, Schlegel exclaims that "how little, and how very unsatisfactorily does he himself speak of the pieces considered as a whole!" (*Course of Lectures,* 360). On Johnson's role as the

key antagonist for Schlegel's criticism, see G.F. Parker, *Johnson's Shakespeare* (Oxford: Clarendon Press, 1989), 12–13, and 126–155.

54 *Course of Lectures,* 414. Schlegel's remark here is aimed at the three Roman history plays: *Coriolanus, Antony and Cleopatra,* and *Julius Caesar,* the latter two of which he considers to be a linked pair (416).

55 Ibid., 416.

56 Ibid., 419.

57 Ibid., 419, 420.

58 Ibid., 435.

59 Ibid., 378. Schlegel notes that Malone himself "only gives out the result of his labours for hypothetical," but, in a footnote, demures from disproving his conclusions in any detail, since the lectures were not immediately intended for an English audience – and, more pressingly, since "the interruption of intercourse with England" had "rendered it impossible to procure any other than the most common English books" (379).

60 Ibid., 442.

61 Ibid., 81.

62 Ibid., 421.

63 See Mary Thomas Crane, "The Shakespearean Tetralogy," *Shakespeare Quarterly* 36 (1985): 282–99. Crane's valuable survey notes the lack of contemporary dramatic models for the idea of a "tetralogy" in Elizabethan England.

64 Examples are too numerous to mention here, but the OED entry for "trilogy" does provide apt instances of both uses of the term: the entry for "trilogy" in W.T. Brande's *A Dictionary of Science, Literature, & Art* (London, 1842) concludes by stating that "all the plays of Æschylus, and the *Henry VI.* of Shakspeare, are examples of a *trilogy,*" while Edward Dowden, in his influential *Shakspeare Primer* (1877), used the term to refer to the two *Henry IV* plays and *Henry V* (OED *Online,* Oxford University Press [accessed August 20, 2015]).

65 A theatrical notice for February 11, 1838, refers to *Richard III* as "the last of a magnificent tetralogy; a section of a grand cycle; yet having its beginning and end as distinct as the hour is marked from the day of which it is an integral portion" (*John Bull* 896 [1838]: 70).

66 *Notes and Lectures upon Shakespeare and some of the Old Poets and Dramatists with other Literary Remains of S.T. Coleridge,* ed. Mrs. H.N. Coleridge (London: Pickering, 1849), 163. On Coleridge's unacknowledged use of Schlegel, see Paulin, *Critical Reception,* 294–96; on Schlegel's influence in England, see Thomas G. Sauer, *A.W. Schlegel's Shakespearean Criticism in England, 1811–1846* (Bonn: Bouvier, 1981).

67 Coleridge continues by saying that such a custom "could not but tend to counteract that mock cosmopolitanism, which under a positive term really implies nothing but a negation of, or indifference to, the particular love of our country" (164). Burns, in "Shakespeare's Histories in Cycles," characterizes Coleridge's wish as one for "an education in patriotism, of a kind which reminds us that its context is the aftermath of the French Revolution, and the beginning of the Napoleonic wars" (153).

68 Schiller ended his letter with a brief but revealing mention of "My *Wallenstein,*" which "is day by day acquiring more shape" (*Correspondence between Schiller and Goethe, from 1794 to 1805,* vol. 1, *1794–1797,* trans. L. Dora Schmitz [London: George Bell and Sons, 1877], 433. The letter is dated November 28, 1797; Schiller mentions reading *Julius Caesar* with Schlegel on April 7 of the same year.

69 The series included only seven plays, *1 Henry VI* being largely abandoned, over an eight-day period. For an account of this

performance in the context of Dingelstedt's career, see Robert K. Sarlos, "Dingelstedt's Celebration of the Tercentenary: Shakespeare's Histories as a Cycle," *Theatre Survey* 5 (1964): 117–31. See also Simon Williams, *Shakespeare on the German Stage,* vol. 1, *1586–1914* (Cambridge: Cambridge University Press, 1990), 153–54.

70 Williams notes that Dingelstedt's practice has been seen "as an actualisation of Wagner's theory of the total work of art" (*Shakespeare on the German Stage,* 156).

71 *Opera and Drama,* 145.

72 "It was the nation itself—in intimate connection with its own history—that stood mirrored in" the drama of the Greeks, which Wagner called "the abstract and epitome of all that was expressible in the Grecian nature" ("Art and Revolution," in *Richard Wagner's Prose Works,* vol. 1, *The Art-Work of the Future, &c.,* trans. William Ashton Ellis [London: Kegan Paul, Trench, Trübner, 1892], 52); cf. 141 for Wagner's direct comparison of Shakespeare to the Greeks.

73 John Bell Henneman, "The Man Shakespeare: His Growth as an Artist," *The Sewanee Review* 5 (1897): 105.

74 The Shakespeare Memorial Theatre in Stratford opened just three years after the debut of the *Ring,* in 1879, with Bayreuth serving as a model for the enterprise. See Sally Beauman, *The Royal Shakespeare Company: A History of Ten Decades* (Oxford: Oxford University Press, 1982), 14.

75 For an overview of English cycle productions, see Grene, *Shakespeare's Serial History Plays,* 31–62. For an account of the politics of performing the histories as a cycle, see Anita Hagerman, "Monumental Play: Commemoration, Post-War Britain, and History Cycles," *Critical Survey* 22 (2010): 105–18. On the Wagnerian tenor of the 2008 cycle, see Alice Dailey, "The RSC's 'Glorious Moment' and the Making of Shakespearian History," *Shakespeare Survey* 63 (2010): 184–97, esp. 185n8.

ie v. vnderschaid von den monatn Jst der
ain vnd insunderhait der tage
nner Freitag nach dem newē iar vor mitag
stund xiij minutem zů finsterung der lufft
veuug ď wind vñ feüchtnuß des schnös ge
wirt Tailichē geschicht vff tauūg verhar
Vol Jenner samstag am tag anthoni vor
g ix stund iij minuten Die natur seins ne
galtē wirt doch teylichē bedeütung so vil
cht ist zů clarung genaigt wirt
eine tag Am dem neüen iar auffs minst
ckung den tag darnach wind Samstag
dē neüen iar feüchtnuß villeicht des schnös
wind Bey dem tag der hailegen drei künig
lenden auffsauūg erscheinen wirt wärm vñ
ie wind bewegt werden mit starcken regen
velliche iter leichtlich dē eiusl vß haben don
werdē Dornstag nach ď hailgē drei küng
ugs minst gewülcken mit etlicher keltin fre
darnach vff die nacht gewülcken mit wind
enden feüchtnuß nachuolgen wirt Son
ach ď hailigen drei küng tag wind mit et
berrůbung der lufft Mitwoch vor antho
nd dornstag vor anthoni kelten mit gewül
am aben anthoni vnd am tag auch bei di
gen veuug der wind in etlichē endē feücht
des schnös nachuolgen wirt Sonntag am
riske vff die nacht feüchtnuß des schnös von
tag fabion biß vff das new viertel weter zů

AFTERWORD

PETER STALLYBRASS

In the third book of the *Aeneid,* Virgil wrote about the failure of historical memory when, with nothing to bind them together, the leaves of the Sibyl's verses were scattered by the wind:

> What she commits to Leafs, in order laid,
> Before the Caverns Entrance are display'd:
> Unmov'd they lie, but if a Blast of Wind
> Without, or Vapours issue from behind,
> The Leafs are born aloft in liquid Air,
> And she resumes no more her Museful Care:
> Nor gathers from the Rocks her scatter'd Verse;
> Nor sets in order what the Winds disperse.[1]

The Sibyl's scattered leaves were a recurring topos from late antiquity. Petrarch imagined his *Rime Sparse,* or scattered rhymes, as similarly cast to the winds of fortune, even as he helped to establish new forms of the book in which they would be gathered together as the materials of immortality.

But Virgil's account of the Sibyl's leaves had taken on a radically new meaning by the time that Petrarch was writing. For Virgil, the Sibyl's leaves could not be the leaves of a book for the simple reason that the "books" he read and on which his own poem was preserved were scrolls. Although scrolls are glued together in segments (*membrana*), they do not have leaves. *Folium,* a leaf, only took on the new meaning of the leaf of a book in the fourth century C.E. – by which time the codex was rapidly becoming the dominant material support for pagan texts, as it had been for Christians from the beginning of the second century, if not earlier. Far from being a dead metaphor, the Sibyl's leaves could now be reinterpreted as the constituent elements of a book. The leaves of parchment or paper on which an author wrote might indeed be literally scattered. But the *folia* or leaves could be gathered together and preserved in what would later be called a *folio* – the form of book that would best preserve a work for posterity. Just as the limbs of Shakespeare's scattered body were brought together in the First Folio, the textual leaves that time had scattered could be brought together in the material form of a book.

Dante made the gathering of scattered leaves the telos of his *Commedia,* conceiving of Paradise itself as being organized like a book. Paradise so overwhelms him that his "memory fails"; indeed his "vision almost wholly fades away" just as, "in the wind, on the light leaves, the Sibyl's oracles were lost" [*così al vento ne le foglie levi / si perdea la sentenza di Sibilla*]. But all is not lost. For in Paradise, Dante sees "ingathered, bound by love into a single volume, what is scattered through the universe in pages":

> Nel suo profundo vidi che s'interna
> legato con amore in un volume,
> ciò che per l'universo si squaderna.[2]

Paradise is preserved, as Dante's poem about it will be, because the "scattered" leaves have been "ingathered" and bound. According to Boccaccio, Dante published his poem in a series of pamphlets [*quadernetti*] of six to eight cantos, but the final pamphlet was unpublished at his death. If Dante wrote about a gathering together of scattered fragments in Paradise, the gathering together of his own leaves was a dream that had not yet come true. Perhaps the very precariousness of his poetic gatherings led him to envisage Paradise all the more powerfully as a bound book. Dante's word for binding together, *legato,* is derived from the Latin *legere,* which means both to gather and to read. Gathered together, the leaves that had previously been scattered become legible or readable.

Equally specific is the word that Dante uses to describe the scattering that precedes the gathering: *squaderna.* The verb *squaderna* suggests the active process of ungathering the quires [*quaderni*] out of which a bound book [*volume*] is composed. A *quaderno* was literally the four sheets of parchment or paper that, folded together, make a folio gathering of eight leaves or sixteen pages – either a small pamphlet or one of the units out of which a book is composed. The prefix "*s*" in *squaderna* negates the meaning of "*quaderna*," like the prefix "un-" in English. "Un*quaderno*ed," not even held together by the provisional sewing that creates a pamphlet, the separate leaves will be scattered by the wind unless they are brought together *in un volume,* "in a single volume."[3]

In 1623, the editors of the First Folio brought together the "remains" of Shakespeare "in a single volume" so as to repair the author's body, his corpus. Before they gathered up his scattered limbs into a bound book, Shakespeare had survived, they claimed, only in "diuerse stolne, and surreptitious copies, maimed, and deformed." They were now preserving Shakespeare's "owne writings," "offer'd to [the reader's] view cur'd, and perfect of their limbes."[4] It was, of course, in Heminge's and Condell's interest to emphasize just how bad all previous editions of Shakespeare had been. But one thing they were certainly right about: the pamphlets that were the material form in which Shakespeare circulated during his lifetime were peculiarly subject to the ravages of time. The First Folio "cur'd" Shakespeare's limbs by securely sewing the folded sheets of his plays, quire by quire, onto cords and protecting them with wooden boards, covered in calfskin.

The relation between the "single volume" of the 1623 Shakespeare First Folio and the multiple other forms in which Shakespeare has been disseminated, from sixteenth-century stab-stitched pamphlets to twentieth-century comic books, is central to David Scott Kastan's argument that "literature exists, in any useful sense, only and always in its materializations, and that these are the conditions of its meanings rather than merely the containers of it."[5] At the same time, to analyze the transformative materializations of Shakespeare clearly, we need to examine "the book" as itself a peculiar historical artifact that was, Kastan notes, hard to see until recently because of its very centrality: "[w]hile the book's monopoly over the written word was unchallenged, its ubiquitous presence seemed natural and inevitable; but the book itself was largely invisible."[6] Kastan characterizes the view that a work transcends any possible material incarnation as "platonic," in contrast to the "pragmatic" view that no text exists apart from the material forms and practices through which it is read or heard.[7] These contradictory conceptions of the text divide both literary criticism and editorial practice, opposing those who attempt to restore the author's immaterial intentions by repairing the "wounds" inflicted in the course of copying the work and setting it in type to those who argue that we must respect the irreducible diversity of a work's historical states.

Those historical states included the range of forms in which Shakespeare circulated not only after the First Folio but also prior to it. On the one hand, this has led to a renewed attention to the impermanence of the stab-stitched *quaderni* or gatherings through which unbound pamphlets were produced. On the other, it has stimulated recent work on how *readers,* and particularly *women* readers, both read and collected plays. We know, for instance, that Frances Wolfreston owned a large number of plays in their original state, "uncut and unbound, stitched as issued, but [by 1856] sadly damaged by damp, decay and possibly rats and mice."[8] "Uncut" is a technical bibliographic term, meaning that the edges of the plays had not been trimmed (as they would usually be when bound for a book); it does not mean that they were "unopened," which would imply that Wolfreston had never used a paper-knife to open the gatherings, a necessary step for reading the plays.[9] Undoubtedly, Wolfreston had opened and read the plays and, at the top of the first page of her copy of *Othello,* she records: "frances wolfreston her bouk," before later adding in the same hand but a different ink: "a sad one."[10] But the fact that her plays were "unbound" is an extraordinary testimony to Wolfreston's transmission of the pamphlets in their original state.

Much more commonly, play-pamphlets were preserved by being bound together with each other. As Heidi Brayman Hackel emphasizes in her fascinating account of the catalogue of the Countess of Bridgewater's London library, it was mainly through such composite volumes that the countess preserved her playbooks. Although the countess does not specify the number of plays in each volume, we can get some sense by the statement in one entry that "Diuerse Playes" are bound in "5 *thicke* Volumes" [italics mine]. At the same time, it is clear that preserving plays by binding them together is seen as a distinctive practice. Apart from a New Testament "in turlcish Leather guilte," the *only* bindings mentioned at all in the countess's catalogue of 241 separate volumes are for the composite collections of plays: the five thick volumes "in Velum"; another volume of "diuerse Playes in Velum"; and a "Booke of Diuerse Playes in Leather."[11] In other words, it was thought worthy of record not only *that* these "diverse" plays were preserved but also *how* they were preserved: "in Velum"; "in Leather."

Women played a particularly important role as readers of plays. In 1647, Humphrey Moseley wrote in his preface to the Beaumont and Fletcher folio that, if he had included plays that had already been printed, "it would have rendred the Booke so Voluminous, that *Ladies* and *Gentlewomen* would have found it scarce manageable, who in Workes of this nature must first be remembred."[12] Collections of plays could be large, but not so large as to be unwieldy like lectern Bibles. As Lena Orlin Cowen has reminded us, "Moseley said not that women readers in this genre must be remembered, but that they must be remembered *first*." She adds:

> Prynne adopted the superlative, as well. Railing against the "prophaneness of...playbooks," he described "the female sex" as taking "*most* pleasure in them" [emphasis added]. In a commendatory poem to the Beaumont and Fletcher volume, Thomas Peyton suggested that the "huge tome of wit" was destined for "ladies' closets."[13]

Such "tomes," huge in wit if not in size, were, in the case of Shakespeare at least, the work of readers, editors, booksellers, and printers, not the author.

Theatrical scripts, as Kastan has argued, are particularly resistant to theories of the immaterial intentions of the author, "dispersing authority for the play among various agents – collaborators and revisers, bookkeepers and prompters, musicians and carpenters, and, of course, the actors themselves – all of whom bear some responsibility for the play's eventual shape and success."[14] At the same time, the transformation of theatrical scripts into pamphlets and books for readers has been the condition both of the wide dissemination of a readerly Shakespeare and of new theatrical adaptations. Our own obsession with discovering traces of the author's hand, and thus above all with lost manuscripts, has led to a rewriting of Shakespeare within the new regime of authorship that the invention of literary archives made possible in the eighteenth and nineteenth centuries.[15] Goethe, for example, employed a team of secretaries and archivists to organize and catalogue the materials for the complete edition of his works that he was working on at the end of his life. Those secretaries and archivists increasingly preserved every trace of the master's own hand as the basis for a *printed* edition that would be the public face of a *manuscript* archive, the manuscripts both foreshadowing and legitimating the printed text.[16]

From the perspective of this new regime, it was almost inconceivable that the greatest writers of the past, writers like Dante, Cervantes, and Shakespeare, had not left to posterity the material traces of their greatest works. On the one hand, every scrap that they had written (even if only in legal documents in the form of signatures) must now be hunted down and reproduced in facsimile (at first through the use of tracing and lithography); on the other, forgeries increasingly provide the texts and material relics that an insatiable hunger for authorial presence demanded.[17] The Ireland forgeries have long been exposed – but the fantasy of Shakespeare's "foul papers," the earliest drafts of his play, written in his own hand, continues to play a dominant role in the editing of his plays. As Paul Werstine has conclusively demonstrated in his recent *Early Modern Playhouse Manuscripts and the Editing of Shakespeare,* nothing even approximating to Greg's concept of "foul papers" can be found in any dramatic manuscript from Renaissance England.[18]

In fact, English Renaissance theaters and the contemporary London printing houses alike undoubtedly preferred texts that *were at the furthest possible distance* from the author's hand – ideally, texts that had been copied by a professional scribe or, even better, that had already been printed. The second quarto of *Romeo and Juliet* is very much the exception in being set from a different manuscript than the first quarto, although even here, as was common, the "manuscript" that was the printer's copy for the second quarto was a cut-and-paste job that included at least one lengthy passage of printed text from the first quarto. More typically, in 1609, the third quarto reprinted the second; in 1623, the fourth quarto and the First Folio independently reprinted the third quarto; in 1632, the Second Folio reprinted the First Folio; and in 1637, the fifth quarto reprinted the fourth. In other words, printers usually used the most recent edition of the play, and therefore the one most distant from the authorial hand, as printer's copy for a new edition. An important exception to this rule is the fourth quarto, which we now know from the evidence of the paper to have been printed in 1623. Although the basis for this printing was indeed the third quarto, an editor at a variety of points collated it with the first quarto of 1597, thus introducing into the transmission process important corrections and new readings.[19] Note, however, that at no point after the second quarto of 1599 was there ever an attempt to use a manuscript of any kind in the making of a new edition. Collation here meant the collating of one printed edition with another.

Of the surviving "manuscripts" specifically marked up for the theater, all of the seventeenth-century Shakespearean promptbooks that were edited by Blakemore Evans were made from *printed* copies of the play.[20] And of the fifty theatrical "manuscripts" that Edward Langhans analyzes in his superb *Restoration Promptbooks,* forty-eight are made from printed copies and a mere two from manuscripts, both of which were made by professional scribes.[21] It is, of course, true that the great majority of plays were never printed and would have therefore required manuscript promptbooks to be performed. But the crucial point remains clear: whenever printed copies of a play were available, the London theaters preferred to use them rather than manuscripts, and particularly rather than authorial manuscripts. Printed copies were both cheaper and more legible, and it must often have been possible to get rapid access to multiple printed copies for actors and backstage personnel that would have taken considerable time for copyists to prepare. Far from fetishizing authorial manuscripts, acting companies and printers alike avoided them whenever possible.

In the wake of Lukas Erne's influential *Shakespeare as Literary Dramatist,* there has been a renewed emphasis upon the work of the author in building a literary reputation.[22] Against this emphasis, Kastan, rightly in my view, has insisted that the construction of Shakespeare as an author was primarily the work of others, starting with the printers who belatedly added his name to the title pages of his plays. It was William Jaggard and Thomas Pavier who in 1619 first published some of Shakespeare's plays in a bound volume, followed by the Jaggards, Edward Blount, and others who published the First Folio in 1623. It is nevertheless striking how early it was that readers appreciated the distinctiveness of Shakespeare. Indeed, to my knowledge, the first volume that collected together Shakespeare's plays under his name was made in 1602. It is the only volume of "diverse" plays in the Countess of Bridgewater's catalogue that was gathered together under the name of an author: "Diuers Playes by Shakespeare 1602."[23] As Roger Chartier has emphasized, the gathering of a writer's works together under his or her name in a bound volume is a crucial step in the construction of "the author"[24] – but that construction of Shakespeare as an author while he was alive was primarily the work of readers, while, after his death, it was the work of booksellers and readers alike.

At the same time, I would stress what I consider to be the major limitations on Shakespeare's canonicity not only before his death but also throughout the seventeenth century. In his essay in this volume, Alan Farmer has rightly emphasized the significance of the *length* of a book (as opposed to its format) to its chances of survival, and he argues that play-pamphlets in quarto cannot be considered ephemeral in comparison to, say, folio broadsides. But my own preference would be to argue for both the bibliographical and the cultural ephemerality of pamphlets and broadsides alike in comparison to larger bound books, whatever their format. We may recall here that the Countess of Bridgewater owned "Diuerse Playes in 5 thicke Volumes in Velum."[25] Indeed, if the countess's volumes of plays were anything like the majority of other such volumes bound up by readers, they would have contained between six and twelve plays. Such "thicke Volumes" were designed for survival on a library shelf in a way that a single stab-stitched pamphlet was not. It was, I believe, much harder to make short texts "stick" as canonical works – hence what happened to Shakespeare's 1609 *Sonnets* when they were reprinted in 1640 as part of a miscellany – but a miscellany in book form. You needed *more* than the *Sonnets* to make a book – and so Benson added more so as to create what we now consider a noncanonical collection.

Lope de Vega provides a striking contrast to the failure or lack of interest in establishing Shakespeare as a canonical book-author during his lifetime. Unlike Shakespeare, Lope began to be sold in bound volumes early in his career. The first such volume, printed in Valladolid in 1604, was a collection of twelve plays in quarto. The volume was reprinted in Antwerp in 1607 (in octavo), in Valladolid in 1609, and in Milan in 1619. In 1611, this first volume of Lope's plays was retrospectively transformed into part 1 of his collected theatrical works by the publication in Antwerp of the *Segunda Parte,* again a collection of twelve *comedias* in quarto. The latter collection was reprinted in Lisbon in 1612 and in Madrid in 1618. Successive collections followed, usually first published in quarto in Barcelona or Madrid. Whatever his early role in publishing his own plays, Lope certainly started to use the numbering system to "authorize" his collections against possible rival ones. The last such volume to be published in his lifetime was the twenty-seventh, printed in Barcelona in 1633 and yet again consisting of twelve plays.[26]

The contrast between Lope and Shakespeare goes well beyond their contrasting fortunes as book-authors in their own lifetimes. Shakespeare was published only in London, a city relatively marginal to the European book trade. Lope was published not only in Madrid, Barcelona, Valladolid, Pamplona, Zaragoza, Valencia, and Cordoba but also in Lisbon, Antwerp, Milan, and (in the case of his religious plays) Brussels. Translations and adaptations of Lope were also made during or shortly after his lifetime, nearly a century before Shakespeare began to have a significant impact in Europe. In the early seventeenth century, English and Shakespeare were on the outer margins of Europe; Spanish and Lope were not. Certainly, books traveled, and a now-famous copy of the Second Folio made its way to Spain, where it was censored and used by the English College in Valladolid.[27] But the Inquisition throughout Europe had difficulty in finding censors who were fluent in English apart from native speakers. By contrast, a wide range of contemporary Spanish books was translated into English. The Countess of Bridgewater's catalogue that we examined above includes translations from the Spanish not only of religious works like "Mount Caluary by Guevara 1595" and "Prayers and Meditacions 14 by Lewis de Granada 1602" but also of fictional works like the recently published "Don Quixot by Shelton."[28]

Of course, once Shakespeare was established as a canonical book-author, he could then be transformed back into myriad less canonical forms. This is a point beautifully illustrated (in the literal sense) in David Kastan's and Kathryn James's *Remembering Shakespeare*. The first illustration (the frontispiece) is of an engraved broadside of the Jubilee at Stratford, published in 1769; the second is the cover of the music and lyrics for Cole Porter's *Kiss Me Kate,* published in 1949.[29] Neither is "a book" in the conventional sense and neither is the work of Shakespeare. But together they suggest how image and music as much as word, how illustrations and score as much as "literary" text, have shaped and transformed "Shakespeare." "BRUSH UP YOUR SHAKESPEARE" is printed at the top of the Cole Porter title page. But "brushing up" Shakespeare turns out to be less a return to a cultural origin than a transformation of that origin under the pressures of the present – and of the entanglements of the past with both the present and imagined futures. Far from advocating a naive return to the past, Kastan demonstrates how past and present alike are composed of multiple and conflicting temporalities: Pistol and gunpowder in a "Renaissance" play about the "Medieval" past; *Hamlet* acted at Covent Garden together with *The Invasion or, All Alarm'd at Brightelmstone* (October 21, 1793) or with *The Death of Captain Cook* (November 2, 1795) or with *Peter Wilkins, or The Flying Indian* (May 26, 1828).[30]

These multiple temporalities, however, are not just features of the texts that we study; they are equally features of our own entanglements with them. To quote Kastan quoting Random Cloud (Randall McLeod), "the struggle for the text is the text."[31] And when Kastan quotes Edward Said, who argues that "[i]t is the critic's job to provide resistance to theory, to open it up toward historical reality," neither Kastan nor Said is suggesting that such a "resistance to theory" is an *avoidance* of theory.[32] To the contrary, it is an argument that we need to resist simply assimilating the past to our own assumptions: assumptions about the individual and his or her detachment from "mere" things; about authorship and print culture; about originality and intellectual property; about the relations between identity and economic property. Kastan's work attends in detail to all of these issues, but it does so dialectically, so as to challenge the categories that we take for granted.

The two dominant tendencies in twentieth-century literary criticism – close reading/new criticism and various forms of historicism – depended upon unexamined assumptions about the Shakespearean texts that they studied. Both schools examined a text (and a set of presuppositions about authorship) that, as Margreta de Grazia has argued, was constructed by Edmond Malone at the end of the eighteenth century.[33] When close readers read "Shakespeare," they were reading a series of texts that had been reordered by date so as to construct and conform to a speculative biography of the author and in which many of the very details that close reading depends upon had been transformed. Close readers, in other words, reproduced the presuppositions of the 1790s, even as they claimed to be addressing the complexities of Shakespeare's language. At the same time, historicists tended to historicize everything except for the text itself. The result was that they tried to contextualize Shakespeare's plays without sufficient awareness that the texts that they were studying were in a crucial sense a post-Enlightenment construct.

The implications of this problem are, I believe, massive. Close readers turn out to be unconsciously reproducing a particular historicity that only extends back to the eighteenth century; historicists become as ahistorical as their opponents by conflating two different periods (the Renaissance with post-Enlightenment editorial practices). It is for this reason that we need, as András Kiséry and Allison Deutermann argue above, to refuse to "distinguish sharply between literary and bibliographical form." At the same time, we need to recognize the changing contours of the "literary" as much as of "bibliographical form." One example of the analysis of the "literary" as a site of struggle is Jesse Lander's *Inventing Polemic*. Lander outlines his project as follows:

> In the first instance, I seek to demonstrate the way in which polemical concerns mark even those texts from the period that we have found most emphatically literary. In the second instance, I hope to show how the modern notion of "the literary" is in part constituted through a repudiation of polemic that imposes a historical amnesia, a willful forgetting of the polemical engagements of the past.[34]

Any adequate attempt to articulate "the literary" will necessarily involve a struggle with the fits, non-fits, and half-fits between our own categories and those of the changing texts and contexts that we study.

Let me take one concrete study of what that means in practice. Nearly every modern editor parades his or her understanding of the Renaissance by glossing the sexual pun in Hamlet's "country matters." As a teacher, I have done so for many years. In the process, I, like other Shakespeareans, articulate the history of the Renaissance with a history of (post)modernity: the Renaissance proleptically and we retrospectively join hands across the "Middle Ages" of Victorian prudery. But, as Zachary Lesser has shown, in the whole history of editing prior to the nineteenth century, even when editors found much that was obscene to censor (for instance, the question of what lies between a maid's legs), no editor had any problem at all with "country matters," nor did they take it to be a sexual quibble. When Samuel Johnson examined the phrase, he thought that it might be a misprint for "country *manners,*" but "country" didn't cause him a second thought. It was, Lesser argues, only *after* the discovery of the first copy of Q1 in 1823, where the phrase reads "*contrary* matters" that editors began to detect a sexual reading in "country matters" and to express a preference for Q1's "non-sexual" reading.[35] In other words, it was the Victorians who implanted a supposed sexual secret that they then tried to erase – and that we, we other Victorians, have "uncovered" as a supposed key to Renaissance philology and sexuality alike.

The entanglements of present and past, like the entanglements of "the book" and "history," require more than a simple opposition between now and then; they require an understanding of the multiple temporalities in which we ourselves live, move, and have our being. It is to an understanding of those entanglements that David Kastan has made such an important contribution, from *Shakespeare and the Shapes of Time* (1982) to *A Will to Believe* (2014).[36] It is to such an understanding that this volume, the work of those he has mentored in more ways that can ever be acknowledged, makes such a significant contribution.

NOTES

1 John Dryden's translation of Virgil, *Aeneid,* 3.567–74 in *The Works of Virgil* (London: Jacob Tonson, 1697), 284. The passage in Virgil reads:
quaecumque in foliis descripsit carmina virgo / digerit in numerum atque antro seclusa relinquit: / illa manent immota locis neque ab ordine cedunt. / verum eadem, verso tenuis cum cardine ventus / impulit et teneras turbavit ianua frondes, / numquam deinde cavo volitantia prendere saxo / nec reuocare situs aut iungere carmina curat: / inconsulti abeunt, sedemque odere Sibyllae.

2 Dante, *Paradiso,* in *The Divine Comedy,* ed. and trans. Charles S. Singleon (Princeton: Princeton University Press, 1977), 33.55–66 and 33.85–87. My account of this passage is deeply indebted to John Ahern, "Binding the Book: Hermeneutics and Manuscript Production in *Paradiso* 33," PMLA 97 (1982): 800–809.

3 These opening paragraphs are taken from what Roger Chartier and I have written about the long history of the book in "What Is a Book?" in *The Cambridge Companion to Textual Scholarship,* ed. Neil

Fraistat and Julia Flanders (Cambridge: Cambridge University Press, 2013), 188–204.

4 *Mr. William Shakespeares Comedies, Histories, & Tragedies Published According to the True Originall Copies* (London: William Jaggard et al., 1623), A3.

5 David Scott Kastan, *Shakespeare and the Book* (Cambridge: Cambridge University Press, 2001), 4. See also "The Mechanics of Culture: Editing Shakespeare Today" and "Shakespeare in Print" in Kastan's *Shakespeare after Theory* (New York: Routledge, 1999), 59–70 and 71–92; and, most recently, Kastan and Kathryn James, *Remembering Shakespeare* (New Haven: Beinecke Rare Book and Manuscript Library, Yale University, 2012).

6 Kastan, *Shakespeare and the Book*, 1.

7 Ibid., 117–18.

8 Sotheby's 1856 auction catalogue, quoted in Paul Morgan, "Frances Wolfreston and 'Hor Bouks': A Seventeenth-Century Woman Book-Collector," *The Library*, 6th ser., 11 (1989): 197–219 (198).

9 I am grateful to James N. Green for pointing out to me this crucial distinction between "uncut" and "unopened."

10 William Shakespeare, *The Tragoedy of Othello, the Moore of Venice: As it hath beene divers times acted at the Globe, and at the Black-Friers, by His Majesties servants written by William Shakespeare* (London: W. Leak, 1655), University of Pennsylvania Rare Book & MS Library, Furness Collection EC Sh155 6220c.

11 Heidi Brayman Hackel, "The Countess of Bridgewater's London Library," in *Books and Readers in Early Modern England: Material Studies*, ed. Jennifer Andersen and Elizabeth Sauer (Philadelphia: University of Pennsylvania Press, 2002), 138–59 (149, 154). See also Brayman Hackel's *Reading Material in Early Modern England: Print, Gender, and Literacy* (Cambridge: Cambridge University Press, 2005) and Heidi Brayman Hackel and Catherine E. Kelly, eds., *Reading Women: Literacy, Authorship, and Culture in the Atlantic World, 1500–1800* (Philadelphia: University of Pennsylvania Press, 2008).

12 Humphrey Moseley, "The Stationer to the Readers," in *Comedies and Tragedies Written by Francis Beavmont and John Fletcher Gentlemen* (London, 1647), A4r.

13 Lena Cowen Orlin, "Shakespeare's Earliest 'Armchair Interpreters'" (paper presented at a conference in honor of Harry Berger, University of South Carolina, October 14, 2006).

14 Kastan, *Shakespeare after Theory*, 73.

15 Roger Chartier, "The Author's Hand," in his *The Author's Hand and the Printer's Mind* (Cambridge: Polity Press, 2013), 73–86. See also Margreta de Grazia, *Shakespeare Verbatim: The Reproduction of Authenticity and the 1790 Apparatus* (Oxford: Clarendon Press, 1991), 107–9.

16 See Siegfried Unseld, *Goethe and His Publishers*, trans. Kenneth J. Northcott (Chicago: University of Chicago Press, 1996), esp. 244–90. For an account of the Schiller archive, see Bernhard Zeller, "The National Schiller Museum in Marbach on the Neckar," *The Modern Language Review* 63 (1968): 886–96.

17 See de Grazia, *Shakespeare Verbatim*.

18 Paul Werstine, *Early Modern Playhouse Manuscripts and the Editing of Shakespeare* (Cambridge: Cambridge University Press, 2013).

19 On printer's copy for the Quartos of *Romeo and Juliet*, see Jill L. Levenson in her edition of *Romeo and Juliet*, The Oxford Shakespeare (Oxford: Oxford University Press, 2000), 103–25; and above all Sonia Massai, *Shakespeare and the Rise of the Editor* (Cambridge: Cambridge University Press,

2007), 174–79. On the dating of Q4, see R. Carter Hailey, "The Dating Game: New Evidence for the Dates of Q4 *Romeo and Juliet* and Q4 *Hamlet*," *Shakespeare Quarterly* 58 (2007): 367–87. On the editing of Q4, see Lynette Hunter, "Why Has Q4 *Romeo and Juliet* Such an Intelligent Editor?" in *Re-constructing the Book: Literary Texts in Transmission*, ed. Maureen Bell et al. (Aldershot: Ashgate, 2001), 9–21; and the important revisions to Hunter's arguments by Massai (above).

20 G. Blakemore Evans, ed., *Shakespearean Prompt-Books of the Seventeenth Century* (Charlottesville: Bibliographical Society of the University of Virginia, 1960–96).

21 Edward A. Langhans, ed., *Restoration Promptbooks* (Carbondale: Southern Illinois University Press, 1981).

22 Lukas Erne, *Shakespeare as Literary Dramatist* (Cambridge: Cambridge University Press, 2003).

23 Brayman Hackel, "The Countess of Bridgewater's London Library," 149.

24 Roger Chartier, "Foucault's Chiasmus: Authorship between Science and Literature in the Seventeenth and Eighteenth Centuries," in *Scientific Authorship: Credit and Intellectual Property in Science*, ed. Mario Biagioli and Peter Galison (New York: Routledge, 2003), 13–31.

25 Brayman Hackel, "The Countess of Bridgewater's London Library," 149.

26 My remarks on Lope are based upon a study of the collection of his works at the University of Pennsylvania, which includes autograph manuscripts of two of his plays. I am profoundly indebted to the analysis and comments of Roger Chartier and John Pollack. See also Alejandro García Reidy, "From Stage to Page: Editorial History and Literary Promotion in Lope de Vega's *Partes de Comedias*," in *A Companion to Lope de Vega*, ed. Alexander Samson and Jonathan Thacker (Rochester, NY: Tamesis, 2008), 51–62.

27 William Shakespeare, *Mr. William Shakespeares Comedies, Histories, and Tragedies* (London: John Smethwick, 1632), Folger Shakespeare Library, STC 22274 Fo. 2 no. 7.

28 Brayman Hackel, "The Countess of Bridgewater's London Library," 148, 151, 149. Bishop Antonio de Guevara's *Monte Calvario* was published in Spain from 1545 to 1549, and first published in English in 1594; the countess owned the second edition: *The Mount of Caluarie* (London: Edward White, 1595). Luis de Granada's *Libro de la Oracion y Meditacion* was first published in Spain in 1554; the countess owned *Of Prayer and Meditation. Contayning Foure-teene Meditations* (London: Edward White, 1602). Cervantes published the first part of *Don Quixote* in 1605 and the second part in 1615; Thomas Shelton translated part 1 into English in 1612 and part 2 in 1620. Because the two volumes of the translation were published separately in 1620, it is presumably the 1612 translation of part 1 alone that the countess owned: *The History of the Valorous and Wittie Knight-errant, Don-Quixote of the Mancha, Translated Out of the Spanish* (London: Edward Blount and William Barret, 1612).

29 Kastan and James, *Remembering Shakespeare*, 2, 6.

30 I take the latter collations from the University of Pennsylvania's large collection of eighteenth- and nineteenth-century playbills.

31 Kastan, *Shakespeare after Theory*, 93.

32 Edward Said, *The World, the Text, and the Critic* (London: Faber and Faber, 1984), 242. Quoted in Kastan, *Shakespeare after Theory*, 17.

33 Throughout this paragraph, I draw upon de Grazia's brilliant *Shakespeare Verbatim*.

34 Jesse M. Lander, *Inventing Polemic: Religion, Print, and Literary Culture in Early Modern England* (Cambridge: Cambridge University Press, 2006), 5.

35 Zachary Lesser, "Contrary Matters: The Power of the Gloss and the History of an Obscenity," in *Hamlet after Q1: An Uncanny History of the Shakespearean Text* (Philadelphia: University of Pennsylania Press, 2015), 72–113.

36 David Scott Kastan, *Shakespeare and the Shapes of Time* (Hanover, N.H.: University Press of New England, 1982) and *A Will to Believe: Shakespeare and Religion* (Oxford: Oxford University Press, 2014).

Th' Archangel ſtood, and from the other Hill
To thir fixt Station, all in bright array
The Cherubim deſcended; on the ground
Gliding meteorous, as Ev'ning Miſt
Ris'n from a River o're the mariſh glides,
And gathers ground faſt at the Labourers heel
Homeward returning. High in Front advanc't,
The brandiſht Sword of God before them blaz'd
Fierce as a Comet; which with torrid heat,
And vapour as the *Libyan* Air aduſt,
Began to parch that temperate Clime; whereat
In either hand the haſtning Angel caught
Our lingring Parents, and to th' Eaſtern Gate
Led them direct, and down the Cliff as faſt
To the ſubjected Plain; then diſappear'd.
They looking back, all th' Eaſtern ſide beheld
Of Paradiſe, ſo late thir happy ſeat,
VVav'd over by that flaming Brand, the Gate
VVith dreadful Faces throng'd and fiery Arms:
Some natural tears they dropt, but wip'd them ſoon;
The VVorld was all before them, where to chooſe
Thir place of reſt, and Providence thir guide:
They hand in hand with wandring ſteps and ſlow,
Through *Eden* took thir ſolitary way.

One common pace they trod and Mourn'd one comm
instead of the last Line

THE END.

Contributors

HEIDI BRAYMAN is associate professor of English at the University of California, Riverside. She is the author of *Reading Material in Early Modern England: Print, Gender, and Literacy* (Cambridge University Press, 2005) and the co-editor of *Reading Women: Literacy, Authorship, and Culture in the Atlantic World, 1500–1800* (University of Pennsylvania Press, 2007) and *Teaching Early Modern English Literature from the Archives* (Modern Language Association, 2015). She is currently completing a cultural history of muteness, deafness, and manual gesture in early modern England.

BIANCA F.-C. CALABRESI teaches in the Department of English and Comparative Literature at Columbia University. She is the author of "Read Blood: Rubrication from Marlowe to Milton" (manuscript under revision) and articles on Renaissance typography and on alternative sites of women's literacy in early modern Europe.

ALLISON DEUTERMANN is assistant professor of English at Baruch College. She is the author of *Listening for Theatrical Form in Early Modern England* (Edinburgh University Press, 2016) and, with András Kiséry, the co-editor of *Formal Matters: Reading the Materials of English Renaissance Literature* (Manchester University Press, 2013).

MARIO DIGANGI is professor of English at Lehman College and the Graduate Center, City University of New York. He is the author of *Sexual Types: Embodiment, Agency, and Dramatic Character from Shakespeare to*

Shirley (University of Pennsylvania Press, 2011) and *The Homoerotics of Early Modern Drama* (Cambridge University Press, 1997). He is currently working on a project that examines affective politics in early modern history plays.

ALAN B. FARMER is associate professor of English at the Ohio State University. He is the co-editor, with Adam Zucker, of *Localizing Caroline Drama: Politics and Economics of the Early Modern English Stage, 1625–1642* (Palgrave Macmillan, 2006) and the co-creator, with Zachary Lesser, of *DEEP: Database of Early English Playbooks*. He is currently working on two book projects, one on playbooks, newsbooks, and the politics of the Thirty Years' War, and the other on "Print, Plays, and Popularity in Shakespeare's England" (written with Zachary Lesser).

THOMAS FESTA is associate professor of English at the State University of New York, New Paltz. He is the author of *The End of Learning: Milton and Education* (Routledge, 2006) and the co-editor of *Early Modern Women on the Fall: An Anthology* (MRTS, 2012).

ADAM G. HOOKS is assistant professor in the Department of English and the Center for the Book at the University of Iowa. He is the author of *Selling Shakespeare: Biography, Bibliography, and the Book Trade* (Cambridge University Press, 2016). He also runs a book history website called *Anchora* at www.adamghooks.net.

SARAH A. KELEN is professor of English and dean of the College of Liberal Arts and Sciences at Nebraska Wesleyan University. She is the author of *Langland's Early Modern Identities* (Palgrave Macmillan, 2007) and the editor of *Renaissance Retrospections: Tudor Views of the Middle Ages* (Medieval Institute, 2013).

ANDRÁS KISÉRY is assistant professor of English at City College of New York. He is the author of *Hamlet's Moment: Drama and Political Knowledge in Early Modern England* (Oxford University Press, 2016) and, with Allison Deutermann, the co-editor of *Formal Matters: Reading the Materials of English Renaissance Literature* (Manchester University Press, 2013).

JESSE M. LANDER is associate professor of English at the University of Notre Dame. He is the author of *Inventing Polemic: Religion, Print, and*

Literary Culture in Early Modern England (Cambridge University Press, 2006), and he has edited *Macbeth* for the Barnes & Noble Shakespeare and *1 Henry IV* for the Norton Shakespeare, third edition.

ZACHARY LESSER is professor of English at the University of Pennsylvania. He is the author of *"Hamlet" after Q1: An Uncanny History of the Shakespearean Text* (University of Pennsylvania Press, 2015) and *Renaissance Drama and the Politics of Publication: Readings in the English Book Trade* (Cambridge University Press, 2004). With Peter Holland and Tiffany Stern, he is General Editor of the Arden Shakespeare, fourth series.

ZOLTÁN MÁRKUS is associate professor of English at Vassar College. He is completing a monograph entitled "Shakespeares at War: Cultural Appropriations of Shakespeare in London and Berlin during World War II," a comparative study of Shakespeare's cultural reception in the two cities. He has published widely on Shakespeare, European drama and theater, and performance theory.

CLAIRE MCEACHERN is professor of English at the University of California, Los Angeles. She is the author of *The Poetics of English Nationhood, 1590–1612* (Cambridge University Press, 1996) and the forthcoming *Believing in Shakespeare: Studies in Longing;* co-editor of *Religion and Culture in Renaissance England* (Cambridge University Press, 1997); and editor of *The Cambridge Companion to Shakespearean Tragedy* (2002). She has edited *Much Ado About Nothing* for the Arden Shakespeare, and several of Shakespeare's plays for other series, including *Twelfth Night* (Barnes & Noble), *King Lear* (Longman), and, for the Pelican Shakespeare, *1&2 Henry V, King John,* and *All's Well that Ends Well.*

BENEDICT S. ROBINSON is associate professor of English at Stony Brook University. He is the author of *Islam and Early Modern English Literature: The Politics of Romance from Spenser to Milton* (Palgrave Macmillan, 2007) and the co-editor, with Zachary Lesser, of *Textual Conversations in the Renaissance: Ethics, Authors, Technologies* (Ashgate, 2006); his work has appeared in *Shakespeare Quarterly*, ELH, SEL, *Journal for Early Modern Cultural Studies,* and elsewhere. He is currently completing a book on the language of emotion in the seventeenth century.

WILLIAM H. SHERMAN is head of research at the Victoria and Albert Museum and professor of English at the University of York (UK). He is the author of *John Dee: The Politics of Reading and Writing in the English Renaissance* (University of Massachusetts Press, 1995) and *Used Books: Marking Readers in Renaissance England* (University of Pennsylvania Press, 2007). He is the co-editor of *"The Tempest" and Its Travels* (Reaktion Books, 2000), as well as numerous journal special issues, including *On Editing* (*Performance Research*), *The Complete Shakespeare* (*Shakespeare Quarterly*), and *The Renaissance Collage* (*Journal of Medieval and Early Modern Studies*).

PETER STALLYBRASS is the Walter H. and Leonore C. Annenberg Professor in the Humanities and professor of English at the University of Pennsylvania. Among numerous other works, he is the author of *The Politics and Poetics of Transgression* (Cornell University Press, 1986; with Allon White) and *Renaissance Clothing and the Materials of Memory* (Cambridge University Press, 2000; with Ann Rosalind Jones), winner of the James Russell Lowell Prize from the MLA. For the past twenty-five years, he has directed Penn's Seminar on the History of Material Texts, a foundational series that has done much to shape the field of book history.

DANIEL VITKUS holds the Rebeca Hickel Chair in Elizabethan Literature at the University of California, San Diego. He is the author of *Turning Turk: English Theater and the Multicultural Mediterranean, 1570–1630* (Palgrave Macmillan, 2003) and the editor of *Three Turk Plays from Early Modern England* (Columbia University Press, 2000) and *Piracy, Slavery, and Redemption: Barbary Captivity Narratives from Early Modern England* (Columbia University Press, 2001).

CHLOE WHEATLEY is associate professor of English at Trinity College. She is the author of *Epic, Epitome, and the Early Modern Historical Imagination* (Ashgate, 2011) as well as articles on *The Faerie Queene* and early modern print culture.

Note on Illustrations

All unnumbered illustrations are from the Beinecke Rare Book and Manuscript Library and the private collection of David Scott Kastan, as follows:

PAGE 8
William Shakespeare, *Mr. William Shakespeares Comedies, Histories, & Tragedies* (London, 1623), frontispiece. Beinecke Rare Book and Manuscript Library, Yale University, 1978 +83

PAGE 26
Certaine sermons or homilies appointed to be read in churches (London, 1623), 2Z4r, with early bookmark made from a tanned shrew. Private collection of David Scott Kastan

PAGE 28
Francis Bacon, *The Twoo Bookes of Francis Bacon. Of the proficience and aduancement of Learning* (London, 1605), title page. Beinecke Rare Book and Manuscript Library, Yale University, Ih B132 605

PAGE 64
William Shakespeare, *The most excellent Historie of the Merchant of Venice* (London, 1600 [1619]), A2r. Beinecke Rare Book and Manuscript Library, Yale University, Eliz 181

PAGE 86
Thomas Tomkis, *Albvmazar* (London, 1615), front cover. Beinecke Rare Book and Manuscript Library, Yale University, Ih T596 615am

PAGE 126
Edmund Spenser, *The Faerie Qveene* (London, 1609), Q5r, with ownership signature. Private collection of David Scott Kastan

PAGE 128
George Herbert, *The Temple* (Cambridge, 1633), A9v. Beinecke Rare Book and Manuscript Library, Yale University, Ih H414 632Cb

PAGE 150
Euclid, *The Elements of Geometrie* (London, 1570), *1r. Beinecke Rare Book and Manuscript Library, Yale University, Z90 013

PAGE 184
Ralph Rabbards, *Inventions of military machines and other devices* (ca. 1591), f. 26r. Beinecke Rare Book and Manuscript Library, Yale University, Osborn a8

PAGE 206
John Foxe, *Actes and Monuments of these latter and perillous dayes* (London, 1563),

*3r. Beinecke Rare Book and Manuscript Library, Yale University, Mey34 F83 +1563

PAGE 232
William Fulke, *The Text of the New Testament of Iesvs Christ* (London, 1589), endpaper opposite title page. Private collection of David Scott Kastan

PAGE 234
Geoffrey Chaucer, *The Workes of our Antient and Learned English Poet, Geffrey Chavcer, newly Printed* (London, 1598), 4A1r. Beinecke Rare Book and Manuscript Library, Yale University, Idz +598B

PAGE 256
John Milton, *The Reason of Church-governement* (London, 1641 [1642]), errata page. Beinecke Rare Book and Manuscript Library, Yale University, 1977 2507

PAGE 274
William Hill, *Commonplace Book* (ca. early 17th century), f. 93v. Beinecke Rare Book and Manuscript Library, Yale University, Osborn b234

PAGE 300
Samuel Daniel, *The Whole Workes of Samvel Daniel Esquire in Poetrie* (London, 1623), internal title page with signature and disclaimer: "Thomas Sedgewick it is not his book." Private collection of David Scott Kastan

PAGE 302
William Shakespeare, *Mr. William Shakespeares Comedies, Histories, & Tragedies* (London, 1623), I6r. Beinecke Rare Book and Manuscript Library, Yale University, 1978 +83

PAGE 324
Wille und Macht (Berlin: Baldur von Schirach, 1940), 2. Sterling Memorial Library, Yale University, A85 151

PAGE 340
Richard Wagner, *Attente* (ca. early 1840s). Beinecke Rare Book and Manuscript Library, Yale University, GEN MSS 601 Box 336, folder 42

PAGE 374
Johann Engel, *Practica auf das Jahr?* (Strasbourg, ca. 1485), proof sheet. Beinecke Rare Book and Manuscript Library, Yale University, ZZi 07

PAGE 390
John Milton, *Paradise Lost* (London, 1678), Y6r, with manuscript emendation of final line by William Molyneux. Private collection of David Scott Kastan

Index

Figures and images are indicated by italicized page numbers and figure numbers.

A

B

D

E

F

K

L

N

O

P

Q

R

T

U

V

W

Y

Z

Copyedited by Lesley K. Baier
Designed & set in Yale typefaces by Rebecca Martz
Office of the Yale University Printer

Printed by EBS Editoriale Bortolazzi Stei, Verona, Italy
on Fedrigoni papers

Distributed by Yale University Press